The State of Civil So

For all the obstacles that remain, civil society is burgeoning in Japan, and the idea of civil society is at the core of the current debate about how to reinvigorate the country. The only volume of its kind, this book gathers the insights of American and Japanese scholars from the fields of political science, sociology, social psychology, and history to investigate the nature of associational life and the public sphere in Japan. It goes beyond assessing the condition of civil society to explore the role of the state in shaping civil society over time, and its broad, comparative framework is useful for thinking about civil society not just in Japan but elsewhere in the contemporary world. Given its wealth of original research and the uniform strength of its individual chapters, this book will appeal to a broad audience of social scientists, practitioners, and policy makers.

Frank J. Schwartz is the Associate Director of Harvard University's Program on U.S.-Japan Relations. At Harvard, he graduated Phi Beta Kappa, magna cum laude in Social Studies, and earned a Ph.D. in political science. He has been the recipient of Fulbright, Foreign Language and Area Studies (FLAS), and Rotary Foundation scholarships, among others. He is the author of *Advice and Consent: The Politics of Consultation in Japan* (1998).

Susan J. Pharr is the Edwin O. Reischauer Professor of Japanese Politics and Director of the Program on U.S.-Japan Relations at Harvard University. She has been a visiting research scholar at Tokyo, Keio, and Sophia Universities (all located in Tokyo), a guest scholar at the Brookings Institution, and a Fellow at the Woodrow Wilson International Center for Scholars. She held the Japan Chair at the Center for Strategic and International Studies and has been the recipient of grants from, among others, the National Science Foundation, Ford Foundation, Rockefeller Foundation, Center for Global Partnership, U.S.-Japan Friendship Commission, and Mellon Foundation. She was a Woodrow Wilson Fellow and graduated Phi Beta Kappa. Her most recent book is *Disaffected Democracies: What's Troubling the Trilateral Countries*? (edited with Robert D. Putnam, 2000).

The State of Civil Society in Japan

Edited by

FRANK J. SCHWARTZ

Harvard University

SUSAN J. PHARR

Harvard University

CAMBRIDGE
UNIVERSITY PRESS

CAMBRIDGE UNIVERSITY PRESS
Cambridge, New York, Melbourne, Madrid, Cape Town, Singapore, São Paulo

Cambridge University Press
40 West 20th Street, New York, NY 10011–4211, USA

www.cambridge.org
Information on this title:www.cambridge.org/9780521827300

First published 2003
Reprinted 2004, 2006

Printed in the United States of America

A catalogue record for this book is available from the British Library.

Library of Congress Cataloguing in Publication Data
The state of civil society in Japan / edited by Frank J. Schwartz and Susan J. Pharr.
p. cm.
Includes bibliogrpahical references and index.
ISBN 0-521-82730-2 — ISBN 0-521-53462-3 (pb.)
1. Civil society — Japan. I. Schwartz, Frank J. (Frank Jacob), 1958— II. Pharr, Susan J.
JQ1681.S69 2003
300'.952—dc21 2003043505

ISBN-13 978-0-521-82730-0 hardback
ISBN-10 0-521-82730-2 hardback

ISBN-13 978-0-521-53462-8 paperback
ISBN-10 0-521-53462-3 paperback

Contents

Tables and Figures

Tables

Figures

Contributors

Andrew Barshay is a professor of history at the University of California at Berkeley. He is the author of *State and Intellectual in Imperial Japan* (1988) and the forthcoming book *The Social Sciences in Japan: Historical Essays, 1890–1990.* His current research concerns Russian-Japanese cultural interactions since the mid-nineteenth century.

Robert Bullock is a professor of political science at the University of California at Riverside. He is the author of "Japan: The Politics of Late Development" (2000), "Reregulation, Deregulation, and Market-Opening in Japan: A Cross-Sectoral Analysis" (2000), and the forthcoming book *Politicizing the Developmental State: Rice Agriculture and the Conservative Coalition in Postwar Japan.*

Margarita Estévez-Abe is a professor of government at Harvard University. Among other works, she is the author of "A Forgotten Link: The Welfare-Finance Nexus in the Japanese Welfare State" (2001), "Social Protection and Varieties of Capitalism" (2001), and the forthcoming book *Unwinding Japan: A Study of Japanese Welfare Capitalism.*

Laurie Freeman is a professor of political science at the University of California at Santa Barbara. She is the author of "Japan's Press Clubs as Information Cartels" (1996), *Closing the Shop: Information Cartels and Japan's Mass Media* (2000), and "Media" (2002). She is currently working on a book project titled *Information Technology and Democracy: A Comparative Study of Japan and the United States*.

Sheldon Garon is a professor of history and East Asian studies at Princeton. His numerous publications include *The State and Labor in Modern Japan* (1987), *Molding Japanese Minds: The State in Everyday Life* (1997), and "State and Society in Interwar Japan" (2000). He is currently finishing the book *Fashioning Cultures of Thrift: Promoting Saving in Japan and the World.*

Helen Hardacre is a professor of Japanese religions and society at Harvard University. Most recently, she is the author of *Shinto and the State, 1868–1988* (1989), *Marketing the Menacing Fetus in Japan* (1997), and *Religion and Society in Nineteenth-Century Japan* (2002).

David Johnson is a professor of sociology at the University of Hawaii at Manoa. He is the author of *The Japanese Way of Justice: Prosecuting Crime in Japan* (2002).

Patricia Maclachlan is a professor of Asian studies and government at the University of Texas at Austin. In addition to the book *Consumer Politics in Postwar Japan: The Institutional Boundaries of Citizen Politics* (2002), her publications include "Protecting Producers from Consumer Protection: Japan's New Product Liability Regime" (1999) and "Information Disclosure and Center-Local Linkages in Japan" (2000).

Robert Pekkanen is a professor of political science and Asian studies at Middlebury College. His publications include "Japan's New Politics: The Case of the NPO Law" (2000), "The Legal Framework for Voluntary and Not-for-Profit Activity" (2002, coauthored), "The Politics of Regulating the Nonprofit Sector" (2002), and the forthcoming book *Civil Society in Japan.*

Susan Pharr is a professor of government and the director of the Program on U.S.-Japan Relations at Harvard University. Among her works are *Losing Face: Status Politics in Japan* (1990), *Media and Politics in Japan* (1996, with Ellis Krauss), and *Disaffected Democracies: What's Troubling the Trilateral Countries?* (2000, with Robert Putnam).

Kim Reimann is a professor of political science at Georgia State University. She is the author of "Building Networks from the Outside In: International Movements, Japanese NGOs and the Kyoto Climate Change Conference" (2001).

Frank Schwartz is associate director of the Program on U.S.-Japan Relations at Harvard University. His publications include "Trading Dangers: Japanese Security in the Post–Cold War World" (1993), *Advice and Consent: The Politics of Consultation in Japan* (1998), and "Civil Society in Japan Reconsidered" (2002).

Suzuki Akira is a professor at Hosei University's Ōhara Institute for Social Research. Among his articles are "The Transformation of Visions of Labor Unionism: Internal Union Politics in the Japanese Steel Industry in the 1960s" (2000) and "Studies of Industrial Relations in the Steel and Auto Industries Since 1980" (2001).

Tsujinaka Yutaka is a professor of political science at the University of Tsukuba. His many publications include *Comparing Policy Networks: Labor Politics in the U.S., Germany, and Japan* (1996, coauthored) and *Interest Group Structure and*

Regime Change in Japan (1996). He is now editing the six-volume series *Civil Society and Interest Groups of the World.*

Yamagishi Toshio is a professor of social psychology at Hokkaidō University. His recent publications include *The Structure of Trust: The Evolutionary Game of Mind and Society* (1998), *From Assurance-Based Society to Trust-Based Society: Where Is the Japanese System Heading?* (1999), and "Social Exchange and Reciprocity: Confusion or Heuristic?" (2000).

Preface

Susan Pharr

"Civil society" is a term with deep historical roots and surprising resilience. Well known in the drawing rooms of early modern Europe, it fell into disuse in the mid-nineteenth century and regained currency only in the 1970s, when a transfixed world sought ways to talk about resurgent social forces that were challenging totalitarian governments across Eastern and Central Europe. The outpouring of academic works and popular writing since then on civil societies, past and present, across the world's disparate regions attests to the power of the concept and its ability to transcend national boundaries. Coupled with the related concepts of social capital and the public sphere, civil society offers a powerful analytical tool for thinking about ways in which people, individually and in groups, link to broader political, social, and economic arrangements, whatever the country.

As the term is used in this book and as most scholars today would agree, *civil society consists of sustained, organized social activity that occurs in groups that are formed outside the state, the market, and the family*. Cumulatively, such activity creates a public sphere outside the state, a space in which groups and individuals engage in public discourse. But given the extraordinary range of settings – from cafes and dinner parties to union halls, trade associations, and charities – in which people in any nation come together, it should come as no surprise that the term has been applied in a variety of ways, even when it comes to Western countries with liberal democratic systems in common and similar institutional arrangements and civic traditions. Extending the term still further to illuminate developments in nondemocratic systems presents still greater challenges. Indeed, efforts to apply the term to all these various settings highlight how important it is not only to develop a conceptual framework that travels well but to consider how, in any given context, civil societies emerge in the first place and become transformed over time.

Building on the wealth of recent research on civil society, this book seeks to respond to these needs and to make three main contributions.

First, it traces the rise of civil society in modern Japan. If we consider the whole sweep of Japan's history from the country's accession to modern statehood in

1868 to the present, it offers a unique laboratory for thinking about how organized social life outside the state fares under conditions ranging from authoritarianism to quasidemocracy to fascism to liberal democracy. Although the primary focus of the volume is contemporary Japan, several chapters (by Sheldon Garon, Andrew Barshay, and Tsujinaka Yutaka) look explicitly at the post-1868 evolution of civil society and thought about it in Japan, and many other authors examine aspects of the country's civic legacy as it affects civil society today.

Second, this book goes beyond assessing the *condition* of civil society to explore the role of the *state* in shaping civil society over time – hence, its title. Largely because the resurgence of interest in civil society stemmed from developments in Eastern and Central Europe, where social groups and movements emerged to challenge disintegrating socialist regimes, most media accounts and, indeed, a sizable share of academic writing have tended to cast civil society in an oppositional role in relation to the state. And, of course, glimpsing civil society in a country such as Poland when it is in the midst of a profound regime shift can lend credence to such a view. But once one's perspective encompasses lengthy periods of time and a host of countries, the critical role played by states in setting the parameters within which social groups arise, organize, and operate – even if and when they challenge state authority – becomes obvious.

This book thus extends the work of Nancy Bermeo (2000), Jonah Levy (1999), Theda Skocpol (1996, 1999), and other scholars who have emphasized the state's role in shaping civil society in America, France, and Europe more generally. The book fully acknowledges, and indeed explores in the Japanese context, the dynamic forces (e.g., rising education levels, technological change, international norms) that deeply affect the nature of civil society, independent of state policies. But its central contribution is its focus on the role of state policy in contouring the associational landscape over the long haul.

Third, the book seeks to clarify the concept of civil society. In any country, the range of nonstate, nonmarket activities is quite large, and scholars debate what to include. "Who likes may snip verbal definitions in his old age, when his world has gone crackly and dry," Arthur Bentley (1908: 199) once observed, but the fact is that civil society's continued utility as an analytical term hangs on whether it will come to be applied in consistent ways across widely varying political systems, Western and non-Western alike. Based on the extensive research conducted by our contributors as well as a broad survey of the relevant literature, this book argues that understanding how civil societies take shape over time requires the inclusion of a broad range of actors and activities. Thus, unlike some previous authors (but like many others), our conception of civil society actors embraces the nonmarket activities of economic actors (e.g., business organizations and trade associations, labor unions, consumer groups) and the societal activities of religious groups, and also includes groups that stand at varying distances from the state. At the same time, our long time horizon leads us to focus on sustained, organized group activity rather than spontaneous, informal activities such as coffee klatches or outings with friends. Although informal activities obviously influence the nature of social life and are important for generating social capital (Putnam 2000), the central dynamic in modern, complex nation-states is between communities of interests that seek to shape the larger political and social reality around them, on the one hand, and governments, on the other.

The book is divided into five parts. Its first part, like the concluding chapter, deals with the theoretical and historical context of our topic. In the volume's introduction, Frank Schwartz makes the case of applying the concept of civil society in the Japanese context. In Chapter 1, he then situates our use of the term among the myriad meanings other contemporary Western authors have assigned to it. Next, Sheldon Garon surveys the evolution of civil society over the course of Japan's modern history. He traces its role in shaping the state and, conversely, the state's role in shaping society from Japan's rise as a modern state in the Meiji era (1868–1912) to the democratic interlude of the Taishō era (1912–26), the period of fascism and wartime control, and the postwar era, in which civil society grew and diversified. Given that Japan's civil society arose in a non-Western context in which words such as "rights," "public," and even "society" were hard to translate, no discussion of civil society in Japan would be complete without an account of the discourse among Japanese themselves on the subject, which intellectual historian Andrew Barshay provides in Chapter 3. As he shows, it was not until the collapse of the imperial system that accompanied Japan's defeat in the Pacific War that the concept of civil society eclipsed the notion of imperial subjecthood and gained moral legitimacy in Japanese discourse.

Part II investigates the nature of associational life in Japan. Tsujinaka Yutaka puts the organizational aspects of Japan's civil society in perspective by comparing them with those of the United States and South Korea in Chapter 4. Drawing on longitudinal data for the period from 1951 to 1999, he presents a relatively optimistic view of Japan as a well-functioning democracy with multiplying and diversifying interest groups, albeit with vestiges of business dominance of the associational landscape. There is a lively tension between his analysis and that of Robert Pekkanen, who in Chapter 5 argues that Japan's regulatory environment has sculpted a pattern of civil society development in which public advocacy groups have ended up smaller, more local, less independent, and more poorly funded than their counterparts elsewhere in the industrial world. Helen Hardacre in Chapter 6 analyzes a fundamental anomaly in postwar Japan: despite few restrictions on religious activities, organized religion has had a remarkably weak position in Japanese society. And in Chapter 7, Margarita Estévez-Abe illuminates the role Japan's state plays in promoting civil associations by detailing the close state-society partnership that has developed in the domain of social welfare provision.

Although the common formula "between state and market" generally excludes economic actors from civil society, producer interests figure prominently in the associational life of any capitalist country and in Japan have played an exceedingly important role. Thus, Part III examines the *non*market activities of some of those actors in Japan. In Chapter 8, Robert Bullock details how producer groups in the agricultural and small-retail sectors have won the state protection on which their survival depends. Along the way, his account mounts a fundamental challenge to those who hold that only democracies can give birth to civil societies, because he demonstrates how even organizations originating from top-down directives of an authoritarian state can succeed in winning independence over time. Suzuki Akira focuses on the failure of Japanese labor unions to establish a distinctive associational life in Chapter 9, and in Chapter 10, Patricia Maclachlan reviews the mixed success enjoyed by consumer groups in their quest to build a consumer society independent of state and market control.

Part IV is concerned with institutional linkages between the state and civil society in Japan. Laurie Freeman both clarifies the domination and/or neglect of the public sphere by the mass media and considers the possibility that the Internet might serve as an alternative public space in Chapter 11. So far, she argues, the state's use of its regulatory power and "guidance" in the development of the Internet casts doubt on whether this potential will be realized. In Chapter 12, David Johnson explores how the state regulates interests by examining its role in prosecuting corruption and contrasts how differing balances between magisterial accountability and independence have affected the prosecution of corruption in Japan and Italy. Although the rule of law is firmly entrenched in both countries, Japanese prosecutors enjoy far less independence than their Italian counterparts. Thus, in this domain, as in so many others examined in this book, the Japanese state retains considerable latitude to control its relations to private interests – in this case, business interests that seek privileged and illicit access to state actors.

How globalization is affecting Japan's civil society is the subject of Part V. Obviously, taking the measure of any nation's civil society requires far more than merely doing a head count of groups and organizations that collectively make up associational life. As Robert Putnam's work (2000) suggests and as Japanese intellectuals themselves have long recognized in their heated debates about the "internal democracy" of labor unions and other organizations, the interior dynamic is essential. Thus, any inquiry into the nature of civil society ultimately comes to focus on values and how they may be changing. In Chapter 13, social psychologist Yamagishi Toshio, using experimental methods to compare the nature of social trust in America and Japan, offers strong support for the view that values associated with a vibrant civil society are, in fact, gaining ground in Japan. While the levels of generalized social trust (i.e., trust in people outside one's own group) are lower in Japan than in America, globalization and other forces are transforming Japan from a security-based society in which individuals pursue commitment-forming strategies within closed groups to a more outer-directed, trust-based society in which they pursue more open, opportunity-seeking strategies. In Chapter 14, Kim Reimann explores a different kind of norm change. Turning to the international arena, she focuses on Japan's emerging community of international development nongovernmental organizations (NGOs). Although state policies constrained their growth until the late 1980s, changing international norms, mediated through state policies, help account for a major turnaround since that time.

Finally, the concluding chapter offers a broad comparative framework for thinking about civil societies in Japan and elsewhere by contrasting "pathways to civility" in Japan with those in Western Europe and America. States, it holds, can be either activist or permissive in their basic orientation toward civil society, but with quite different effects depending on whether policies apply broadly or are targeted (i.e., vary by group). Except for a relatively brief period prior to and during wartime, when it imposed broadly applicable restrictions on civil society, the chapter suggests, Japan has had an activist state with targeted policies under which economic interest groups have thrived while other organizations have encountered widely varying – and, in most cases, more restrictive – policies. More broadly, the chapter proposes a framework for analyzing the evolution of associational landscapes in other countries, including those elsewhere in Asia.

This book grew out of a major international project on "Civil Society in the Asia-Pacific" organized under the auspices of the Program on U.S.-Japan Relations of Harvard's Weatherhead Center for International Affairs, in which Susan Pharr serves as director and Frank Schwartz as associate director. Founded in 1980, the program has long included domestic issues within its purview. In recent years, a number of scholars associated with the program as speakers or postdoctoral Fellows have usefully applied the concept of civil society to the study of Japan, so the idea for a collective research endeavor gradually took shape. Generous funding from the Japan Foundation Center for Global Partnership (CGP), which is based in Tokyo and New York, and the Japan-U.S. Friendship Commission, which is based in Washington, D.C., as well as Harvard's Reischauer Institute of Japan Studies made this project and volume possible.

The overall project, which was conducted jointly with the East-West Center of Honolulu and was developed in cooperation with Keio University of Tokyo, has two stages. Brought to completion with this book, the first focuses on Japan in comparative perspective. The second, which is under the direction of political scientist Muthiah Alagappa of the East-West Center, focuses on "Civil Society and Political Change in Asia" and embraces Bangladesh, Burma, China, India, Indonesia, Japan, Malaysia, the Philippines, Singapore, South Korea, Sri Lanka, Taiwan, Thailand, and Vietnam.

The present volume grew out of an international conference held at the East-West Center in January 2000 that brought together some twenty leading scholars on contemporary Japan and other specialists with a deep knowledge of how the civil society framework has been applied to the United States, Western Europe, and elsewhere in Asia. We express appreciation to Charles Morrison, the president of the East-West Center; to Muthiah Alagappa; and to the center staff, especially Carolyn Eguchi and Ralph Carvalho, for their help and gracious hospitality. We also extend our thanks to Andrew Gordon, director of the Reischauer Institute; Chano Junichi, Wada Yoshihiro, Ishida Takashi, Susan Hubbard, Oshida Yukio, and Takahashi Rikimaru of CGP; Eric Gangloff and Margaret Mihori of the Friendship Commission; as well as many others who helped us along the way.

In addition to the contributors to this volume, Muthiah Alagappa, Helmut Anheier, Andrew Gordon, Hagen Koo, Charles Morrison, Sone Yasunori, and Patricia Steinhoff took part in the Hawaii conference and made many invaluable suggestions. We thank Laurie Freeman, who proposed the title for the book, and Gary Allinson, Jeffrey Broadbent, Gerald Curtis, Larry Diamond, Inoguchi

Takashi, and Richard Samuels for the input they offered to this project. Before and after the Hawaii conference, the project convened, sponsored, or otherwise facilitated or encouraged our members' participation in a large number of seminars, colloquia, and workshops, and also panels at professional meetings – including annual meetings of the American Political Science Association, the International Political Science Association, and the Association for Asian Studies – on topics relating to the project's themes. These events, which took place in venues from Cambridge, Massachusetts, to Ulaanbaatar, Mongolia, sought to spur research and thinking on civil society and to provide feedback to our authors. Staff members of the Program on U.S.-Japan Relations – Jana Van der Veer, Kenneth Marden, Andrew Dusenbery, Laurie Gagnon, Jeffrey Newmark, Amy Demarest, and John Kuzcwara – provided many hours of assistance in planning and running the Honolulu conference, administering our grants, and pulling this volume together. Finally, we express warmest thanks to Mary Child and Frank Smith of Cambridge University Press for their enthusiastic support of this book project.

Except for the most familiar names (e.g., Tokyo), the Japanese forms of proper nouns are used here. Japanese individuals' names are thus written surname first. Given constant and considerable fluctuations in the exchange rate, conversions from yen to dollars are made at a constant rate of ¥100 to the dollar. Newspaper citations always refer to morning editions unless otherwise noted.

The State of Civil Society in Japan

Introduction: Recognizing Civil Society in Japan

Frank Schwartz

Academics, politicians, journalists, foundation executives, development assistance officials, regimes and their opponents alike throughout the world – they have all joined the civil society bandwagon. Civil society's most ardent advocates could not be more effusive: it is the "hitherto missing key to sustained political reform, legitimate states and governments, improved governance, viable state-society and state-economy relationships, and prevention of . . . political decay" (Harbeson 1994: 1–2). Its detractors, on the other hand, dismiss civil society as a "new cult" (Wood 1990: 63), an idea that "is seductive but perhaps ultimately specious" (Kumar 1994: 130).

It was not always so. Although the origins of the idea of civil society, a realm independent of the state, go back to classical antiquity and it was central to the intellectual debates of early modern Europe, it virtually disappeared from political discourse in the mid-nineteenth century before being resurrected in the 1970s. A term that became "the motherhood-and-apple pie of the 1990s" (McElvoy 1997: 30) made no appearance in the *International Dictionary of the Social Sciences* written in the 1960s. The renewed popularity of civil society resulted from a variety of overlapping and sometimes contradictory forces (Keane 1988b: 1; 1998: 35).

Given the twentieth-century penchant for ideologies such as fascism, communism, socialism, and social democracy, a reaction against centralized state power should have come as no surprise, but civil society explicitly reentered political discourse during the struggle against totalitarianism in Eastern Europe. Some intellectuals there saw in civil society the solution to all their problems, and it became a rallying cry throughout the region after Poland's Solidarity movement invoked it. Although this did prompt many thinkers in the West to reconsider its applicability to their own societies, there were also endogenous forces propelling the civil society framework to prominence. On the left, the search was on for an alternative to a discredited socialism and an increasingly unviable welfare state. On the right, antistatist values were ascendant. On the ground, market-oriented policies alone were insufficient to address state failures; older forms of associational life seemed at risk; and new social movements and other private, voluntary activities began mobilizing previously passive citizens.

But what exactly do we mean by "civil society"? Because it touches on so many critical themes, "few social and political concepts have traveled so far in their life and changed their meaning so much" (Pelczynski 1988: 363), and even when they strive for rigor – which they rarely do – different contemporary thinkers stress different aspects, to say nothing of traditions, of the concept, making for ambiguity and outright confusion (Seligman 1992: ix). Of course, there is no one way in which civil society "should" be defined; the test of any definition is whether it illuminates a particular problem at hand. For our purposes, contributors to this volume gravitate around a conception of civil society as that sphere intermediate between family and state in which social actors pursue neither profit within the market nor power within the state. As defined here, civil society is occupied by associations – including economic actors such as employer associations and labor unions when they are active outside the market – and by a "public sphere" of institutions that encourage debate among private persons on matters of common concern (see Habermas 1989). Although such a definition rests squarely within the contemporary Western mainstream, most Japanese commentators take a less inclusive approach, focusing on civic and advocacy groups, private foundations and philanthropies, and research institutions. And that is one of the contributions of this volume: examining Japan's civil society from a broader perspective than has usually been the case.

The Historical and Cultural Specificity of Civil Society

From the perspective of 5,000 years of civilization, Jenö Szücs (1988: 295) aphorized, "For any sector of society to exist autonomously, independent of the state (even when functionally connected with it) is a rare exception. And exceptions are the luxury products of history." Rather than an inevitable and invariable concomitant of human existence, civil society was the result of a specific historical process. As Sheldon Garon writes in this volume, "the idea of 'civil society' is rooted in a time and a place." In the modern sense of the term, it first emerged in Europe on the basis of some fundamental institutions and cultural dispositions of Western civilization. The most important of these were the existence of several competing sources of authority and identity that were separate from the state – and one another (Eisenstadt 1995: 240–41). An autonomous legal system that distinguished between public and private spheres was one of the legacies of Rome, and the endless competition attendant on the removal of Rome's centralized authority penalized states for relying too heavily on sheer coercion vis-à-vis their populations (Wood 1990: 61; Hall 1998: 60–61). The independence of the church helped differentiate society from the state by separating the spiritual and ideological from the temporal and political (Szücs 1988: 300; Taylor 1990: 102), and the subsequent split in the Latin church further pluralized society. Medieval trading cities demonstrated a capacity for self-governance and defended such local control (Schmitter 1997: 255).

Feudalism bore an ambiguous relationship to civil society. On the one hand, fragmentation replaced old relations of states and subjects with new social ties of a contractual nature, and decentralization frustrated "descending" mechanisms of exercising power. Collective rights legitimated by custom extended to the lowest levels (Szücs 1988: 301, 302, 306; see also Taylor 1990: 102–3). On the other hand, the modern conception of civil society could not emerge without the corresponding emergence of the modern conception of the state as a separate entity, yet feudalism dispersed the modern state's functions throughout society and conferred a directly political character on institutions that are today regarded as socioeconomic.[1] The rise of absolutism provided European states with a corporate identity of their own (Wood 1990: 61), and with the rise of capitalism, the elements of civil society threw off what Marx characterized as "the political yoke."

In explaining the modern distinction between state and civil society, some theorists (e.g., Marx, Ellen Wood) emphasize the growth of capitalism; others (e.g., John Keane, Charles Taylor) portray it as a political development, a defense against the threat of despotism. In any event, the distinction took root in late eighteenth- and early nineteenth-century Europe. Because it developed in distinctively Western milieux, applying the civil society framework across cultures is controversial. Some commentators deny its applicability to non-Western societies altogether. "The current vogue [is] predicated on a fundamental ethnocentricity," complained Chris Hann (1996: 1). As Hann (ibid.: 10, 19–20) himself conceded, however, the idea of civil society exerts an obvious attraction to large numbers of people around the world, and it is not the unique product of the West. Let us examine these normative and analytical aspects of the civil society debate in turn.

In their zeal to defend other cultures, extreme relativists underestimate the extent to which those cultures have borrowed from abroad in the past and overestimate the extent to which they constitute harmonious unities in the present, thus denying their members the fruits of other societies (Keane 1998: 55–56). Defying abstract considerations of authenticity and universality, ideas and institutions are constantly spreading beyond their place of origin to take root elsewhere, where they may be reconceived in local terms (Bayart 1986: 109–10; Iokibe 1999: 57). Although Middle Eastern societies have been sensitive to Western influence, for example, civil society "has entered the discourse of the Arab world and become a central concept in current Arab debate over the direction of politics in the region. State officials use it to promote their projects of mobilization and 'modernization'; Islamists use it to angle for a legal share of public space; and independent activists and intellectuals use it to expand the boundaries of individual liberty" (Bellin 1995: 121). President Mohammad Khatami galvanized voters with his explicit calls for creation of a civil society in Iran. In another society wary of Western influence, civil society is "almost a mantra in Russian politics these days" (*New York Times*, June 22, 2000).

[1] What exactly constitutes "the modern state" is an enormous question in itself, of course. For a clear and concise introduction to the subject, see Poggi (1978).

As for analytical uses of the term, the (in)applicability of a concept such as civil society cannot be assumed a priori but must be determined in each individual case empirically (cf. Weber 1949: 90). The Western origins of the concept are thus irrelevant; applying it elsewhere is less an imposition of alien values than the posing of a set of research questions that may or may not prove illuminating (Norton 1995: 10). It is important to appreciate the historical specificity of civil society, to avoid treating it "as a static and transhistorical concept, supposedly generative of empirical generalizations about society-state relations across time and space" (Blaney and Pasha 1993: 5). Nevertheless, if the contemporary concept of civil society arose out of theorizing about the specific historical experience of the modern West, aspects of it can be found in other cultural milieux, whether as the result of indigenous developments or foreign influence. Although the spread of the concept outside the West has mobilized what might have remained "undeveloped possibilities" elsewhere (Weller 1998: 236, 242; see also Hefner 1998: 20), it is not necessary for other societies to Westernize to boast their own civil societies.

In other words, civil society is not a dichotomous variable, a phenomenon that is either wholly present or wholly absent (Gold 1990: 20). When defined broadly, as it is here, "civil society exists, even if in defensive or underground form, under all types of political regimes. . . . There are always uncaptured social groupings that enjoy a sphere of autonomy beyond the reach of the state" (Bratton 1994: 57; cf. Stepan 1988: 4; Gold 1990: 25; Carapico 1996). We proceed, then, on the assumption that in all but the most totalitarian of modern contexts, there is some kind of civil society that can be identified and compared cross-nationally.

Why Japan?

That said, Japan may not strike the casual observer as the most fertile ground for such an investigation. It is not a country that celebrates diversity. Even foreigners who know little else of the country are familiar with the proverb "the nail that sticks out gets hammered down" (*deru kugi wa utareru*). Moreover, state-centric ideas are deeply rooted. The word *okami*, which has long signified the government or authorities, literally means "those above." That a modernizing Japan had to coin new words for "society" and "public" is telling, and although it came to be translated as "public," the word *ōyake* originally referred to the house of the emperor and still has strong connotations of "governmental" (Deguchi 1999: 15, 19; Yoshida 1999: 26).[2] Neatly encapsulated by the maxims "sacrifice self in service to the public" (*messhi hōkō*) and "respect for authorities, contempt for the people" (*kanson minpi*), the traditional attitude (the attitude traditionally sustained by power holders, at least) called for the subordination of what were regarded

[2] On the subject of nomenclature, how to translate "civil society" itself is a subject of dispute among Japanese. Although the term *shimin shakai* (literally, "citizen society") was generally used in the past, the word *shimin* (citizen) carries so much ideological baggage that it is becoming common simply to transliterate the English word as *shibiru sosaeti*. Given its novelty and foreignness, this term is more neutral if less familiar.

as necessarily partial when not downright evil private considerations to public interests that only the bureaucracy could discern and act on. The public sphere was also impoverished by individual attention to immediate connections within one's in-group (*uchi*) rather than to more anonymous, collective interests.

In this respect, modernization brought fewer changes than might have been expected. Because it centralized state power and heightened officials' prestige, the Meiji Restoration of 1868 reduced what vigor private nonprofit activities had enjoyed during the preceding feudal Tokugawa period (Deguchi 2000: 18–19). Fukuzawa Yukichi (1835–1901), the preeminent intellectual of his age, refused to accept any government appointment precisely because he saw a pressing need to set an example of independence in a country whose citizens relied so heavily on the state (Iokibe 1999: 67–68). Prewar Japan was marked by a "failure to draw any clear line of demarcation between the public and private domains," asserted Maruyama Masao (1963: 6). The fact that the development of a modern state in Japan was prompted and guided in response to external necessity encouraged the assumption that "the state is a prior and self-justifying entity, sufficient in itself," and the external imposition of democracy after the Pacific War permitted that mentality to survive (Matsumoto 1978: 38, 36).

Even in the postwar period, when ministerial bureaucrats have retired to assume what are typically higher-ranking and more lucrative jobs outside government, they are still said to "descend from heaven" (*amakudari*). Jealously guarding their authority over the provision of public services, officials have regarded private associations as useful only to the extent that they cooperate with the government or perform functions insufficiently important for the state to shoulder. Even when nongovernmental organizations (NGOs) have gained recognition as service providers, they have commonly been slow to take on advocacy functions vis-à-vis the state. Independent and voluntary nonprofit activities have long been suspect, with Japanese often viewing NGOs as "exotic, unique, different, strange and bizarre entities" (Yamaoka 1999: 30).

Several of the contributors to this volume have previously emphasized how narrow is the sphere that lies outside state and market in Japan. Sheldon Garon (1997: xiv) has pointed to "a powerful pattern of governance in which the state has historically intervened to shape how ordinary Japanese thought and behaved – to an extent that would have been inconceivable in the United States and Britain, and would probably have strained the limits of statism in continental Europe." Because Japan's state and business have been inextricably joined since the beginning of the Meiji era, Helen Hardacre has argued (1991: 219), "both have shaped and molded public discourse on the public good in such a way that it is extremely difficult to discern the existence of a public sphere standing between the two. The scope for a public sphere in the classic, liberal sense, therefore, has throughout modern Japanese history been extremely limited, in addition to being dominated by marketplace issues."

Should we thus conclude that it would be unproductive to investigate Japan's civil society? On the contrary, these observations highlight how setting bounds to the state and market and freeing space for plurality – the foci of a civil society approach – are key issues for Japan, and they have been intensely and widely debated by Japanese themselves as well as by foreign scholars. In Japan, such debates flared during the Occupation (1945–52), a major goal of which was to establish and strengthen institutions operating outside the state; during a period of citizens' movements and popular protests in the 1960s and early 1970s; and during a period of renewed civic engagement that has continued unabated since the mid- to late 1980s (Bestor 1999: 2; cf. Deguchi 1999: 11). As a matter of fact, although it went unnoticed in the West, the contemporary revival of the language of civil society began *in Japan* during the second half of the 1960s with the work of such Marxists as Uchida Yoshihiko and Hirata Kiyoaki (Keane 1998: 12–14), of whom Andrew Barshay writes below.

There are many other theoretical justifications for an examination of civil society in Japan. Western theories require broad, cross-national testing to determine the scope of their applicability; "with its Western institutions but Eastern cultural background, Japan represents the perfect case of 'experimental' variation" (Broadbent 1998: 6). Recent research has emphasized the complementarity of state and civil society, and even Europeanists (e.g., Levy 1999) pay homage to the instructiveness of the Japanese example in this regard. Theories of social capital, which have provided such a stimulus to the study of civil society, lay at the heart of many analyses of Japanese politics long before that term came into vogue.

To apply concepts that are Western in origin is not to deny the distinctiveness of Japan, and, indeed, every contributor to this volume has something to say on that issue. Many observers have presumed that the development of civil society in Japan has been handicapped by what they regarded as an unusually strong state and that stereotype is not devoid of empirical support. In the aftermath of Aum Shinrikyō's attacks, for example, state monitoring of religion has tightened, undermining its position in Japan's civil society and effectively nullifying any capacity it had to restrain the state (Hardacre). Although the Internet has the potential to alter the situation, the mass media have frequently worked together with, or on behalf of, Japan's political core to delimit rather than augment the discursive realm (Freeman). The Japanese state has not only adopted an activist stance vis-à-vis civil society as a whole, it targets policies at specific groups and sectors (Pharr). On a micro level, the informal discretion enjoyed by Japanese bureaucrats permits them to advantage some associations at the expense of others (Estévez-Abe). Thus, state influence in Japan has served primarily to shape rather than suppress civil society, resulting in a plethora of small, local groups and a dearth of large, professionalized, independent organizations (Pekkanen). State policies accounted for both the way Japanese international development NGOs long lagged behind their Western counterparts and for the way they have boomed since the mid-1980s (Reimann).

Nevertheless, it would be a mistake to overemphasize state primacy. Although much of this volume explores the influence of the state on civil society in Japan, this is by no means to suggest that civil society should be treated as a dependent variable vis-à-vis the state. Max Weber (1952: 183) concluded his seminal investigation of the influence of the Protestant ethic on the spirit of capitalism with the following caveat: "It is, of course, not my aim to substitute for a one-sided materialistic [i.e., vulgar Marxist] an equally one-sided spiritualistic causal interpretation of culture and of history. Each is equally possible, but each, if it does not serve as the preparation, but as the conclusion of an investigation, accomplishes equally little in the interest of historical truth." Correspondingly, neither the accountability of Japan's state nor the voice of its civil society can be ignored. Portions of the state apparatus such as public prosecutors are actually more accountable in Japan than elsewhere (Johnson). Even in the extreme case of organizations originating from top-down directives of the Japanese state, they may succeed in winning independence over time by taking advantage of the countervailing leverage offered by competitive elections (Bullock). The bottom line is that the Japanese state's considerable capacity to manage society has rested on the active cooperation of groups in civil society (Garon).

If civil society is conceptualized as a sphere apart from the state and the market, its relationship with the latter is logically as important as its relationship to the former. Although the Western literature tends to be state-centric, postwar Japanese discussion of civil society has been inseparable from debates about the nature of Japanese capitalism (Barshay). The hegemony of corporate management and the integration of workers as members of corporate communities rather than as citizens of political society as a whole have prevented Japanese labor unions from becoming important actors in civil society (Suzuki). Japan's consumer movement has struggled not only to represent the interests of its constituency to state authorities, but also to educate individuals about their rights and responsibilities as consumers and citizens in order to build a consumer society that is independent of market as well as state control (Maclachlan).

What of the future? Civil society in Japan is expanding and becoming more pluralistic, gradually moving away from the predominance of business associations typical of a developmental state (Tsujinaka). Japanese society as a whole is moving from a security-based society in which individuals pursue cautious, commitment-forming strategies to a trust-based society in which individuals pursue more open, opportunity-seeking strategies (Yamagishi).

An examination of Japan's civil society has strong practical as well as theoretical justifications. Explorations of the role of civil society in governance are taking place around the world, and building civil society has joined the encouragement of democracy and the promotion of liberal capitalism as a basic policy objective shared by the United States and Japan in their dealings with the developing world. Only comparative study will permit in-depth analysis of the diverse factors stimulating and constraining the growth of civil society, and Japan's experience offers a useful reference for other countries (Yamamoto 1999: 8), particularly in East Asia, where Japan's demonstration effect is profound.

A better understanding of civil society in Japan can make an important contribution to international dialogue. As the history of U.S.-Japan relations has demonstrated time and again (Iriye 1967), Americans and Japanese continue to operate on the basis of distinct images of one another that color how they approach issues of common concern. When the subject has arisen, it is often presumed that Japan is a civil society laggard (e.g., Wolferen 1991; Carothers 1999: 23), but such criticism rarely proceeds from a systematic analysis that is put in historical and comparative perspective. As Gerald Curtis (1997: 141) observed, "In terms of traditions of self-rule and the existence of a multitude of voluntary organizations, Japan has always had a stronger civil society than neighboring countries (and a much stronger one than is often presumed to be the case, by both Japanese and foreigners)." Given the growing importance of the civil society framework as a guide for policy around the globe and the importance of Japan as an international actor, it is essential that the debate over civil society in Japan be well informed.[3]

The most compelling reason to study Japan's civil society, however, is that it has been burgeoning. Although the rest of this volume gathers a variety of evidence for – and against – this claim, it would not be out of place to touch on a few recent developments here.

Beginning with sectoral organizations rooted in key industries and followed by "policy-beneficiary" organizations concerned with the distribution of government resources and finally "value-promotion" organizations devoted to particular ideas or movements, interest groups proliferated in Japan over the first two decades of the postwar period (Muramatsu, Itō, and Tsujinaka 1986). Tsujinaka Yutaka (1996: 18) has found strong trends toward even greater participation and pluralization since then, with Japan's level of associational activity steadily catching up with America's (which has changed little). In 1960, Japan's density of nonprofit associations was only one-third that of the United States (11.1 associations per 100,000 people vs. 34.6). By 1991, however, Japan had reached a level more than 80 percent of America's (29.2 vs. 35.2). Although the density of employees in Japanese associations was only a little over half the U.S. figure in 1991, it had increased even more quickly than associational density over the previous three decades (3.3 times vs. 2.6 times), and that growth accelerated in the 1990s. Aggregate pluralization aside, the composition of the interest group sector has shifted as the dominance of business groups has weakened. A growing divergence of interests has hollowed out established federations of businesses (and labor unions), and increasing moderation among formerly ideological and confrontational groups has enhanced their access to the policy-making process and reduced the leverage of traditional interest groups.

The uneven distribution of resources may still favor established interest associations, but Tsujinaka (1996: 57) has found that newer, citizen-initiated movements enjoy a dynamism and mass appeal that the former lack. Because the citizens' or resident movements (*shimin* or *jūmin undō*) that mobilized large numbers of ordinarily apolitical Japanese from the 1960s through the early 1970s tended to

[3] Scholars are increasingly applying the civil society framework elsewhere in East Asia. See, e.g., Robert Weller's *Alternate Civilities: Democracy and Culture in China and Taiwan* (Boulder, Colo.: Westview Press, 2001) and Hagen Koo's *State and Society in Contemporary Korea* (Ithaca, N.Y.: Cornell University Press, 1993).

be locally based and limited to protesting against specific grievances, ameliorative government policies dampened their activity, and many disbanded once they achieved their immediate goals. Civic involvement experienced a resurgence in the mid- to late 1980s, however, and has grown substantially since then. Coinciding with a decline in confidence in government among virtually all the advanced industrial democracies (Pharr and Putnam 2000), the general public – and some leaders – in Japan have concluded that the state lacks the flexibility and resources to cope with increasingly complex socioeconomic issues, and more and more citizens have responded with their own initiatives.

Thanks in large part to exogenous developments, NGOs and nonprofit organizations (NPOs) have become household words in Japan.[4] In a watershed event, many Japanese got involved in helping Indochinese refugees in 1979, and NGOs gained visibility in the late 1980s, when many of the dramatic changes sweeping Japan were attributed to the country's internationalization (*kokusai-ka*). They have benefited from exposure to and cooperation with foreign organizations at home and abroad, and Japan's NGO movement gained new momentum thanks to a series of United Nations conferences held in the 1990s. Although they often regarded NGOs as interlopers in what should remain affairs of state, Japanese officials were faced with the reality of these organizations' playing a substantive role in shaping international treaties and with the international expectation that they, too, should include representatives of NGOs in their delegations and even subsidize their activities. The move away from patron-client relations that began in the government's treatment of internationally oriented organizations is now being extended to more and more domestic groups (Menju and Aoki 1995: 143–46; Yamamoto 1998: 131, 140, 151; Yamamoto 1999: 99–103).

Since the early 1970s, Japan has undergone continuous structural transformation. Increasing affluence and diversity have enhanced the ability of private groups to organize independent of the state and make demands on it, resulting in a qualitatively different type of political interaction. Japanese politics now has a "more competitive, strenuously negotiated character" (Allinson 1993: 48). As the grip of the nation-state and a system of production based on massive mobilizations of capital and labor weakens, Japan seems poised to move in the direction of the decentralization that characterized its history until the late nineteenth century, a decentralization that would reinforce civil society (Inoguchi 2000: 103, 105). But as Tsujinaka contends in this volume, the optimism of a pluralist analysis must be tempered by the greater caution of an institutionalist analysis. For all the growth that civil society has enjoyed in Japan, it still faces many obstacles, foremost among them a strict regulatory environment.

[4] In Japanese usage, these terms have narrower meanings than in English. Because they were the first organizations to adopt the label, Japanese tend to use "NGO" for groups that are active in international relations, especially civic groups involved in international development cooperation. They are thus distinguished from NPOs, by which Japanese mean less the totality of nonprofit organizations than *domestically* active civic groups, especially voluntary groups not incorporated as public-interest corporations (Wada 1999: 173, 181).

Japan's Strict Regulatory Environment

Japanese enjoy a high degree of freedom – in recent years, Freedom House (www.freedomhouse.org) has consistently rated their political and civil rights as (a high) 1 and 2, respectively, on its seven-point scale – but Japan may be the strictest of all advanced industrial democracies in regulating the incorporation of NGOs. Organizations must obtain the status of "legal person" (*hōjin*) to have legal standing. Although it is possible to operate without that status, groups lacking it cannot sign contracts, and that makes it impossible for them to do such things as open a bank account, own property or sign a lease for office space, undertake joint projects with the government, or even lease a photocopy machine (Pekkanen 2000b: 113). The lack of legal standing may also deprive organizations of social recognition they would otherwise win.

Although Article 21 of the Meiji Constitution guaranteed freedom of association, Article 33 of the Civil Code of 1896 required that all legal persons be formed in accordance with its regulations. And while Article 35 of the code provided for the establishment of for-profit organizations, rather than provide for a corresponding category of nonprofit organizations, Article 34 provided only for the much narrower category of "public-interest corporations" (*kōeki hōjin*). Specifically, "an incorporated association or foundation[5] relating to worship, religion, charity, science, art or otherwise relating to public interests and not having for its object the acquisition of gain may be made a juridical person subject to the permission of the competent authorities."

As Robert Pekkanen (2000b: 116–17) forcefully argues, "This creates a legal blind spot – most groups that are nonprofit but not in the 'public interest' had no legal basis whatsoever to form.... There was simply no legal category for these groups to exist in and, as a result, they were reduced to operating as informal, voluntary groups, or perhaps even becoming [limited liability] corporations."[6] Occupation pressure and a movement for revision of Japan's civil law in the early postwar period resulted in several reforms. Separate, less restrictive laws were enacted to regulate such specialized organizations as private school corporations (*gakkō hōjin*), social welfare corporations (*shakai fukushi hōjin*), religious corporations (*shūkyō hōjin*), and medical corporations (*iryō hōjin*), and governors were empowered to approve the incorporation of organizations that operated within the borders of a single prefecture. Otherwise, that part of the Civil Code regulating public-interest corporations remained unchanged into the 1990s.

The important points here are that a public-interest (or "civil-code") corporation had to operate for the public good and had to win the permission of the competent state authority to gain legal recognition. First, activity for "the public interest" was interpreted to mean for the benefit of society in general or of many and unspecified

[5] The difference between incorporated foundations (*zaidan hōjin*) and incorporated associations (*shadan hōjin*) is more legal than practical.

[6] On the basis of an examination of the framing of Japan's Civil Code, Pekkanen (2000b: 117) goes further to argue that "this disincorporation by categorization was deliberate."

persons. Activity for the benefit of specific groups was ipso facto regarded as for a private interest (Amemiya 1998: 64), and this legal interpretation actually narrowed over time. National ministries and prefectural governments reached an agreement in 1972 that only nonprofit organizations with clear, unambiguous, and direct public benefits were to be granted the status of public-interest corporation. Those corporations approved before 1972 retained their legal status, but so-called intermediate organizations (*chūkan hōjin*) such as business organizations, sports clubs, and alumni associations, which do not necessarily have public benefit among their primary objectives, no longer qualified for incorporation as public-interest corporations (Amenomori and Yamamoto 1998: 4). The incorporation of organizations that were set up for neither the public interest nor economic gain required passage of a special, separate law for that purpose. Second, "the competent authorities" who granted incorporation were normally officials of the ministry with jurisdiction over the field in which an organization was active. But because of a lack of explicit and standardized criteria, bureaucrats decided on a case-by-case basis at their own discretion whether to approve or reject applications for incorporated status, and groups whose activities cut across ministerial jurisdictions were in a special bind.

Unless the government itself took the lead, winning state approval as a public-interest corporation was a very difficult process. The Civil Code stipulated that successful applicants had to have "a sound financial basis," and government agencies generally interpreted that clause to require an endowment of at least ¥300 million (about $3 million). In addition, they had to have an annual budget of ¥30 million (about $300,000), an activity plan, and a board consisting of publicly respected individuals to be eligible for incorporation. Even when these demanding conditions were met, it normally took from several months to a year to explain the application to the appropriate ministry before it granted incorporation. Just as firms often hire retired bureaucrats to maintain relations with their government regulators, there was a trend for organizations to employ officials who could expedite the application process thanks to their ministerial connections, but that practice also had the potential to compromise an organization's independence. Once registered as a legal entity, an organization was then obliged to submit a budget and a plan of proposed activities before the start of each fiscal year and a financial report and description of its activities after the end of the year. These reports were closely scrutinized, and accounting procedures required adherence to rigid guidelines. A ministry could revoke incorporated status if, in its judgment, an organization failed to fulfill its requirements (Yamamoto 1999: 108; see also Menju and Aoki 1995: 150).

Such an exhaustive application process and such intrusive supervision discouraged organizations from registering. In contrast to the 1,140,000 groups to which the Internal Revenue Service had granted nonprofit status in the United States, only 26,089 Japanese groups had attained legal status as public-interest legal persons by the mid-1990s (Pekkanen 2000b: 113). As a result, unincorporated associations (*nin'i dantai*) greatly outnumber public-interest corporations. Positively encouraged by the state, community organizations are extremely numerous. Throughout the country, there are an estimated 275,000 local mutual-help organizations (*jichikai* or *chōnaikai*), 150,000 children's associations (*kodomokai*), and 130,000 clubs for the elderly (*rōjin kurabu*), as well as youth clubs (*seinendan*) and women's organizations (Amenomori and Yamamoto 1998: 12–13).[7] A survey (Economic Planning Agency 1997b) conducted at the end of 1996 turned up 85,786 nonprofit "citizen activity organizations" (*shimin katsudō dantai*) that undertook social activities on a continual and voluntary basis but lacked corporate status, and this category included many of Japan's most dynamic associations.

Unincorporated organizations labor under financial handicaps, however. Public-interest corporations are exempt from the corporate income tax and the taxation of interest income, and beyond a certain percentage, their business activities are taxed at a reduced rate.[8] Unincorporated organizations do not enjoy these abatements. As for contributions, "the treatment of individual and corporate donations to nonprofit organizations is uneven and seemingly arbitrary" (Yamamoto 1998: 124). Winning financial privileges is even more difficult than incorporating, and those privileges must be renewed every two years. As of 1996, contributions to a mere 3.4 percent of all public-interest corporations were tax deductible. Donations are eligible for different levels of tax deductibility depending on the status of the recipient organization. In the absence of a unified treatment for contributions, the Ministry of Finance can extend two designations of special tax status at its own discretion: "special public-interest-promoting corporation" (*tokutei kōeki zōshin hōjin*, or *tokuzō*) and "designated donation recipient" (*shitei kifu*). Most of the former are created by government agencies, staffed by seconded officials, and financed with state subsidies. Only recently was an organization free of government control and acting as something other than an auxiliary for the public sector granted the status of special public-interest-promoting corporation (Yamamoto 1998: 123, 134; 1999: 109). What tax incentives exist encourage corporate philanthropy more than citizen initiatives, and unincorporated organizations are altogether ineligible for tax-exempt contributions.

The severe restrictions on tax-deductible contributions make it difficult for some private organizations to maintain their autonomy vis-à-vis the state. Coming on the heels of strong national regulation (and Japan's unhappy experience with State Shintō) during the prewar and war years, Article 89 of the postwar constitution rendered private organizations ineligible for state funds: "No public money or other

[7] Inclusion of these organizations yields extremely high membership rates in Japan. Even in the late 1960s, before associational activity began to decline in the United States, 72 percent of Japanese belonged to some sort of private organization versus only 61 percent of Americans, and almost twice as many Japanese as Americans (59 percent vs. 30 percent) belonged to nonpoliticized organizations (Verba, Nie, and Kim 1978: 100–101). As Garon points out in Chapter 2, however, the extent to which these community organizations can be regarded as "private" is open to debate.

[8] Japan and the United States are opposites in this regard. In Japan, public-interest corporations do not gain tax exemption by means of a uniform process, but by virtue of being incorporated by the ministry with jurisdiction over their particular field. In the United States, on the other hand, tax-exempt status is determined solely by the Internal Revenue Service in compliance with laws that are not directly related to the granting of corporate status (Yamaoka 1999: 24).

property shall be expended or appropriated for the use, benefit or maintenance of any religious institution or association, or for any charitable, educational or benevolent enterprises not under the control of public authority." This stipulation was intended to establish a clear legal divide between the public and private sectors, freeing the latter from the former's control and interference. At the same time, however, Article 25 committed the state to promoting social welfare, and Article 89 was eventually reinterpreted to permit government support for private organizations that supplement public services under strict supervision.[9] Although the state is thus obliged to provide social services, private organizations are expected to supplement public services where necessary, and most social welfare corporations are heavily dependent on public support, which constitutes an average of 80 to 90 percent of their income. As a result, social welfare corporations may be private nonprofits from a legal perspective, but they operate as quasigovernmental organizations, subcontractors that are established to perform tasks entrusted to them by the national and local governments (Amenomori and Yamamoto 1998: 6; Pekkanen 2000b: 119).[10]

Social welfare corporations lie at one end of a spectrum: nearly all government subsidies flow to either health or social service programs, and private revenue in the form of fees, sales, and charges far outweighs government subsidies for every other type of organization (Yamamoto 1998: 126).[11] In 1995, public-sector payments accounted for 86.9 percent of the revenue of groups concerned with health, 71.6 percent of those concerned with social services, 37 percent of those concerned with development and housing, 27.2 percent of those concerned with civic issues, 26.5 percent of those concerned with the environment, 19.2 percent of those concerned with international affairs, 13.1 percent of those concerned with education, 6.9 percent of those concerned with culture and recreation, and 0.2 percent of professional associations (Yamauchi et al. 1999: 257). It should be pointed out, however, that a relatively small number of organizations receive a relatively large share of government subsidies, and the presumption is that these organizations enjoy a patron-client relationship with their ministerial sponsors (Yamamoto 1998: 127). Furthermore, most of the organizations that do not currently receive government subsidies wish they did. According to a comprehensive survey conducted in 1997 (Wada 1999: 178), 34.5 percent of citizens' groups had annual expenditures

[9] Although most public-interest corporations have resulted from private initiatives, they became associated with public services, and the word *kōeki* – public interest – came to have a connotation of *government* interest. Those bodies that do not substitute for the government have had to fight an uphill battle to prove that they do in fact represent private initiatives (Imata 2001).

[10] In contrast to this critical assessment, Inoguchi Takashi (2000b: 77, 84) maintains that nonprofit organizations started as local government affiliates are established "to create and maintain social space for civic engagement on the grass-roots level with resources made available on the non-profit principle. This constitutes one arm of local governments' empowerment policies that have been underway for the last two decades or so."

[11] Because of "the unusual private character of health care" found there, Lester Salamon and his colleagues (1999: 20–21; Yamauchi et al. 1999: 249–51) categorize the nonprofit sector of Japan (and the United States and the Netherlands) as "health-dominant."

under ¥300,000 ($3,000) and 21.2 percent under ¥100,000 ($1,000). Only 23 percent of the groups had full-time paid staff and fewer than 7 percent their own office. It is not surprising, then, that over 80 percent of these groups regarded government support as necessary.

The 1990s as a Watershed

Although there is no end to arguments over whether Japan is "really" changing, it is not much of an exaggeration to say that in the 1990s, Japan underwent "a massive political and economic transformation as has never been seen before in the post–World War II era . . . [and] the topic of civil society is at the core of the current debate about how to reinvigorate Japan politically and socially" (Imata 1999: 25). As noted above, political discontent has been spreading in Japan. Due to recurrent corruption scandals, the Liberal Democratic Party (LDP) was finally (if temporarily) thrown out after thirty-eight years in power in 1993, and as political turmoil continued, voter identification with parties plunged. Distrust of politicians was nothing new, however. What was new was plummeting confidence in the central bureaucracy. An officialdom that had long been credited with Japan's rapid climb to prosperity and prestige demonstrated inflexibility, incompetence, and occasionally downright malfeasance in a long string of failures that included the distribution of HIV-tainted blood, the bursting of a speculative bubble, the bailing out of housing loan companies (*jūsen*), systematic bill-padding and toleration of lavish entertaining at the taxpayers' expense, and inadequate management of several nuclear accidents. By the start of 2001, the confidence of Japanese in their Diet and national bureaucracy had fallen to 9 and 8 percent, respectively. The comparable figures for the United States were 63 and 51 percent (*Daily Japan Digest*, January 19, 2001).

The most dramatic demonstration of the limitations of the state and the growing prominence of civil society came in 1995. On January 17 of that year, the Great Hanshin-Awaji Earthquake struck the Kōbe-Ōsaka area, killing 6,430 people and forcing another 310,000 to evacuate their homes. The disparity between public and private responses to the disaster could not have been starker. Despite the devastation, jurisdictional disputes and red tape paralyzed the government's relief efforts; dismayed by the disorganization of the government's efforts, about 1.3 million volunteers converged on the affected area and spontaneously organized themselves. Apart from emergency relief on the heels of the earthquake, official financial assistance did not go beyond low-interest loans and the provision of public housing; private donations amounted to ¥160 billion ($1.6 billion). The disparity extended to incorporated versus unincorporated NGOs. Because the former require authorization for their activities from bureaucratic agencies that are themselves highly compartmentalized and turf-conscious, they could not escape the straitjacket of sectionalism. A group that sought permission from the Ministry of Foreign Affairs to establish an organization "to help the children of the world" was warned that activities in Kōbe would be inconsistent with its objective because "children of the world" refers to children overseas (Deguchi 1999: 12). Although that may have been an extreme case, few of the groups that assisted with the relief effort enjoyed any legal status (Yamamoto 1999: 109; Pekkanen 2000b: 114).

"In the face of that horrific disaster and that marvelous outpouring of voluntary effort, people began to imagine the potential of civil society in Japan" (Bestor 1999: 7). Celebrating an "NPO boom" and a "volunteer [*borantia*] revolution," the mass media repeatedly, graphically, and invidiously compared the public and private responses to the catastrophe.[12] The media had started paying attention to the importance of civil society prior to the earthquake, but Kōbe added an extra fillip to such coverage. The combined number of articles on NGOs and NPOs in the *Asahi Shinbun*, *Yomiuru Shinbun*, and *Mainichi Shinbun*, three major dailies, soared from 178 in 1990 to 1,455 in 1994. After the earthquake, the number jumped to 2,151 in 1995 and continued to rise, reaching 2,868 in 1997 (Yamamoto 1999: 101–2). This media attention raised people's consciousness about the contributions unincorporated groups could make, thereby replacing the antigovernment, antibusiness reputation they had inherited from the citizens' movements of the 1960s and 1970s with a much more favorable image (Deguchi 1999: 15).

Citizen groups and NPOs had established a coalition in 1994 to support new legislation that would enable private groups to incorporate outside the jurisdiction or influence of government agencies. Because the obvious lesson of Kōbe was that the existing legal framework hampered the growth of a vibrant civil society in Japan, pressure immediately mounted for such a change, and only ten days after the earthquake, the government itself spoke publicly of the need to redress the situation. With as many as eighteen government ministries and agencies rushing to respond, officials formed a liaison committee for volunteer groups. Although bureaucrats normally draft legislation in Japan, all the country's political parties submitted or amended legislation regarding private nonprofit groups between 1995 and 1998, and not only did citizen groups participate actively in the debate, but their lobbying substantively affected the contents of the bills under consideration (Pekkanen 2000b: 112). This level of dialogue among government officials, political parties, and citizens' groups over pending legislation was unprecedented.

After long and heated deliberations, the so-called NPO Law (*Tokutei hieiri katsudō sokushin hō*, or Law to Promote Specified Nonprofit Activities – some conservative politicians objected to the progressive connotations of its original name, the Law to Promote Citizen Activities) finally passed with the unanimous consent of the Diet on March 25, 1998, and went into effect in December of that year. Under the new law, incorporation is not much more than a formality for nonprofit groups that conduct most of their activities in one of twelve specified

[12] Even before the quake, the mass media had tarnished the image of incorporated public-interest corporations. They were portrayed as "one of the last sacred places where bureaucrats can do anything they want without being exposed to public scrutiny." Stories about *kōeki hōjin* typically focused on mismanagement, the improper use of funds, a lack of transparency, or some kind of collusion with government (Imata 2001).

fields.[13] Prefectural authorities (or, in the case of organizations operating in more than one prefecture, the Economic Planning Agency, which is now part of the Cabinet Office) have little choice but to grant corporate status to these organizations when they are established in conformance with the provisions of the law – it is no longer left to the discretion of bureaucrats in the national ministries – and they must normally decide on applications within four months, clearly explaining any decision to withhold certification.

Government officials fought tenaciously to retain their right to supervise private organizations, and some politicians, particularly within the ruling LDP, were skeptical of civil society's playing a greater role (Yamamoto 1999: 115). It did not help that 1995 was also the year Tokyo's subways were gassed by the cult Aum Shinrikyō, which was itself an incorporated nonprofit organization. Thus, the NPO Law failed to satisfy reformers' expectations, to say nothing of their hopes. One scholar (Deguchi 2000: 20) went so far as to charge that "the government's NPO measures still fall short of those provided by the Tokugawa government in the Edo period [1600–1868]." Rather than clarifying the status of citizens' groups in general by amending the Civil Code to provide for organizations that are neither profit-making nor public-interest bodies, the law only facilitated the operation of a fraction of those groups by slapping a complicated patchwork of provisions onto the inadequate, preexisting legal framework (Deguchi 1999: 16).

Fearing tax evasion and a diminution of their power to allocate resources, bureaucrats adamantly opposed the granting of tax deductibility for contributions to NPOs (Yamamoto 1999: 110). The NPO Law offered no tax privileges, but it did provide for a review of the issue within three years of the time it went into effect, and the government finally began to permit the deductibility of contributions to "approved specified nonprofit corporations" (*nintei NPO hōjin*) in 2001.[14] Although this reform represents a big symbolic step, approval by the National Tax Administration is so difficult to win that most NPOs will not benefit from these exemptions (Kuroda Kaori, personal communication). As of April 2002, a total of eleven organizations had applied for the new status, and only five out of a

13 The law explicitly listed activities for the promotion of health, medical, and welfare services; the promotion of social education; the promotion of community building; the promotion of culture, arts, or sports; the preservation of the natural environment; disaster relief; regional security; the protection of human rights or promotion of peace; international cooperation; building a participatory society that treats both sexes equally; the promotion of sound rearing of children; and communication, advice, or assistance for organizations that perform any of these activities.

14 Once the National Tax Administration Agency approves a specified nonprofit organization: (1) individual donors may deduct contributions of up to 25 percent of their annual incomes, minus ¥10,000; (2) apart from the amount allowable for general contributions, the deductibility of corporate contributions is computed in accordance with the formula: half of the sum of 0.25 percent of capital plus 2.5 percent of income; and (3) when individuals contribute inheritances, those donations are excluded from calculations of inheritance tax. See *Nintei NPO hōjin seido no tebiki* [A Guide to the System of Approved Specified Nonprofit Corporations] at the National Tax Administration's website, www.nta.go.jp/category/npo/npo.htm, and the NPO C's website, www.npoweb.gr.jp/topic02.html.

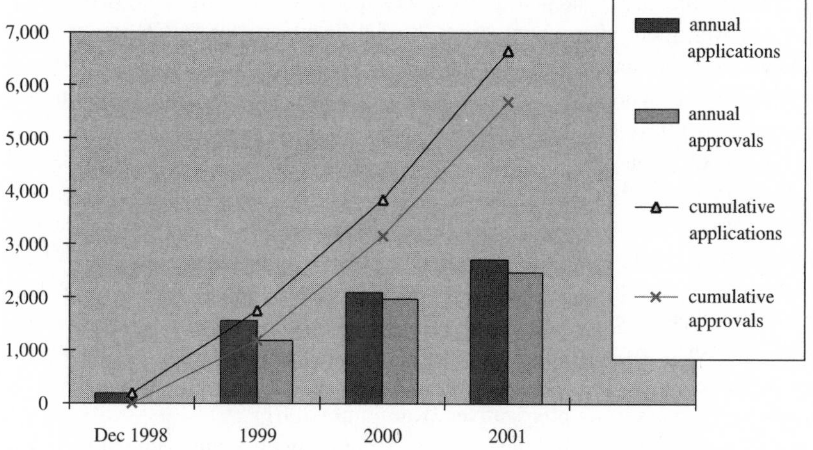

Figure I.1 The incorporation of nongovernmental organizations under the NPO Law. *Source:* Cabinet Office website (www5.cao.go.jp/j-j/npo/history.txt), accessed February 22, 2002.

universe of 6,700 organizations – 0.075 percent – had been certified (Matsubara 2002: 2–3). The Diet was expected to reconsider and perhaps ease the law in 2002.

Pekkanen (2000b) is hopeful that the NPO Law represents a milestone. With its citizen group lobbying, Diet member bills, and devolution of authority to prefectural officials, passage of the law may erode central bureaucratic decision making. It will enable thousands upon thousands of organizations to win legal status without subjecting themselves to stifling state regulation. By the end of 2001, some 6,547 organizations had applied, and 5,625 of those organizations had already been certified (see Fig. I.1). "Perhaps most importantly," Pekkanen (2000b: 112) concludes, "the law legitimates a new kind of social group and, by implication, a shift in the state-society power balance." The NPO Law undermines the idea that the state has a monopoly over matters bearing on the public interest even as it confers on nonprofit activities the official imprimatur that has so long been necessary and lacking (Deguchi 2000: 19–20). Less well-established groups in particular can gain quick recognition by incorporating under the new law, and Japanese are also more likely to acknowledge the many groups that do *not* seek legal status (Yamaoka 1999: 31).

What does the future hold? There is no question that many bureaucrats and conservative politicians are learning to talk the talk. Although the idea first arose in deliberations among international NGOs in the early 1990s, the proposal to proclaim 2001 the International Year of Volunteers (IYV) emerged at a U.N. policy forum held in Japan in 1996, it was the Japanese government's proposal that was put on the U.N. agenda in 1997, and Japan was the first country to establish an IYV national committee in 1999 (see the IYV website at www.iyv.org). The

G-8 Summit that Japan hosted in 2000 was the first to include NGOs formally, and the government even appointed a special "Ambassador in Charge of Civil Society" (*shibiru sosaeti tantō taishi*) for the occasion (Kim Reimann, personal communication). The LDP's Foreign Policy Council proposed the creation of a permanent "Ambassador in Charge of NGOs" in April 2002.

Even an exception proves the rule: when an influential LDP politician pressured the Ministry of Foreign Affairs in January 2002 to bar two Japanese NGOs from an international conference held in Tokyo on the grounds that their leader had publicly criticized the government, a great hue and cry followed. The prime minister reversed the decision, and the politician came under scathing attacks. National actors aside, assertive local governments collaborated with civil society organizations in the 1990s to challenge the central government even on the kinds of national security issues (e.g., U.S. military bases, nuclear ship visits) over which the state is most eager to assert its prerogatives (Kamimura 2001).

Are state actors sincerely interested in encouraging civic engagement and civil society organizations as positive ends in themselves or solely as inexpensive means for delegating governmental responsibilities and quieting their critics? Time will tell, but Patricia Maclachlan (2000: 10, 27–28) reminds us that the NPO Law was only one of several pieces of legislation passed in the 1990s that have the potential to rework relations between state and civil society in Japan. Other examples of laws initiated by and for average citizens include the Administrative Procedures Law (1993), the Products Liability Law (1994), and the revised Code of Civil Procedure (1996). The Information Disclosure Law (1999) is especially noteworthy for enhancing government transparency and accountability. Although it made no mention of citizens' right to know, it did entrench their rights to request information from the national government and to seek redress through the judicial system when information is refused.

Even if the Japanese state is (hesitantly and grudgingly) opening up space for civil society, will nonstate actors step in to fill this opening? Regarding the so-called volunteer revolution, for example, the evidence is ambiguous. On the one hand, Japan ranked lowest among all the developed countries included in a 1996 study of the subject (Atoda, Amenomori, and Ohta 1998: 108; cf. Yamauchi et al. 1999: 248), and there was unquestionably an element of faddish romanticization to volunteerism that faded with Kōbe's return to normalcy. Moreover, in the provision of social services, at least, the state is "highly involved" in Japanese voluntarism, Mary Alice Pickert (1999) cautions us: "The central government defines the boundaries of volunteer activities, the scope of their involvement, and the nature of their work environment through regulations and guidelines. . . . A volunteer in Japan is someone who is unpaid, not necessarily someone who is independent from the state." On the other hand, the number of volunteers more than tripled between 1980 and 1997 (rising from 1.6 to 5.5 million); two 1997 surveys revealed that 21.5 percent of all adults and 40.7 percent of college students had engaged in volunteer activities; and 270,000 people offered their help when thousands of tons of crude oil leaked from a Russian tanker off the Japanese coast that year (Sōrifu 1998: 608, 567; Yamauchi 1999: 123; Yoshida 1999: 42).

The evidence for Japanese participation in international NGOs (INGOs) is similarly ambiguous, John Boli (1999: 100–103) found. When countries are ranked by the total number of INGOs to which their citizens belonged in 1997, Japan comes in at seventeenth despite its large population and high level of economic development (the United States comes in at thirteenth). Japan not only ranks behind leaders France, Germany, and Britain, which might not be surprising given the depth of European regionalism, but also behind all the small West European democracies, including Norway, whose population is less than one-fortieth of Japan's. On the other hand, however, Japan's ranking by this measure has been stable since 1960, so Japanese engagement in INGOs has risen as fast as elsewhere, which is to say extremely rapidly. Although Japan ranks eighteenth, below all the other advanced industrial democracies, in the number of INGO headquarters, it ranks ninth in the number of regional offices. Finally, "we should bear in mind that Japan is clearly the most prominent Asian country in all types of INGO involvement, . . . and by good measure" (Boli 1999: 103).

Whatever we conclude from this conflicting evidence, one of the primary messages of this volume is that the spotlight now focused on voluntarism, NPOs, and INGOs should not blind us to the continuing relevance of preexisting civil society organizations such as religious bodies, social welfare corporations, farmer and consumer cooperatives, and the like. Victoria Bestor (1999: 7–8) offers the most sanguine interpretation of the current situation. "What is happening is a reimagination of civil society. . . . Through the popular media and other means civil society is being reimagined into an indigenous Japanese concept to bring about changes that are barely being considered by increasingly marginalized bureaucrats, elected leaders, and corporate elites. This reimagination is carving out newly legitimate roles for a true civil sector in Japan." The degree to which this "reimagination of civil society" is realized will determine the face of twenty-first-century Japan.

I
CONTEXT

1

What *Is* Civil Society?

Frank Schwartz

Salvador Giner (1985: 254) wrote of civil society that "the imprecision of the notions used may perhaps be more symptomatic of the object described by them than a reflection of carelessness on the part of its interpreters. In stark contrast to the clearly defined boundaries of its 'opposite' entity, the state, those of civil society must always remain unclear. For the state, demarcation is all, whereas for civil society ambiguity – the ambiguity that stems from a certain kind of freedom – is all." I disagree. Many contemporary commentators define civil society in determinedly idiosyncratic ways. The boundaries of the state are anything but clear. And neither is it clear why the concept of civil society must remain ambiguous. It *is* notoriously difficult to define, however.

John Keane has written eloquently of this difficulty. "Civil society has no natural innocence; it has no single or eternally fixed form," he observes (1988a: 14; cf. Harbeson 1994: 23), and even when investigations focus on the present alone, "modern civil societies have comprised a constellation of juxtaposed and changing elements that resist reduction to a common denominator, an essential core or generative first principle" (1988b: 19). The very concept of civil society is contested, and the problem has only worsened over time: "The 'language' of civil society . . . increasingly speaks in tongues, in accordance with different rules of grammar and conflicting vocabularies" (1998: 52). This confusion has led some scholars (e.g., Honneth 1993; Kumar 1993) to question the usefulness of the term. The answer, though, is not to discard it, but to clarify it and formulate it in such a way that it illuminates a specific problem at hand.

Although there is no unanimity among the contributors to this volume, we did arrive at what might be called a "median" definition of civil society. Whether individual authors take a somewhat more or less restrictive view, for our purposes, we gravitate around a conception of civil society as that sphere intermediate between family and state in which social actors pursue neither profit within the market nor power within the state. Rather than defending that particular formula here – readers of this volume will judge its usefulness for themselves – this chapter situates that definition among the welter of meanings other contemporary Western authors have assigned to civil society.

Contemporary Uses of the Term

Although some authors regard it as a "package deal" (Hall 1995: 2), civil society can be understood in several complementary yet distinct ways. Adam Seligman (1992: 201; cf. Keane 1988b), for example, distinguishes among political uses of civil society as a slogan, normative uses of the term as a vision of the good life, and social scientific uses as an analytical concept to describe or explain social phenomena.

Although not unimportant, political uses of the term are of least concern to us here. Simply to list a few examples, it was opponents of despotism who initiated the modern debate about civil society in the late eighteenth century. Nineteenth-century socialists aimed at – and twentieth-century communists nearly succeeded in – abolishing civil society as an autonomous sphere because of the capitalist connotations it held for them. In recent years, on the other hand, Western neo-conservatives and East European radicals alike have raised the banner of civil society to justify the unleashing of market forces. Orthodox Marxists deplore today's civil society debate for downplaying what they take to be the totalizing logic of capitalism, while postmodernists join it in order to disaggregate society along the lines of personal identity. Westerners call for the cultivation of civil society as a prerequisite for democratization, but Third World elites smell an imperialist project of questionable appropriateness to their countries (Bellin 1995: 120–21). State actors themselves have taken to extolling civil society actors as vehicles for the devolution of governmental functions and the reduction of state expenditures. Because each of these projects advances or attacks a different aspect of civil society, political use of the term tends to reduce its determinacy. Sometimes, that result is intentional. Whether in the eighteenth-century battle against absolutism or the twentieth-century battle against totalitarianism, there was a practical advantage to vagueness: the broader the concept of civil society, the broader the swath of society that might be rallied (Honneth 1993: 19; Alexander 1997: 126).

I must also be brief in illustrating normative uses of civil society. Seligman (1995: 205) himself declares that "the tradition of civil society is . . . first and foremost an ethical edifice" that has wrestled with modernity's problematic relation between public and private. Finding democratic, socialist, capitalist, and nationalist accounts of the good life lacking, Michael Walzer (1991: 304) defends civil society as a corrective to these ideologies because its inhabitants are *simultaneously* citizens, producers, consumers, members of a nation – and much else besides. "The projects have to be relativized and brought together, and the place to do that is in civil society, the setting of settings, where each can find the partial fulfillment that is all it deserves. . . . Civil society is a project of projects" that provides the testing ground for all versions of the good. In a similar vein, Keane (1998: 53) provides a "post-foundationalist" justification for civil society that "recognizes, and actively reinforces respect for, the multiplicity of often incommensurable normative codes and forms of contemporary social life."

Social scientists typically use the term "civil society" analytically. Víctor Pérez-Díaz (1995: 81; cf. 1993: 55) advocates an ideal type whose expansive multidimensionality helps structure this account. After acknowledging that it is "interconnected with some key *cultural dispositions*," he defines the "institutional core" of civil society as "a *government which is limited* and accountable and operates under the rule of law; a *market economy* (implying a regime of private property); an array of free, voluntary *associations* . . . ; and a *sphere of free public debate*. At the same time, real, historical civil societies have always been specific *nations* . . ." (emphasis added). In addition to exploiting the concept's rich connotations, the advantage of this broad ideal type for Pérez-Díaz (1998: 212–13) is its emphasis on the mutual dependence of its components; his premise is that "its different parts tend to fit together." Precisely because they deny the existence of systemic links between these "parts," other theorists defend narrower understandings of civil society. At the opposite end of the spectrum, Jeffrey Alexander (1997: 128), for example, limits civil society to "the sphere of universalizing social solidarity." Having a logic, interests, and discourses of its own, he argues, it should be differentiated not only from the state and market, but also from the spheres of religion, science, and so on. Boundary relations are marked by "destructive intrusions" that distort and compromise these discrete spheres as well as by "facilitating inputs" (Alexander 1998).

Proposed Boundaries

I begin with the nation and discuss increasingly circumscribed frontiers assigned to civil society on the basis of Pérez-Díaz's ideal type.

A Nation

Although it is possible to point to stateless nations (e.g., Scotland) and nationless (e.g., Prussia) or multinational (e.g., the Soviet Union) states, nineteenth-century nationalism identified the two in the nation-state (Bryant 1995: 139). To the extent it instills people with a sense of belonging and a security in themselves and each other, nationalism can encourage the toleration of diversity. To the extent it sharply sets off Self and Other, it can also lead to the repression of internal differences, let alone antagonism toward foreign rivals (Keane 1998: 87, 97). Because of its ambiguous and variable nature, nationalism has a complicated relationship to civil society.

Civil society and the nation began as allies. Nationality provided the cohesion that might otherwise have been lacking in nascent civil societies; it enhanced the ability of individuals to combine into effective institutions (Shils 1991: 7; Gellner 1995: 43–45). Both ideas served as rallying cries of early modern assertions of popular sovereignty. But if popular sovereignty is compatible with civil society in its assertion that the people have an identity and purposes outside any political structure, this notion of a people's prepolitical identity took a much more powerful form in the nation than in civil society (Taylor 1990: 111).

Given that nations and nationalism can be conceived of in various ways, Christopher Bryant (1995) contends that national society need not be the enemy of civil society. He distinguishes between a "civic nation," which integrates disparate populations into an association of human beings living in a common territory under the same government and laws, and an "ethnic nation," which seeks to bring together presumed kinsmen into an organic unity. Although even ethnic nations can and do develop one, civil society is aligned with civic nations insofar as it is conceived of as inclusive, he claims. It may not be that simple. Civic and ethnic nations can be distinguished in theory, but they tend to be entangled in fact, and the twentieth century witnessed the repeated repression of civil society in the name of the popular will as embodied in the nation (or proletariat). "A strange and horrifying reversal has taken place, whereby an idea whose roots lie in a pre-political conception of society now can justify the total subjection of life to an enterprise of political transformation. And in less spectacular form, the power of the state has often been enhanced by its self-identification as the instrument of the national will" (Taylor 1990: 113).

Cultural Dispositions

Among other things, Shmuel Eisenstadt (1995: 240) enumerated as cultural influences on the structure of civil society

> the major symbols of collective identity, especially the relative importance of primordial (tribal, ethnic, national), religious, and ideological components among those symbols; the prevailing conceptions of the arena of political action, the scope of the state, the nature of statehood, and the desirable relationship between state and society; the conception of public authority and accountability prevailing in the principal sectors of society; the place of law in political discourse and activity; the concept and practice of citizenship. . . .

"Prevailing conceptions" aside, subcultures and alternative discourses contribute to the autonomy and pluralism that are essential to civil society (cf. Fraser 1992: 121–28).

Seligman sharply differentiates between the civil society conception of the moral order and that of the civic virtue tradition. In the latter, morality "is less a private attribute and more a public or communal enterprise. It is realized by the active and continual participation of collective members in communal affairs . . . " (Seligman 1995: 203–4; cf. Taylor 1989). In this vision, because it is the community itself that is moral, the relationship of the member to the whole is as important as possible, that relationship should be totally unmediated, and "private interests" and "partial associations" are condemned. In the civil society tradition, on the other hand, virtue is a private matter for morally autonomous individuals who can legitimately seek to realize their own ideas of the good life outside the public arena.[1]

In addition to autonomy and pluralism, civil society has been linked to such specific values as participation, publicity, solidarity, toleration, generalized social trust, voluntarism, and, of course, civility. It is not physical violence, but our ability to live together in peace that requires explanation, and Norbert Elias (1978) attributes it to a centuries-long "civilizing process." The state formation that began in the sixteenth-century West required would-be sovereigns to disarm competitors by centralizing power resources and creating a monopoly of force within a given territory. As a result, he argues, subjects internalized stricter yet more temperate standards of conduct and sentiment as self-restraints. If internal pacification and the concentration of the means of violence formerly functioned to the benefit of its controllers – and still permit mass cruelty – the balance of power has now shifted in at least a few states to the advantage of those whom they rule (Elias 1988: 180).

A Limited State

Harking back to the philosophers of the Scottish Enlightenment, Pérez-Díaz includes limited government as a *component* of civil society, but the vast majority of commentators today consider it a *prerequisite* of civil society that lies outside it.[2] Granted, state activism over the last century has resulted in both a "state-ification of society" and a "societalization of the state" (Habermas 1989: 142). Franz-Xaver Kaufmann (1991: 158–59) goes so far as to assert that, given their growing interdependence, "the old distinctions of 'state' and 'society' or of 'public' and 'private' as *separate domains* is meaningless. . . . 'Public' and 'private' are not separate domains, but *distinct perspectives* that apply in various mixtures to the social, economic, and political reality" (emphasis in the original). Nevertheless, the interpenetration of state and society has not rendered the analytical distinction between the two obsolete.

The recent history of Eastern Europe colors a great deal of thinking about civil society, and not always to advantage. Whatever the differences within Poland's democratic opposition, Andrew Arato (1981: 24) famously observed during the early heyday of Solidarity that "one point unites them all: the viewpoint of civil society against the state." Because communism constituted a "Caesaro-papist-mammonist" regime that "fused the political, ideological and productive hierarchies into one single unified *nomenklatura*" (Gellner 1991: 495), a head-on confrontation with the state would have been suicidal. The opposition thus turned its

[1] Rather than opposing the civic virtue to the civil society tradition, Kai Nielsen (1995) interprets the former's argument to be that *civil society itself* would not be viable without a commonly recognized idea of the good life.

[2] Jonah Levy (1999: 329–30), on the other hand, argues that independently elected *local* governments merit inclusion in civil society when they exist apart from the central state and serve to disperse state power, bringing it within the reach of ordinary citizens.

back on the state in an attempt to build a civil society that aspired to be a "parallel society." Although useful as a slogan, so adversarial a conception has encouraged many people in the West as well as the East to picture the relationship in simplistic, Manichaean terms: state bad, civil society good (Kumar 1993: 386–88; White 1994: 376–77; Keane 1998: 79).[3]

Civil society cannot be understood in isolation, but it must be understood *in relation* to the state, not *in opposition* to it. And the nature of that relationship must be assessed empirically rather than presumed on the basis of theory. It can be engaged as well as disengaged, collaborative as well as conflictual (Bratton 1989: 418), collusive (i.e., corrupt) as well as cooptative. Put differently, interaction between the two need not be a zero-sum game: it can be reciprocal, whether positive- or negative-sum (Stepan 1985: 318). Although there are cases, such as the emergence of Solidarity, in which civil society's gain is the state's loss, given their interdependence, it is far more common for strength (or weakness) in one to be associated with strength (or weakness) in the other (Putnam et al. 1993: 176; Keane 1998: 26, 67–68).[4] It is a truism that civil society and the state must be protected from one another, but neither can function effectively without the countervailing force and support provided by the other.

Totalitarianism is only a temporary option. "No state can survive for long if it is wholly alienated from civil society. It cannot outlast its own coercive machinery," Walzer (1991: 301) cautions. "The production and reproduction of loyalty, civility, political competence, and trust in authority are never the work of the state alone, and the effort to go it alone . . . is doomed to failure." State capacity is enhanced by linkages to private actors, not isolation from them (Evans 1992; Levy 1999). Only a state that is immersed in civil society can devise policies that respond to problems perceived by private actors, have those policies regarded as legitimate, and rely on nonstate actors for help with implementation.

As Hobbes observed centuries ago, anarchism is not even a temporary option. "Civil society, far from acting as a substitute for the state, is integrally tied to its fortunes" (Chazan 1992: 304). Civil society generates inequalities and conflicts that only the state can mediate and ameliorate. On a more mundane level, it depends on the state for certain preconditions of its existence like political order, an adequate physical infrastructure, and essential services (Bratton 1989: 427–28). Not least among these services is a reliable legal system. On the one hand, the autonomy of civil society is enhanced by the state's respecting the rule of law, guaranteeing those freedoms (e.g., of association) that facilitate its operation, and establishing a clear and nurturing regulatory framework for extragovernmental organizations. On the other hand, the autonomy of civil society actors is limited by the necessity

[3] Eastern Europeans and students of the region were not alone in assuming that the relationship between civil society and the state is necessarily antagonistic, of course. The Africanist Jean-François Bayart (1986: 117), for example, insisted that "civil society exists only in so far as there is a self-consciousness of its existence and of its opposition to the state."

[4] Attention to the *strength* of civil society must not obscure the importance of its *composition*. Actual existing civil societies are diverse, and this heterogeneity cannot help but affect their nature and influence (Bermeo 2000: 237–38).

that they, too, respect the rule of law, and they daily look to the state to protect private property, enforce contracts, adjudicate disputes, and the like (Shils 1991: 9, 15). Although social capital is typically regarded as conducive to good governance (e.g., Putnam et al. 1993; Putnam 2000), the state itself can serve as a source of social capital (Levi 1996: 49–50; Tarrow 1996: 395–96).

Evidence of the state's ability to empower as well as tolerate or make room for civil society leads Jonah Levy (1999: 8, 295) to defend the possibility of voluntarism against the determinism attributed to Robert Putnam (1993). "Look not simply to the legacies of the past but also to the politics of the present," he writes:

> (1) societal and local institutions have been organized, reconstructed, and redirected far more frequently and in far less time than prevailing depictions of civil society would deem possible; (2) by and large, such transformations have been the product not of state withdrawal but on the contrary, of repeated, aggressive projections of state power . . . ; (3) political considerations have figured prominently in the capacity and willingness of state authorities to provide the necessary intervention.

Of course, *dirigiste* policies can damage civil society, and any direct linkage to the state (e.g., explicit state sanction, private-public partnerships, financial assistance) carries a risk of dependency and decreased organizational autonomy (Hadenius and Uggla 1996: 1634; Bermeo 2000: 243), but deliberate state intervention to strengthen societal and local institutions is not only possible, it is often necessary (cf. Schmitter 1997: 248–49, 254; Carothers 1999: 26–27).

It is important to note that this discussion has focused on a *limited state* as a precondition of civil society and not on *democracy*. Because it is sometimes defined so loosely, critics (e.g., Seligman 1992: 203; Kumar 1993: 391) charge that the concept of civil society as a type of institutional order is unnecessary given the more familiar ideas of democracy, liberalism, constitutionalism, and citizenship. Civil society complements these ideas without being subsumed into them (Bryant 1993: 399). It has a greater need for what T. H. Marshall (1977: 78) labeled civil rights – "liberty of person, freedom of speech, thought and faith, the right to own property and to conclude valid contracts, and the right to justice" – than for a panoply of political rights, let alone social rights. If civil society were to be equated with full-blown democracy, the category's applicability would be limited to little more than a sparse set of present-day advanced industrial countries.

Jean-François Bayart (1986: 118; cf. Ehrenberg 1999: 241; Trentmann 2000: 15–16) recognized that "there is no teleological virtue in the notion of civil society. The advance of a civil society which does not necessarily contain the democratic ideal does not in itself ensure the democratisation of the political system." Depending on the circumstances, different elements of civil society will fight for (different versions of) democracy, remain politically inactive, tolerate authoritarian rule, or positively support it (White 1994: 380). Thus, democracy is only one possible outcome of emergent civil societies (Schmitter 1997: 242; Keane 1998: 40), and they are sometimes "more the beneficiary than the wrecking ball" of democratization

(Norton 1995: 7; cf. Kumar 1993: 387–88). They can also benefit from processes of political liberalization that fall well short of democracy. Regimes can, and often do, limit the arbitrary exercise of power, permit associations, and open outlets for the free expression of opinion without welcoming popular participation in political life and staging freely contested elections that determine who governs (Stepan 1988: 6; Norton 1995: 5). Conversely, elites can turn to formal democracy to preempt and demobilize civil society. The electoral competition of political parties normally helps protect civil society from encroachment by the state. Writing of the rocky transition to democracy in Eastern Europe, however, Arato (1990: 31) warns that "the move to electoral parties with their less intense, more inclusive, more abstract form of political identification as well as lower degree of direct participation tends to devalue and replace movements and associations with their more particular, but also more intense and participatory forms of organization."

Drawing on the rise of Nazism, Sheri Berman (1997) attacks the easy identification of civil society with democracy head-on. Depending on the political context, she contends, there can even be an *inverse* relationship between the two. Associational life flourished in Weimar Germany, and many of those organizations were horizontally organized and civic-minded. Nevertheless, "because weak national political institutions reinforced social cleavages instead of helping to narrow them, . . . associational activity generally occurred within rather than across group lines. Under these circumstances, associational life served not to integrate citizens into the political system, as neo-Tocquevilleans would predict, but rather to divide them further or mobilize them outside – and often against – the existing political regime" (ibid.: 411).[5] Although participation in civil society organizations provided individuals with political and social skills, linked them together, and lowered barriers to collective action, the Nazis succeeded in turning those consequences to antidemocratic ends. Even in established regimes with strong political institutions, many commentators (e.g., Crozier, Huntington, and Watanuki 1975; Olson 1982; Rauch 1994; Carothers 1999) have cautioned, the proliferation of particularistic interest groups can undermine democratic governability.

All that said, however, civil society is "the icon of the global trend of democratization" (Norton 1995: 7–8), and the two have an elective affinity: democracy is the form of government most nurturing of civil society, and a vibrant civil society is indispensable to a vital democracy (e.g., Diamond 1999: 239–50).

A Market Economy

Reinhard Bendix (Bendix, Bendix, and Furniss 1987: 14; cf. Alexander 1997: 126) was not alone in postulating that "families are one cornerstone of civil society."

[5] Putnam, who helped revive interest in the role played by voluntary associations in sustaining democracy, has come to emphasize the distinction between "bonding" and "bridging" forms of social capital out of just such considerations. While the former are "inward looking and tend to reinforce exclusive identities and homogeneous groups," the latter are "outward looking and encompass people across diverse social cleavages" (Putnam 2000: 22).

It has been the convention since Hegel, however, to exclude households and to situate civil society between kin groups and the state. A far more contentious issue is whether the market economy should be included.[6] Marx, of course, *reduced* civil society to the market, and many non-Marxist theorists (e.g., Keane, Pérez-Díaz) continue to regard the latter as an important component of the former.

Civil society is constituted by economic as well as political processes: the market economy provides the material basis for independence from the state. Historically, the emergence of an autonomous economy was an essential precondition for the conceptual differentiation of civil society from the state. For the early modern thinkers who championed civil society, it was the rise of self-regulating markets that conclusively demonstrated the possibility, even the necessity, for certain spheres to organize themselves apart from the state (Calhoun 1993: 270–71; Varty 1998: 29). Those thinkers and their modern followers (e.g., Friedrich Hayek, Milton Friedman) believed – and it remains to be disproved – that a free market is as necessary as free association to narrow the bounds of state authority (Pérez-Díaz 1995: 92).[7] Adam Ferguson pointed out in the eighteenth century that institutions such as the rule of law are, in themselves, insufficient defenses of liberty (Varty 1998: 46); more than just a bulwark against state encroachment, private property offers a means for citizens to sanction an overweaning state. Dating back to classical antiquity, the evolution of concepts of civil society "has been from the beginning bound up with the development of private property as a distinct and autonomous locus of social power" (Wood 1990: 61), and the birth of indigenous business classes independent of the state often strengthens emerging civil societies in Third World countries today (Bayart 1986: 116). The process of marketization drives associational development. On the positive side, the state's withdrawal from a direct role in economic life decentralizes resources, making them more widely available for associational life. On the negative side, marketization exacerbates fears and conflicts that spur people to organize (Bermeo 2000: 250).

Nevertheless, the most influential twentieth-century theorists of civil society excluded the market economy from their definitions. Antonio Gramsci conceived of civil society as a set of cultural institutions (in the broadest sense of the word) that mediate between and reinforce an economy structured by class and a state apparatus based on coercion, and this view has almost become a new Marxist orthodoxy (Giner 1985: 253–54). Offering a similar tripartite division, Jürgen Habermas interprets modernization as a process of differentiation among a polity

[6] Although they are to some extent interchangeable here, it is preferable to speak of the market economy rather than capitalism because capitalism can also take state-led forms that are antithetical to civil society (Beetham 1998: 78).

[7] This argument requires some qualification, of course. One lesson Alfred Stepan (1985: 324, 339) draws from authoritarian regimes in Latin America's Southern Cone is that reducing the state's capacity for economic intervention can be a positive goal for officials who pursue a "small-state, strong-state" project for the *domination* of civil society. By politicizing "economistic" issues, state intervention can increase the potential for political organization in civil society. Conversely, deliberate efforts to extricate the state from the economy can lessen the possibility of mounting political opposition.

based on power, an economy based on money, and a "lifeworld" based on personal relationships and (at its best) free communication. Left to itself, a market economy exacerbates inequalities, undermines solidarity, and generates a structure of power relations that is all the less accountable for existing in the private rather than the public sphere, so it is the norm today to define civil society as a combination of the associational and public spheres independent of the market as well as the state (e.g., Wolfe 1997).

These opposing arguments are difficult to resolve. David Beetham (1998: 91), for one, doubts whether it is worth debating at all: "Whether we . . . say that the market is itself a part of civil society, or only a facilitative condition for it, or only in some respects, seems to me fairly arbitrary." There are, however, ways to square the circle and overcome an overly rigid demarcation of market and civil society. Just as "political society" (more of which below) is conceived of as mediating between civil society and the state, Jean Cohen (1995: 38) has proposed the concept of "economic society" as mediating between civil society and the economy. Larry Diamond (1999: 224), on the other hand, notes that "confusion about the boundaries of civil society and the location of particular actors derives in part from the multiple and shifting nature of organizational goals. . . . Many times, organizations based in one sphere temporarily cross the boundary into another." Thus, another approach – one adopted here – is to distinguish among activities rather than institutions. Defining civil society as a "sphere" rather than a set of specific institutions permits the inclusion of such actors as employer associations, labor unions, consumer cooperatives, and perhaps even individual firms when they are active *outside* the market (e.g., seeking and implementing public policies).

One caveat is in order: if civil society is conceived of as a sphere apart from the state and the market, its relationship with the second is logically as important as its relationship to the first. The civil society literature tends to be state-centric, however. For John Ehrenberg (1999: 144, 234), it is precisely its "disregard of the material processes of civil society" that helps account for the contemporary popularity of Tocqueville's notion of civil society as local voluntary activity and civic norms. That notion "performs a normalizing function by making it difficult to see the economic roots of contemporary problems and blinding us to the political avenues for their resolution." Whatever the merits of this charge, ignoring the influence of the market economy will clearly vitiate any understanding of civil society.

Associations

Although a few thinkers limit civil society to the public sphere alone (e.g., Alexander 1997; cf. Calhoun 1993: 269), associations are an essential part – and perhaps the least controversial part – of civil society. It remains open to question whether the connection between associational activity and the consolidation of civil society is axiomatic (Chazan 1992: 281–83; Berman 1997), but it is not much of an exaggeration to say that "the independence of private associations is a synonym for civil society" (Bendix et al. 1987: 14). (What follows applies, *mutatis mutandis*, to interest groups and social movements.)

Associations come in many shapes and sizes, and it is common for theorists to make invidious distinctions, to privilege certain types of association as somehow more representative of or important to civil society than others. Some analysts (e.g., Wesolowski 1995) argue that groups held together by ties of rational interest are more civil than those held together by communal ties of subjective feeling. Many authors (e.g., Diamond, Keane) emphasize the importance of civil society actors' being self-organized, voluntary, democratically structured, tolerant, and civic-minded as well as autonomous from the state. Although he writes of "civic community" rather than civil society, perhaps the most influential distinctions today derive from Putnam's writings on social capital. After attributing superior governmental effectiveness to dense "networks of civic engagement" fostered by "civil associations" of all kinds, Putnam (1993: 174) contends that "a vertical network, no matter how dense and no matter how important it is to its participants, cannot sustain social trust and cooperation." Narrowing his focus still further, he (ibid.: 175) maintains that "dense but segregated horizontal networks sustain cooperation *within* each group, but networks of civic engagement that cut across social cleavages nourish wider cooperation." Thus, the civil associations that are most likely to achieve the beneficial effects attributed to civil society are horizontally structured groups that bridge social cleavages.

All such distinctions become problematic when they prejudge the issue, excluding aspects of associational life from civil society by definition (Kasfir 1998: 5; cf. Garon, this volume). Although communal groups are frequently vilified for their divisiveness, they supply social capital that can facilitate intragroup cooperation and overcome external opposition (Hadenius and Uggla 1996: 1626; Putnam 2000: 22–23), and where formal organizations tend to be weak or coopted, such as in Africa and the Middle East, it can be tribal, ethnic, religious, or regional associations that promote societal autonomy and pluralism in the face of authoritarian states (Bayart 1986: 115; Carapico 1996: 289). While most of us would agree that it is desirable for associations to be self-organized, voluntary, democratically structured, tolerant, and civic-minded, these traits are discrete. "A given association might enjoy sufficient autonomy from the state to countervail its power but be too authoritarian in its internal workings to school members much in the art of compromise," observes Eva Bellin (1995: 125; cf. Berman 1997; Trentmann 2000; Bullock, this volume). "Conversely, an association might be subject to state control and hence incapable of hedging state power yet be sufficiently mobilizational to school citizens in public spirit and political participation." Associations frequently depend on state protection, subsidization, guarantees of access, and so on, Philippe Schmitter (1997: 248–49, 254) notes, and "there is no a priori reason why initially state-dependent organizations might not develop greater autonomy if offered the opportunity." Although Putnam's work has spawned a scholarly growth industry unto itself, his every assertion is disputed.

The effect of participation is more important than its guise. As Gordon White (1994: 378–79) emphasizes, any approach that makes invidious distinctions "carries with it the characteristic problems and limitations of [its] particular paradigm and each runs the risk of pressing analysis into a manichean evaluative mould, with 'civil society' taking on distinct and usually favourable moral connotations." And it is one specific paradigm that is usually being invoked: the conventional notion of civil society has a relatively narrow and normative meaning because it "has been shaped to serve the goal of better governance, particularly democratic reform, rather than a deeper understanding of the relationship between social formations, the associations that represent them and the state" (Kasfir 1998: 1). It is entirely appropriate to distinguish among different kinds of associations and to examine their varying impacts on significant issues of the day such as democratic reform, but if we are to deal in analytical concepts rather than normative models, to explain rather than prescribe, we need inclusive definitions that keep our minds open and embrace the diversity of actual existing civil societies.

Given that the defining feature of civil society is its empowering of individuals to resist the totalizing pretensions of state, market, and family, we can say that one attribute of associations (in addition to autonomy) *is* essential: multiplicity. "The term 'civil society' is a signifier of plurality," Keane (1998: 53) declares. Although extreme fragmentation poses dangers of its own, civil society can be undermined by the monopolization of power bases or domains of interest by a small number of associations or by associations that monopolize the representation of all their members' interests and encapsulate those members within a totalistic environment of their own (Gellner 1991: 1995; Eisenstadt 1995: 240; Diamond 1999: 223, 232).[8] A strength during its period of opposition, the lionized Solidarity movement's encompassing scope became a weakness after its defeat of communism; it came to inhibit the creation of a genuine pluralism of opinions and interests (Kumar 1993: 387).

Level of analysis cannot be ignored, and vertical as well as horizontal linkages are vital for civil society to flourish (Chazan 1992: 291). Given disappointment with aspects of the welfare state, the advocacy of local, grassroots activism represents the accepted wisdom in America today, but Theda Skocpol (1997a: 17–18) attacks that consensus to emphasize the importance of America's federal government and federally structured associations to promoting civic activism. "Contrary to the conservative view that federal social policies are harmful to voluntary groups, popularly rooted voluntary associations have often grown up in a mutually beneficial relationship with federal policies. . . . Just as it is a mistake to see the federal government as automatically opposed to a healthy civil society, so too is it wrong to imagine that most American voluntary groups have been self-contained local efforts." In fact, most popularly rooted groups in the United States have belonged to multitiered national federations. Although cooperation is certainly easier in small groups, vertical linkages sustain both intimate solidarities and connections to wider worlds, thus permitting more effective claim making (Hadenius and Uggla 1996: 1626–27; Skocpol, Ganz, and Munson 2000: 541).

[8] This is not to say that (societal as opposed to state) corporatism is necessarily antithetical to civil society. Schmitter (1997: 249) hypothesizes that the more corporatist a system, the greater the contribution of civil society to the consolidation of democracy, for example.

It bears repeating that any conception of civil society as a sphere of intermediate associations pure and simple, as something that can be analyzed without regard to context, will inevitably obfuscate more than it illuminates. That sphere is constituted by both politics and economics (Ehrenberg 1999: 174, 231).

A Public Sphere

Tocqueville interposed a third region, "political society," between the state and civil society. Inhabited by local self-government, parties, newspapers, and public opinion, political society is the realm of citizens' involvement in politics or public affairs. But Tocqueville conceived of political society expansively because he defined civil society narrowly, identifying it with private, mostly economic activities based on self-interest (Pelczynski 1988: 379). Few contemporary commentators would deny that civil society organizations consider and act on public as well as private interests. These two dimensions of actors' behavior are not necessarily incompatible (Pérez-Díaz 1993: 58; Ehrenberg 1999: 235), and they are inextricable to the extent that actors are motivated by passions and values rather than material advantage. If anything, the tendency now is to *equate* the activities of some civil society organizations with the public interest. Several commentators (e.g., Chazan 1992: 283; Diamond 1999: 223) relegate groups that serve exclusively private interests to a "parochial" sphere, outside civil society altogether. In reaction, Thomas Carothers (1999: 21) feels obliged to point out that "although many civic activists may feel they speak for the public good, the public interest is a highly contested domain. . . . Struggles over the public interest are not between civil society on the one hand and bad guys on the other but within civil society itself."

Thus, although political society might usefully be defined as the arena in which actors compete to assume power within the state – in a democracy, that would include political parties, elections, and legislatures (Stepan 1988: 4) – civil society is generally regarded as combining a public sphere along with an associational one. It is the inclusion of a public sphere that most clearly distinguishes civil society from the nonprofit (or "third") sector, two concepts (if not scholarly literatures) that otherwise overlap to a great extent (Helmut Anheier, personal communication).

Habermas (1989), the best-known theorist of the public sphere, links its evolution to broad historical trends. As the rise of national and territorial states on the basis of early capitalist economies led to the idea of a separate public realm, civil society came to include institutions that encouraged debate among private persons on matters of common concern, including the exercise of political authority. "All sorts of topics over which church and state authorities had hitherto exercised a virtual monopoly of interpretation were opened to discussion" within "an arena of deliberative exchange in which rational-critical arguments rather than mere inherited ideas or personal statuses could determine agreements and actions. It was an operationalization of civil society's capacity for self-organization" (Calhoun 1992: 13; 1993: 273).

Given their scale and levels of participation, Habermas himself finds no institutional basis for an effective public sphere in advanced industrial welfare democracies,[9] but other commentators are more sanguine. If the mass media can commodify and distort communication, enhancing possibilities for centralized social control, Arato and Cohen (1988: 51) maintain, they also expand and create new publics, and today's electronic media offer the possibility of nonhierarchical and autonomous forms of media pluralism. In place of a unified public sphere bound to the territorial nation-state, Keane (1998: 169) asserts, there are now developing "a multiplicity of networked spaces of communication . . . , a complex mosaic of differently sized, overlapping and interconnected public spheres that force us radically to revise our understanding of public life."

The public/private distinction and the exclusion of the family from civil society raise an issue that theorists have only begun to address: What are the consequences of a gendered approach to civil society? Carole Pateman (1988: 102) charges that "political theorists argue about the individual, and take it for granted that their subject matter concerns the public world, without investigating the way in which the 'individual,' 'civil society' and 'the public' have been constituted as patriarchal categories in opposition to womanly nature and the 'private' sphere." When social contract theorists recounted the creation of civil society as a universal realm that (at least potentially) includes everyone, they remained silent about the conjugal (husband/wife) dimension of patriarchalism even as they rejected its paternal (father/son) dimension. This had the effect of portraying the subjection of women as nonpolitical or natural, Pateman contends, relegating women to the privacy of the household, outside the male-dominated public sphere. Civil society came to be idealized as a realm of liberty, equality, and *fraternity*, which means exactly what it says: the ties that bind a community are man-to-man ties of brotherhood.[10] Although at odds with traditional thinking, such a feminist critique cannot be ignored.

A *Global* Civil Society?

It is thus difficult to oppose the declaration of Pérez-Díaz (1995: 88) that "one of the clearest challenges of our time (for those attached to the institutions of civil

9 For Habermas (1989), the liberal model of the public sphere presupposes the strict separation of the public and private realms, and it was structurally transformed, "refeudalized," by the gradual interpenetration of the two. As compromise among particularistic interests supplanted the notion of an objective general interest, negotiations that only sporadically included the public replaced critical debate, ultimately resulting in depoliticization of the public sphere and the rise of a more passive culture of consumption. In addition, he complains, growing democratic inclusiveness has led to a reliance on mass media and vulnerability to public-relations manipulation.

10 Habermas (1992: 428) concedes Pateman's point: "The exclusion of women has been constitutive for the political public sphere not merely in that the latter has been dominated by men as a matter of contingency but also in that its structure and relation to the private sphere has been determined in a gender-specific fashion." Nevertheless, the universalistic discourses of the bourgeois public sphere have the potential for self-transformation, he believes, and they have, in fact, been transformed as a result of feminism.

society) consists of making the very powerful forces of nationalism compatible with the development of a variety of plural societies, and the emergence of a world-wide civil society." For him, the growth of an international civil society necessarily implies the growth of what he takes to be its various components, and that includes an international public authority able to address critical issues and an international public sphere to debate them at the citizen as well as elite level. For all its supranational bureaucracies, common markets, and associations, however, even the European Union only partially corresponds to his ideal type because its public sphere remains undeveloped (Pérez-Díaz 1998). If it is premature to speak of a nonnational civil society in Europe, which is unique in its wealth of supranational institutions, where *could* it possibly exist?

Despite the anarchy of international politics (i.e., its absence of an overarching sovereign to maintain order), we do not see a chaotic war of all against all; there exists an international society of sorts with its own rules and norms (e.g., international law and sovereignty). And if Hedley Bull (1977) and his followers characterized this as a society of states, economic globalization and the end of the Cold War have led more and more commentators to take this analysis from the *inter*national to the *trans*national level to focus on relations among organizations and citizens as well. (The term "transnational" refers to regular activity across national borders that involves at least one nonstate actor.) The transnational approach is much more accommodating to the idea of international civil society than that of Pérez-Díaz. As Paul Wapner (1995: 313) has posited: "The interpenetration of markets, the intermeshing of symbolic meaning systems, and the proliferation of transnational collective endeavors signal the formation of a thin, but nevertheless present, public sphere where private individuals and groups interact for common purposes. Global civil society as such is that slice of associational life which exists above the individual and below the state, but also across national boundaries."

According to Ronnie Lipschutz (1992), global civil society arises from the conjunction of a variety of interacting changes on both the macro, structural level and the micro, agency level: the fading away of anarchy among states and its replacement by an individualistic liberalism as a global "operating system"; the leaking of state sovereignty upward to supranational institutions and downward to subnational ones; the passing of the Cold War, which, rather than ending history, let it recommence; the decreasing ability and willingness of states to deal with certain social welfare problems, resulting in increased efforts by nonstate actors to address them; and the crumbling of old forms of political identity centered on the state and the growth of new forms of identity.

As Wapner's oft-cited definition indicates, most authors concentrate on associations and transnational networks. Recent years have witnessed a striking global upsurge in organized voluntary activity and the creation of nonprofit or nongovernmental organizations (NGOs). Transnational NGOs have been accumulating at an unprecedented and accelerating rate since the end of the Second World War. The Union of International Associations (www.uia.org) now lists over 15,000 transnationally oriented NGOs. The scale and scope of this phenomenon are so immense,

Lester Salamon (1994: 109–10) asserts, that it is fair to say "we are in the midst of a global 'associational revolution' that may prove to be as significant to the latter twentieth century as the rise of the nation-state was to the latter nineteenth. The upshot is a global third sector: a massive array of self-governing private organizations . . . pursuing public purposes outside the formal apparatus of the state." Third-sector activity is flourishing, he posits, because perceived crises of the welfare state, economic development, the environment, and socialism converged with revolutions in communications and the birth of sizable urban middle classes in the Third World to diminish the hold of the state and stimulate private initiative. Jessica Mathews (1997) paints a similar picture of an epochal "power shift." By favoring decentralized networks over other modes of organization, new information technologies have dispersed power from national governments to businesses, international organizations, and NGOs: "The steady concentration of power in the hands of states that began in 1648 with the Peace of Westphalia is over, at least for a while" (ibid.: 50).

Because conventional wisdom assumes that that is where the state ought to be most autonomous, security policy represents a particularly hard case for demonstrating the influence of nonstate actors. For that very reason, Richard Price (1998) analyzed the campaign to prohibit antipersonnel land mines. The key impetus for normative change came from transnational nonstate actors, which succeeded in socializing states to redefine their interests. "Transnational campaigns like that against mines provide novel answers to . . . questions that lie outside of the ambit of a single and exclusive center of politics territorially structured by the state. They constitute a transnational civil society . . ." (ibid.: 627).

To focus solely on transnational groups' influence on state policy is to adopt an unnecessarily narrow understanding of politics, however. Wapner (1995: 312) contends that a more expansive understanding of politics brings into focus the additional dimension of "world civic politics," "the attempt by activists to shape public affairs by working within and across societies themselves. . . . Activist organizations are not simply transnational pressure groups, but rather are political actors in their own right." When it promises to be more effective, activist groups try to effect widespread changes in behavior by conducting research, raising awareness through media stunts, empowering local communities, exposing corporate misdeeds, and so on without directly pressuring states. Thus, "the forms of governance in global civil society are distinct from the instrumentalities of state rule" (ibid.: 337).

Anne-Marie Slaughter (1997: 184) has attacked the "power shift" thesis, countering that it is *trans*governmental rather than *non*governmental organizations that are the most widespread and effective mode of international governance: "The state is not disappearing, it is disaggregating into its separate, functionally distinct parts. These parts – courts, regulatory agencies, executives, and even legislatures – are networking with their counterparts abroad, creating a dense web of relations that constitutes a new, transgovernmental order." Because international networks of bureaucrats expand the regulatory reach of their respective nations, they serve to *strengthen* the state as the primary player in the international system.

International institutions are not essential to the coordination Slaughter points to, but John Boli and George Thomas (1999: 29) have found that many intergovernmental organizations rely on NGOs for support and that NGOs themselves can lead to the formation and expansion of such organizations. Boli and Thomas come out of the "world-polity institutionalism" school championed by John Meyer, which takes an unusually strong stand on the existence of an international society: "Modern states, economies, and cultural systems are obviously ongoing constructions of worldwide processes. . . . Clearly, the economy, political system and culture of the world system penetrate all societies, structuring their internal institutions in response. . . . Properties of national units are acquired by the diffusion of the structures of the wider system" (Meyer and Hannan 1979: 12). This distinct, global level of social reality is thought to have begun to crystallize organizationally in the second half of the nineteenth century and to have played an authoritative role in constituting the identities, interests, goals, and means adopted by states, corporations, groups, and individuals since the Second World War. Boli and Thomas (1999: 6) regard international NGOs as "the primary organizational field in which world culture takes structural form."

If Boli and Thomas adopt a top-down perspective that focuses on the mundane work of intellectual, technical, and economic rationalization, Margaret Keck and Kathryn Sikkink (1998) adopt a bottom-up perspective that focuses on transnational advocacy networks in the high-profile sectors of human rights, women's rights, and the environment. And while world polity theorists concentrate on the process of adhering to norms that have already gained wide acceptance, Keck and Sikkink explore the earlier stages of creating and institutionalizing new norms, stages characterized by intense conflicts that highlight human agency and indeterminacy. Thus, they believe (ibid.: 33) that their findings "do not yet support the strong claims about an emerging global civil society. We are much more comfortable with a conception of transnational civil society as an arena of struggle, a fragmented and contested area."

According to Ann Florini (2000: 211), "The power of transnational civil society manifests itself at virtually every stage of policy making, from deciding what issues need attention to determining how problems will be solved to monitoring compliance with agreements." On the heels of this sweeping assertion, however, Florini herself (2000: 213) acknowledges that "there are clear limits" to this power. Transnational civil society lacks a single, coherent agenda; it works indirectly, by means of persuasion; and national governments and intergovernmental organizations retain considerable power to fight back, regularly objecting to what they characterize as illegitimate usurpations of their authority and prerogatives. Although international NGOs and networks try to leverage the moral authority they often enjoy, global acceptance of that authority should not be exaggerated. As on the national level, there is nothing inherent in transnational civil society to ensure the representation of broad public interests: "The neo-Nazi hate groups that exchange repugnant rhetoric over the Internet are just as much transnational civil society networks as are the human rights coalitions" (ibid.: 231).

On the basis of their examination of U.N. world conferences, Anne Marie Clark, Elisabeth Friedman, and Kathryn Hochstetler (1998: 5) conclude: "we do find evidence that the construction of a global civil society is under way but is far from complete." Although the number of participating NGOs has increased significantly, representation remains imbalanced in favor of the North. Although new rules facilitate NGO access, NGOs have acquired new repertoires of participation, and there is greater interaction among NGOs, states continue to limit NGO participation and their own interaction with NGOs. And although mutual understandings regarding their relationships and substantive issues are developing among NGOs, sovereignty claims block substantive agreement between NGOs and states.

More research is necessary before we can assess the applicability of the notion of global civil society with any confidence, but as M. J. Peterson (1992: 377–78; cf. Shaw 1994: 655) judiciously observes, it would be as serious an error to overestimate the impact of transnational activity as to underestimate it: "Today, anything that could be labelled 'international society,' operates in a decentralized political system where loyalty to the world as a whole is insignificant. . . . Analyzing events as if one international society exists is premature. It is not premature, however, to conceive of several interlinked national civil societies." Regardless of whether hope for the world depends on the continued growth of an "extraordinary international relations" of transnational undertakings to complement and challenge the ordinary international relations of traditional state undertakings, it remains true that "the assertion that global civil society 'exists' is an act of faith, an expression of political will, and a statement of conviction" (Falk 1993: 221, 232, 230) – not a verifiable statement of fact.

Real-World Civil Societies

Civil society cannot offer any usefulness as an analytical concept if it is romanticized, but precisely because civil society is often idealized as an unconditionally good thing (e.g., Harbeson 1994: 1–2), the concept's more astute friends no less than its foes take pains to highlight its shortcomings. "Civil society is, no more than state power, a panacea," complains skeptic Kumar (1993: 389–90). "A robust civil society isn't a cure-all and never was" echoes advocate Jean Elshtain (1997: 14–15). The social theorists who have examined real-world civil societies over the last several centuries have been as impressed with their vices as their virtues. The arbitrariness, confusion, disharmony, egotism, exclusivity, fragmentation, inequality, oppression, prejudice, and violence that we observe every day are endemic to actual existing civil societies, undermining their autonomy and pluralism and necessitating state agency.

Even where civil society "works," the results will not please all people all the time. When Jordan's civil society found its voice during the Gulf War, for example, the government had to respect the pro-Iraq activities of professional associations even when those activities went against its own official position (Norton 1995: 17). An increasingly strident and public "antinormalization" movement subsequently drafted a blacklist to ostracize Jordanians who had cordial or collaborative relations with Israel. "The anti-normalizers are not marginal figures: Their backers include such bastions of the establishment as the national bar association. A gathering of anti-normalization forces in September drew more than 400 representatives of leading unions and business associations, and 13 of Jordan's 20 registered political parties" (*New York Times*, October 15, 1999).

Whatever the demerits of real-world civil societies, the idea of civil society unquestionably has merit in having stimulated fruitful debate in the social sciences. We hope to contribute to that debate in the pages that follow with a many-sided and in-depth analysis of one particular civil society: that of Japan.

2

From Meiji to Heisei: The State and Civil Society in Japan

Sheldon Garon

"Civil society" may well be the Holy Grail of our time. Scholars and statesmen seek it with a fervor that borders on the spiritual. And recognizing it among the more mundane chalices has stymied many in their quest. For a historian of state-society relations like myself, the charge of investigating civil society in Japan raises a thorny set of problems. Civil society has occupied an important place in modern Japan, I argue. Yet if we are to appreciate its complexities, we must first consider the limitations of ahistorically applying "civil society" to Japan.

The idea of civil society is rooted in a time and a place. Both are distant from modern Japan. Its origins are distinctly European, dating back to the classical Greek term *koinonia politike* and the Roman *societas civilis*. For much of European history, civil society referred to self-governing towns or cities. The emphasis was on the word "civil," which connoted a "citizen," or a member of the polity endowed with certain rights to participate in governance. The concept of civil society assumed its present-day meaning, most scholars agree, during the latter half of the eighteenth century and the early nineteenth century in Western Europe. Particularly in the Anglo-American world and France, "civil society" began to describe a society or space that not only lay outside the control of the state but whose vibrant exchange of ideas monitored and limited state authority. Against the backdrop of the American and French revolutions, this new type of civil society grew out of a "fear of state despotism" (Keane 1988b: 35–39, 65). In this sense, civil society was composed of voluntary, self-organized associations, such as learned and reading societies, moral reform groups, and Masonic lodges (Trentmann 2000: 1). Closely related was the emergence in this same period of a "public sphere" within which people came together to discuss politics and other matters of the day. Political journalism, salons, and coffeehouses were favored venues (Habermas 1989). In such contexts, "civil" retained the meaning of belonging to a self-regulated body, but the word also implied "civility" – that is, openness, equality among members, tolerance, and cultivation of oneself and others (Trentman 2000).

Is it helpful to analyze modern Japan in terms of a historically rooted Western phenomenon? It may be, if Japanese themselves invoked that Western concept in contemporary debates, as they did in the cases of fascism, socialism, or industrialization. However, whereas European and North American thinkers often wrote of "civil society" between 1750 and 1850, few Japanese promoted or even discussed the idea of civil society from the late nineteenth century to 1945. Indeed, its translation (*shimin shakai*) did not appear in common Japanese parlance until the postwar era.

During the prewar era, most Japanese would have regarded "civil society" as inappropriate and illegitimate. The sticking point was the term "civil." While many Japanese embraced the Western word "society," the vision of a society governed by "citizens" (*shimin*) explicitly challenged the fundamental notion of imperial sovereignty. Put simply, there were no "citizens" in prewar Japan – only "subjects" of the emperor.

Then there is the problem of time. Fresh from the Meiji Restoration of 1868, Japan became a part of the modern world order during the latter decades of the nineteenth century – when Westerners themselves had lost interest in establishing a civil society that would exist autonomously from the state. In Western polities, state and society increasingly penetrated each other (Habermas 1989: 142–46). To protect "society" from capitalists' harmful pursuit of self-interest, socialists and other progressives necessarily looked to the state. States, for their part, granted private groups the public authority to educate the populace, supervise welfare provision, and police everyday life. Idyllic images of an autonomous civil society became all the more anachronistic amid the international rivalries and "national efficiency" movements of the early twentieth century. The advent of Bolshevism, fascism, and the New Deal seemingly sounded its death knell. From 1868 to 1945, few Japanese – whether on the left or right – would have regarded civil society as an attractive "trend of the world" that their nation should follow to become modern.

Moreover, scholarly attempts to examine civil society in prewar Japan have been impeded by tendencies to focus on either the state or society to the exclusion of the other. At one extreme lies the dominant body of Japanese historical analysis. A powerful "emperor-system state," argue most Japanese scholars, crushed or coopted popular movements from 1890 to 1945. This emperor system is often characterized as the "source of all moral, religious, cultural, and aesthetic values" (Gotō 1976: 113–14). Indeed, Japanese historians pointedly distinguish prewar Japan's lack of civil society from the late eighteenth-century European experience. While contemporary Western European civil societies weakened or destroyed absolutist monarchies, the Meiji oligarchy is said to have *established* an emperor-centered absolutism, which collapsed only with defeat in 1945. Some observers, such as Karel van Wolferen (1989), argue further that imperial governance bequeathed legacies to *postwar* Japan in the form of a "submissive middle class," a "house-broken press," and coopted environmental, labor, and women's movements. Remarked Wolferen (1991) about contemporary Japan: " 'civil society' – the part of the body politic outside the active Government and power system – is virtually unknown."

At the other extreme are those historical studies that single-mindedly seek out evidence of a vibrant society, a public sphere, or a consumer culture operating outside the state apparatus. Frustrated by the attention paid to the state, some historians have sounded the call to study society instead (e.g., Gluck 1992: xvii). Others reduce "society" to those groups, such as feminists, who resisted state power and ideology (e.g., Sievers 1983). Still others attempt to tell the story of the democratic spontaneity of "the people," as contrasted with conservative elites (e.g., Dower 1999). Regrettably, these accounts assume rather sharp distinctions between society and the state. They also tend to define civil society as necessarily progressive. Few scholars consider the possibility that assertive individuals or groups might cooperate with the state on some issues, while criticizing it on others.

To sum up, the question of civil society may be productively discussed in the Japanese context, but not if we associate it exclusively with late eighteenth-century Western European limitations on monarchical states or with the unfolding of democracy. A more inclusive definition is needed. Accordingly, some scholars of Europe and Japan wisely begin their analyses by examining the thought and behavior of a *variety* of groups outside the state rather than prejudge whether each qualifies as part of civil society (e.g., Berry 1998; Trentmann 2000).

For the sake of analysis, this essay similarly defines civil society to include groups and public discourses that exist in spaces between the state and the people. Institutionally, civil society may consist of formal associations at either the national or local level or looser networks. Various forms of media, in which contemporary issues are debated, also form a part of civil society. These associations and media are usually established independently of the state, but not always. In cultural terms, they must offer, at least occasionally, alternatives to official discourses and values – even if they agree with the state on other matters.

My quest is not to seek the Holy Grail of civil society in Japan, but to utilize the concept to better understand historical relations between state and society. To begin our analysis, let us suppose that Japan lacked all traces of a civil society. That is, suppose the state ruled, top-down, over a compliant, passive populace incapable of independently exercising any power or formulating any values outside those licensed by the regime. In the total absence of civil society, would the state have developed differently from the way it actually did? I believe it would have. Though able to narrow the parameters of acceptable discourses and activities within society, the state in prewar and even wartime Japan did not impose totalitarian control. Journalism and publishing flourished; public debate could be lively; and hundreds of thousands of Japanese belonged to associations that advanced various demands. There were times when societal pressures compelled the regime to loosen its controls. More often, groups in society worked with officials to modify and modernize state policies, invariably becoming active agents in new state programs to manage the rest of society. These patterns continued into the postwar era (Garon 1997).

Thus, this essay explores: (1) the evolution of civil society in Japan, (2) its role in shaping the state, and (3) the state's role in shaping this society.

An Early Modern Public Sphere

Civil society in the West did not suddenly erupt in the eighteenth century, but evolved from institutions and discourses of previous centuries. The same could be said for civil society in modern Japan. Developments during the early modern or Tokugawa era (1600–1868) both constrained and encouraged the evolution of a public sphere following the Meiji Restoration.

The constraints are generally understood. Under the Tokugawa shogunate, Japanese towns and religious institutions did not retain various "liberties" vis-à-vis overlords, as had occurred widely in medieval and early modern Europe. Politics was, for the most part, restricted to the *shōgun*, a few powerful *daimyō* (i.e., lords of domains), and high-ranking samurai advisers. Reinforcing these restrictions was a status system in which all people were expected to function within a given hereditary status, be it samurai, peasant, artisan, merchant, or outcaste. The status system prohibited peasants and other nonsamurai from taking part in governance above the local level. Although the shogunate could not systematically censor all public discussion of current political events, it did successfully prevent the periodical publication of the type of news seen in eighteenth-century Britain (Berry 1998: 154).

Nonetheless, as the Tokugawa era wore on, significant spaces opened up for public discussion and associational life. Numerous academies of learning and martial arts brought together samurai of different domains and diffused political knowledge throughout Japan. Some of these samurai openly challenged the shogunate in the 1860s. In the cities, merchants organized philanthropic and learned societies. The best known was the Osaka merchant academy, the Kaitokudō, whose founders proposed reforms in agriculture, banking, prisons, and the regulation of markets (Najita 1987). Fueling the circulation of information was the remarkable growth of literacy among well-to-do commoners in town and country. At least 5,000 publishing firms operated during the early modern era. Though publications generally avoided political topics, they – like their counterparts in Western civil society – promoted techniques of self-improvement, thrift, and profit-making (Berry 1998).

We do not usually think of rural society as a prime site of civil society. However, in the waning decades of Tokugawa rule, prosperous farmers and rural entrepreneurs (*gōnō*) increasingly crossed village boundaries to form regional and even national networks of production, credit, and sociability. Alliances of wealthy farmers also sponsored visits by itinerant technologists, notably Ninomiya Sontoku (1787–1856), who instructed villagers in methods of moral and material improvement (Smith 1970; Pratt 1999). Rich peasants took to studying the Chinese classics, Japanese history, and Japanese classical poetry. Indeed, during the 1850s and 1860s, poetry circles afforded wealthy farmers (and sometimes rural women) the opportunity to exchange ideas with samurai and court nobles (Walthall 1998).

Although some participants in the emerging public sphere of Tokugawa Japan did help overthrow the shogunate, few overtly challenged the old regime. On the contrary, as would happen again and again in the modern era, the social elites' improvement activities generally served to manage the populace and stabilize the rule of higher authorities.

A New Society

Nonetheless, the early modern growth of a public sphere proved crucial to the dramatic rise of new social forces in the wake of the Meiji Restoration of 1868. Japan became exposed to new currents of Western liberalism, which valued a freer society and economy outside of government. Equally important, during the last three decades of the nineteenth century, the modernizing regime dismantled many of the earlier barriers to a civil society and associational life. The hereditary status system was abolished, and all Japanese became equal before the law. Henceforth, a merchant or peasant had as much right as a former samurai to take part in governance or discuss public issues. The new freedom of physical mobility, together with better transportation and communications, enabled associations to operate on regional and national scales.

The result was a flurry of public discussion and popular organization within a few years of the Restoration. Privately owned newspapers sprang up in the big cities and provincial centers. Although the new state initially supported the establishment of newspapers in some locales, many dailies took to lambasting the government. The Meiji regime's efforts to censor publications were relatively mild and easily evaded (Kasza 1988: 4–6). By 1889, some 647 newspapers and magazines were in print, 164 of them treating current events. Working-class Japanese and ordinary villagers increasingly consumed print media as universal elementary education brought mass literacy. On the eve of World War I, Japan boasted 1,500 to 2,000 magazine titles. The number of book titles published annually was double that of the United States (Gluck 1985: 12).

The Meiji era also saw the rise of Western-style learned societies and other associations that aimed at debating contemporary issues and enlightening the public. The most influential may have been the Meirokusha (Sixth Year of Meiji Society), established in 1873. Although members included several government bureaucrats, the Meirokusha functioned as a voluntary association that encompassed the urban public and civil society of the time. Leading independent publicists introduced Western liberal theory. The best known was Fukuzawa Yukichi, a former shogunal translator who had toured the United States and Europe and subsequently wrote the widely read book *Seiyō Jijō* (*Conditions in the West*, 1867). The society's magazine reached hundreds in government and the intelligentsia in Tokyo, Osaka, and beyond. "Civil society" itself was not a topic for discussion. Rather, most members argued for the freedom and autonomy of *individuals* from the state. Some were equally concerned about protecting individuals, especially women, from oppressive societal practices. Nevertheless, the Meirokusha intellectuals implicitly demanded autonomous public spaces in which individuals could freely exchange and refine ideas. To Fukuzawa, this public sphere should be based on private institutions, and to that end, he founded an academy that later became Keiō University, one of Japan's leading private universities. Advising scholars to work outside the government, Fukuzawa declared: "independent individuals make for an independent country" (Braisted 1976; Irokawa 1985: 61).

As in the Tokugawa era, exuberant manifestations of civil society were often found in the countryside, where the vast majority of Japanese lived. Wealthy peasants who had previously formed networks for the study of Chinese classics or indigenous "national learning" now added Western learning. During the 1870s and 1880s, translations of liberal British and French tracts circulated in the countryside in the tens of thousands of copies. Among the most popular were books by John Stuart Mill, John Locke, Herbert Spencer, Jeremy Bentham, and Jean-Jacques Rousseau. In many a town and village, literate men – landlords, headmen, priests, and teachers – debated political questions in ad hoc societies. Some societies wrote draft constitutions for the nation (Irokawa 1985).

Political and intellectual ferment in the countryside led many rural notables into political associations and sometimes opposition to the government. What became known as the Freedom and Popular Rights movement initially formed around political associations of disaffected samurai in the mid-1870s. In the late 1870s, the opposition movement expanded to include journalists, merchants, and wealthy peasant entrepreneurs. By 1880, the movement had garnered a quarter of a million signatures in some sixty petition drives for a national assembly. One year later, leading figures founded the first opposition party, the Liberal Party (Jiyūtō), with 149 local branches (Howell 2000: 101–2). Popular rights groups demanded representation in the government, but they also insisted on the freedom to associate, assemble, and express their opinions. After the Meiji Constitution (1889) established a national parliament, opposition activists adamantly defended their new public sphere from government encroachment. During the 1890s, opposition parties introduced numerous bills in the House of Representatives to liberalize the censorship provisions of the Newspaper Ordinance of 1887 (all such bills failed in the House of Peers). The House of Representatives also passed several bills aimed at relaxing or eliminating the government's restrictions on the freedom of association and assembly.

In the cities at the turn of the century, "society" or the public sphere became particularly identified with the growing "new middle class." Initially, the new middle class was comprised primarily of those working in the free professions: lawyers, teachers, physicians, nurses, and civil servants (Flaherty 1999). They soon organized themselves into professional associations that discussed contemporary issues and advanced common interests. During the 1910s and 1920s, legions of salaried employees in large companies and government offices swelled the ranks of this new class. Middle-class individuals became the principal spokespeople for Japanese civil society in large part because their status derived not from property but from their higher education and exposure to Western knowledge. Eager to distinguish itself from the "decadent" upper classes and the "backward" masses, the new middle class proclaimed its mission to be the "civilization" of the rest of society. Middle-class people avidly produced and consumed urban journalism, and they constituted the core audience for family and housewives' magazines, which first appeared in the early twentieth century (Ambaras 1998).

In addition, middle-class society was defined by the progressive politics and Christian convictions of its prominent publicists. At the turn of the century, many Japanese social reformers possessed multiple identities as Protestant, international, middle-class, liberal, and socialist. Although Japanese Christians comprised less than 1 percent of the population, they exerted substantial influence on thought and official policy. Inspired by "social gospel" thinking in Britain and North America, middle-class Japanese Christians founded private charities, orphanages, and reformatories. The Christians also established the first Japanese chapters of major international organizations, notably the Women's Christian Temperance Union, the Salvation Army, and the YMCA. In the late 1890s, Protestant politicians and reformers attempted to integrate the nascent working class into society. They taught workers the virtues of self-help and supported the formation of early labor unions. Moreover, the middle-class Protestant vision of a "civil" society had no place for Japan's pervasive state-managed system of licensed prostitution and sexual enslavement. From the Japan Women's Christian Temperance Union to pioneer socialist leaders, Japanese Protestants sharply criticized the state in their decades-long struggle to abolish the licensed brothels (Garon 1997: chap. 3).

Compared with the new middle class, with its many associations and journalistic spaces, the lower-middle and working classes of the cities were less organized and articulate. However, as literacy and political knowledge spread, they, too, entered the public sphere during the early twentieth century. More than 95 percent of school-age children attended school by 1905, and the percentage actually completing compulsory education (four years until 1907 and six years thereafter) rose rapidly. Newspaper readership among the working poor was surprisingly high. Various surveys after 1918 suggested that a majority of workers in Tokyo regularly read newspapers. Much of what ordinary people read attacked the government. In a series of urban protest rallies and riots between 1905 and 1918, the urban crowd surfaced as a volatile actor in Japanese civil society. Rickshaw drivers, artisans, and small proprietors rubbed shoulders with maverick politicians and journalists to oppose the policies of oligarchic cabinets (Gordon 1991: 18–19, chap. 2).

The Intertwining of Civil Society and the State

The rise of new social forces did not necessarily occur in opposition to the state. By 1900, civil society and the state were considerably more intertwined than they had been during the first three decades of the Meiji period. In retrospect, the civil society of those earlier decades strikes us as anomalous in its autonomy and its often spirited resistance to the government. Thereafter, most societal groups preferred to work *with* the state to realize their objectives, while state officials increasingly sought to mobilize society for the purposes of governance.

The interpenetration of state and society is evident in several realms. During the 1880s and early 1890s, the political parties (or "popular parties" as they were then called) fought to safeguard the autonomy of society from official intrusions. Gradually, the parties entered into cooperative relationships with the oligarchic cabinets. In exchange for their party's approval of government budgets, party leaders eventually served as ministers of state. In all but two years between 1918 and 1932, the two major parties alternatively organized the cabinet itself. In terms of economic base, the major parties increasingly represented the interests of big business, abandoning their earlier back-country aversion to the central state (Masumi 1968: 230, 267, 293).

After 1900, most erstwhile champions of freedom in the Diet accepted, even welcomed, state policies that restricted membership in civil society to bourgeois males like themselves while excluding many others. In that same year the House of Representatives overwhelmingly passed the repressive Police Law (*Chian Keisatsu hō*). The law maintained previous bans on women's joining political associations and their sponsoring and attending any meeting at which "political discussion" occurred. But more than the specter of politicized women, bourgeois politicians feared the rise of labor and socialist movements. Accordingly, they turned to the state to control radicalism and collective labor activity. The same Police Law of 1900 that categorically excluded women from political life also empowered officials to disband threatening popular organizations. Its Article 17 further outlawed the act of "instigating" or "inciting" others to strike, join unions, or engage in collective bargaining (Garon 1987).

Nor should we regard the growth of the new middle class as entirely autonomous from the state. As products of the newly established universities and experts in Western knowledge, middle-class leaders shared much in world view and lifestyle with the government's higher civil servants. They may have battled the state over the issue of licensed prostitution or sought greater freedom to practice Christianity, but middle-class activists solidly allied with the state in matters of "civilizing" the Japanese people. In the associations of early-nineteenth-century Western Europe, *civil* society normally implied that societal groups would themselves bring civility to the masses. In a late-developing military power like Japan, however, the middle classes invariably looked to the state to use its vast resources to enlighten the nation systematically and rapidly. Beginning in the first decade of the twentieth century, Christian social reformers and charities worked closely with the interventionist Home Ministry to relieve poverty and cultivate self-help (Garon 1997).

Finally, the turn of the century marked the beginning of the state's efforts to organize society on its own terms. Prior to that time, the countryside and urban neighborhoods had been sites of diverse, indigenous, and strongly autonomous associations. In the 1870s and 1880s, rural elites organized numerous agricultural discussion societies to explore new techniques and often criticize government policies (Pratt 1999: 39). Confraternities (*kō*) combined the functions of sociability, religion, and credit societies. Village youth associations could be quite raucous.

A series of concerted measures gradually enabled the central bureaucracy to reorganize local associational life. Officials began with laws designed to incorporate small agricultural and industrial producers into increasingly compulsory associations. Such associations, they reasoned, offered effective means of disseminating information and technology, improving quality control, and establishing cooperative arrangements in credit, buying, and selling. Chambers of commerce were legally mandated in each locale in 1890. Trade associations (*dōgyō kumiai*) in important export industries were given legal standing in 1897 and 1900. Regulations in 1899 governed the formation and operation of village agricultural societies (*nōkai*), which formed the lowest rung in the state-run Imperial Agricultural Association. The 1900 Producers' Cooperative Law (Sangyō Kumiaihō) served as the springboard for a massive government drive to establish agricultural cooperatives in every village. In each case, the regime provided associations and cooperatives with subsidies and other benefits. In exchange, the associations surrendered their autonomy, becoming part of hierarchical organizations intended to further official policies (Pempel and Tsunekawa 1979: 249–50; Pratt 1999: 43–45).

Under the intrusive Local Improvement Campaign (1906–18), the Home Ministry and Ministry of Agriculture and Commerce implanted semiofficial associations not only among producers but in several other areas of everyday life. The Hōtoku societies, which had previously flourished as a genuine peasant movement among followers of the Tokugawa-era reformer Ninomiya Sontoku, came under the bureaucratic control of the Central Hōtokukai in 1906. Officials thereupon introduced government-issue Hōtoku societies throughout Japan. Various ministries of state similarly reorganized indigenous associations of reservists, young men, and young women into bureaucratically administered national federations (Pyle 1973).

The imposition of semiofficial associations impeded the development of an autonomous civil society. Even so, we should not assume – as many have – that officially organized associations lacked all capacity to differ with the state. The trade associations (*dōgyō kumiai*) are a case in point. Although the state organized trade associations to do its bidding, small businesses soon utilized the associations to assert their own demands. During the 1910s and 1920s, federations of trade associations forced the government to repeal the Business Tax (1896) and institute a more favorable form of taxation. The Tokyo Federation of Business Associations, which boasted 99,000 members in 1930, led the opposition. In 1937, a similar coalition of retailers' trade associations successfully lobbied a reluctant government to enact the first anti–department store law (Garon and Mochizuki 1993: 149–50).

Likewise, the young men's associations (*seinendan*) frequently spun out of bureaucratic control. At the time of the Rice Riots of 1918, local young men's associations frequently spearheaded the protests (Lewis 1990: 26, 128, 161). During the 1920s and early 1930s, a number of young men's associations founded independent newsletters and espoused radical politics of both left and right (Wilson 1997). In short, the lines between civil society and the state often blurred after 1900, but they hardly disappeared.

Civil Society and "Taishō Democracy"

Historians conventionally divide the period between 1918 and 1945 into two distinct eras. During the rapidly democratizing interwar era (1918–31), civil society appears to flourish. Under Japan's "Fifteen Years' War" (1931–45), on the other hand, civil society dies a dramatic death as the regime disbands nearly every autonomous body and reorganizes the populace into state-run organizations. As generalizations, these interpretations are reasonable. Yet they exaggerate the autonomy of civil society under interwar democratization, while overlooking the continued development of society during wartime.

Without question, the 1920s and early 1930s witnessed the unprecedented appearance of new sociopolitical forces and cultures that lay outside state domination. The greatest challenge to the authority of the state and big business came from the political left, labor unions, and affiliated social movements. Although employers and the government had easily marginalized labor unions before World War I, the booming wartime economy emboldened workers to strike and organize in record numbers. By 1931, Japanese unions had organized nearly 8 percent of the industrial work force movement, or 369,000 workers. Similarly, tens of thousands of tenant farmers took part in disputes against landlords to lower rents by the early 1920s. Aided by socialist and labor activists, tenants formed their own unions. Established in 1922, the underground Communist Party adopted the most radical stance, advocating the overthrow of the capitalist order and the emperor system. Its affiliated labor federation, the Hyōgikai, mounted a series of highly politicized strikes against major companies during the mid-1920s.

More moderate labor leaders and their rank and file disavowed the tactics of the far left, but they, too, embraced a counterhegemonic "dispute culture" (Gordon 1991: 3). Increasingly, workers rejected employers' claims of paternalistic management. They demanded better treatment in the workplace and a higher status in society. In some heavily unionized urban areas, workers forged their own subculture – complete with consumer cooperatives, newsletters, night classes, and theatrical groups. During disputes, these subcultures occasionally swelled to include sympathetic shopkeepers and other nonworkers in the neighborhood. Politically, trade unionists allied with intellectuals, liberal politicians, and tenant-farmer unions. Together they organized socialist parties, demanded labor and social legislation, and insisted on the workers' right to vote. In response, the governing bourgeois parties enacted universal manhood suffrage, the period's greatest democratic reform, in 1925. In the 1937 parliamentary elections, a united leftist party, the Social Masses Party, emerged as the third largest political party with a total of thirty-seven seats in the House of Representatives (Garon 1987).

The advent of an urban mass culture during the 1920s and 1930s furthered the growth of civil society and public spaces. Several newspapers had circulations in the hundreds of thousands, with Osaka's two big dailies each surpassing one million (Young 1998: 59–60). Even high-brow magazines such as *Chūōkōron* (*Central Review*) and *Kaizō* (*Reconstruction*) achieved large readerships, their pages filled with spirited commentaries on contemporary issues by leading Marxists, liberals, and feminists. Marxist discourse itself attained the status of a mass commodity. Publishers sold huge quantities of the translated works of Marx, Engels, and others at attractive prices (Silverberg 1990: 64–67). Much of interwar consumer culture was apolitical, of course. City people indulged in the new delights of department stores, the cinema, and cafés. Nonetheless, consumer culture itself challenged the regime, thwarting official efforts to mold self-denying subjects who saved their money for the good of the nation.

Less obvious but no less significant was the development of new centers of policy expertise and "social knowledge" outside the administrative state. Prior to World War I, bureaucrats had dominated policy making on the basis of greater access to information (e.g., statistics, Western models). During the 1920s, some nongovernmental institutes surfaced to rival the state's research capacities. The best known was the Ohara Institute for Social Research, which was established by a philanthropic industrialist to survey and improve labor conditions. Marxian social scientists soon assumed control of the institute and formed close ties to the labor movement (Garon 1996: 282–84).

The interwar era was also a time when the gendered composition of civil society changed dramatically. Whereas associational life and the public sphere had theretofore been largely the preserve of males, women began entering public life in a number of realms. Their new activism was related in part to rapid increases in girls attending secondary schools and colleges. Growing numbers of educated women chose careers in teaching, medicine, nursing, journalism, and social work. Many formed women's professional associations, such as those of teachers and midwives, which lobbied the government to promote common interests (Newell 1997). State officials and the political parties, for their part, softened their previous opposition to the political and social inclusion of women. They became convinced of the benefits of women's public roles after observing women's contributions to the war efforts of Western belligerents in World War I. Indeed, in 1922, the Diet repealed the infamous clause in the 1900 Police Law that had barred women from sponsoring and attending political meetings (Garon 1997: chap. 4).

Women took advantage of the more tolerant environment to influence political and social discourses as never before. After securing the right to hold political meetings, several women's organizations campaigned for universal women's suffrage (the House of Representatives twice passed local suffrage bills in 1930 and 1931, although they were quashed in the House of Peers). Some groups stepped up demands on the government to abolish licensed prostitution, and most agitated for state assistance to mothers and children in fatherless families. At a less politicized level, there emerged a new public sphere dedicated to the discussion of housewives' concerns. Established in 1917, *Shufu no tomo* (*Housewife's Friend*) became the most successful of several housewives' magazines, with a circulation of 850,000 in 1935, while the family magazine *Kingu* reached 750,000 readers. Some magazines, notably *Fujin no tomo* (*Woman's Friend*), developed loyal readers' groups nationwide (Saitō 1988; Itagaki 1992: iii). The new "women's culture" undoubtedly influenced women's groups to concentrate on extending women's domestic roles into the public sphere in such areas as protection of mothers and children, educational reform, and campaigns to improve daily life.

Historiography tends to overlook the era's other social forces because they were not associated with progressive political movements. Yet their rise is further evidence of the vibrancy of interwar civil society. Each of these groups contested upper-class or state domination while creating a distinctive subculture. Developing independently of the officially recognized Shintō and Buddhist sects, the so-called new religions mushroomed during the 1920s and 1930s. Some claimed hundreds of thousands of believers and maintained their own newspapers, adult classes, and even paramilitary corps. In the countryside, "middling farmers" displaced wealthier landlords as village leaders, and they often led tenant unions in the 1920s (Waswo 1988). In the cities, small proprietors not only organized themselves nationally to demand state protections against big business, but likewise assumed leadership positions in their neighborhoods.

Despite its vitality, civil society did not develop as autonomously from the state as historians commonly portray in their accounts of interwar Japan. In case after case, groups criticized the government concerning some issues while working closely with the bureaucracy on others. This pattern holds true particularly for the middle classes and women's groups. Interwar democratization did little to sunder the ties between middle-class activists and the state. On the contrary, the 1920s were years of glaring social problems. Slums proliferated, the gap between the cities and countryside grew, and workers' dissatisfaction frequently erupted in strikes and riots. The middle classes made common cause with the state to modernize what they regarded as the backward and unruly elements of Japanese society. They eagerly joined in official "moral suasion" campaigns to promote thrift, improve hygiene, and eradicate popular "superstition." In urban neighborhoods, small proprietors headed officially established moral reform associations, and they became state-appointed district welfare commissions, whose duty it was to guide and improve the poor. Middling farmers played similar roles as the state's agents, "rehabilitating" depressed villages in the 1930s.

Most women's groups, too, allied with the bureaucracy in interventionist campaigns to "improve the daily lives" of the Japanese people. Their eagerness to inculcate habits of thrift and "scientific" homemaking meshed with the state's interest in encouraging high household savings that could be invested in industry and the military. In many cases, women's groups owed their origins to the state. The vast majority were based on residential "women's associations" (*fujinkai*), which officials had aggressively organized after 1920.

Nor did some of society's most independent associations maintain significant autonomy vis-à-vis the state. The labor movement could not unite on a strategy to build up workplace organizations from which to challenge the elites. Instead, labor fragmented, and its mainstream "realists" allied with the government to isolate left-wing militants. Also, because the surviving unions believed themselves too weak to struggle against employers on their own, labor relied on the state and its police to mediate disputes. This strategy might have succeeded in a polity in which labor unions enjoyed influence within the state, but not in Japan, where the regime's interests were not necessarily those of the workers.

On balance, the interwar alliances between societal activists and bureaucrats served to enmesh popular groups, making it difficult for civil society to challenge the state. At the same time, these associations could be quite assertive, and the state was forced eventually to include many societal actors in the apparatus of governance. In this sense, the interwar expansion of civil society altered and, ironically, "popularized" the state's management of society (Garon 1997).

Society under "Total War"

Japan's "Fifteen Years' War" began with the occupation of Manchuria in 1931–32 and escalated to full-fledged hostilities with China in 1937 and the Western powers in 1941. If civil society during the interwar era was not as autonomous as it has often been portrayed, the wartime regime's attempts to eradicate it were not as successful as we commonly suppose.

To be sure, the state obliterated the independent organizations of those elements deemed so heterodox as to obstruct the war effort. The "new religions" and labor movement bore the brunt of this assault. In 1935, the police launched a campaign to "eradicate the evil cults." Beginning with the enormous Ōmotokyō sect, several large new religions were brutally disbanded, their shrines smashed and their leaders imprisoned (Garon 1997). Although the police had already crushed the remnants of the Communist Party and far-left unions, government officials grew intolerant of all trade unionism after 1936. Inspired by Nazi Germany's Labor Front, bureaucrats replaced unions with labor-management councils at the plant level. In 1939–40, the authorities coaxed and coerced the remaining unions into dissolving themselves. The regime thereupon established the Greater Japan Industrial Patriotic Association, which encompassed enterprise-level councils and nearly all Japanese workers (Garon 1987).

The Industrial Patriotic Association was one of many state-run organizations that together aimed at absorbing every autonomous group in society. In 1940, officials, maverick politicians, and others founded the Imperial Rule Assistance Association (IRAA) with an eye toward creating a single mass party on the model of the Nazi Party. In short order, most nongovernmental associations – whether business federations, women's groups, farmers' leagues, or writers' guilds – were forced to disband and become part of "patriotic associations" under the IRAA.

Officials of the powerful Home Ministry were especially keen on imposing a command structure on local life that would displace the existing patchwork of community organizations ranging from obstreperous youth groups to fairly autonomous residential associations. To mobilize the populace at the grassroots more systematically, the ministry in 1940 ordered the creation of new organizations in every Japanese neighborhood. Block associations (*chōnaikai*) were established in town and city wards, while each village was divided into hamlet associations (*burakukai*). At the lowest level, the authorities organized every ten households into neighborhood associations (*tonarigumi*). Officials charged the neighborhood associations with civil defense, mutual surveillance, distribution of rations, and extracting household savings and curbing consumption (Braibanti 1948).

In spite of its totalitarian designs to obliterate civil society, the wartime regime could not roll back many ongoing developments in society and the public sphere. Japanese society in the 1930s was far more diverse and politically literate than it had been at the turn of the century. The democratic currents of the 1920s continued to influence people. They actively participated in the war effort, but often insisted that their lives improve in return (Yoshimi 1987). Although the government tightened up censorship and other controls over the media, an impressive variety of magazines continued to publish into the last years of World War II. Leftist publications had long since disappeared, but the public could still read leading middle-class magazines – even the journal of the Japan Women's Christian Temperance Union. Rather than shut down the private media, officials recognized that the nation's lively public sphere might rally people behind the war more effectively than government propaganda. Following Japan's seizure of Manchuria in the early 1930s, newspapers and the entertainment industry took the lead in stirring up "war fever" in large part for commercial reasons. With little prodding from the regime, the media offered sensationalist coverage of the fighting, and newspapers and nongovernmental associations sponsored promilitary rallies throughout the nation (Young 1998).

Likewise, the popular housewives' magazines of the 1920s (notably, *Shufu no tomo*) neither folded nor simply became mouthpieces of the wartime state. While they cooperated with the regime to preach war saving and austerity, the magazines cast their messages in the self-interested language of the emerging "women's culture." Women's magazines occasionally chided the government for cavalierly demanding that housewives save without making it worth their while. Readers were advised not simply to save for the nation, but also to enrich one's own family, elevate one's position as a clever homemaker, and give one's children the best education (Saitō 1993; Garon 2000).

As for the previously autonomous associations of the interwar era, authoritarian incorporation often had the unintended effect of relocating civil society's spirited debates and competition within the state itself. The political parties dissolved themselves in 1940, yet their Diet members continued to align themselves against rival factions in the IRAA (Berger 1977). For those people further from the centers of power, the wartime structure opened up new opportunities to participate in national life. Resident Koreans and Japan's outcastes (*burakumin*), whom society had theretofore shunned, became members of state-organized associations (Neary 1989; Chung and Tipton 1997).

Ironically, leaders of the interwar women's movement became more publicly influential after 1937 than ever before. They sat on mobilization boards and advised officials on improving conditions for women working in munitions factories. Women's leaders also worked for the Ministry of Finance, exhorting ordinary women to save money and give up "luxuries." For a former suffragist such as Ichikawa Fusae, the war represented a unique opportunity to advance women's causes as an agent of the state. Rather than resist the official incorporation of all women's groups, Ichikawa prominently supported the creation of the nearly 20-million-member Greater Japan Women's Association in 1942 (Garon 1997).

At the grassroots level, as well, the imposition of neighborhood associations did not obliterate all other forms of associational life. In most villages, the existing local women's association continued as the new wartime women's chapter, and in the cities, leaders of the previous women's groups commonly led the neighborhood associations. Moreover, the neighborhood associations frequently created networks of communal solidarity among wives that would survive the war. With their men at the front or in the factories, women headed many neighborhood associations for the first time (Fujii 1985: 202–3).

Of course, the unwillingness of wartime associations and the media to challenge the regime diminished their worth as a public sphere. Yet one could argue that the state itself was transformed by its absorption of evolving society. Officials were compelled to "democratize" their managerial apparatus, deputizing previously powerless elements. Wartime campaigns modernized their appeals, using the tools of the interwar public sphere (e.g., posters, magazines, and motion pictures). And in giving people incentives to support the war, leaders were forced to negotiate with society.

Postwar Civil Society: Expansion and Limits

From 1868 to 1945, two seemingly contradictory developments shaped relations between Japan's state and society. On the one hand, the public sphere and associational life steadily expanded. At the same time, many of the new social forces entered into rather intimate relations with the state that impeded the emergence of a truly autonomous civil society. The two tendencies continued to influence state-society relations long after Japan's defeat in World War II, but they necessarily interacted with a new external force of monumental significance. Dominated by the United States, the Allied Occupation of Japan (1945–52) introduced a series of reforms aimed at promoting the independence and assertiveness of civil society. Many of these reforms endured, even as indigenous presurrender relationships reasserted themselves.

Japan was occupied by the Western power that best preserved the late-eighteenth-century ideals of civil society. Beginning with General MacArthur himself, Americans burned with a passion to decentralize Japanese governance and encourage participation by communities and popular groups. Occupation reforms decentralized the police, established local school boards, and dismantled the Home Ministry, the command center of the imperial state.

Occupation authorities also strove to sever the historic ties between the Japanese state and popular associations, believing that these cozy relationships stifled the growth of democracy. The wartime IRAA was dissolved, as were its patriotic associations. The Americans, above all, sought to eliminate the officially created associations in each locale: the hamlet, block, and neighborhood associations, plus local chapters of the national youth and women's federations. Such organizations, complained the occupiers, compelled all residents to join, and they became the bailiwicks of bosses. Residential organizations, moreover, supplanted truly voluntary associations. Instead, the Americans encouraged the formation of nonresidential groups in which like-minded individuals could associate freely (Supreme Commander for the Allied Powers 1951; Garon 1997).

Toward that end, the Occupation removed the worst of the legal-constitutional restraints on collective action. It ordered the abrogation of presurrender laws –

notably, the Peace Preservation Law of 1925 – that had enabled officials to disband popular organizations and censor publications. Under the Trade Union Law of 1945, Japanese workers gained the long-sought rights to organize unions and collectively bargain. And in terms that were close to unconditional, the new postwar constitution of 1947 guaranteed the freedoms of religion, speech, press, assembly, and association (Beer 1984).

For a society long accustomed to active associational life and a lively public sphere, defeat and occupation served as potent catalysts. Many Japanese lambasted the elites who had led them into a losing war. People not only became free to organize against their leaders, they were often encouraged to do so. Famished housewives and disillusioned veterans formed grassroots associations throughout the nation. Periodicals representing a tremendous variety of opinions and groups appeared and disappeared at a frenetic pace. From 1945 to 1949, Occupation censors dealt with some 13,000 different periodicals and 16,500 newspapers (Dower 1999: 182).

Liberated from the worst of state repression and employers' union-busting, the political left emerged as the cornerstone of early postwar civil society. By the end of 1949, labor unions had organized more than 3 million workers – an extraordinary 56 percent of the industrial work force. Enjoying a brief ascendancy within the labor movement, the newly legalized Communist Party dared to question the continuities between the old and "New Japan" that the general public preferred to overlook. The Socialist Party was not nearly so bold. Yet as the largest opposition bloc from 1948 to the mid-1990s, the Socialists took it upon themselves to contest many of the policies and values of the ruling conservative parties. Especially during the 1950s, the Socialist Party fought furiously against conservative efforts to recentralize the police and education, restore some of the emperor's prewar powers, and weaken the constitution's Article 9, or "no war," clause. The left's opposition peaked in 1960, when millions protested the revision of the U.S.-Japan Security Treaty. Within the workplace, the early postwar unions struggled for a substantial role in management. They generally failed, but unions did wrest from employers an enduring commitment to job security for regular employees. In addition, the labor movement succeeded in persuading society of the enterprise's obligation to maintain its workers (Gordon 1998; Suzuki in this volume).

The postwar era's more active civil society also rests on the unprecedented autonomy of religious organizations, especially the new religions. After suffering decades of persecution, the new religions have flourished under the American-imposed freedom of religion. By the late 1980s, Sōka Gakkai may have had 12 million members, while Risshō Kōseikai claimed 5 million. In 1964, Sōka Gakkai organized its own political party, the Kōmeitō (Clean Government Party), which has since exerted influence as the third largest party. Although the new religions are not united on a political agenda, they generally act as watchdogs against conservative efforts to subordinate religion to the state. Formed in 1951, the Union of New Religious Organizations has thwarted the Liberal Democratic Party's efforts to grant state support to Yasukuni Shrine, the Shintō memorial to Japan's war dead. Moreover, Sōka Gakkai, its Kōmeitō, and other religions have passionately resisted measures to give government greater power to monitor religious organizations (see Hardacre in this volume; Garon 1997).

Another challenge to the political establishment came from the revitalized women's movement. The Occupation not only introduced women's suffrage and removed legal barriers to their joining political parties, but also actively encouraged the organization of women as a key democratic force. Some of the newly formed groups, notably the Women's Democratic Club (Fujin Minshu Kurabu), associated themselves with Socialist and Communist critiques of the political order. They resolutely called for gender equality and castigated conservative women's associations for their collaboration with the wartime state. Housewives, too, organized to overcome the hardships of early postwar life. Founded in 1948, the Housewives Association (Shufuren) protested faulty merchandise and the high prices of rationed goods. In recent decades, the association has spearheaded campaigns against price-fixing and unsafe products (Maclachlan in this volume). In perhaps their greatest postwar victory, disparate women's groups banded together to press the Diet into enacting the Antiprostitution Law in 1956. Women's power forced the government to abandon the system of licensed prostitution after some eighty years of operation (Robins-Mowry 1983).

A more assertive civil society unquestionably emerged during the early postwar years. At the same time, many seemingly autonomous groups remained intertwined with the state. As I argue elsewhere (Garon 1997), several elements constrained the development of a more independent civil society in postwar Japan.

First, despite its efforts to implant the American ideal of voluntary associations devoid of state interference, the Occupation failed to alter the basis of local associational life. Try as the occupiers might to eliminate the wartime neighborhood associations and block associations, local people – aided by officials – maintained block associations (*chōnaikai* or *chōkai*) in form and often name (Dore 1958: 272–75). Similarly, the residentially based women's associations (*chiiki fujinkai*) and youth associations of wartime continued with minor changes. Employing de facto compulsion, the residential associations enrolled members from nearly every household. The Americans were no more successful in their efforts to prevent the reestablishment of prefectural and national federations that vertically integrated the local women's associations. No sooner had the Occupation ended in 1952 than women's leaders formed the National Federation of Regional Women's Organizations (Zen Chifuren). In the countryside, most women also belonged to women's sections of the nationally federated Agricultural Cooperatives (Nōkyō). These federations are nominally autonomous from government ministries, but in fact they have cooperated closely with the bureaucracy and conservative parties.

What is more, many of the burgeoning popular organizations of the postwar era espoused right-wing nationalism and were not in the least interested in defending the autonomy of civil society. Harking back to the pre-1945 imperial order, they crusaded for *greater* state intervention in forming a national morality among Japanese. Prominent among them have been the Association of Shintō Shrines (Jinja Honchō) and the Society of Bereaved Families of Japan (Nihon Izokukai). Such groups have repeatedly pressed relatively moderate ruling-party leaders on behalf of conservative causes, including the reinstatement of Kigensetsu, the prewar commemoration of Japan's mythical founding by the first emperor, and the revival of state support for Yasukuni Shrine, which enshrines the spirits of the war dead. Employing the tactics of postwar democratic mobilization, grassroots rightist groups may be considered as much a part of civil society as progressive organizations (Ruoff 2001: chap. 5).

Nor were the self-styled progressive forces averse to working with the bureaucracy in campaigns aimed at managing society. Progressives and conservatives may have been at loggerheads over Article 9 of the Constitution, the role of the emperor, and the Ministry of Education's control of schools. But when it came to matters of modernizing people's daily habits or enhancing Japan's productive capacity, left and right generally agreed on the use of state power to socialize and mobilize the populace. With the notable exception of the Communists, progressive groups actively participated in official campaigns on behalf of social education, "New Life," and the promotion of household saving.

A few examples should suffice. The Socialist Party, which briefly participated in coalition governments in 1947–48, wholeheartedly supported the early postwar "National Salvation Savings Campaigns" despite their uncanny resemblance to the wartime state's intrusive drives. Moreover, the Socialist prime minister, Katayama Tetsu, was the one who in 1947 kicked off the New Life campaign, in which he exhorted Japanese to "work harder by bearing all present hardships with the idea of sacrificing the present for a better future" (Garon 1997: 164). In large firms from the 1950s to the 1970s, the wives of labor unionists flocked to company-sponsored New Life programs that taught them how to keep household budgets, improve children's nutrition, and bring "science" to daily life. Such programs enabled employers to incorporate working-class families into Japan's emerging "enterprise society," thus eroding the autonomy of labor's subculture (Gordon 1997).

Within the women's movement, most groups eagerly cooperated with bureaucratic agencies that seemingly shared their mission of encouraging ordinary women to be frugal and rational homemakers. Even the assertive Housewives Association has had few qualms about formally participating in the Central Council for Savings Promotion or the New Life Campaign Association. As late as 1958, Housewives Association members cruised in sound trucks, haranguing passersby to exercise self-restraint in end-of-the-year spending.

Another element in the often incestuous relations between Japanese society and the state revolves around the official practice of granting subsidies to nongovernmental organizations. In part because the Japanese bureaucracy is relatively small, agencies and local governments subsidize private associations to assist in implementing public policies. Under the revised Social Education Law of 1959, governments freely subsidize "social-education-related organizations." To this day, myriad organizations of women, youths, and others receive such subsidies. Social education activities range from traffic safety campaigns to recycling drives. The subsidies rarely amount to much, but most Japanese associations have had difficulty funding themselves, and many a group became dependent on official subsidies at the expense of its autonomy. Particularly in the 1950s, national or local officials routinely vetoed politically objectionable speakers or imposed their own lecturers at events they cosponsored with private associations. In one noteworthy case in 1957, when the government sought to rationalize the nationwide campaign to promote saving, officials granted a sizable sum to the National Federation of Regional Women's Organizations, which duly reorganized itself into seven regional blocs. Lamented Housewives Association leaders a year later: "When one takes money [i.e., subsidies], one cannot say what one would like. That's the state of the supposedly autonomous women's associations" (Garon 1997: 195, also 160, 189).

The generally close ties between society and the state became strained in the late 1960s and early 1970s. The government's high-growth industrial policies resulted in both worsening pollution and a public less willing to tolerate the environmental consequences of a rising GNP. Thousands of local groups arose to protest pollution and other quality-of-life problems. As many as 6 million people participated at any given time in the early 1970s (McKean 1981: 7). Intellectuals and journalists dubbed these groups "citizens' movements" (*shimin undō*), envisioning them as the core of a new grassroots democracy in which ordinary citizens took part in decision-making. Citizens' movements were distinguished from protest movements of the 1950s and the opposition to the 1960 revision of the U.S.-Japan Security Treaty: in those cases, leftist parties, labor unions, and intellectuals took the lead. For the first time, Japanese spoke explicitly of cultivating "civil society."

To what extent did the explosion of citizens' movements strengthen civil society in the long run? On the one hand, the movements emboldened ordinary residents and community leaders to question state policies and bureaucratic hegemony. They also introduced a new form of grassroots organization that citizens could apply to resolving other problems (Krauss and Simcock 1980). To the historian of state-society relations, however, they failed to overcome key constraints of the past. Many of the constituent groups were based on block associations or other residential organizations. Although some groups moved beyond their previous role as "subcontractors" for local and national governments, most remained embedded in the administrative nexus. A majority of their leaders were politically conservative, and they continued to support the Liberal Democratic Party after the heyday of citizen activism in the early 1970s (McKean 1981). Thereafter, by all accounts, citizens' movements lost much of their dynamism. Once local pollution issues were resolved and the Diet enacted antipollution legislation, most of the ad hoc groups disappeared without establishing themselves as a democratic force. Equally important, the oil shock of 1973–74 raised the specter of national economic collapse. Public attention again shifted, this time from environmental concerns back to economic growth (Krauss and Simcock 1980). Opposition parties, which had earlier captured mayoral and gubernatorial offices thanks to support from citizens' movements, gave up most of their gains in urban areas during the latter half of the 1970s.

Finally, optimistic observers of citizens' movements commonly underestimate the Japanese state's ability to accommodate and incorporate civil society. Although segments of the government originally took a dim view of civic activism, officials soon found ways of harnessing popular energy to achieve national goals. Once the first oil shock struck, environmental groups and bureaucrats discovered common ground in the causes of conservation and restraints on mass consumption. The National Federation of Regional Women's Organizations, the Housewives Federation, and housewives' magazines cooperated with the government in campaigns to encourage recycling and economizing on water and energy usage. While pleasing the environmentalists, these campaigns advanced official policies to reduce Japan's dependency on foreign energy sources, dampen inflation, and boost household savings.

At the grassroots, governments appropriated the language and organization of citizens' movements to reintegrate a great many civic groups into local administration. As the passions of the early 1970s cooled, citizens' movements often turned to assisting local governments in tidying up parks, furnishing school-crossing guards, or helping the elderly. Although we commonly speak of Japanese "volunteerism" as an autonomous development of the 1990s, officials began *recruiting* volunteers for these projects in the late 1970s. To address the problem of Japan's rapidly aging society, the Ministry of Health and Welfare spearheaded efforts to muster ever-increasing numbers of community "volunteers" to assist the elderly and others during the 1980s and 1990s. The ministry now reports more than 5 million officially registered volunteers. Of course, many of these people have decided on their own to help out. Still, we should not forget that the core of these so-called volunteers are members of existing local associations that have long cooperated with the authorities (Garon 1997: 172, 228).

Conclusion

Surveying state-society relations from the late Tokugawa era to the late twentieth century, this chapter uncovers ample evidence of a vibrant public sphere and civil society. Yet this is not to say that leading elements in civil society have generally insisted on autonomy from the state. Nor were activists in civil society necessarily tolerant and liberal toward other members of society, as the Western ideal (but not the reality) would have it. For the most part, groups in civil society – particularly middle-class ones – have worked closely with the state to "civilize" the rest of society. In many respects, the twentieth-century Japanese state's formidable capacity to manage society rests on the active participation of groups in civil society. Ironically, had Japan possessed a less vigorous civil society, its state would have remained an ineffective autocratic regime, unable to manufacture consent.

As Japan begins the twentieth-first century, we see many developments that portend a more autonomous civil society. The number of true volunteers grows, as does the number of Japanese NGOs that act on the world stage. Consumers' groups are becoming more independent of the national government and business. These and other important changes are documented in this volume. Nevertheless, it is in the historian's nature to sound a cautionary note. This is not the first time that observers have equated the expansion of the public sphere and associational life in Japan with a genuinely autonomous civil society. Today, no less than in the past, the political system is being transformed by an infusion of new social forces. Even so, we must ask: Has civil society finally reined in the managerial Japanese state, or has that state once again enmeshed a new generation of popular associations?

3

Capitalism and Civil Society in Postwar Japan: Perspectives from Intellectual History

Andrew Barshay

In postwar Japan's intellectual world, discussion of civil society has been inseparable from the tradition of Marxian thought and from debates about the nature of Japanese capitalism and, more broadly, about the significance of the imperial system and its failure for Japan's historical development. Such was the context in which the explicit discussion, and advocacy, of civil society as such began early in the postwar years. But for reasons explored here, these discussions reached critical mass only in the 1960s, leaving a considerable "afterlife" as well. The seemingly intractable malaise that has marked the Heisei era (1989–) in its turn has prompted a reconsideration of that earlier episode, but what legacy did that long-ago efflorescence leave to those now witnessing the apparent decay of Japan's postwar order?

Civil Society: Promise and Problem

The redoubtable dictionary *Kōjien* defines civil society (*shimin shakai*) as a "modern society composed of free and equal individuals, having abolished all privileges, control by status or relations of subordination. Advocated in the 17th and 18th centuries by Locke and Rousseau." In other words, the notion of civil society was European in origin and had to be translated, indigenized. Did that happen? Did the translated *term* itself come to refer, for a broad generality of Japanese, to something identifiable in their own experience and political *Weltanschauung*?

Allow me to sketch an answer. The "revolutionary Restoration" of 1868, the narrative would begin, did nothing if not create the political and legal framework, the formal preconditions, for such a society. One would then call attention to the early Meiji discourse of natural rights, to Protestant social criticism and activism, and especially to Fukuzawa Yukichi's attempt to pry loose the consciousness of his fellow Japanese from the habit of turning to the state for moral validation. All of these were currents of thought and action in which the central role was taken by former samurai, many of them political "losers" whose values and livelihood seemed to have been cast onto history's trash heap along with the Tokugawa regime. Fukuzawa argued that he and his fellow "scholars of Western learning" could serve as Japan's "middle class," albeit a virtual one, because its sociological requisites were still lacking. The point is that for Fukuzawa, and not only Fukuzawa, the "middle class" was the maker of history in the modern world. One could point out, further, the Spencerian arguments of Tokutomi Sohō to the effect that, yes indeed, the middle class was the maker of history, but that Fukuzawa's version of it belonged to the "old men of Tenpō" (Fukuzawa was born in 1835, the fifth year of the Tenpō era). The samurai values of that generation, Tokutomi held, availed nothing; former warriors had no claim to the role of history maker. Japan's commoners (*heimin*) could and would assume the honor. So said Tokutomi in 1887 (Scheiner 1970: 188–224).

And yet, amid the profusion of neologisms that sought to stabilize the categorical flux of Meiji society, "citizen" does not stand out. "Nation," rendered as both *kokumin* and *minzoku*, "people" rendered as *heimin*, *jinmin*, or *shomin*, and "middle class" – all had their champions in the age of Civilization and Enlightenment. But citizen? It may be only a slight exaggeration to say that "citizen" was at best the conceptual and moral stepchild of Japan's modernization. Instead, the official bearer of the tasks of development, and in this sense of making history, was the imperial subject, *shinmin*, clad in a neo-traditionalist mantle of loyalty, filial piety, and self-sacrifice on behalf of the national community. Installed hegemonically over these other designations for modern Japanese, it nevertheless failed to displace them. Vis-à-vis that of "subject," other collective identities were to be negotiated from positions of unequal strength, their descriptors reflective of greater or lesser consciousness of difference from official subjecthood, with difference extending by degrees toward more radical estrangements.

Legally speaking, not every subject was as free an individual as every other: the household (*ie*) system enshrined a patriarchy that remained in force until 1945. And in any case, rights did not inhere in nature but were granted by the state, which had been elevated to an object of worship. Kawakami Hajime would later put this in binary terms: "In the democratic lands of Europe, human rights are granted by heaven, and the state's rights by the people. . . . In Japan, the state's rights are granted by heaven, and human rights by the state" (quoted in Uchida 1993: 217–18). By the 1890s, "society" (*shakai*) emerged on the scene, but as a problem, the seedbed of conflict and strife and division *among* the emperor's subjects. With urbanization and industrialization, gifts in some sense of Japan's successful imperialism, "society" came all too soon to be captured by that most polarizing notion of "class," especially ominous when it bore the adjective "propertyless" (*musan*).

A propertyless class, of course, implies a propertied one. A considerable distance was traveled from the age of Fukuzawa's "virtual" middle class to the unmistakable reality of concentrated, industrially based wealth in the bourgeoisie of the

1920s. Indeed, at first sight, the former would have found the latter unrecognizable. Fukuzawa's vision was of a morally independent, nationally minded class of individuals who subsisted on their modern skills. Japan's Marxists, notoriously divided though they were in their assessments of the nature of Japan's capitalism and over revolutionary strategy, were united in the perception that the Japanese bourgeoisie was a signally sycophantic class. It depended on state favor for its position and remained so weak politically that the coming revolution – one that would usher in socialism – would nevertheless require the working class and its party to carry out the "bourgeois democratic tasks" left unfinished after 1868. Capitalism there may have been in Japan, but never a fighting bourgeoisie and perforce no "bourgeois" or "civil" society. The tasks of civil society were delegated, as before, to a virtual class, this time of reformist officials, incipient "free" professionals, intellectuals (especially university-educated and -based), journalists, and social activists. Particularly after World War I, their achievements were real. Japanese civil society, even without the hegemony of the "citizen" in political and social discourse, was not the "primordial and gelatinous" morass that Antonio Gramsci perceived in Russia (Gramsci 1971: 238).

Even so, this civil society did not enjoy broad moral or conceptual legitimacy until the massive failure of the imperial system associated with military defeat significantly eroded the moral stature of the state and the attendant category of imperial subjecthood. And to the extent that "one cannot understand prewar Japan without looking at the villages," it must also be said that as long as the landlord-tenant relation remained the crux of rural society, the "citizen" would have to wait in the ideological shadows (Yamada 1994: 69). Notwithstanding its compelling prehistory, the moment for the articulation of citizenship as a positive ideal did not come until 1945, and it would take still longer for it to assume the status of an "objective" category for social analysis. From either point of view, the history of civil society in Japan – that is, a "self-conscious" or "self-aware" history – belongs to the postwar era.

With this starting point, I turn now to an examination of three thinkers whose work gave voice to that moment. Two of these, Uchida Yoshihiko (1913–89) and Hirata Kiyoaki (1922–95), were economists and historians of economic thought who, while profoundly influenced by Marxism, were little constrained by considerations of dogma. Known as "civil society Marxists," their conception of civil society combined moral, political, and critical moments, each of which, they thought, had to be brought to bear in concert with the others in order to intervene effectually in contemporary social debate.[1] The third thinker, Maruyama Masao (1914–96), was a historian of East Asian, especially Japanese, political thought and a working political scientist. Far better known outside Japan than Uchida or Hirata, Maruyama was in fact personally close to Uchida and shared with both of them a strong conviction that the task facing socially conscious intellectuals was to contribute to the

[1] Note that "moral, political, and critical" readily translates into the "normative, strategic, and analytical" orientations discussed by Schwartz in Chapter 1 of this volume.

fullest possible realization of Japan's "modernity," which had been left tragically incomplete at war's end.

In this respect, all three were critical legatees of the "particularist" Marxism of the "Lectures Faction" (Kōza-ha), whose influence over Japanese social science and social thought extended well into the postwar era. In the famous "debate over Japanese capitalism," this group of Marxist social scientists had argued that the Meiji Restoration ushered in an "absolutist" imperial regime whose social foundation was a "semi-feudal" peasantry. In dissent, the so-called Worker-Farmer Faction (Rōnō-ha) contended that, however pusillanimous, Japan's bourgeoisie had in fact triumphed in 1868 and that the Meiji regime rested on a properly capitalist, if nonetheless backward, foundation. From this perspective, it might be said that for the Kōza-ha, Japan was a nation of subjects, while for the Rōnō-ha, it was already, if incipiently, a society of citizens.

Maruyama differed from Uchida and Hirata in one striking respect: he deliberately avoided the use of the term "civil society," into which Uchida and Hirata invested serious moral and intellectual capital. As should become clear, the fact that he avoided it is significant for the understanding of both Maruyama and postwar Japanese conceptions of civil society as it was, is, and ought to be.

The Crucible of Wartime Thought

In the words of his intimate colleague Hirata (1989: 3), Uchida was "first and foremost an economist," and in its turn, economics was first and foremost a "moral science." For Uchida, the ethical and social element preceded but did not displace the analytical. What produced the economic phenomena that form the object of analysis in a particular society? Uchida's sophisticated intellectual culture, wide range of involvements, and his close attention to form and the high literary quality of his expositions were all directed toward situating economic analysis in the dual context of history and his self-examination as a "producer" of economic knowledge. In this regard, Uchida's work evokes that of Kawakami Hajime, the founder of Marxian economics in Japan, but, more important, a founder determined to impart to Marxism that very ethical perspective he found lacking in its official, party-authorized formulations. It was, in fact, Uchida who first gave proper scholarly attention to Kawakami's work (Hirata 1989: 3–10).

The vectors of a critical, ethical, and national perspective were in place in Uchida's thinking from an early point, and as a graduate student in economics at Tokyo Imperial University, he would have been especially sensitive to the demands of status. Indeed, Uchida had left off his studies to take a position as a researcher at the East Asia Institute (Tō-A Kenkyūjo) from 1940 to 1942, conducting surveys of rice production and the "monoculturalization" of the Malay economy under British rule. As Sugiyama Mitsunobu observes (1993: 217), Uchida's work, like that of the Kōza-ha theorist Yamada Moritarō on Chinese paddy agriculture, drew on Marxist critiques of Western imperialism and to that extent coopted Marxism into the functional support of Japan's own imperial project. From January 1943 to August 1945, Uchida was affiliated with the World Economy Institute (Sekai Keizai Kenkyūshitsu) at Tokyo Imperial. Such was his contribution to "contributionism," the peculiar compulsion felt by social scientists, in their capacity as public intellectuals, to offer their services to the state and the national community in a time of crisis. But his work was interrupted, first by a brief period of conscripted service in the navy and then by four months' imprisonment under suspicion of having violated the Peace Preservation Law.

Sugiyama (1993: 217–20) also points to the dramatic difference between the efforts of Uchida and Yamada, on the one hand, and the "true-believing" embrace of Japan-centered pan-Asianism by Hirano Yoshitarō, the influential author of *The System of Japanese Capitalist Society* (*Nihon shihonshugi shakai no kikō*, 1934), on the other hand. That work, together with Yamada's *Analysis of Japanese Capitalism* (*Nihon shihonshugi bunseki*) of the same year, had virtually laid the foundation for the Kōza-ha Marxist analysis of contemporary Japanese society and political economy, one centered on the notion that the modern imperial system was an absolutist regime along the lines of post-1905 Russian tsardom. The rural "community" as the cell form of a persistent semifeudalism was matched at the elite level by the dominance of absolutist elements in the state and the corresponding fragility and sycophancy of the bourgeoisie. In the Kōza-ha perspective, Japan had no citizens, no autonomous individuals, and perforce no civil society, or only the barest beginnings of each, but it *had* developed a species of capitalism. Capitalism, in other words, was not the same thing as civil society.

Under the circumstances of political repression and wartime mobilization, Kōza-ha Marxism was bound to be taken in unwonted directions. In his pathbreaking 1934 analysis, Yamada had left open the possibility that skilled workers in *zaibatsu*-run firms could "use the judgment and discipline they developed on the job to good advantage in a revolutionary movement," that even with the legal left and union movement suppressed, wartime industrial rationalization might produce "dissident elements" – dissident, that is, by virtue of their modernity itself (Yamada Moritarō 1992: 198–99; Sugiyama 1995: 148). Following his *volte-face* (*tenkō*) to Greater East Asia-ism, by contrast, Hirano Yoshitarō argued that Western economic forms had to be prevented from penetrating any further into the region lest they undermine small-holder communitarianism with bourgeois individualism (Hirano 1934: 156; Hirano 1944; Sugiyama 1993: 207–20). The typical Kōza-ha insistence on the need for Japan to complete its bourgeois revolution, in other words, now became an assertion that revolution was no longer necessary or that Japan was *itself* the necessary revolutionary force.

As if to split the difference between these two views, the labor economist Ōkōchi Kazuo advanced the notion that wartime labor policy, by bringing about a vast increase in the number of highly skilled and "self-activating" workers, might effectively transcend the spuriously paternalistic social policy of the "Prussian-model" of capitalism typical of prewar – absolutist – Japan. Through this enhancement of the "productive forces" – labor power's being recognized as a crucial element of those forces – the social *relations* of production would be altered and the profit motive and "blind greed" of individual capitalists would be overcome. The "total social capital" could be directed to a rationalized end as a by-product of war mobilization; the active agency (*shutaisei*) of workers and managers alike would be dedicated to the greater national good. In place of its earlier and backward form of capitalism and the impossible burden of realizing socialism, Ōkōchi hoped, the Japan of what he termed the "third way" could become a "productive-forces-rational" society (Sugiyama 1995: 146–50).

That did not, could not, happen. Wartime Japan, Ōkōchi recognized, was not yet a "productive-forces-rational" society. Virtually as soon as the war ended, Uchida assumed the role of sympathetic critic and legatee of the Kōza-ha, and from that position he followed a research trajectory that refined his perspective, adjusting it to radically changing circumstances of failed total war, fitful recovery, and rapid growth. In a 1948 article, he ([1948] 1989: vol. 10, 109–18) assessed, even championed, Ōkōchi's "productive-forces theory" as a form of antifascist "contributionism"-cum-resistance, a position greeted with widespread skepticism. Beyond that, he argued, the "contradictory development" (*mujunteki tenkai*) of Japan's economic structure had indeed pushed the country's "Prussian-type" capitalism into its last phase, that of an unwinnable war. In some sense Japan had defeated itself. And finally, with that defeat, with the powers of reaction in abeyance, it was possible to contemplate the creation of a new society.

Redeeming *Homo economicus*

A new society: civil society. In one of those "slighter gestures of dissent" (Merton 1966: 162) that loom so large in historical reconstructions of wartime experience, Uchida had apparently been deeply reading Adam Smith. And following the surrender, in the face of a dramatically renascent Marxism, Uchida, like Kawakami in an earlier era, tried forcefully to link his affirmation of structural transformation with a concern for the form of subjectivity needed to make it effectual. For his orthodox contemporaries, "civil society" was a term of opprobrium, a rationalization of bourgeois egotism and acquisitiveness, a theodicy of exploitation. Developmentally, civil society was at best a pre-stage to or instrument for ushering in socialism and would not continue in any substantial way once socialism was achieved. But for Uchida, freed from the distorting – and demoralizing – effects of wartime coercion and violence, civil society was the very instrument of positive social transformation.

From his reading of Smith, Uchida drew the basic notion that real *Homo economicus* was not just a cold calculator, but the individual constituent of civil society, in which market relations and the social division of labor itself must be, and in fact are, underlain by a basic human sympathy between equals who recognize the "sanctity" of each others' good-faith efforts, their labor. Uchida invested great moral significance in the notion of "one commodity, one price" (*ichibutsu ikka*), of equality in the market. For Uchida, here was a vital "moral sentiment" without which social life clearly becomes intolerable and that must be restored to consciousness. Even as he came to immerse himself in the "early Marx" and the *Grundrisse* (texts that had become available only after the 1930s), Uchida held fast to a reading of Smith's civil society that was strongly oriented to a kind of national productivism, one far more positive than the *laissez-faire* individualism of the stereotype (Uchida [1953] 1989: vol. 1).[2]

As an inheritor of the Kōza-ha perspective on Japanese capitalism, Uchida understood that while Smith may have "used the term 'civil society' to refer in a positive sense to the society in which he lived" (Sugiyama 1995: 152), in France and even more in Germany, "civil society" meant more than what Smith imagined: in those countries it functioned critically in relation to actually existing capitalism. And beyond such relatively advanced "late starters," in Russia and Japan, where capitalism retained its semifeudal agrarian base and "Prussian" characteristics, civil society was something still to be achieved. Indeed, in an early postwar essay, Uchida writes of the Russian populists, or *narodniki*, those opponents of capitalist industrialization who had done so much to educate Marx himself on conditions in Russia, as the very bearers of Russian civil society thinking. Why? Because insofar as they envisioned a liberated peasantry now possessed of land and following the lead of local large owners toward upward mobility – what Lenin called the "American path" – "the *narodniki* were advocating capitalism in the name of anticapitalism" (Sugiyama 1995: 151–54; Uchida [1946] 1989: vol. 10, p. 79). Such considerations were intensely topical: just as Uchida, along with many others, was turning his scholarly attention to the history of Russia's peasantry, Japanese villages were on the verge of being transformed in a strikingly similar direction.

And here, certainly, lay the key to Uchida's ideas on civil society and the key to their appeal. Civil society in Japan could not possibly be the mere ideological reflex of bourgeois hegemony because that hegemony had never formed. No, the problem with Japan's bourgeoisie was its continued failure to internalize the principle of "one commodity, one price" and its premise of equality in the market and, indeed, in society more generally. If anything, Uchida pointed out, "bourgeois thought," particularly literary thought, from the Meiji period onward was antieconomistic. Its criticism of the economic world was not so much a recoil from the cold calculation of a (misunderstood) *Homo economicus* as it was of advancement through worldly success (*risshin shusse*). Uchida (1967: 81, 96) uses the example of Ozaki Kōyō's novel *The Golden She-Devil* (*Konjiki yasha*, 1897–1902) and its portrayal of those who advance by making use of personalistic connections (*kane wa kone nari*) to arraign Japanese capitalism for its lack of a healthy, modern ethos.

So, too, for the domain of labor. In the early postwar years, Uchida's views seemed fully corroborated by works such as John Bennett and Ishino Iwao's (1955)

[2] *The Birth of Economics* (*Keizaigaku no seitan*, 1953) is generally regarded as Uchida's masterpiece, albeit a flawed one (cf. Hirata 1989: 7–8). Of this work, Hirata (1989: 6) writes:

> The era in which *The Birth of Economics* appeared was one in which workers carried out factory control and people's control in the railways, in which managers formed Keidanren and other organizations in order to establish managerial rights, and various efforts were made to speed the process leading to the alliance of conservative forces. Articles reporting that Tokyo University graduates were becoming union officials appeared in the papers; at Hitotsubashi – I graduated from there – there were even those who burst out, determined to become revolutionaries. That was the age in which *The Birth* was written.

study of boss-*protégé* (*oyabun-kobun*) relations in industry, which was based on research done during the Occupation, or the legal sociologist Kawashima Takeyoshi's influential study (1948) of the "family-like structure" of Japanese society. For Uchida, the problem with capitalist society in Japan was that, although (as in feudal society) the sanctity of ownership was recognized, the sanctity of labor had not been. In a system based on status or personalistic differences, the best workers could hope for was status-appropriate "fairness," never equality. And under those circumstances, institutional (i.e., state or corporate) interest, clad in the mantle of service to the community, could be used to justify unending demands for labor. In other words, the principle of "one commodity, one price" did not apply to labor power, either.

> With the mediation of the principle of "one price per commodity," i.e., of the law of value, capitalist acquisition [of property] comes into being. However, even if the law of value is not fully realized, capitalist acquisition does in fact materialize. Japanese capitalism may be capitalism in this latter sense, but it does not constitute civil society in the first sense. The inclination toward civil society . . . contains within it an inclination toward pure *capitalism*. But at the same time, pure capitalism is a society in which, via the mediation of the law of value, property acquired through labor is definitively converted into *capitalist acquisition*, and as that occurs, demands for *earnings proportional to ability* are suppressed. In this sense, the question inevitably arises as to whether capitalist society can be called a society of citizens. To the extent that the issue of acquisition *not through status or connections, but according to ability* is forced out, civil society takes on an abstract character and drops away from *pure capitalism*. (Uchida 1967: 92–93, emphasis in the original)

In Uchida's thinking, civil society was a future-oriented but immanent critique of Japan's capitalism and, more broadly, of the complex of institutions at all levels of society that perpetuated the hold of premodern values over social life and relations. In the economic realm, the "objective correlative" of this premodernity was the much-discussed "dual structure" of the industrial economy. In the face of such circumstances, Uchida became a "pure capitalist" in the domain of thought, but instrumentally. All social relations have to become commodified first – under the aegis of a large and active labor movement – such that the "one commodity, one price" principle can be made to reward labor "according to ability." Thus would capitalist society in Japan also become civil society. Yet insofar as Uchida was a Marxist as well as a devout Smithian, the development of civil society relations would necessarily generate contradictions in the form of antagonistic relations between capital and labor. The supersession of the "purely capitalist" values of civil society is implicit in their own development. Such is the Marxian logic of his position.

Two questions arise at this juncture. First, to what extent was Uchida's position Marxist? That is, to what extent did he look to the intensification of contradictions, leading to socialist revolution, as the medium of development? And second, to what extent did the actual trajectory of Japanese capitalism accord with his expectations for the realization of civil society? Or, to be less coy about it, how did Uchida respond to the remarkable spurt of growth in the Japanese economy, and did that growth affect his basic stance as a "moral economist"?

In a sense the two questions resolve into one. Uchida had never lost the concern for the "subjective" or moral dimension of production relations. It will be recalled that he began to ponder the issue of civil society in the context of the mobilization of the economy for total war as in part a covert act of protest against his own "contribution" under duress of professional knowledge to that misbegotten process. Yet he had never championed egotism or self-interest as such, either during the war or in its aftermath. Like Kawakami, Uchida was uncomfortable with the "self," and he regarded civil society as a space, or place, for genuine, that is, autonomous and uncoerced, self-transcendence.

But whether from this elevated perspective or one that was more affirmative of attempts by "the masses" to defend their everyday lives and hard-won comforts, civil society was clearly operative in the heated ideological struggles of the 1950s. In striving to settle accounts with the old order represented by Prime Minister Kishi Nobusuke and his drive to "discipline" Japanese society as part of a program to restore the country's role as a military power, the movements leading up to and including the anti-Security Treaty (*Anzen Hoshō Jōyaku*, or *Anpo*) demonstrations of 1960 represented for Uchida the collective action of a self-aware citizenry. Its like had not been seen before. The galvanized and convergent energies of a range of quite disparate social groups, the huge scale and variety of protests, the sense that individual commitment and engagement need not come at the price of ideological subordination to any party – all of this was new. This was civil society.

Civil Society in the Wake of *Anpo*

The outcome of these struggles is well known. The so-called 1960 *Anpo* led to an epochal political defeat for the left that fixed the category of "citizen" in a variety of modes of protest. In this sense, the 1960 *Anpo* was the ne plus ultra of Japanese civil society. It also prompted a shift toward a full-court press of government policies designed to maximize the economic growth that was already under way, accelerating the rate of urbanization and the state-dependent *embourgeoisiement* of the countryside. Uchida clearly understood that the success of the government's income-doubling policy could not be ignored, but it was not merely to be celebrated. It had to be explained and anatomized – defetishized. But how?

In this context, a gap opened between the realities of the new affluence – including popular attraction to it despite the steady accumulation of social and environmental costs – and the capacities of received progressive thought and "old left" institutions to offer a credible critique. Would the critics of the "old left" do better? This was the moment, Sugiyama observed (1995: 142–43, 160), in which civil society discourse attained critical mass in the Japanese intellectual world. Why? One can see the 1960 *Anpo* in quasigeological terms, almost as if two tectonic plates, after having become closely aligned, slowly begin to pull apart.

In one sense, discussions and arguments over "organizing the spontaneous" (in Takabatake Michitoshi's memorable phrase) or the activities of the antiwar movement Beheiren (Betonamu ni Heiwa o! Shimin Rengō) point toward the emergence of the so-called new social movements, in which class and status, and indeed the notion of productive labor, recede in favor of a neocommunitarian ideal of residency as the basis for shared identity and collective action. "Community" here, however, has nothing in common with local chauvinism, but could support, as in Beheiren, a kind of "counternetwork" of local, autonomous nodes in a national, or even international, movement. Along with this came critiques (such as that of Kitazawa Masakuni 1968, 1975) of "managed" or "administered" society. Rather typically, Takabatake (1975; Sasaki-Uemura 2001) betrayed strong fears that the infinitesimally fine net of "administration" would all too soon insinuate itself into every movement, even as he understood that "spontaneity" could subsist only through organization.

On the other hand, for early postwar proponents of civil society such as Uchida, the 1960 *Anpo* was an end, and the role it played was increasingly that of Minerva's owl. Indeed, Uchida's own interests shifted away from labor unions and their struggles to passionate involvement in the salon of intellectuals that formed around Yamamoto Yasue, an actress of the (prewar) Tsukiji Little Theater and patroness of the oppositionist elite (Sugiyama 1995: 160). Yet because the cleavage between Uchida's vision of civil society and that of the not-yet-articulated new social movements was still relatively slight, Uchida's writings in fact found, if anything, even larger audiences as the 1960s wore on. Furthermore, the critical tasks of the post-*Anpo* years accorded well with Uchida's long-standing approach, one that had already separated him from Marxist orthodoxy. This was another point in his favor. Not for the first time, he would raise the question of the moral worthiness of the collective on behalf of which the efforts of labor were being claimed and whether those efforts were receiving just recompense. In a classic essay from 1967, "Japan Today and *Das Kapital*," Uchida summed up his thinking, using the coincidence of the centenaries of the Meiji Restoration and Marx's great work to allow the one to illuminate the other.

The fact was, he recognized, that "'*Das Kapital* – 100 Years' sheds a wan light in comparison with the luster (bluster) of '100 Years of Meiji.'" Japan had advanced far beyond the "developing countries" that might see socialism as a goal to be attained. "If Europe is headed from the modern to the 'supermodern,'" Uchida remarks, "then Japan is running still further ahead . . . toward the 'super-super modern'" (*chōchōkindai*). What constitutes this "super-super" modernity of Japan, however, appears to be its greatest debility:

> A kind of old patriotism is being dredged up, not as a cultural or sentimental thing, but as a politically useful andiron in forging Japan's super-modernization. The central themes are production and development. Both democracy as a humanizing factor in industrialization and European modernity as something to be admired are being played down by the super-modernizers who are trying instead to counter-balance the "excesses of democracy" in postwar Japan by

> mass-producing the antidote – patriotism. We are paying a big price in the loss of democratic freedoms in order to build our super-modern machine.[3] (Uchida 1970: 14–16)

Underlying this political criticism lay a series of linked historical claims concerning modern Japan read against and through the threefold schema of social development as Marx outlined it in his *Grundrisse*. Since the Meiji period, local autonomy in Japan had been drastically sacrificed to centralization, and a virulent statism – conflated with emperorism – subordinated both local autonomy and individual (or human or natural) rights to the "needs of the state, *for the development* of the state" (emphasis in the original). Finally, Uchida asserts, in the absence of "natural law thinking and the labor theory of value," a species of "pseudo-Darwinism" was mobilized to ensure that "the right to live" was given only to those able to survive. As a corollary, "sanctity of ownership as a widely-held concept was never broken by a belief in the sanctity of labor" (ibid.: 19–25).

In this "sanctity of ownership" Uchida saw a fundamental continuity with Japan's feudal "premodernity," the "irrational" perpetuation of personalism in spheres where it did not truly belong, such as in the exercise of public or corporate authority, but combined with a more than requisite share of "impersonal" values. This could take the form, for example, of hyperidealization, or fetishism, of material indices of performance. The result, on the one hand, was that "premodernity assumed a kind of viscous tenacity in common thinking that has never entirely disappeared." On the other hand, under unprecedented postwar conditions, this modernized premodernity had clearly fostered in the industrial work force, both blue- and white-collar, an extraordinary ethos of "service to enterprise." As he puts it (ibid.: 15–16):

> If you look beneath the surface of our social and economic life, there is a degree of premodernity in both social relations and thinking patterns. It is precisely this premodernity that has made our startling leaps in production possible, while at the same time, this same factor has rendered it extremely difficult to understand the basic nature of the problems confronting our society. . . . Among the reasons it has been possible to supermodernize so super-quickly is, I think, that Japan has not eradicated her premodernity but has sustained it in her institutions and in her thinking. Far from impeding modernization, this left-over premodernity has *helped create* what I call supermodernity at an unprecedented rate of speed. (emphasis in the original)

Or, as one commentator (Yamada 1987: 40) on Uchida succinctly observes, "paradoxical though it may seem, . . . in Japan, capitalism has developed thanks to the weakness of civil society."

Civil society, then, was the vital *medium* (literally, between state and enterprise) that enabled resistance to the overdetermined forces of "supermodernity." These

[3] The English version quoted here (Uchida 1970) is a considerably abridged version of "Shihonron *to gendai – Meiji hyakunen to* Shihonron *hyakunen*," originally published in *Sekai* no. 262 (September 1967) and reprinted in Uchida 1967: 315–60.

were forces that should be resisted because, at least at the height of Japan's high growth, they threatened to strip Japanese workers of any genuine autonomy, society of its incipient democracy, and the physical environment of its elemental livability. In putting matters this way, Uchida had both inherited and transcended the Kōza-ha perspective. The problem now was *not* simply that of "overcoming community," but of overcoming its coopted modern forms. The officialized discourse, whether at the state or corporate level, that sought to diminish the sphere of individual rights, equality, and justice in the name of "community" ignored the basis in real human sympathy that in fact sustained any viable market or society modeled on the market.

Yet Uchida was no mere proponent of enlightened self-interest. To this extent, one can say that his notion of the market, of civil society, and of "civil society capitalism" is reminiscent of the "anticapitalist capitalism" of the Russian populists. Just as the appeal of the *narodniki* to an anachronistic notion of the village community led Lenin to see them as "petit-bourgeois democrats," so, too, Uchida, mutatis mutandis, appears to rest his arguments on an idealized, and similarly anachronistic, mode of preindustrial, or at least premonopoly, capitalism. In this respect it is slightly *amattarui* – ever so sweet at the core. At the same time, he does not flee into cultural exceptionalism and resolutely rejects any attempt to "relativize" the issue of the rights of persons under the guise of resisting Western imperialism. No synonym for contemporary bourgeois society, let alone capitalism, neither is civil society fated to disappear with the advent of socialism. For Uchida, civil society possesses a virtually transhistorical status. More abstract and with a longer history than the "modern West," civil society is a slowly and painfully built up "society composed of self-aware individuals" that must – as its historical condition of possibility – be "educed" out of resistance to the process by which "civil society is incessantly converted into capitalist society" (Yamada 1994: 49; Sugiyama 1995: 144).

Civil Society and Socialism/Socialism without Civil Society

As noted, Japanese discussions of civil society peaked in intensity in the 1960s, in part as an effort among progressive social scientists to catch up with a Japan for which their conceptual legacy had not really prepared them, and in part as an effort to revitalize that legacy. In that context, the work of Hirata Kiyoaki is of central importance, fully complementary to Uchida's in that for both writers, Japan's late-developing capitalism had in fundamental ways warped its civil society, and both regarded the task of social science to be helping to push the ne plus ultra of that civil society beyond its current point. For both, civil society was a reality and a "category" for its critique: to act on that critique was to enact civil society.

But to what political end? As of the late 1960s, to inquire into capitalism (including the issue of its relationship to civil society) was to inquire into the prospects for socialism. We have already seen that for the orthodox Marxist, civil society was, if not a term of abuse, then no more than history's unworthy instrument in the inevitable transition from capitalism to socialism. Uchida had sought to detach civil society from this allegedly inevitable transition, focusing on the internal dialectics of the capitalism–civil society relation rather than on its putative resolution. For his part, Hirata took up the task of critically examining "actually existing socialism" from the point of view of Marx's own texts, but also in terms of an affirmation that socialism in crucial ways meant the continuation and full realization of civil society. Although such a reconsideration had long been delayed in Marxist circles, with the Sino-Soviet split and the Russian invasion of Czechoslovakia, the contradictions of state socialism had grown too obvious and too dangerous to ignore.

In an influential 1968 essay, "Civil Society and Socialism," Hirata (1969: 73–125) worked through exegeses of a number of key passages to restore to Marx his proper status as a critical legatee of the notion of civil society rather than its implacable antagonist. The work is notable for its sometimes brusque manner, its embattled and personal tone: "Speaking as one who has in his own way pursued economic research for all he is worth, the thought of the situation facing us today brings pain to my heart." Hirata (1969: 75) wrote in full awareness of the gap that separated him from his opponents.

Marxism today, Hirata begins, is facing an "internal collapse of values," and it is by no means clear that its adherents are capable of responding at the necessary level of depth and intellectual sincerity to the crisis: "Descartes's *cogito* must be revived *now*." The "basic categories" of *Capital*, Hirata argues, have been "lost." Property, commerce (*Verkehr*; *kōtsū*), and civil society have all fallen victim to the pernicious influence of "'Marxist-Leninist' cant." Yet they constitute a system that must be restored as such: property has its origins in productive labor (the making of things) and in the acquisition of that product by others. The "intercourse" of ordinary people in civil society as they exchange what they make actualizes both "property as production" and "property as property," introducing the dialectical moment in which the fateful alienation of work from property occurs and is ceaselessly reproduced. Civil society is the place where this exchange takes place, it is the act itself: "'Citizens' refers to ordinary, concrete human beings in their quotidian, economic life; they are the real foundation of the free and equal subjects of law." Capitalism developed, and ceaselessly continues to develop, from civil society as its partial negation. "Individual private property . . . founded on the labor of its proprietor," Marx had said, is transformed into capitalist private property. For Hirata, here lay the basis of the "private exclusiveness and mutual indifference" that "soiled" the quotidian sensibilities of "bourgeois" society. But through its own mode of (re)production, that society would generate its own negation.

This "negation of the negation" does indeed reestablish "individual property on the basis of . . . cooperation and the possession in common . . . of the means of production produced by labor itself." This foundational Marxian tenet, Hirata argued, had been misunderstood for a variety of reasons as meaning the final elimination of civil society. But for Hirata, this was an unwarranted reading. The legacy of capitalist civil society to what followed, he contended, consisted of "cooperative labor" in mechanized industry in contradiction with "dispersed" – privatized – production. The resolution of that contradiction was a synonym for socialism. But insofar as it was premised on the restitution to workers of individual ownership of their product and the continuation of legal rights to individual property and life, socialism was also a synonym for the fulfillment of civil society. "Only those who can positively value the freedom and equality of civil society – only they may criticize them. That which substantiates such criticism is civil society itself" (Hirata 1969: 73, 74, 77–93; Marx [1867] 1990: 929).

By this measure, the system of contemporary state socialism was "socialism without civil society" and therefore not genuinely socialist. Such a system was incapable of resolving long-term problems such as the continued limits on the absolute volume of wealth that would lead to inequality and conflict or the continued functionality of the division of labor and how it is to be prevented from "ossifying" as in capitalist society. Socialist society will continue to require some "internal" measure of work (such as labor time) to determine reward and aid in the planning of production, but it need not perpetuate the money fetish. Relations will, as promised, be direct, with both individuality and communality fully restored. But a socialist Leviathan had emerged that combined, in a perverted form, the "suppressive compulsion of the state under the dictatorship of the proletariat" with the "external regulative standards of the civil state." Less abstractly, Hirata (1969: 110–25) was speaking here of the use of "socialist legality" as a weapon in bureaucratic oppression and terror.

Hirata concludes with a discussion of the "theocratic tendencies" of socialist systems that have arisen in backward societies, where solidarity among individuals – premised upon a requisite development of productive forces – is lacking. Here, both the individuality and communality of the human being is alienated in the deification of the leader. The ultimate cause, Hirata argues, lies in the "backwardness" at society's base, the fatal weakness of those checking mechanisms that civil society alone can provide a people in the course of their political development. Such a pathological alienation, Hirata suggests, can end only with the "overcoming" (*yōki* or *Aufhebung*) of both the vestiges of old community relations and the immaturity of new, individually based communal forms.

When one considers Hirata's conclusions, it is no wonder his essay met with bitter criticism by those vested in the belief that actually existing socialism was already genuine. But it can hardly have been more comforting for those who believed that it might yet be made so.

Contemporary Civil Society

Earlier, I quoted an observer's remark that one cannot understand prewar Japan without looking at its villages. The observer in question was Yamada Toshio, an economist and student of Uchida's and a devotee of the French *régulation* school and its "neo-Marxist" approach to the analysis of capitalism (see Kenny 1999). In the remark cited, Yamada continued (1994: 69): "One cannot understand postwar Japan without looking at corporations." I would like to modify that statement to read: "One cannot understand civil society in Japan without looking at corporations." As noted, following his period of greatest influence in the 1960s, Uchida turned increasingly toward the intellectual life of the salon. In wondering how he might have reacted to the apparently epochal shifts in Japan's political economy since 1989, however, we may turn to Yamada's work, along with that of Hirata in his last years. An important indicator is *Contemporary Civil Society and the Enterprise State* (Hirata et al., 1994), which included a keynote essay by Hirata and contributions by five scholars, including Yamada.

Hirata identifies the "enterprise state" (*kigyō kokka*) as a hegemonic formation distinct to postwar Japan. Its contours are familiar: strong bureaucratic guidance over economic decision making, the presence of networks of massive firms with highly elaborated internal labor markets dominating a deeply segmented work force, and so on. The notion of mutually imbricated state organs and corporations seeks to bring together the micro and macro aspects of political-economic analysis that other treatments have tended to leave in isolation. I cannot assess their arguments here except to note that both Hirata and Yamada express some skepticism that Japan can be usefully described as "post-Fordist" because it never *had* been "Fordist." Yet it was only under the "Fordist compromise" of the decades after 1945 that "sustained economic growth based on high productivity was realized through the fair distribution of productivity." The lesson of Fordism was "without fairness, no efficiency." Under the "enterprise state" (or "Toyotist" regime), it was "no fairness, yet efficient," leading to "unfair, therefore efficient" (Yamada 1994: 51–58). Here was a theodicy of exploitation of a different stripe.

This point bears on the issue of civil society, "a world," as Hirata (1994a: 33) puts it, "of value, law, and sign." How does one capture the quality of civil society under the regime of the "enterprise state"? By pointing out that individual and community life are accorded no innate significance, only instrumental value for the corporations that employ "labor" but do not, as Uchida put it, recognize the labor theory of value. Instead, tremendous "cultural" work goes on within firms to shape the subjectivity of employees in such a way that no demand for labor can be refused (as opposed to being subverted) because its performance is perceived as a direct expression of that subjectivity. At its most effective, this system produces "workers vested with the soul of capital (of self-expanding value)" (Yamada 1994: 70). At its extreme, worker "subjectivity" under this regime takes the form of "death by overwork" (*karōshi*) brought about by excessive, and unremunerated, overtime. The link to civil society is cruelly empirical: when workers lack free time, they lack an essential requisite of civic or associational life. The measurement of free time, correlated with patterns in the instances of *karōshi*, speaks volumes about the condition of civil society in Japan: such is the argument of the contribution by the sociologist Katō Tetsuro (Hirata 1994b: chap. 3).

To be sure, the enterprise state has been challenged since the late 1960s by local residents', women's, citizens', and other new social movements. The range of these movements has expanded dramatically, forcefully placing the continuing operation of discriminatory structures under scrutiny. In so doing, they have certainly relativized the "location" of the large minority that makes up the corporate employee segment of the national population within actually existing civil society in Japan. The historian and political scientist Maruyama Masao (1998: 127) once noted that "unless the army is revolutionized, the revolution will not succeed. And the army is the last element to be revolutionized." If an analogy may be permitted, it is one thing to have even strong social movements active outside the corporate "core." But unless the "army" of workers within it is revolutionized, no revolution will succeed.

In modern times, Japan had gone from "semi-feudal" to "supermodern" through the agency of war, reconstruction, and growth, but without the full realization of civil society. Would Uchida have found in the decadence of the postwar system a chance for a fundamental redefinition of Japan's civil society? Or would he have thought that in the name of globalization, civil society was again being sacrificed to the gods of capital? On the one hand, while severe competition eroded profits, technological innovation also created new possibilities for their realization by reducing "socially necessary labor time." In this situation, some workers could find themselves with less (or shared) work but increased "time sovereignty" and the chance for enhanced participation in civic life as the collective narcissism of the enterprise gave way to a more mature and diversified perspective. Alternatively, in a society that has tended to equate the status of "human being" (*ningen*) with enterprise membership, greater unemployment would surely bring pervasive anomie or worse, while those who retain their identity as corporate employees might find themselves subject to still greater demands for unrewarded labor (Hirata 1994a: 41–43; Yamada 1994: 66, 70–73). As far as civil society is concerned, Uchida would say, capitalism promises nothing that it cannot also take away.

As an active category in Japanese social thought, civil society belongs to the postwar era; only then did it combine the analytical and moral force necessary to make it meaningful as more than a translated term. And yet, this new discursive status did not constitute a new hegemony. That honor, if such it was, went to the "enterprise community." As Takashima Zen'ya wrote (1950), social science must be more than the "science of civil society": it must also serve as its critique. But that is because civil society itself, in Japan as elsewhere, has a dual character. It *is* by virtue of what ought to be; it is affirmed and valued to the extent that it is self-critical. As Hirata argued, once the historical process was completed by which civil society was "articulated" by (*bunsetsu sareta*) and separated from the state, that same civil society was destined to act as a counterweight to the state. The task for contemporary analysis, however, lies in grasping the many and complex ways in which the two are being reconnected, particularly through economic institutions. In his final work, Hirata (1994a: 21–22) noted that despite the "hollowing out" of its substance by the capitalist economy from the 1960s onward, the state in Japan – in the form of the enterprise state – "remains in full force." Is the category of civil society empirically rich, analytically acute, and morally centered enough to be brought to bear on the contemporary reality of Japan? Uchida and Hirata thought it was.

Postscript: Maruyama Masao and Civil Society

Critics though they were of received versions of Marxism in Japan and elsewhere, Uchida and Hirata belong to that tradition as they did to no other. At the same time, their "faithful departures" from orthodoxy in their conceptions of civil society were attractive to thinkers more clearly outside, if not antagonistic to, Marxism. As critics within of Marxist notions of civil society, they gained prestige both from the imprimatur of that system and from the fact that they sought to challenge it. Such was the intellectual context, the peculiar symbiosis, through which Japanese civil society thought, which had achieved its first serious and self-conscious articulation only in the postwar era, was mediated to the non-Marxist intellectual world.

Among the luminaries of that world, none shone brighter, perhaps, than Maruyama Masao. An intimate of Uchida Yoshihiko, Maruyama was also a political thinker in a way Uchida was not; this seems to have been a difference of some consequence. It is interesting indeed to note that Maruyama, apart from a scattering of instances in his early writings, seems deliberately to have avoided the term "civil society." Not because he and Uchida did not share similar concerns: one has only to recall his role in the 1960 *Anpo*; his lifelong immersion in the work of Fukuzawa; his remorseless examination of what he regarded as the moral pathology of an "ultranationalist" state that arrogated to itself the authority to define its subjects' values; his declaration in 1946 that "it is precisely the 'petit-bourgeois character' that has formed the core of all that is most precious in the spiritual legacy of the West," or decades later that he "would never lower the flag of liberalism" (Maruyama [1946] 1966: 222; Maruyama, Satō, and Umemoto 1983: 142–43). Why then not speak of the Japan he envisioned as one in which civil society had "matured" and become able to support the "permanent revolution" of democracy?

One reason appears to be Maruyama's sense that in the twentieth-century West, civil society had become a "mass society" capable of producing fascism (an argument that is suggestive of Maruyama's own engagement with Marxism). Even the United States had seen McCarthyism – "fascism in the name of democracy." Given these historical – and contemporary – realities, "civil society" smacked too much of an idealized West and was too lacking in social and national specificity to be accorded the position of jewel in his lexicon. For Maruyama, civil society could not be the answer to mass society, including its postwar Japanese incarnation. The road to overcoming the contradictions of mass society – social atomization, hyper- or total politicization – lay rather in the self-conscious combination of "radical democracy with spiritual aristocracy." This was what had enabled a politically awakened Thomas Mann to turn in the depths of his being against the Germany that had produced Nazism (Maruyama 1961: parts 3–4; Ishida and Kang 1997: 11–23, 87).

To be sure, Maruyama never ceased to affirm a modern, democratic, and open society as his critical ideal. But in the end, he was most concerned with its "spirit" or "gut feelings," speaking of a "sense of the other" (*tasha kankaku*) as essential to the kind of society that Uchida, looking through idealizing lenses at a purified market relation, would call "civil." Yet as Ishida Takeshi and Kang Sangjung have remarked, Maruyama's sense of the "other" was compromised by his quest to uncover the "deep substrata" – with ethical, historical, and political dimensions – of a single national consciousness. It was as if Maruyama, while rejecting "civil society" for its economic assumption of homogeneity among its constituent members, then assumed just such a political homogeneity for Japan. But as Ishida goes on to say – and as is easily forgotten – Maruyama's final major work was a profound, even loving, exposition of Fukuzawa's *Outline of a Theory of Civilization* (Ishida and Kang 1997: 24–25, 29–37, 47–51, 98). If any figure deserves to be called the *fons et origo* of "civil society thought" in Japan, it is surely Fukuzawa, whose thought so effectively bridged the categories of the economic and the political. Even with Maruyama, then, the dilemma of civil society remains: how, in the modern world, to be both different from, and the same as, the others among whom we live, and who we ourselves are.

II
THE ASSOCIATIONAL SPHERE

4

From Developmentalism to Maturity: Japan's Civil Society Organizations in Comparative Perspective

Tsujinaka Yutaka

Introduction

The size and quality of civil society organizations are key measures of a democracy's health. Associational life in any country can be approached theoretically from three different angles: from the viewpoints of the state, of society, and of the groups themselves. I empirically operationalize these three viewpoints using the indices of state-recognized institutions, social establishments, and active groups (Tsujinaka 2002: 230–50). The state always tries to mold and influence civil society organizations to its liking by means of state-recognized institutions. Society provides such organizations with the resources to hire employees and establish offices. Regardless of institutions and establishments, citizens in practice form groups, communicate with other groups, and lobby for public policies. Analyzing the role of civil society organizations within a democracy requires this three-pronged approach if it is to comprehend fully the holistic nature of associational life.

Portraying Japanese civil society in this manner has been problematic since the dawn of modern Japan. As Frank Schwartz suggests in the introduction to this volume, Japan's civil society has been analyzed from two contrasting perspectives. First, the institutional-statist perspective emphasizes the relatively strict regulatory environment created either by a strong, interventionist state (Wolferen 1989; Sugimoto 1997) or, conversely, by a socially penetrative public administration that requires maximum mobilization of social organizations to compensate for its weak jurisdictional power (Muramatsu 1994). According to this perspective, which focuses on institutions such as public-interest corporations (*kōeki hōjin*), (mainly public) institutions play an important role in regulating civil society organizations. Studies by Lester Salamon and Helmut Anheier (1994, 1997)[1] that compared the

[1] Salamon's group projects in 1994 and 1998 compared the economic strength of the nonprofit sector in seven European countries. In terms of the financial size of this sector, Japan (2.5 percent share of

nonprofit sectors of twelve countries appear to take this perspective because of their reliance on governmental data. From this perspective, Japan's civil society is relatively small and under rigid state control.

Second, the social-pluralist perspective focuses on emerging citizen activities and movements by nongovernmental organizations (NGOs) and nonprofit organizations (NPOs) since the late 1980s (Yamamoto 1995; Dentsū Sōken 1996; Yamamoto et al. 1998; Nakamura and Nihon NPO Sentaa 1999). A kind of "NGO-NPO boom" and "volunteer revolution" was clearly observable in the 1990s (Honma and Deguchi 1996), at least in terms of media and scholarly coverage (Tsujinaka 2002: 30–34). This trend culminated in the passing of the Law to Promote Specified Nonprofit Activities (1998 Law No.7, or the NPO Law).

A social-modernization perspective that regards as natural the differentiation of societies supports the pluralist perspective: the number of interest groups, voluntary citizen groups, and other citizen-initiated social actors is thought to be directly proportional to a society's level of modernity, industrialization, and affluence (see Dahl 1991 and Huntington 1991). When viewing Japanese civil society from this perspective, it appears to be very mature, active, and pluralistic. Japan has boasted the second largest economy in the world since the 1970s and has embraced liberal democracy for more than half a century.

The path to modernization has not been completely linear: there have been several booms and waves of vitalization among civil society organizations in Japan. Corresponding to Samuel Huntington's (1991) three waves of democratization in the world's nation-states, these periods within Japan roughly correspond to Taishō democracy of the 1920s, the postwar Occupation democracy of 1945 to 1950, and the progressive municipality and citizen movements of the 1970s. The recent NGO-NPO boom of the 1990s may represent a fourth wave. Despite, or because of, the existence of these wave-like periods every twenty-five years, evaluations of Japan's civil society tend to be ambiguous and ambivalent, as are evaluations of Japan's democracy.

Clearly related to the independent foci of the institutional-statist and social-pluralist models are two vectors that are driving Japan's civil society in different directions: interventionist state control and spontaneous social drives. My main concern is how to comprehend their points of convergence empirically and comparatively and to evaluate the resulting equilibrium. To that end, my purpose here is to objectively measure and structurally characterize the organizational aspects of Japan's civil society at the turn of the twenty-first century in comparative perspective by examining the United States and South Korea as well as Japan.[2] To follow

GDP) ranks fifth between Germany and Italy and is slightly below the average of 3.4 percent. Japan recorded a higher than average proportion in four of eleven subcategories, however. This study highlighted the unsolved problem of how adequately to compare societies with different cultures and historical patterns, so differences should not be exaggerated in the fashion of some statist authors.

2 To overcome the problem of cross-cultural applicability of the concept of civil society (see Schwartz's introduction to this volume), we must compare Japan with other non-Western, industrialized societies. Here, the comparison with Korea serves that purpose.

the definition of civil society proposed by Schwartz in this volume, my objective is to delineate those intermediaries[3] located between the state and individuals or families that seek neither profit within the market nor power within the state.

I mainly base my observations and analyses on three empirical sources:

1. State-recognized institutions. I use statistics found in government directories for such institutions as associations, foundations, cooperatives, unions, NGOs, and NPOs. This material covers approximately 420,000 formally incorporated entities existing in Japan's nonprofit sector in the mid-1990s.
2. Social establishments. This refers to that category entitled "membership organizations" (Korea and the United States) and "political-economic-cultural associations" (Japan) in establishment censuses and related statistics provided by the respective governments. This category covers a narrower range of intermediaries (fewer than 40,000 associations, clubs, unions, and so on) that serves as the core of sociopolitical activities in Japan.
3. Active groups. My comprehensive Japan Interest Group Survey (JIGS) project conducted a cross-national survey of civil society organizations and interest groups in the latter part of the 1990s (Japan and Korea in 1997 and the United States in 1999) using telephone directories as population samples.[4] The most recent (2000) Japanese directory contains the category "unions and associations," which includes approximately 200,000 groups. This category offers coverage intermediate between the other two, enumerating active groups that have telephones to communicate with other actors.

Ranging from business associations to purely ideological advocacy organizations and from established think-tanks with many professional members to voluntary neighborhood groups without any staff, my definition and its operationalization as described above may entail one of this volume's most inclusive approaches to Japan's civil society. In addition, this chapter discusses the present situation, history, and structural nature of Japan's civil society organizations in comparison with those of Korea and the United States. Without this kind of systemic and

[3] According to Kasza (1995), these intermediaries are not always civic. According to his analysis, there are many administered mass organizations that work for and under authoritarian or state corporatist regimes.

[4] For further information regarding these surveys, see Tsujinaka 2002 and the codebooks contained in Tsujinaka 1999a, 1999b, 2001a, and 2001b. In a word, based on random sampling of commercial telephone directories, the survey had a sample size of approximately 4,000 to 5,000 in each country. It was conducted by mail. Differences in response rates may have affected the survey results. The highest response rate was attained in Japan (38.5 percent), followed by the United States (34.3 percent), and finally Korea (12.4 percent). The Korean data may thus represent groups that are more active and elitist than those in Japan or the United States. The author conducted similar surveys in Germany (2000) and China (2002).

structural comparison of a wide range of organizations, any debate concerning statist versus pluralist aspects of civil society would be fruitless. Because civil society organizations are not easily isolated from the state and society at large, it is very difficult to distinguish which organizations are "civil." A phenomenon such as civil society must be examined within its cultural and historical context. Therefore, it is crucial to compare Japan with other non-Western and Western societies.

The Present Configuration of Civil Society Organizations in Japan

As noted above, the present configuration of civil society organizations in Japan can be approached from the three different angles of state, society, and groups. Empirically, I examine state-recognized institutions, social establishments, and active groups.

The State and Civil Society Organizations: An Institutional Perspective

Robert Pekkanen (2000a: 77) lays out the institutional-statist understanding of the relationship between the state and civil society in Japan as follows:

> Japan has managed its civil society organizations with one of the most severe regulatory environments in the developed world. Japanese law stipulates that such groups can acquire legal status only through the explicit permission of the competent bureaucratic authority, and grants this authority continuing powers of supervision and administrative guidance. This combination of a discretionary screening function, close supervision of operations, and sanctioning power has compromised the vitality of the civil society and NPO sector in Japan. Moreover, the legal blind spots have impaired the legitimacy of many groups and the sector as a whole.

In addition to the relative strictness of the Japanese regulatory environment, he (ibid.: 76) also refers to "the comparative immobility in the pattern in Japanese regulation."

The statists, represented here by Pekkanen and Salamon and Anheier (1994, 1997), tend to focus narrowly on the system of public-interest corporations (see Sasakawa 1992 and Hayashi 1997 for a comprehensive and analytical profile of these corporations), which is based on the Japanese Civil Code. Pekkanen (2000a: 77) sharply contrasts Japan and the United States, noting that "under Japan's Civil Code system, only 26,089 groups gained legal status as nonprofit 'public interest legal persons,' versus the 1,140,000 American groups to which the IRS has granted nonprofit status."

Given these figures, the ratio of American to Japanese groups appears to be 44:1. As Pekkanen (2000a: 100) himself observes, however, there are more than 130 varieties of public-interest corporation based on ninety special laws (Minkan Kōeki Sekutaa Kenkyūkai 1997: 21–22). In Japan in the mid-1990s, the total number of groups in this category that had attained legal status reached 420,000. (See notes to Fig. 4.1, which also includes organizations without legal status, which are referred to as "nonjuridical organizations" and shown in gray, and most "political organizations.") Further complicating any analysis is the potential confusion concerning the status of such bodies under the American taxation system (as prescribed by the Internal Revenue Service) and the Japanese legal system (as delineated by the Civil Code). We must also consider the difference between America's and Japan's federal and unitary political systems, differences in size (e.g., area, population, population density), and historical patterns of state-society relations (continuity in the United States versus discontinuity in Japan as a result of its defeat in the Second World War). Given these considerations, the original figures provide an incomplete portrait of the actual state of civil society organizations in the two countries.

An adequate institutional analysis is thus very complicated, requiring at the very least elaboration of legal status in terms of what constitutes a corporate "legal person," the nature of the taxation system (e.g., taxation of different sources of income, possible deductions for contributions and donations, the status of the receivers and contributors of such tax deductions), public administration (e.g., regulations pertaining to group formation and operation, administrative subsidies and trust systems), and the role of the courts (e.g., the extent of their influence in adjudicating these problems).

Figure 4.1 illustrates the spatial configuration of civil society organizations in Japan from the institutional perspective of legal institutionalization and taxation. The horizontal axis distinguishes between organizations legally regarded as contributing to the "public good" and for-profit organizations. The vertical axis distinguishes between organizations that are regarded as foundations or having a property nature and those that emphasize human associations as sets of persons (National Institute for Research Advancement 1995: 21–32).

As pointed out by statist analysts, organizations lacking any legal status occupy a large gray zone in the middle of Figure 4.1. Associations, unions, and any other organizations that fall within this zone are called "voluntary associations" (*nin'i dantai*) in Japan, and they amount to roughly 380,000 groups in the map. These organizations are legally considered "nonjuridical associations or foundations and the like" when they have a formal organizational structure including representation, observe the principle of majority rule, demonstrate a continuous existence regardless of membership changes, have rules of representation, and hold general meetings and the like. Organizations that meet these conditions can enjoy almost the same privileges as public-interest corporations in terms of taxation on income of less than ¥8 million ($80,000) earned by means of nonprofit activities.[5]

This concept of "nonjuridical associations or foundations and the like" gradually developed within legal theory from the 1920s in response to the first surge of social

[5] See the Corporation Tax Law, Articles 7 and 66 (National Institute for Research Advancement 1994: 24–25). Article 7 clearly describes the tax exemptions available to nonjuridical associations and foundations for their nonprofit activities.

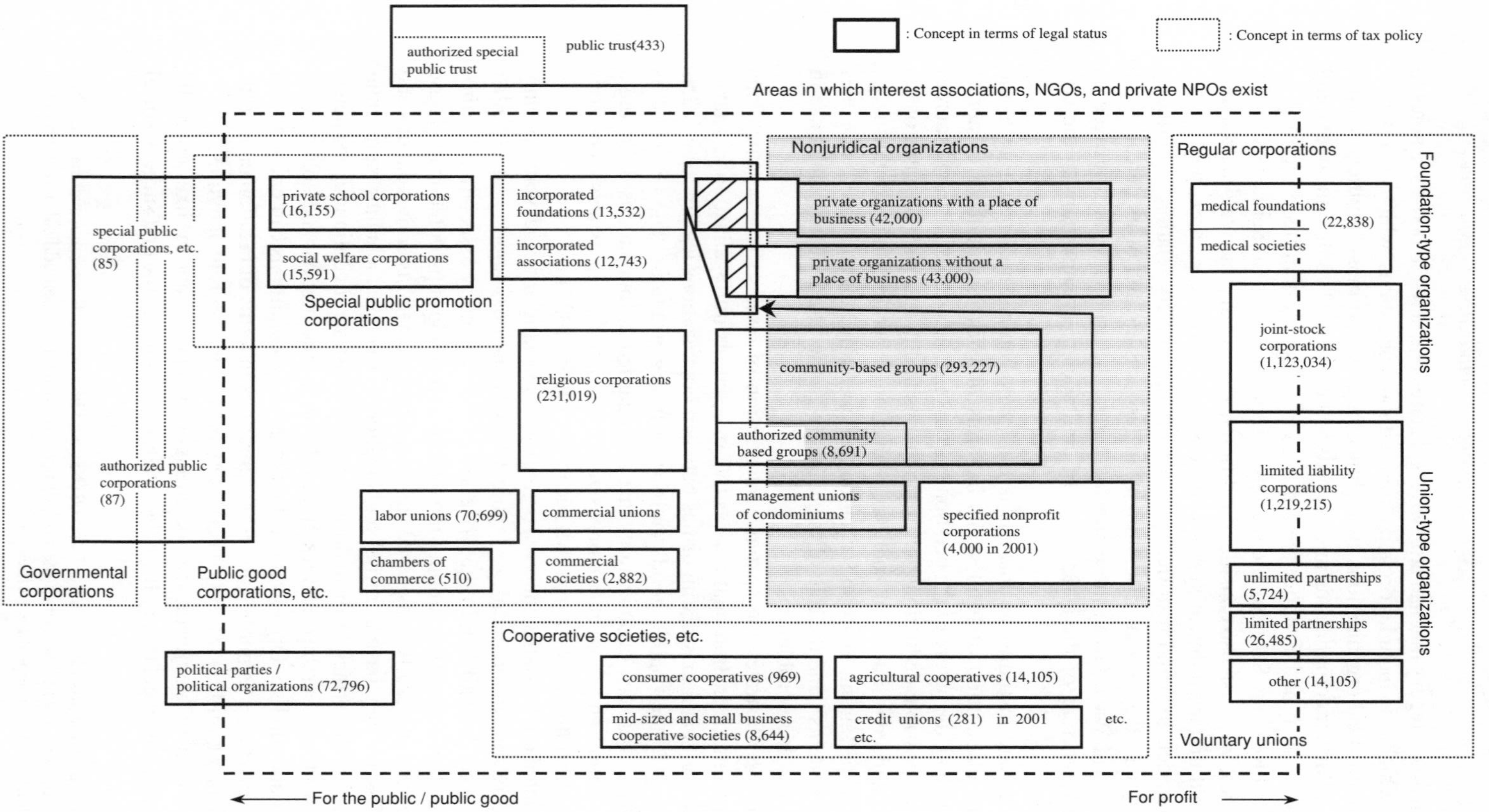

Figure 4.1 Japanese civil society organizations in institutional perspective. *Note*: These figures are for 1996 or 1997. Groups and organizations are positioned on the basis of the National Institute for Research Advancement's Report No. 980034, *Research Report on the Support System for Citizen's Public-Interest Activities* (in Japanese), 1994, p. 27. The author has revised the section "For-Profit Groups." The figures for each type of organization are based on the Economic Planning Agency's *Minkan hieiri katsudō dantai ni kan suru keizai bunseki chōsa* (Economic Analysis of Private Nonprofit Organizations), 1997, p. 10 (internal material), with additional material supplied by the author. *Source*: Tsujinaka and Mori 1998.

Table 4.1 *Number of Incorporated Organizations in the United States, Japan, and Korea by Type (per 100,000 persons)*

	United States	Japan	Korea
A. State-related	31	–	–
B. Party-related	–	58	–
C. Public-interest corporations, nonprofit organizations	511	273	65
D. Profit-making and general corporations	8,184	1,906	366
Total	8,726	2,237	431

Note: Different classification methods are used in each country for the "state-related" and "party-related" categories.
Source: Compiled by the author from government sources from the mid-1990s.

associations during the era of Taishō democracy. The concept was finally embodied in law by means of a Supreme Court decision in 1964.[6] Thus, this theory is itself a product of the development of civil society organizations and democratization in Japan.

Aside from nonjuridical associations and foundations are many incorporated nonprofit organizations. Table 4.1 shows precise per capita figures for the United States, Japan, and Korea. The figures for category C, public-interest corporations and (incorporated) nonprofit organizations, are especially interesting. This category includes a variety of civil society organizations (see Fig. 4.1; for data and data sources, see Yamauchi 1999 and Nakamura and Nihon NPO Sentaa 1999). Japan's figure of 273 per 100,000 persons is more than half that of the United States (511) and more than four times that of Korea (65). I expected that this sector would be smaller in Japan than in the United States, but it is noteworthy that the ratio of incorporated nonprofit organizations to all corporations in Japan is double that of the United States because of the huge size of America's for-profit sector.

The total number of incorporated organizations in Japan is rather small when compared with the United States. This does not mean that nonprofit organizations are significantly discriminated against in terms of legal status. In fact, the opposite is true. When Japan's figures are compared with Korea's, it seems remarkably easy for Japanese organizations to incorporate. This does not detract from the significance of the enactment of the NPO Law in 1998 and the introduction of a bill concerning the Intermediate Corporation Law to the Diet in 2001. Below I try to answer why this law and bill were introduced at this time.

6 For the Supreme Court decision, see November 14, 1964, in *Saikō saibansho hanreishū* [*The Supreme Court Case Report*], vol. 18, no. 8, p. 1671. See also Hoshino 1970: 227–314.

Table 4.2 *Incorporated Associations in the Survey Instrument (Japan, the United States, and Korea)*

	Japan	United States	Korea
Associations (capital)[a]	60.3%	86.8%	58.2%
Sample size	1,438	748	371
Associations (region)[a]	67.5%	85.4%	44.5%
Sample size	197	752	110

[a]Percentage of incorporated associations out of total samples.
Note: Japan and Korea data from 1997, U.S. data from 1999.
Source: Surveys conducted by Tsujinaka Yutaka as part of the Japanese Interest Group Survey (JIGS) Project.

Focusing on active groups, Table 4.2 shows the proportion of incorporated associations examined in the JIGS Project surveys in each country. Once again, the ratio is highest in the United States, followed by Japan, then Korea. From an institutional-statist perspective, the United States seems to be more open and generous in incorporating broad groups. The U.S. figure is only 1.5 to 2 times higher than that of Japan, however (see Table 4.1, category C). In Japan, advocacy groups such as citizen-led groups concerned with the environment and welfare demonstrate lower rates of incorporation than groups in other categories, but the potential inconvenience of their status should not be serious except in terms of legitimacy. It is interesting to note that nonprofit organizations constitute a larger share of all corporations in Japan and Korea than in the United States. In this context, Japan's severe regulatory policies do not target nonprofit organizations.

Society and Civil Society Organizations: Social Establishments

Although the institutional-statist approach successfully highlights the vector of state policy, its reach is limited to formal civil society organizations. Examination of the Establishment Censuses of Japan and Korea and the County Business Patterns of the United States[7] yields information on how many actual offices these organizations maintain and how many people work for them. By means of these statistics, we can understand both the organizational reality of society and the social outcomes of state policy.

In this context, an "establishment" is defined as "an economic unit, generally at a single physical location, where business is conducted or where service or industrial operations are performed" (Executive Office of the President 1987: 12). For a place of business to be considered an establishment, it must serve as an enduring location for a specific group's activities and have more than one employee. Each

[7] Conducted every three to five years, Japan's Establishment Census has been the government's second census since 1947. Comparable data are available since 1951 in Japan, since 1959 in the United States, and since 1981 in Korea.

country's statistics offer categories that merit further study: in Japan, Category No. 94 (Political, Economic, and Cultural Associations, which comprises four subcategories but excludes religious association); in the United States, Category No. 86 (Membership Organizations, which comprises six subcategories, of which I exclude religious associations to make the statistics more comparable with those of Japan); and in Korea, Category No. 91 (Membership Organizations, which comprises six subcategories, of which I exclude religious associations). Civil society organizations with establishments embody social capital in general terms, if not as specifically defined by Robert Putnam (1993). In comparison with those for institutions and active groups, the range of these statistics is fairly narrow.

For each country, Table 4.3 compares the absolute number of civil society establishments, the relative weight of different subcategories, and their standardized density per 100,000 persons. The first noteworthy fact is the similarity in density (Japan, 30.3; the United States, 35.6; and Korea, 29.2)[8] of associational establishments among the three different countries in the mid-1990s. Despite their differences in culture and the amount of time they have enjoyed democratic regimes, they are now similar inasmuch as they all boast liberal-democratic regimes and highly industrialized societies. These similarities belie the institutional differences analyzed above.

Nevertheless, it is easy to divine differences among the three countries in their paths to the present. On a per capita basis, Japan's figures for civil society establishments were less than one-third of America's in the 1960s and half in the 1970s before approaching the U.S. figure during the 1980s. Korea recorded a distinct up-and-down pattern during the 1980s and a major surge in the 1990s.

Differences also exist among the countries' subcategories[9] and in their compositions. The Japanese pattern is very simple: a long-lasting predominance by business associations, which accounted for one-third to one-half of the total in all periods. This can be labeled civil society developmentalism (Johnson 1982; Tsujinaka 1996: 5–9). Since the late 1980s, however, the supremacy in numbers long enjoyed by business has been eroded by the category "not elsewhere categorized" (NEC).

This NEC category includes many civic associations and semipublic organizations (mostly membership associations), such as alumni associations, fraternal associations, social clubs, taxpayer associations, parent-teacher groups, foreigners' ethnic federations, sport and hobby federations, YM/YWCAs, and so on (see Tsujinaka 1988: 80–85; Tsujinaka 1996: 36–41; Tsujinaka 2002: 85–87). The JIGS survey of active groups based on Japanese telephone directories also includes a large category titled "other (NEC)." This category contains a variety of semipublic associations and federations (30 to 40 percent of the total), ranging

[8] Based on these surveys, Japan's *employee* density in the associational sector is still only 60 percent of America's, and Korea, too, was behind in the late 1990s.

[9] Japan lacks the categories "civil" (as does Korea) and "professional." The former is included in the category not elsewhere classified (NEC), and the latter is dispersed among the business, academic-cultural, and NEC categories.

Table 4.3 *The Absolute Number, Composition, and Density per 100,000 Persons of Associations, 1960–1996*

	Japan, 1996			United States, 1995			Korea, 1996		
	Number	%	Density	Number	%	Density	Number	%	Density
Total	37,982	100.0	30.3	93,754	100.0	35.6	13,078	100.0	29.2
Business	14,728	38.8	11.8	14,643	15.6	5.6	1,230	9.4	2.7
Labor	5,248	13.8	4.2	18,819	20.1	7.2	1,552	11.9	3.5
Political	840	2.2	0.7	1,897	2.0	0.7	827	6.3	1.8
Civil				41,764	44.5	15.9			
Professional				5,871	6.3	2.2	875	6.7	2.0
Academic	942	2.5	0.8						
NEC[a]	16,224	42.7	13.0	10,760	11.5	4.1	8,594	65.7	19.2
	Japan, 1991			United States, 1990			Korea, 1991		
Total	36,140	100.0	29.2	88,725	100.0	35.5	4,103	100.0	9.5
Business	13,798	38.2	11.1	12,677	13.4	5.1	1,946	47.4	4.5
Labor	5,116	14.2	4.1	19,246	23.4	7.7	497	12.1	1.2
Political	828	2.3	0.7	1,653	1.4	0.7	645	15.7	1.5
Civil				39,999	44.8	16.0			
Professional				5,480	6.0	2.2	703	17.1	1.6
Academic	878	2.4	0.7						
NEC	15,520	42.9	12.5	9,670	10.7	3.9	312	7.6	0.7
	Japan, 1986			United States, 1986			Korea, 1986		
Total	33,668	100.0	27.7	84,989	100.0	35.2	5,604	100.0	13.5
Business	13,386	39.7	11.0	11,637	13.6	4.8	3,309	59.0	8.0
Labor	4,816	14.3	4.0	20,577	24.1	8.5	146	2.6	0.4

Political	790	2.3	0.7	1,315	1.5	0.5	352	6.3	0.9
Civil				37,067	43.3	15.3			
Professional				5,236	6.1	2.2	733	13.1	1.8
Academic	679	2.0	0.6						
NEC	13,997	41.6	11.5	9,157	10.7	3.8	1,064	19.0	2.6
	Japan, 1975			United States, 1976			Korea, 1981		
Total	20,614	100.0	18.4	80,224	100.0	37.3	4,962	100.0	12.8
Business	10,027	48.6	9.0	12,077	15.6	5.6	3,576	72.1	9.2
Labor	2,268	11.0	2.0	22,265	27.6	10.3	186	3.7	0.5
Political	532	2.6	0.5	1,371	1.7	0.6	207	4.2	0.5
Civil				33,854	42.0	15.7			
Professional				3,746	4.6	1.7	254	5.1	0.7
Academic	455	2.2	0.4						
NEC	7,332	35.6	6.5	6,911	8.6	3.2	739	14.9	1.9
	Japan, 1960			United States, 1962			no data available		
Total	10,357	100.0	11.1	62,542	100.0	34.6			
Business	4,698	45.4	5.0	11,141	17.8	6.2			
Labor	1,572	15.1	1.7	18,976	30.3	10.5			
Political	169	1.6	0.2	815	1.3	0.5			
Civil				25,236	40.3	14.0			
Professional				1,558	2.5	0.9			
Academic	147	1.4	0.2						
NEC	3,771	36.4	4.0	4,816	7.7	2.7			

[a]NEC: Not elsewhere classified

Sources: Japan: Establishment Census, Statistics Bureau, Management and Coordination Agency; United States: County Business Patterns, U.S. Bureau of Census; Korea: Report on Establishment Census, National Statistical Office.

from Traffic Safety Associations under the supervision of the Police Agency (an extreme case) to the benefit society for local public servants and a variety of civic associations (35 to 50 percent), such as sport or hobby clubs, academic societies, international and fraternal societies, social clubs, residential groups, and miscellaneous organizations that cannot be otherwise classified. Now the largest of the five categories, NEC is thus equally comprised of civic and semipublic organizations. For the purposes of international comparison, we could rename the category "civic and other."

Thus, in terms of social establishments, Japan's associational sector is a steadily expanding part of civil society as a whole, and there now exists an equilibrium between this expanding sector of civic and semipublic organizations and the relatively stagnant sector of business associations.

Active Groups in Practice

As explained above, associations with establishments account for only a limited number of civil society organizations. Many associations without establishments (i.e., that lack a permanent office or employees) are nonetheless active.[10] The challenge is how to delineate these groups. One answer is to investigate associations listed in the telephone directory and conduct a random-sampling survey. This method is more comprehensive than surveying groups that are listed in association directories or the Establishment Census (Tsujinaka 2002: 50–60). It should offer a clearer approximation of the reality of active groups because a group cannot be active today without a telephone. My survey was conducted in one metropolitan capital area and one nearby local region in each country.[11] Table 4.4 compares the number and density of associations listed in the metropolitan capital and regional telephone directories in each of the three countries.[12]

The metropolitan capital areas confirm my preliminary ideas concerning the pluralistic associational world of the United States: the per capita figure for

[10] The Economic Planning Agency conducted a comprehensive survey of Japanese citizen groups other than public-interest corporations to grasp the background situation for the NPO Law. It found that only 7 percent of all groups have a permanent office (whether rented or owned), and only 18 percent have more than one salaried staff (Shakai Chōsa Kenkyūjo 1997; see also Tokyo Metropolitan Government 1996).

[11] One local region (*ken* in Japan, *do* in Korea, and state in the United States) was selected in each country using the criteria of location relatively near the metropolitan capital area, a regional nature mixing urban and rural areas, and a certain representative character. The hope is that these factors will permit inferences about other regional locales.

[12] According to database information that has recently become available on NTT's website, 198,000 unions and associations were listed in Japan's telephone directories in July 2000. The union and association category includes more than 20 subcategories. This coverage is slightly broader than the survey population targeted in my JIGS surveys. According to NTT's database, Tokyo ranks first in absolute number and 37th in density (per 100,000 persons) out of Japan's 47 prefectures. Ibaraki ranks 25th in absolute number and 41st in density. Because the average density throughout Japan is 156, the average density during the survey period (1997) might have been higher than in Tokyo and Ibaraki.

Table 4.4 *Number of Associations in the Telephone Directory*

	Japan		Korea		United States	
	Tokyo	Ibaraki	Seoul	Gyeonggi-do	Washington, D.C.	North Carolina
Associations per 100,000 people	181.5	59.5	80.2	37.8	596.9	54.4
Number of associations	21,366	1,762	8,647	2,874	3,122	4,106
Population (10,000)	1,177	296	1,078	761	52.3	755

Notes: Japanese and Korean data from 1997, U.S. data from 1999. The population for the surveys is the number of associations in the telephone directory. See Tsujinaka 1999a, 1999b, and 2001a.
Source: Surveys conducted by Tsujinaka Yutaka as part of the Japanese Interest Group Survey (JIGS) Project.

Washington, D.C. (close to 600), is more than three times Tokyo's (182) and more than seven times Seoul's. Tokyo hosts the greatest absolute number of associations (21,366), however, followed by Seoul (8,647) and Washington, D.C. (3,122).

Differences among these capitals should not be ignored. Although Washington, D.C., is famous for specializing in politics, the other two metropolitan capitals are huge cities. In this sense, Seoul and Tokyo might be more comparable. Although the same problem may apply to the local regions of Japan's Ibaraki, Korea's Gyeonggi, and America's North Carolina, it is interesting to find similarities among them. Ibaraki has the most associations per capita (59.5), followed by North Carolina (54.4) and Gyeonggi (37.8). The first two figures are quite close, and the second is less than 1.6 times the third. As was true of social establishments, it seems likely that a similar number of groups are active in each of these local regions.

Table 4.5, which is also based on the JIGS survey, permits further analysis of the composition of active groups in each country. The survey asked target organizations to choose one of eleven classifications (one of ten in the Japanese survey; see note *e* in Table 4.5). To simplify the resulting data, I integrated the responses into three major and two residual categories: the producer sector (original classification: agriculture, business, or labor), the social service sector (educational, governmental, social welfare, or professional), the advocacy sector (political/public and citizen), religious associations, and not elsewhere classified.

Japanese organizations tend to cluster in the business, labor, governmental, and NEC categories (see section B of Table 4.5); Japan's professional sector is smaller than Korea's and America's. When gathered into broader categories (section A of Table 4.5), a larger share of groups fall into the producer and NEC categories in Japan than in the other two countries, and a smaller share into the social service and advocacy categories. This is the same developmentalist configuration as we saw in the Establishment Census, with business associations or the producer category clearly predominating.

Table 4.5 *The Proportions of Different Types of Civil Society Organizations in Japan, the United States, and Korea (5 major sectors and 11 categories, percentage)*[a]

	A		
Organization type	Tokyo	Seoul	Washington, D.C.
Producer	29.8	18.7	22.3
Social service	34.1	41.4	40.7
Advocacy	6.3	10.5	8.7
Religious	0.9	9.9	4.3
NEC[b]	28.9	19.5	24.0
Total	100.0	100.0	100.0
N	1,403	353	715
	B[c]		
Agricultural	2.5	3.7	1.5
Trade, business	19.5	11.0	17.4
Labor union	7.8	4.0	3.4
Education	8.8	8.5	18.7
Govermental	9.7	4.8	2.1
Social welfare	6.1	14.4	4.9
Professional	9.6	13.6	15.0
Political, public	2.1	2.5	6.6
Citizen	4.3	7.9	2.1[d]
Religious[e]	0.9	9.9	4.3
Other	28.9	19.5	24.0
Total	100.0	100.0	100.0
N	1,403	353	715

[a]Respondents were asked, "Which one classification best describes your organization?"
[b]Not elsewhere classified.
[c]The U.S. survey has fifteen categories that were later collapsed into eleven for purposes of comparison with other countries.
[d]Only environmental groups are included in this category.
[e]Japan's survey has no category for "religious groups," but the "not elsewhere classified" (NEC) category includes some religious associations.
Source: Surveys conducted by Tsujinaka Yutaka and the Japanese Interest Group Survey (JIGS) Group.

Summary

With regard to the number of civil society organizations in Japan in the late 1990s, institutional groups numbered more than 400,000, followed by about 200,000 active groups listed in telephone directories and about 40,000 establishments (the ratio among the three types of groups is thus 10:5:1).

From the institutional-statist perspective, there is a sizable difference among the three countries in incorporated nonprofit organizations: the United States has the most organizations of this type, followed by Japan (with about half as many on a per capita basis), and finally Korea (with about one-eighth the U.S. figure). From the social establishment perspective, all three countries enjoyed similar organizational densities in the late 1990s. From the active-group perspective, although there are clear differences among the metropolitan capital areas, the local regions are remarkably similar. I emphasize the similarities rather than the differences in social establishments and those groups that are active at the local level to correct statist portrayals of an exaggerated gap between the United States and Japan.

There was a major dichotomy among the three countries in the composition of their social establishments. In sharp contrast to the United States, Japan displays developmentalism, having many business associations, as Korea did in the 1980s. Japan also displays a gradual pluralization, however, which I elaborate below. Surveys of active groups confirmed these observations.

Historical Paths: Development by Waves, Shifting Emphases, and Maturity

Along which historical paths have Japan's characteristics been formed? I first trace these paths descriptively and then analyze the data within a historical framework.

Overview

Although verifying causal relations is difficult, there is an interesting parallel between the global waves of democratization that Huntington (1991) perceived and waves in the vitalization of civil society organizations in Japan.

Throughout the long period (1826–1926) of the first democratization wave (Huntington 1991: 16), Japan progressed through the stages of building a nation-state (from the Meiji Restoration of 1868), establishing a modern constitutional system (1889), forming a party-led government (1918, 1924–32), and granting universal manhood suffrage (1925). As shown in Figures 4.4 and 4.5 below, several brief upsurges of civil society organization formation occurred before the Second World War: around the turn of the century, from 1921 to 1933, and around 1940. The period of 1921 to 1933 coincided with Taishō democracy and the early Shōwa era. Even during this relatively democratic period, however, the state did not approve of the institutionalization of voluntary, society-led organizations in social or political processes (Miyazaki 1984; Muramatsu, Itō, and Tsujinaka 1986; Tsujinaka 1988). This was symbolized by the failure to enact a labor union law during the 1920s. Civil society organizations could maintain a de facto existence through social activities alone. Nevertheless, because almost all kinds of social organizations did in fact exist in the Taishō period, it can be regarded as the formative period of Japan's civil society.

Throughout the tsunami-like second wave (1943–62) of democratization (Huntington 1991: 18–19), Japan institutionalized and consolidated its civil society by enacting a democratic constitution (1947) and a variety of laws legitimatizing labor unions, agricultural cooperatives, consumer cooperatives, small- and medium-sized business cooperatives, and business associations. Japan went through a period of mass movements that culminated in a number of watershed events during the late 1950s and 1960s. This period carved the highest and sharpest notch in the record of establishing civil society organizations. Ultimately, the state simultaneously (1964) abandoned revision of the constitution and formally accepted wide-scale collective bargaining (the spring wage offensive, or *shuntō*) by the labor movement. As noted above, the Supreme Court finally ratified the legal theory of "nonjuridical associations or foundations and the like" in the very same year to provide unincorporated voluntary associations a status that was almost equal to that of public-interest corporations.

During this era, civil society organizations' participation in the political process gained legitimacy. Core organizations were mainly employers' associations and their labor union rivals, which supported the Liberal Democratic Party (LDP) and the Japan Socialist Party (JSP), respectively, under the so-called 1955 regime. Under this regime, Japan became a fully participatory and cooperative developmental state (Johnson 1982; Tsujinaka 1996; see also the discussions of "welfare corporatism" by Dore 1989 and "corporatism without labor" by Pempel and Tsunekawa 1979 and Pempel 1998).

During the third wave (1974 to the present) of democratization (Huntington 1991: 23–25), nonproducer sectors gained significance. Japan's policy-making process has been intermittently disturbed by emerging citizen-led movements of consumers, students, women, and opponents to pollution since the end of the 1960s. This tide led to the election of many progressive local governments in urban areas during the 1970s, which in turn pushed the national government to change environmental and welfare policies.

Since the 1980s, under the combined pressures of globalization, liberalization, and deregulation (Pempel 1998), such ruling actors as governing-party politicians, bureaucrats, and business leaders have gradually realized the need for and utility of citizen-led voluntary organizations (Yamamoto et al. 1998). This rethinking by old actors and the emergence of new citizen-led organizations suddenly became visible after the mass media focused on NGOs and NPOs in the 1990s (Kawakami 1999). Japan's civil society matured in terms of organizing the citizen-led nonproducer sector. The 1998 NPO Law was a symbolic event starting this trend. In the late 1990s, civil society organizations rapidly acquired legitimacy as actors in the policy-making process (Yamamoto 1998).

The effects of the second and third waves of democratization – the consolidation and maturation of Japan's civil society – can be traced to different patterns in civil society organizations. On the basis of previous studies (Muramatsu et al. 1986; Tsujinaka 1988; Tsujinaka 1996), I inferred as a tentative hypothesis that civil society organizations were established in Japan in the following order:

1. associations and political organizations created among the elite, and professional associations and major business firms (in the producer and social service sectors);
2. business circles and economic organizations (producer sector);

3. industry associations and labor unions (producer sector);
4. policy-taker groups and pressure groups (producer and social service sectors); and
5. citizen movements, international NGOs, public interest–promoting organizations, and citizen lobbies (advocacy sector).

In other words, groups developed in the order of elite organizations, producer organizations, policy pressure groups, and civil advocacy organizations, or, in broader terms, in the order of the producer sector, the social service sector, and the advocacy sector. This cycle can be observed over the long or mid-term, and in both the pre- and postwar periods. When regimes changed, existing organizations were abolished or reorganized and the cycle repeated itself. Comparative studies should verify whether this is a universal tendency or one that is distinctly Japanese. This should also relate to the logic of organizational capital (Walker 1991) or more broadly to the logic of path dependence and the institutional complementarity of Japan's sociopolitical system (Aoki and Okuno 1996). In any event, if there is truth to this observation, NGO- or NPO-type citizen-led organizations surfaced as a transient phenomenon in the past, but they have gradually increased their resources and expanded their networks in the same manner as other social organizations: first acquiring legitimacy in the social process, then in the political process, and finally in the policy-making process.

This hypothesis derives from a variety of empirical evidence that I have collected over time (see especially Tsujinaka 1988, 1996). The task at hand is to verify this hypothesis more empirically and systematically. To that end, I analyze establishment data for the postwar period, establishment income data for private nonprofit associations for the 1980s and 1990s, and data on the formation years of active groups (JIGS).

Postwar Developmentalism Among Civil Society Organizations in Japan

In comparison with the United States and Korea, Japan's establishment data paint a picture of steady growth punctuated by waves of vitalization of civil society organizations. On the basis of Figure 4.2 for organizational density and Table 4.3 for absolute numbers, we can describe each country's development as follows. In general, the American situation has been very stable. Year by year, the number of organizations has gradually increased. The absolute number of organizations grew 46 percent between 1959 and 1998, an average annual increase of 0.97 percent. With density per capita almost stagnant at approximately 35 organizations per 100,000 persons, America's civil society seems to have been saturated for four decades. The composition figures reveal a continuous predominance of civil citizen-led organizations. Although the density figures for labor have gradually decreased, those for the business sector, in decline at one point, show a moderate increase in recent years. With civil society in the United States changing moderately in terms of content but stagnant in terms of density, change appears to have a zero-sum quality.

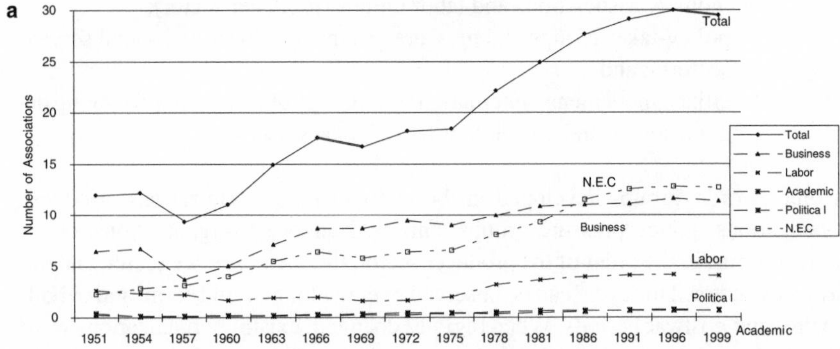

Figure 4.2a The number of associational establishments by subcategory, Japan, 1951–99 (per 100,000 persons). *Source*: Establishment Census, Statistics Bureau, Management and Coordination Agency.

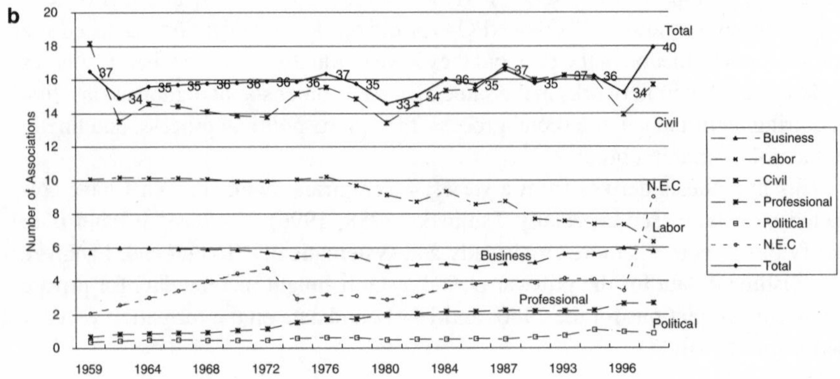

Figure 4.2b The number of associational establishments by subcategory, United States, 1959–98 (per 100,000 persons). *Source*: County Business Patterns, U.S. Bureau of the Census.

By contrast, Korea displays drastic fluctuations in the limited period of 1981 to 1996. The number of organizations decreased in the late 1980s until 1991, then tripled during the brief period of 1991 to 1996. Korea's organizational density also increased from one-third of Japan's level in 1991 to equality in 1996. With explosive growth occurring in the NEC (consisting substantially of citizen-led organizations) and labor categories, the composition of civil society shifted from the predominance of business to dominance by NEC organizations. The Korean situation since 1991 appears to be revolutionary, but interpretation is problematic: Do we see an associational bubble, well-established pluralism, or elite-led pluralism (Tsujinaka, Lee, and Yeom 1998)?

In comparison to these two societies, Japan's civil society has demonstrated steady growth in numbers. Between 1957 and 1999, the absolute number of civil society organizations more than quadrupled, growing at an annual average rate of 3.6 percent. Per capita density grew at an annual average rate of 2.7 percent until

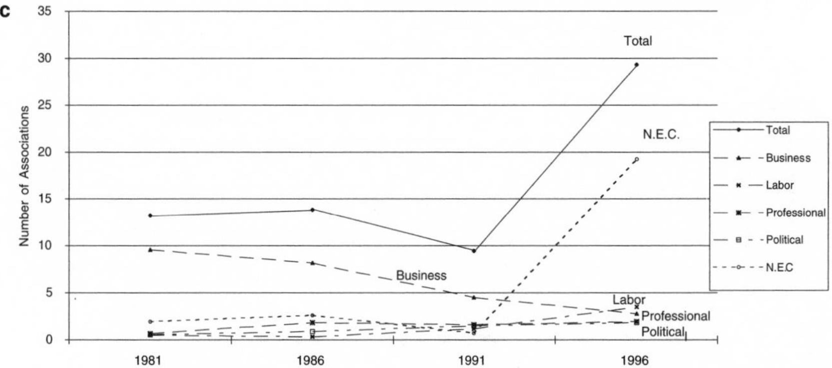

Figure 4.2c The number of associational establishments by subcategory, Korea, 1981–96 (per 100,000 persons). *Source*: Report on Establishment Census, National Statistical Office.

density reached about 85 percent of the U.S. figure in the mid-1990s. Although business associations still predominate, their position has gradually weakened, falling ten percentage points from their peak. In addition, the NEC category has continuously increased in strength – since 1986, it has been the largest category – but its growth apparently stagnated in the late 1990s.

Although the steady growth of Japan's civil society organizations is remarkable, it seems that the locus of association establishment has been influenced by economic expansion. Using density figures, Figure 4.3 graphically portrays the relationship between changes in the total number of establishments in all industries (mainly companies), which represent business cycles and general economic conditions, and changes in association establishment.

In contrast to the situations in the United States and Korea, it is very clear that in Japan there is a parallel between the two: the economy and associations have grown in proportion to one another. Because this observation is still impressionistic, I calculated for Japan and the United States the simple correlation coefficients between the per capita number of associational establishments and total establishments in all industries, between the per capita number of employees in associational establishments and total establishments in all industries, between fluctuations in the per capita number of associational establishments and total establishments in all industries, and between fluctuations in the number of per capita employees in associational establishments and total establishments in all industries (see Tables 4.6–4.9).

The results are telling. On every score, Japan's associational world exhibits stronger correlations than does America's. Except for fluctuations in the number of associations, total figures for association establishment correlate significantly with all industry-related figures. The same is true for the number of associational employees. There are many interesting variations in the correlation coefficients of subcategories.

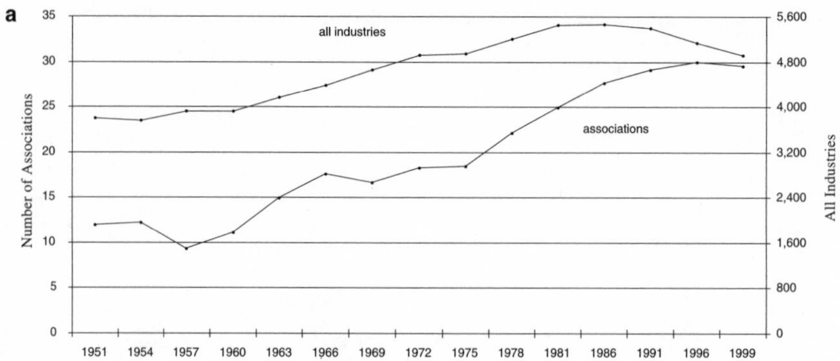

Figure 4.3a Associational establishments versus total establishments in all industries, Japan, 1951–99 (per 100,000 persons). *Source*: See Fig. 4.2a.

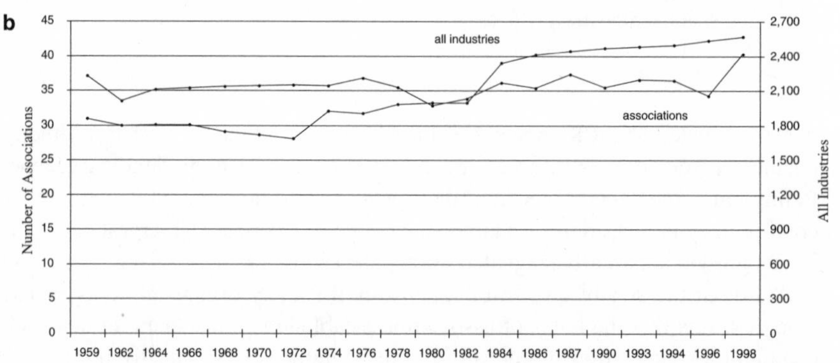

Figure 4.3b Associational establishments versus total establishments in all industries, United States, 1959–98 (per 100,000 persons). *Source*: See Fig. 4.2b.

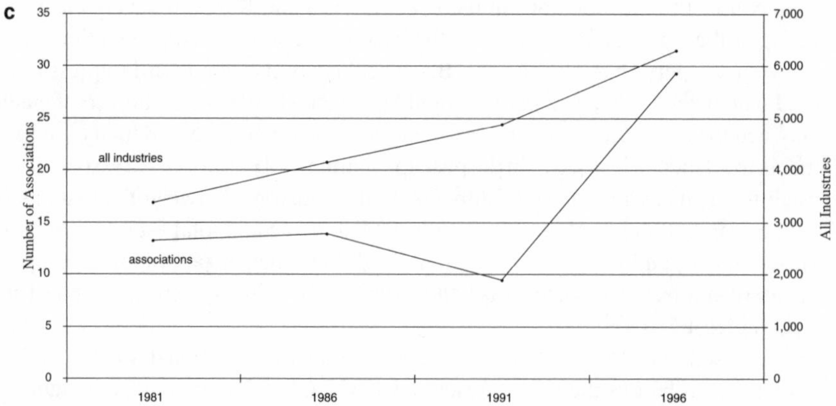

Figure 4.3c Associational establishments versus total establishments in all industries, Korea, 1981–96 (per 100,000 persons). *Source*: See Fig. 4.2c.

Table 4.6 *Correlation Between the per Capita Number of Associational Establishments and Total Establishments in All Industries*

		Organizations							
	Period	Total	Economy	Labor	Science/Civil[a]	Political	Other	Agricultural/Professional[a]	Religion
Japan	1957–99	0.865**	0.909**	0.733**	0.772**	0.955**	0.800**	−0.433 (−0.770**)[b]	−0.891**
United States	1959–98	0.367	−0.388	−0.899**	0.438	0.734**	0.408	0.900**	0.974**

[a]The organizations on the top refer only to Japan and the organizations on the bottom refer only to the United States.
[b]The correlation coefficient is for the period 1960–99.
**A coefficient with two-tailed observed significance levels less than 0.01. This means that the probability that a correlation coefficient would be obtained when there is no linear association between variables in the population is less than 1 percent.
Source: Japan: Establishment Census, Statistics Bureau, Management and Coordination Agency; United States: County Business Patterns, U.S. Bureau of Census.

Table 4.7 *Correlation Between the per Capita Number of Employees in Associational Establishments and Total Establishments in All Industries*

			Employees						
	Period	Total	Economy	Labor	Science/Civil[a]	Political	Other	Agricultural/Professional[a]	Religion
Japan	1957–99	0.930**	0.979**	0.751**	0.884**	0.802**	0.858**	0.707** (0.473)[b]	0.762**
United States	1959–98	0.598**	0.900**	0.351	0.924**	0.846**	−0.127	0.978**	0.968**

Notes: See Table 4.6.
Source: See Table 4.6

Table 4.8 *Correlation of Fluctuations in the per Capita Number of Associational Establishments and Total Establishments in All Industries*

		Organizations							
	Period	Total	Economy	Labor	Science/Civil[a]	Political	Other	Agricultural/Professional[a]	Religion
Japan	1957–99	0.559	0.552	0.331	0.007	0.770**	0.377	−0.109 (0.193)[b]	−0.079
United States	1959–98	0.172	−0.083	0.318	0.335	0.057	−0.178	0.287	0.683**

Notes: See Table 4.6.
Source: See Table 4.6.

Table 4.9 *Correlation of Fluctuations in the Number of per Capita Employees in Associational Establishments and Total Establishments in All Industries*

		Employees							
	Period	Total	Economy	Labor	Science/Civil[a]	Political	Other	Agricultural/Professional[a]	Religion
Japan	1957–99	0.672*	0.759**	0.327	0.390	0.259	0.449	0.746** (0.811**)[b]	0.241
United States	1959–98	−0.039	−0.012	0.092	0.293	−0.134	−0.153	0.128	0.354

Notes: See Table 4.6.
* A coefficent with two-tailed observed significance levels less than 0.05. This means that the probability that a correlation coefficient would be obtained when there is no linear association between variables in the population is less than 5 percent.
Source: See Table 4.6.

This statistical analysis suggests that Japan's associational world is strongly influenced by trends in the business cycle and economic conditions. In part, this is because of the high proportion of business groups, but other categories are also influenced by business conditions. In this context, Japan's associational world continues to display developmentalism.

The Formation of Active Groups

From my telephone directory data concerning active groups, we can construct a more detailed representation of the associational world. Because the data were collected in 1997 (Japan and Korea) and 1999 (the United States), we must remember that the data reveal the "birth years" of only those associations that existed at the time of these surveys. These are not data concerning the actual volume of group formation,[13] but they are informative nonetheless because they suggest trends of association formation and represent the sudden, gradual, and eventual appearance of associations that has been illustrated by other sources (see Tsujinaka et al. 1998). In addition, these statistics indicate which generations of associations have been long lasting. Figure 4.4 shows the birth year frequency statistics of civil society organizations in five major sectors.

Each of these graphs displays a distinctive peak-formation period: the period 1946–50 for Japan, the 1970s and 1980s for the United States, and 1991–95 for Korea. These periods of eruptive association formation are closely related to regime change in each country. One reasonable inference is that regime change inevitably causes the formation of new associations and pressures old associations to restructure and realign. Another inference is that the new associations that appeared immediately after such changes were strong enough to survive until the time of the survey.

Subcategories of associations display their own patterns (for the five categories, see Table 4.5). Figure 4.4 is based on figures that indicate not only patterns, but also the relative scale of each sector. The three nations underwent distinctive waves of association formation, with each sector following a pattern that confirms the differences among the three countries (Fig. 4.5 articulates these patterns even more clearly). In Japan, for example, fewer organizations form in the advocacy sector than in other sectors (except the religious one), and the formation figures in the social service sector are consistently large in both the United States and Korea.

To simplify our analysis, we can concentrate on just the producer, social service, and advocacy sectors. Figure 4.5 illustrates what percentage of each sector's organizations formed during each period. In Japan, the producer sector peaked immediately after the Second World War, with a subsequent tendency to decline;

[13] Birth-year statistics differ from the actual volume of group formation because they exclude groups that disappeared prior to the year of the survey. These statistics also differ from establishment statistics that illustrate the total number of existing associations. Regardless of these issues, birth year statistics offer many analytical insights. As a good example of this kind of analysis, see Walker 1991.

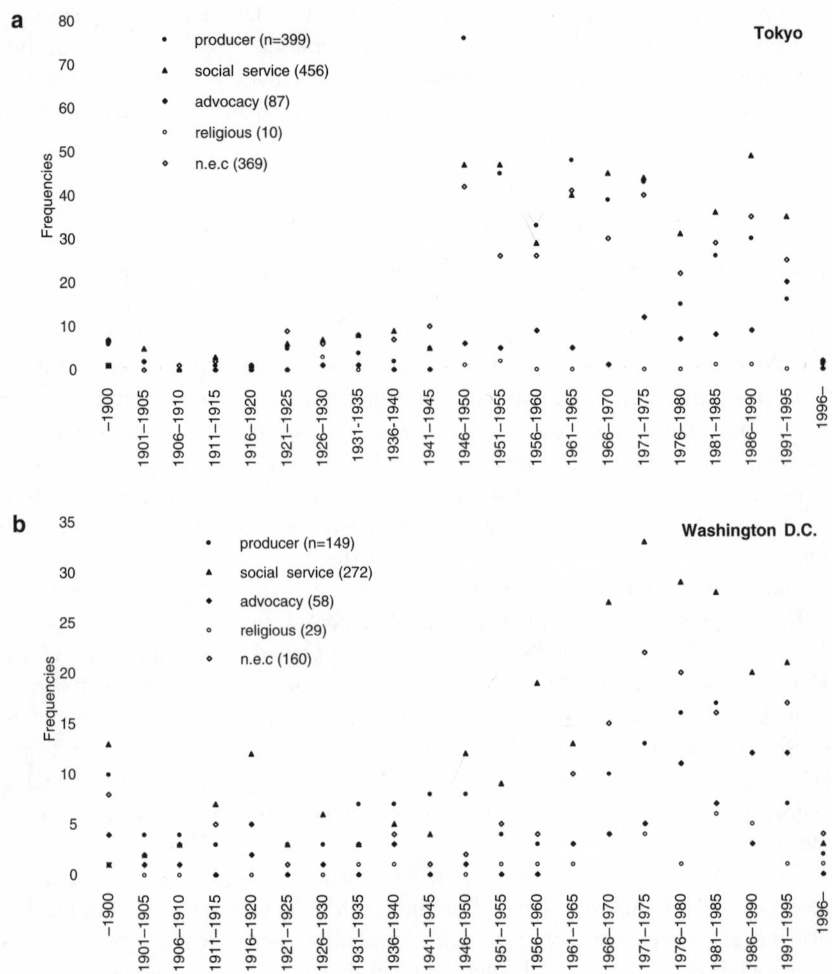

Figure 4.4 Formation of civil society organizations in five sectors in Japan, the United States, and Korea (capital city comparisons, number of foundations, five-year totals). *Note*: Japanese and Korean data from 1997, U.S. data from 1999. *Source*: Surveys conducted by Tsujinaka Yutaka and the Japanese Interest Group Survey (JIGS) Group, Cross-National Survey on Civil Society Organizations and Interest Groups (Japan), 1997; Cross-National Survey on Civil Society Organizations and Interest Groups (U.S.A.), 1999; and Cross-National Survey on Civil Society Organizations and Interest Groups (Korea), 1997.

the social sector's curve is relatively flat and tends to plateau, but the accents are moderately high immediately after the Second World War, between 1960 and 1975, and throughout the 1990s; and the advocacy sector peaks during the periods immediately after the war to 1960, around 1970, and between 1985 and 1995, with a further tendency to increase in recent years. In the United States, the

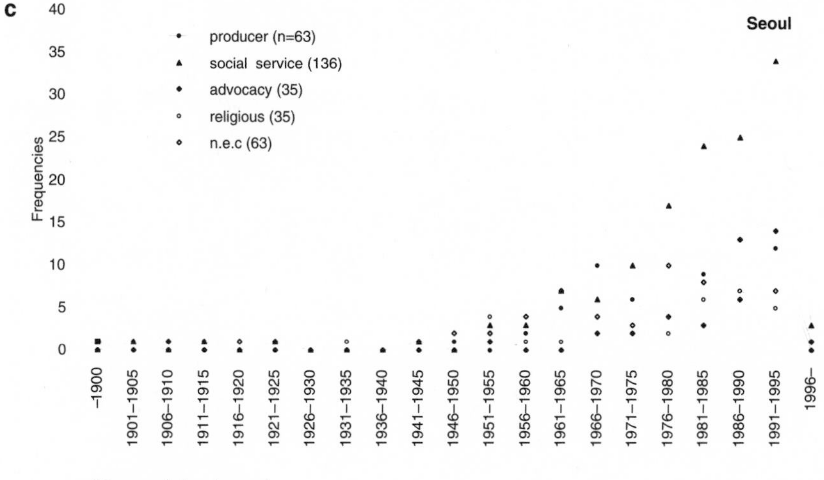

Figure 4.4 *(cont.)*

producer sector features a low hill in the 1930s and 1940s and a moderate, gently waving curve with some surges between 1970 and 1990; the social service sector shows a moderate curve with small peaks in the periods 1910–20 and 1945–60 and some surges between 1970 and 1990; and the advocacy sector surges throughout the 1970s and the 1990s. In Korea, the producer sector peaks around 1970 and between the 1980s and 1995; the social service sector shows a big surge between the 1970s and 1995; and the advocacy sector surges strongly between the late 1980s and 1995.

Why did association formation surge during each of these periods? And why did associations that appeared during these surges succeed in surviving to the time of the survey? This could be related to the nature and mechanisms of the political regime in each state. In terms of cross-national similarities, only the advocacy sectors of the three countries follow comparable paths, with accents during the 1970s and the 1990s.[14]

Japan's path is distinctive. It alone shows sharp contrasts among the producer, social service, and advocacy sectors. An "age of producers" immediately followed the Second World War and continued until 1975. The social service sector has maintained a stable association formation pattern. And the advocacy sector, while consistently accounting for less than 10 percent of all associations except during the short period of 1926 to 1930 and throughout the 1990s, has been expanding gradually but with waves throughout the postwar era, especially since 1990. Thus, the emphasis has gradually shifted from the producer to the social service sector,

[14] This similarity may be due in part to the vulnerability of the advocacy sector in any country because of its relative shortage of organizational resources. On the other hand, each peak is pronounced enough to remind us of certain eras marked by democratic movements in these three countries. These curves thus have specific meanings.

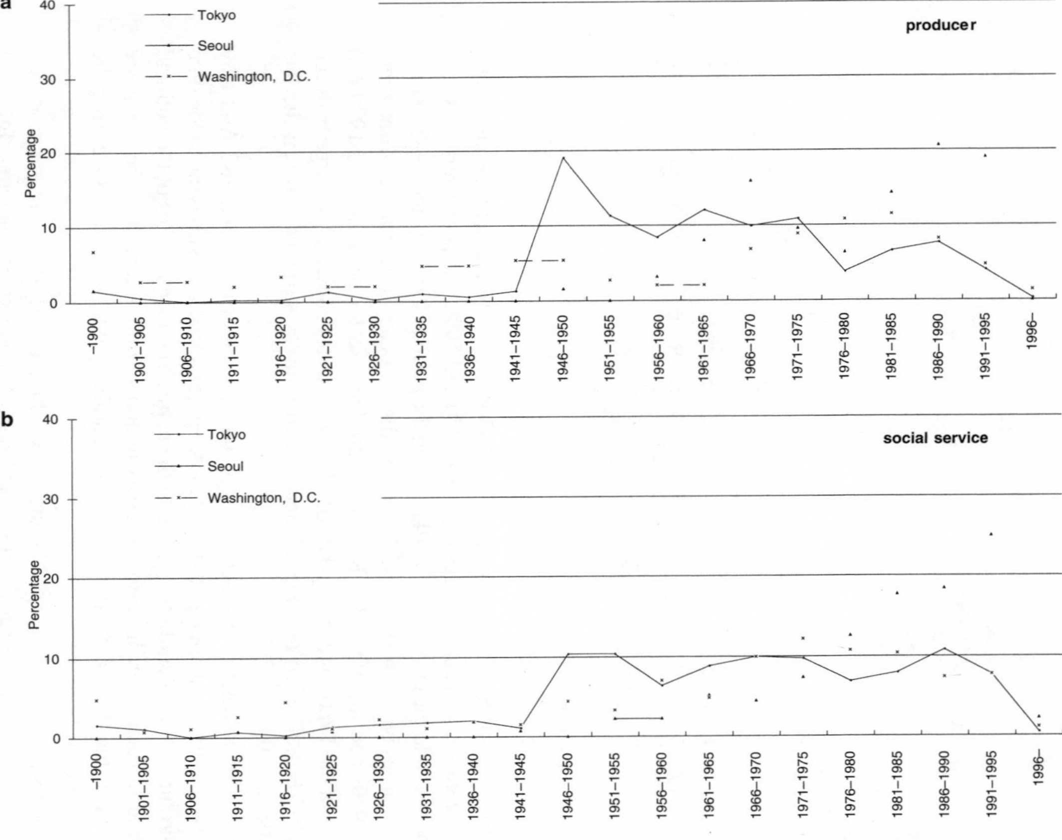

Figure 4.5 Formation of civil society organizations in the producer, social service, and advocacy sectors in Japan, the United States, and Korea (capital city comparisons, five-year totals (%)). *Source*: See Figure 4.4.

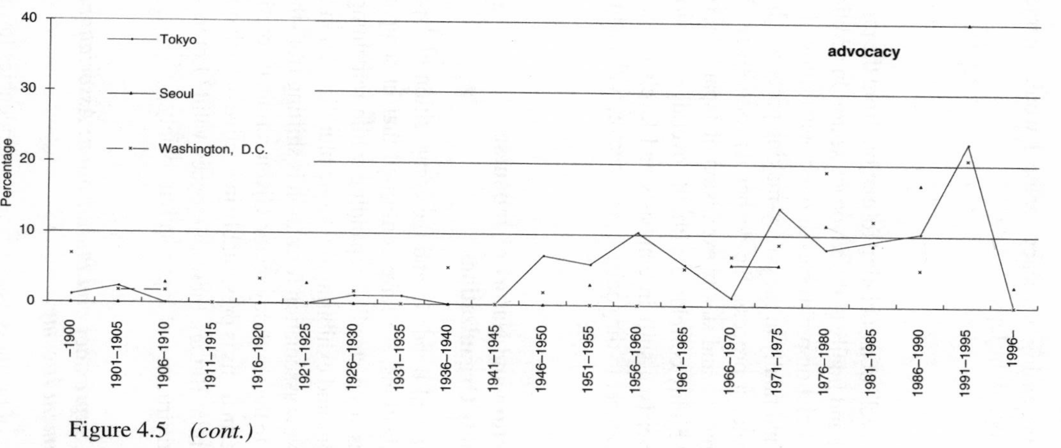

Figure 4.5 *(cont.)*

with a moderately increasing advocacy sector. I would characterize this as the maturation of civil society in Japan.

Summary

Above I proposed a cycle of association formation: from the producer sector to the social service sector and finally to the advocacy sector. In addition, I hypothesized that each type of association progresses through penetration of social processes to political processes and finally to the policy-making process. The earlier the sector appears and penetrates a process, the deeper its roots there. The establishment data reveal an impressive and steady expansion of Japan's associational world in comparison to, and highly correlated with, the overall expansion of industry. The active group data verify a shift in emphasis and levels of maturity within civil society from the producer to the social service sector, with an increasing advocacy sector.

The Structure and Nature of Japanese Civil Society Organizations

Documenting numerical trends in and the composition of Japan's population of civil society organizations, we have confirmed that in comparative perspective, its civil society has been steadily expanding while remaining weighted toward business associations and exhibiting moderate pluralization in the NEC (civil and related) category. New association formation is shifting from the producer and social service sectors to the advocacy sector. Given certain theoretical inferences, this kind of quantitative analysis is presumably indicative of such qualitative change as regime transformation. But are these inferences valid? Let us delve more deeply into the quality and structure of Japan's civil society.

Business Supremacy and Pluralization: Associational Establishment Income

Can the supremacy of business associations or tendencies toward pluralization be interpolated by examining the income statistics of associational establishments? Available statistics (Economic Planning Agency 1981–98) cover business, labor, culture/academic, and NEC associational establishments between 1981 and 1998. This coverage is close to that of the preceding two sections but excludes political associations.[15]

[15] The statistics of the *Report on the Conditions of Private Nonprofit Organizations* (*Minkan hieiri dantai jittai hōkoku*) have been collected annually since 1981 by the Economic Research Institute of the Economic Planning Agency (EPA; located since 2001 in the Cabinet Office). They are based on random-sampling surveys of approximately 2,000 samples, including all nonprofit establishments employing more than fifty persons. See also EPA 1998 for estimates of their financial size. For NGOs, see Japan NGO Center for International Cooperation 1996b.

The statistics show a rapid and steady expansion of associational income. From 1981 until 1996, total associational income increased from ¥2,335 billion ($23.35 billion) to ¥5,035 billion ($50.35 billion), an aggregate growth of 116 percent, which translates into an annual average growth of 5.3 percent. This growth rate is far higher than those of the number of establishments and the number of employees in associational establishments.[16] Even after Japan's economic bubble burst, civil society organizations maintained high rates of growth in income, with total income peaking in 1996. The data also illustrate the interesting fact that labor's income peaked in 1996 and dropped 43 percent the following year, and the income of the NEC (civil and other) category similarly peaked in 1997 and suddenly declined 32 percent the following year.[17] These facts remind us of the significance of the enactment of the NPO Law in 1998. After civil society organizations had increased in number of establishments and employees and radically expanded their incomes, they faced serious barriers to future growth in the period 1996–97, and they may have felt anxious about future budgetary problems.

The contrast between the 1980s and 1990s in income distribution is remarkably clear. First, the business sector maintained a continuous superiority in both periods, with a share in excess of 40 percent, which was slightly larger than its share of associational establishments and employees. Nevertheless, the 1990s saw a reduction in business's share from 50 to 43 percent, while the share of NEC (civil and other associations) increased from 34 to 42 percent. Meanwhile the share of labor and academic/culture associations shrank over this period.

These income statistics offer more qualitative evidence for both the tenacious developmentalism and the gradual pluralization (maturity) hypotheses.

The Relative Strength of Civil Society Organizations

While we have consistently confirmed the coexistence of both tenacious developmentalism and an emerging mature pluralism in Japan, one remaining area of controversy is the relative strength of civil society organizations, especially within the advocacy sector (i.e., civic, political, and public-interest groups). The statist perspective emphasizes this sector's vulnerability and dependency, but is this portrayal accurate?

I tested this in terms of organizational resources in the active groups data drawn from the JIGS telephone directory surveys of the metropolitan capital and a local region. To discern organizational resources, I focused on membership figures,

[16] The number of associational establishments in all four categories increased from 28,579 to 37,142, an aggregate growth rate of 30 percent, which translates into an annual average of 1.8 percent. The number of employees in the four categories of associational establishments increased from 155,119 to 232,033, an aggregate growth rate of 50 percent, which translates into an annual average of 2.7 percent.

[17] There appear to be lags between the business cycle, the budgets of business organizations, and the budgets of labor and NEC organizations. Several years after Japan's long downturn had begun, business organizations suffered budgetary declines from 1993 until 1997. Several years after business organizations had begun to suffer, labor and NEC organizations followed suit.

permanent staff size, and income. First, I compared the overall strength of civil society organizations.

In the three countries' capitals, we find obvious similarities in the distribution of membership (the modes are the categories 100 to 500 and 1,000 to 5,000 members) and staff size (three to thirty employees). The United States lies at the top of a ladder-shaped pattern among the three countries, followed by Japan and then Korea. As for income, the United States and Japan show clear similarities (the modes are the categories ¥30 million to ¥100 million ($300,000 to $1 million) and ¥200 million to ¥1 billion ($2 million to $10 million)), but the ladder-shaped pattern is even more evident: the United States leads again, followed by Japan and Korea.

It is interesting to note that in the local regions, Japanese groups demonstrate the most organizational resources as measured by all three indices, followed by the United States and Korea.[18] I contrasted staff size in the metropolitan capitals and the local regions. Staff size is regarded as the most important index for comparative purposes because differences in purchasing power and other organizational characteristics can be ignored. Japan ranks second in its capital, but first in its region. Regional civil society organizations in Japan seem to be richer in resources than in the United States and Korea.

Turning now to the advocacy sector, Table 4.10 compares its organizations' strength to the average strength of all civil society organizations in the three countries. Generally, membership figures for the advocacy sector are above average in the three countries. As for staff size and income, civil associations in Japan are weaker than the average, but political associations are typical of all civil society organizations. In Korea, neither civil nor political associations are unusual. In the United States as well, they are either typical or slightly above average.

It is necessary to point out that the survey had a higher response rate in Japan, so it is possible that small groups are more heavily represented there due to the comprehensiveness of the survey. Regional figures are for reference rather than for exact comparisons because of the small sample sizes.

In conclusion, our data on active groups do suggest the relative vulnerability of civic but not political associations in Japan in international perspective.

Conclusion

Because the size and quality of civil society organizations are key measures of the health of a democracy, I have attempted to measure the associational life of Japan and compare it with that of the United States and Korea from three angles: those of state-recognized institutions, social establishments, and active groups. My main purpose here was to provide fully documented evidence to contribute to further

18 The Japanese region of Ibaraki contains more producer sector associations than the American and Korean regions studied here.

Table 4.10 *Relative Strength of Advocacy Associations in Terms of Organizational Resources*[a]

	Japan		Korea		United States	
	Civil	Political	Civil	Political	Civil	Political
Capital						
Individual members	No difference	High	High	High[b]	High	High
Paid full-time employees	Low	No difference	No difference	No difference[b]	No difference	No difference
Finance	Low	No difference	No difference	Slightly low[b]	High	No difference
Region[c]						
Individual members	No difference	No difference	No difference	–[d]	High	High
Paid full-time employees	Low	Low	Low	–[d]	Slightly high	No difference
Finance	Low	Low	Low	–[d]	High	No difference

[a]"Relative strength" refers to five degrees of difference between survey figures and the average, ranging from "low" (the survey figures are much lower than the average) to "no difference" (the survey figures are close to the average) to "high" (the survey figures are much higher than the average).
[b]The sample size is small.
[c]The sample size of each item in each region is small.
[d]The sample size is zero.
Source: Surveys conducted by Tsujinaka Yutaka and the Japanese Interest Group Survey (JIGS) Group.

debate on the nature of civil society in Japan, whether from the institutional-statist or the social-pluralist viewpoint.

Regarding the size of civil society in terms of state-recognized institutions, my survey found that Japan has half as many nonprofit corporations as the United States (on a per capita basis), but about four times as many as Korea. In terms of their share of all corporations (including for-profit companies), however, Japan's figures are twice those of the United States. There is a large sector of unincorporated "voluntary groups" in Japan, mainly in the advocacy field. In terms of social establishments (permanent places of business with full-time employees), on the other hand, we found a similar density of associations in all three countries. And in terms of active groups, there is no large difference among the countries' local regions. Whatever the expected differences, we can thus conclude that the size of the population of civil society organizations in the three countries was quite similar in the late 1990s.

Despite this similarity in numbers, we found sharp differences in the composition of the associational worlds of these three countries. Japan in particular continues to display a numerical superiority in business associations, which account for approximately 40 percent of all associational establishments (a plurality) and more than 40 percent of all associational income. Although its proportion is smaller among active groups (around 20 percent), even this share is larger than in the United States and Korea. The producer sector in the active group category (which includes business, labor, and agricultural associations) is also the largest in Japan. This developmentalist configuration was confirmed by correlating the history of associational establishments with that of all establishments. Unlike the American pattern, the growth of Japanese associations has been strongly influenced by economic growth.

In determining whether this developmentalism is permanent, trends in the NEC category indicate a transformation since the 1980s. The growth experienced by Japanese civil society organizations during the 1980s and 1990s was due mainly to organizational and financial expansion within the NEC category, which combines civic advocacy, semipublic, and miscellaneous groups. Given the data on years of formation of active groups, there has been a distinct shift in emphasis from the producer sector to the social service sector and finally to the advocacy sector in Japan.

Finally, focusing on the advocacy sector, civic associations demonstrated the most vulnerability, being weaker than the average association in Japan, if not in the United States and Korea. Even so, political associations exhibited average strength in Japan, not unlike the situation in the other two countries.

Japan has undergone waves of democratization that have stimulated civil society organizations, and it was through these waves of democratization that civil society organizations have come to gain greater access and acceptance in the postwar era. Throughout this period, civil society organizations in Japan have carried the imprint of a developmental state (Johnson 1982) in that the producer sector (including industry associations, business groups, and even labor and agricultural associations) has been overrepresented, at least in comparison with the United States, while civic advocacy groups have been underrepresented and organizationally and financially weak. This imprint has maintained an institutional and sociopolitical structure that includes related legal codes, state agencies, party-political liaisons, and so on, which demonstrate (using neoinstitutionalist terminology) an institutional complementarity and path dependence in postwar Japan's sociopolitical system (Aoki and Okuno 1996: 24–36; Tsujinaka 2002: 334–35).

Nevertheless, supported by the government and business, a mixed sector of civic and semipublic associations began booming in the 1980s and especially in the 1990s. Just as this boom started to face budgetary constraints, the NPO Law was passed in 1998, making it somewhat easier for citizens' advocacy groups to obtain legal status and gain legitimacy. There is additional evidence that NGOs and NPOs may increase significantly in number and resources in the decades ahead to occupy a greater area of the gray zone of nonjuridical organizations in Figure 4.1. By any measure, we can find evidence of increasing pluralization and growing maturity in Japan's civil society, regardless of what happens to its economy.

The pattern of growth of Japan's civil society is distinctive in its gradual transition from developmentalism to pluralistic maturity. In this context, both statist and pluralist models are misleading. While the former focuses too much on the institutional dimension, the latter limits its focus to the surface of emerging bubbles. Because the statist viewpoint overemphasizes the system of public-interest corporations, it cannot grasp the dynamism evident from the perspective of social establishments and active groups. Because the pluralist model overemphasizes the advocacy sector, it cannot comprehend the structural nature of Japan's civil society.

At the turn of the twenty-first century, Japan displays a unique mixture of both tenacious developmentalism and emerging pluralism (Tsujinaka 1997). In examining this turning point in the fourth wave of democratization in modern Japanese history, I predict that pluralism will finally advance one more crucial step thanks to the NPO Law and related structural reforms in public-private relations that should result from today's harsh economic conditions.

5

Molding Japanese Civil Society: State-Structured Incentives and the Patterning of Civil Society

Robert Pekkanen

What is the role of the state in the development of civil society?[1] Rather than a simplistic, oppositional relationship, the state's influence has typically been to shape, not suppress, civil society. Through its direct and indirect structuring of incentives, the state promotes a particular pattern of civil society organization; political institutions structure the "rules of the game," which in part determine who plays and who flourishes. This pervasive influence can be overt or subtle. Legal, regulatory, and financial institutions and instruments create varying incentives for the organization of civil society by the processes of group formation and development and institutionalization of social movements.[2] Rules on what kind of groups are allowed to form have clear implications, but less obvious are the implications of bulk-mailing discounts for nonprofit organizations, which promote mass memberships, or a difference in access points for interest groups in the policy-making process. In making this argument, this chapter joins an emerging trend of more sophisticated understandings of how the organizational dimensions of civil society are influenced by state action and political institutions (e.g., Carapico 1998; Skocpol 1999; Levy 1999; Chessa 2000).

State structuring of incentives accounts for the pattern of civil society development found in Japan today, with state actions promoting one type of group at the same time they have hindered another. Specifically, small, local groups such as neighborhood associations have been promoted by the state; large, independent, professionalized groups such as Greenpeace have faced a much more hostile legal environment. While few observers would dispute the existence of this pattern, it

[1] The author thanks John Campbell, Steven K. Vogel, Jonah Levy, Saadia Pekkanen, Richard Samuels, Apichai Shipper, and the participants of the "Global Perspectives on Civil Society in Japan" conference of January 2000 for comments on this text. The author also gratefully acknowledges the support of the Aspen Institute Nonprofit Sector Research Fund.

[2] This is the meaning of the word "molding" in the title, which also acknowledges Sheldon Garon's important study (1997) on the relationship between groups and the state in several spheres.

is not often recognized that this state of affairs exists in large measure because of state action.

The distinctive pattern of many small, local groups and few large, professionalized groups has a variety of consequences. Small, local groups can contribute to stocks of social capital and perhaps to the performance of local governments. They form a crucial basis of social life. These groups lack professional staffs, however. Unlike small, local groups without full-time employees, professionalized groups that have a large core of full-time employees can develop expertise, institutionalize movements, and influence policies and other outcomes down the road; they change the political landscape.

Compare the many old people's clubs in Japan with the American Association of Retired Persons (AARP) in the United States. The AARP claims 30 million members, 160,000 volunteers, 1,837 employees, and, through its dozens of registered lobbyists and more than 150 policy and legislative staffers, an important influence on policy making (Karen Stewart, AARP staff; telephone interview, July 31, 2000). Although Japanese old people's clubs might improve the quality of life of many aged people by providing them opportunities to socialize, they are neighborhood affairs with limited membership, no professional staff, and no impact on policy making. The distinction is not in the number of members or volunteers,[3] but rather in the concentration, in the U.S. case, of membership in one organization with professional staff. Original research made a crucial contribution to the success of the Nobel Prize–winning International Campaign to Ban Land Mines, which compiled gruesome statistics such as the fact that one in every 236 Cambodians is an amputee, compared with one in every 22,000 Americans (Price 1998: 620). Beyond research, the message must be put out. Greenpeace, for example, has its own media facilities and can distribute photographs to newspapers and circulate video news spots to television stations in 88 countries within hours (Wapner 1995: 320). The point is not that one organizational configuration is more effective or "better" than the other, but rather that these institutional forms have many implications for politics, policy formation, and government performance.[4]

In short, it is clear that different configurations have different consequences. Japan has many of the small, neighborhood watch–type groups, and relatively few large, independent groups like the AARP, and state action in large measure

[3] Although volunteers as a percent of the population are higher in the United States than in Japan (48.8 percent in 1995 vs. 26.9 percent in 1996), they are numerous in Japan, too (Yamauchi 1999: 59). Two important new studies that investigate the volunteer phenomenon in Japan are Pickert 2001 and Kage 2001.

[4] With a focus on the organizational level, Shimizu Hiroko (2000) demonstrates the importance of the distinction between paid staff and volunteers. She argues that paid staff are crucial to the development of organizational capacity in the nonprofit sector and that they cannot be replaced by volunteers. Compared with the United States, however, few Japanese organizations have paid staff. See also the work of Jeffrey M. Berry (1998), whose research indicates a correlation between the size of professional staffs in citizens' groups and their political influence as measured by citations in news media, appearances to testify before Congress, and citations of research produced by these groups as authoritative.

accounts for this pattern. The Japanese state has structured incentives to promote this pattern of development because it seeks to nurture social capital–type civil society groups and to discourage pluralistic, lobbying-type civil society groups. Although democratic theory sometimes conflates these types of groups, they can be analytically distinguished for greater theoretical leverage.[5]

Defining Civil Society

Too often, vagueness plagues discussions of civil society. To clarify causal claims about the patterning of civil society, we must be clear as to exactly what we mean by civil society. For my purposes, *civil society is the organized, nonstate, nonmarket sector*. This definition encompasses voluntary groups of all kinds, such as nonprofit foundations, charities, think tanks, and choral societies. It includes nonprofit organizations (NPOs), nongovernmental organizations (NGOs), and other voluntary or tertiary associations. It is larger in scope than the category of civic groups, which more narrowly comprises participatory organizations. It is also broader than the nonprofit sector, which at the least excludes unincorporated voluntary groups and which is also sometimes limited to groups performing public purposes (Hall 1987). On the other hand, it does *not* include labor unions, companies, or other profit-oriented groups.[6] It also excludes government bureaucracies, parastatal organizations, and political parties as well as the family. Under this definition, the Japanese pattern of few large, professionalized, nonprofit organizations and many smaller, grass-roots organizations snaps into focus.

Civil society is not a dichotomous variable. Rather, attention should be paid to the *types* of organizations that exist as well as to participation in organizations and their numbers. Civil society can vary in level and composition from time to time and from place to place. Because civil society comprises a motley crew, there should be theoretical gains from disaggregating the concept. Unpacking also allows us to fine-tune our analysis of the relationship between state and civil society. Rather than search for either the suppression or nurturing of civil society, we can examine the patterns that the state creates in civil society and the patterns of state–civil society relations that emerge. This chapter thus adopts this perspective on the pattern of development of civil society organizations in Japan before linking this pattern to causal arguments about state influence.

Direct versus Indirect State Influence

State institutions shape civil society in Japan both directly and indirectly. "Direct" refers to purposeful attempts to influence the configuration of organized civil soci-

[5] I am indebted to John Campbell for this observation. See also Theda Skocpol's argument (1999) distinguishing the advocacy and membership dimensions of voluntary associations.

[6] See Cohen and Arato (1992) on the exclusion of market organizations from definitions of civil society. Although I have excluded unions and other economic associations from this analysis to maintain definitional consistency, their inclusion would only provide additional evidence in favor of my central argument. The importance of the legal context for labor organization is well documented.

ety. This can consist of regulation of groups' legal status or activities, tax benefits, or direct financial flows such as grants, contracts, and the like. Legitimation is another important resource the state can often give or withhold from a group. This could be especially true in Japan, where the state's historical and cultural weight is often regarded as greater than in other nations. Legitimation comes from legal recognition of the social value of civil society groups through the creation of a special class of groups or through recognition of a particular group's belonging to that sanctioned category. Intriguingly, preliminary evidence from implementation of the so-called NPO Law of 1998 suggests that legitimation may be *the* key resource for new groups (Pekkanen 2000b).

Examination of the regulatory framework and state actions provides compelling evidence that the state has shaped civil society in Japan into its distinctive pattern. That may reflect an attempt to foster groups intended to safely harness the energy of the population in directions helpful for administration while discouraging the formation of groups that could challenge the bureaucracy by monitoring policy outputs or providing an alternative source of expertise. As Frank Upham (1987: 17) writes, one of the "major instruments for such control is the manipulation of the legal framework within which social change and its harbinger, social conflict, occur."[7]

"Indirect" refers to unintentional influences on civil society's organization that are the by-products of institutional structure. Japan's institutional structure has had a large indirect influence. A relatively insulated bureaucracy and uninfluential parliament have shaped how groups that seek to influence the state must form in order to be effective. Although exceptions such as the farm lobby exist, close coordination with ministries is typically more important than mass membership (Richardson and Flanagan 1984; Richardson 1997; Schwartz 1998). Susan Pharr (1990) argues that the state's response to social conflict has typically been to seek to privatize it. Preemptive concessions and the privatization of conflict also have the effect of making group formation less likely. This can have long-term consequences in shaping the nature of protest in two senses. First, lack of institutionalization raises collective-action problems should another potential conflict emerge, thus making such conflict more manageable for the state. Working conditions can become much worse before a strike will occur if workers must reestablish a union every time conditions deteriorate, for example. Second, Charles Tilly (1979) has shown how state responses to protest can over time structure the nature of protest itself.

An electoral system (e.g., proportional representation vs. single-member districts) might have an effect on how interests are structured (e.g., into small, ideological parties vs. pressure groups). Theda Skocpol (1998) argues that the increase in U.S. congressional staffers from 6,255 in 1960 to 20,000 in 1990 was a key factor in the rise of advocacy groups in the United States. Her reasoning is that the presence of more staffers translated into more opportunities for advocacy groups to lobby and get their message across. Compared with twenty-six staffers for a U.S.

[7] Upham (1987) meticulously documents the importance of the legal framework in a number of social realms. This chapter is in line with his overall approach to the study of law in society and many of his conclusions about the way law has structured social conflict (for me, civil society) in Japan.

senator, Japanese Diet members can hire only three, and there are correspondingly fewer opportunities for lobbyists to get their message across to legislators.

The political opportunity structure is clearly important for the development of advocacy groups, but even seemingly unimportant regulations can have an important effect in structuring incentives for organizational development. Indirect influences may include such factors as the lack of a bulk postage discount for nonprofits in Japan. Although this might seem a trivial example, in the United States, this discount is important in promoting large membership organizations, which can deliver a letter to your door for less than a nickel (*total* cost, including printing and sorting if done internally). They rely on the discount to attract and communicate with wide membership bases. In Japan, on the other hand, the lack of this discount can make the operation of groups aiming at large memberships quite expensive and thus less likely to succeed.

The head of a small citizens' group in Tokyo confessed to me that he has actually found it cheaper on occasion to pack a suitcase full of mailings, fly to Korea, and mail them from there because the cost of mailing from Korea to Japan is less than the cost of mailing within Japan – even when the additional expense of an air ticket is included (Watanabe Bungaku, TOPIC; personal interview, November 22, 1996). Incidentally, this gentleman heads an antismoking group in Tokyo of which he is the sole full-time employee. I could not help but contrast the image of him laboring alone with that of the plush office space of the American Cancer Society.

Competing Explanations

The state directly and indirectly structures incentives for the formation and development of civil society organizations. This insight allows us to understand why Japanese civil society is distinctive in international comparison by reference to the regulatory framework that Japanese civil society organizations face. Let me detail that argument, then briefly review two competing explanations.

The Political-Institutional Hypothesis

My political explanation focuses on how institutions structure incentives to explain which groups form and operate in civil society. It does not claim that civil society is a product of what state agencies or politicians want to happen, but rather that institutions have effects through structuring action. The focus here is on the regulatory framework as an independent variable, and no attempt is made to distinguish between bureaucratic intentions and politicians' desires in shaping this framework.

It would be useful to describe Japan's laws and regulations and how they apply to civil society groups. Japan's nongovernmental organizations (hereafter NPOs[8])

[8] In Japan, domestically active groups are called "NPOs," while "NGOs" usually refer to groups involved in international activities. I use the Japanese term "NPO," which, while technically referring to all nonprofit organizations, in practice overlaps significantly with the meaning Americans attach to NGO.

face one of the most severe regulatory environments in the developed world (Salamon and Anheier 1996). In the United States, it is an uncomplicated procedure for groups to register as nonprofits and qualify for tax exemptions. Because authorities apply the technical definition of nonprofit – an organization that does not distribute profits to shareholders – the procedure of gaining this legal status is straightforward. Rather than using the concept of "nonprofits," however, Japanese law uses the category of "public-interest legal persons" (*kōeki hōjin*). This begs the question of who decides what is in the public interest. In Japan, the bureaucracy has a legal monopoly on this decision, and it cannot (legally) err in making this determination. Furthermore, Japanese law stipulates that public-interest legal persons can acquire legal status only through the explicit permission of the competent bureaucratic authority, and it grants this authority continuing powers of supervision and administrative guidance. This combination of discretionary screening, close supervision of operations, and sanctioning power is one of the essential causes for the Japanese pattern of civil society development, and it has compromised the vitality of that development.

This strict regulation is based mostly on Article 34 of the Uniform Civil Code, which was promulgated in 1896. Although Article 21 of Japan's Constitution provides for freedom of association, Article 33 of the Civil Code requires that all legal persons be formed in accordance with its regulations, which in practice limit that freedom. "Legal persons" (*hōjin*) are groups or organizations that are legally provided with an independent existence and attendant rights and obligations. Without this status, groups have no legal existence. Articles 34 and 35 flank Article 33's general provisions to create two classes of legal persons. Although Article 35 provides for the establishment of for-profit organizations, Article 34 does not provide for a corresponding category of nonprofit organizations, but rather for a much more restrictive category of public-interest legal persons (PIPs).[9] This creates a legal blind spot: most groups that are nonprofit but not in the public interest have no legal basis to form. Needless to say, there are many such groups, especially when the "public interest" is interpreted by the bureaucracy in a narrow or arbitrary manner. There is simply no legal category for such groups to occupy, and as a result, they are reduced to operating as informal, voluntary groups, or even to becoming corporations if they can.

Still other groups are prevented from becoming legal persons because of another legal peculiarity. The Civil Code left the handling of PIPs to the "discretion of the competent ministry." This provision has been interpreted in such a way that each ministry or agency handles the PIPs in its bailiwick. In addition to having been established by funds from that ministry, many PIPs will also host a large number of retired bureaucrats and receive operating income from that same ministry. Groups whose activities cut across ministries, on the other hand, such as those involved in education or the environment, have extreme difficulty in winning legal status.[10]

[9] Public-interest legal persons include both foundations (*zaidan hōjin*) and associations (*shadan hōjin*).

[10] Special laws have established a number of subcategories of PIPs, mainly as part of the liberalization imposed by Occupation authorities. Such groups include education legal persons (first established

Table 5.1 *Civil Society Groups in Japan*

	Type of group	Numbers
With legal status	Education legal persons	16,155
	Social welfare legal persons	13,000
	Public-interest legal persons (*zaidan*)	13,476
	Public-interest legal persons (*shadan*)	12,451
	Religious legal persons	183,894
	Medical legal persons	22,838
	PIP subtotal – broad definition[a]	(261,814)
	Cooperatives	23,718
	Political groups	72,796
	Think tanks (not counted elsewhere)	449
	Neighborhood associations (with legal status)	8,691
Legal status subtotal		367,468
Without legal status	Neighborhood associations	292,227
	Children's groups	130,000
	Elderly people's groups	150,000
	Other civic groups	598,000
	Voluntary groups with offices	42,000
Without legal status subtotal		1,212,227
Total		1,579,695

[a]See note 10.
Sources: Yamauchi 1997: 218, 227; Tsujinaka and Mori 1998: 298; Japanese government documents.

Even for those groups that do fit into the appropriate category, bureaucrats have raised high financial hurdles. Citing the Civil Code's call for a "sound financial base," bureaucrats have frequently insisted on an aspiring PIP's possessing at least ¥300 million ($3 million) in capital.[11] Many viable groups can not accumulate such funds. Although the United States has 1,273,000 tax-exempt nonprofit organizations registered with the Internal Revenue Service (the great majority of which have budgets of at least $100,000 a year and which collectively employ 10 million full-time workers), Japan has about 260,000 public-interest legal persons (see Table 5.1).

Japan's authorization system has been implemented in such a way that groups whose objectives or styles differ from those of the authorizing ministry find it very difficult to gain approval. These groups are de facto denied legal status by a system

in 1947), medical legal persons (1948), religious legal persons (1951), and social welfare legal persons (1951). These should be considered special categories within Article 34. Together with the *shadan hōjin* and *zaidan hōjin*, these groups constitute PIPs under my broad definition. The latter two groups alone constitute PIPs under my narrow definition.

[11] This provision is theoretically open to a liberal interpretation. I contend that bureaucrats' narrow interpretation results from political will rather than a close reading of the relevant laws.

reliant on bureaucratic discretion. Due to this screening mechanism, bureaucrats select which groups are allowed to organize and which are not (*Jurisuto* 1997; NIRA 1995).

For whatever reason, many NPOs can not qualify as legal persons, and this puts them at a significant disadvantage. The logistical difficulties should not be underestimated, especially for groups that seek to become large, professionalized organizations. Tales abound among civil society organizations of the problems created by a lack of legal status. Tanaka Naoki (personal interview, March 12, 1998), director of Wonderful Aging Club, told me that before his group became a PIP in 1988, "Without legal status, the officials at the Ministry of Welfare wouldn't even give me their business cards. In companies, I couldn't even get past the reception desk." The *Asahi Shinbun* (March 23, 1998) reported how a citizens' group in Kyūshū could not receive the donation of a car from a local company for over a year because, without the group's enjoying legal status, the donation would look as if it went directly to the group's leader. As another group leader put it, "to relate to other bodies, legal status is a necessity." The *Asahi Shinbun* (March 25, 1998) also cited the example of an aged-care group that would receive about ¥12 million ($120,000) a year from the government if it had legal status. Because it had no legal status, however, it received no money at all.

These examples demonstrate that it is hard for independent groups to become large in Japan. Legal status is just one part of the equation, and other important resources that the state can direct to favored groups include legitimation (mainly through legal status), public funds, and tax breaks. Not only is it hard for independent groups to grow large in Japan, but it is hard for large groups to remain independent. The latter is due primarily to an institutional arrangement that confers significant monitoring and sanctioning powers on a single bureaucratic ministry or agency. Even in the abstract, it is easy to understand that if a single agency grants permission to a group to form, monitors it, is able to punish it, and can even dissolve the group entirely, often without effective legal challenge, that agency will hold significant power over the group.

In Japan, a PIP must report to the competent ministry, which retains the power to investigate the group or even to revoke its legal status. Attendant tax benefits are not as generous as those of other industrialized democracies, either. Even worse, bureaucrats have insisted on continuing administrative guidance. This supervision is established by Article 67 of the Civil Code. Paragraph 2 establishes a "supervision system" (*kanshi seido*) by the "competent supervising ministry" (*shumu kanchō*). Article 84 makes further provisions for fines on directors of PIPs who violate the directions of the competent ministry.

Backed by the power to punish, this administrative guidance forces licensees to comply with bureaucrats' preferences and impairs the independence of civil society organizations. It has been employed in such a heavy-handed way that many observers regard social welfare legal persons, for example, as little more than cheap subcontractors for the government, bereft of the independence necessary to qualify as true NPOs. As Iriyama Akira, director of the Sasakawa Peace Foundation (a PIP), put it, "even those like us who make it through and get permission have to suffer from very severe control and guidance from authorities. If I start to talk about the notorious administrative guidance, it'll take days" (Pekkanen 2000b: 119).

Despite the great logistical problems it creates, foreign groups such as the Asia Foundation sometimes choose not to become a PIP precisely to avoid bureaucratic interference. In a nationwide Economic Planning Agency survey of Japanese NPOs, the most common reason cited for not applying for legal status was that accounting and finance reporting requirements were too onerous (61 percent of groups cited this reason), and the third most common reason (cited by 45 percent) was the fear that the objective of the NPO or the content of its activities could be controlled by bureaucrats (*Jurisuto* 1997). PIPs must submit reports on annual activities, lists of assets, accounts of changes in membership, and financial statements for the past year, as well as planned activity reports and budget estimates for the coming year.

An authorizing agency is empowered to investigate PIPs. The agency can make on-site inspections and audits. Article 68 of the Civil Code provides that a PIP can be dissolved if its authorizing agency cancels its authorization of incorporation, and Article 71 states that the authorizing agency may cancel its approval if a PIP has engaged in activities outside its purposes as defined in its articles of association, has violated the conditions under which its establishment was approved, or violates supervisory orders issued by the agency. Article 25 of the Civil Code Enforcement Law requires an inquiry by the authorizing agency and also requires that the agency indicate the reasons for dissolution to the affected parties, who then have the right to a legal proceeding and appeal. It is interesting to note that cancellation of authorization is interpreted as a response to changed circumstances and not as a mistake by the authorizers as to the degree to which the PIP was in the public interest to begin with. Despite the possibility of appeal, the legal deck is stacked in favor of the authorizing agency, in part because of the considerable discretion attached to its evaluation of the public interest (Hayashi 1972: 192–93; Pekkanen and Simon 2003).

Two recent legal changes improve the legal environment: the 1998 Law for the Promotion of Specified Nonprofit Activities (or "NPO Law") and the 2001 granting of tax privileges (in the Fiscal Year 2001 Tax Reform). Designed to limit administrative guidance and bureaucratic discretion in the granting of legal status and allow many more civil society groups to gain that status, the NPO Law created a new category of PIPs by means of a special law attached to Article 34 (Pekkanen 2000a, 2000b). On the one hand, there is some evidence that administrative guidance continues, and a survey of the 1,034 groups granted NPO legal person status by November 1999 (to which 463 groups responded) found only 5.2 percent "satisfied" with the law (C's 2000: 9). On the other hand, as of April 27, 2001, some 3,933 of the 4,626 groups that had applied had been granted the status of NPO legal person (http://www5.cao.go.jp/seikatsu/npo/index.html). The 2001 tax changes created a subcategory of NPO legal persons (tax-deductible (*nintei*) specified nonprofit activities legal persons) to which individuals or corporations can make a contribution that is deductible from their income tax. Although implementation had yet to occur at the time of this writing, the change will not lower tax rates for NPOs and allows only some NPO legal persons to receive tax-advantaged charitable contributions. Those groups must be certified by the commissioner of the National Tax Administration of the Ministry of Finance as meeting a number of stringent criteria, including a requirement that one-third of the organization's budget derive from donations. This "public-support test" alone could disqualify as many as 90 percent of NPO legal persons (Pekkanen 2001a).

Recent changes notwithstanding, the status, number, and independence of NPOs have been severely curtailed in Japan as a result of the regulatory environment. Groups can form as corporations or remain voluntary groups without legal status, of course, but the legal system has a heavy bias against such NPOs. This bias is, again, an essential element in the structuring of incentives that helps to create the pattern of civil society development found in Japan. It makes it difficult for many groups to grow, especially those seeking to be independent of the state.

It is important to keep in mind that the negative role of the state is only one part of the equation. The Japanese state also *promotes* many groups it deems cooperative. Although that does include some PIPs, neighborhood associations are an excellent example of the civil society organizations positively promoted by the Japanese state. Neighborhood associations benefit from de facto legal recognition, the devolution of powers and jurisdiction, the conferral of a monopoly of legitimacy (tantamount to the repression of rival organizations), and state funds. Japan's civil society is characterized by few large, independent organizations and many small, local groups for reasons that are flip sides of the same coin.

To frame my political-institutional hypothesis more formally:

> **Hypothesis**: Groups facing less favorable regulatory conditions will be smaller. Groups with access to greater resources from the state (e.g., legal status, financial flows, tax benefits, legitimation) will ceteris paribus be larger.

My independent variable is the regulatory framework, including licensing, tax, and operational provisions and financial support. As a dependent variable, civil society is operationalized by the measurement of group numbers and group membership. Large and small groups are distinguished by the number of professional, full-time staff they employ.

The Culturalist Hypothesis

Culturalist hypotheses make two claims. First, they explain the level of civil society organization by proclivities to join or form certain kinds of organizations. Second, they uniformly posit a *low* level of civil society activity in Japan because of distinctive cultural characteristics. A richer understanding of the importance of culture in shaping civil society emerges from a longitudinal study of the interplay of institutions and culture, of how institutions themselves structure cultural expectations (e.g., about the public sphere and legitimate social activitiy) that in turn instruct actors within that cultural framework. For the purposes of this chapter, however, I extract the following claim:

> **Hypothesis**: There will be few civil society groups in Japan, and groups that espouse abstract ideals or involve aid to unknown third parties will be especially small in number.

Cultural constructs influence individuals' framing of social problems and provide a repertoire of organizational responses. By themselves, however, cultural explanations fail to explain the pattern of civil society organizations that has developed in Japan. Although the culturalist hypothesis would predict few instances of volunteerism, for example, it is contradicted by the outpouring of volunteerism in the aftermath of the 1995 Kōbe Earthquake, when 1.2 million volunteers went to that city to join relief efforts and nearly ¥160 billion ($1.6 billion) was donated. The difficulties these spontaneous groups faced in gaining legal status and in institutionalizing, on the other hand, are consistent with the political-institutional explanation.

The Heterogeneity Hypothesis

An abundant literature explains the size of a nonprofit sector by relating it to the distribution of preferences in a population. In short, where there is greater heterogeneity of preferences regarding a good, the nonprofit sector will be larger. Many analysts (e.g., Weisbrod and Schlesinger 1986; Weisbrod 1988; James 1989) argue that residual unsatisfied demand for public goods exists and can be supplied by nonprofits because governments provide public goods only at the level demanded by the median voter. An observable implication of this explanation should be that in sectors or nations where greater heterogeneity and intensity of preferences exist regarding public goods, the market share of nonprofits versus government should be higher (James 1987, 1989).

> **Hypothesis**: The greater the residual unsatisfied demand for public goods (i.e., the heterogeneity of preferences), the larger the size of the nonprofit sector.

Even a cursory review of a single sector, education, reveals problems with this explanation. In Japan, it is not nonprofits, but rather private, for-profit educational institutions – the cram schools (*juku*) – that meet the surplus demand for education. This is true of both catch-up schools and those schools that prepare students to get ahead in the university entrance exams. In fact, Thomas Rohlen (1980: 38) observes that "[n]o other country in the world comes close in the percentage of their populations involved in buying private educational advantage." Moreover, stratification begins in high school. This is due not to a feature of demand, but rather to the historical legacy of an acute space shortage among high schools in the postwar period. Although the social heterogeneity explanation offers helpful insights, it fails to explain important elements of the development of civil society in Japan.

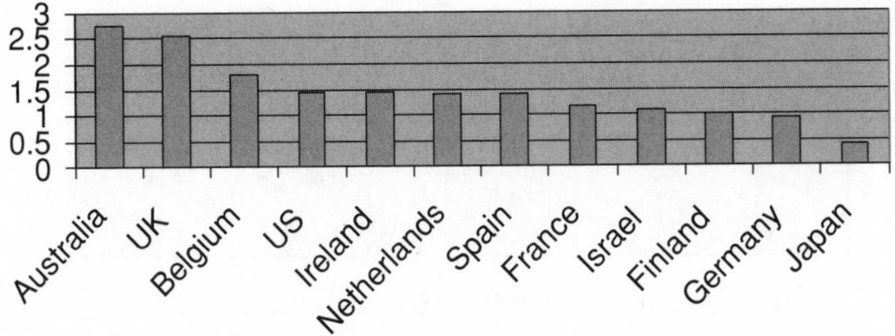

Figure 5.1 Civic group employment as a percentage of total employment. *Source*: Author calculations based on 1995 data supplied by the Johns Hopkins Comparative Nonprofit Sector Project.

The Evidence

Although support is also found for the cultural hypothesis, evidence from a variety of cases supports the political-institutional hypothesis.[12]

The Pattern of Groups

As predicted, the evidence confirms that groups without access to state resources are smaller and that less provocative groups have easier access to state resources. This is true cross-nationally as well as across sectors in Japan. As a percentage of their total revenue, public-sector support of civic/advocacy groups is small in Japan compared with other industrialized nations (Salamon and Anheier 1997). As the political-institutional hypothesis predicts, these groups are quite small, averaging 3.35 employees and expenditures of ¥36.12 million yen ($361,200), only 22.7 percent of the average for all nonprofits in Japan (Atoda et al. 1998: 105). Civil/advocacy groups are an especially good example because of their frequently oppositional relationship to the state. In other words, it is precisely these troublesome groups among which we would expect to find the least state support.

Figure 5.1 shows the proportion of the total work force occupied by civil society organization. (These figures exclude workers in education, health, and social services, whose figures vary widely because of state policies, but they do include workers in all other civil society groups.) This represents the professionalization of civil society organizations. Proportionally, Japan's 73,500 civil society professionals are fewer than half the number of the next lowest nation (Germany) and fewer than a third of the average for these developed nations. Even those groups with the most secure financial bases are small in Japan. Figure 5.2 shows how the overwhelming majority of PIPs have only a handful of employees.

[12] See also Reimann, this volume, who shows how changed government policies toward international development NGOs (IDNGOs) influenced the growth of these groups in the 1990s.

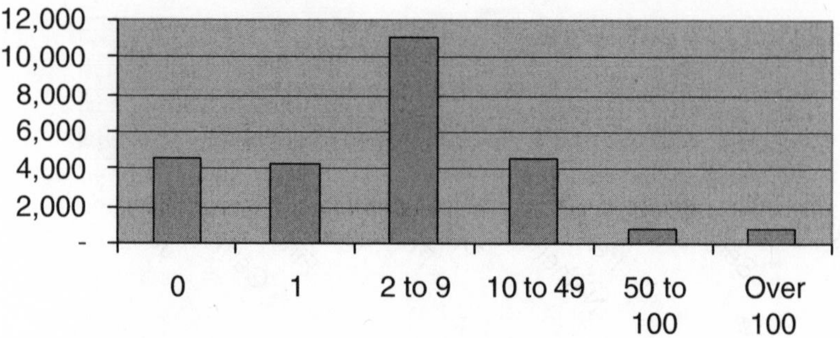

Figure 5.2 Public-interest legal persons by number of employees. *Source:* Prime Minister's Office, *Kōeki hōjin hakusho 2000*, p. 361.

Table 5.2 *Citizens Groups' Main Activities (%)*

Social welfare (aged care, child services, disabled services, other)	37.4
Local groups (crime prevention, traffic safety, disaster prevention)	16.9
Environmental	10.0
Other (e.g., consumer issues, human rights, gender issues, supporting citizens activities, peace promotion)	5.7
Medical	4.7
Education, sports, culture (education, research, sports, nurturing youth, arts, culture)	4.6
No answer	4

Source: Economic Planning Agency, "*NPO ni tsuite no shiryō*" Data on NPOs), 1998.

The status of independent groups formed by citizen activists provides another example. These groups typify what Americans would regard as "real" civil society groups. They engage in a wide range of activities (see Table 5.2), and the very category implies independence from the state. Citizen groups are small; very few have large staffs. A recent survey of several thousand such groups found that only 1.6 percent of them have more than five full-time paid employees, and as a category, they average only 0.5 full-time paid employees (Yamauchi 1997: 220). As might be expected, very few of these groups have legal status. Tokyo-area citizen groups, for example, are almost all (82 percent) voluntary associations without legal status (Tsujinaka 1998: 19).

The flip side of cutting off resource flows to provocative groups is that the state often seeks to coopt or supervise those groups that do earn legal status. Intense supervision and personnel transfers compromise the independence of many groups. The price of gaining legal status is often a de facto agreement to employ ex-bureaucrats of the authorizing ministry. Besides providing a cozy refuge for these erstwhile denizens of Kasumigaseki, this practice also confers on ministries substantial influence over the group's operations. This is especially true when the bureaucrats assume posts on a group's board of directors. The former practice occurs in over one-third of PIPs supervised by the national bureaucracy, the latter in about one-sixth (Prime Minister's Office 1998: 124).

The pattern of tax benefits also supports the political-institutional hypothesis. In general, charitable contributions by individuals or corporations are not tax-deductible in Japan. There is a subcategory of Special PIPs, however, to which contributions are deductible.[13] Of the 232,776 PIPs incorporated in 1997, only 17,000 held this status. In contrast, the government has been promoting social welfare legal persons in an effort to deal with such social issues as the aging society, and not surprisingly, every one of the 14,832 social welfare legal persons held Special PIP status (Yamauchi 1997: 198).

Social Movements

Where social movements of comparable size arise in different countries, their institutionalization in different forms offers a means to test the political-institutional hypothesis. In general terms, that hypothesis predicts that social movements similar in scope will not take similar institutional forms because of the direct and indirect influence of state institutions. In Japan, large social movements do not tend to result in large civil society organizations that institutionalize their aims. This supports the interpretation that political-institutional barriers are higher in Japan than in other advanced industrialized democracies, preventing the development of large, independent civil society organizations.

The United States now possesses large, professional, and entrenched environmental NGOs that are involved in almost every feature of environmental policy. These include such organizations as the Environmental Defense Fund, Friends of the Earth, Environmental Action, and Greenpeace USA (Gelb and Palley 1982). Although a German-style Green Party is (with apologies to Ralph Nader) unlikely to succeed in the United States due to its single-member electoral districts, the plethora of lobbying opportunities and easy rules for formation make the creation of NGOs an attractive option. The American and Japanese environmental movements involved roughly the same percent of the adult population (6 percent) at their zenith (McKean 1981; Broadbent 1998), yet the Japanese groups have melted away. The reasons for this divergence have more to do with differing incentives for institutionalization than with variation in the nature of the movements or national culture.

[13] Given its civil code system, Japan's tax laws differ in many respects from America's. PIPs are taxed at a lower rate than corporations on activities subject to taxation; the United States uses a system of "related activities" instead. Donations are not tax-deductible in Japan, however, except for those made to a very select and numerically small group of Special Public Interest Increasing Legal Persons (*tokutei kōeki zōshin hōjin*, commonly called *tokuzō*). Differences in tax privileges are more complex, and include deductible contributions, reduced taxation, and tax-free activities for PIPs.

Neighborhood Associations

Certain cases pose harder tests for some explanations than for others. With roots in the spontaneous self-organization of Japanese communities, neighborhood associations (NHAs) present a difficult case for the political-institutional explanation. Accordingly, NHA-related facts that support the political-institutional hypothesis represent important evidence. To support the political-institutional hypothesis, the spread of NHAs would have to have been actively promoted by the state, and this promotion would have to have been important for the success of NHAs as an organizational form.

Perhaps Japan's most widespread group, there are a total of 298,000 NHAs, which enjoy extremely high participation rates. Although many NHAs formed spontaneously by the first decade of the twentieth century, especially in rural areas, up to 90 percent of modern NHAs exist as a result of government promotion (Pekkanen 2002a, 2002b). Culturalist explanations might predict the maintenance of the authentic, early NHAs and even expect some NHAs to form in urban areas (as "surrogate villages"), but only government support can explain the spread of NHAs throughout Japan.

Unlike other civil society organizations, these groups have been actively promoted by the government. Although they are independent entities, they often work with branches of local government in disseminating information or maintaining public facilities. Government funds flow to NHAs for these and other purposes. The services are provided quite cheaply, yet the money is important to hold these locality-based groups together and may also create social capital-type externalities. When the government pays a neighborhood association to clean or maintain a local park, for example, the work is done more cheaply and better than if professionals were employed. At the same time, civic community is strengthened as local people work together to maintain the area. Despite strong efforts at cooptation, however, it is the state's support for and promotion of the NHAs that stand out in contrast to its treatment of other civil society organizations. Definitionally limited to small geographic areas, NHAs cannot challenge the state (e.g., in providing alternative sources of information).

Legal History

Additional corroboration of the political-institutional hypothesis can be found in documentary evidence and interviews. Thirty years after the Meiji Restoration (1868) put Japan on the path to modernization, the framers of the Civil Code made clear choices about legal frameworks to regulate civil society organizations. Legal documents, including the framers' notes and a comparison with the original German and Swiss laws that served as their models, indicate that the Civil Code was written with the intention of creating high hurdles for the organization of civil society groups. This is confirmed by evidence from the explanatory notes attached to Article 35 of the Civil Code and to an earlier draft of the code. There was a conscious shift from nonprofit to public-interest legal persons, for example, as part of an attempt by the Meiji oligarchy to place strict limits on the formation of civil society groups. This was done not so much to cripple civil society as to prevent people from frittering away their energy in private organizations and to steer them instead toward the state's goals of nation building under the slogan "rich nation, strong army." Regulating civil society has always been a political process. Another example can be found in my research (Pekkanen 2000a, 2000b, 2003) on implementation of the NPO Law, which relies on documents as well as interviews to uncover the motives and interests of bureaucrats, politicians, and group leaders in negotiating the most significant change in the regulation of civil society in a century.

Accounting for Variation

Regulatory frameworks matter. They structure incentives, both directly and indirectly, that profoundly influence the development of civil society. But why do different countries regulate civil society in different ways? More narrowly, what accounts for variations in the regulation of civil society organizations across advanced industrialized democracies? Specifically, why does Japan regulate its civil society organizations so strictly? By shaping the "rules of the game," states determine who can and cannot play (and develop policy expertise, and so on), and this affects policy outputs.[14] The rules of the game also determine the strength of players seated at the table in future games. What is at stake are state-society relations in their raw form. What, then, determines the rules of the game?

Several factors are important. First are political parties. With passage of Le Chapelier Act, associations were actually outlawed in France from 1791 until 1901. This policy may best be explained by people's equation of the state with the Rousseauan "general will," which led to a distaste for the intrusion of secondary associations between state and citizen. When France's Socialists came to power in 1981, however, they supported the creation of a number of associations. They promoted the concept of the "social economy" at domestic and European levels, even to the point of briefly appointing a Secretary of State for Social Economy under Prime Minister Michel Rocard. Measures to encourage peak nonprofit organizations were also implemented. The party took these policies because it regarded the nurturing of nonprofits as an essential part of decentralization (Archambault 1997; Ullman 1998; Levy 1999).

In general, conservative political parties are less likely to promote permissive regulation of civil society organizations. Analysis of Japan's NPO Law (e.g., the existence of a credible opposition inspired LDP compromise, and progressive parties pushed hardest for change) and the French example demonstrate that the Liberal Democratic Party's long dominance of Japanese politics from 1955 until 1993 and the party's ideology explain in part the regulatory stasis of the postwar period (Pekkanen 2000a, 2000b).

[14] Regulation of civil society groups fits what some authors have seen as a typical pattern of the Japanese bureaucracy's giving in on issues, but in a fashion that does not allow institutionalization of opposition claims. See Upham (1987) and Pharr (1990).

Second, interest groups have also been active in lobbying for change in regulatory frameworks. In the United States, for example, while the charitable deduction for individuals was incorporated into the tax code in 1917, it was not until 1936 that firms received the same privilege. President Franklin Roosevelt opposed this deduction, but acquiesced after intensive lobbying by the Community Chest (Hall 1987). In Japan, the severity of the Civil Code has meant that fewer groups have been around to lobby for change and that these groups have often been coopted or tied into close relationships with ministries.[15] The rise of new NPOs such as C's was important in passing the NPO Law (Pekkanen 2000a, 2000b, 2003). In general, the more conducive a political system is to interest group lobbying, the more likely it is that the regulatory framework will promote civil society organizations.

Third, institutional factors are clearly important in determining the regulatory framework for civil society organizations. Passage of the NPO Law demonstrates how a change in electoral institutions can alter incentives for politicians and have important consequences for policy toward civil society (Pekkanen 2000b). In historical perspective, however, it is opposition from the bureaucracy that has accounted for Japan's regulatory pattern. Similarly, institutional factors explain the Japanese bureaucracy's reluctance to promote vibrant, autonomous civil society organizations.

Subgovernments, or policy communities, are of particular importance in the Japanese political system (on subgovernments, see Walker 1977; Heclo 1978; Kingdon 1984; Campbell 1989; Campbell et al. 1989). Although the term "iron triangles" is of American coinage, Gerald Curtis notes (1999: 54), "[P]olicy making in Japan, more than in the United States, is characterized by the existence of disaggregated policy communities, of a multiplicty of iron triangles." As John Campbell (1989: 6) noted, this is because the "governmental system of Japan is quite fragmented and compartmentalized" due to a weak chief executive, parties that participate in policy making most heavily at the specialized level, bureaucratic power that is concentrated at the ministry level, and an absence of corporatist bargaining across policy areas.

Although there are exceptions (e.g., the LDP–Japan Medical Association–Ministry of Health and Welfare triangle is politicized), Japan's policy communities are generally marked by bureaucratic primacy. In part because of the fragmentation of policy making, getting items onto the agenda requires an unusual degree of consensus in the policy community. Given the high salience of policy communities, bureaucratic primacy within them, and the importance of consensus to getting items on the agenda, the bureaucracy has a strong incentive to back regulations that retard the formation of autonomous civil society groups.[16] Although Campbell (1989: 93) was writing in the abstract, observers might be forgiven for mistaking his general characterization of defensive subgovernments as an apt de-

[15] Perhaps not coincidentally, the number and composition of Japan's civil society groups has recently begun to change. See Tsujinaka (1996, 1997) and Tsujinaka et al. (1998).

[16] But it has perhaps a *greater* incentive to push for the formation of auxiliary organizations (*gaikaku dantai*), which are another striking feature of Japan's associational world.

scription of the attitude of Japanese ministries toward civil society regulation: "A 'cozy little triangle' trying to hold onto its own can often rely on monopolizing information, manipulating procedures, delaying decisions, simple stubbornness and other means of passive resistance. . . ."

The very fragmentation that renders policy communities important in Japan made a fundamental rewriting of the Civil Code unlikely. Meanwhile, Article 34's delegation of authorization for incorporation to ministries promotes interest groups and experts who are less capable of independent action and creates firmer boundaries for policy communities, thus diminishing the likelihood of there emerging looser issue networks (on issue networks, see Heclo 1978).

Conclusion

The Japanese regulatory framework for civil society does not prevent all groups from forming. Rather, some groups face greater difficulties in formation, operation, and growth than do others. Although small, local groups such as neighborhood associations are promoted by the government, it is hard for autonomous groups to become large and hard for large groups to be autonomous. The issue of professional staff is critical. Only groups with full-time professional staff can develop the expertise necessary to participate in a policy community (see Pekkanen 1999, 2000d, 2001b, 2002a, 2002b; Shimizu 2000). Another critical issue is independence. Although no satisfactory metric for this exists, the regulatory framework for civil society groups in Japan included many institutional features that diminished the independence of civil society groups, at least until passage of the NPO Law.

State regulation shapes the development of civil society more than any other single factor. Understanding the sources of variation in state regulation across nations and over time is thus a critical task. The case of the NPO Law and comparative insights reveal that the support bases for Japan's regulatory regime are the long dominance of a conservative party and interest groups that are often coopted or compromised by bureaucratic supervision. Above all, we must examine institutional arrangements that promote policy communities characterized by bureaucratic primacy, high political salience, and ministerial jurisdiction over groups.

Although it is beyond the scope of this chapter to discuss the likely results of Japan's distinctive pattern of civil society development, we may speculate on its implications (see also Pekkanen 2002b for a discussion of, and some evidence on, these implications). Recall for a moment the two strains of democratic and civil society theory touched on at the start of this chapter, the social-capital strain and the pluralism strain. In Japan, social capital–type groups have been promoted, while pluralist-type interest groups have been discouraged. To turn Skocpol's observation on the United States (1998) on its head, what we see in Japan are members without advocates, which might be of even greater concern to proponents of liberal democracy than its opposite. Preliminary evidence indicates that the direct elements of the state's effort have been targeted in this way partly out of a desire to nurture social capital. At the same time, bureaucrats are concerned about groups that have large professional staffs because it is precisely these groups that develop policy and informational expertise that could rival or undermine the bureaucracy. This argument contributes to the increasing recognition in the civil society literature of the complexity of the relationship between civil society and democracy.

6

After Aum: Religion and Civil Society in Japan

Helen Hardacre

Introduction

Religious organizations are powerful, vocal participants in America's civil society, and they enjoy a high level of public trust based on their many, widely known contributions.[1] Among other things, they collect funds and perform volunteer services for the poor, the homeless, the unemployed, refugees, and victims of war and natural disaster; they manage hospitals, hospices, schools, and universities; they consult with policy makers at all levels of government; and they assist international bodies such as the United Nations in resolving ethnic and religious disputes. It is on the basis of this public trust and contributions to the public good that religious bodies enjoy tax privileges. Japanese religious organizations also serve the public good in manifold ways. They operate schools, museums, parks, and hospitals; homes for orphans, the elderly, and the handicapped; rehabilitation facilities for the infirm and released prisoners; and a host of volunteer social services (Bunkabu shūmuka 1997). The United Nations officially recognizes some Japanese religious organizations for their international development programs and peace work. But far from enjoying public trust, religion's position in Japanese society is vulnerable. Recent opinion polls show that only a minority of the population regards religious organizations as trustworthy, while a majority believe that there is no justification for continuing religions' tax privileges (Ishii 2000).

This study identifies several factors accounting for Japanese religions' weak status within civil society: politicization of public opinion regarding religion; the post–oil shock emergence of a new sector of the religious world, leading to a spectacular confrontation involving one religion of that sector, Aum Shinrikyō; and the resultant tightening of government regulation of all sectors of religion. Because these factors must be understood in historical perspective, this essay begins with a brief review of prewar regulation of religion, followed by a discussion of the

[1] Mark Ramseyer and Michael Oh provided extensive comments on an earlier draft of this chapter.

postwar legal framework and the present-day religious world in Japan. This material forms the basis for a general discussion of religion and civil society and of religion and the public sphere up to 1995. An examination of Aum Shinrikyō's clashes with society follows. Revision of the Religious Corporations Law, passage of the New Aum Laws, and the intervention of the Public Security Investigation Agency and the Japan Federation of Bar Associations are also addressed. A concluding section summarizes changes in religion's position in Japan's civil society.

At one level, the events related here are part of a trend toward the expansion of the religious world, which is seen also in the United States (Wood 1993), and the attempts of government and society at large to comprehend the change and respond appropriately. Contemporary public opinion about religion has emerged in tandem with the history of religion's relations with media over the twentieth century. Reacting in part to public opinion, government agencies, religions, political parties, and civil society associations such as the Japan Federation of Bar Associations have become involved in complex ways with sometimes unintended, but nevertheless highly consequential, results. To preview my main findings, the principal result has been the tightening of state monitoring of religions and changed perceptions that have generally chilling effects on the religious world. At another level, this study also reveals important aspects of Japan's modern history that could be seen as the repudiation of democratic reforms inaugurated by the American-led Occupation or from another perspective as part of a broader attempt to replace foreign-dictated legal frameworks with measures more in keeping with Japan's history. One effect of religion's changed position within civil society is the diminution of its capacity to restrain the state.

State Regulation of Religion Before 1945

The Meiji Constitution of 1889 granted freedom of religion to the extent that its exercise did not interfere with one's duties as subject. Article 1 stated that the emperor was "sacred and inviolable." Buddhism, Christianity, and thirteen sects of Shintō were recognized, allowing them to undertake missionary activities freely. Religious organizations were recognized as working for the "public good" (*kōeki*). The status of shrine Shintō (as distinct from its sectarian varieties) continued to be debated, as it had been from the beginning of the Meiji period. Shrine priests held that Shintō constituted a suprareligious entity responsible for carrying out the rites of state, especially those in which the emperor participated, such as paying tribute to the war dead enshrined at the Yasukuni Shrine. In this view, religions were the "mere" creations of human founders, and it was these that subjects were free to follow. The implication was that Shintō *shrine* observances, unlike those of Shintō *sects*, Buddhism, and Christianity, were incumbent upon all imperial subjects and above criticism.[2]

Although these ideas were not clearly expressed in law, they nevertheless shaped the repressive ways in which religions and individuals were disciplined during the

[2] For a useful source on religion in prewar Japan, see Murakami (1980). For a detailed study of the Meiji constitution's provisions regarding religion and related regulation, see Inoue (1969).

prewar period by means of charges of lèse majesté. In a celebrated event, when Uchimura Kanzō declined on Christian principles to pay obeisance at a ceremonial reading of the Imperial Rescript on Education in 1890, he was accused of lèse majesté, precipitating public debate on whether Christianity, a foreign religion, could be patriotic. Likewise, when Kume Kunitake, a historian at Tokyo Imperial University, published an essay in 1891 entitled "Shintō: The Remains of a Cult of Heaven" (*Shintō wa saiten no kōzoku*), he was forced from his post for insulting Shintō. The Home Ministry ordered the dissolution of a religion called Honmichi and charged 180 of its members with lèse majesté in 1928, when its founder Ōnishi Aijirō publicly denied the emperor's divinity. In a similar incident, the new religion Hito no Michi was disbanded in 1936 on charges of lèse majesté on the basis of a doctrine identifying the Shintō goddess Amaterasu Ōmikami (the first ancestor of the imperial house, according to Shintō mythology) with the sun, a position taken to insult the imperial house.

The Peace Preservation Law of 1925, which gave the state wide-ranging powers to restrict speech and public assembly, was used in combination with charges of lèse majesté to suppress minority religions that conflicted in some way with Shinto. Three new religious movements were effectively silenced and their leaders jailed until the end of the war through combined charges of lèse majesté and violation of the Peace Preservation Law: Ōmoto in 1935 (following an earlier suppression of this religion under the Newspaper Law in 1921); Honmichi in 1938 for its pacifism and renewed denial of imperial divinity; and Sōka Gakkai in 1943, when its leaders refused to enshrine a talisman from the Ise Grand Shrines. Although some cases targeted traditional Buddhist sects, the majority of prewar incidents of religious suppression involved either Christianity or new religious movements. The highly repressive Religious Organizations Law of 1940, whose stated purpose was to clarify the state's role to "protect and supervise" (*hogo-kantoku*) religion, labeled all religious organizations except Buddhism, Shintō sects, and Christianity "pseudo-religions" (*ruiji shūkyō*). Shintō shrines remained outside the purview of state regulation (Satō and Kinoshita 1992: 274–80).

We can summarize the nature of prewar state regulation of religion as follows. Christianity incurred lasting suspicion of insufficient patriotism. Other targeted groups were typically new religious movements that had grown quickly and contravened Shintō. Public opinion was easily mobilized against them, and the specific nature of the formal charges was less important than an amorphous sense that newly arisen religions were suspect and liable to harbor seditious tendencies. The press consolidated negative public opinion against new religious movements, as is discussed below. Assertions of the state's prerogative to regulate religion gradually replaced recognition of religions' work for the public good.

The Postwar Religious World

Since the 1947 promulgation of a constitution that was largely authored by the Allied Occupation, Japanese religions have been protected from the intrusive regulation characteristic of the prewar era. Article 20 of the constitution reads: "Freedom of religion is guaranteed to all. No religious organization shall receive any privileges from the State nor exercise any political authority. No person shall be compelled to take part in any religious acts, celebration, rite or practice. The State and its organs shall refrain from religious education or any other religious activity." The Occupation linked the anomalous status of Shintō under prewar law to militarism and the unfair persecution of other religions. Thus a central goal of Article 20 was to put all religions on the same footing and to sever Shintō's ties to the state irrevocably.[3]

The Religious Corporations Law (RCL) of 1951 allows religions to incorporate, giving them a legal right to own property and business enterprises. Around 184,000 religious bodies – Buddhist temples, Shintō shrines, Christian churches, and new religious movements' churches – are now incorporated under this law. When a religion incorporates under the RCL, it receives two kinds of official recognition: a certification that it is a religious body, as opposed to some other kind, and a certification that it conforms to the standards of a corporation. The law incorporates religions without questioning whether they conform to some extralegal standard of "genuine religions." This is the significance of incorporation through certification (*ninshō*) rather than some other mechanism, such as the issuing of a license. In recognition of religions' work for the public good, income from for-profit enterprises (e.g., sale of religious publications) is taxed at a lower rate. Religions are exempt from taxation on income from believers' contributions and from nonprofit activity (e.g., the performance of rituals). Included in the law's interpretation of work for the public good are the operation of schools, the sponsorship of academic research, and social welfare work.[4]

Judicial interpretation of Article 20 and the RCL broke sharply with prewar law by emphasizing the rights of the individual and the need to protect religions from excessive state regulation. So long as they do not violate public morals or the public welfare, religious organizations are recognized as self-governing bodies with which the state should not interfere. Out of respect for religions' autonomy, the courts have typically refrained from intervening in disputes arising within religious organizations or between organizations and former members. Thus, religious organizations have enjoyed virtually complete freedom from state supervision during the postwar period (Nakane 1996: 193–202).

The religious world in Japan today can be divided into three main sectors that differ in their history and patterns of affiliation. The first sector is the "established religions" of temple Buddhism, shrine Shintō,[5] and Christianity. Affiliation in the established religions is typically based on family tradition or residence. That is, most members do not undergo adult conversions but are born into families that are already affiliated. Because religious education for lay people tends to be

[3] Article 89 provides further protections against state sponsorship of religion. See Woodward (1972) and Ikado (1993).

[4] See Inoue (1969). The RCL is composed of 10 chapters, 89 articles, and 28 addenda. On the legal interpretation of religions' work for the public good, see Kobayashi et al. (1996: 170–74).

[5] It is conventional to distinguish between "shrine Shintō," which is nonsectarian, and "sect" or "sectarian Shintō," which refers to new religious movements based on Shintō doctrines, especially a group of thirteen such organizations founded in the nineteenth century.

weak, adherents tend to have little understanding of elementary matters such as how their sect of Buddhism differs from any other or the identity of the god of the neighborhood shrine. While this is not to deny the existence of highly knowledgeable and committed members, the proportion of affiliations arising from informed conviction is probably small. Except for Christian churches, communal life focuses on annual ritual or the timing of ancestral memorial services that differ for each family, so congregational life is not especially active. The religions themselves seldom become involved in public debate; they show little activism within Japan and only a low level of international activity, mainly in the form of missionary work.

National statistics on religion are collected by the Culture Agency (Bunkachō) of the Ministry of Education, and these reveal a persistent phenomenon of dual religious affiliation. Although families typically have a tie with the Buddhist temple that performs its funerals and maintains the family's grave, they may also be counted among the "parishioners" of a Shintō shrine located near the family residence. Dual affiliation is reflected in national statistics figures; when the membership figures for all Shintō-affiliated organizations are added to those for Buddhism, the total regularly exceeds Japan's entire population (Bunkachō 1998).

The second sector is composed of new religions, also called new religious movements (NRMs), whose doctrines may be derived from Buddhism, Shintō, Christianity, or revelations to a founder not directly stemming from traditional religions. Although it is conventional to speak of them as "new," this terminology originally pointed to the beginnings of some of them as *sectarian* developments within Shintō or Buddhism, and not to the *time* of their founding. Thus, a group founded as early as 1814 can, confusingly, be spoken of as a "new religion," even though it has existed for nearly two centuries. Membership in these groups is estimated at around one-quarter of the national population. The largest organizations are Sōka Gakkai (around 12 million members), Risshō Kōseikai (around 6 million), Reiyūkai Kyōdan, Tenrikyō, and Busshō Gonenkai (just under 2 million each), and Perfect Liberty Kyōdan and Myōchikai Kyōdan (around 1 million each). Several hundred smaller organizations are also considered NRMs. The older the new religion, the more likely it is to have generations of members born into it, but new religions continue to proselytize and a large proportion of their members are relatively recent converts. Because religious education and frequent meetings characterize these religions, their group life is much more active than that of the established religions. Sōka Gakkai and Risshō Kōseikai are active in a variety of peace and development activities that are coordinated with the United Nations as NGOs.[6] The new religions tend to be highly optimistic and "world-affirming." They believe that all things are possible with effort and that the supernatural world (however conceptualized) is benevolent.

Sōka Gakkai is the most prominent religion within the second sector. Because its first president, Makiguchi Tsunesaburō, died in prison, Sōka Gakkai has consistently opposed any state interference with religion. Imprisoned along

[6] On Risshō Kōseikai's recent NGO work in the former Yugoslavia, see Nishimura (2000).

with Makiguchi, Toda Jōsei, Sōka Gakkai's second president, presided over the religion's most rapid growth in the 1950s. Under his successor, Ikeda Daisaku, the religion founded the political party Kōmeitō (translated as Clean Government Party) in 1964. At the time, Sōka Gakkai proclaimed a goal of converting the majority of the population and was conducting a campaign of aggressive proselytization that earned it society's lasting dislike. Originally, there was an interlocking directorate between the religion and the party. Although they are now formally separate, Sōka Gakkai remains Kōmeitō's main support. Kōmeitō's base is broadening; it favors the expansion of social welfare and has no explicit religious agenda. As Japan's third largest party, it is a powerful organization able to mobilize as many as seven million votes. Its connection to Sōka Gakkai remains controversial, however, as a possible violation of the constitution's principle of separation of religion and state.

A Third Sector?

Founded or flourishing since the mid-1970s, a cluster of "new-new religions" (*shinshin shūkyō*) emerged alongside widespread commercialization of a variety of new religious goods and services. The new-new religions differ from their predecessors in their more pessimistic, "world-rejecting" outlook, tending to believe either that humanity does not know what forces rule human destiny and/or that human effort is powerless to influence them, that the supernatural world may not be benevolent, and that divination in various forms is more important than self-effort. One new-new religion, the Science of Happiness (Kōfuku no kagaku), has grown to five million members. Founded in the 1980s, Aum Shinrikyō belongs to this category of new-new religions. Some, including Aum, require a high degree of commitment, leading to conflict with family and communities (Hardacre 1996). Friction between society and high-commitment new-new religions such as Aum and the Unification Church of Japan (Sekai Kirisutokyō Tōitsu Shinrei Kyōkai, or UCJ) increased from the 1970s. Religions that require a high level of commitment from their members discourage contact with nonmembers (including family) and have come to be regarded as "cults" (*karuto*).

The appearance of new-new religions was accompanied by the emergence of a host of commercialized religious rituals and services. A prominent type, which actually appeared in both established religions and new religions as well as among independent religious entrepreneurs, was commercialized rituals to appease aborted fetuses (*mizuko kuyō*). Temples specializing in healing or *mizuko kuyō* advertised widely and drew their clienteles from around the country. Bookstores devoted special sections to "The Spiritual World" (*seishin sekai*), featuring apocalyptic best-sellers such as *Japan Sinks* and the works of Nostradamus. Fortune-telling parlors sprouted up in all cities, and they were patronized enthusiastically, especially by the young.

The current climate of negative public opinion about religion and post-1995 changes in government regulation are mainly responses to religions (or new forms of religious activity) that date from 1970 or have grown to prominence since then.

For that reason, post–oil shock religions and religious activity are disproportionately influential in shaping religion's current position in civil society, and it is useful to examine them as a separate sector.[7]

Religion and Civil Society

"Civil society" refers to a part of society located beyond the primordial ties of kinship and community, between the state and the market, lying outside the scope of state control, composed of voluntary associations in which people come together to advance some common interest. One effect of these associations is to monitor and limit state authority. In this parlance, religions might be considered one of the types of voluntary associations composing civil society.

But religion also differs from voluntary associations in significant ways. Although membership in voluntary associations typically arises from a choice made by adults, the majority of religious affiliations probably arise from being born to parents who are already affiliated. This means that there is a significant overlap between kinship and religious ties, though it is of course true that other religious affiliations result from adult choices made as a result of proselytization and/or conversion, making this type of affiliation more like that involved in voluntary associations. Beyond this difference, religions place obligations on their members that are not generally regarded as matters of choice, such as belief in a deity (or supreme being(s)), commitment to a moral code or an ideal vision of community, or following some path toward salvation, however conceptualized. Here, too, there may be overlap with voluntary associations, but the fit is not perfect. The nature of leadership also differs, and the elevation of religious leaders above the rest of humanity facilitates a concentration of authority and power in them exceeding that typical of secular voluntary associations. Obedience to a leader's command may not be a matter of choice. Finally, it is significant that the very idea of religious affiliation as a matter of choice is a distinctly modern phenomenon, one that rests on the existence of a modern society, a separation between religion and state, and a pluralistic religious culture.

Of the three sectors of the contemporary religious world in Japan, the established religions are the least engaged in civil society because most affiliations there arise from kinship or territorial connections and because of their weak communal life and generally low level of religious education and activism. Buddhism and Shintō have long traditions of allying themselves with the state and investing their connections to government or the imperial house with the highest prestige. It is difficult to think of a single modern example of their restraining the state.

It is the second sector that most resembles the voluntary associations of civil society because proportionately more of its affiliations arise from nonkinship,

[7] For discussion of the issues surrounding the new-new religions, see Kokugakuin Daigaku Nihon Bunka Kenkyūjo (1990). Scholars are divided in their assessment of religious change since the oil shocks, and not all would agree that the period of 1970 to 2000 is radically discontinuous with the previous era, or that the nature of religious organizations and activities appearing during this time deserve special categorization.

nonterritory-based ties and adult choices. Kinship ties reinforce religious ties in second and succeeding generations of members, while the vitality of the separate organizations is continually renewed by proselytization, religious education, and group life. The second sector demonstrates the highest level of engagement in civil society voluntarism and the highest level of international engagement. The prewar history of persecution in some second-sector religions has facilitated their capacity to contemplate restraining the state, though public advocacy of such a function is rare outside Sōka Gakkai and Kōmeitō.

The high-commitment groups of the third sector resemble voluntary associations in their voluntary nature, but those groups exhibiting strong alienation have not usually sought to contribute to civil society in the many ways typical of the second sector. Although they have been the source of the most confrontations, it is difficult to regard them as effective restraints on state power. If anything, the controversies they engender have arguably facilitated the *extension* of state power.

Religion and the Public Sphere

No consideration of the place of religion in civil society would be complete without an examination of the distinctive relation between religion and the public sphere in Japan. Religion is almost absent from the public sphere, a situation resulting from antagonism toward religion among journalists and timidity among religionists about media exposure. In much of the developed world, the relation between media and religion is generally positive, with major newspapers retaining a religion editor or similar expert on staff. By comparison, coverage of religion in the Japanese media is limited and, in the case of new religious movements, generally negative. Traditional print and broadcast media in Japan maintain an informal taboo on reporting good news about religion or even legal verdicts favorable to religion (Murō 2000: 138).[8]

We can distinguish four historical stages in the relation between media and religion. New religious movements first appeared in the pages of Japanese newspapers as material for scandalous exposé articles at the end of the nineteenth century. The religion Renmonkyō was destroyed by one such attack in the 1890s, and the religions Tenrikyō, Hito no Michi, and others were badly damaged by press campaigns that gave them no chance to respond. When newspapers were first expanding to achieve nationwide readership, sensationalist exposés of religion were used to boost circulation and to present media as the champions of science, medicine, rationality, and modernity. Journalists constructed religion as a straw man representing the opposite qualities of superstition, irrationality, and opposition to modernity. At this first, early stage, religion had neither effective access to media nor media of its own, so it was unable to defend itself or to influence the terms of its relations with media.

[8] On October 7, 1999, in Tottori District Court, the media were present for a landmark verdict against parents and Christian ministers-deprogrammers who had kidnapped members of the Unification Church in Japan and held adults against their will for months. The verdict was not reported, however.

Soon, however, new religions began to create media to promulgate their point of view. Since the early decades of the twentieth century, new religions have experimented with operating alternative media of their own, sometimes owning newspapers with wide circulations. Until 1945, these efforts were heavily regulated by the state through the Newspaper Law, and this law was used to suppress the newspaper and to imprison the leaders of the new religion Ōmoto. State regulation was the central characteristic of this second stage, and of course the state still licenses television and radio stations. In that sense, elements of the second stage remain.

In addition to using radio, network television, cable television, and audio and videotape, religions developed many print media vehicles after 1945. Although nominal state regulations remain in effect, constitutional protection of freedom of expression has protected the postwar use of media by religions. And with the exception of Sōka Gakkai's newspaper *Seikyō Shinbun*, whose circulation rivals that of the major dailies, religions have not sought to use media to address the nation as a whole, but rather for proselytization and to convey information to existing members. The development of the Internet has recently opened a fourth stage in the relation between religion and media, and new religions in particular are enthusiastic creators of new web media. This creativity has been made possible by the absence of state regulation. The equality of all voices that characterizes the Internet is changing the relation between religion and media, though the change is difficult to assess as yet (Hardacre 1999).

For the most part, religions have shunned the limelight and maintained a self-imposed media blackout. As organizations, all sectors of religion share a need to hold together people affiliated by various ties of variable strength, all of whom are extremely sensitive to criticism. Christianity is sometimes an exception to the rule, but just as they generally counsel their believers to accommodate themselves to circumstances rather than attempt to change society, the first and second sectors of Japanese religions tend to regard public protest as unbecoming a "proper" religion. These sectors have peaked in growth and see a greater need to maintain membership than to engage in debate on the media's terms. Whenever subjected to media attack, religions have typically reacted passively and waited for media attention to shift away. This "ostrich approach" is based on *Realpolitik*. Whenever religions *have* counterattacked or resorted to the courts for redress, the criticism they incurred outweighed the benefits of rebuttal or legal vindication. The media are just too big to fight, and religions' uses of independent media are too few and isolated to counter mainstream media, though adoption of the Internet could change that slightly. Sōka Gakkai's newspaper *Seikyō Shinbun* constitutes the single exception; it probably can effectively counter mainstream media condemnations, but only for the already converted (Hardacre 1991).

The media's negative attitudes prevent promulgation of positive news about religion, thus preventing the public from forming positive opinions. "Straight" news coverage of religion (as opposed to the entertainment shows described above) is almost entirely restricted to coverage of public rituals or works of art and architecture connected with the first sector or reports of scandal or illegal activity in the second and third sectors. The media do not assume an ongoing responsibility for informing the public about religion as a service that could build up a fund of information for making informed choices. Only third-sector religions consistently challenge the media. Paradoxically, it could be argued that this absence of balanced media coverage of religion has left Japanese particularly vulnerable to the appeal of unscrupulous religionists.

Aum Shinrikyō Clashes with Japanese Society, 1985 to 2000

Asahara Shōkō (born Matsumoto Chizuo in 1955) opened a natural food store and yoga school in Chiba Prefecture in 1978. In 1982, when he was a follower of the new religion Agonshū, he was arrested for manufacturing fake medicine. He traveled to India for the first time around 1986, returning to claim that he had experienced enlightenment. From this time on, his yoga practice evolved into a syncretic religion that incorporated aspects of Hinduism and esoteric Buddhism.[9] Aum believers were increasingly pressured to leave their families and abandon secular employment in favor of all-volunteer labor for the religion, frequently in the religion's computer-manufacturing business. Ordained members were expected to donate all their resources. Alarmed relatives banded together to force Aum to permit regular contact with ordained members who had cut off relations with their families and to compel Aum to return family assets. Around 1988, conflicts over land purchases also emerged in several locales.[10]

In October 1989, the tabloid *Sunday Mainichi* began an exposé of Aum, but whereas other religions might have responded passively, Aum fought back with its own attempt to embarrass the paper's editor. This breach of religion's customary relations with the media was so striking that Aum was able to get television coverage to present its side of the story. Thereafter, Aum retaliated forcefully against all media criticism.

The relation between religion and the public sphere then entered new territory, in which a network protected its access to a religion at the expense of its duty to inform the public and the police. On October 26, 1989, the Tokyo Broadcasting Service (TBS) television network filmed interviews with Sakamoto Tsutsumi, a Yokohama attorney who represented a newly formed group of aggrieved relatives of Aum members, Aum Shinrikyō Higaisha no Kai (The Victims of Aum Association), for inclusion in a TV program on Aum to be called "The Underwater Powers Experiment." The program was to feature one segment showing Asahara demonstrating supernatural power by remaining underwater for thirty minutes without air; another segment was to focus on Sakamoto's criticisms of Aum.[11] On the evening of October 26, three Aum leaders appeared at TBS offices and met with the producers in charge of the program. They demanded to be shown the segment on Sakamoto, and at that time they learned that he was calling the religion a fake,

[9] The timing of Asahara's journeys to India remains somewhat unclear. See Hardacre (1995).

[10] The points of tension between Aum and Japanese society at this time were entirely comparable to social conflicts between NRMs and American and British society. See Beckford (1985).

[11] In the event, it was not Asahara, but a disciple, Inoue Yoshihiro, who performed the underwater exercise, and it lasted not thirty minutes, but eleven. A third segment was to have featured the *Sunday Mainichi* incident.

charging it with kidnapping, extortion, and other crimes, and generally debunking it. The three demanded that the broadcast be canceled. A deal was struck, granting TBS an exclusive interview with Asahara in return for the cancellation of the damaging critique by Sakamoto.[12]

On November 4, Sakamoto, his wife, and infant son disappeared without a trace. An Aum badge was found in their apartment, but it was not until eleven days later that the Kanagawa Prefectural Police began an official investigation into the disappearance. Although TBS broadcast this news along with footage of people distributing handbills calling on anyone with information to come forward, the network kept silent about having shown Aum the video of Sakamoto threatening to expose the religion. Later, Asahara granted the promised interview, but the interviewer made no inquiries into the possibility of an Aum connection with the Sakamoto affair. TBS remained silent about this event for six and a half years, until March 20, 1996, when a Diet investigation was held. By that time, the bodies of the Sakamotos had been found buried in drums, the sites identified by the Aum members who murdered them at Asahara's personal orders. TBS General Director Ōkawa Mitsuyuki apparently perjured himself in Diet testimony, denying that the network provided an advance showing of the program to Aum leaders, only to reverse himself a week later and admit that the network *did* show the video to Aum and subsequently covered up the affair. Two staff members were dismissed, and Ōkawa was eventually forced to resign.

In keeping silent about Aum leaders' violent reaction to Sakamoto's views, TBS withheld information that could have led to the exposure of criminal activities in Aum a full six years before the Tokyo subway attack, probably preventing that disaster and the 1994 attack in the city of Matsumoto, to say nothing of numerous kidnappings and unlawful confinements, the manufacture of weapons and illegal drugs, and the use of those drugs to silence dissidents.

Meanwhile, the police response to the Sakamoto family's disappearance was similarly revealing. The investigation stalled almost immediately, with the police unwilling to pursue the connection suggested by the Aum insignia found at the scene. The police explanation was that they feared accusations of persecuting religion if they investigated Aum too vigorously. Viewed historically, police inaction in this case reflected both the postwar pattern of assuming that religions act to promote the public good and the habit of protecting religions' autonomy. Adopting a more politicized perspective, Sakamoto's coworkers attributed police sluggishness to reluctance to assist their left-leaning law firm. Either way, police inaction enabled Aum to commit further crimes.[13]

[12] Two of the Aum representatives, Hayakawa Kiyohide and Aoyama Yoshinobu, made careful notes of the contents of the 1989 video, and their notes match up with its content, down to exact wording. The 1989 video affair came to light in connection with criminal prosecutions of these two. The third man was Jōyu Fumihiro.

[13] The media did not pursue Aum any more than did the police, perhaps fearing a barrage of embarrassing counterattack like that received by *Sunday Mainichi*. Likewise, scholars of religion, themselves largely dependent on the media for information about Aum, showed naiveté in their largely positive statements about Aum. When criminal trials began in 1995, exposure of this naiveté led to the disgrace of a single scapegoat, followed by a general silencing. See Shimazono (1995).

In February 1990, Asahara lost a bid for election to the Diet, as did the several other adherents of Aum who also stood for election. Having predicted victory, Asahara was shocked to find that society rejected him overwhelmingly. His reaction revealed increasing isolation from public opinion.[14] Thereafter, Asahara gave up the idea of peaceful coexistence with society in favor of creating an alternative government with himself as theocrat. On the night of June 27, 1994, he celebrated the completion of this new system with his closest leaders and ordered them to carry out the religion's first attack using sarin gas. The attack was aimed at the District Court of Matsumoto, which was conducting a trial challenging Aum's purchase of land. It later emerged that Aum had been developing weapons technology through a science and technology team that had experimented with sarin gas on an Australian sheep property since 1993. Police investigation of the Matsumoto sarin attack, which left several dead and others with life-long injuries, focused on a local man unrelated to Aum who was later vindicated.

Fearing a police investigation, Asahara ordered the March 20, 1995, attack on the Tokyo subway system as a diversionary tactic. Five Aum members boarded subway trains bound for Tokyo's government center. Each man got off his train a station or two in advance, dropping two small plastic bags to the floor, piercing them with the sharpened tip of an umbrella, and mingling the contents to produce sarin gas. Terror struck as fumes rose, sickening everyone nearby and spreading to the platform when the doors opened at the next stop. Stricken subway workers fell to the ground as they tried to help fleeing passengers. With thousands of people flooding street-level exits, ambulances and paramedics could not reach the sick and dying. Once outside, people collapsed on the street in droves. Miraculously, only twelve were killed, but 5,000 required hospitalization, and many sustained life-long trauma. A police investigation began two days later, leading to Asahara's arrest on May 16. Since that time, trials of Asahara and others have led to numerous convictions, with sentences including the death penalty.

Revision of the Religious Corporations Law

The vast majority of Aum members apparently had no idea of the criminal activity of their leaders. Neither had almost anyone else, with the single exception of freelance reporter Egawa Shōkō, who from 1989 to 1995 tirelessly prodded the Kanagawa police to interrogate Aum about the disappearance of the Sakamotos. Aum's status as a religious corporation, which carried the presumption that Aum was working for the public good and won it the privileges of autonomous operation, undoubtedly retarded impartial investigation by the police, media, and scholars, and RCL status evidently restrained the state.

On October 30, 1995, Aum was stripped of this status, and it subsequently declared bankruptcy. This was the first time corporate status had ever been withdrawn

[14] In early 1990, Aum's membership was about 5,000, of whom 800 were ordained. The membership in 1995 was estimated at 10,000 members, of whom around 1,200 were ordained.

from a functioning religion.[15] Although loss of corporate status was far too mild a punishment to fit the crimes, the RCL was the state's only instrument for disciplining a religious body *as an organization*, as opposed to charging individuals. To address what some critics regarded as a legislative loophole, a move began to enact legislation that would facilitate the punishment of religious bodies as organizations, beginning with revision of the RCL, continuing with a failed attempt to invoke the Anti-Subversive Activities Law, and leading in late 1999 to the creation of two so-called New Aum Laws. Before Aum, there had been no impetus for any such initiative.

On December 15, 1995, several amendments to the RCL were adopted that called for all religions to be registered with the Ministry of Education, required greater financial transparency, expanded the membership of the ministry's advisory body, the Religious Corporations Council (Shūkyō Hōjin Shingikai), and gave the ministry authority to question religions suspected of violating the law (Kisala 1997: 63). These apparently innocuous provisions struck fear into the hearts of religious bodies of all kinds because they clearly signaled the end of the previous presumption that religions are a positive force in society that should not be subjected to invasive regulation and the beginning of the RCL's use not to restrain the state, but to strengthen it.

No group felt so chilling an effect as Sōka Gakkai, which views the revisions as a "blatant opportunist attempt by the ruling coalition to exploit the Aum affair for political gain" (LoBreglio 1997: 39). This charge derived from the LDP's opposition to Sōka Gakkai's support for the New Frontier Party (Shinshintō). Quite apart from anything related to Aum, Kōmeitō merged with other opposition parties to form the New Frontier Party in late 1994. Sōka Gakkai delivered six or seven million votes in the Upper House elections of July 1995 for New Frontier Party candidates, allowing the party to increase its representation from thirty-five to fifty-six seats. Although the LDP retained its majority, it was clear that Sōka Gakkai was in a position to undermine it significantly in the more important Lower House elections. Alarmed at this prospect, the LDP hit on a brilliant strategy for dividing the New Frontier Party from Sōka Gakkai, its most formidable supporter.

The LDP convoked public hearings on the RCL to investigate what it called "increasingly aggressive political activities by a giant religious organization" and demanded that Ikeda Daisaku, Sōka Gakkai's honorary chairman, appear for interrogation. This had the public relations effect of associating Sōka Gakkai with Aum and problematizing Sōka Gakkai's political influence. This ploy to force a Sōka Gakkai official to testify before the Diet was only thwarted by New Frontier Party men physically blockading the room and preventing the meeting from being held. This was a Pyrrhic victory, however, because an association in the public mind had already been created among the New Frontier Party, Sōka Gakkai, and Aum (LoBreglio 1997: 39–40).

[15] There had, however, been previous instances of corporate status being withdrawn from religions that had ceased to operate.

The public was so inflamed against Aum that only the Communist Party was prepared to oppose revision of the RCL. Given Sōka Gakkai's history of opposition to state regulation of religion, its members could not consistently support revising the RCL, but the alternative was to be seen as supporters of Aum. Although established religious bodies now oppose the revisions that resulted, with the exception of Christian churches, they did not publicly question the process of revision as it was happening. In short, those most knowledgeable about and most likely to be affected by revision were too intimidated by the tide of public opinion to dissent.

The attempt to revise the RCL thus became a political tool for LDP intimidation of Sōka Gakkai and Kōmeitō. Aum's crimes provided the occasion, but the effects for the religious world will be pervasive. Although religions had previously been largely *protected from* state scrutiny of their finances and membership lists, revision of the RCL creates a *mandate for* state monitoring. Before revision, the RCL was premised on a view of religions as working for the public good, and the law was a neutral mechanism assisting them to do so, without state interference. By contrast, the revised law presumes religions' potential to do harm and casts the state as a monitor of religion to protect the populace. Widely perceived as preparing the groundwork for further state intervention, the new law hangs over all religions like the sword of Damocles.

Aum and Japanese Post–Cold War Intelligence Gathering

Since 1995, Japan's Public Security Investigation Agency (Kōan Chōsachō, or PSIA) has become involved in regulating religion through its connection to the Anti-Subversive Activities Law (*Hakai katsudō bōshi hō*, or ASAL) of 1952. The ASAL was intended to control political organizations sponsoring Communist demonstrations. Its drafters never envisioned enforcing it against a religion, and several of its provisions underline that it must never be used to infringe on religious freedom. To date, it has never been applied against an organization.[16] Attached to the Ministry of Justice, the PSIA is charged with making recommendations regarding use of the ASAL.[17] If investigation establishes a danger of subversive activity, a group can be dissolved or its activities restricted for a specified period of time. The group is allowed an opportunity to answer the charges at a hearing before the Public Security Council (Kōan Shinsa Iinkai), an advisory body appointed by the PSIA, but no judge or neutral adjudicator presides.[18]

Before the subway attack, religions were not among PSIA monitoring targets, and it had no files on Aum. The PSIA began seeking authorization to apply the ASAL against Aum in 1995, specifying in early 1996 the manner in which it

[16] Of the eighteen individuals charged and brought to trial under the ASAL, twelve have been convicted.

[17] The PSIA, the membership and budget of which are never made public, exists only to investigate groups in connection with the ASAL. Because its sole function is investigation, it has no powers of arrest or detainment.

[18] Implementing the law, however, would have had no immediate effect on the question most troubling to local governments: how to rid themselves of Aum buildings, businesses, and meeting places.

proposed to do so. All Aum proselytization and fund raising would be banned. Individual worship would be permitted, but receiving guidance from group leaders or meeting together at a residence would be prohibited. Although communal life would not be prohibited, working or undergoing religious discipline under the guidance of a leader or leaders would be prohibited. Many other prohibitions were enumerated.

The PSIA's proposals were widely seen as arbitrary and infringing directly on constitutional guarantees.[19] Individual faith and belief are constitutionally protected, and forbidding proselytization (a manifestation or "exercise" of belief) impinges on this freedom. In fact, much of the prohibited activity overlaps with freedom of religion, speech, and assembly. The Japan Federation of Bar Associations (Nihon Bengoshi Rengōkai, or JFBA) argued that Aum's crimes are best addressed under existing laws of the criminal code and that to invoke the ASAL would be to react hysterically to public opinion (*Asahi Shinbun*, September 28, 1995, p. 4; see Okudaira 1996). For these reasons, the plan to invoke the ASAL against Aum was eventually dropped in January 1997.

The PSIA's defeat came as intelligence agencies around the world were struggling to articulate a new, post–Cold War rationale for their continued existence. The PSIA persisted in the attempt to make itself an agency indispensable for the surveillance of religions. On August 26, 1997, the PSIA published a report on Aum that cited its expansion and the continued threat it posed. A PSIA "Cult Squad" was established in 1998 for wide-ranging information gathering on religious bodies. Sōka Gakkai reportedly became an object of such monitoring, as did the Unification Church and some rightist Shintō groups. It was around this time that efforts began to revise the ASAL to eliminate the constitutional problems that had prevented its implementation against Aum. Working with the PSIA, the Ministry of Justice drafted two new laws for use against Aum that were enacted in December 1999 (Noda 2000: 82).

The "New Aum Laws"

Media coverage of Aum from 1996 to 1999 prepared the public to accept – even desire – its complete extirpation. Strange stories of Aum kidnappings circulated all through 1999, only to be repudiated by the alleged victims, one of whom eventually admitted that she had staged her own disappearance to strengthen the view that Aum was as bad as ever. Over 1999 and early 2000, clashes with Aum broke out on a daily basis in which local governments refused to provide official registration of residence or permission for Aum children to enter schools or in which locals

[19] Japanese newspapers expressed various views on the relation between public sentiment and the imposition of the ASAL. The *Hokkoku Shinbun* said that use of the ASAL "could not be helped." The *Kōbe Shinbun* wrote, "Considering the innumerable evil acts Aum has committed, the numerous victims and their families, the people's sentiment that the ASAL should be imposed is unavoidable." The *San'in Shinpō* said, "It is certain that the great anger against Aum's crimes has fueled the sentiment in favor of applying the ASAL." See "*Aum e no habō hō benmei tetsuzuki*," *Asahi Shinbun* (February 27, 1996), p. 21.

simply blockaded buildings where Aum members were living and demonstrated against them, demanding that they get out, brandishing signs, shouting, and deploying loudspeaker trucks. In a bizarre twist apparently signaling a schism, two of Asahara's teenage daughters kidnapped their younger brother, the eldest son and heir apparent. An Aum accountant was taken into custody when he protested against a bank's refusal to open an account for Aum. Each of these stories added fuel to the public's belief that Aum had not changed and sparked the public into a fury for vengeance. In this climate of public opinion, it was not difficult to pass two laws that further advanced the state's mandate to regulate religion.

The two "New Aum Laws," as they are popularly known, establish mechanisms for the compensation of victims of crimes of mass murder (informally known as the *Higaisha kyūsai hō*, its official title is *Minji saisei hō*) and for the control of organizations whose members and leaders have been convicted of mass murder (informally known as the *Dantai kisei hō*, its official title is *Musabetsu dairyō satsujin kōi o okonatta dantai no kisei ni kansuru hō*). The Victims Compensation Law (VCL) is intimately connected to the Organizations Control Law (OCL): resources identified by inspections authorized under the OCL can be designated for compensation of victims (and payment of Aum's bad debts). The VCL's provisions are premised on the OCL's having been implemented, and they mainly enumerate how property may be identified and transferred to victims. Under the OCL, the PSIA and the police are to work together in inspecting Aum facilities for three years; the first inspection began in February 2000. Aum is required to submit lists of its assets and its members' names and addresses every three months. These lists will be shared with local authorities as appropriate (e.g., in areas where an ongoing dispute about land or residence exists). The police may not forcibly enter any locked facility, but if Aum refuses them entrance, the PSIA may prohibit Aum from using or renting the facility or from acquiring any new facilities for six months. The same penalties will be exacted if it is found that members are being held against their will or if the investigation is obstructed in any way. Significantly, the Japan Federation of Bar Associations does not object to the OCL/VCL, although opposition-party politicians point out that existing laws were entirely adequate to deal with Aum crimes and that passage of the New Aum Laws was mainly a response to public opinion.

The Role of the Bar Association (JFBA)

By the mid-1990s, the JFBA had accumulated significant experience with third-sector religious organizations. Commercialization of third-sector religious or semi-religious practices in a plethora of new forms inevitably spawned abuses, and many people took their problems to an attorney. A group of attorneys formed a task force on "consumer problems" related to religion and counseled numerous plaintiffs seeking the return of money they had donated to the Unification Church in Japan or to a group of temples headed by one called Myōkakuji.[20] Deceptive

[20] Myōkakuji is currently slated to be stripped of corporate status under the RCL, the second application of this law to remove recognition following a criminal prosecution.

methods of proselytism and fund raising, accompanied in the worst instances by systematic fraud and extortion, lay at the heart of these cases.

The publications of the Consumer Problems Task Force within the JFBA are beginning to clarify the conditions under which religious proselytization should be regarded as violating the rights of those targeted for conversion, a perspective differing significantly from the previous understanding of proselytization as a constitutionally protected exercise of religious belief (Shūkyō to Shōhisha Bengodan Nettowaaku 1996; Nihon Bengoshi Rengōkai Shōhisha Mondai Taisaku Iinkai 1999). From the verdicts discussed in these publications emerges the view that threats of spirit retribution, heavy pressure to prevent a prospective convert from reconsidering, demands for amounts of money that would be financially ruinous, deceptive approaches, quotas for proselytizers, and the compilation of manuals endorsing any of these elements constitute coercive proselytization and that such proselytizing can be punished by law. The Task Force also started issuing warnings about minority religions, saying, "The [exploitative] features to be seen in Aum are not necessarily limited to that religion. Those tendencies can frequently be seen in religions referred to as 'cults,' even if not to the same degree or the same kinds seen in Aum" (Shūkyō to Shōhisha Bengodan Nettowaaku 1996: 75; on Myōkakuji, see 30–61).

The Task Force issued guidelines for the handling of legal problems involving religion in a March 1999 report. Focusing on the rights of a person targeted by a religious group for proselytization or fund raising, the "target" is regarded as a consumer of services offered by the religion, which is held to have the duty of full disclosure from initial contact. Thus, proselytizers must clearly tell the target what religion they represent and what its doctrines are. If they are soliciting funds, they may not intimidate the target – for example, by prophesying that the targets or their ancestors will go to hell if funds are not donated – nor may they press the target for an amount that would cause economic hardship. Proselytizers failing to observe these requirements can be regarded as guilty of violating the human rights of targets as well as their rights as consumers.[21]

The recommendations of the Task Force are eminently reasonable and measured, but two ideas on which they are based point toward an important shift in the postwar understanding of religion's position in civil society. First is the presentation of religious organizations as if they were businesses offering services to consumers whose rights should be codified and defended against "excessive sales pressure" or "misleading advertising." Second is the framing of this consumer-versus-seller perspective in terms of human rights – not the religion's right to freedom or the proselytizer's right to manifest religious belief through proselytization, but instead an emphasis on the need to protect the "human rights" of potential converts from excesses or abuses perpetrated by religions. In a significant departure from postwar judicial traditions of nonintervention, the guidelines share the changed viewpoint

[21] Nihon Bengoshi Rengōkai, "Ikensho: Han-shakaiteki na shūkyō katsudō ni kakawaru shōhisha higai nado no kyūsai no hōshin" (Position Paper: Guidelines for the Relief of Victimized Consumers in Cases of Anti-Social Religious Activity) (March 26, 1999).

also seen in the revised RCL and the New Aum Laws, advocating greater government monitoring of religion to protect people from abuses.

A prosecution adopting the Task Force's perspective on coercive proselytizing has begun against a religion called Hō no Hana ("The Dharma Flower"). This new-new religion is best known for its founder's claim to be the only human being capable of hearing "the voice of Heaven" (*tensei*) and its unique divination practice of "sole diagnosis" (*ashi-ura shindan*), in which the soles of the feet are "read" (like a palm) to diagnose sickness. Police investigation uncovered manuals instructing local leaders how to extort money from followers through intimidation. They were to say the person would contract cancer if large sums were not forthcoming, for example. Without awaiting a verdict on the extortion charges against founder Fukunaga Hōgen and eleven other leaders, the Ministry of Education has initiated the process of stripping the religion of its corporate status (*Asahi Shinbun*, May 9, 2000, p. 1, and May 10, 2000, pp. 1, 23).

Conclusion

Discussion at a symposium sponsored in early 2000 by the ecumenical religious newspaper *Chūgai Nippō* succinctly summarized religions' position in Japan's civil society today as deeply intimidated by the public's newly energized skepticism. The symposium brought together Buddhist leaders, noted scholar of the new religions Professor Inoue Nobutaka of Kokugakuin University, and attorney Yasui Yūji, a member of the JFBA's Consumer Problems Task Force. Inoue pointed out that the first sector of the religious world, which was represented at the symposium by sectarian leaders, remains ignorant about and prejudiced against the second and third sectors. The usual timidity of religions facilitates uncensored media sensationalism about brainwashing, mind control, and "cults." Buddhist leaders expressed extreme frustration at being tarred with the same brush as Aum, and they joined Inoue in expressing dismay at the process of the RCL's revision and the lightning-quick passage of the New Aum Laws, which gave the religious and academic worlds no opportunity for consultations with the legislative or judicial branches of government. Yasui tried to persuade the Buddhist leaders to accept Task Force guidelines willingly, implying that failure to do so could result in the forcible imposition of them in the future, further damaging religion's tarnished image. Unfortunately, there was no indication that his attempts at suasion succeeded. All participants agreed that the climate of public opinion toward religion is becoming increasingly negative.[22]

Future researchers may come to regard the liberal period of 1945 to 1995 as a brief, foreign-dictated abnormality in Japan's long history of state monitoring of religion. From 1945 until the oil shocks, they may say, Japan's prewar legacy of repressive regulation was repudiated. Religion secured an acknowledged place

[22] "*Zadankai: Ima shūkyō ni nani ga towarete iru ka*?" *Chūgai Nippō* no. 26025 (March 23, 2000), pp. 1, 6; no. 26026 (March 25, 2000), p. 6; no. 26027 (March 28, 2000), p. 6; no. 26028 (March 30, 2000); no. 26029 (April 1, 2000), p. 6.

in civil society as a force for good that worked in the public interest. With the assistance of Occupation-authored provisions, second-sector religions' prewar experience of persecution enabled them to function like the voluntary associations of civil society to restrain the state. Controversies were few and mainly arose from second- or third-sector groups experiencing huge growth rates that made them mass movements, from religions that seemed to blur the constitutional mandate for separating religion and state, or from exposés of religious leaders' personal indiscretions.

The appearance in the 1970s of a third sector in the religious world, with a rapid proliferation of novel practices and high-commitment organizations "advertised" through intensively commercialized forms of recruitment, fueled a widespread perception of a need to protect society by regulating religion. First- and second-sector religions have not countered this opinion, and all sectors of the religious world are increasingly regarded as existing on a continuum of "cults." The public sphere is now thoroughly poisoned against religion.

In the aftermath of Aum Shinrikyō's attacks, religion has come under intense scrutiny, and its position in civil society has been significantly undermined, with any capacity it had to restrain the state effectively nullified. The revised RCL mandates increased state monitoring of religion, and it has been made a tool for the power struggles of political parties. Families and communities have become politicized in opposition to Aum and are becoming vocal participants in civil society by means of an increasingly generalized opposition to religion. The media promote the notion that only a thin line divides "proper" religions from "cults," as does the PSIA, rescued from obsolescence by its new-found role in gathering intelligence on religion. The guidelines issued by the Consumer Problems Task Force of the JFBA are strangely at odds with the constitution's presumption of a need to protect religion from excessive state regulation and the individual from violations of religious freedom. Perhaps future researchers will see the reimposition of greater regulation as an anti-imperialist attempt to dismantle the machinery of "victors' justice," paralleling rhetorical assaults on Article 9, the "no-war, no-arms" clause of the constitution. However that may be, a changed position for religion within Japanese civil society may be Aum's most enduring legacy.

7

State-Society Partnerships in the Japanese Welfare State

Margarita Estévez-Abe

For Alexis de Tocqueville (1988: 515–16), "The morals and intelligence of a democratic people would be in as much danger as its commerce and industry if ever a government wholly usurped the place of private associations. It is therefore necessary that [government] should not act alone." Was he right? Japan provides an important perspective on this question.[1]

This chapter argues that intermediate associations can play roles that neither Tocqueville nor contemporary Tocquevilleans have recognized. If Tocqueville emphasized intermediate associations' roles as an external check on government and as a means of civic education, contemporary Tocquevilleans seem more interested in the effect of associations on what Tocqueville called democratic *mores*. They attribute a good economy, public health, effective governance, and democracy to the aggregate psychological state of a community.[2] In particular, they value associations because they are thought to promote social capital (e.g., Putnam et al. 1993; Fukuyama 1995; Putnam 1995, 2000; Brehm and Rahn 1997). Associations, whether formal or informal, presumably help citizens connect to and trust their fellow citizens. This kind of trust, Robert Putnam (Putnam et al. 1993; Putnam 2000) asserts, can improve both governmental effectiveness and the quality of democracy. Trust between citizens and government officials, so the argument goes, makes government more effective by making it more responsive (Putnam et al. 1993; Pharr and Putnam 2000). Putnam (2000: chap. 21) also claims that associations serve as a locus for deliberative democracy. People who come together in

[1] The author thanks Andrew Gordon, Sheldon Garon, and Frank Schwartz for their feedback on an earlier draft of this chapter, and especially John Campbell for his usual thorough comments on the final draft. Generous financial support from the Kanagawa Foundation for Academic and Cultural Exchange was indispensable for conducting the research that served as the basis for this chapter.

[2] See Berkman and Kawachi (2000) for examples of recent applications of social psychological arguments to new areas.

associations express their views, which get amplified to form public opinion, and associations make people more public-spirited, too (ibid.: 338–39).

These roles are indirect: they do not refer to such roles as associations' participation in state decision making or implementing policy tasks. In contrast, scholars of comparative political economy have accumulated significant knowledge about the *direct* roles played by intermediate associations. Many of these scholars have argued that patterns of societal organizations and networks affect economic performance. They emphasize the role that formal associations and informal networks play in self-regulation of the market at both the sectoral and national levels (e.g., Schmitter 1977; Streeck and Schmitter 1985; Hall 1986; Hollingsworth, Schmitter, and Streeck 1994; Berger and Dore 1996). Others go so far as to argue that the presence of economic organizations such as business associations is a crucial component of successful industrial policy (Tilton 1996; Doner and Schneider 1999; Levy 1999). In more general terms, these scholars assert that to be effective, states require reliable counterparts in society to cooperate in policy making and implementation (Evans 1995; Tilton 1996; Johnson 1999; Levy 1999).

Despite its own concern with associations' role in promoting economic performance and effective public policy, recent works in the civil society literature rarely take advantage of the insights political economy has to offer. The focus on close relationships between intermediate associations and governments often found in the political economy literature seems to have driven away contemporary Tocquevilleans because of their distrust of government. They do not pay sufficient attention to the direct roles intermediate associations play and to the consequent blurring of the distinction between state and society. The relationship goes both ways: not only does the state shape civil society, but civil society also takes part in affairs of state. This situation poses a set of questions Tocquevilleans do not ask. Does this participation of intermediate associations in affairs of state affect government effectiveness and economic performance? Does it contribute to democracy?

This chapter is intended to contribute to the debate about the roles of associations in promoting democracy and effective governance by exploring the more direct roles associations can play. Japan is an important case because it has been known for its close state-society partnerships (Samuels 1987; Garon 1988, 1997; Allinson and Sone 1993; Schwartz 1998). I want to argue here that the pattern of societal organizations and the needs and resources of government officials are critical to understanding the direct roles that societal organizations play. Inquiries into the direct roles played by associations are indispensable to answering the questions that concern contemporary Tocquevilleans, namely, the impact of associational life on democracy, governmental effectiveness, and economic performance. Most important, an examination of the direct roles played by intermediate associations helps us recognize the difficulty of determining the effects of civil society apart from the nature of the relationship between government and intermediate associations. In other words, I place equal emphasis on government in trying to understand what intermediate associations do (Levi 1996; Berman 1997; Skocpol 1997b).

This chapter examines state-society partnerships in the realm of social welfare services. Although there is a great deal of research about state-society partnerships in Japan, most studies pay attention only to the close working relationship between the state and business in industrial policy (e.g., Dore 1987; Samuels 1987; Okimoto 1989). In contrast to industrial policy, social welfare policy involves individual citizens more directly. Individual citizens and intermediate associations have played an important role in the making and implementation of social welfare policy just as businesses and their associations have in Japan's industrial policy.

This chapter is organized into five sections. First, I identify the range of groups that form partnerships with the state. Second, I explore the characteristics of organizations that long had a monopoly on administrative partnerships in the realm of social welfare. Third, I compare the traditional state-society partnership in social welfare policy to state-society partnerships in industrial policy. Fourth, I ask why the government formed partnerships with new types of voluntary groups in the field of social welfare in the 1990s. Finally, I place Japan's state-society partnership in social welfare in a comparative context.

Who Become Societal Partners of the Japan State?

Potential administrative partners for the state in the area of social welfare services include individual citizens, participatory civic groups, professional nonprofit organizations, for-profit enterprises, and quasigovernmental organizations that are created by the state outside its formal structure. In Japan, individuals and nonprofit organizations have been the traditional partners of the state in social welfare policy. These traditional partners often appear very much like governmental agencies because of strict regulation and bureaucratic discretion over who can qualify for nonprofit organization status and because of their roles as subcontractors of government services.

Let us contrast the United States and Japan to illustrate this point. In the United States, Internal Revenue Service regulations specify the conditions under which associations qualify as nonprofit organizations, regardless of whether they offer welfare or other services. In Japan, on the other hand, organizations need to seek the approval of the ministry with jurisdiction over its particular activities. Two requirements for nonprofit status merit attention: "service to the public interest" and adequate financial assets. It is bureaucrats who define what constitutes the "public interest" and the amount of assets necessary to guarantee the organizational continuity of a nonprofit-to-be. Traditionally set at the level of a few million dollars, the asset requirement served to prevent most grassroots civic groups from becoming nonprofit organizations. Although the recent Nonprofit Organization Law enacted in 1998 significantly deregulated the granting of that status, nonprofits still must go through the traditional channels to attain tax advantages (Nenkan Jiten Henshūshitsu 2000; Pekkanen 2000b). Thus, Japanese regulations allow for significant bureaucratic discretion.

Until recently, Japanese bureaucrats were legally permitted to hire only nonprofit organizations as subcontractors, but it was they who controlled entry to and exit from the nonprofit sector. Working with societal actors with nonprofit status also helps sustain the bureaucracy's image of political neutrality. As a result, bureaucrats make it possible for associations of private firms and individuals to attain legal status and thus become state partners by deciding they serve the public interest. Strange as it might sound, most of the civic groups providing nonprofit services for the elderly do not qualify as nonprofit public-interest corporations in Japan, while almost all industrial associations do.

What are the criteria Japanese bureaucrats use to decide which organizations contribute to the public interest? Bureaucrats gauge whether societal actors can perform such functions as gather information, serve as interest groups, and implement policy (Lynn and McKeown 1988; Yonekura 1993; Kikkawa 1995). These criteria tell us as much about bureaucrats as they do about societal partners. That is, bureaucrats need societal resources like extra personnel to implement their policies. The career civil service is not flexible enough to adjust its personnel to policy needs because it promises officials long-term employment (cf. Inoki 1995). This is where societal partners enter the picture, subcontracting the implementation of such policies as providing public services and determining the eligibility of citizens and firms for public services.

Societal partners economize state resources in other ways. They reduce the cost of government by gathering information about society and monitoring compliance. Because bureaucrats suffer from information asymmetry vis-à-vis the society they are supposed to regulate and service, societal partners can serve as conduits to monitor new demands and levels of compliance. Paradoxically, they also help legitimate bureaucratic activities by getting involved in the policy process in their capacity as representatives of society. Bureaucrats, who draft most legislation in Japan, need societal counterparts that authoritatively represent societal interests in their jurisdictions to legitimate their activities vis-à-vis parliament (cf. Pempel 1974, 1982).

The bureaucratic requirements for societal partners noted above explain why civic groups have traditionally fared badly: they have had little to offer bureaucrats. Such qualities of civic groups as the relative absence of barriers to participation, which many of us regard as a virtue, do not necessarily make them attractive as administrative partners. From the bureaucratic point of view, easy entry means easy exit, reducing the reliability of such organizations as partners. In fact, once bureaucrats grant nonprofit status to groups, regulations make it difficult for public-interest organizations to exit. The assets of a nonprofit must be turned over to the government when it is dissolved. Another critical deficiency of civic groups in the eyes of bureaucrats is that, due to their diversity, they are more difficult to organize into umbrella organizations capable of authoritatively representing a specific segment of the population under a particular ministerial or local jurisdiction. Societal groups with more tangible and common material incentives are more reliable and easier to organize.

Bureaucratic discretion over the granting of legal status to groups makes the Japanese nonprofit sector appear quasigovernmental. Not only does the Japanese state rely on societal partners, it also directly creates what Japanese call "auxiliary associations" (*gaikaku dantai*) outside the formal state structure.[3] Legally, these associations are also public-interest corporations, so under Japanese law they are part of the nonprofit sector.[4] Auxiliary associations nevertheless differ from other voluntary nonprofit associations in that they carry out such tasks as issuing product standard certificates or conducting research; they do not represent society. This difference is important because auxiliary associations do take part in the policy process as authoritative representatives of society.

In short, the kind of civic associations on which Putnam et al. (1993) focus – horizontally organized associations in which citizens learn participation and mutual trust – are not the kind of associations in which bureaucrats have traditionally been interested. Segments of Japanese society neglected by the bureaucracy do not simply remain passive, however. Some civic groups use innovative means to secure organizational continuity and mobilize personnel and expertise, thus emerging as viable societal partners for the government.

Traditional Administrative Partners in Social Welfare

Four groups stand out as key postwar partners of the Japanese state in the field of social welfare: welfare commissioners (*minsei iin*), social welfare councils (*shakai fukushi kyōgikai*), social welfare corporations (*shakai fukushi hōjin*), and seniors' clubs (*rōjin kurabu*).

In the prewar period, the Japanese government appointed private individuals as district commissioners (*hōmen iin*) – unpaid social workers (Garon 1997: chap. 1) – and in spite of the intentions of Occupation officials, postwar Japan reintroduced this type of state-society partnership. Typically, local notables had served as commissioners. Although their attitude toward people in need of public help was more paternalistic than democratic, they served as the Japanese equivalent of social workers. The postwar government gave welfare commissioners (*minsei iin*) the dual role of representing fellow residents and implementing policy. Commissioners are responsible for an average of 200 households in the neighborhood where they reside.[5] Although it appoints them, the government treats them as formal representatives of residents in each administrative unit. As described

[3] These auxiliary associations multiplied with the fiscal crisis of the 1970s and the government's decision to set a ceiling on the size of the national civil service (Prime Minister's Office 1998: 152–53). Not only did auxiliary associations provide ministries an outlet for bureaucrats who retire early to make room for new recruits, but they also frequently provided them with quick ways to respond to demands in new sectors. A major national newspaper, *Asahi Shinbun*, ran a front-page story (October 6, 2000) on how these auxiliary associations continue to hire retired civil servants. For an important related argument, see Johnson (1978).

[4] Salamon and Anheier (1998) emphasize that nonprofit organizations should be voluntary to be regarded as part of civil society. Clearly, Japanese auxiliary associations are not nonprofits in Salamon and Anheier's use of the term.

[5] Currently, there is one welfare commissioner per 270 households in heavily populated urban areas such as the twenty-three wards of Tokyo. In smaller towns, there is one per 120 households. See the administrative notice (*tsūchi*) dated May 22, 1972, from the former Social Bureau in the Ministry of Health and Welfare titled "*Minsei iin no teisū oyobi haichi kijun ni tsuite*."

below, commissioners are further organized into local and national associations and integrated into the policy process.[6]

The Occupation encouraged the formation of a more democratic source of revenue for charitable activities. In an effort to make the Japanese state more directly responsible for social welfare, Article 89 of the new constitution that the Occupation imposed prohibited the government from channeling public funds to private charitable and welfare associations (Tochimoto 1996: 82). (The Occupation also feared that a dependence of civil associations on public funds would inhibit the development of a democratic society in postwar Japan.) As a result, the government created a Japanese version of United Way, called Kyōdō Bokin, to channel private money to charitable activities.

Social welfare councils were originally established to reflect the voices of local residents in the allocation of funds in Kyōdō Bokin. In other words, both the national donation organization and social welfare councils were organized in a top-down manner so the government could "represent" citizens in local- and national-level deliberative councils that allocate public resources. Social welfare councils are regionally organized on the basis of a Social Welfare Enterprise Law (*Shakai Fukushi Jigyō Hō*) enacted in 1951. Clause 47 of that law mandates that social welfare councils include as members the majority of social welfare providers in the locality, government officials, welfare commissioners, and medical personnel and other specialists, with no group to exceed 10 percent of the total membership (Tsujinaka 1989: 170–72). Regional social welfare councils are themselves organized into the National Social Welfare Council (Zenkoku Shakai Fukushi Kyōgikai). Social welfare councils have generally been conservative in their political and social orientation.

Let us look at the actual delivery of welfare services. Because the postwar constitution made it the government's responsibility to care for the needy (Milly 1999), Japan has the so-called *sochi* system, under which the national government had to provide means-tested care to people who were incapable of taking care of themselves (Gyōsei Kenkyūkai 1981). Although regulatory and legislative authority is centralized in its hands, the Ministry of Health, Labor and Welfare (MHLW) – formerly the Ministry of Health and Welfare – does not do much in terms of actual service provision or policy implementation. The ministry relies on local governments to carry out nationally determined welfare services, and local governments, in turn, establish public facilities and subsidize private organizations to provide actual services. Because public funds paid for all services contracted out to private welfare providers, MHLW required that those providers be licensed as social welfare corporations, a type of nonprofit public-interest corporation (Social Welfare Enterprise Law, section 4).

The licensing process for social welfare corporations allows significant discretion. First, applicants need to donate a significant portion of their assets (in most

[6] Officials often meet welfare commissioners in their locality to consult them on policy matters. Interview with Mr. Fujita Jōji, chief, Office of Planning and Coordination for Women, Civic Affairs Bureau, Yokohama city government (summer 1995).

cases, real estate) to the social welfare corporations they want to create. Although there is an administrative guideline for the amount of assets required, local officials sometimes settle for less when they want to approve a specific application.[7] Second, applicants must prove they possess prior agreements with the relevant local governments to become subcontractors of public services (i.e., for child care, elderly care, care for the disabled).[8] The need for such prior agreements reveals that once local government officials decide to use specific groups as new service providers, they are able to secure social welfare corporation status for those groups. Once licensed, social welfare corporations subcontract public social welfare services. All social welfare corporations must follow detailed regulations regarding hours of operation, building regulations, and staffing, among other things. In turn, the state guarantees these corporations future subsidies and government payments. More than 65 percent of nonprofit social welfare organizations' revenue came from the government in the late 1980s (Atoda et al. 1998: 113).

In short, for most of the postwar period, local governments decided who participated in the policy process and who subcontracted public services. Administrative partnerships were three-tiered. Welfare commissioners took care of means testing and monitoring abuse of public services. Social welfare corporations built welfare facilities such as nursing homes and child daycare centers to offer in-facility services. Finally, social welfare councils, whose members included both welfare commissioners and social welfare corporations, served as representative and consultative organs in which public-service subcontractors joined public officials to share views on social welfare policy.[9]

Although the four types of partners described here are essentially subcontractors of public services, the state has not created subcontractors alone. The Japanese government also helped form more civic seniors' clubs, subsidizing groups of fifty or more citizens beyond the age of sixty. There exist about 133,000 seniors' clubs nationwide with close to 9 million members (Kawamura 1996: 92). The involvement of local governments has been crucial in organizing them, but these clubs are nonetheless participatory. They welcome all local residents beyond a

[7] Interviews with the following people, who were involved in successful applications for social welfare corporations, revealed the discretion enjoyed by government officials: Mr. Ōhashi Takamine and Ms. Hotta Eiko, board members for the social welfare corporation Yūyū in Hoya (June and January 1995, respectively); Ms. Mataki Kyōko, Atsugi city assembly representative (July 1995); Mr. Katayama Masaru (January 1995), policy staff, Policy and Planning Section, Kanagawa Livelihood Club Cooperative; and Ms. Uno Mizue, president, Consulting Sō (July 1997). Ōhashi, Hotta, and Katayama stated that support from Diet members and officials from the upper echelon of the government helped their cases go forward. Although an official we interviewed (at the Seniors Policy Section of the Seniors Policy Promotion Department of the Tokyo Metropolitan Government, December 1997) denied that such intervention takes place or is effective, a subsequent scandal revealed frequent intervention by ministerial officials in favor of chosen applicants. Ōhashi and Hotta indicated that their negotiations with local officials enabled them to settle for a smaller amount of assets than previously required. Similarly, they reported how they had acquired a letter of agreement for subcontracting from a sympathetic mayor.

[8] Ibid.

[9] Legally speaking, MHLW awarded social welfare councils the status of social welfare corporation.

certain age, and they operate more like hobby clubs, where the elderly to socialize. They also function as channels through which local gove get in touch with local residents who are no longer accessible through occu based groups. In this sense, these clubs complement other neighborhood-based associations, such as *jichikai* and *chōnaikai*.

The Japanese experience suggests that intermediate associations do not merely check the state from without; at least some associations directly communicate with the government and carry out public tasks. As participants in the policy process, they offer a channel other than political parties to represent residents. As service providers, they offer a cheaper means to construct the Japanese welfare state.[10]

Before we examine the diversification of societal groups participating in the social welfare policy process that occurred in the 1990s, let us contrast traditional state-society partnerships in social welfare with those found in industrial policy. The contrast helps illuminate similarities across policy areas as well as unique features of the traditional pattern in social welfare.

Industrial Policy versus Social Welfare Policy

Both policy areas share three important similarities in the way bureaucrats interact with societal partners. First, both the Ministry of Economy, Trade and Industry (METI) – formerly, the Ministry of International Trade and Industry – and MHLW choose as counterparts societal organizations that are authoritatively organized. By authoritative, I mean that each trade or industry possesses one association, which does not compete with other associations for members (Lynn and McKeown 1988). I have already discussed how the state interacted with such hierarchically organized societal representatives as social welfare councils. Similarly, METI bureaus work closely with authoritative organizations that represent the industries they oversee. The organization of firms into authoritative trade associations provides the bureaucracy with legitimate representatives of each industry to work with.

Second, METI, like MHLW, regulates associational activities by deciding which groups can attain the status of public-interest corporation along with the attendant tax benefits. METI bureaucrats possess discretion over what constitutes the "public interest" within their jurisdiction, and, like social welfare corporations, trade associations gain legal status only when the ministry decides they serve some public interest.[11] Thus, those business associations that work closely with METI all possess nonprofit tax status because they have been licensed as public-interest corporations by METI. Furthermore, METI has created numerous auxiliary associations. Unlike trade associations, which are voluntarily set up by private firms

[10] These service providers also offered an alternative to expanding the size of public-sector employment. Politically speaking, this mattered a great deal to the Liberal Democratic government because public-sector workers tended to be highly organized in leftist unions.

[11] This is not to say that business associations are founded by the government; I am referring here to their legal treatment. For the history of business associations in Japan, see Curtis (1975), Fujita (1988), Garon (1988), Miyamoto (1988), Kikkawa (1988), Gordon (1989), Yonekura (1993), and Tilton (1996).

within the same product market or industrial sector, auxiliary associations are more explicitly tools of the ministry.

I discussed above how Japanese bureaucrats tap private resources by creating associations that are neither fully part of the state nor part of civil society. Along with MHLW, METI is one of the ministries that relies most heavily on these organizations.[12] Although there are no data on the number of auxiliary associations, there are data on the number of public-interest corporations within each ministerial jurisdiction. METI ranks third after the former Ministry of Health and Welfare (MHW) – which merged with the Ministry of Labor to create the new MHLW – and the Ministry of Agriculture, Forestry and Fisheries, with 1,883, 5,239, and 1,945 corporations, respectively (Prime Minister's Office 1998: 258–59). As of the late 1990s, METI and the former MHW were also among the ministries with the most former bureaucrats occupying top positions in public-interest corporations they oversaw (ibid.: 281).

Third, despite the term "public-interest corporation," bureaucrats appear to favor societal groups that represent specific sectoral interests. Ironically, this means that societal groups with strong vested interests in public policy are better represented than groups that pursue a public interest that is not necessarily linked to their sectoral interests. METI has traditionally worked very closely with business associations but less closely with consumer groups, for example (Maclachlan, this volume). Similarly, MHLW (by which I mean the former Ministry of Health and Welfare bureaus that are now part of MHLW) has worked more closely with service providers than with representatives of beneficiaries. Although all ministerial advisory committees have so-called public-interest representatives, they tend to be academics chosen by bureaucrats themselves, so these public-interest representatives clearly differ from the representatives sent by industries (Sone et al. 1985; Schwartz 1998). Consumers and citizens have been conspicuously absent in the postwar history of state-society partnerships until very recently.

Of course, there are differences between state-society partnerships in various policy domains. Industrial policy traditionally aimed at eliminating counterproductive, "excessive" competition and encouraging collective efforts among domestic producers to catch up with foreign competitors (Johnson 1982; Okimoto 1989; Tilton 1996; Noble 1998). Providers of social services have faced a different situation. Because social welfare services have long been heavily regulated, very little competition existed in service delivery, and there were no rewards for innovation, so the only way to increase revenue was to seek more public funding.[13] Relations

[12] As of 1996, a total of 151 "designated corporations" (*shitei hōjin*) existed within the twenty-two ministries and independent agencies. Over one-third of these were subcontractors for METI (Prime Minister's Office 1998: 153). Because designated corporations are legally entrusted with governmental activities, they account for only a fraction of all auxiliary associations. Two METI officials stated in an interministerial study group that METI could not carry out its daily activities without auxiliary organizations (Policy Network Study Group, October 1996).

[13] Atoda et al. (1998) calculate that an average of 65 percent of nonprofit social service providers' revenue comes from public payments, compared with only 11 percent of business associations' revenue.

among service providers and between providers and the government were thus rather different from those in competitive industries.

Furthermore, societal partners in industrial policy have been embedded in denser societal networks. Business associations in related sectors interact closely with one another (Lynn and McKeown 1988; Tilton 1996). These associations operate in the context of formal and informal corporate networks such as financial, manufacturing, and retail *keiretsu*. Thus, societal partners in industrial policy do not function merely as arms of the government; they also play an important coordinating role within society independent of government. As mentioned above, scholars in the field of political economy have paid particularly close attention to how formal trade associations and informal corporate networks regulate the Japanese market (e.g., Asanuma 1985; Gerlach 1992; Aoki and Dore 1994). Traditional societal partners in social welfare, on the other hand, have little in the way of a private realm because they exclusively carry out public services. As a result, coordination of vested interests among service providers required government involvement; mutual interaction among the societal partners did not develop outside the realm of public policy.

Before we examine the implications of state-society partnerships for effective governance and democracy, we need to discuss how a greater variety of associations began to assume these roles in the 1990s. This was an important development because it demonstrates that a diversity of associations does not necessarily inhibit close working relationships between the state and intermediate associations. Depending on the type of problem to be solved, government officials may actively seek to diversify their partners beyond traditional, more corporatist arrangements.

New Problems and New Partnerships at the Local Level

The rapid aging of Japan's population and the declining capacity of families to cope with elderly care began to increase citizen demands for public social welfare services for frail seniors in the 1970s (Campbell 1992). The demands of middle-class families gradually exposed the limitations of means-tested services, which failed to meet the needs of middle-class seniors who required nonmedical assistance (Estévez-Abe 2002).

Policy changes in the late 1980s and the 1990s expanded the scope of service provision beyond means-testing and liberalized the rules governing who could provide services.[14] Various local governments broke away from a strict reliance on means-tested services to help middle-class residents on a fee-for-service basis.[15] The relatively high cost of institutionalized care and the more diverse demands

[14] Although attacks on social welfare began in the late 1970s for fiscal reasons, social services for the elderly, if anything, expanded (Campbell 1992).

[15] A fee-for-service system (*fukushi no yūryōka*) introduced in the late 1980s allowed governments to provide services to middle-class citizens outside the means-tested *sochi* system. In fact, care for the elderly was the most active social welfare issue area under MHLW's jurisdiction in the 1980s and 1990s (Campbell 1992).

from middle-class citizens led to the expansion of such in-home services (*zaitaku kea*) as assistance with household chores and bathing and daycare services for frail seniors.

The Elderly Health and Welfare Law (*Rōjin Hoken Fukushi Hō*) of 1990 and the Gold Plan of 1992 made it compulsory for local governments to draft a long-term plan for how they would meet increasing demands for elderly care (Campbell 1992; Etō 1996). Plans involved an assessment of the potential need for specific services, an assessment of the resources available in each locality, a feasibility study of future service expansion, and concrete plans by local governments. Most local governments formally invited citizens' groups and existing welfare providers to participate in different stages of the drafting process. According to a national survey, about half of all local governments involved residents from the initial stage of the drafting process, and about 80 percent of local governments invited representatives of residents to participate in the deliberation process for the draft. As for the *type* of local residents involved, 90 percent of local governments contacted "official" groups such as welfare commissioners and seniors' clubs, while about 50 percent also contacted citizens' volunteer groups. More than 60 percent of large cities brought in citizens' groups (Eto 1996: 6). John Campbell (personal communication; see also Campbell and Ikegami 1999), however, notes that much of the civic participation at this stage was on paper and formalistic. Real civic participation began with preparations for the introduction of the new Long-Term Care Insurance (*kaigo hoken*) program (effective in 2001).

This was a radical step. In the past, the rule was for the national government to plan and legislate and for local governments to carry out national decisions. The decentralization of policy making and fiscal responsibility challenged local officials: they had to deal with new tasks with limited personnel and revenue.[16] The variegated representation found in metropolitan areas reflects more than the diverse needs of a heterogeneous community. Local governments in urban areas needed to establish new relationships with residents in planning and providing social welfare services for middle-class residents because traditional welfare commissioners were no longer effective there. They did not know people in their neighborhoods well enough to provide local officials with useful feedback.[17] Moreover, the recruitment of welfare commissioners itself was becoming difficult in urban areas.[18]

The drafting of local plans revealed a serious inability of local governments to meet social service demands. More social welfare corporations were necessary to build more nursing homes and daycare centers, and more welfare workers were required to staff new centers and provide in-home services. Most local governments turned to their traditional partners, asking social welfare councils to find ways to mobilize residents, but when officials realized that regional social welfare councils were inactive and ineffective, they searched for other means. Some local

[16] Similar challenges took place in urban planning. See Gelb and Estévez-Abe (1998).

[17] Again, there were fewer welfare commissioners per capita in urban areas. See note 5.

[18] Interview with Mr. Fujita (see note 5).

governments created quasigovernmental organizations called welfare authorities (*fukushi kōsha*). Others began to form working relationships with participatory civic groups (Takechi 1993; Yamaguchi and Takahashi 1993; Shakai Hoshō Kenkyūjo 1996).

Indeed, citizens' groups began to play prominent roles as new entrants in the social service sector. Liberalization rapidly expanded the number of welfare providers in the 1990s. Although entry into traditional in-facility services was somewhat more regulated, the government broadened the range of private providers qualified to subcontract government services. It also created a less regulated version of welfare facilities. In addition to nursing homes, which institutionalized the elderly, there were now daycare centers, too. And in addition to the traditional contractor, social welfare corporations, providers now included social welfare councils, quasigovernmental welfare authorities set up by local governments, agricultural cooperatives (*nōkyō*), and consumer cooperatives (*seikyō*). As a result, a new area of welfare service developed, so-called citizen-participatory in-home welfare services (*jūmin sankagata zaitaku fukushi saabisu*).

Great regional variations emerged in the combinations of new providers even within Greater Tokyo. Chōfu and Fuchi, two suburbs, came to be known as examples of regional social welfare councils that successfully mobilized their communities. Musashino and Yokohama created quasigovernment agencies so that they could hire "paid volunteers" to deliver in-home services. Although it falls beyond the scope of this chapter, the emergence of the concept of "paid volunteers" in Japan itself merits analysis. Takechi (1993: 121) notes that the use of paid volunteers reduces the psychological burden on welfare clients, who would otherwise feel too indebted or ashamed for "being taken care of by strangers."[19]

Government initiatives do not imply lack of civic efforts. For instance, in Yokohama, the city depended heavily on a preexisting private nonprofit network for social service delivery to make the new quasigovernmental agency work. Other municipal governments more directly sought to support participatory civic groups. Machida, Kawasaki, Hoya, Fujisawa, and Atsugi all licensed the creation of daycare centers for frail seniors run by participatory residents' groups. Machida is well known in the Tokyo metropolitan area for its partnership with civic groups. Its officials supported civic groups and built ties with them without taking over their activities.[20] The city surveys the activities and needs of citizens' groups in the social services sector, and officials stay in close touch with large citizens' groups in the area.[21] The Tokyo Metropolitan Government, which stands between local governments in Tokyo Prefecture and the national government, does not have

[19] In a survey of 3,600 citizens in 300 localities all over Japan, two-thirds of the respondents replied that volunteers should be compensated for the actual costs they pay (e.g., transportation fares) to deliver volunteer work (Takechi 1993: 120–21).

[20] Interview with Mr. Tsuchiya Yutaka, Senior In-Home Sevice Section, Welfare Bureau, Machida city government (June 1995).

[21] Interviews with Mr. Tsuchiya Yutaka, Senior In-Home Sevice Section, Welfare Bureau, Machida city government (March 1997); Ms. Kawashima Tatsuko, Machida assembly representative; and workers' collective members (March 1997).

close ties with service providers because city-level and ward-level governments directly oversee service delivery. Nevertheless, it began to provide untied grants to volunteer groups in the 1990s. The grant system devised by the metropolitan government stands in contrast with the way the government subsidizes social welfare corporations.[22]

Most citizens' groups involve only a few dozen residents, however. Many of these groups have chronic financial difficulties, and there is little interaction among civic groups, which suggests that they do not aggregate local residents' views the way business associations aggregate sectoral interests.[23] These limitations often make their activities too uncertain for local officials to rely on them as potential resources for policy implementation. When citizens' groups are organizationally solid – with their own offices, financial resources, and a large membership – local governments seem to find it easier to interact with them in a more routine way. One good example of an organizationally solid group is the Livelihood Club Cooperative (Seikatsu Kurabu Seikyō) and its offshoot, the workers' collectives. The Livelihood Club is a participatory consumer cooperative run by its members. A major aim of the cooperative is to raise civic awareness regarding local affairs. It has an expansive membership in the Tokyo and Kanagawa metropolitan areas, and it began to venture into welfare services in the late 1980s (Yokota 1995).

The Livelihood Club Cooperative successfully obtained social welfare corporation status in such localities as Fujisawa, Atsugi, Hoya, and Kawasaki. This means local officials promised to contract out public services to the cooperative, which now both subcontracts public services and itself contracts out such tasks as food services to worker collective offshoots that are independently run by groups of local women.[24] This subcontracting was carried out with governmental approval, which suggests a significant change from the highly regulated social welfare services in which participatory citizens' groups played hardly any formal role.[25]

In suburbs where the Livelihood Club Cooperative and workers' collectives operate, city officials have become increasingly familiar with these groups (Gelb and Estévez-Abe 1998). The resourcefulness of these voluntary associations has created an incentive for officials to create a channel of regular interaction. In

22 Interview with Mr. Miyakawa Yoshiaki, director, Ability Club Tasukeai (a volunteer group), Setagaya Ward, Tokyo (June 1995).

23 It is interesting to note that in the case of Machida, it was a local government survey (Machida City 1997, 1998) that revealed the desires of citizens' welfare group leaders to learn about what other civic groups and traditional partners do to coordinate their efforts.

24 Unlike other grassroots organizations, which rely on members' fees, donations, and occasional fund-raising events such as bazaars, workers' collectives offer services for a fee. Some local branches (e.g., Miyamae Ward of Kawasaki) have begun a mutual help network, Fukushi Alta Net, in which volunteers can cash in points they receive for time they have provided. Interview with Ms. Kitahara Shigeko, Alta Net, Miyamae Ward branch, Kawasaki (January 1995).

25 The most successful workers' collectives deliver meals to individual seniors unable to cook for themselves and to nursing homes run by social welfare corporations and elderly care centers. These workers' collectives consist of volunteer housewives (some of them paid below the market rate) and are managed as nonprofits.

other words, these participatory citizens' groups have made inroads into the traditionally conservative policy network linking city welfare officials and local social welfare councils, networks that have generally excluded participatory civic groups.[26]

Critics argue that the new governmental emphasis on civic participation is intended only to secure cheap personnel (e.g., Itō 1996).[27] The actual organization of participatory service provision has by no means been top-down, however. In most cases, mobilization of citizens involved leadership from within civil society. Although it is true that "paid volunteers" do not earn a market wage, a survey indicates that most residents who have served as paid volunteers do so primarily out of a sense of public purpose rather than for financial reasons (Takechi 1993; Takano 1996).

Although all local governments now try to tap residents as volunteers (or paid volunteers), an interesting difference has emerged between conservative and progressive governments. Local governments that have actively sought collaboration with new types of participatory civic groups tend to be those in which conservative parties do not have a firm electoral base at the level of the local assembly or mayor. City governments with many socialist representatives in local assemblies and those headed by nonconservative mayors (e.g., Hoya, Kawasaki) were among the first to grant social welfare corporation status to spin-offs from the participatory Livelihood Club Cooperative. They were also the first to allow workers' collectives to subcontract out social services.[28] Machida, Hoya, and Kawasaki had relatively progressive local governments when they extended the scope of partnerships to citizens' groups. Progressive mayors, who rely on the support of loosely organized civic groups, encourage or permit local government officials to interact more with civic groups (Gelb and Estévez-Abe 1998). Nevertheless, the general weakening of the conservative electoral base in urban areas makes it increasingly difficult for conservative local governments to rely solely on traditional societal partners for effective policy implementation.

The contrast between national and local governments is also interesting. At the national level, bureaucratic politics as usual continues. Despite the encouragement of volunteer work and civic participation in welfare services, MHLW has not interacted with civic groups. It has, however, met regularly with private enterprises interested in cultivating the business of elderly care.[29] The deregulation of social welfare services opened the way for for-profit providers to subcontract government services. Moreover, the infusion of new public funds in the 1990s to expand the scope of elderly care raised business expectations of profit in providing services for the elderly. According to one MHLW official, "The Silver Service

[26] In Kanagawa Prefecture, the Livelihood Club Cooperative has formed its own social welfare council by mobilizing participatory citizens' welfare groups as members.

[27] Matsui (1997) shows how civic provision of care is cheaper than other methods.

[28] Interviews with Ōhashi, Hotta, and Katayama (see note 7) and Mr. Minegishi Tadao, Urban Policy Research Section, Planning and Finance Bureau, Kawasaki city government (July 1994).

[29] Interviews at MHLW (July 1997) and Dasukin (December 1997).

Industry – health-related and nursing services for the elderly – is a growth industry" (interview at MHLW, July 1997).[30]

Indeed, MHLW's approach to the Silver Service Industry was what METI's had been to infant industries in manufacturing; it looks more like industrial policy than social policy. MHLW established a public-interest corporation (i.e., a nonprofit organization) called the Association for the Promotion of the Silver Industry. The association's task was to determine whether for-profit and nonprofit organizations met a certain standard. Those organizations that met the standard received a "silver mark" – de facto ministerial endorsement. This silver mark mattered greatly to service and equipment providers because MHLW required subcontractors of governmental social welfare services to possess it.

MHLW's intention was to institutionalize its influence over private service providers even after the liberalization of services and to help insiders combat competition from new entrants.[31] Providers who sought a silver mark had to join the private trade association, the National Bathing and Welfare Service Providers' Council (Zenkoku Nyūyoku Fukushi Jigyō Kyōgikai), and receive recommendations from two other members (*Asahi Shinbun*, October 27, 1995, p. 11). The silver mark requirement for subcontracting was revoked, however, when a series of ministerial scandals broke out. Indeed, the scandals reveal a weakness in state-society collaboration: when private firms rely on public funds, there arises an incentive for these firms and their bureaucratic overseers to collude. In any case, the actual growth of the Silver Industry proved to be disappointing even after the introduction of Long-Term Care Insurance; it did not expand as much as MHLW officials and industrial analysts had expected (John Campbell, personal communication).

State-Society Partnerships, Effective Governance, and Democracy

The preceding sections demonstrate that intermediate associations can play important direct roles in addition to the indirect roles on which contemporary Tocquevilleans focus. Intermediate associations in Japan directly represent societal views in policy making and help implement policies. The Japanese state, in turn, helps establish associations, strengthens some associations, and relies on them as administrative partners.

Japan is not exceptional in its state-society partnerships. States in other countries sometimes encourage the formation of civil associations (e.g., Levy 1996; Skocpol 1997b; Skocpol et al. 2000). Similarly, the comparative political economy literature suggests that Japan is not the only country with close working relationships between associations and the state: close state-society partnerships characterize states such as Sweden and Germany, too (Schmitter 1977; Streeck

[30] It is interesting to note that private businesses were wary of the emergence of quasigovernmental service providers (*Nikkei Health Business*, January 25, 1993, p. 11).

[31] Steven Vogel (1996) notes that "liberalization" in Japan has often led national bureaucrats to exercise their influence in new ways.

1983). As in Japan, societal interests in Sweden and Germany are authoritatively organized into single, sectoral associations that take part in both policy making and implementation (Curtis 1975; Wilson 1985; Fraser 1992). In other words, variants of corporatism – such as neocorporatism in Sweden and mesolevel corporatism in Germany – all involve societal interests that are monopolistically represented by associations that interact and cooperate closely with the state.

Does the direct participation of societal partners contribute to economic performance and effective governance? Many commentators argue that the participation of intermediate associations in public policy making improves government effectiveness and economic performance (e.g., Samuels 1987; Garon 1988, 1997, this volume; Gordon 1989; Tilton 1996; Doner and Schneider 1999; Johnson 1999; Levy 1999). Sheldon Garon (1997, this volume) doubts that the Japanese state could ever have achieved what it did had it not been for its civil society.[32] At the same time, however, he is skeptical about the democratic implications of the role Japanese civil associations have historically played. Garon (this volume) reminds us that the civil society is not always progressive or democratic. This view is also echoed by Sheri Berman (1997), who demonstrates that a vibrant civil society did not protect democracy in Weimar Germany.

The most important contribution of intermediate associations to effective governance appears to be a reduction in the information asymmetry from which bureaucratic actors suffer and thus an improvement in the quality of industrial policy (Lynn and McKeown 1988; Yonekura 1993; Kikkawa 1995). These associations also coordinate interests within relatively homogeneous segments of society, becoming agents for further interest aggregation and negotiation at higher levels. Trade associations for specific products can get together to work out policy requests for their industry as a whole, for example (Lynn and McKeown 1988). This type of interest articulation and intermediation complements interest intermediation via the party system by institutionalizing multiple channels of policy input that reflect the complexity of societal and governmental activities.

Nonetheless, we cannot conclude that direct participation by intermediate associations will always be welfare enhancing. Although these associations can function as good sources of information and vehicles for the coordination of private actions that is necessary for successful policy making and implementation, they also protect vested interests. A combination of vested interests well represented within the executive and the bureaucracy can cause a rigidity that negatively affects both the economy and the government. Jonah Levy (1999), for example, contrasts France with countries such as Germany and Japan to argue that the vibrant associational networks among businesses in the latter countries strengthened the capacity of their states to tackle economic problems. But Germany and Japan, the two success stories of the 1980s, staggered in the 1990s, and unlike Germany after unification, Japan experienced no major changes in its business associations.

[32] The role of intermediate associations in social control, which Garon (1997) details, is reminiscent of conflict and cooperation between states and social forces in developing countries establishing a new system of authority and domination (Migdal et al. 1994).

Do intermediate associations contribute to effective governance in areas other than economic performance, such as the provision of social welfare services? Because the criteria for success are more ambiguous, such an assessment is difficult. In industrial policy or neocorporatist arrangements, effectiveness can be evaluated in terms of national industrial competitiveness; in social policy, governmental objectives vary across countries and across time. Indeed, if we were to interpret the goal of the Japanese government to be the delivery of social services cheaply or the enhancement of people's self-reliance, then the appointment of conservative petit-bourgeois residents as social workers may indeed have been highly effective (see Garon 1997: chap. 1).

As middle-class demands for social services increased, the goals of social welfare policy gradually changed during the 1980s. The growing demand for elderly care and the attendant need to contain the cost of such care impose two conflicting pressures on the state (Campbell 1992). In this context, any new measures that enhance the supply of less costly care for the elderly or prevent frail seniors from crowding medical facilities to receive nonmedical care contribute to effective governance. Performance can thus be measured in part by relative changes in the overall supply of nonmedical care for frail seniors, for example. Civic participation in the provision of services certainly helps increase the supply of services, and the participation of associations of nonprofit social welfare service providers improves policy makers' knowledge.

The direct participation of intermediate associations is not always beneficial, however. Especially in heavily regulated sectors, close state-society partnerships can lead to mutual cooptation and corruption, with public policy significantly benefiting few at the expense of many. The problem is exacerbated when the state develops close ties with potential rent seekers and not with groups that represent broader interests such as those of consumers or environmental safety. In the case of social welfare services, heavily subsidized providers are likely to hang on even after reforms. Regardless of their merits, these providers have a privileged position in the formal policy process due to their partnership with the state. Such inertia due to the way vested interests are institutionally represented hardly contributes to effective governance.

What can we say about the implications of intermediate associations' playing direct roles in a democracy? The Japanese experience strongly suggests that we cannot reach a conclusion by focusing on intermediate associations alone. More important is the scope of bureaucratic discretion over societal participation, which affects how democratic the participation of intermediate associations can be. As discussed above, bureaucratic discretion over who becomes a public-interest nonprofit organization is greater in Japan than in the United States. In the United States, the criteria are specified by the Internal Revenue Service, which does not supervise or interact with nonprofit organizations on a daily basis. In Japan, the introduction of the Nonprofit Organization Law in 1998 opened a way for citizens' groups to gain legal status, but it still does not grant new NPOs tax privileges. Only the old type of public-interest corporation enjoys the luxury of tax benefits. Not only does the simplicity of the procedure make the formation of new associations easier in the United States, but it also makes it impossible for a particular bureaucratic unit to manipulate the procedure to favor those organizations that cooperate with the government over those that may not.

Another comparison, that of Japan with Germany, illuminates the very elusive nature of bureaucratic discretion in Japan. In Germany, while authoritatively organized societal actors take on such public functions as running the vocational system and providing welfare services, legal codes clearly specify the terms of a division of labor between civil society and the state (Katzenstein 1987). In Japan, state-society cooperation is more ambiguous.[33] Bureaucrats modify the rules of the game as they go along to accommodate the activities of their societal partners. Although some observers might characterize such ambiguity as a capacity to adjust flexibly to new policy demands that potentially contributes to effective governance, such ambiguity is highly problematic from the point of view of democracy. The elusive nature of bureaucratic regulations makes contestation more difficult, exacerbating the political disadvantage of groups that do not currently have ties with the government.

In short, state-society partnerships are not undemocratic or ineffective in themselves. Rather, it is the nature of bureaucratic involvement that is critical. Bureaucratic discretion over licensing, regulation, and subsidies can turn otherwise useful societal cooperation into a corrupting alliance. Such bureaucratic discretion depoliticizes issues that should not be depoliticized and thus reduces the scope of public debate.[34] Discretion also serves as a political resource for bureaucrats in their political exchanges vis-à-vis party politicians: public interests may be compromised to favor the party in power or to promote the organizational interests of the bureaucracy (cf. Ramseyer and Rosenbluth 1993). Again, the more heavily regulated a sector, the stronger this tendency will be. In Japan, the combination of bureaucratic discretion and the direct participation of intermediate associations in the policy process segmented public debate into smaller, more private debates, turning Japan into a kind of "managed democracy."

We need not be too pessimistic, however. The recent development of new partnerships in social welfare services demonstrates how "managed democracy" may change. Decentralization and liberalization diversified participation in policy making. Their relatively limited policy-making and implementation capacities made it more urgent for local governments to rely on private actors for help. The urban middle class challenged the government's traditional societal partners as it became increasingly clear that the latter's capacity to represent salaried employees and their families was diminishing. Unlike the situation in national politics, this opened a political window of opportunity for civic groups, and they succeeded in making inroads into local policy making in metropolitan areas in the 1990s.

[33] This ambiguity resembles what Frank Upham (1987) calls "informality of law" in Japan.

[34] Hiwatari Nobuhiro (1991) argues that bureaucratic partnerships with leading firms created a regulatory system that protected oligopoly. Protected markets had the capacity to deal with most economic and social issues internally, without politicizing them. He attributes the longtime dominance of a single party in Japan to this depoliticization of issues.

Finally, Japan's state-society partnerships confirm that intermediate associations play important roles dealing directly with the state. Although contemporary Tocquevilleans emphasize the indirect, psychological contributions of intermediate associations to effective governance and democracy, this chapter has focused on the more direct roles intermediate associations may play. The most important lesson to be drawn from this analysis is that we cannot focus on civil society alone when we think about democracy. The level of informal discretion that bureaucrats possess strengthens some associations at the expense of others, making them "insiders" vis-à-vis the government. Although the impact of such discretion on governmental effectiveness is not necessarily negative, its implications for democratic participation are worrying.

III

THE NONMARKET ACTIVITIES OF ECONOMIC ACTORS

8

Redefining the Conservative Coalition: Agriculture and Small Business in 1990s Japan

Robert Bullock

Introduction

In the *Prison Notebooks*, Antonio Gramsci writes that "the counting of votes is only the final ceremony of a long process" (quoted in Przeworski and Sprague 1986: 7). Although one can interpret this remark in many ways, for my purposes it means two things: first, that politics – winning and keeping power – is a structured process in which votes are only occasional indicators of continuing, long-term struggles. The study of electoral outcomes alone never suffices because the greater part of politics – institution building, agenda setting, coalition formation – happens well before voters go to the polls. Second, elites consciously shape those processes, making deliberate choices within and about them. Politics, then, concerns both "long processes" and the strategies pursued by the political actors who drive them.

This chapter explores the "long processes" of Japanese politics. In particular, it takes up the puzzle of long-term conservative rule and its petit-bourgeois social bases, the groups that would seem likely to be among the greatest *enemies* of the conservatives and their pro-industry policies. Rice agriculture and small retail served as the chief social bases of conservative rule from the 1950s into the 1990s. Together, agriculture and retail supplied some three-quarters of the vote of the ruling Liberal Democratic Party (LDP) in the 1950s and nearly one-half in the late 1980s. The two sectors owed their electoral clout not only to their numbers but to their high turnout, stable conservative support over time, organizational strength, and bloc-like voting behavior. Their support has enabled continual postwar rule by a grand conservative coalition of the LDP, bureaucracy, and big business. This coalition ruled Japan from 1955 to 1993 and reemerged in little-altered form in 1994. As the coalition's chief social bases, agriculture and small business made possible the long-term political stability that has served as a necessary (though not sufficient) condition for rapid, long-term development. Even so, long-term ties have not led to state capture or escalating rents. Both conservative elites and the two sectors retain a measure of independence to preserve bargaining leverage and flexibility.

The two sectors survived decades of industry-led growth, rapid demographic change, and mounting pressures to open their markets. During the 1990s, however, small business was squeezed out of the coalition, while agriculture assumed new primacy within it. This constitutes perhaps the most dramatic coalitional shift of the postwar era, and none of the prevailing approaches to Japanese politics can explain it. Prima facie, we would expect policy change to follow a similar path in each sector. Both are economically weak but well organized and central to postwar conservative dominance. If anything, prevailing approaches would predict that agriculture is the more likely to be sacrificed: the Uruguay Round (concluded in December 1993) was seen in Japan as virtually synonymous with agricultural liberalization; farmers' political power was a central target of electoral reforms in 1994, which substantially reduced malapportionment favoring rural districts; and agricultural payoffs depend more heavily on budget outlays than do small-business payoffs (which depend more on barriers to entry), making agricultural more vulnerable to attack amidst Japan's long recession and mounting fiscal deficits. Where they differ, however, is in their position in the domestic economy, particularly vis-à-vis big business: small-business protection and support has become too costly for big-business interests, while that for rice agriculture has not.

To understand why this difference is so consequential, we must think about the position of social bases in the conservative coalition. If we conceive of civil society as organized, politically active interests – interests that may be created by and overlap with the state, but nonetheless make claims on it – it is here, in agriculture and small retail, where civil society has been most powerful in Japanese politics. Organized agriculture and small retail stand in the gray area between state and society, representing the power of organized producer interests and their centrality not simply in the marketplace but in social and political life. Each is central to local community life in Japan, helping to organize festivals, sponsor youth groups and culture circles, settle disputes, implement state policy, and direct political action. And even where such organizations originate as the result of statist, top-down directives (this is clearest in the case of the Nōkyō agricultural cooperatives, which were created by the state during the Pacific War), they may succeed in "going independent" over time and, indeed, have every incentive to do so.

Even as agriculture and small-business organizations receive state subsidies and help implement national policy, they have resisted *amakudari* appointments (of retired officials) by the central bureaucracy, built up independent financial bases, and wielded political clout, especially at the polls. Groups that depend on state protection for their survival typically obtain that protection only via the countervailing leverage that is enabled by organizational independence and, of course, competitive elections. Without it, their protection would surely decline or disappear. Broadly, that independence derives from the long-term legacies of small-business and agricultural organization, the shocks of Japan's defeat in the Pacific War and subsequent democratization, and, most important, the enduring political bargains struck between these organized interests and postwar Japan's ruling elites (see Bullock n.d.).

This chapter begins by reviewing what Robert Wade (1992: 307–9) calls the "thin politics" of existing work on East Asian political economy and the need to "politicize" our understanding of the developmental state. Even in a state said to be focused on achieving economic growth, politics necessarily comes first. The chapter then develops my argument about the centrality of politics in postwar Japan, introduces the two sectors, and takes up recent policy change.

Competing Perspectives

There are three main groups of scholars working on domestic Japanese politics and political economy: developmental state theorists, pluralists, and scholars of the postwar conservative coalition. Theorists of the developmental state study the state and economic policy, but show little interest in electoral politics.[1] To the extent these scholars address the issue of LDP rule at all, they tend to reduce its role to playing defense for a dominant bureaucracy, attributing the party's success primarily to Japan's impressive economic performance. This approach faces a number of difficulties, starting with the fact that conservative dominance in Japan emerged almost a decade before the "economic miracle" and still persists today after a decade-long recession.

Pluralists (e.g., Muramatsu and Krauss 1987; Allinson 1989; Richardson 1997) focus on electoral politics. For them, power is diffused and political relations are relatively open, unstructured, and becoming more so as modernization proceeds. This approach has trouble explaining the structured process by which Japanese votes are cultivated and cast, notably the long-term loyalties of certain occupational groups to the conservatives and the use of distributional policy to cement these ties. In particular, it cannot explain why farmers and small businesspeople remained the core of conservative support for forty years despite industry-first economic policies and the steady economic decline of both sectors.

The third group of scholars, led by T. J. Pempel (1978, 1993, 1998) and Masumi Junnosuke (1985), has pioneered work on Japan's postwar conservative coalition. Their research works best as macrodescription, spelling out coalitional lines, policies, and the growing domestic and international pressures for change. What has drawn less attention in this work are the conditions for coalitional stability or change and microlevel analysis of bargaining and conflict inside the coalition.

Building on the "creative conservatism" that Pempel stresses, several American scholars have recently offered bold new theories to explain change in the conservative coalition. Kent Calder (1988) attributes long-term conservative dominance

[1] It is worth stressing, however, that Chalmers Johnson's (1982: 23–24) conception of the developmental state is fundamentally political: "[I]n the developmental state, economic institutions are explicitly subordinated to political objectives. The very idea of the developmental state originated in the situational nationalism of the late industrializers, and the goals of the developmental state were invariably derived from comparisons with external reference economies."

to elite responsiveness in times of political "crisis," but he defines this term in a post hoc manner and treats Japanese politics as a series of reactive responses to international, economic, or other shocks. Mark Ramseyer and Frances Rosenbluth (1993) attribute LDP change to postwar demographic transformation, but this approach cannot account for the staying power of agriculture and small business within the coalition. More fundamentally, neither of these approaches treats politics as an autonomous force in its own right. For all these scholars' attention to LDP resourcefulness, the party essentially best gets along by going along. These theories of politics are oddly apolitical.

This chapter combines the political focus of the second and third groups with the institutional focus of the first to offer a positive theory of coalition formation and change. My focus is the sociopolitical underpinning of conservative rule by organized agriculture and small retail. Even as Japanese civil society has somewhat pluralized and organizations like consumer groups and international NGOs have become more prominent (see Tsujinaka, Maclachlan, and Reimann in this volume), organized agriculture and small retail remain the two most powerful and enduring sectors of civil society in contemporary Japan.

Elections and the Developmental State

Many analysts, especially those focused on the state and industrial policy, believe it was economic growth that kept the LDP in power. The party was too corrupt and ineffectual to be responsible for its own success, but it was able to ride the coattails of bureaucratic leadership and Japan's world-historical success. Although there are a number of problems with this approach, let me highlight two. First and most fundamentally, this approach neglects the centrality of distributional politics in electoral democracies, even those in which policy making is dominated by the bureaucracy (Tsebelis 1990; Knight 1992). In early postwar Japan, double-digit growth was only a fantasy and even recovery looked a long way off; in the meantime, elections had to be won somehow. From the perspectives of big business and the bureaucracy, it was the conservatives who had to win. Only conservative rule was conducive to long-term economic guidance by the economic bureaucracy and productive, long-term investment by the private sector. The left, in contrast, threatened to pursue redistributional policies and the nationalization of key industries. In the February 1947 election, support for the left totaled 49 percent, with 36 percent of the vote going to the Japan Socialist Party (JSP) alone. Concern over the threat from the left was thus far from academic.

The second problem for the economic-success thesis is that it soon became clear that industry-first policies actually undercut the conservative coalition once they began to show results. Indeed, the most precipitous declines in the LDP vote came during the years of highest economic growth, the mid- and late 1960s. During the boom years, Japan's largest cities grew rapidly and the "new middle classes" – the salaried urban workers multiplying under the economic miracle – were proving the least likely of any socioeconomic group to vote for the LDP.

Faced with these demographic transformations, LDP strategists such as Ishida Hirohide (1963) foresaw defeat by the end of the 1960s.

Indeed, the conservative coalition faced serious problems from its very outset. True, at the elite level, the LDP, big business, and bureaucracy were made for each other. Together, they had the leadership, expertise, coherence, and political-economic agenda to rule. Their union was, in Kozo Yamamura's words (quoted in Pempel 1993: 114), a "match made in heaven." What the conservatives lacked, however, were the votes, the mass base, necessary to win and retain power under the new conditions of universal suffrage and regular, competitive elections.

Big business, the bureaucracy, and the conservative politicians who joined in 1955 to form the LDP are conservative elites virtually by definition. They constitute the conservative core, and there are no substitutes for any of them. Put simply, big business supplies the capital, the bureaucracy supplies the policy expertise, and the LDP supplies political stability. Their preferences are sufficiently close that cooperation, while neither frictionless nor assured, is likely. By contrast, the mass base of the LDP, or of any conservative party, is not predefined or fixed. For a conservative party to win electoral majorities, its first task must be to identify and win additional, mass bases of support. In early postwar Japan, however, options were limited. Rural landlords, the mainstay of prewar conservative politics, had been expropriated by Occupation land reforms, which resulted in 80 to 90 percent of tenanted landholdings changing hands (Dore 1959). Most of the labor movement was left-dominated and economic reconstruction depended on low wages. The urban middle classes were inchoate and politically weak, and they, too, tended to vote left. Given these conditions, farming communities and urban small-business districts (*shōtengai*) were the conservatives' only hope.

Winning the farm vote was especially important. Following land reform, the new masses of smallholder farmers constituted a swing vote of huge proportions. Nearly 40 million people – almost half of the country's electorate and twice the size of its industrial labor force – lived on farms. As smallholders with a history of tenant grievances, they could side with the left. But as newly propertied producers, they could also back the right. Indeed, Socialist and Communist tenant unions had already organized millions amidst early postwar instability. To win elections and to pursue policies of reconstruction, winning over farmers was the conservatives' only real option. The conservatives' strategy for doing so was exactly what Samuel Huntington (1968) would later advocate: implement land reform, organize farmers, marginalize urban interests and labor, and use the political space thus gained to consolidate the new regime and focus on development. By the mid-1950s, the bargain had been made. Land reform, increases in the state-set rice price and farm subsidies, and Nōkyō consolidation (aided by massive state subsidies) served as key instruments of incorporation. Since then, agricultural support for conservatives has been significantly and consistently higher than the national average (Ishikawa 1984: 215).

Construction of a conservative mass base is not a one-shot deal; there is nothing immutable about a social base or the terms of membership. In postwar Japan, economic transformation of world-historic proportions would seem almost to guarantee change, whether welcome or not. But such transformations must be investigated, not assumed. Unfortunately, many prominent Japan analysts (e.g., Murakami 1984; Satō and Matsuzaki 1986; Calder 1988; Ramseyer and Rosenbluth 1993) make this epistemological leap to become what we might call "demographic determinists." The urbanization of Japan and the emergence of the new middle classes, the argument goes, led *naturally* to a new, urban-based politics. Politicians seek majorities, and the majorities are now in the cities. But what such a numbers-based approach lacks is a positive theory of politics, a theory of how coalitions are formed, how partners are chosen, and what are the conditions under which they change over time. Political parties are not condemned simply to react to economic, demographic, or other changes. Sometimes they have good political reasons for accepting some changes while resisting others. As we see below, there is nothing neutral, natural, or indefeasible about these choices.

Politics as Alliance Capitalism

Let me clarify what I mean by "social base." Social base refers to a political relationship fundamentally different from the more fluid, ad hoc, voter-party relations that are said to characterize a pluralist polity. Instead, the position of a social base is *long-term*, *institutionalized*, and *valued*. As Phillip Selznick (1957: 94, 104–5) puts it, a social base serves as "a training ground for loyal and self-conscious adherents" sharing both interests and values. "Choosing a social base," he continues, "is a *choice for leadership*, a developmental problem for the institution" (emphasis in the original).

Relations between conservative elites and their social base constitute a political analogue to what Michael Gerlach (1992) calls "alliance capitalism." In politics as in economics, alliances are institutionalized networks of cooperation and support. These differ from, but perform functions similar to, the short-term, individualized, market-driven relations of free-market capitalism or pluralist politics. In other words, free-market politics represent one form of organization, while alliance politics represent another. In alliance politics, relations between core and base are hierarchical: organized agriculture and small business were *junior* partners in the coalition from the start, their interests subordinate to those of senior members. If there is, say, substantial, zero-sum conflict between big business and a segment of the social base, big business is likely to win. (On the primacy of big business, see Garon, Hardacre, and Suzuki in this volume). Consequences range from renegotiation of coalition terms to, more rarely, redefinition of coalition membership.

But while agriculture and small business may be junior partners, they are not *silent* partners. If challenged by other coalition members, they fight back, and not with "voice" alone: they are fully capable of defecting. Following U.S.-forced liberalization of the beef and citrus markets in 1988, just 54 percent of farmers backed LDP candidates in the 1989 Upper House election, down from 77 percent in 1986. Small retail has long held close ties to the Japan Communist Party (JCP) as well as the LDP and repeatedly clashed with the conservatives during the 1980s and 1990s. Put generally, credible commitment is balanced by credible threat and helps keep players honest, limiting rents and rent seeking. Threats of defection by a social-base member probably cannot be taken seriously over the long term. The LDP remains Japan's predominant party even today, and striking alliances with the "eternal opposition" (*mannen no yatō*) is politically short-sighted. But because elections are won and lost in the short run, short-term threats are likely to suffice. Consider the comments of a JCP official on farmers' defection in 1989: "Flight from the LDP is not the same thing is same thing as JCP support. This is how the phrase is used [among rural voters]: 'instilling imaginary fears in the LDP.' By 'imaginary,' I mean that this strategy is used only to punish [the party] temporarily and that LDP support persists" (Zadankai 1989: 42).

Why is a social base so important in Japanese politics? To answer this question, we must look beyond the functional needs of the conservative party to Japan's political environment, particularly electoral institutions, and Japan's social structure, particularly the size, organization, and political availability of agriculture and small business versus those of other groups. First, the importance of the social base derived from the multimember electoral district system that prevailed until the 1994 electoral reforms (Yamaguchi 1997; Curtis 1999). This system resulted in chronically weak grassroots organization among political parties, particularly the LDP. Multimember districts placed a premium on organized voters who vote predictably (Ramseyer and Rosenbluth 1993), and such votes are concentrated in producer groups, especially in agriculture and small business. Because these sectors are economically vulnerable and bureaucratically well connected, they tend to be tightly organized and politically active.

These sectors appeal to the LDP for several reasons. First, even if farmers and small businesspeople tend to back candidates over parties, and even if their doing so is contingent on continued material payoffs, the candidates they back are overwhelmingly from the LDP. Eighty percent of both sectors have routinely supported the party, and these shares have been significantly and consistently higher than for any other social or producer group. Despite the LDP's industry-first economic policies, it is these petit-bourgeois groups that have supplied the "hard vote" (*koteihyō*) for individual candidates and, by extension, for the LDP as a whole. The second appeal of these sectors is that their high degree of organization helped the party leadership to divide the district vote, that is, to spread the vote among several competing party candidates to maximize seats won.

The hard vote's appeal is especially immediate for individual candidates. As one LDP politician put it, "With a single handshake, farmers and small shopkeepers will support you until death. In contrast, *salarymen* often move and simply cannot be depended on" (*Asahi Shinbun*, December 8, 1990). In this way, organized support bases mean lower transaction costs, less effort and uncertainty, in wooing voters and winning elections (on transaction costs, see Eggertsson 1990). Even senior Diet members with comfortable levels of support can be wary of openly challenging these sectors. Concerning a proposed land tax increase, another LDP Diet member observed, "[I]f I agree with the plan to tax agricultural land the same as housing land, the number of agriculture-related votes lost would be at most

5,000 to 10,000. That is not enough to defeat me. But how many *salaryman* votes would come to me in return? It's impossible to know – that's what's difficult" (*Asahi Shinbun*, May 30, 1987). In other words, there is uncertainty and risk in dropping the old for the new (on the driving force of uncertainty in politics, see Fenno 1978). Doing so might work out in the long run and is probably in the party's collective, long-term interest, but there are elections to be won in the meantime. Winning elections is particularly important for a party such as the LDP, dependent as it is on government largesse to reward its supporters.

Unfortunately for LDP politicians, the farm and small business votes are also swing votes. As one well-known Nōkyō adage puts it, "We may not have the votes to see that a particular candidate is elected, but we do have the votes to see that he is defeated." Although farmers are inclined to back the LDP, they do not do so automatically. In the past, roughly one-quarter of the farm population has voted for opposition parties, especially the Socialists. For the remainder, voting for the LDP remains conditional on the provision of the subsidies and market protection necessary for economic survival.

Agriculture and Small Retail: Numbers and Social Structure

Let me describe each sector in more detail. Japanese agriculture remains overwhelmingly rice agriculture. Rice is grown by over 80 percent of Japan's 4 million farm households, occupies half of Japan's farmland, and provides one-third of agricultural income. Agriculture has been rationalized largely through the spread of part-time farming (now 90 percent of the total) rather than by the exit of the inefficient. The average farm size in Japan today is just over two acres, virtually the same as in the 1930s. The logic is both economic and political: smallholder farming remains economically rational for individual farmers (if not for the economy as a whole), and farmland consolidation would reduce both the vote of the LDP and the constituency of the powerful Ministry of Agriculture, Forestry and Fisheries (MAFF) and Nōkyō cooperatives.

Ninety-nine percent of farmers belong to Nōkyō. Total Nōkyō membership, nearly 9 million in 1995, is *increasing* despite agricultural decline, which makes the cooperatives one of the largest mass-membership organizations in Japan as well as one of the country's biggest economic concerns. With help from the LDP (which wants votes) and MAFF (which wants support for its policies), Nōkyō has worked to build what Domon Takashi (1996: 211) calls an "untouchable world, an independent kingdom" over the postwar period. The cooperatives invoke a farm-village "communalism" (*kyōdōtai*) as a core principle of the organization, but they are hardly governed by it: many critics charge that the cooperatives, increasingly bureaucratized and focused on lucrative operations in finance and insurance, are turning their backs on the rank and file. Still, agriculture is its raison d'être and the membership vote its most powerful political weapon. It has used this weapon to win two state policies in particular: a virtual ban on rice imports (partly lifted in 1993) and a state-set rice price some seven to twelve times that found on world markets.

Retail shopkeepers are by far the largest and most politically active subcategory of small business. Like agriculture, small retail engages about 8 to 9 percent of the labor force today (with about 4 million workers in each). Unlike agriculture, small-business organizations are not combined into a single peak association. Instead, hundreds, even thousands, have proliferated. Minshō, with close ties to the JCP, has achieved particular success. Local chambers of commerce (*shōkō kaigisho*) and shopping associations tend to be much closer to the LDP (Higuchi 1977; Garon and Mochizuki 1993). Compared with Nōkyō, small-business organizations are smaller and less centralized, but they tend to be more internally democratic and representative of rank-and-file interests (Bestor 1989).

Small retail has been served by a range of subsidies, mostly low-interest loans, that expanded over the high-speed growth period even as similar loans to big business rapidly declined. The centerpiece of support, however, was the Large Stores Law (Daitenhō, or LSL), which imposed barriers to entry on large retail operations. The LSL was introduced in 1973 to replace the Department Store Law of 1956 (originally 1937). According to Kusano Atsushi (1992: 228), the Ministry of International Trade and Industry (MITI, now the Ministry of Economy, Trade and Industry) had no plans of its own to introduce new legislation, but the opposition JCP and JSP won new small-business support in the 1972 election, so the LDP stepped up its efforts to win back the sector, demanding that the Department Store Law be enhanced or replaced. Under the LSL, local retailers themselves held the power to grant or deny permission for the construction of large retail stores. Typically small shopkeepers, they tended to be unsympathetic to large-store proposals. Many localities imposed effective bans on new large stores ("large" being defined as those with a floorspace of more than 500 square meters). With no time limits set for the process, even successful applicants could be forced to wait ten years or more for approval.

Under the new law, the number of new large- and medium-sized stores dropped to a trickle. In 1974, retail shops with one or two employees accounted for 62.5 percent of the total number of retail stores. By 1988, their share had fallen by just 5 percent. Over the same period, stores with over twenty employees increased their share of the total by just 1.1 percent (Schoppa 1997: 236). Among Western countries, only France has a comparably large small-retail sector (Keeler 1985).

Because the two sectors are highly similar, there is good reason to expect any policy change to be similar in each:

1. Approximately 80 percent of both farmers and small-business people have voted for the LDP, and each sector supplied approximately one-quarter of the LDP's support base in the late 1980s.
2. Each sector is well organized politically. Their organizational structure is not perfectly analogous – that of agriculture is highly concentrated and pro-LDP, while that of small business is more fragmented and politically split – but there is no reason to believe that the divided politics of small business would make the LDP less sensitive to the sector's demands. Indeed, one could well argue the opposite.

3. Both are characterized by a dense, highly organized "old-middle-class" social structure that makes them well suited to serve as the conservatives' hard vote.
4. Each sector has a powerful ministry advocate, MAFF in the case of agriculture, and MITI's Small and Medium-Sized Enterprise Agency (SMEA) for small business. Both are major players in bureaucratic politics.[2]
5. Each has strong, entrenched public support, not least in the cities. This support is strongest and most obvious for agriculture, with domestic rice popularly seen as Japan's "essential foodstuff" (*shushoku*), but it also holds for small retail, given its centrality in everyday neighborhood life (Sōrifu 1997, various years).
6. In terms of international pressure, the United States was at least as aggressive in demanding rice market liberalization as it was in pursuing reform of the LSL. Indeed, in Japanese-media reportage, the Uruguay Round was virtually synonymous with rice market opening. Although the first Bush administration's Structural Impediments Initiative called for LSL reform, that was just one of many issues.

Pressures for Change in the Social Base

The conservative coalition functions as a trading cartel, with narrow lines of membership, rents for both core members and social-base voters, and outsiders (especially consumers and labor) excluded. To be sure, the divide between insiders and outsiders is not absolute. Relations among coalition members are preferential, probabilistic rather than deterministic.

The problem with cartels is that they are prone to breakdown. They are subject to free riding, demands to renegotiate terms, outside attack, and a range of other pressures for change. Remarkably, Japan's conservative coalition persisted from 1955 to 1993 and reemerged in 1994 in little-changed form. Still, pressures for change have only mounted. In particular, conservative elites have faced increasing pressures to reconstitute their social base, to shift away from agriculture and small business and toward the new middle classes of the cities. Indeed, it is common wisdom (e.g., Calder 1988: 270–72, 347–48; Ramseyer and Rosenbluth 1993: chap. 4; Rosenbluth 1996: 145) that the conservatives have cut support for the two sectors and are in the process of redefining their social bases, if they have not done so already.

In pointing out the problems of "demographic determinism," my intent is not to claim the opposite: that the coalition worked in the past and therefore works today due to "path dependence," policy irrationality, or the like despite growing

[2] The SMEA is on equal terms with MITI bureaus that are more devoted to developmental policies. Given that their next posting may well be in the Agency, MITI bureaucrats outside the SMEA stress that attacking it would be foolish (MITI interviews, 1996, 1997).

threats. The question is not, Is there change, but What kind of change and under what conditions?

There are five main pressures for coalition change. First, state capture: a group's demands on the state become so great that they begin (or are perceived to begin) to undermine development or overwhelm government budgets. Second, slow economic growth: reversing the causality of state capture, high levels of protection and support become unacceptable as big-business expansion declines or as government budget deficits grow. Third, profit squeeze: social-base protection cuts into big-business turf or poses a barrier to its expansion. Fourth, trade war: social-base protection becomes the target of foreign pressure and threats of economic sanction, potentially jeopardizing Japanese exports as a whole. Fifth, new politics or new social bases: an altered political incentive structure (due to institutional or demographic change) makes new domestic constituencies available and attractive.

Let me save profit squeeze and trade war for more extensive discussion below. Briefly, they matter only insofar as they filter through domestic political institutions. Japan's poor economic performance in the 1990s helps explain policy retrenchment, but not why it occurred for small business alone. International pressure (*gaiatsu*) played a critical role as a catalyst for reform and helped to determine its timing, but it fails when unaccompanied by the support of domestic allies (Schoppa 1997), and even when it succeeds, it cannot explain the particular forms reform has taken.

State Capture and Recession

With Japan's ongoing economic difficulties, it is no surprise that a range of state subsidies and protection programs have come under challenge. Small business and agriculture are routinely singled out for their extreme dependence on state supports. I review the budget cuts carried out under Prime Minister Nakasone (1982–87) here and take up more recent attacks below.

With declining economic growth and growing budget deficits, discretionary programs in the budget were challenged by Nakasone's "administrative reforms" (*gyōsei kaikaku*). Although small-business protection was not an explicit target of the reforms, rice agriculture was at their center. Indeed, reform targets were sometimes called the "three k's": *kokutetsu* (the deficit-ridden national railways), *kenpo* (Japan's costly national health insurance program), and *kome* (rice). At first glance, Nakasone's cuts in agricultural spending look like a major victory. After years of steady increases, the general account budget of MAFF was cut by 10 percent between 1982 and 1991. The reduction was greater – 38 percent – for the Food Control Account, which handles rice sales and distribution. Nakasone even cut the state-set producer rice price, the symbol of conservative commitment to agriculture. That price was reduced in 1987, 1988, and again (under the Takeshita administration) in 1990. These were the first cuts since the 1950s.

Nonetheless, we must not confuse such cuts with reductions in payoffs to farmers. Although MAFF, like other distributional ministries, was forced to accept deep budget cuts over the 1980s, because the ministry (with broad support from within the LDP) had no intention of reducing farm supports, it turned to other means. What it did was to shrink and then reverse the gap between low-consumer and high-producer rice prices. In other words, the Japanese people lost as consumers what they gained as taxpayers. In E. E. Schattschneider's (1988 [1960]) terms, this reversal represents a classic "substitution of conflicts." Agricultural protection was privatized and the scope of potential political conflict reduced as the conservative coalition pursued a strategy of cutting concentrated-cost, high-visibility supports and replacing them with diffused-cost, low-visibility supports.

A more accurate indicator of agricultural support is the Producer Subsidy Equivalent (PSE), computed by the OECD for all member nations since 1979. The PSE combines price supports, subsidies, and border protection into a single indicator (OECD, various years). For Japanese rice, the PSE steadily increased from the beginning of administrative reform: it was 80 in 1984, 86 in 1985, 93 in 1986, 94 in 1987, and 90 in 1988. It dropped to 86 for 1989–90, but rebounded to 87 in 1991 and 97 in 1993. In other words, rice supports increased precisely when budget cuts and deficit reduction were supposed to have lowered them.

Growth of the New Middle Classes

This pressure for change restates the demographic-change thesis. In Japan, the most serious problem with the argument is that economic growth has brought not just urbanization but an extremely fickle urban electorate, the so-called floating vote (*fudōhyō*) of the young, urban, well-educated middle classes. Masumi (1988) calculates that it grew from 4 percent of the electorate in 1960 to 20 percent in 1971 to over 30 percent in 1976. The most recent surveys put the number at over one-third of voters (*Yomiuri Shinbun*, June 20, 2000; *Japan Times*, June 22, 2000).

Since the late 1970s, the urban floating vote has become *generally* more conservative, but not *reliably* so. The new middle class (NMC) is marked by low levels of organization, low interest in politics, diffused policy demands, limited participation in party organizations or MPs' individual support groups (*kōenkai*), and a lack of ministry or interest group advocates (e.g., Japan has no Ministry of Consumers or Urban Affairs). Unorganized, uncommitted, and unstable, the NMC vote stands in contrast to the hard vote supplied by farmers and small businesspeople, who consistently turn out at 80 percent levels, with 70 to 80 percent supporting the LDP. It is the NMC of the city, not petit-bourgeois groups like small retail and agriculture, that most closely recall the "potato sacks" of Karl Marx's *Eighteenth Brumaire*.

Policy Change in the 1990s

While outcomes in the two sectors have diverged, the processes of policy change have been strikingly similar in each: *gaiatsu* has played an important role in determining the timing but not content of change; policy change has been managed primarily by bureaucrats rather than politicians; and policy outcomes are marked by reregulation, not deregulation, in support of slow, state-guided liberalization of domestic markets (on reregulation, see Vogel 1996).

Agricultural Reform

Despite the political, economic, and organizational similarities of agriculture and small retail, the conservative coalition has increased protection and support for rice even as it has cut that for small retail. The Producer Subsidy Equivalent for rice has continued to climb, and the "minimum access" formula for rice imports that Japan accepted as part of the Uruguay Round represented a very minor concession. Under the agreement, imports were controlled by MAFF, which bought them at cheap international prices, sold them at expensive domestic prices, and used the proceeds to fund additional farm subsidies.

Since the Round's 1993 conclusion, the conservative commitment to agriculture has only increased. Back in power in the spring of 1994, the LDP's first priority was to push through a massive ¥6.01 trillion ($60 billion) farm subsidy package that even MAFF found excessive. Some 20 to 30 percent of the annual agricultural budget was simply forwarded into the following year's budget because there was more money than could be spent (*Aera*, April 28–May 5, 1997, pp. 24–27). Soon afterward, the party and Nōkyō won a ¥685 billion ($6.85 billion) bailout for the cooperatives' losses in the housing loan (*jūsen*) debacle, Japan's version of the U.S. savings-and-loan crisis. In 1997, the Ministry of Finance (MOF) organized a study group to consider ways to reduce the growing budget deficit. Although huge farm subsidies were one of the reasons the group was formed in the first place, in the end it recommended cuts in defense and official development assistance rather than in farm grants (*Nihon Nōgyō Shinbun*, February 23, 1997).

Some analysts contend that the 1995 scrapping of the Food Control Law (in place since 1942) and the introduction of the new Food Supply Law (*Shin shokuryō hō*) promise, at last, to free up the farm sector. The new law has won praise as "drastic deregulation" and an important step toward making rice a "normal good" (*Nihon Keizai Shinbun*, October 30, 1995; Francks 1998). Such views, however, mischaracterize these reforms. Market liberalization has occurred domestically, but not internationally, and domestic market liberalization does not mean deregulation. Because MAFF has redefined its control over the rice economy via reregulation, it has reduced that control only marginally.

The new Food Supply Law has five main features. First, MAFF's role as a direct participant in the rice economy has been reduced. Government purchases of rice are now limited to foreign rice imported under the Uruguay Round minimum-access arrangement and domestic rice for stockpiling. Second, there are now two rice distribution routes, those for government rice (*keikaku mai*) and voluntary-marketed rice (*keikaku igai mai*), or what used to be the illegal black market. For voluntary-marketed rice, direct sales by farmers and the Nōkyō cooperatives are now permitted to retailers and wholesalers. After deciding that it could not eliminate the black market, MAFF decided to legalize it, thereby bringing the market under ministerial oversight. It expects about three-quarters of marketed rice to be voluntary-marketed rice, just as under the old law. Third, Japan's rice stockpiles are to be increased to 1.5 million tons. This change reflects, above all, the "rice riots" of 1993–94, when a 25 percent shortfall in the rice harvest produced shortages, panic, and spectacular price increases on the black market.

Fourth, formerly ad hoc in nature, rice production control has been incorporated into the legal framework. Coercive measures such as withholding subsidies from areas that do not fulfill their reduction quotas have been abolished. Concern remains, however, that the law leaves room for informal pressure, particularly from Nōkyō. And fifth, in what appears to be the most significant measure of the new law, rice retailing has been substantially deregulated. Prospective retailers are no longer required to apply for permission to enter the market; they need only register with the Food Control Agency (FCA). Registration applications are being approved almost automatically, and the number of stores selling rice is projected to triple. By the end of 1996, the number of retail rice outlets had already reached 175,600, nearly twice the number a year earlier (*Japan Agrinfo Newsletter*, August 1997, p. 2). Many analysts have remarked on the new "warring states period" (*sengoku jidai*) in the rice trade, with the number of wholesalers as well as rice specialty shops likely to plummet (*Asahi Shinbun*, April 2, 1996).

Retail aside, the new law is a clear case of reregulation. The *Shūkan Tōyō Keizai* (April 20, 1996, p. 72) dismissed the MAFF-proclaimed "deregulation" in production and distribution as a "big lie." The new law constitutes a "new form of control from above. . . . MAFF has introduced new, clever mechanisms." Price controls remain, and with domestic rice prices at least ten times international prices, production control is still essential. MAFF withdrawal from production control has been matched by Nōkyō's advance. Indeed, one common criticism of the new law reads "from government food management to Nōkyō food management" (Ouchi and Saeki 1995; Nōsei jaanarisuto no kai 1996, p. 14). Again, 99 percent of Japan's farmers are members of the quasistatist Nōkyō, and the cooperatives overwhelmingly dominate rice distribution and marketing. Overall, the new law represents far more an accommodation to long-term changes in the agricultural economy than a positive program for reshaping it (MAFF interviews, May 1997).

MAFF handling of rice imports since 1993 is also best characterized as reregulatory and of limited significance for market opening. In December 1993, under the auspices of the Uruguay Round, Japan agreed to a U.S. minimum-access formula for rice imports: Japan would import 4 percent of its rice demand in 1995 and increase the share to 8 percent by the year 2000, with renegotiation to follow. Although the market-opening deal is a clear case of managed trade in terms of both who sells to Japan (see below) and how the imports are handled (via state trading), the United States and GATT accepted this as a step toward complete liberalization. The results, however, have not been encouraging for would-be free traders.

The Food Control Agency is responsible for importing rice, and the import system will remain "state trading until the very end," in the words of one FCA bureaucrat (Saitō 1995: 14). And while the agency is required to buy foreign rice, it is not required to sell it to Japanese consumers. Because selling foreign rice at anywhere near international prices would mean stiff new competition for domestic producers, MAFF decided to set foreign-rice prices at nearly domestic levels. It is unsurprising, then, that very little foreign rice has appeared on the table-rice market. Most imports are being diverted to processing (e.g., rice crackers), food aid for developing countries, and even animal feed. Of the 940,000 tons imported in fiscal year 1995–96, for instance, 38 percent was used for processing, 31 percent for animal feed, and 13 percent for overseas food aid – just 7 percent was sold as table rice. The remainder (11 percent) lay in storage (*Nihon no kome shijō*, April 8, 1998).

Under the minimum-access agreement, Japan has had to import increasing shares of foreign rice even as domestic production (the 1993 shortfall aside) has continued to exceed demand, leading to mounting rice surpluses. An increasing share of the backlog is of foreign origin. Between 1995 and 1997, Japan imported 920,000 tons of rice; just 200,000 tons of this had been sold by May 1997. Over 700,000 tons (about half from the United States) remained in government warehouses. Between the fall of 1996 and the summer of 1998, Japan's total rice stock jumped 40 percent to 3.7 million tons, with imports constituting at least one million tons (*Asahi Shinbun*, July 26, 1998). The new Food Supply Law was billed as introducing market principles into rice agriculture, that is, as allowing prices to reflect the laws of supply and demand. These numbers make it clear that the attempt has failed and that Japan's farmers enjoy more protection than ever.[3]

In early 1999, Japan converted its import policy from minimum access to tariffication, the original U.S./GATT demand. It did so not because of U.S. pressure, but because tariffication would allow Japan to import even less rice, MAFF bureaucrats determined. In effect since April 1, 1999, the tariff amounts to ¥351.17/kg, translating to a rate of 300 to 400 percent. Although the price of foreign rice ranges from ¥60 to ¥100/kg, with the tariffs added, it is more expensive than every brand of rice in Japan except one: Uonuma Koshihikari, which is grown in a single village. For the time being, there is thus a virtual ban on imports (*Nikkei Ryūtsū Shinbun*, April 6, 1999; *Nikkei Weekly*, April 12, 1999).

The United States has protested the high tariff rates and the methods used to calculate them. It has not, however, lodged a formal complaint with the World Trade Organization, perhaps for fear of jeopardizing its current market share. Rumors abound that the United States has negotiated a secret market-share agreement under the new arrangement, just as it allegedly did in 1993 for half the minimum-access market (*Mainichi Shinbun*, March 24, 1999).

Retail Reform

By contrast, protection of small retail has declined dramatically. Reforms to the LSL in 1990 returned authority to grant large-store operating permits to MITI, and the approval process was limited to a maximum of eighteen months. The reforms also increased permissible hours and days of operation for large stores

[3] With even MAFF calling their goals unrealistic, Nōkyō and the LDP began pushing in 1998 for new farm income supplements to increase Japan's overall food self-sufficiency from 42 percent to 50 percent by 2010 (*Nihon Keizai Shinbun*, December 18, 1998). The figure was ultimately negotiated down to 45 percent and approved by the Obuchi cabinet in March 2000.

and improved the transparency of the approval process (unpublished MITI report, 1997). As a result, the number of large-store openings jumped from 132 in 1989 to 617 in 1990. The 1990 figure exceeded total openings for the previous five years combined. Following the initial burst of pent-up demand and due also to economic recession, annual openings subsequently declined somewhat, but they exceeded 2,000 in 1995 and 1996 before falling to 1,928 in 1997 (*Sankei Shinbun*, April 15, 1997; Tsūsanshō 1998). Meanwhile, the number of small retailers dropped more than 19 percent between 1991 and 1999 (*Nihon Keizai Shinbun*, February 27, 1998; May 19, 2000). The Japan Small Retailers' Association (Nihon Kouri Gyokai) predicts that their numbers will drop 30 percent by 2010 (*Nihon Keizai Shinbun*, February 27, 1998; May 19, 2000).

There were no major new subsidies to compensate for relaxation of the LSL. The only new package (for shopping-district revitalization, computers, parking facilities, and other physical improvements) provides just ¥10 billion ($100 million) per year. A MITI official specializing in small business agreed that the amount was both minuscule and insufficient compared with what rice farmers received (again, $60 billion over six years) in compensation for a far less significant market opening (MITI interview, August 1997; Tsūsanshō 1997: 50).

The reforms have provoked cries of distress from small retail that neighborhood stores will collapse. Surveys show steady declines in the number of small businesses and small-business districts' vacancy rates (*Yomiuri Shinbun*, March 15, 1997). Contemplating these changes, even the conservative *Nihon Keizai Shinbun* (May 12, 1997, eve. ed.) was moved to quote from Karl Polanyi's *The Great Transformation* on the destructive power of the market and the need for society to limit its influence. As MITI moved toward further relaxation (and later, abolition) of the LSL with new reforms in 1992 and 1994, even some big-business beneficiaries thought this was adding insult to injury. When LSL abolition was being considered in late 1993, leading chain stores and supermarkets made no calls whatsoever in support of the proposal. One retailer observed, "It would be unwise to provoke small- and medium-sized retailers by touching the LSL, which [now] has little impact" (*Nihon Keizai Shinbun*, December 15, 1993, eve. ed.). And despite its early enthusiasm, MITI itself grew ambivalent about further relaxation given that the changes to date seemed to be working (MITI interviews, June 1998, November 1999).

Not surprisingly, small businesspeople have been defecting from the LDP in droves. An *Asahi* survey on party preferences conducted just after the October 1996 Lower House election found that, on a preference scale ranging from −6 to +12, the LDP's scores were as follows: farmers, 6.0; small business, 3.8; industrial labor, −0.5; commercial labor, −1.8; and office/administration, −4.5 (*Asahi Shinbun*, October 24, 1996). While small-business support for the party remained positive, it had been approximately equal to farmers' support in previous elections. Meanwhile, membership in the Communist-affiliated Minshō was said to be surging (MITI interviews, June 1997).

In the spring of 1998, retail reform went a step further – or backward, critics said – with abolition of the LSL and introduction of the new Large Store Location

Law (*Daikibo kouri tenpo ritchi hō*, or LSLL). The new law, dubbed the "crown jewel of deregulation" by the *Sankei Shinbun* (May 28, 1998), was passed by the Diet in May 1998 and took effect in June 2000. It specifies transparent store-opening procedures and sets a one-year time limit on the application approval process. The intent, MITI claims, is to shift emphasis from protection of small retailers to a positive program of community development that includes large retail. Even so, large retailers worry that the new law means a return to the old days. In early 1998, the small business–dominated Chamber of Commerce had a "terrible reaction" to the proposed LSLL and stepped up its lobbying of the LDP and MITI. It succeeded in persuading MITI to place regulatory authority back in the localities, where small-retail power is most potent. "With [the changes], the group's influence was clearly written into the final draft of the law as vested interests crept into the process" (*Asahi Shinbun*, March 12, 1998).[4] This devolution of authority, along with strict new regulations on parking lots, garbage removal, and noise, poses new hurdles for large stores and constitutes more, not less, regulation. As one large retailer put it, "the regulatory means have simply become more ingenious" (*Nihon Keizai Shinbun*, February 28, 1998).

Still, it is easy to overstate the backlash. Small retailers see the new law as a poor substitute for the old LSL. They turned against the LDP in the July 1998 Upper House elections just as they had in 1996. Although Prime Minister Hashimoto Ryūtarō and the Japanese media were confident of an LDP victory, the party won just 25 percent of the vote. The loss was due to dissatisfaction (especially among floating voters) with Hashimoto's weak, contradictory program for economic recovery, but also to small-business defections. One small-retail specialist at MITI believes this was the single most important cause of the LDP's loss (MITI interview, July 1998). Still, it is unclear, stated the same MITI official in a November 1999 interview, that the LDP made the wrong choice in pushing through the law. "If the LDP had failed to pass the law, that would have been damaging, too" (see also Kabashima 1999).

While the media has widely publicized the new ¥1 billion funding package to revitalize shopping districts, only 10 percent of the monies are actually new: the remainder had already been appropriated. On balance, MITI officials seem to be committed to regulatory opening and claim to be more concerned about large retail interests overpowering localities with money, business savvy, and so on than the reverse (MITI interview, November 1999).[5] More concretely, tens of thousands of

[4] In the Lower House, 1994 replacement of multimember, medium-sized districts with single-member, small-sized districts has made politicians even more beholden to local interests, including small retail (*Nihon Keizai Shinbun*, May 14, 1999). Backbenchers in the Upper House are also wary. As one put it in early 1998, "We're facing elections this summer and it is taboo to oppose the views of the large vote base of the small retailers" (*Nihon Keizai Shinbun*, February 28, 1998). See also Yamaguchi (1997).

[5] But even MITI bureaucrats are unsure what the new law will mean. When I asked another official whether he thought the law marks a return to the old LSL, he replied, "As a MITI bureaucrat, no, but as a political scientist, yes" (MITI interview, June 1999).

large stores have opened over the 1990s, hugely changing the balance of power in the sector. No regulatory tightening can reverse these changes.

Explaining Policy Change

How do we account for this divergence between agricultural and small-business policy? As noted above, the two sectors are similar in political clout, ministry representation, public attitudes, and external threat. And given the 1994 electoral reforms, which significantly reduced rural-urban malapportionment and replaced multimember districts with a mix of single-member and proportional-representation districts, we might expect agriculture, not small business, to be the loser.

The most striking difference between the two sectors lies elsewhere: their position in the overall economy, particularly vis-à-vis big business. From big business's perspective, protection of small-retail is considerably more zero-sum than that of agriculture. In the latter, concentrated producer gains from protection are balanced by diffused losses that are borne by millions of poorly organized, politically weak consumers. There are no Japanese agribusinesses scheming to enter the agricultural sector, especially in rice, and no foreign powers have ever threatened to target Japanese industrial exports in retaliation for agricultural protection. The only significant agriculture-related industry is food processing. That sector is highly concentrated, has very low productivity by manufacturing standards, and is the most protected of all manufacturing sectors in Japan (McKinsey Group 1993). Given these advantages, the sector can easily pass high input costs onto consumers. In this way, food processing resembles other Japanese industries that tolerate the protection of intermediate-goods industries, such as concrete, steel, and petrochemicals (Tilton 1996).

In contrast to agriculture, small retail has come under direct assault from powerful domestic business interests, particularly from the late 1980s. The timing owes in part to a slowing economy and in part to the emergence of chain stores as the most dynamic force in Japanese retail. Significantly, big-business pressure *predates* the 1990 U.S. demand for changing of the LSL. In other words, Japan's inefficient distribution system was not an issue for Americans alone: it represented a huge opportunity for aggressive Japanese retailers, one that became all the more tempting in a time of sluggish sales. This new generation of retailers was eager to win new markets. Convenience store chains such as 7-Eleven were among the most dynamic and aggressive Japanese firms of the 1980s and 1990s (Kawabe 1994; Yahagi 1994), and what small retail gained or retained represented a loss for these stores. The chains tend to open small- or medium-sized stores that are the closest substitutes for small, family-owned retail shops. They have directly borne the costs of laws such as the LSL.

Convenience store chains have used their market power to wrest concessions from once-dominant wholesalers and are seen as the principal driving force behind the modernization of Japanese retail. The Japanese press was full of reports on "convenience store wars" and "price destruction" (*kakaku hakai*) over the 1990s. Recent innovations include just-in-time delivery systems, high-tech distribution networks, value-added networks, electronic ordering systems, and point-of-sales systems record keeping. As the number of mom-and-pop stores declines, they are replaced less by large stores than by medium-sized stores, especially convenience and specialty stores.

MITI itself was pressing for LSL reforms from the late 1980s, again predating U.S. demands. In the summer of 1989, MITI proposed the abolition of all local regulations on retail-shop opening, but backed down in the face of opposition from prefectural governments (Kusano 1992: 116). The Economic Planning Agency and the Council on Administrative Reform also issued reports criticizing the LSL. In 1990, a MITI advisory council prepared for the Ministry its "Vision for Distribution in the 1990s," which called for relaxing provisions of the LSL. Although MITI had planned to make the report public well before the June 1990 election, LDP leaders protested, persuading the ministry to delay the report's release and to slow down reforms (ibid.: 161–94).

By 1990, however, Kusano Atsushi (1992: chap. 5) found that the LDP offered no resistance to reform of the LSL. In the late stages of negotiations, LDP officials simply refused to meet with small-business representatives. Business policy specialists (*zoku*) in the party were divided between those supporting small shops and those supporting supermarkets and convenience stores. The more powerful individual *zoku*, such as Noda Takeshi, Watanabe Shuo, Mutō Kabun, and Tahara Takashi, tended to back the latter. While evidence concerning shifts in LDP preferences at this time is thin – the decision was highly controversial – it is clear that the LDP did little to defend small retail. Nor did LDP members publicly object to further LSL reforms by MITI (until 1998, at least).

Finally, while the *timing* of the LSL reform can be attributed in part to U.S. pressure, it was domestic pressure that made the reforms inevitable. Within the conservative coalition, LDP ambivalence was overpowered by big business and MITI's commitment to reform. The latter enthusiastically, if tacitly, supported American pressure. Even after the United States put LSL reform on the back burner, reforms continued apace in the 1990s. Changes in 1992 and 1994 limited the application process period to one year and increased the floorspace definition of "large stores" from 500 to 1,000 square meters, for example. In consequence, observers report declining small-business support for the LDP and a turn toward opposition parties, especially the JCP. The JCP now controls 4,448 seats in local assemblies, more than any other party, including the LDP (JCP campaign handout, June 2000). We can only speculate on LDP misgivings over the downside, but important in its calculations were doubtless the emergence of several new conservative parties, which has made it possible to govern with just 30 to 35 percent of the seats in the Diet's lower house, and the fact that any lost small-business votes were expected to go disproportionately to the JCP, the one party that has refused to participate in any coalition opposing the LDP.

Conclusion

This chapter has looked inside Japan's conservative coalition to assert the primacy of politics even in the developmental state. The ruling coalition includes not only conservative elites, but also organized, politically powerful, and ideologically available parts of civil society, even as other parts of society have been systematically excluded. Coalitional relations are arm's-length, not organic. They are negotiated, not fused. Distributional payoffs to agriculture and small retail do not ipso facto constitute "state capture" by rent seekers, nor are they the product of "path dependence" or occasional political crises. Rather, they are the product of mutually beneficial exchanges among fundamentally rational, self-interested actors. And the terms of coalition bargains, of coalition membership itself, are always up for grabs, subject to constant negotiation and mounting pressures for change. But these pressures do not dictate change across the board. This chapter has explored and explained why one of the coalition's social bases, small retail, has been squeezed out even as the other main base, rice agriculture, has been embraced all the more tightly.

Even so, the position of agriculture is far from secure. No longer is it the "sacred ground" (*seiiki*) of Japanese politics, off-limits to all political criticism and attack. But if conservative elites know they must reorient policy toward Japan's urban majorities over the long term, individual MPs, particularly backbenchers, fear that doing so would mean losing office in the short term. These conflicting imperatives make for a daunting collective-action problem, and that is good for agriculture: short-term threats may well suffice to preserve the sector's longer-term advantages.

9

The Death of Unions' Associational Life? Political and Cultural Aspects of Enterprise Unions

Suzuki Akira

Although discounted by some theorists of civil society, labor unions can offer a rich associational life for their members by performing political and social as well as purely economic functions. The potential of labor unions as civil society actors was demonstrated by the crucial role played by Solidarity in reviving civil society in Poland. What role have labor unions played in Japan's civil society? Have they succeeded in establishing their own sphere of activities relatively autonomous from management and the state? To examine this question, I focus here on the political and cultural aspects of labor unions. On the basis of a historical analysis of an enterprise union in one of the major steel firms, I demonstrate that labor unions failed to establish either internal democracy or their own organizational culture distinct from corporate culture. These political and cultural aspects of unions constitute what I call their "associational life." Labor unions in postwar Japan made some significant achievements in their economic activities, winning wage increases and employment security for their members. They nevertheless failed to become important actors in civil society because their associational life came to be dominated by and incorporated into corporate society (*kigyō shakai*), by which I mean the hegemony of corporate management and the integration of workers as members of corporate communities rather than as citizens of political society as a whole.

First, I outline the history and organizational characteristics of Japan's labor unions. Second, I consider the conditions under which labor unions can play a significant role in civil society. I argue that the significance of labor unions as civil society actors depends on the extent to which they perform political and social functions. Third, I discuss the theoretical framework of civil society in the context of Japanese industrial relations. In analyzing the associational life of labor unions in postwar Japan, I posit that we need to take into account the vitiating influence of the market economy, particularly business corporations, on civil society actors. Fourth, I examine the associational life of labor unions at the enterprise level, the focal point of industrial relations in Japan, on the basis of a historical analysis of the Yahata Steel Union from the late 1940s to the 1970s. I show that the enterprise union failed to develop internal democracy and its own distinctive culture because management-dominated industrial relations at the enterprise level limited the union to mainly economic functions at the expense of political and social functions. Finally, I briefly consider the future prospects for labor unions as actors in Japan's civil society.

The History and Organizational Characteristics of Japanese Labor Unions

Japan's first labor union was organized by metalworkers in 1898. The labor movement became active in the 1920s and the 1930s, and the prewar unionization rate peaked at 7.9 percent in 1931. The state did not legally recognize unions; it tacitly acknowledged moderate unions while severely repressing radical ones. Prewar Japan's labor movement came to an end in 1940, when most labor unions were dissolved and reorganized into the wartime labor front Sanpō.

The labor movement was resurrected in 1945 as part of the Occupation's policy to democratize Japan. Labor unions were legalized for the first time with passage of the Labor Union Law that year. The first five years after the war witnessed one of the most active and militant periods in Japanese labor history under the leadership of the Communist-dominated Japan Council of Industrial Labor Unions (Sanbetsu), and the unionization rate reached its postwar peak of 55.8 percent in 1949. With the intensification of the Cold War, however, the Occupation took repressive policies toward Sanbetsu and its affiliates, and the unionization rate declined.

In 1951, the anti-Communist General Council of Trade Unions of Japan (Sōhyō) was established with the Occupation's support. Sōhyō soon began to take militant policies under the dominance of leftist socialists, so in 1954, the Japanese Trade Union Congress (Zenrō) was formed by conservative union leaders. From 1954 to 1987, the labor movement was basically divided between the left-wing Sōhyō and the right-wing Zenrō and its successor, the Japanese Confederation of Labor (Dōmei). Dominated by militant public-sector unions, Sōhyō advocated a class-based union movement. Dōmei, on the other hand, consisted mostly of private-sector unions and advocated labor-management cooperation. Industry-level federations of moderate private-sector unions increased their influence in the labor movement after the mid-1970s and played an important role in unifying the two rival confederations into the Japan Trade Union Confederation (Rengō) in 1989.

In spite of its decline after 1949, Japan's unionization rate remained relatively stable between 32 and 35 percent during the high-growth era from the mid-1950s to the mid-1970s. This rate was not especially low by international comparison. In the 1960s, Japan's unionization rate was about the same as that of West Germany, five to seven percentage points higher than that of the United States, and six to nine percentage points lower than that of Britain. From the mid-1970s, economic growth in Japan slowed, and the unionization rate declined more quickly. It dropped from

34.4 percent in 1975 to 30.8 percent in 1980 to 25.5 percent in 1990 to 21.5 percent in 2000.

The labor movement in postwar Japan has been characterized by its decentralized structure, with enterprise unions constituting the predominant form of union organization. In 1964, enterprise unions accounted for 93.6 percent of all unions, while craft and industrial unions accounted for only 1.6 percent and 3.1 percent, respectively. In 1988, enterprise unions remained the predominant form, accounting for 94.9 percent of all unions (Rōdōshō 1964, 1988). Enterprise unions enjoy autonomous decision-making authority on such issues as their constitutions, finances, and election of officials. Although most enterprise unions belong to industry-level federations, the latter have very limited control over the former (Shirai 1983: 119). Because enterprise unions autonomously negotiate with employers on issues related to wages and working conditions, the enterprise can be regarded as the focal point of industrial relations in Japan.

At the industry and national levels, labor unions do not directly negotiate with employers and their associations. Rather, industry-level federations concentrate on coordinating wage negotiations among their member unions, particularly during the so-called spring offensive (*shuntō*) annual wage negotiations. Industry-level federations in turn form confederations of unions in related industries[1] and national-level confederations. These national-level confederations set broad goals for the union movement and represent the general interests of labor in national politics, but they have no formal authority over member unions.

Labor Unions and Civil Society

Labor unions are actors in the market economy as well as in civil society. In labor markets, unions collectively represent the interests of sellers of labor power and engage in collective bargaining with management for better wages and working conditions. Unions may also play a certain role in product markets by cooperating with management to improve productivity in exchange for wage increases, for example. Unions cannot be regarded as significant actors in civil society, however, if they concentrate exclusively on activities in the economic arena.

As Peter Lange, George Ross, and Maurice Vannicelli (1982) pointed out, unions offer four types of incentives to members in exchange for their support. In addition to material incentives (corresponding to economic functions) are purposive, identity, and sociability incentives. Lange et al. (1982: 221–22, 225) argued that purposive and identity incentives often occupy an important position in the "incentive structure" of unions, and these roughly correspond to the political and cultural aspects of unions. Unions provide purposive incentives to their members by formulating "general policy goals" that they support in their relations with other actors, especially the state, and they provide identity incentives by advocating "a

[1] Seven industry-level federations of enterprise unions in metal industries (e.g., steel, autos, electronics, and shipbuilding) form a confederation called the Japan Council of International Metalworkers Federation (IMF-JC), for example.

system of values" with which members identify. On the basis of this argument, I hypothesize that the significance of unions as civil society actors increases in proportion to their political and social functions.

In their famous study of union democracy, Seymour Lipset, Martin Trow, and James Coleman (1956: 80) posited that secondary associations such as labor unions perform two types of political functions. First, by means of their "external power functions," they oppose "the power of the central body," that is, the state. Second, on the basis of their "internal functions," associations increase "the political involvement of their own members," that is, internal democracy. Although associations lacking internal democracy still perform external power functions, internally democratic associations are arguably more conducive to the development of civil society than oligarchical associations because they aggregate member interests in such a way that the views of dissenters as well as rank and filers are expressed in the process of policy formation.

Social functions are another important condition for unions to become significant civil society actors because they contribute to the development of a union culture autonomous from the hegemonic ideas of the state and corporations. Union culture is based on a system of values shaped by the class consciousness of union members, their sense of justice and fairness, or their idea of "us versus them." Union culture is not necessarily "given": union leaders may consciously promote it through social activities to strengthen organizational unity. Unions' social activities often take the form of culture and sports clubs or "circles," and the more active these groups are, the more likely there will develop an autonomous culture among union members.

A concrete example of a labor union offering members a rich associational life is the International Typographical Union (ITU), whose social and political functions were analyzed by Lipset et al. (1956). They pointed out that union democracy in the ITU was based on an occupational community of printers, that is, a vast internal network of voluntary organizations through which members cultivated their interests and participated in union politics. Another example can be found among Japanese enterprise unions in the early postwar period. Andrew Gordon (1998) demonstrates that the union of Nippon Kōkan (NKK), a major steel firm, had its own political dynamic and distinct culture independent of management. Union politics were active because informal groups within the union, ranging from company loyalists to Marxists, engaged in policy debates. Cultural circles (e.g., a chorus) of union members were also active, and the union and cultural circles reinforced one another: "the circles were nurturing union activities of the future, and the union was protecting circle leaders from discriminatory treatment by managers" (ibid.: 99).

Civil Society in the Context of Japanese Industrial Relations

In analyzing the associational life of Japanese labor unions, we need to pay attention to the relationship between civil society and the market economy. Previous discussion of this has focused on the issue of whether the market should or should not be considered part of civil society (see Beetham 1997). Some observers argue that an unregulated market "intensifies economic and social inequalities" and emphasize the need for political constraint of the market (e.g., Walzer 1992; Beetham 1998; Asano and Shinoda 1998). Weighing both the supportive and undermining effects of the market on democracy, David Beetham (1997) argues that the relationship between the two is ambivalent, and that what actual effect the market has on democracy (and therefore civil society) depends on how the market and politics are institutionally mediated.

In the context of Japanese industrial relations, that mediation has been institutionalized in such a way that the focal point of labor-management interaction is at the enterprise level rather than at the industrial or national level. Under these institutional arrangements, I posit that the market has a vitiating rather than supportive effect on civil society actors. More specifically, given the market imperatives to which they are exposed, business corporations limit enterprise unions' action to the economic arena, particularly at the corporate level, at the expense of their role in civil society. And as I noted above, the fewer the political and social functions unions perform, the less important their role in civil society. I also posit that the relationship between business corporations and labor unions is dynamic and that enterprise unions' functions change over time.

This theoretical framework is in line with the point of view taken by critical observers of civil society and industrial relations in Japan, who point out the weak regulatory power of societal actors such as labor unions on the economic activities of corporations (Tabata 1991). Some of these critics also emphasize the detrimental effects on civil society of the deep integration of workers into corporate society, where they are expected to be strongly committed to corporate goals. This is because workers are deprived of opportunities to engage actively in social movements outside corporations and because corporate management represses workers who question or oppose corporate goals (often violating their civil rights) and union officials and activists who advocate militant and/or political unionism (Kumazawa 1989; Yamamoto 1991; Yamada 1994).

The Political and Cultural Aspects of the Union Movement: The Case of the Yahata Steel Union

Let us examine the associational life of labor unions in the context of enterprise-level industrial relations, focusing on their internal democracy and cultural activities. Concerning union democracy, I discuss relations between union factions advocating different policies, relations between union leaders and rank-and-file members, and the influence of management on the factional balance of unions. Concerning union culture, I discuss how enterprise unions attempted to develop a distinctive workers' culture to counter the hegemony of corporate culture, what kind of discourses they used in invoking an autonomous identity for union members, and how policies of culture promotion changed over time. My analysis is based mainly on a case study of the Yahata Steel Union. Although one might question the generalizability of the case of one union, the Yahata Steel Union is representative of enterprise unions in large, private-sector firms because of its large size and influential position not only in the steel industry but in the entire private-sector union movement.

Yahata Steel Works is located on the northern tip of the island of Kyūshū. Yahata Steel had been part of the state-owned steel company in the prewar period, but in 1950, the state-owned company was privatized and divided into Yahata Steel and Fuji Steel. With a 20 to 30 percent market share, Yahata Steel was the largest producer of crude steel in the 1950s and 1960s; it was closely followed by Fuji Steel. (Beside the two largest steel firms, there were four major companies: NKK, Sumitomo Steel, Kōbe Steel, and Kawasaki Steel.) Under the guidance of the government, Yahata Steel and Fuji Steel joined once again to form the giant Nippon Steel in 1970. The government wanted to control competition for capacity expansion among steel firms by creating an oligopolistic market structure.

The Yahata Steel Union was one of the largest enterprise unions in Japan. Although the average enterprise union in the manufacturing sector had a membership of only 225 in 1964 (Rōdōshō 1964), the Yahata Union's membership ranged between 43,000 and 46,000 in the 1960s. In the early 1970s, membership decreased to 25,000 because locals at steel works other than Yahata Steel Works established their own unions. Nevertheless, the Yahata Union remained one of the largest unions in the steel industry. The union also played an influential role in the private-sector union movement. The enterprise unions of the major steel companies were federated into the Japan Federation of Steel Workers' Unions (JFSWU) in 1951. The Yahata Union was the most influential union among affiliates of the JFSWU, which, with its affiliate unions, played an important role in the development of Japan's postwar labor movement. From the mid-1960s to the mid-1980s, wage settlements in the steel industry *shuntō* set a standard for wage negotiations in other industries, and from the mid-1970s, the JFSWU played an important role in restraining the wage demands of private-sector unions. It also played a key role in the movement to unify the politically divided labor movement that led to the formation of Rengō.

Union Politics in the 1950s

In the 1950s, industrial relations in major private-sector industries were adversarial. The union movements in industries such as steel, coal, paper, auto, and ship building adopted militant policy lines and engaged in prolonged conflicts with employers over wage increases and control over the shop floor (Gordon 1993; Ohara Shakai Mondai Kenkyūjo 1999; see Garon, this volume). The JFSWU was affiliated with the left-wing confederation Sōhyō, and its leftist leadership tried to transform the federation of enterprise unions into an industrial union. It attempted to strengthen its authority over member unions by leading joint strikes for wage increases by its five major unions. Although the strikes of 1957 and 1959 were the largest and the longest, respectively, the unions lost both disputes (Matsuzaki 1991). These defeats discredited the strategy of industrial unionism advocated by the JFSWU.

Reflecting conflicts between advocates of the militant, industry-based strategies of the JFSWU and advocates of moderate, enterprise-based strategies, the enterprise unions of the major steel firms were factionalized. The Yahata Union was split into two rightist factions, which advocated economic unionism and took a cooperative stance toward rationalization, and one leftist faction, which was oriented to political unionism, was antagonistic toward rationalization, and advocated strike-based strategies.[2] The leftist faction was the largest in the forty-member executive committee in the mid-1950s, but its influence declined after the union's defeat in the labor dispute of 1957. By the early 1960s, members of the two rightist factions formed an overwhelming majority of the executive committee (Gibbs 1980; Suzuki 2000: 80–81).

The volatility of internal union politics indicates two things. First, the Yahata Union represented diverse interests. While most members seemed to agree that the union should be independent from management control, they disagreed among themselves over such fundamental issues as the organizational base of the union (industrial vs. enterprise unionism) and the basic direction of the union movement (political vs. economic unionism). Second, in spite of these disagreements, the Yahata Union maintained its organizational unity and tried to represent its members' diverse interests by mediating them in relatively democratic ways. (Although they were common in other industries, there were no union splits in the other steelworkers' unions, either.)

If the mediation of members' diverse interests was a sign that the Yahata Union enjoyed a certain degree of internal democracy, we can say that the union succeeded in performing political as well as economic functions during this period. It succeeded because the management of Yahata Steel did not wield as much influence over the union during the 1950s as it came to later. Management started to promote the union's rightist factions systematically from the mid-1950s by providing them with financial and other forms of support (Morita 1967: 62). This management policy was not influential enough to depoliticize internal union politics under the hegemony of these factions, however. The policy was implemented indirectly by the foremen and subforemen of work teams. Although they were expected to pressure their subordinates to vote for promanagement candidates in union elections, leaders of work teams did not seem to implement the policy as consistently as management expected.

Union Culture in the late 1940s and the 1950s

In the 1950s, the tenor of the union movement as a whole was militant and political.[3] The militancy of labor unions derived not only from grievances over wage levels and working conditions, but also from members' strong antiwar sentiments. In fact, the theme of "peace and democracy" dominated the discourse of antiestablishment movements, including the labor movement. Labor and other social movements

[2] In the 1950s, there were two small factions in addition to the three major factions, but I leave them out of this discussion for the sake of simplicity.

[3] My analysis of union culture is based mainly on the trimonthly newspaper of the Yahata Union, *Neppū* (Hot Blast).

strongly opposed the conservative government, which tried to rearm Japan and restore at least some elements of the prewar regime by revising the constitution and introducing reactionary laws (see Shimizu 1982). Workers regarded corporations as part of the establishment. At the enterprise level, workers in many firms created what Gordon (1993) calls a "union-dominated workplace culture" on the basis of which they sought to regulate the pace and extent of rationalization of the production process. This context provided fertile ground for development of a union culture independent from corporate culture.

The Yahata Union formally started its cultural policies in 1948 with establishment of a Council of Cultural Circles (*Bunka saakura kyōgikai*). Cultural circles were voluntary groups of union members interested in fields like poetry, literature, art, and musical and theatrical performance. At the start, seventeen circles belonged to the council. By establishing the council, the union aimed to promote cultural activities of union members by providing them with subsidies. Although it largely refrained from interfering in the activities of these circles, the union also aimed to "direct" members' cultural activities as part of its educational program (*Neppū*, July 23, 1951; January 3, 1955). In addition to supporting the activities of its member circles, the council organized its own activities. It organized such events as a cultural festival for May Day, lectures by prominent writers and artists, public performances of plays and music, and exhibitions of paintings and other art (*Neppū*, September 23, 1960). The youth and women sections of the union organized their own activities, such as a cultural festival in celebration of peace in 1954 (*Neppū*, July 23, August 13, 1954).

In 1950, the council faced a major crisis. With the sanction of the Occupation, whose anticommunism intensified after the outbreak of the Korean War, the management of Yahata Steel dismissed 230 communists and their sympathizers (Gibbs 1990: 231). The so-called Red Purge that swept Japan led to the dismissal of most of the leaders of the cultural circles, and half of the circles dropped out of the council. Criticism of the council mounted, and its budget was slashed by 40 percent. Due to both the reduced budget and the "low posture" the union adopted after the Red Purge, cultural circles became inactive, but by the mid-1950s, the union had recovered from the damage, and cultural circles became active again (*Neppū*, December 5, 1950; January 3, 1955; September 23, 1960).

The discourse of union culture was militant in this period, especially before the Red Purge. Articles of the union newspaper *Neppū* (Hot Blast) from this period indicate the union regarded cultural circles and their council as means to political ends. For example, a 1949 article in the newspaper defined the historical mission of the council as the promotion of a working people's culture on the basis of which Japan would realize a democratic revolution (*Neppū*, March 28, 1949). Immediately after the Red Purge, the union dropped its politicized understanding of cultural activities. A 1951 article in *Neppū* stressed that the role of the council should be to assist union members in their efforts at "moral improvement" (*Neppū*, April 25, 1951).

In the second half of the 1950s, the discourse of union culture once again became militant. The union still stressed the promotion of members' class consciousness as one of the main goals of cultural activities, but it no longer saw these activities as a means to broad political ends like revolution. The union stressed economic struggles within the existing political system and seemed to regard cultural activities as a sort of counterweight against an excessive orientation toward economic unionism and the absorption of union members into mass culture (*Neppū*, November 13, 1954; March 13, 1956; July 13, 1957; January 3, 1960).

During this period, the union started to be concerned about the vitiating effects of corporate labor and education policies on union culture and the class consciousness of union members. All employees of Yahata Steel belonged to an organization called the Fraternal Society, or Shinwakai. Shinwakai was established by the company in 1945 to succeed the Yahata branch of Sanpō, the wartime labor front. Its purported goals were to "manage and promote cultural and athletic activities of employees in autonomous and democratic ways" (Yahata Steel 1980: 552; Gibbs 1980: 23). *Neppū* articles pointed out that Shinwakai had the upper hand over the union in sponsoring cultural activities. They also warned that the company inculcated enterprise consciousness and the ideology of labor-management cooperation in union members through its "PR activities" (*Neppū*, March 3, April 13, 1958; July 23, 1960). The influence of management on union culture seemed to be limited, however, because most union members, regardless of the faction they supported, had an identity as blue-collar workers and generally perceived their relationship to management as one of "us versus them."[4]

Union Politics in the 1960s

In the 1960s, labor unions in many private-sector manufacturing firms experienced a change in union leadership or a split that resulted in the dominance of "procompany" union leaders (see Gotō 1996: 348). The steelworkers' unions were no exception to this trend. The internal politics of the Yahata Union and other major steelworkers' unions were largely settled in favor of economic unionism by the early 1960s, but the procompany stance did not immediately dominate their policy orientation. Although reduced to a minority status, leftists maintained their presence within the leadership of these unions, criticizing policies based on union-management cooperation. In the case of the Yahata Union, some rightist leaders advocated militant economic unionism: even as they advocated union-management cooperation in rationalization, they pursued the economic interests of union members through mobilization-based policies such as strikes (Suzuki 2000: 82–89). The steelworkers' unions staged joint strikes during annual rounds of wage negotiations in 1961, 1963, and 1965.

By the end of the 1960s, the executive boards of the major steel unions excluded most leftists. Among rightist leaders, those who advocated cooperative economic unionism, or what Gordon (1998) calls an "ultracooperative stance,"

[4] Gordon (1998: 99) makes a similar point. NKK and other corporations in the 1950s had "limited control over workers after hours," and the union's cultural circles provided "sites of employee activity independent from and opposed to the company."

became dominant within the union leadership. In the Yahata Union, one of the two rightist factions, the Liaison Council of Labor Unionists (Renkyō), steadily increased its influence over the union's leadership. It absorbed the other rightist faction and took complete control over the executive board in the union election of 1968. Although the faction advocated militant economic unionism in the first half of the 1960s, it reoriented its policy toward cooperative economic unionism after the defeat of the union in the 1965 strike (Suzuki 2000: 88–91).

After the mid-1960s, the principles behind the dominant faction's policies were documented in its "Platform of Labor Unionism," which was announced in 1968 by a group of rightist union leaders in the Yahata Union and other major unions of the JFSWU. According to the platform, the steelworkers' union movement should oppose class struggle, accept the existing capitalist system, and absolutely oppose communists and their sympathizers in the union movement. Furthermore, the platform set forth a type of economic unionism that was very cooperative vis-à-vis corporate goals. It stated that union-management relations should be based on mutual trust and that unions should resort to a strike only when that mutual trust was betrayed by management. Unions should support rationalization and contribute to the prosperity of corporations, on the basis of which unions would demand a fair share of the economic reward. In sum, the dominant rightist faction no longer took a mobilization-based policy, and it sought the economic interests of union members solely within the framework of corporate interests (Japan Federation of Steelworkers Unions 1981: 183–85; Miyata 1991: 180). It should be noted that this type of economic unionism came to be embraced by the leadership of the other major steel unions by the late 1960s, and that the Yahata Union and the other unions did not stage any strikes after 1965.

The dominance of advocates of cooperative economic unionism did not mean that most Yahata Union members supported the policy line of their leaders. A substantial minority of union members (26 to 37 percent) voted for leftist candidates for union president and vice president in the elections of 1968 and 1970 (Serizawa 1988). Moreover, there were dissenters who remained within the framework of economic unionism. Some young, lower-ranking union officials were critical of top leaders who gave priority to mutual trust with management over the mobilization of union members, and they advocated a mobilization-based economic unionism (Morita 1967: 68). The monopolization of the executive board by rightist officials did mean that the union no longer represented those union members who advocated either class-based or militant economic unionism. In addition, the union leadership repressed or discouraged the expression of dissent against its policy of cooperative economic unionism.[5] In this sense, the internal democracy of the Yahata Union declined during the 1960s.

[5] The union leadership repressed leftists, making great efforts to isolate leftist activists in workplaces, to prevent their running in union elections and, if they did run, to ensure that an overwhelming majority of union members voted against them (Suzuki 1997: chap. 4). The leadership did not take as repressive measures against dissenters who remained within the framework of economic unionism, but they were discouraged from openly expressing dissent, which led to their removal from union posts (Morita 1967).

What accounts for the decline of union democracy? Management played an important role in transforming the union from a politicized but relatively democratic institution into a depoliticized and oligarchical one. As noted above, the management of Yahata Steel started to intervene in union politics in favor of the rightist factions from the mid-1950s. It intervened regularly in union elections thereafter and reportedly increased its intervention in the union election of 1968 (Tekkō Rōdō Tsūshin 1968: 2; Saki 1969). Management wanted to ensure that the merger of Yahata Steel and Fuji Steel scheduled for 1970 proceeded smoothly by excluding all union officials opposed to the merger – that is, leftists. As a result of heavy intervention in the union election, rightists took all of the forty posts on the executive board (Michimata 1974: 73). In this way, the union's factional balance was strongly affected by power relations between the union and management.

Equally important were personnel policies that indirectly helped the dominant rightist faction to consolidate its power. The management of Yahata Steel and other steel firms adopted new personnel policies in the first half of the 1960s that affected the shop-floor hierarchy, wages, and education and training programs (Japan Federation of Steelworkers Unions 1980: 115), and these policies had a significant impact on internal union politics. The most important of them was the new foreman system (*sagyōchō seido*) that was introduced to Yahata Steel in 1963. According to a Yahata manager in charge of labor relations, one of the important goals of the system was to clarify the position of foremen in union-management relations. Foremen were deunionized and assigned the task of enforcing the labor policies of management at the workplace level (Komatsu 1968: 230–33). The new system also increased management's control over work teams, not only with respect to production-related issues, but also in personnel management. For example, according to the job description used at Yahata Steel, foremen were to pay particular attention to the maintenance of "harmonious human relations" on the shop floor and should ensure that the "shop-floor discipline" of their subordinates (*shokuba kiritsu*) was strictly observed (ibid.: 224–25). Although the job description did not specifically mention leftist union activists, it seems that foremen were to tighten control over such activists at the shop-floor level in order to maintain "harmonious human relations" and "shop-floor discipline" (Serizawa 1984: 115–17). The introduction of the new foreman system arguably made the shop-floor activities of leftists very difficult, thus contributing to the decline of the leftist minority's influence over internal union politics and to the repression of those members who might challenge the legitimacy of cooperative union leaders.

Why did the management of Yahata Steel seek to transform the nature of its enterprise union in the 1960s? What were the market imperatives that drove management to intervene in internal union politics? Management policies toward the union reflected the intense rationalization program that the management of Yahata Steel undertook from the mid-1960s, which in turn reflected intense market competition among the major steel firms.

In the 1960s, the steel industry expanded rapidly, and the major firms competed for market share. Market competition was closely linked to investment competition among the firms in new integrated steel works. Four new steel works began operations between 1961 and 1965 and five more between 1966 and 1970. In the

1960s, Yahata Steel built two new integrated steel works (the Sakai and Kimitsu Works), which started operations in 1965 and 1967. In conjunction with the construction of the two steel works, the management of Yahata Steel started in 1963 a rationalization program that was more intense than previous programs. The program aimed to retrench the number of workers at Yahata Steel Works by means of intense rationalization of the production process and to transfer those workers who became redundant to the new steel works. The rationalization program cut about 8,000 workers at Yahata Steel Works between 1963 and 1968, and the new steel works were manned mostly by employees who were transferred from there (Hyōdō 1982: 240; Tanaka 1982: 68–69).

The intense rationalization program affected working conditions through both the intensification of the work process at Yahata Steel Works itself and the large-scale transfer of workers from Yahata Steel Works to distant new steel works. Because the success of the rationalization program depended on the union's cooperation, management tried to eliminate any possibility of unpredictability in its behavior by adopting policies to depoliticize internal union politics and by constraining the union to act only within the framework of cooperative economic unionism.

Union Culture in the 1960s

The general context of union culture became less favorable in the 1960s. The opposition of labor and social movements to the conservative government reached its peak in 1960, when these movements staged protests on an unprecedented scale against revision of the U.S.-Japan Security Treaty. At the time, many social scientists regarded this mass movement as the beginning of the full-scale development of civil society in Japan (see Yamaguchi 1992: 11), but the government subsequently shifted its focus from controversial political issues to economic growth, and the tenor of the times changed drastically under rapid growth (Masamura 1990).[6] As people became less concerned with political issues and more concerned with issues related to their private lives, such as the improvement of living standards, the labor movement toned down its antiestablishment stance and instead stressed economic issues, particularly wage increases. In addition, the 1960s witnessed the full-scale development of a mass culture that diluted the distinctiveness of unions' cultural activities (see Ivy 1993: 241). At the enterprise level, the union-dominated workplace culture of the previous period was decisively weakened with the defeat of militant unions in labor disputes and replaced by a management-dominated workplace culture. The decline of union-dominated workplace culture was symbolized by the defeat in 1960 of a powerful union in a prolonged and bitter dispute against the Mitsui Miike mine that lasted 313 days (Gordon 1993).

Union culture at Yahata stagnated in the 1960s. The union continued to support cultural activities of its members by subsidizing the Council of Cultural Circles.

[6] During the 1960s, the Japanese economy enjoyed real growth rates of more than 10 percent every year except 1962 and 1965. Average nominal wage settlements amounted to about 12 percent.

The council tried to revitalize union culture by organizing events, the most important of which was a Cultural Exhibition and Performance of Workers that was held annually from 1962. It also organized a cultural festival that was held during spring offensives from 1964 to stimulate the interest of union members in economic struggles (*Neppū*, June 3, 1962; February 23, June 3, 1964; February 23, 1965), but the attempt to revitalize union culture failed because only a limited number of members participated in these events (*Neppū*, March 23, October 3, 1965).

As a result of a change in the union leadership in that year, it seems, the union reevaluated its cultural policy in 1968. As noted above, rightist officials who advocated cooperative economic unionism took complete control of the executive board, and the new leadership criticized the activities of the existing cultural circles because they attracted only a small minority of union members. It emphasized that the union's cultural activities should have popular appeal. The union thus took the position that it would no longer automatically subsidize cultural activities; instead, it would support only those activities that contributed to the solidarity of union members (*Neppū*, September 14, December 13, 1968). In reaction to this change in policy, at least one leader of the cultural circles expressed apprehension that the union leadership would start to intervene in cultural activities (*Neppū*, December 13, 1968). While it did not intervene directly, the leadership seemed to tighten its control over cultural activities. In its plan for the 1971 business year, the executive board stated it would "manage cultural activities under its strong leadership" while respecting the autonomy of cultural circles (*Neppū*, September 17, 1970).

In the 1960s, the union emphasized the solidarity of its members and the promotion of union consciousness. If the discourse of union culture survived in this period, it was characterized in these terms rather than by the class consciousness of the previous period. The union invoked solidarity and union consciousness mainly in reaction to management's systematic introduction of educational programs from around the mid-1960s (see, e.g., *Neppū*, August 27, 1969). It regarded these programs with suspicion because they would potentially inculcate a strong enterprise consciousness in union members and lead to a stricter system of labor management (*Neppū*, July 3, 1965). To counter management's educational programs, the union provided its own educational programs from 1962 on "knowledge about labor unions and techniques for union activities" (*Neppū*, August 27, 1969). These programs consisted mainly of lectures on topics of labor economics and industrial relations, however, and union members learned the importance of labor unions and union consciousness only theoretically (see *Neppū*, July 3, 1965). Thus, the programs offered by the union were ineffective in countering the more systematic and extensive programs provided by management.

The stagnation of union culture in the Yahata Union can be explained by changes in the general economic and social context, such as the rapid economic growth and the full-scale development of mass culture. Management's educational programs may constitute another factor. Moreover, the decline of the union's political functions seems to be related to the stagnation of its culture. As noted above, the union was depoliticized under the dominance of a faction advocating cooperative economic unionism, and it became undemocratic with the suppression of dissenting opinions. It can be argued that cooperative economic unionism has a strong affinity to the logic of the market economy, and because the union leadership adopted that strategy as its *only* policy line, the union was ineffective at countering the enterprise consciousness promoted by management's educational programs. If the union had left some space for policy debate involving advocates of different types of unionism, it might have been able to maintain some form of union culture longer than it actually did. In other words, the performance of its political function might have served as a bulwark against the undermining effect of management policy on its social function.

Union Politics in the 1970s and Thereafter

In the 1970s, the Yahata Union and other steelworkers' unions continued to advocate cooperative economic unionism. On the basis of this principle, they increased their commitment to union-management cooperation when steel and other major industries suffered a structural recession after the oil crisis of 1973. Forced to reduce capacity by 20 to 30 percent to ease oversupply, the steel industry closed old and unprofitable facilities and transferred redundant workers to newer plants (see Rōdōshō 1978: 586–88).

The steelworkers' unions actively cooperated with management on production-related issues and accepted sacrifices for rationalization in the form of intensified labor, intracompany transfers, and the "loaning" of workers to outside firms (see, e.g., Kamada 1994; Yamagaki 2000). The unions also began to cooperate on wage-related issues. They had demanded wage increases in return for their cooperation on rationalization until the mid-1970s. After that, however, they adopted the principle of "economically rational wage demands" and restrained their wage demands – which were often used by unions in other industries as a reference point for their own demands – in order not to hurt the performance of the Japanese economy. As a result, the real wages of steelworkers remained almost static after 1975. Although their real wages had increased by an annual average of 6.5 percent between 1965 and 1974, that rate fell to 1.0 percent between 1975 and 1984 and to 0.8 percent between 1985 and 1994 (Yamagaki 2000).

In the 1970s and thereafter, rightist leaders and officials consolidated their dominance within the steelworkers' unions as rightist candidates increased their share of votes in biennial union elections. In the case of the Yahata Union, their share of votes in the presidential election increased from 65 percent in 1970 to 84 percent in 1988 (Serizawa 1988). Did the electoral success of rightist union leaders indicate that an overwhelming majority of members actively supported their policies? The responses of Yahata Union members to opinion surveys suggest that their interests were not as homogeneous as indicated by union elections. In 1984, a presidential candidate of the dominant Yahata faction received about 85 percent of the votes. In a survey conducted that same year, on the other hand, union members asked to evaluate activities of the Yahata Union were evenly divided (at 48 percent) between those who were "satisfied" or "somewhat satisfied" and those who were "dissatisfied" or "somewhat dissatisfied" (Nippon Steel Union 1985: 192). The 1984 survey also revealed that a substantial minority of union members (about 30 percent) had a critical or cynical attitude toward the union.[7]

If about half of union members were dissatisfied with their leadership and its policies and if a substantial minority of them even took critical or cynical attitudes toward them, why did they vote for rightist union leaders? Why did internal debate over union policies remain inactive even as the economic context of industrial relations changed drastically after the first oil crisis? These union members no longer regarded the union as an association that represented their interests to management, and they "exited" from union activities by becoming indifferent to them rather than "voicing" their critical opinions (see Hirschman 1973). The extent of their exit was indicated by a 1984 survey of Yahata Union members in which 53 percent of respondents stated that they were unwilling to participate in union activities (Chōsa Jihō 1985: 184). Behind the exit of these members was the blurred boundary between union and management at the workplace level, a phenomenon widely observed in the industrial relations of major private-sector firms. The organizational boundary was blurred because leaders of work teams such as subforemen, who enforced management's labor policies, frequently became union officials, such as local presidents (Nitta 1979: 263; Kurita 1994: 187–88). For unranked workers, the experience of serving as a local union official became an important requirement for their promotion to a lower managerial position, such as subforeman or foreman (Fujisawa 1978: 146–47).

In sum, even though the interests of union members remained diverse, the interests actually represented by the Yahata Union were defined not by internal policy debate but by union leaders who shared management's perspective.[8] This absence of internal democracy was not limited to the Yahata Union. A decline in unions'

[7] The survey found that 53 percent of Yahata respondents were unwilling to participate in union activities. To explain their unwillingness, the largest proportion of them (36 percent) answered that they questioned the stance of the union leadership. This answer was followed by "I want to spend more time on personal matters than on union activities" (24 percent), "Union activities are meaningless" (14 percent), "My opinion is not reflected in union activities" (8 percent), and "I want to concentrate on my job" (8 percent). About 19 percent of all union members thus questioned the stance of their leadership, and another 11 percent took cynical, if not critical, attitudes toward union activities and/or leaders (i.e., the proportion of respondents who found union activities meaningless or did not find their opinions reflected in union activities). In other words, 30 percent of the members of the Yahata Union were unwilling to participate in union activities because they had a critical or cynical attitude toward the union (Nippon Steel Union 1985: 185–86).

[8] Although this discussion has not given much consideration to the "consent" aspect of union politics, this is not to downplay the efforts of leaders to generate the consent of union members. Leaders were concerned with the maintenance of their legitimacy among union members. When the Yahata Union and other steelworkers' unions restrained wage demands, leaders appealed to the long-term economic interests of union members to defuse their discontent, for example. The support of about half of all members for the union leadership may be due to the fact that they were convinced by the leadership's economic-interest argument. (The other half, however, did not seemed to be convinced by it.)

representational function was observed in other enterprise unions in the steel industry and in other private-sector industries, such as autos and electronics (e.g., Yamamoto 1981, 1990; Gordon 1998).

Union Culture in the 1970s

The cooperative economic unionism advocated by the leadership of the Yahata Union became the dominant ideology of the labor movement as a whole by the end of the 1970s. Although public-sector unions, particularly the unions at Japan National Railway, advocated militant unionism and opposed the government's prohibition of strikes by public-sector workers, the influence of militant political unionism declined drastically after public-sector unions lost a "Strike for the Right to Strike" in 1975. With the declining influence of these unions, the last legacy of oppositional culture virtually withered away in the labor movement. During this period, many private-sector unions actively cooperated with management in rationalizing and restructuring corporations to cope with the economic recession that followed the oil crisis of 1973. Enterprise unions were subsumed under the hegemony of corporate society and were more constrained than before in the economic sphere, which deprived them of most opportunities to develop a distinct culture.

In the 1970s, the Yahata Union no longer stressed the importance of building its own culture through sponsored activities. The Council of Cultural Circles survived and regularly held cultural festivals. A cursory look at the union newspaper *Neppū*, however, suggests that the number of articles – whether supportive or critical – on union culture and the space allocated to this topic decreased during this period. This suggests the growing indifference of the union to its members' cultural activities.

What the union stressed from the late 1960s was "the management of leisure hours [*yoka kanri*] of union members" through recreational activities. Behind the union's attention to leisure hours lay a major change in the working environment. In 1970, Yahata Steel introduced a new system in which three shifts were manned by four teams, replacing the old shift system in which three shifts were manned by three teams. The number of regular days off per year increased from 68 to 84 days (and later to 91 days) under the new system.[9] Concerned that many members did not know how to spend their increased leisure hours except by "lazily watching television," the union attempted to organize their recreational activities so that

[9] Although the number of regular days off per year increased under the new shift system, management made up for increased labor costs by intensifying the labor process. When the new shift system was introduced, management reorganized the work process on the basis of an extensive reevaluation of the number of workers required for a certain set of jobs, and in many cases it reduced the number of workers in a shift team. The fourth-shift teams were staffed mostly by those workers who became redundant as a result of the reorganization. Management also intensified the labor process by reducing the break time from one hour to forty-five minutes (which was then divided into two separate breaks) and by managing working hours much more strictly than before (Matsuzaki 1982; Kawanishi 1992: 48–51).

they would spend leisure hours in more "meaningful" ways, by which it meant activities that not only benefited individual members, but also contributed to the organizational unity of the union and to successful wage struggles (*Neppū*, July 3, 1969). In other words, the union promoted the recreational activities of its members for the instrumental purpose of promoting its own organizational interests. It should also be noted that the union adopted this policy not as a result of its own strategic thinking but in reaction to a similar management policy that aimed to promote the enterprise consciousness of workers through recreational activities (*Neppū*, August 27, 1969).

How did the union try to "manage" the leisure hours of its members? The union established a special committee to discuss measures to be taken for recreational activities. It also appointed one "recreation leader" per local and provided that leader with training programs on recreational activities. They were supposed to lead recreational activities at the local level (*Neppū*, August 27, 1969; September 17, 1970). Training programs consisted mainly of lectures on issues related to leisure and recreation, but also included folk songs, folk dances, and games (*Neppū*, August 13, 1971; July 3, 1973; July 3, 1974). Thus, the union managed the leisure hours of its members only indirectly, via its recreation leaders, and it seems that the union concentrated on providing training without doing much follow-up on exactly how recreation leaders practiced what they had learned in their respective locals (*Neppū*, July 13, 1974). Moreover, recreational activities at the workplace level were apparently carried out mainly at the initiative of Shinwakai, the organization established by the company for the promotion of employees' cultural and athletic activities (*Neppū*, April 13, 1979). Thus, it can be argued that the union was ineffective in carrying out its leisure policy and ended up making itself more bureaucratic by adding yet another committee to its organization.

Two points should be noted about the leisure hour policy of the union. First, its logic was similar to that of management's personnel policies. Both management *and* the union used "management" as a key concept. While management, through its personnel policies, managed workers' behavior in the workplace, the union, through its leisure policy, attempted to manage workers' behavior outside the workplace. In other words, if it is defined in a broad sense to include leisure policy, the discourse of union culture was influenced by the hegemonic discourse of corporate management. Second, this union policy had implications for civil society as a whole because the management of leisure hours might have deterred members from participating in social movements outside the company. The union's policy aimed at promoting workers' identity as members of an enterprise union, not as participants in labor or social movements at the industrial, regional, or national level. Thus, whether the union intended it or not, its leisure policy was not incompatible with management's policy for employees' recreational activities because they both tried to promote workers' sense as members of corporate society.[10]

[10] The compatibility of the two policies is indicated by the fact that representatives of the union served as officers of workplace units of Shinwakai, which organized recreational activities at the workplace level (*Neppū*, April 13, 1979).

Conclusion

This chapter places labor unions in an analytical framework focused on the relationship between civil society and the market economy to examine how the market economy can undermine civil society. I analyzed union-management relations at the enterprise level as an arena where the forces of civil society confront those of the market economy in a concrete way. Because I hypothesized that the more unions perform political and social functions, the more important is the role they are likely to play in civil society, I examined the internal union politics and cultural activities of the Yahata Union from the late 1940s to the 1970s. History shows that the union tried but eventually failed to develop a sphere of political and cultural activities autonomous from management and therefore from the constraint of the market economy. By means of its labor and personnel policies, management limited the union to mainly economic functions within the framework of enterprise-level industrial relations. As a result, the union was transformed from a politicized but relatively democratic institution into a depoliticized and oligarchical institution under the dominance of leaders advocating cooperative economic unionism. Along the way, union culture declined. Although the union promoted its own culture through the use of militant and class-based discourse in the 1950s, it dropped such discourse in the 1960s, and it subsequently failed to find any alternative discourse to support an autonomous union culture. With its growing inclination toward economic unionism, it stopped supporting cultural activities for their own sake, instead supporting them only to the extent that they would contribute to its economic goals. In this way, the union's role in civil society declined as it faced difficulty performing political and social functions within the framework of enterprise-based industrial relations.

The problem of the underdevelopment of labor unions as civil society actors remained latent as long as the Japanese economy performed well. In the 1980s, many observers regarded the enterprise as a "community" in which union and management shared a common interest in improving corporate competitiveness. The underdevelopment of unions' associational functions due to the blurred boundary between unions and management was thus perceived as a source of strength. With the onset of a severe recession in the early 1990s, however, many companies started a drastic restructuring of their organizations by closing plants and reducing their work forces. Moreover, the diversity of the interests of union members has become more pronounced than before in terms of their gender, age, and employment status (see Shinoda 1989: chap. 3). Working women have become more assertive in demanding equality in pay and job assignments. Because workers in their forties and fifties are specifically targeted in the restructuring of corporate organizations, they are far more concerned with employment security than are younger workers. In addition, management's labor policies contribute to the diversity of union members because they no longer treat regular employees uniformly and have begun to divide them into different groups enjoying varying degrees of employment security.

Due to the drastic changes in the context of industrial relations, observers have begun to regard the underdevelopment of unions' associational functions as a serious issue. In spite of the changes, many labor unions remain passive, continuing or even strengthening their policy line of cooperative economic unionism (Kawanishi 1998). Because existing unions have not been sufficiently responsive to the increasingly diverse interests of workers, a new type of union has been formed outside enterprises to represent the interests of special categories of workers, such as women and middle managers (Ohara Shakai Mondai Kenkyūjo 1999: 496, 504). It remains to be seen whether Japanese labor unions will assume (or resume) associational functions by effectively representing the diverse interests of members vis-à-vis management and the state. Unless labor unions do perform political and social functions by means of active internal policy debates among union members with diverse interests and by creating their own "identity incentives" autonomous from corporate society, they may not be able to overcome their underdevelopment as civil society actors.

10

The Struggle for an Independent Consumer Society: Consumer Activism and the State's Response in Postwar Japan

Patricia L. Maclachlan

In a country where the state was at one time viewed as all-encompassing, the public interest equated with the interests of producers and the private sphere dismissed as the locus of greed, disorder, and incivility (Harootunian 1974), the very notion of civil society (*shimin shakai*) as a realm of autonomous individuals connected to neither the market nor the state is imbued with almost radical overtones. Be that as it may, many postwar social movement activists have upheld *shimin shakai* not only as a wellspring of their protests against the lingering supremacy of state and producer interests in Japanese politics, but also as the ultimate beneficiary of that activism. This has been particularly apparent within the organized consumer movement – a movement that, since its inception during the immediate aftermath of World War II, has struggled not only to represent the interests of the country's expanding consumer constituency to state authorities, but also to educate that constituency about their rights and responsibilities as consumers and citizens (*shimin*). Their ultimate aim in this regard has been to build a consumer society that is independent of both state and market control. In the face of a traditionally passive political culture and a strong, pro-producer state, however, their efforts have met with mixed results.

My purpose here is to explore the political intellectual history of postwar consumer activism as an illuminating case study of the development of Japanese civil society and its relationship to the state. To that end, I focus on the following sets of interrelated questions. First, how have historical, political, and economic circumstances shaped movement views of the consumer's place in society, and how have those views reflected and/or influenced the goals, tactics, and alliances pursued by consumer groups in their efforts to wrest concessions from the state? Second, how have consumer advocates contributed to enhanced awareness about civil and consumer rights within the public at large? Third, how have state laws and institutions constrained consumer movement activism, and how have activists compensated for those constraints? Finally, how and why has consumer activism changed over the past decade or so, and what do those changes suggest about the future of Japanese civil society more generally?

Before progressing, a few theoretical observations are in order. First, a word about definitions. By equating *shimin shakai* with a realm of individuals that is neither of the state nor of the market, I am adopting a definition[1] of civil society that, from the vantage point of consumer activism, may strike some as too narrow or simplistic. Consumers are, after all, indispensable market actors who have a significant stake in the processes of production. My decision to situate consumer *movements* within civil society, on the other hand, reflects the fact that consumer activists in advanced industrialized democracies are concerned with far more than just consumption – the straightforward act of purchasing and consuming goods and services in the marketplace. As the experiences of the American and other Western consumer movements highlight, activists are also concerned, to varying degrees, with notions of citizenship and the promotion of governmental accountability, the health and safety of the family, environmental protection, and a host of other "quality-of-life" issues that transcend the simple dynamics of supply and demand in the marketplace and often involve the assertion of individual rights vis-à-vis state (and market) representatives. Put simply, consumer activists have at least one foot rooted in that nonmarket, nonstate sector where free association of citizens, citizen group autonomy, and individual rights are among the operative concepts.[2] These observations, as we see below, ring particularly true for the Japanese consumer movement.

Second, it is important to justify my selection of the consumer movement as representative of both Japanese social movements and civil society more broadly. To do so, it is helpful to begin with a general definition of social movements. In the political science literature, it is customary now to define the term as collectivities of individuals who rely at least in part on noninstitutional tactics in order to "make claims" against governments (Tarrow 2000: 337). As such, social movements serve as noninstitutionalized instruments for changing the distribution of rewards (McCarthy and Zald 1977: 1218) within a political system to the benefit of members and, in some cases, nonmembers as well. Thus, social movements can be viewed as political representatives of otherwise apolitical individuals within civil society that are designed to wrest favors from state and/or market institutions of which they are not a part.

Social movements are also interested in issues of social and political identity insofar as they seek to change how individuals in society view such key democratic principles as freedom of expression and association, political equality, and individual rights. Social movements, in other words, can be transformative as well as instrumental in their political orientation.[3] For civil society, this means

[1] This definition is similar to that of Alan Wolfe (1997).

[2] In keeping with this definition, households can be regarded as integral parts of civil society insofar as they participate in consumer cooperative movements and other social networks related to quality-of-life issues.

[3] Perhaps the best examples of the dual nature of many social movements are the feminist movements of many Western countries. These movements have been influential not only in changing public

that social movements serve not only as conduits for citizen influence over those in political and economic authority, but also as vehicles for attitudinal changes within civil society itself.

As the following pages attest, the postwar Japanese consumer movement has performed both kinds of functions for civil society. Since the late 1940s, consumer groups have pursued instrumental objectives vis-à-vis the business community by pressuring individual firms or industries for safer products, more consumer-friendly business practices, and the like. During the postwar period, those groups have also been increasingly involved in nationwide political campaigns designed to leverage from state authorities such consumer-related public goods[4] as stricter antitrust and food safety policies, laws governing door-to-door sales, and products liability legislation. In addition, many Japanese consumer groups also work to strengthen the very attitudes and beliefs that are so integral to a vibrant and autonomous civil society – one that is not, in other words, coopted or controlled by state and/or market institutions.

Finally, it is worth noting that the consumer movement embraces two of the most significant strains within the postwar Japanese social movement environment. The first is "citizens' groups" (*shimin dantai*), those grassroots, horizontally organized, nonpartisan voluntary associations that engage primarily in protest and other noninstitutionalized forms of interest articulation (see McKean 1981). These groups, which have been particularly prevalent within the environmental and student movements since the 1960s and have proliferated within the consumer movement at the local level, embody many of the organizational traits and quality-of-life objectives that scholars now associate with so-called new social movements. The second is advocacy groups: vertically structured voluntary organizations that carry out both institutionalized (e.g., lobbying, participation in governmental advisory commissions) and noninstitutionalized forms of interest articulation. Although such groups can also be found within the women's, environmental, and other Japanese movements that seek access to the political system in order to instigate change, they have grown particularly prevalent within the consumer movement. Over the years, these groups grew to resemble the "public interest groups" that came to prominence in the United States during the 1960s (see Berry 1977).[5] For the purposes of this study, I focus on the activities of both organizational types, except for those that fall under direct governmental control.[6]

policies toward women, but also in transforming the attitudes of both men and women toward the position of women in society.

4 For consumers, examples of public goods would include safe products and lower prices, both of which benefit not only the members of consumer groups but society more generally.

5 The relative strength of "public interest" groups within the Japanese consumer movement can be explained in part by the severity of free-rider problems within consumer movements. For more on this topic, see Maclachlan (2002: chap. 1).

6 Many local groups have been so closely allied with local governments that they have come to be viewed as administrative arms of those governments. At the national level, there are a number of groups that are subject to governmental control: the Japan Consumers' Association (Nihon Shōhisha Kyōkai), for instance, is a prominent organization affiliated with MITI. While these organizations

The Politics of Survival: The Early Postwar Period

Many scholars date the outbreak of citizen activism from the 1960 Security Treaty Crisis and the wave of environmental protest movements that exploded onto the political scene shortly thereafter (McKean 1981; Apter and Sawa 1984). Although these scholars are certainly correct in assuming that the 1960s and early 1970s constituted the high point of postwar social movement activity, I would argue that the story of postwar social movements is rooted in the Occupation period (1945–52). For the consumer movement, this was an era of unprecedented political opportunities that were to condition the nature of movement activism for years to come.

As others (e.g., Tsujinaka 1988: 73) have shown, Occupation authorities granted Japanese citizens a number of basic rights and freedoms that sparked a veritable explosion of both citizen and interest group activity. Among those who took full advantage of these developments were the country's newly enfranchised women, a significant number of whom swelled the ranks of labor unions and political parties (Garon 1997: 181). Others established their own grassroots women's groups – in some cases even before the occupiers had set foot on Japanese soil.[7] Still others flocked into the country's nascent consumer groups and consumer cooperatives.

Unlike Ralph Nader's network of consumer groups in the United States, which, since their establishment from the mid-1960s, have focused on quality-of-life problems resulting from economic affluence, early Japanese consumer groups were primarily concerned with restoring a sense of material well-being to the general population at a time of mass poverty and severe economic scarcity. Accordingly, their efforts were collectively referred to as "The Movement to Defend Livelihoods" (Seikatsu Bōei no Undō). Most of these groups, which were overwhelmingly dominated by women, formed spontaneously at the local level in response to intense consumer-related grievances in much the same way that citizens' groups organized during the 1960s and 1970s in reaction to the spread of environmental pollution (see McKean 1981; Broadbent 1998). Some of those groups went on to form the nuclei of the housewives' organizations and consumer cooperatives, both of which have played a leading role in the organized movement at the national and prefectural levels throughout the postwar period.

One of the most prominent features of the early consumer movement was a structural overlap with the country's nascent women's movement. In the context of economic scarcity, many of the problems that plagued women as consumers were closely linked to their roles as mothers and housewives. One of the most important tasks performed by housewives during the early Occupation period was to collect their families' daily rations (Kobayashi 1994: 41; Garon 1997: 181). When the rationing system did not function properly (a frequently occurring consumer

perform important educational functions for consumers, they tend to avoid the kind of overt political activities pursued by independent housewives' organizations and consumer cooperatives.

7 Ichikawa Fusae, one of Japan's foremost feminist activists, organized the postwar precursor of the Japan League of Women Voters (Nihon Fujin Yūkensha Dōmei) only ten days after the surrender (Kokumin Seikatsu Sentaa 1997: 5).

problem), housewives' ability to fulfill their family-related responsibilities was correspondingly weakened. Thus, it was no coincidence that many of the organizations that we now associate with the women's movement, such as Ichikawa's League of Women Voters (Fujin Yūkensha Dōmei), became involved in consumer-related campaigns during the Occupation. This practice continues to this day, although to a much less significant degree. Meanwhile, organizations such as Shufuren (The Japan Federation of Housewives' Associations), which have assumed prominence since World War II primarily as consumer advocacy organizations, have simultaneously pursued objectives designed to promote the status and protection of women. In contrast to, say, the American or British consumer movements, there were virtually no organizations at this time that focused exclusively on consumer issues (Maclachlan 2002: 79).[8]

As consumer-related groups fought to restore the supply of basic goods and services to the marketplace, a loose consensus gradually emerged about the consumer's place in society, a consensus that reflected the social, political, economic, and even gender-related context of consumer activism and that was to have a significant impact on movement tactics throughout the next several decades. This process of defining the consumer identity within a particular socioeconomic context is an example of what social movement theorists have referred to as "framing": the fashioning by movement activists of "shared understandings of the world and of themselves that legitimate and motivate collective action" (McAdam, McCarthy, and Zald 1996: 6). Because the process is highly symbolic of the relationship between the consumer movement as representative of a broad cross-section of civil society and other actors in the polity, it warrants detailed attention.

The Consumer Identity in Postwar Japan

The concepts of "consumer" (*shōhisha*) and "consumption" (*shōhi*) have never been as widely accepted in Japan as they have in the West. During the 1920s, for example, the country's first consumer cooperativists were often struck by the negative responses of Japanese citizens to such seemingly mundane phrases as "buyers' cooperative" (*kōbai kumiai*) and "consumer cooperative" (*shōhisha kumiai*), phrases that connoted passive, not-for-profit economic activities that were of benefit to self-seeking individuals rather than the economy as a whole (Yamamoto 1982: 674). These negative reactions can be at least partly attributed to the very linguistic make-up of the term *shōhi* (consumption): the ideograph for

[8] This has changed. The late 1960s witnessed the formation of a handful of organizations at the national level that are solely concerned with the affairs of consumers, the Japan Consumers Union (Nihon Shōhisha Renmei) being the most well-known case in point. Similar but much smaller groups proliferated at the local level during the mid- to late-1970s as an attempt by local citizens to solve consumer-related problems resulting from the 1973 oil shock. From a national perspective, however, the movement continues to be dominated by the housewives' organizations and the consumer cooperatives.

shō means "to extinguish," while *hi* connotes "waste." In the context of a political-economic system that was struggling to catch up both economically and militarily with the West, it was difficult to legitimize the interests of the *shōhisha* – literally, "one who extinguishes and wastes."

In the immediate aftermath of the war, use of the term "consumer" as a category of individuals in their consuming and, by logical extension, nonproductive capacities struck many activists as particularly inappropriate in the context of sweeping economic destruction. Recognizing that Japanese citizens were struggling with economic adversity not only as consumers, but also as farmers, laborers, and small businesspeople, many activists in the Movement to Defend Livelihoods stood up on behalf of *all* these groups against governmental negligence and the harmful activities of big business (Maclachlan 2002: 79–80).

To avoid some of the controversies inherent in the concept of *shōhisha*, newly formed consumer cooperatives labeled themselves *seikatsu kyōdō kumiai* (lifestyle cooperative unions, or *seikyō*, for short). The term *seikatsu* (lifestyle, livelihood) appealed to many co-op organizers in part because it legitimized membership by representatives from the agricultural and fisheries cooperatives, organizations that one would normally associate with producer interests. The incorporation of both producer and consumer interests under a single organizational banner was greeted warmly by activists elsewhere in the nascent consumer movement, including Oku Mumeo, a leading member of the prewar feminist, labor, and cooperative movements and the founder of Shufuren (see Oku 1988: 167).

The activities of the consumer cooperativists are just one manifestation of a growing willingness on the part of consumer activists more generally to ally with other downtrodden groups in society in opposition to big business interests and their government allies, who were the perceived perpetrators of inflation, the black market, a dysfunctional rationing system, and other examples of economic inefficiency that proved harmful to citizen livelihoods. Indeed, the early postwar period is peppered with instances of cooperation between consumer activists and small firms, labor unions, and the fisheries and agricultural cooperatives in support of objectives designed to raise general living standards. In some cases, as we see below, activists were even willing to cooperate with governmental officials at both the local and national levels when the situation warranted it.

These examples suggest that Japan's early postwar consumer activists were assuming a far more holistic view of the role of consumers within the political economy than has been common in the more confrontational political cultures of the United States and other Western countries. Indeed, if the objectives and alliances pursued by the movement are any indication, these early activists were fashioning a kind of consumer gestalt that situated the consumer within a nexus of interdependent identities that in turn characterized the individual in his or her efforts to build a meaningful and sustainable lifestyle or livelihood. According to this line of thinking, an individual is at once: (1) a human being in pursuit of survival and well-being, (2) a worker or small producer (or the spouse or dependent of a worker or producer), (3) a consumer who purchases and consumes goods and services in the marketplace, (4) a citizen of a particular country (*kokumin*), or "nationalist," and, finally, (5) a citizen (*shimin*) of civil society (*shimin shakai*) (see Shimizu 1994: 15–16). In many ways, these categories are mutually reinforcing: one must consume in order to survive and produce or work (or obtain sustenance from someone who does) in order to consume. Needless to say, conflict is also inherent among these identities. The protection of one's position as a producer, for instance, may prove detrimental to one's consumer identity, and vice versa. Meanwhile, promotion of the consumer's preference for competitively priced products conflicts with one's interest as a Japanese nationalist (*kokumin*) in shielding the economy from foreign imports – an economic specter that in turn jeopardizes access by the "human-being-as-survivor" to an indigenous and hence reliable source of rice and other food staples.[9] By recognizing the integral interrelationships among these identities, the consumer gestalt stressed the need for balance among them (Maclachlan 2002: 80).

This emerging consumer identity, which enveloped the concept of consumer within a broad web of interdependent sociopolitical relationships, symbolizes an important difference between the Japanese and American consumer movements. During the heyday of the U.S. consumer movement, the consumer-as-citizen and producer identities were manufactured as almost polar opposites by consumer advocates intent on distinguishing themselves from producers in their quest for enhanced consumer protection (Maclachlan 2002: 81). This conceptualization made sense in the United States in the 1960s and early 1970s, where civil society was based on an adversarial culture and a deeply entrenched respect for individual rights within the population at large and where an affluent economy had produced no pressing need for consumers to defer to the interests of producers for the sake of overall economic growth. It would not have made much sense in early postwar Japan, however, where a consensus-oriented, assimilative political culture still held sway and where the severe economic conditions of the period had created a moral imperative for otherwise conflicting socioeconomic groups to cooperate with one another, sometimes in deference to producer interests. Finally, manufacturing consumers and producers as polar opposites did not mesh well with the fact that the vast majority of consumer activists in early postwar Japan were not sophisticated public-interest lawyers, but rather housewives married to workers or producers who needed to strike a workable balance between the interests of consumption and production for the sake of long-term family survival. Thus, the early postwar consumer gestalt was a distinctly Japanese conceptualization that embraced not only the newly granted rights and freedoms of democratic citizenship, but also the need for compromise between the assertion of those rights and freedoms and the subordination of individual interests to the pressing social and economic imperatives of the times.

[9] The postwar consumer movement's support for national self-sufficiency in the production of rice is largely a product of the movement's establishment in the context of postwar economic destruction and extreme food shortages. Interestingly, the contemporary British movement has been a staunch supporter of agricultural liberalization. This may be attributable to the fact that it experienced its most formative moment during the mid- to late-1950s and beyond – a period of relative economic affluence.

As such, the consumer *gestalt* of the early postwar period can be compared to the concept of *seikatsusha*[10] that was popularized by the Seikatsu Kurabu Seikyō, a network of local consumer cooperatives launched during the 1960s (see Amano 1996; LeBlanc 1999). According to Seikatsu Club usage, the *seikatsusha* is both a consumer/worker and an autonomous, proactive citizen (*shimin*). In the context of early postwar economic stagnation, by contrast, the term was used in popular discourse to denote the individual in his or her preoccupation with such scarce resources as food, clothing, and shelter (Amano 1996: 58) – the main focus of consumer activism during this period and one of the key dimensions of the consumer's multifaceted identity as defined by movement activists. Although many consumer activists used the term *seikatsusha* in their own conversations, the concept did not yet embrace the multifaceted identities that were part and parcel of the consumer gestalt. These observations notwithstanding, because the consumer gestalt can be viewed as an early postwar prototype of the *seikatsusha* concept used by contemporary consumer activists, for the purposes of analytical simplicity, I henceforth refer to it as the "early *seikatsusha* identity."

The Movement's Tactical Repertoire and Relations with the State

The consumer movement's holistic conceptualization of the consumer identity both reflected and legitimized a distinctive tactical repertoire within the emerging consumer movement that combined various forms of protest against state and market actors with selective cooperation with those actors.

In early postwar Japan, the extrainstitutional tactic of protest was rendered all but necessary by a political system that, despite the recent introduction of democratic principles, excluded the routinized representation of consumer voices beyond the ballot box. Rarely, however, did protest become violent, as it was wont to do during the student uprisings of the 1960s and, to a lesser extent, within the environmental citizens' movement. Generally speaking, protest consisted of boisterous but peaceful demonstrations in public places, product boycotts, face-to-face confrontations with recalcitrant businesspeople and local (and sometimes national) governmental officials, and, in the context of the latter, the "moral suasion" of businesspeople and governmental officials who had failed to fulfill their social obligations (see Garon 1997). In many ways, this tactical repertoire was akin to that of the disenfranchised Japanese of the prewar period. It was to persist, moreover, until 1968, when enactment of the Consumer Protection Basic Law led to the introduction of a comprehensive system of consumer protection policy making and administration that accorded activists more routinized access to the policy process.

Although consumers were quick to protest in the face of blatant abuses of the consumer dimension of the *seikatsusha* identity, they were equally prone to cooperate with their business and state adversaries in support of common goals, a practice that was almost unheard of during the heyday of American consumer activism. Shortly after the war, for instance, the predecessor to the Kansai Shufuren

[10] For a comprehensive history of the term *seikatsusha*, see Amano (1996).

joined forces with the regional branches of the Price Agency (Bukkachō) and the Economic Stabilization Board (Keizai Antei Honbu) and two labor federations in order to combat price gouging and the myriad ill effects of the black market (Kokumin Seikatsu Sentaa 1997: 18). Although short-lived, the alliance had the blessing of the Occupation. In Tokyo, meanwhile, Shufuren activists allied with the owners of public bathhouses on behalf of a public health objective: educating consumers about proper bathing hygiene. Through direct confrontation and advertising campaigns, these and countless other campaigns often succeeded in pressuring business into curbing their opprobrious commercial practices and citizens into fulfilling their potential as responsible consumers (see Maclachlan 2002: 76–77).

A more controversial example of cooperation between consumer groups and state and business authorities was the so-called New Life Movement (Shin Seikatsu Undō),[11] a state-sponsored "grassroots" movement that included participation by *fujinkai*, Chifuren (The National Federation of Regional Women's Organizations),[12] Shufuren, and, to a lesser extent, the consumer cooperatives. Although the specific themes of the movement varied from region to region, the ultimate aim as eventually envisioned by governmental authorities was the promotion of modernization through the "free" association of citizens at the local level, an end to the hold of tradition on the lives of individuals within the household and local community and at election time, and the encouragement of a strong work ethic (Nihon Hōsō Shuppan Kyōkai 1980: 45; see also Garon 1997).

Consumer-related groups were most conspicuous in New Life Movement campaigns that addressed indigenous movement goals, such as efforts to improve access to quality food, clothing, and housing and to teach women about modern household accounting and child-rearing methods. There were even joint public health programs to curb the incidence of disease by reducing the production of household garbage and eliminating flies and mosquitoes in local communities (*Shufuren dayori*, August 1955, p. 1). Many of the local organizations that cooperated with state and business representatives in support of such goals eventually grew into bureaucratic appendages of local governments; the housewives' organizations, on the other hand, were able to keep the state at a distance. On several occasions, moreover, the housewives' organizations managed to use these campaigns as opportunities to promote pet projects that were not directly related to the New Life Movement, such as the push for more female politicians at the local and national levels (*Shufuren dayori*, June 1955, p. 1).

The diverse experiences of consumer groups within the New Life Movement were representative of the early postwar movement's relationship with business and state authorities more generally. In keeping with the principles of cooperation and compromise that were implicit within the early *seikatsusha* identity and as a result of their lack of routinized representation within political and business circles, consumer groups were quick to cooperate with business and governmental

[11] For a historical analysis of the New Life Movement, see Garon (1997).

[12] Formed in 1952, Chifuren serves as an umbrella organization for local *fujinkai* (women's groups). For a history of the *fujinkai*, see Kobayashi (1995a, 1995b) and Garon (1997).

authorities when their interests overlapped. At the same time, however, a significant number of consumer groups were equally willing to put those actors on the political defensive when those interests worked at cross-purposes to one another (Maclachlan 2002: 77).

The question that then arises is: Why would consumer representatives cooperate with governmental authorities *at all* given the potential impact of such cooperation on their reputation as independent representatives of the nonstate, nonmarket sector? One possible explanation is that consumer organizations felt morally obligated to do so by a state that was purportedly acting in the best interests of the "people's economy" (*kokumin keizai*). Although there is certainly some validity to this argument, it does not explain why some consumer groups cooperated with the state while others did not and why those that did cooperate often did so very selectively. A more convincing explanation is that cooperation served several legitimizing functions for movement activists in a country where democratic customs and institutions are still relatively new and where a traditional penchant for obedience to authority and lingering public distrust of protest has rendered the extrainstitutional activities of citizen-based groups somewhat suspect. Even more compelling is the fact that cooperation often provided consumer groups with scarce financial resources. This explains why the consumer cooperatives, which have historically been the most financially well-endowed consumer organizations, cooperated with state and business actors far less frequently than the less fortunate housewives' organizations (Maclachlan 2002: 78).

Partial dependence on governmental coffers in turn compelled the housewives' organizations – particularly the conservative Chifuren – to tone down some of their political rhetoric to make it more palatable to governmental authorities. Many of the small consumer groups at the local level that had virtually no financial resources of their own, meanwhile, grew so dependent on local governmental largesse that they completely lost their organizational independence. I would not, however, go so far as to argue that the housewives' organizations have been subjected to this fate. Activists in those organizations are determined not to sacrifice their organizational integrity to state control, and they continue to protest vociferously against governmental authorities when they feel the consumer (or *seikatsusha*) interest has been violated.

These observations suggest that the emerging consumer gestalt served as a cultural "frame" for movement activism that reflected not only the social and economic needs of the times, but also some of the more practical financial and political challenges faced by the country's newly formed citizens' groups as they struggled to improve the lot of Japanese consumers. Selective cooperation continues today. Over the past twenty years or so, for example, consumer groups have allied with small retailers in support of the Large Scale Retail Store Law and in opposition to the introduction of the controversial consumption tax. They have also continued to ally with rice farmers in support of agricultural protectionism, which is perhaps the most conspicuous manifestation of the nationalist dimension of the *seikatsusha* identity. As the next section shows, however, activists have also been increasingly willing since the 1960s to resort to conflict with those allies on behalf of the consumer and citizen (*shimin*) dimensions of that identity.

The High-Growth Era

The high-growth era (1955–73) witnessed a proliferation of social movement types. In many cases, those movements embraced a style of political activism that involved aggressive confrontation with business and state representatives in a confrontational and "accusatory" manner (*kokuhatsugata*). A few of those movements were profoundly ideological in orientation. The Citizen's Alliance for Peace in Vietnam (*Betonamu ni Heiwa o! Shimin Rengō*, or Beheiren), for instance, resorted to mass demonstrations and other forms of protest in opposition to the U.S. presence in Vietnam and the principles of the U.S.-Japan Mutual Security Treaty, while the student movement of the late 1960s called into question the very principles of the postwar political economy, including rapid growth and consumerism (Soranaka et al. 1991: 186; see also Krauss 1974). Another example of ideology-based activism that erupted onto the political scene toward the end of the 1970s was opposition to the construction of Narita Airport by local farmers and their radical student supporters. As Apter and Sawa (1984) showed, the often violent antiairport demonstrations can be characterized as a confrontation between a progrowth, forward-looking state, on the one hand, and local residents seeking to preserve a more traditional way of life, on the other.

Most of the *kokuhatsugata* social movements that appeared during the high-growth era, however, were opposed to the negative side-effects of rapid economic growth rather than to economic development per se, and were interested in strengthening the quality of life and political rights of average Japanese citizens rather than advancing some particular ideological agenda. Examples of such movements included, of course, the well-documented environmental citizens' movements (see, e.g., McKean 1981; Broadbent 1998), campaigns against the development of nuclear energy (Hasegawa 1991), and opposition to Shinkansen expansion (Groth 1996). The proliferation of consumer groups – both advocacy and grassroots groups – during the 1960s and 1970s was also a reflection of this phenomenon.

In addition to "making claims" on governmental decision makers in support of more citizen-friendly public policies, consumer groups, as well as other nonideological *kokuhatsugata* social movement groups, were also determined to reform the way in which those policies were made. Within the more grassroots-oriented branches of the movement, consumer groups conveyed their opposition to the reigning decision-making customs of the day through the force of example. In keeping with the principles of new social movements that were proliferating in the West at this time, for example, they eschewed hierarchical bureaucratic structures and promoted democratic decision-making norms among rank-and-file members. Advocacy organizations within the movement, including Shufuren, Chifuren, Shōdanren,[13] and Seikyōren,[14] proved less capable of adhering to

[13] The Nihon Shōhisha Dantai Renrakukai (The National Liaison Committee of Consumer Organizations) was established in 1956 as a national umbrella committee of consumer organizations interested in influencing national public policy. The organization has led many of the issue-specific political campaigns of the postwar consumer movement.

[14] The Nihon Seikatsu Kyōdō Kumiai Rengōkai (Japan Consumer Cooperatives Union) is the nonpartisan national umbrella organization and foremost political representative of the Japanese cooperative movement.

such organizational principles because their focus on influencing policy making and close association with state representatives over time contributed to the professionalization of consumer activists, the bureaucratization of movement organizations, and a growing gap between leaders and rank-and-file members. For these groups, opposition to the government's exclusionary decision-making norms was conveyed through both protest and more conventional lobbying tactics. For guidance on how to carry out those tactics, some of these groups looked to the experiences of Ralph Nader in the United States.[15]

No matter what their organizational characteristics, many consumer groups, like their environmental counterparts (see McKean 1981: 5), served as mechanisms for the assertion of democratic principles from the grassroots level to the state. More specifically, these groups lent new meaning to the *shimin* dimension of the early *seikatsusha* identity by constantly asserting that citizens are autonomous individuals with certain rights and responsibilities that should be pursued in the political sphere (Soranaka et al. 1991: 185). At the same time, they served as important mechanisms for the education of Japanese citizens about those rights and responsibilities. These points demand further scrutiny given their implications for Japanese civil society.

The **Shimin** *and the Notion of Individual and Consumer Rights*

In the words of one Japanese scholar, a *shimin* can be defined as an "autonomous human being who, ideally, embodies the republican spirit of freedom and equality" (Matsushita 1978: 173). Integral to the notion of *shimin* among both consumer activists and their allies in the legal community[16] is the notion of individual rights: powers or privileges that are vested in the individual and, ideally in the case of rights in the political-economic sphere, that are protected by law. Many Japanese social movement activists believe that without rights (*kenri*), individuals cannot be autonomous, free, or equal. Without rights, in other words, *shimin* cannot exist; and without *shimin*, there can be no civil society.

Japanese consumer activists also believe in the inviolability of consumer rights (*shōhisha no kenri*). Since 1962, when President John F. Kennedy delivered a

[15] Since the late 1960s, Ralph Nader has served as a model consumer advocate for a small number of advocacy groups within the Japanese consumer movement and has also informally advised some of those groups. It is important to note, however, that while the Japanese movement has learned a great deal from the experiences of foreign consumer movements, international trends in the consumer realm had virtually no impact on the movement before the late 1960s. Today, a handful of consumer groups at the national level belongs to and participates in the so-called Consumers' International (known until recently as the International Organization of Consumer Unions), an international network of consumer groups that coordinates movement policies on global consumer trends, consumer rights, the impact of national economic policies on foreign consumer populations, and comparable issues. Aside from these links and a commitment to ally more closely with international consumer groups, the Japanese consumer movement has developed primarily in response to indigenous historical and economic trends and remains largely nationalist, as opposed to internationalist, in scope.

[16] In contrast to the United States, the sphere of consumer law is well represented within Japanese universities. Consumer activists often work closely with scholars in this field in support of consumer protection legislation.

speech to Congress articulating the notion of basic consumer rights, activists have consistently upheld the consumer's rights to product safety and choice, access to consumer information, representation in governmental decision making, and, more recently, redress for consumer-related damages.[17] In the United States, Britain, and Germany, acceptance of these rights within state, market, and societal circles developed relatively quickly, in large part because they had been grafted onto a preexisting awareness and acceptance of basic individual rights and responsibilities. In Japan, by contrast, where the birth of the postwar consumer movement *preceded* the entrenchment of such an awareness in society (Shōda 1989: 118), widespread acceptance of consumer rights materialized slowly, which impeded the development of the organized consumer movement as a powerful force in Japanese politics (Inaba et al. 1979: 7).

The promotion of consumer rights during a period of rapid economic growth and in a country that had not yet digested the more general notion of individual or civil rights[18] proved challenging for consumer activists. This was, after all, an era of "growth at all costs," of pro-producer policies generated by a political system that was committed to catching up economically with the West. In keeping with tradition, meanwhile, consumers were inclined to leave the resolution of consumer problems to governmental authorities (*okami ni makaseru*) or to passively "cry themselves to sleep" (*nakineiri suru*) as mere victims of producer-instigated abuse. As might be expected, these habits were hard to break for those who had been educated under the yoke of prewar authoritarianism (Maclachlan 2002: 103).

These challenges were further complicated by a distinctive conceptualization of governmental responsibility vis-à-vis consumer protection. In many Western countries, governments assume the role of guarantor or caretaker of consumer rights that are vested in the individual and that entitle consumers to legal redress on demand. In Japan, by contrast, the task of protecting consumers from the negative side-effects of production during the rapid growth period was approached primarily as an obligation of a paternalistic government. The implications of this tendency were at least twofold. First, it cast doubt on the legitimacy of consumer activists' taking political issues into their own hands when those issues were widely perceived as falling under the purview of an experienced and benevolent state. Second, although the state was certainly beholden to fulfill its obligations in those few consumer-related areas that were defined by law, the absence of legally – or even socially – entrenched consumer rights gave it the upper hand when dealing with consumer issues that had yet to be formally defined. In those cases, the state, in its preoccupation with economic growth, tended to champion the interests of producers over those of consumers (Maclachlan 2002: 103). The end result of this

[17] In keeping with international trends, advocates nowadays also endorse the rights to consumer education and to a clean and safe natural environment, among others.

[18] Indeed, Japan lacks an indigenous equivalent to the concept of "right." According to Koschmann, the term *kenri* (right) was invented at the end of the Tokugawa period (1603–1867) to correspond to the Dutch notion of *regt* (Koschmann 1978: 15).

state of affairs was a self-perpetuating cycle of irresponsibility in the consumer realm.

Breaking that cycle has been one of the key objectives of consumer activists. To accomplish that objective, advocates became not only representatives of the "consumer interest" within state decision-making processes, but also vehicles for the dissemination and articulation of the concept of "citizenship" – the weakest link of the early *seikatsusha* identity. Accordingly, education about consumer rights in particular and individual political rights more broadly became one of the most important responsibilities shouldered by consumer groups during the high-growth era and beyond (Kimoto 1986: 35). To that end, activists in some of the more politically independent groups put great store in the cultivation of "active consumers" (*kōdōsuru shōhisha*) (ibid.: 45), that is to say, consumers who were willing to stand up on behalf of their interests and exercise their rights as both consumers *and* citizens. This task was carried out not only through the dissemination of movement literature, but also via product boycotts, street demonstrations, and petition drives. Throughout the various stages of legislative campaigns, moreover, advocates devoted considerable attention to "issue definition" (*mondai teigi*), the task of publicly defining consumer-related issues in relation to consumer rights (Maclachlan 2002: 127). This process of educating consumers about their rights and responsibilities involved much more than just disseminating information to the attentive public. It was, in many instances, a politically contentious undertaking that involved open defiance of both business practices and governmental policies (Maclachlan 2002: 102).

Consumer Protection Law at the National and Local Levels

By cultivating "active consumers" who were willing and able to assert their individual and consumer rights vis-à-vis state and market actors, activists hoped to institutionalize consumer rights within the political and legal frameworks of both the national and local levels of government. Their record on this score, however, has varied markedly according to level of government.

At the national level, there are virtually no national laws of any significance that clearly stipulate the individual's *right* to consumer protection. The 1968 Consumer Protection Basic Law (*Shōhisha hogo kihon hō*), the so-called constitution of Japanese consumer protection, strives to "secure the stability and improvement of consumer lifestyles" by defining the responsibilities of the state, localities, business enterprises, and consumers themselves toward the "interests" of consumers (Keizai Kikakuchō and Kokumin Seikatsu Kyoku 1999: 154), but it makes no mention of consumer rights. This feature of the law reflects the power of business interests within government decision-making circles and has been the focus of a great deal of criticism from both consumer activists and scholars of consumer law.

The nature of the Consumer Protection Basic Law has had profound implications for the representation of consumer society within the national consumer protection policy-making process. As I have shown elsewhere, consumer representatives frequently sit on ministerial advisory councils (*shingikai*) that deliberate on consumer policy, but that presence is largely symbolic in scope (Maclachlan 2002: 121–22). In keeping with a close government-business relationship that places a heavy premium on the generation of pro-producer policies and with the government's approach to consumer protection as a responsibility of the state rather than a right of individual consumers, the various rules and operating procedures that govern the consumer policy process often exclude meaningful participation by citizen representatives. In many cases, the results are consumer policies that go to great lengths to shield producers from the negative side-effects of consumer protection and, in the process, perpetuate the consumer's long-standing dependence on governmental initiatives.

Japan's 1994 Products Liability Law serves as an illustrative case in point (see Maclachlan 1999). Although the law fails to specify the consumer's *rights* to product safety and consumer redress, it nevertheless improves consumer access to both by institutionalizing the concept of strict liability, which lessens the burden of proof shouldered by the victims of defective products, and providing economic and legal incentives for producers to manufacture safer products. The trouble with the new products liability regime is the extensive network of low-cost alternative dispute resolution (ADR) facilities that were either established or expanded by the government after 1994. Situated within the bureaucracy and the business sector, these facilities, which are closed to public scrutiny, are staffed in part by bureaucrats and businesspeople whose neutrality is open to question. By deflecting products liability cases away from the courts – the ultimate arbiter of consumer rights, some might argue – and into the cloistered confines of the bureaucracy and the business community, this system subjects the protection of "consumer rights" to the decision-making discretion of pro-producer (or potentially pro-producer) interests. Consumers may be much better off in terms of access to safer products and more efficient redress procedures under the new system, but their long-standing dependence on state and, to a lesser extent, market interests for consumer protection remains intact. As might be expected, the system has been the target of criticism from consumer advocates.

While consumer representatives have had a tough time carving out an independent political niche for themselves and their constituents at the national level, they have made significant headway in this regard at the local level. Indeed, consumer rights have not only been championed by local officials and politicians, they have, in many cases, been legally entrenched through the enactment of local ordinances. The 1975 Tokyo Consumer Ordinance, for instance, initially specified five consumer rights, and a sixth was added in the amendments of 1994. This official recognition of consumer rights mirrors a level of direct consumer participation in local political affairs that distinguishes localities from the national policy-making system. Representatives in Tokyo, Hyōgo, Ōsaka, Hokkaidō, and Kanagawa prefectures, to list just a few, are frequently consulted by prefectural officials on important consumer-related policies and are active and *equal* participants in local *shingikai* deliberations, which, it should be noted, have long been open to the public. Consumer advocates who have sat on these committees and dealt with local policy makers on a regular basis view their experiences in a relatively favorable light, noting that in many instances their contributions have made a significant difference in the local policy process.[19] One would be hard-pressed to find this level of satisfaction with the structure of citizen participation in national policy making.

These almost radical differences in the relationship between the organized consumer movement and governmental officials at the national and local levels can be explained with reference to both the history of party politics and the specific policy objectives of those two levels. Although party politics at the national level have, until recently at least, been characterized by close cooperation between the conservative Liberal Democratic Party (LDP) and well-organized producer and agricultural interests in support of policies that benefit those groups, party politics in many localities since the late 1960s and early 1970s have been far more fluid and eclectic. Following the spread of environmental pollution during the 1960s and the resulting rise of progressive local governments (see McKean 1981; Broadbent 1998), many of those governments actively encouraged dialogue with local residents and routinized citizen participation in local affairs. Together, these moves entailed a repudiation of the kinds of elitist, bureaucratic politics that had long characterized decision making at the center (Matsushita 1978: 172). For consumer activists, they opened an unprecendented window of opportunity both to assert the *shimin* dimension of the *seikatsusha* identity and, in the process, to press for the recognition of consumer rights. As a result of these divergent political trends, the lion's share of consumer movement activism since the enactment of the Consumer Protection Basic Law has been local in orientation.[20]

Recent Developments

As consumer activists themselves are often quick to acknowledge, the dual nature of Japan's consumer society is currently showing significant signs of change. At the heart of those changes is the end of one-party dominance in 1993 and the increasing fragmentation of the institutional, policy, and socioeconomic context of Japanese politics (see Pempel 1998: 167). These developments in turn helped spark a number of legal and institutional changes at the national level that have had a significant impact on both consumer society and the representation of consumer interests in politics.

Not all of these changes have been popular among movement advocates. The movement toward deregulation, for instance, was viewed with nothing short of apprehension. Since the early 1980s, when the central government first began to toy with the notion of deregulation, and particularly after 1993, when the pace of reform accelerated, numerous advocates opposed the process for fear that it would

[19] Interviews, consumer activists, 1992–94, December 1997, and July 1998.

[20] Consumer activists have used their inroads into the local policy process not only to influence local consumer protection programs, but also to influence policy-making trends at the national level. For more on these political dynamics, see Maclachlan (2002).

directly expose consumers to the negative side-effects of business activities. Advocates were not championing continued dependence on governmental deregulation for its own sake. On the contrary, many supported deregulation provided it was accompanied by civil law protections of consumer access to safe products, redress, and the like.[21] More specifically, advocates wanted to see the entrenchment of basic consumer rights in consumer protection law as the consumer's primary safeguard in a deregulated economy. Now that some of those demands have been met, many advocates have softened their opposition to deregulation.[22]

Their trepidation notwithstanding, advocates have reason to be optimistic about other manifestations of governmental reform. For starters, the strong government-business relationship at the national level that stifled consumer voices in the past has weakened. As a result, post-1993 governments have paid considerably more attention to broad consumer needs than in the past. For parties other than the LDP, sympathy for the consumer appeared to reflect, to varying degrees, a bona fide policy preference. For the LDP, increased attention to the consumer interest can be attributed to electoral uncertainty, the party's tenuous presence in the Diet, and the concomitant need to cooperate more closely with other political parties (Maclachlan 2002: 253). No matter what their origins, these policy shifts have been enthusiastically welcomed by consumer activists.

The erosion of many of the political alliances of the conservative era has also led to a series of small changes within the institutional context of consumer protection policy making. First, politicians have become significantly more accessible to nonbusiness lobbyists as the parties – including the LDP – pay more attention to the wishes of average Japanese citizens. Second, starting in 1995, the veil of secrecy shrouding national *shingikai* proceedings has been gradually lifted. Members of the public can now apply to attend many of those proceedings, and *shingikai* documents are now more open to public perusal than ever before. Third, many ministries have introduced the so-called Public Comment system, a procedure that allows average citizens to voice their opinions on specific policy issues to relevant bureaucratic organs over the Internet. Although officials are by no means obligated to act on that feedback, the system facilitates citizen-state dialogue on policy-related matters (Maclachlan 2002: 244–46).

One of the most important developments for consumers in particular and the relationship between civil society and the state more generally has been the May 1999 enactment of the Information Disclosure Law (see Maclachlan 2000). Implemented in 2001, the law subjects all forms of bureaucratic information, with a few notable exceptions, to disclosure. What is particularly significant about the law is the fact that it encourages greater levels of accountability by a bureaucracy

[21] Interviews with representatives of Shōkaren (Consumption Science Federation), Shufuren, Shōdanren, and the consumer cooperatives, December 1997 and June–July 1999. Concern about the negative side-effects of deregulation was one of the main motivating forces behind the organization's push for products liability legislation.

[22] These safeguards include the Products Liability Law (1999) and the Consumer Contracts Law (2000). Neither of these laws openly acknowledges the existence of consumer rights, however.

that has long been notorious for hoarding information. In theory, at least, this is an empowering development not only for consumer advocates, but also for Japanese citizens more generally.

Together, these institutional changes have enhanced the leverage of consumer groups over the agenda-setting and formulation stages of the policy process. For example, activists played a significant role in the recent strengthening of laws regulating payment plans based on installments (*Wappu hanbai hō*) and door-to-door sales practices (*Hōmon hanbai hō*). The impact of "citizen power" in the 1990s is even more tellingly illustrated by the legislative process surrounding the enactment of the Information Disclosure Law. Since 1993, networks of consumer and citizen groups helped elevate the issue onto the national political agenda by filing for information pertaining to corrupt bureaucratic practices under local disclosure ordinances, testing the redress mechanisms of local governments when their requests were refused, and even resorting to the courts. Over time, their campaign heightened the public's awareness of governmental corruption, the lack of governmental disclosure, and the need for more comprehensive disclosure rules at *both* the national and local levels. In response to intense media and public pressure, the LDP finally presided over the enactment of the law in the spring of 1999. Widely hailed as a rare piece of "citizen legislation," the law meets many of the demands of consumer and citizen advocates and, in an interesting and surprising twist, actually surpasses many of the disclosure standards set by prefectural and city ordinances (Maclachlan 2000).

The disclosure case is also a noteworthy illustration of qualitative changes not only within the consumer movement, but also within civil society more broadly. Whereas in the past most consumer-related legislative campaigns were spear-headed by national consumer advocacy organizations, the disclosure movement was in many ways a bottom-up affair led by highly politicized grassroots consumer and human rights groups. It also appears that many of these grassroots groups consisted not of the middle-aged or elderly housewives who have played such an important role in the national advocacy groups, but rather young women *and* men, many of them college students (Maclachlan 2000). The implications of the disclosure case are at least twofold. First, it suggests that as the context of national politics changes and many of the country's most glaring economic and consumer problems have been solved, the consumer movement is expanding qualitatively to embrace issues pertaining not only to consumer protection per se, but also to good governance and, by logical extension, enhanced citizen participation in national politics. In the parlance of the movement itself, activists are placing more emphasis on the *shimin* dimension of the *seikatsusha* identity than ever before and, in the process, are willing to assume a much more combative stance vis-à-vis governmental officials.

Second, it is very likely that we are now experiencing the demise of advocacy consumer politics and the beginning of a more mass-based approach to consumer participation in national politics. Although these developments do not bode well for the future of the housewives' organizations, consumer cooperatives, and political umbrella groups that have led the movement at the national level in the past, these organizations can certainly find solace in the fact that their decline is in and of itself a sign of ultimate movement success. Put simply, the upsurge of grassroots citizen initiatives vis-à-vis both the localities and the national government can be interpreted as a clear sign that the movement has made considerable headway in instilling a deeper awareness of individual and consumer rights within the public at large (Maclachlan 2002: 253). Consumers, in other words, are growing far more independent and assertive in their relations with national governmental actors – so much so, in fact, that the gap between the local and national dimensions of consumer society may finally be closing.

Conclusion

The evolving history of the postwar consumer movement serves as a revealing example of citizen activism as both cause and reflection of Japan's ever-changing civil society. During the early postwar period, as we have seen, the movement exploded onto the political scene as a direct result of the introduction of basic democratic rights and freedoms by the Occupation authorities. In an interesting twist of historical fate, consumer activists assumed a surprisingly cooperative stance toward many of their theoretical adversaries in response to the unique political, social, and economic circumstances of the era – a stance that became embodied intellectually in a distinctive consumer gestalt propounded by movement activists. As the pro-producer policies of the rapid-growth period assumed a preeminent position in national politics, however, many groups within the movement eschewed cooperation in favor of a more combative stance toward state and market actors, while simultaneously encouraging consumers to fulfil their potential as autonomous citizens. Over time, the institutional context of Japanese politics helped shape the development of a dual structure within consumer society, one marked by passive dependence on governmental initiatives at the national level and a more active and independent stance at the local level.

Thanks, in part, to the relentless efforts of consumer activists to deepen awareness of individual and consumer rights within the public and to arouse a greater level of political activism among consumers as citizens, there are now signs that the national government is becoming more receptive to an independent and assertive consumer society. Against this backdrop, the citizenship dimension of the *seikatsusha* identity is as strong as ever, but in response to a different set of political and economic circumstances. Consumers are much better off politically and economically than they were even twenty-five years ago and, consequently, seem more willing to broaden the scope of their activism to include not only consumer protection narrowly defined, but also issues of good governance. If we accept the premise that the consumer movement is a manifestation of civil society, then these developments can only bode well for the strengthening of Japanese civil society in the years to come.

IV

STATE-CIVIL SOCIETY LINKAGES

11

Mobilizing and Demobilizing the Japanese Public Sphere: Mass Media and the Internet in Japan

Laurie Freeman

As long as in the public sphere the mass media prefer . . . to draw their material from powerful, well-organized information producers, and as long as they prefer media strategies that lower rather than raise the discursive level of public communication, issues will tend to start in, and be managed from, the center, rather than follow a spontaneous course originating in the periphery.

Jürgen Habermas (1998: 380)

In a recent theoretical tome examining the relationship between law and democracy, Jürgen Habermas (1998) suggests that it is possible to evaluate the quality of a democracy on the basis of the extent to which *formal* institutions of deliberation and decision making (such as the parliament and ministries) are open to input from *informal* public spheres. For Habermas (1998: 359), the political public sphere is an important discursive component of civil society that acts as a "sounding board for problems that must be processed by the political system because they cannot be solved elsewhere." While Nancy Fraser (1992: 110) has described the public sphere as "a theater . . . in which political participation is enacted through the medium of talk," Habermas (1998: 359) reminds us that, as a discursive realm, the public sphere should not just amplify the pressure of problems in society, but must also "convincingly and *influentially* thematize them, furnish them with possible solutions and dramatize them in such a way that they are taken up and dealt with by parliamentary complexes" (italics in the original; underlining added).[1] In Habermas's view (1998: 373), the concepts of the "political public sphere" and "civil society" are not mere normative postulates; they have empirical relevance.[2]

[1] It is noteworthy that these functions closely resemble the normative roles that another, related component of civil society – the mass media – ascribe to themselves.

[2] Habermas (1998: 366) provides the following definition: "Civil society is composed of those more or less spontaneously emergent associations, organizations and movements that, attuned to how societal problems resonate in the private life spheres, distill and transmit such reactions in amplified

Indeed, one of the great contributions of the idea of a public sphere, as Michael Schudson (1992: 147) has noted, is that "it insists that an ideal democratic polity be defined by features beyond those that formally enable political participation. It is not only the fact of political involvement but its quality that the concept of the public sphere evokes. . . . The more people participate as citizens in politics, the closer one comes to the ideal of a public sphere."

Many observers (e.g., Pharr and Krauss 1996; Garon 1997; Machlachlan, this volume) have argued that in both qualitative and quantitative terms, Japan falls short of this theoretical ideal. Throughout the postwar period, public communication and the public sphere have been largely demobilized and denatured; Japanese civil society has only infrequently exhibited the level of vitality that Habermas (1989, 1998: 352) and others have suggested is necessary for bringing conflicts from the periphery to the center of the political system. While there is no denying that Japan has seen periods of civil activism, including the environmental and consumer movements of the 1960s and other more recent examples noted elsewhere in this volume, the prevailing scholarly image of Japan nevertheless remains that of a country with a strong state and a decidedly weak civil society.

Although the causes of this state of affairs are difficult to disentangle and multifarious, ranging from the historical-social to the legal-institutional, I argue that a decisive factor has been the domination and/or neglect of the public sphere by the mass media and mass media–linked state organizations. In this view, the responsibility for civic vitality lies largely (though not solely) with the *discursive* realm: for civil society to be properly mobilized, it must first have a voice and an effective means of extending that voice. The democratic mass media are presumed to be the natural allies of the public sphere, broadcasting issues discussed within it, providing it with the information needed for the cultivation of topics requiring larger deliberation, and transmitting the requisite information for making informed choices about political candidates, parties, and policies. But this view of the mass media is not entirely accurate. The reality in Japan, for example, is that the mass media have frequently worked together with, or on behalf of, the political core – capturing, subverting, misleading, or alternatively ignoring the political periphery represented by the public sphere. As a result, one finds in Japan not only limited societal inquiry into the political process but a public that no longer believes that it has the power to bring about political or social change. Ironically, this has been the case even during historically promising moments: Japan experienced its lowest voter turnout rate in the postwar period in the first election held under its new and more democratic electoral system in 1996.

Until quite recently, it was thought that the institutions responsible for the emasculation of the Japanese public sphere were so well embedded in the political core that there was little civil society could do to unseat them. The rise of the Internet, however, suggests an alternative mechanism through which civil society and the

form to the public sphere. The core of civil society comprises a network of associations that institutes problem-solving discourses on questions of general interest inside the framework of organized public spheres. . . ."

public sphere might independently be able to influence the political process, supplementing rather than supplanting the traditional relationships and procedures of the mass media and the state. Whether, and in what contexts, the Japanese public uses this potential and what impact resultant political discussions and other Internet-aided behavior may have on the larger political process are important empirical questions. I address these possibilities in the remainder of this chapter, first by examining the ways in which the mass media and mass media–linked state organizations have delimited rather than augmented the discursive realm in Japan and then by considering what possibilities the new electronic media of the Internet might serve as an alternative or parallel public sphere to the mass media– and state-dominated one.

Mass Media and the Public Sphere in Japan: An Overview

Japan has some of the highest levels of newspaper readership and television viewership in the world, but its "information society" has been characterized by a lack of diversity, and its public sphere has had only limited and occasional access to the formal decision-making apparatus of the political core. The mass media are at least partially to blame. Although Japan is considered a functioning democracy with few formal restrictions on freedom of expression, it has long operated with a media system in which access to official news sources and information has been limited to a handful of elite media outlets, notably, national newspapers and broadcasting stations that have cartel-like relations among themselves. By limiting access in this way, official sources and the mainstream media have been able to promote and benefit from the establishment of what I call "information cartels": institutionalized rules and relationships guiding press behavior with sources and with each other that serve to limit the types of news that get reported and the number and makeup of those who do the reporting. As I have argued elsewhere (Freeman 2000), three key institutions provide the underpinnings for this collaborative news-management process: the *kisha* (press) clubs, the newspaper industry *kyōkai* (trade association), and media *keiretsu* (business groups).

Most important in the cartelization process have been the press clubs. They define the basic relationship that exists between journalists and their news sources: bureaucrats, politicians, business leaders, and the police. One of the things making *kisha* clubs so powerful is their very pervasiveness: virtually all major business, local, state, and political organizations throughout Japan are covered by them. As members of press clubs, journalists from the powerful mainstream media cultivate close ties with news sources, drawing from them the material for their news stories and collectively making decisions about how this information is to be presented. The rigid rules of access and conduct established by the clubs impose powerful constraints on the impact, content, and slant of the media's messages. In assigning the lion's share of available journalists to these clubs, the large and powerful national news organizations virtually guarantee that the activities and deliberations occurring at the political periphery (e.g., within civil society and the public sphere) are all but ignored.

Helping to ensure that alternative media do not gain access to the political core are the *kyōkai* and *keiretsu*. Throughout its history, the Japan Newspaper Publishers and Editors Association (Nihon Shinbun Kyōkai, or NSK) has striven to assert exclusive access for its members to the clubs – and thereby to the news itself. It has not only kept out the foreign press (with some recent exceptions), but has also excluded other domestic media organizations, including news magazines, which are frequently the most aggressive at pursuing political anomalies. Finally, and perhaps most egregiously, it has served as the key representative for the entire industry during negotiations with important official sources when these sources have wanted to muzzle the press. A well-cited example of this occurred vis-à-vis the Imperial Household Agency during the crown prince's search for a wife in 1992. These negotiations resulted in a total ban on news reports that lasted almost an entire year.

Media groups (*keiretsu*) organized around Japan's national newspapers ensure that other news outlets, especially television broadcasting, are brought into the club system and follow its news gathering and reporting rules. Japan's core print media include five national papers: *Yomiuri*, *Asahi*, *Mainichi*, *Nikkei*, and *Sankei*, each of which is among the world's ten largest newspapers as measured by readership, with individual circulations ranging from 3 to 14 million. Combined, these papers control more than half of the total newspaper market share in Japan. Although there appear to be a number of mainstream alternatives to these dominant papers, many local newspapers and magazines maintain close financial and information ties to the national dailies. Likewise, each of the nation's five national commercial television networks (and many of its regional broadcasting stations) is also tied to a major national daily: Nippon Television Network with *Yomiuri*, Asahi National Broadcasting with *Asahi*, Tokyo Broadcasting System (albeit in a somewhat limited manner) with *Mainichi*, Television Tokyo with *Nikkei*, and Fuji Television Network with *Sankei*. Among the major broadcasters, only the "gargantuan, semiautonomous public entity" (Hall 1998: 49) of NHK retains financial independence from this industry structure, though it has its own set of limiting political and financial ties (Krauss 2000) and remains an active member of the *kisha* clubs. These media groups' substantial control over many of the alternative sources of information available to the public amplifies the impact of the relationships outlined above. By limiting the number of participants in the marketplace of ideas, the media *keiretsu* play an important role in the homogenization of views across media and among the general public.

How Japan's Media Institutions Impact the Public Sphere: Five Outcomes

The three institutional arrangements discussed here – *kisha* clubs, the newspaper *kyōkai*, and media *keiretsu* – reinforce each other in ways that have profoundly shaped the nature of news reporting in Japan, the role of the media in the Japanese political process, and the nature of its relationship with and coverage of the political public sphere. Working within this excessively cartelized media system, the mainstream media have, however unintentionally, served to lower rather than raise the level of public communication. On the basis of the writing of well-known American political leaders, Supreme Court opinions, and First Amendment scholars, Doris Graber (1986: 258) argues that the five basic functions of a democratic media are to serve as a marketplace of ideas, a source of political information, the voice of public opinion, a guardian of minority rights, and a policer of errant politicians.[3] In Japan, however, reporting is characterized by the five outcomes described below: a hyperreliance on credentialed facts, a lack of a political auditing function, a limited agenda-setting role, the marginalization of alternative sources of information, and an overall homogenization of news (Freeman 2000).

Credentialing of Facts

One important consequence of the cartelization of information in Japan is the extreme reliance on "credentialed facts," or information from official sources (Bagdikian 1987: 213). The dependence on official sources for information gives the news an aura of objectivity and makes it difficult to accuse journalists of bias. But this reliance also dissuades journalists from reporting "unofficial" facts or circumstances and from going outside the *kisha* club in search of the voices and opinions of groups on the political periphery. It also leads to an overall conservative cast to the news and a view of the world that largely mirrors that of officialdom (ibid.: 214). Although credentialed facts constitute a large proportion of political news reporting in all democratic countries, many media organizations elsewhere have rigid rules requiring journalists to balance their stories. In Japan, however, journalists are much less likely to leave the information-gathering base provided by the *kisha* club to seek out opposing viewpoints, and their editors are less likely to ask them to do so. It is not just that Japanese journalists tend to rely more heavily on official sources for information and on official versions of events. More importantly, they frequently limit themselves to a very small subset of the official sources available without attempting to provide alternative perspectives (Feldman 1993).

Weakening of the Political Auditing Function

A second consequence of Japan's information cartels is the nearly wholesale elimination of what Graber refers to as "policing" and what James March and Johan Olsen (1995: 164) have labeled the "political auditing" function of the mainstream media: the process of monitoring the powers that be against dishonesty and corruption. Political auditors – mostly the mass media, but also the courts – are supposed to serve as agents of civil society, accessing information and providing it to those who cannot be as well informed. The biggest problem these auditors face, however, is remaining independent of those whom they audit (ibid. 1996: 164). The lack of

[3] Graber (1986: 258) is skeptical about how effectively *American* media play each of these roles.

a political auditing function among the Japanese media and the Japanese judiciary has long been noted by scholars. In a detailed study of the politics of scandal, for example, Maggie Farley (1996: 149) finds that scandals are rarely uncovered by the mainstream press. In many cases, it is only after the investigative process has already been initiated by the marginalized news weeklies or the foreign press that the mainstream media pick up these stories and pursue them. In some cases, such as the 1976 Lockheed bribery scandal involving former Prime Minister Tanaka Kakuei, which was first uncovered by a newsmagazine, mainstream journalists later admitted that they had known about improprieties, but had not felt it necessary to write about them. Even when Japanese journalists follow the lead of the newsmagazines and report such stories, they frequently focus on minutiae, following stories so closely that they miss policy implications and appropriate reforms, thus reducing their potential impact (ibid.: 149). There are a number of reasons why Japanese reporters have not been effective political auditors, but loyalty bred by proximity to their sources in the *kisha* clubs is certainly one.

Limiting the Agenda-Setting Process

A third consequence of Japan's information cartels is the fundamental shift in the relationship between news makers and news organizations in the overall agenda-setting process. Even more than elsewhere, the evidence in Japan suggests that the mainstream media do not report many important details (such as the names of individuals or companies involved) when they do report major news stories or scandals. Neither do they independently set political agendas nearly as often or as forcefully as elsewhere.[4] In contrast to the recent rise in the United States of a more participatory journalism (so-called civic journalism) in which reporters are unabashed supporters of certain causes, the Japanese press still adheres to the rigid policy of "impartiality and nonpartisanship" (*fuhen futō*) that it adopted in the late nineteenth century. But this "neutrality" and "objectivity" have not given the Japanese press greater power vis-à-vis the state because nonpartisan in theory has meant progovernment in practice – in the nineteenth century and today. It was a "nonpartisan" Japanese press, for example, that failed to write forcefully about the corruption of the ruling Liberal Democratic Party (LDP), a vastly unfair electoral system, and organized crime, thereby helping to perpetuate almost four decades of LDP rule. This is not to say that the Japanese media never report or support social issues or protest movements. What is clear, however, is that this is often done *within the context of the state and not against it* (Reich 1984; Campbell 1996; Groth 1996). By showing institutionalized means of conflict resolution in a neutral light while casting opprobrium on more confrontational, grassroots activities, the mass media stifle potential action on the part of many segments of

[4] The argument that the Japanese media have not played an exceptional role as agenda setters is supported by others, including the media historian Yamamoto Taketoshi (1989), political scientists Ofer Feldman (1993) and Ellis Krauss (1996, 2000), and journalist and media critic Ivan Hall (1998).

civil society (Groth 1996: 233–34). This view of the media as important "social managers" in Japan stands in sharp contrast to their normative image as agenda setters.

Marginalizing Alternative Media

A fourth consequence of cartelization is the marginalization of the outside or "alternative" media, which are regarded as untrustworthy because they are not living in the corridors of power and do not have direct access to the all-important credentialed facts discussed above. When we speak of the "alternative" press in Japan, we are not referring to radical or leftist publications but to weekly magazines (both serious and scandalous), opinion monthlies, localized publications such as community papers, industry and "sports" papers, religious organs, "mini media" (a term used to denote the "nonmass" media, including nonregularly published, issue-based broadsheets and pamphlets), and the work of freelance journalists. All of these are excluded from the *kisha* clubs. It is important to keep in mind that much of the aggressive and adversarial reporting in Japan is found in these alternative media. If the problem of the mainstream media is an overreliance on credentialed sources, the problem of the alternative press is its insufficient access to the same.

Homogenizing News and Opinion

One final consequence of Japan's information cartels is the homogenization of news and consequently of public opinion. Observers of Japan's mainstream newspapers have frequently noted that they look pretty much the same, report pretty much the same stories, and offer up pretty much the same innocuous editorial opinions. This results in part from the way journalists in the clubs coordinate their activities, often writing stories as a group, and is encouraged by the limited opportunity for bylined stories. But the press clubs and these related features are not the sole cause of uniformity in Japan. As outlined above, the ownership and control structure of the Japanese media has also helped this along through *keiretsu* linkages among the key players.

This analysis has suggested ways in which information – and therefore political choices – have been narrowly controlled in Japan for an especially long time. The selective reporting of news and information from the political core and the simultaneous neglect of the political periphery have resulted in the creation of an informationally inferior product. People do not always get "all the news that's fit to print." Although political news and information are conveyed to the public in Japan, they are conveyed in a highly delimited fashion that narrows the range of societal inquiry into the political process. It is not simply an issue of the extent to which the mass media define the agenda of society as a whole, either. It is also important to note, especially in the Japanese case, how the state can, through its institutionalized linkages with the mass media, explicitly or implicitly define the media's agenda and in the process circumscribe – and in a very real sense lead – the discursive realm of civil society.

As long as the *kisha* clubs remain the primary mechanism for news gathering in Japan, and as long as journalists and media companies continue to draw most of their material from the credentialed sources to whom club membership gives privileged access, political and social agendas will continue to be set in the core of the political system and not in its periphery. Unless, of course, the Japanese public discontinues or reduces its singular reliance on the mainstream media for most of its information, analysis, and interpretation about its political and social world. The institutions that have largely been responsible for the demobilization of the public sphere in Japan – *kisha* clubs, the *kyōkai*, and *keiretsu* – are not likely to disappear soon. Still, recent developments in information technology suggest that there may be alternative paths for information and ideas to move between center and periphery in Japan. One potential alternative is the Internet.

Can the Internet Mobilize and Empower the Political Public Sphere in Japan?

The political potential of the Internet and other new information technologies for both democratic and authoritarian societies is that they make it possible for citizens to bypass formal political organizations, the scrutiny of government authorities, and the often predictable fare of the mainstream media to create an *unmediated* space within which information and ideas can be debated and exchanged. As Steve Case, the chair of America Online, has put it (Politics Online 1998), the Internet "offers an unprecedented opportunity to reconnect people to the political process – by helping people become more informed citizens, by helping our elected representatives to be more responsive to those citizens, and by engaging more people in public policy discussions and debate." It is precisely the unmediated nature of the Internet that gives the medium its potential as a tool for nurturing the development of the political public sphere and distinguishes it from traditional mass media.

Early studies of the political implications of the Internet conducted in a variety of countries have produced mixed results on whether this potential is being realized. Some observers, such as Nicholas Negroponte (1995), have tried to show the ways in which the Internet promotes global democracy and increases political participation. Whereas civic participation in the past was undermined by constraints on time, distribution, access, and knowledge, Negroponte (Wheeler 1997) argues, the Internet removes many of these constraints, providing "the electronic landscape for a reinvented civil society." Other observers, such as Mark Poster (1995: 42–43), have suggested that the Internet can actually retard citizenship as much as aiding it. Unlike the community gathering places that Habermas believes helped give rise to civil society in the West, he and other critics charge that the Internet is a socially isolating technology: it replaces face-to-face interaction. In addition, these skeptics argue, as it becomes increasingly commercialized, it may undergo the same kind of centralizing tendencies as traditional media: a limited number of large corporations may be allowed to frame political and social agendas on the Internet as they have in other media. As an example of this, one need look no further than Case's own AOL, which announced a merger in early 2000 with media giant Time-Warner.

We can imagine at least three broad ways in which the Internet might empower the political public sphere. First, it can be used for grassroots activism by allowing activists and volunteers – both local and global – to broadcast information about their causes, increase their memberships, and gain financial support. As an example of this, the extensive use of the Internet in the international campaign for the elimination of land mines ultimately had a direct impact on the decision-making apparatus of the political core of many nations. At the level of the nation-state, it was activist use of the Internet in the United States that largely led to the defeat of the U.S. Communications Decency Act in 1999.

Second, the Internet provides a potentially important information link between the public and government. State and local governments can use the Internet to let the public become more informed about their activities and policies and to interact with the public in the policy-making process through e-mail and other means. In the United States, community networks have been established in cities such as Santa Monica, California, and Blacksburg, Virginia, in order to give citizens more direct access to the policy-making process at the local level. State agencies everywhere have established home pages through which citizens can obtain up-to-date information about ongoing deliberations and register their opinions and complaints. Additionally, many nations, including Japan, have passed legislation to further the process and development of electronic government.

Finally, the Internet can be used as a means for individuals, groups, and candidates to carry out meaningful exchanges of information and views during election periods. Here, the Internet provides the means for individuals selectively to obtain, and candidates and parties to broadcast, information relevant to the election of representatives to legislatures. Conversely, voters can create their own sites to influence other voters' decisions. Parody sites and the creation of blacklists of unsatisfactory candidates are just two of the tools such individuals have used. Given its low cost compared with other types of media, including advertisements in traditional print and broadcast media, the Internet is also considered to be especially useful for smaller parties or marginal candidates. Some countries have even taken this a step further in allowing online voting as well. I consider each of these potential Internet functions below in the context of Japan.

Japan Online: Who Surfs?

Before detailing the ways in which information technology might serve as a means to foster alternative public spheres and increase political participation and awareness in Japan, we first need to examine the rate of diffusion of the Internet and outline who is using it. Two decades ago, Japan and the United States were the undisputed leaders in the development of the "information society," but Japanese have been slower in making the Internet a part of their lives than individuals in many other advanced industrialized (and newly industrializing) nations. Although Japan has the world's second largest economy, according to a

January 2002 NUA survey of how many people are currently online in the world (www.nua.ie/surveys/how_many_online/index.html), it ranks fourteenth in terms of the percentage of the population online, at 38.9 percent. Not only is Japan's diffusion rate behind that of the United States (58 percent), Sweden, Norway, Denmark, and other industrialized nations in North America and Europe, it is also behind that of many nations in the Asia-Pacific region, including Korea (46 percent), Taiwan (51 percent), and Singapore (50 percent).

As individual nations and regions have gone online, people have worried about the rise of a "digital divide" and the creation of information "haves" and "have-nots" both within nations and between nation-states (Norris 2001). Concerned about this possibility, the U.S. Department of Commerce in 1995 carried out the first of a series of surveys to evaluate computer and Internet use in the United States. Initially entitled "Falling Through the Net" (www.ntia.doc.gov/ntiahome/digitaldivide), these surveys revealed considerable disparities in Internet access and use, especially in terms of race, household income, gender, age, education, and location (rural vs. urban users). Similar analyses carried out by the Japanese government (Nihon Intaanetto Kyōkai 2001) have likewise found that higher rates of Internet use are directly related to age of household head (younger), size of the city (larger), household income (higher), gender (male), and education level. These results are not so different from the pattern found earlier in the United States, particularly in terms of gender and age gaps, which have begun to narrow in Japan much as they have elsewhere. On the other hand, while the income divide is less severe in Japan than in the United States and other nations (due to the existence of a large and well-educated middle class in Japan), there is some concern that the lack of connectivity among Japanese schools and the limited number of teachers with technical skills might exacerbate existing disparities. In 2001, for example, only 10 percent of Japan's classrooms had Internet access, compared with 77 percent of those in the United States in the fall of 2000 (Nihon Intaanetto Kyōkai 2001: 182; U.S. National Center for Education Statistics, nces.ed.gov/pubs2001/internetaccess/2.asp).

While Japan lags behind other nations in percentage terms, when it comes to the overall number of users, with 50 million people connected to the Internet in January 2002, Japan ranks second behind the United States (NUA, www.nua.ie/surveys/how_many_online/index.html). Moreover, between February 1997 and February 2001, Japanese Internet use increased 5.7 times, and it continues to climb (Nihon Intaanetto Kyōkai 2001, 32). Thus, the potential for the Internet to serve as an alternative or parallel public sphere to the mass mediated one is real. *How* it is used is an altogether different question. As I suggest below, it may well be that the issue with respect to Japanese Internet use (and Internet use everywhere) is not just a quantitative one. Japan will probably catch up in numerical terms, and the gap between its haves and have-nots is expected to narrow. What recent studies of Internet use have begun to show, however, is that "localization" and particularism will be important factors in determining the ultimate rate and trajectory of Internet development and use. As just one example of how this might play out, an increasing number of Japanese now say that their only means of connecting to the Internet is their web-enabled cell phone (Nihon Intaanetto Kyōkai 2001: 32). This leads to the possibility that there may be an additional layer to the digital divide in some nations, one determined by the technology platform individuals use to connect to the web. Other examples of qualitative factors and their impacts in Japan are discussed below.

The Internet and Grassroots Activism

As other authors have noted in this volume and in contrast to the American case described by Robert Putnam (2000), there is evidence of *greater* citizen participation and diversity in Japanese associational life in recent years when measured by the number of nongovernmental, nonprofit, and other voluntary organizations and by the apparent greater openness of the state bureaucracy. These changes are the result of a catastrophic event – the Kōbe earthquake of 1995 – that awakened a volunteer spirit among Japanese, and the passing of laws designed specifically to facilitate greater democratic participation, including the Nonprofit Organization (NPO) Law of 1998, which makes it easier for nonprofits to win corporate status, and the Information Disclosure Act of 1999, which gives private citizens the legal right to access certain categories of public information.[5]

What role has the Internet played in this process, and what role can we expect it to play in the future? How does the experience of Japan differ from that of other countries? It is clear that the Internet is being used by activists and volunteers everywhere in their efforts to improve citizens' quality of life. There are numerous examples in Japan of the ways in which the Internet and computer-mediated communication have been used by activists, volunteers, and organizations to gain support for their activities, including those intended to alter or challenge government policy.

One of the earliest examples of the use of computer-mediated communication by Japanese activists goes back nearly as far as the earliest examples in the United States. In 1985, the Japanese government came up with a plan to construct 1,000 housing units for American military personnel in the Ikego forest surrounding the city of Zushi south of Tokyo. Zushi mayor Tomino Kiichi was himself opposed to the proposal and decided to enlist Aizu Izumi – at that time a young computer enthusiast and today one of the best-known Internet intellectuals in Japan – to help him use computer networks to garner international opposition to the project. Because Japanese communication networks were still in their infancy at that time (the first academic network had been established only a year earlier by network pioneer Murai Jun), Aizu contacted some American computer network pioneers, notably Lisa Carlson and Frank Burns. They let him use their newly established "Meta Network" to send out an international plea for support. Ultimately, according to

[5] It is important to note that by the time the national government had finally gotten around to passing the Information Disclosure Act in 1999, all forty-eight prefectural governments had already enacted their own IDAs – some as early as 1982. About 300 of Japan's 3,250 municipalities had also introduced similar laws on their own (Okabe 2000).

virtual communitarian Howard Rheingold (1997: 5), "more than one thousand replies came in over a period of months from people in more than fifty countries," and the construction of housing was halted. Reflecting on that campaign years later, Mayor Tomino, who eventually helped establish one of Japan's first city computer networks with Aizu's help, "acknowledged that this computer conferencing campaign had played a major part in the citizens' grassroots movement to stop the development in the forest" (ibid.: 5).

Largely spurred by two events, other grassroots activists in Japan were also beginning to use personal computer (PC) networks to augment their activities right around the time of the Zushi campaign. The first was the passing of the Electronic Communications Business Law in 1985, which denationalized the state telecommunications company, NTT. This move was important because, in addition to ostensibly removing state control over the domestic telecommunications monopoly, the law made it possible for the first time for private individuals to use telephone lines freely for data transmission. Until that time, use of telephone lines was under the strict control of the Ministry of Posts and Telecommunications (MPT, now part of the Ministry of Public Management, Home Affairs, Posts and Telecommunications), and even Japanese computer scientists had considerable difficulty getting permission to use the lines for anything other than voice transmission (Murai 1995: 137).

The second catalyst was the publication in 1986 of what many PC activists in Japan would later refer to as their "bible," a book written by Okabe Aki (1986) entitled *Pasokon shimin netowaaku* (Citizens' Computer Networks). This book described the various ways in which American grassroots activists were using computer networks, especially bulletin boards, in the pre–worldwide web era to achieve political and social goals. These two events led to the establishment of a number of bulletin boards in the period from 1987 to 1989 and to the creation of two of Japan's earliest networks: DAISAN (*Daisan nettowaaku*, or the Third Network), established by NEC in 1987 as a place for the discussion of grassroots activities, and NIFTYserve (now known as @Nifty), established by Fujitsū in 1988 and now Japan's largest fixed-line Internet service provider.

Thus, a number of activist groups were already using computer networks well before Japan's "Internet Year One" in 1994, the year Japan's first Internet service provider (ISP) went into business. For many Japanese, however, the event that first awoke them to the possibilities offered by the Internet was the Great Hanshin-Awaji (i.e., Kōbe) Earthquake of January 1995, which claimed the lives of more than 6,000 people. Indeed, for many individuals, this represented their first real knowledge of the Internet and its potential as a tool for gathering disparate individuals and resources both within Japan and around the world for humanitarian causes.

The Internet played an important role during the earthquake, especially in its immediate aftermath, when most telephones and other traditional communications means were down and the government seemed ill-equipped to handle the crisis on its own. Late on the afternoon of the day the earthquake hit and by the next day, for example, commercial PC networks established special corners on their systems on which information about the earthquake could be exchanged (Furusei and Hirose 1996: 55). Many Japanese relied on information obtained from these sites to organize assistance for survivors and retrieve information about friends and family living in the region. The EFJ (Electronic Frontier Japan) mailing list, which had been established some time earlier for the discussion of information technology issues, was just one of many mailing lists that was used to let individuals in Japan and abroad know about conditions in Kōbe immediately after the earthquake. In fact, according to one source, it was a message sent by an EFJ member in the United States to the White House immediately after the earthquake that first alerted the American president of the disaster, apparently before Japan's own prime minister had that information (ibid.: 46).

Since the Kōbe earthquake, the Internet has been used more extensively by Japanese activists, volunteer groups, and NPOs in a variety of ways. One early post-Kōbe site, launched in July 1995, is called Peer-net (www.peer-net.org) and is based on the idea of peer counseling. Its purpose is to bring together supporters and volunteers to help Japan's disabled learn how to use PCs to access the Internet and improve their quality of life. Other groups and websites have been established to provide computer services and technical support to newly created nonprofits, some of which repair old PCs and give them to NPOs, NGOs, and foreign minorities. One of the best known of these websites is JCAFE (Japan Computer Access for Empowerment, www.jca.apc.org), which was originally founded in 1993 to link domestic activists to one another and to overseas activist organizations. In 1997, the related JCA-NET was set up as a dedicated ISP for NPOs, and in January 2001, the organization itself acquired the status of NPO. A similar, though somewhat more limited, site is TUNAGU-NET (www.tunagu.gr.jp), which also provides technical support and consulting for NPOs and has extensive links to civic activists in Japan. Other sites include the World Nature Network (www.wnn.or.jp), which features environmental information and a number of links to computer volunteer groups; the Forum on Environmental Administration Reform (www.eforum.jp), which aims to make the government more accountable in the area of environmental policy; and the Citizens' Nuclear Information Center (www.cnic.or.jp), which offers information for researchers as well as activists on nuclear issues in Japan. Many similar organizations also have an online presence.

With the passing of the NPO Law in 1998, a web-based information project by the name of Nonprofit Japan (www.igc.org/ohdakefoundation/index/html) was formed to provide information on the Japanese nonprofit sector and grassroots activities in Japan. It is clear from the activities listed on this site that the Internet is becoming a real tool for various activists and volunteers in Japan. At the same time, although computer-aided activism has a long history in Japan, even in the pre-web days and increasingly in recent years, it is apparent that the network-connected activist community in Japan both differs from and lags behind its counterpart in the United States. From January to March 2001, Viva Volunteer-net (viva.cplaza.ne.jp) conducted a survey of the 1,200 organizations listed in the Japan NPO/NGO directory. They found that only 64 percent of the NPOs listed in the directory had official mailing addresses and only 37 percent had their own websites. What's more, those that did have web pages rarely updated them. Still, in spite of their otherwise limited connection to the web, 80 percent of the NGO/NPOs responded that they were using the net in some capacity, if only to communicate with members and gather information. In contrast, a number of American NPOs and NGOs (e.g., eGrants.org, Netaid.org, and CompuMentor) are actively using the Internet to seek out donations from the public, while others match prospective volunteers with NGOs. Impact Online, for example, has successfully recruited several hundred thousand volunteers for several thousand organizations. But as one member of the Japan Citizens' Computer Communication Research Association has pointed out, such practices have yet to take hold in Japan, where NPOs and NGOs still suffer from limited technical support and limited access to web consultants (Intaanetto Hyakusho 2001: 207).

What explains the apparent lag in Internet use by NPOs and NGOs in Japan? First, rates of adoption of the Internet by grassroots organizations have lagged, just as they have more generally in Japan. There are various reasons for this. For one, the high cost of getting online resulting from the NTT monopoly over leased lines severely hinders the spread of computer-mediated communication in Japan. In the early days of computer networking, people who logged on to NIFTYserve or DAISAN forums had to be dedicated activists and/or have deep pockets. Okabe (2000) notes that the local toll charge is "a major obstacle to the proliferation of the Internet in Japan . . . [and] . . . was an obstacle to a wide-spread use of electronic bulletin board systems (BBSs) among citizens. . . . " According to an MPT report released in 1999, it cost six times more to be connected to the Internet in Japan than in the United States (Miyao 2000: 24). And while NTT has introduced new protocols for transmitting data digitally, such as ISDN (Integrated Services Digital Network), that have a number of advantages over analog leased lines, including faster data throughput speeds and connection times, it has steadfastly refused to reduce the costs of the existing leased lines that most Japanese use to access the Internet. Moreover, because NTT controls the "last mile" of underground telephone cable, it is very difficult for any potential rival to compete with NTT on price.

Further hampering the early development of networks was the fact that Japan's major computer manufacturers (i.e., IBM Japan, Fujitsū, Hitachi, and NEC) used proprietary network protocols that made internetworking extremely difficult. Moreover, although TCP/IP (Transmission Control Protocol/Internet Protocol), an open-system, public-domain architecture owned by no one and accessible by all, was created in 1977 and quickly became the global standard for connecting to various computer networks, including the Internet, government management of the development of PC networks delayed its recognition as a standard protocol in Japan. Incompatible methods for encoding Japanese texts were another cause for the lag in PC network and Internet use in Japan. Finally, when considering the slow pace of NPO/NGO Internet usage, we need to keep in mind that until 1995, there simply were not very many NGOs in Japan to begin with. Now that Japan has a law recognizing the special status of such organizations and allows them to incorporate, we can expect that more NPOs will take advantage of these new opportunities and that more of them will take to the Internet to disseminate information, gather donations, and interact with the public at large.

A number of Japanese scholars writing about the history and development of networks and the Internet in Japan have highlighted the efforts by national and local governments to establish community and local area networks (CAN and LAN, respectively) throughout the country. These have included a number of NGOs (e.g., the Community Area Network (CAN) Forum) that have been established for the express purpose of introducing the Internet and computer-mediated communication in various regions to improve the quality of life of local residents. CANs are widespread in other nations as well and serve a useful purpose. But it is important to note that their purpose is less to provide residents with the tools for an *autonomous* and unmediated realm for discussion of social and political issues (i.e., the creation of a public sphere) than it is to build stronger *connections between* citizens, local governments, and local businesses. This distinction is an important one: many of these are government-subsidized and -created "community networks," not the "virtual communities" of a mobilized public sphere. Although efforts to link citizens to government, businesses, and academe have many positive aspects, they also have the potential to limit the autonomy of the public sphere. As noted by Sheldon Garon (1997), Susan Pharr (2000), and others, it is the state's efforts to create such connections between itself and civil society in other contexts in Japan that has resulted in the subsuming of private goals and interests under those of the state.

The Internet as an Information Link Between the State and the Public Sphere

A second way the Internet can empower the political public sphere is to facilitate a two-way flow of information between the state and citizens. This function is already well developed in the United States. By 1998, for example, the House of Representatives was already processing 750,000 pieces of e-mail a week and an estimated 37.5 million messages a year; the Senate was receiving more than 150,000 messages a week (*New York Times*, January 15, 1998).

The Japanese government has also begun taking steps to include the public in its decision-making process by mandating not only that all ministries and agencies make provisions for public comment as they draft bills but that they utilize the Internet as one means to do so. Makino Jirō (1999), the director of the Internet Lawyers Conference, notes that even though Japanese government agencies have used the Internet to conduct surveys in the past, "they have never before been obliged to employ it to learn public sentiment in advance of the preparation of legislation, with accompanying influence on lawmaking." It is hoped that such "request for comments" (RFC) schemes utilizing the Internet will become an effective way of ascertaining the public will in Japan.

Nevertheless, in spite of the many apparent gateways to Japanese government information and the policy-making process, public access to key government databases is still limited, especially when compared with the accessibility of similar databases in the United States (Okabe 2000). Suggesting that access to government information is critical for public participation in decision making, Okabe decries the fact that "Japanese government databases are largely behind firewalls." Included below are a few of the examples he and others have provided of key differences between the U.S. and Japanese governments' use of the Internet to provide information to the public.

Legislative Minutes and the Text of Bills. Although it has been possible since January 1998 to obtain the minutes of Diet sessions on the Internet, until quite recently, only the abstracts of bills were available on the Internet, and then only for a price because they were published by a commercial press, Daiichi Hōki. While it is now possible to obtain full text data of some bills in Japan, the full texts of all U.S. congressional bills going back to the 93rd session (1973–74) are readily available on the Internet without charge.

Legal Codes. In the United States, one can get free on the Internet (or for $37 in CD-ROM format) copies of the United States Code containing the complete texts of major federal laws. In Japan, the text of all laws and regulations (the *Genkō Hōki*, or Current Codes and Regulations) is published by the government. But as Okabe (2000) notes, "though basic and truly public, the law information is behind the firewall." In this case, a quasigovernmental NPO sells a magnetic tape version of the government's database for about $1,000. Commercial publishers purchase this to develop their own CD-ROMs and online products, which they sell for an even higher price. Researchers can access this information through the database of the Ministry of Education's National Center for Science Information, but they must pay ¥50 (about 50¢) a minute and ¥13 (about 13¢) per record accessed. To overcome this limitation, groups of volunteers have been inputting the texts of laws into the Internet on their own.

In 2001, however, access to legal resources on the web was enhanced by the creation of three new official sites: the Current Law Database, the Supreme Court Judgment database, and the Gazette (Kanpō) database (see Ibusuki n.d.). The Current Law Database was established in April 2001 by the Ministry of Home Affairs. This represents the first time that the consolidated code has been available to the Japanese public without a fee. The Japanese Supreme Court database, also launched in 2001, includes full-text data of official case reports. Case reports from lower courts are still unavailable on the web, in part because most lower courts lack the appropriate technological infrastructure to distribute them. Finally, although the Official Gazette (Kanpō), Japan's equivalent of the U.S. Federal Register (which is provided in full text on the Internet), used to be available only on floppy disk for approximately $100 a year (an index was available on the Internet), the gazettte website now includes the details of new legislation as PDF files that are updated weekly.

Securities Reports. The U.S. Securities and Exchange Commission provides free access to corporate financial disclosure data on its EDGAR database. Although Japan's Ministry of Finance collects similar corporate data, it is not available on the Internet. Individuals can purchase the information in CD-ROM format, but only for a hefty price (about $20,000).

Directories of Government Officials. In the United States, directories of government officials that include names, addresses, and telephone numbers can be found on the websites of individual government offices. In Japan, such information is published by the Ministry of Finance Printing Office and sold to the public as a CD-ROM for more than $1,500. Okabe (2000) notes that this is "most irritating to the public" and asks rhetorically, "Why do we have to pay that much for a list of high-ranking government officials?"

The private ownership, management, and sale of what is for all intents and purposes public information is a topic that has begun to gain prominence even in the United States. But the examples offered here suggest that the issue is more urgent in Japan, where basic kinds of public information are still not freely and easily accessible. Although the government appears to be moving forward slowly in placing public information online, the passage of the Communications Interception Law in August 1999 suggests that the government is at the same time trying to obtain greater access to private information. This law, which gives enforcement officials investigating certain types of crimes (including immigration offenses) access to private e-mail accounts, has been challenged by opposition parties and by many civil society actors who claim that it is an unconstitutional violation of privacy rights.

The Internet and Political Campaigning

A third way that the Internet can be used to empower the political public sphere is through its impact on elections. Yet it is here that the power of the Japanese state to hinder this process is most obvious. To borrow a phrase now much in vogue, there is an enormous "digital divide" between the United States and Japan in this regard. Both nations have laws that limit electoral campaigning to reduce corruption and illicit contributions. In the United States, the Federal Election Campaign Act serves this function and is interpreted by the Federal Election Commission (FEC). In Japan, the Public Offices Election Law is enforced by the Ministry of Public Management, Home Affairs, Posts and Telecommunications. Both laws were enacted long before the advent of digital communications, and as a result, government officials, politicians, and individual citizens have been blazing new trails. But the Japanese state has chosen to interpret these laws in ways that are far more draconian in their impact on Internet-based campaigning.

The relatively unregulated nature of the American Internet has resulted in a number of new techniques for campaigning and encouraging political participation. The growth in online political campaigning has been phenomenal, especially in the 2000 presidential election. Although many of the websites in 1996 were quite simple, those of federal candidates in particular are now multimedia affairs, containing embedded video and audio clips as well as links to related sites (Corrado 2000: v). With its growth as a campaign tool in the United States, the

Internet has begun to change the political process. In the 2000 election, for example, "candidates [were] using the new technology to inform voters of their candidacies, to share their policy views, to distribute schedules of events, to raise money, to recruit volunteers, to solicit voter opinions, and to make available audio and video materials, including the advertisements they broadcast[ed] on television" (ibid.: 5). A few politicians even used "campaign cams" that permitted voters to see what was happening in their campaign offices by means of a video camera left on all day (*Politics Online*, August 18, 1998). Adding to the power of the Internet as a campaign tool, online donations in the United States have qualified for federal matching funds since June 1999 (before then, the FEC had required a written document such as a check or a paper credit card receipt to track the donation), and individuals can now make online campaign contributions by credit card.

Most important for our purposes here, the Internet has become a tool by which candidates can reach voters – and voters, candidates – directly, without the intermediation of traditional mass media. As Anthony Corrado (2000: 1) notes:

> Candidates now use web sites to offer voters texts of public statements and detailed information on their policy positions, as well as audio and video material. These sites allow individuals to "customize" information so that they may access materials that are relevant to their particular concerns or interests. Similarly, these sites allow candidates to provide individuals with updated information as it becomes available, facilitating a type of interaction between campaigns and individual voters that was not possible before the advent of digital communications.

The Internet has also proven useful for less prominent candidates. One of the best examples of successful use of the Internet by such a candidate was provided by the 1998 gubernatorial election in Minnesota. The nonincumbent candidate, Jesse Ventura, a former professional wrestler and Reform Party candidate, spent about $600 to establish a website to recruit volunteers and raise money. Victorious in his candidacy, "most knowledgeable observers claim that his innovative use of the Internet earned him an additional 2–4 percent of the vote – about the size of his margin of victory" (ibid.: 6).

Use of the Internet in campaigning is not limited to the United States. Major German parties post important information on their websites, and the sites of some of the larger parties, such as the Christian Democratic Union and the Social Democratic Party, get 2 million hits a month. According to *Politics Online* (August 18, 1998), "In Germany, the most frequently used political Internet features are discussion groups on the party sites." In both Germany and Sweden, prospective voters can answer a series of questions to determine which of the parties' views most closely match their own. The Swedes' Val-Guide is a political "matchmaker" sponsored by the national newspaper *Svenska Dagbladet*. After users complete the survey's thirty-three questions, they are given a weighted index that compares their views with those of the major political parties (*Politics Online*, August 18, 1998).

The situation in Japan is radically different. Even though every major political party and a large proportion of Diet members now have their own (albeit in many cases rudimentary) home pages, campaigning in Japan continues today pretty much as it has for the last seventy-five years. Politicians in Japan still rely on some of the more intrusive means known for getting name familiarity: loudspeaker trucks (actually, a *single* truck per candidate that can be used only between the hours of 8 A.M. and 8 P.M.) and telephone calls. Originally enacted in 1925 and recently revised to permit longer campaign periods and absentee voting, Japan's rigid electoral law allows candidates to distribute a circumscribed number of leaflets (70,000), postcards (35,000), and campaign posters (which must be hung in designated places), and not much else. One of the most restrictive among the advanced industrial democracies, the Japanese campaign law regulates even the size and number of advertisements a candidate or party may post in newspapers and prohibits door-to-door canvassing and many types of speeches and debates that are allowed elsewhere.

And the Internet? While not technically illegal, the Ministry of Public Management, Home Affairs, Posts and Telecommunications (MPHPT) has interpreted the antiquated Electoral Law to mean that cyberspace is off-limits during election periods. In Japan, the law is interpreted in such a way that anything that is not expressly permitted is forbidden. And because that law was enacted well before even television existed, MPHPT's official stance is that the Internet is not to be used for campaigning during election periods. In the election held in October 1996, for example, the ministry did not stop at prohibiting political parties from using the Internet. According to one account, "Behind the scenes and out of public view, bureaucrats . . . [told] campaign staff members for a number of competing parties to take campaign information off their home pages for the duration of the campaign . . ." (*San Jose Mercury News*, October 14, 1996).

In practice, the government ban has meant that once a campaign has officially begun, candidates, as well as some activists, *close their home pages* in order not to break the law. The webmaster for the New Party Sakigake, Okamoto Kenji, complained to an American journalist, "It's so strange. . . . When an election campaign starts, people want to have political information. But because of the ministry's rules, everything disappears from our home pages just as the campaign heats up" (*San Jose Mercury News*, October 14, 1996). In the June 2000 election, some politicians left their pages untouched but up and running because material that had been posted before the election was allowed to remain so long as it was not altered in any way. Still, the rigid election rules and the watchful eye of the ministry have made many politicians reticent to post *any* campaign information and literature on their home pages.

At least as important with regard to the public sphere, it is not just candidates who are afraid to post information during election periods: the Japanese Internet ban has an impact on activists as well as politicians. In an extraordinary example of the ways in which the Internet's potential as a tool for the political periphery can be limited by the state, just prior to the June 2000 election, a number of Japanese activist groups (borrowing a technique successfully used by Korean activists) used the web to post blacklists of candidates they deemed unsuitable for office. At least one such group, however, the Ōsaka-based Alliance to Defeat Unqualified

Parliamentarians, removed from its site for the duration of the campaign a list of thirteen politicians whose reelection it opposed. Why? The group was concerned that their actions might be construed by the Ministry of Home Affairs as campaign-related and thus illegal.

Requesting a ruling from the agency responsible for interpreting the law, the now defunct New Party Sakigake was at the forefront of efforts to open up the campaign potential of the Internet in 1996. In its response, the government dictated that web pages would be handled in the same way as printed pamphlets or posters. The electoral law restricted the number, type, and procedures for distributing these campaign materials. "Because the distribution of such materials on the Web was not something that had been considered in the law," the government agency noted, the Internet could not be used during the campaign period (Nihon Intaanetto Kyōkai 2000: 165). Ironically, one of the reasons the law had been passed in the first place was to minimize the electoral advantage enjoyed by candidates with better access to financial resources. Yet the Internet is much cheaper than the posters and advertisements provided for under the law for the wide distribution of political and campaign information.

Some of the opposition parties, whose members are often younger and more Internet-savvy, tried once again to lift the de facto ban on e-campaigning in 1998, but they were defeated by the majority LDP, which had fewer members with home pages (36 percent vs. 61 percent of Diet members of the Democratic Party of Japan) and cited such issues as the danger posed by hackers and the digital divide as reasons for maintaining the ban (*Los Angeles Times*, June 19, 2000). Although similar attempts to do away with the ban were made in the spring of 2000 and again in 2001, they also failed. In March 2000, the Democratic Party announced as part of its "informatization project" a proposal to begin using the Internet for campaigning by the 2003 election. It even went a step further than other parties in recommending that the public be allowed to *vote* on the Internet by the same year (Nihon Intaanetto Kyōkai 2000: 165). During the June 2000 campaign of that year, one Democratic lawmaker, Shima Satoshi, posted a blank web page to register his opposition to the ban. Visitors to this site who clicked on the page received a voice message from Shima criticizing the restrictions on cyber-campaigning in Japan (personal interview, November 2000).

There appear to be at least two reasons for the ban. First, MPHPT and many politicians are genuinely concerned about the digital divide. In Japan, as noted earlier, many people still do not have ready access to online information, and there is concern that this might create a political divide on top of the existing social one. Second, the LDP leadership is reticent to permit change because more younger, urban individuals are connected than the party's traditional supporters among older, rural individuals. But even the LDP appears divided on this issue: while older Diet members are still suspicious of the Internet's possibilities, their younger colleagues are enthusiastic. Perhaps most important are the fears among LDP and other politicians that the Internet could undermine the already weak "analog relations" or *jinmyaku* (literally, personal connections) that have traditionally been a major source of power and support for candidates at election time. Indeed, recent trends suggest that voters are no longer loyal to parties or individual politicians in the same way they have been in the past. And while the Internet may not be the major source of this transformation of attitudes, nonaligned voters have begun to use it as one of their tools as they take politics into their own hands.

The surprise election of novelist Tanaka Yasuo as governor of Nagano prefecture in 2000 is just one example of what has become an increasingly common phenomenon in Japanese elections, the election of nonaligned, independent candidates who otherwise lack a strong organizational base. How have these candidates succeeded? In part riding on a wave of voter dissatisfaction, many of these candidates have been elected because of the support they have received from individuals who have no direct or official relationship to them. In many cases these "supporters" have not even been sought out by the candidate. Rather, they have, for reasons of their own, decided independently (*katte ni*) to support candidates of their choosing (interview with Nagano Governor Tanaka Yasuo, December 2001). In many cases, like-minded voters have formed "support groups" known as *katteren* and established websites and created mailing lists without having spoken to or met the candidate. In some cases, these websites have eventually been adopted by the candidate and become his or her official site after a successful campaign.

There is some hope that the section of the Public Officials' Election Law that has been interpreted as banning Internet use during the campaign period will eventually be revised. MPHPT is currently sponsoring a research group (*kenkyūkai*) chaired by Tokyo University Professor Kabashima Ikuo to study the issue, and it is expected to make its recommendations soon (the deliberations have been posted online at www.soumu.go.jp/singi/it_senkyo.html). Still, it may be several years before the law is revised, in part because of the ministry's desire that this be a parliamentary bill as opposed to a ministerial one (interview with ministry official, November 2001).

Conclusion

Civil society ideally features high levels of public discourse, a wide-ranging and active network of voluntary associations, tolerance for diversity, and a voice for marginalized groups. Until recently, at least, civil society in Japan has been weak relative to that of other advanced industrial democracies. The reason for this, as some scholars (Pharr 1999, 2000) have argued, might be that it is easier for the state to bring voluntary organizations under its control in Japan because they are vertically rather than horizontally organized.

Yet the Internet (as well as the other "new media" of which it is a part) has the potential to facilitate and spread precisely the kinds of civic connectedness and participation that political scientists see as beneficial for a healthy, functioning democracy and in ways more traditional media cannot. As Susan Herbst (1994) has noted in other contexts, an alternative communications medium such as the Internet does not necessarily replace traditional connections, but it does provide an alternative realm in which civic discourse can occur unmediated and uncontrolled. This presents the possibility of overcoming traditional structural barriers in Japan by creating horizontal linkages and networks of communication and information exchange at a national and international level.

Although the Internet provides a potential parallel public sphere that is much harder to control given its unmediated and horizontal nature, it remains to be seen whether this potential will be realized in Japan. Despite its goal of becoming an "information superpower," Japan still lags behind the United States and a number of other advanced countries in use of the Internet in terms of both overall use and use by activists, NGOs, and NPOs. Will this new technology be regulated and coopted in ways that limit its access and usefulness to civic organizations, including those outside the mainstream? Or will it be allowed to follow free-form and open-ended pathways? It is still too early to make definitive judgments about the future role of the Internet in Japan (or anywhere else, for that matter). On the one hand, the state in Japan has so far played an active role in each of the areas examined here, either through its formal power of regulation (such as its draconian ban on Internet use during elections) or through more informal means by which it has "guided" the development and use of the Internet. On the other hand, we have recently begun to see more examples of citizen (such as in the case of the *katteren*) and activist (NGP/NPO) use of the Internet in Japan, and it is expected that these will increase.

What is clear from this analysis is that it will be qualitative factors rather than quantitative ones that will ultimately shape the development of the Internet in Japan and elsewhere. These qualitative factors include the policies initiated by the government and the mass media, different approaches to cyberspace, different ideologies with respect to Internet use, and even different technology platforms. Although many studies have begun to examine such issues as the digital divide, the impact of qualitative factors, especially on the political divide within nations, has not been given sufficient consideration to date.

12

A Tale of Two Systems: Prosecuting Corruption in Japan and Italy

David Johnson

Independence and Accountability in Japan and Italy

This chapter explores the role and rule of law by telling a tale of two systems for prosecuting corruption. In Japan, prosecutors have "limited independence" from outside political influence. In Italy, prosecutors are largely insulated from the world of electoral politics. This difference makes for a huge difference in the nature and scope of corruption prosecutions.

For example, Japan's Recruit Scandal of the late 1980s "came to symbolize an entire political establishment on the take" (Schlesinger 1997: 236). Prosecutors connected more than forty politicians to dubious Recruit payoffs, including nearly every ranking member of the ruling Liberal Democratic Party. Yet only two Diet politicians were indicted, neither of whom was prominent. In the 1990s, Italy's "Clean Hands" (*Mani Pulite*) investigation in the Tangentopoli ("Bribe City") Scandal also implicated a whole political class, but with radically different results. In all, some 3,000 arrest warrants were issued, and at least 251 members of parliament and five former prime ministers were indicted (Nelken 1996). Ultimately, a small group of Italian prosecutors destroyed or caused the reconstitution of all the major parties of government (Burnett and Mantovani 1998: 6). These two scandals – Recruit and Tangentopoli – arose from similar forms of misconduct – bribery, extortion, and "political financing" – in similarly corrupt societies (Reed et al. 1996; Transparency International 1999). Whether measured by the size of the catch or the consequences of the investigation, however, they had radically different trajectories. This chapter explains why.

This tale of two systems makes three points about Japan. Descriptively, I demonstrate that Japanese prosecutors are neither highly independent nor highly dependent. They instead have what I call "limited independence." Causally, I show that their limited independence arises from two main sources: the legal and institutional "rules of the game" that constitute the framework within which prosecutors work, and events in the 1954 Ship-building Scandal that have cast a long shadow over subsequent corruption investigations. Normatively, I argue that limited or moderate independence is better – because it better balances democratic values – than extreme independence. The Tangentopoli case reveals the high costs of sacrificing too much accountability on the altar of independence.

This chapter is also about corruption and civil society, two of the most notoriously ambiguous terms in the social studies lexicon. Corruption is one linkage among many between civil society and the state. It is a distinctive route by which wealth, as a political resource, influences government policies. As such, corruption may be seen as a special case of influence that is "frequently an integral part of the political system" – a part that analysts ignore at their peril (Scott 1972: 2).

The core meaning of *corruption* is the misuse of public power for private gain (Rose-Ackerman 1999: 1). Since corruption consists of violations of rules governing relations between social interests and state actors, it both reflects and reinforces illicit linkages between social groups and the state. The notion of *civil society* is more slippery still, but nearly all conceptions link it in one way or another to the rule of law (Schwartz, this volume). At its core, the rule of law means government must be ruled by law and subject to it (Raz 1979: 210). Hence, the rule of law has two analytically central aspects: government by law and government under law. *Government by law* means that when governments do things, they must do them according to the rules with which officials are required to comply (Fuller 1969). To the extent that this happens, people can predict what governments will do and what other people will do and can arrange their affairs accordingly. *Government under law* means that even high political officials are confined and confinable by legal rules and challenges. Thus, where the rule of law prevails, law is both a means of exercising power (government by law) and a means of limiting the powers it grants (government under law).

The rule of law generates two imperatives for the prosecution of corruption. To prosecute corruption crimes and thereby secure government under law, prosecutors need some measure of *independence* from the target of their investigation.[1] To ensure that they exercise their powers responsibly, prosecutors must be held *accountable*.[2] These two requisites stand in ineluctable tension, for prosecutors cannot be highly independent and highly accountable at the same time. More of one is purchased at the price of the other. The focus of this chapter fixes on the tension between these two imperatives and on the different balances struck between them in Italy and Japan. Thus, while my focus is Japan, much of the analysis

[1] *Independence* means freedom from control or influence by others, while *dependence* denotes subjection to outside control or influence. The main Japanese term for independence is *dokuritsu* (literally, "standing on one's own"). Cognates include *gensei kōhei* ("strict neutrality") and *fuhen futō* ("nonpartisanship").

[2] *Accountability* means responsiveness to legitimate authority or influence. A survey conducted by Japan's Cultural Affairs Agency found that 88 percent of Japanese respondents believe *setsumei sekinin* ("responsibility to explain") is easier to comprehend than the more frequently used English import *akauntabiritii* (*Asahi Shinbun*, May 3, 1999). Note, however, that the indigenous Japanese expression is narrower in scope than the English import, for the latter connotes an obligation to do, not just to explain.

concerns Italy. To understand what is distinctive and problematic about corruption prosecutions in Japan, one must compare. To know one country is to know no country.

Why Independence Matters: A Model of Corruption Prosecutions

American debates over the various Clinton scandals and over the recently expired Independent Counsel Act avoided a centrally important question: Why is prosecutorial independence a good thing?[3] There are two answers to this question, one jurisprudential and the other practical.

Stated broadly, the jurisprudential reason is that independence serves core democratic values. Two such values are noteworthy. First, independence advances society's interest in seeing that people are treated equally under the law, regardless of their position or power. This value is called equality or impartiality. Without some measure of independence, prosecutors are unduly influenced by wealth, power, and fame. This undermines equality. Second, by serving the value of equality, independence promotes public trust and the voluntary compliance and cooperation that public trust fosters and on which a vibrant civil society depends (Putnam et al. 1993; Pharr 2000: 34). As U.S. Attorney General Janet Reno declared, "It is absolutely essential for the public, in the process of the criminal justice system, to have confidence in the system, and you cannot do that when there is conflict or an appearance of conflict in the person who is, in effect, the chief prosecutor" (Labaton 1999).

Independence also matters practically, for it enables effective law enforcement. Indeed, prosecutors need two things in order to charge crimes of corruption: independence from the target of their investigation and evidence sufficient to charge and convict. When prosecutors lack independence, political elites can quash investigations that threaten them or their allies, or they can use prosecutors to punish and harass enemies or rivals. When prosecutors lack evidence, law (in the form of judicial decisions) and public opinion will declare prosecutor failure, thereby damaging the procuracy's legitimacy and its capacity to investigate future cases. In Japan, both requirements are difficult to meet, the first because law grants prosecutors limited independence from elected politicians, and the second because law imposes an unusually heavy burden of proof without conferring sufficient powers

[3] The Independent Counsel Act was enacted in 1978 in order to insulate criminal investigations from political interference. It was spurred by the Watergate Scandal, in which President Richard Nixon ordered the dismissal of Archibald Cox, a special prosecutor who lacked statutory protection. Controversy over the law prompted Congress to let it lapse for eighteen months, beginning in 1993. President Clinton won its renewal in 1994, but it expired again on July 1, 1999, largely because "it failed, abysmally, in the view of almost every official who has been scrutinized by independent counsels, in its intended goal of extracting politics from corruption investigations" (Johnston 1999). Over the life of the law, twenty independent counsels were named at a total cost of \$167 million, or over \$8 million per prosecutor (as of April 1999).

to shoulder that load.[4] Conversely, Italian magistrates[5] possess greater independence than their Japanese counterparts while also facing smaller problems of proof with more adequate legal powers to develop the evidence necessary to charge and convict. These institutional differences enabled prosecutors in Tangentopoli to issue indictments on a far vaster scale than was possible in Japan's Recruit Scandal.

In sum, independence matters because it implies impartiality, equality, public trust, and effective law enforcement. On the other hand, independence also implies reduced responsiveness to outside influence, which is to say, curtailed accountability. When a prosecutor's independence occasions perceptions of unaccountability, public support sags (Dellinger 1999). Unsurprisingly, proponents of America's Independent Counsel act (and supporters of Kenneth Starr) stressed the benefits of impartiality, while opponents of the act (and Starr's critics) emphasized the costs of unaccountability (Dash 1999; Fisher 1999; Lewis 1999b; Sunstein 1999). Ironically, the act's attempt to depoliticize decision making by promoting prosecutorial independence "seemed only to inject more politics into the process" (Toobin 2000: 69). The act was born because Watergate revealed how much independence matters to American civil society. It died because, as this chapter shows, accountability matters, too (Posner 1999).

Limited Independence Limits Indictments: Japan's Ship-building Scandal of 1954

Some scholars believe Japanese prosecutors possess "almost complete independence" from the political world (Castberg 1997: 39). On this point, the evidence is clear and abundant: they do not. Moreover, it is good that they do not, as Japan's prewar history, Italy's Tangentopoli case, and America's Kenneth Starr debacle all show (Matsumoto 1981; Burnett and Mantovani 1998; Toobin 2000). Other analysts make the converse error by claiming that Japanese prosecutors are either insufficiently independent or, worse still, controlled by and beholden to elected politicians (Kubo 1989; van Wolferen 1989; Tachibana 1993). These claims are also problematic, because they fail to recognize the costs incurred when independence is purchased at the price of accountability. Japan may not have struck the best

[4] Although this chapter focuses on the independence requisite for effective prosecution, the evidence requirement is equally important. The evidence exigency can be understood by analogy to pole vaulting, a sport in which two things matter (besides the skill of the vaulter): the height of the bar and the quality of the pole. In Japan, the evidence bar is set higher than in the United States or Italy by the Diet, which has enacted laws that insulate political parties from legal scrutiny; by courts, which in adopting a narrow interpretation of the "scope of authority" (*shokumu kengen*) element of crimes such as bribery have made it difficult for prosecutors to prove a quid pro quo; and by Japanese culture, wherein the ubiquity of gift giving makes it especially difficult to distinguish gifts from bribes (Johnson 1997). Similarly, Japanese prosecutors have a bad "pole" for getting over the evidence bar, because they are unable to engage in investigative techniques – such as wiretapping, undercover operations, plea bargaining, and immunity – considered essential by corruption investigators in the United States and other countries (Field and Pelser 1998; Johnson 1999).

[5] In Italy, prosecutors and judges belong to the same judicial profession; both are called "magistrates" (*magistratura*).

arrangement between independence and accountability, but it is not a bad balance. To see why Japan has a system of "limited prosecutorial independence" and how limited independence limits indictments, one must begin with the interplay between victors and vanquished that occurred under the American Occupation following World War II.

"Democratizing the procuracy" (*kensatsu no minshuka*) was a primary Occupation aim. Occupation officials, like many Japanese, believed prewar prosecutors had misused their independence by trampling human rights and pursuing political objectives, as in the notorious Teijin investigation of 1934 (Yasko 1979; Mitchell 1996). As a result, Occupation reformers aimed to increase the procuracy's responsiveness to democratic forces, and they advanced a number of proposals to make prosecutors more democratically accountable. Prosecutors resisted, but to no avail. In 1947, one proposal was codified as Article 14 of the Public Prosecutors Office Law. This statute permits the minister of justice (almost always an elected politician) to direct the prosecutor general (Japan's top prosecutor) in the investigation and disposition of individual cases. Because the prosecutor general has authority to supervise and control all other prosecutors, Article 14 creates an institutional structure that leaves prosecution decisions open to outside influence. There was nothing nefarious about this change. The law was designed to make prosecutors accountable, to reduce the risk of "prosecutor fascism" (*kensatsu fassho*) that was all too common in prewar Japan.

The Ship-building Scandal of 1954 – the first major corruption case of the post-Occupation era – demonstrated the procuracy's openness to political influence. In it, Tokyo prosecutors attempted to arrest Liberal Party Secretary General Satō Eisaku for bribery. Satō was one of Prime Minister Yoshida Shigeru's "honor pupils" and a future prime minister himself. Acting through his justice minister, Inukai Takeru, Yoshida used Article 14 to prevent Satō's arrest. This action came to be known as the "exercise of the right to command" (*shikiken hatsudō*). In the short run, Yoshida's action shipwrecked the investigation, outraged the public, forced Justice Minister Inukai's resignation, and humiliated the procuracy. But the more important consequences were long-term. For decades after 1954, the ship-building case cast a "dark influence" over prosecutor efforts to uncover and charge high-level corruption (Murobushi 1981). Indeed, the scandal survives in the procuracy's collective memory because it represents not only the most visible instance of overt political interference in an ongoing investigation, but also the procuracy's biggest postwar failure. All major works on Japanese prosecutors assign primacy of place to this episode, and most agree that over the years since Yoshida intervened, prosecutors have remained "intensely conscious of the 1954 precedent" (Nomura 1988: 154).

The Ship-building Scandal shows that the institutional framework for prosecution, and especially Article 14, the key rule of the prosecution game, matter greatly. Yoshida's directive may have saved Satō, but the resultant public uproar hastened the collapse of his fifth and final cabinet. If the directive had mixed consequences for political elites, the damage it did to the procuracy is "impossible to measure" (ibid.: 115). Prosecutors were harshly criticized for following Yoshida's legal order and for failing to continue the investigation and arrest Satō. The public backlash shaped the working personalities of the main prosecutor participants, Kawai Nobutarō and Itō Shigeki, both of whom went on to become highly influential prosecutors in subsequent decades. In particular, the events of 1954 made both men determined to avoid open confrontations with political elites and to instill the same resolve in their subordinates.

Above all, the Ship-building Scandal taught prosecutors that before driving politicians into a corner, they must anticipate the probable political reaction and "adjust" their decisions to prevent a recurrence of the 1954 calamity. Ironically, these adjustments in response to "unseen commands" (*miezaru shikiken*) enable prosecutors to prevent overt political intervention precisely because they make it unnecessary (Murobushi 1981: 271; Takao 1993: 36; Nomura 1994: 40). Indeed, Kawakami Kazuo, a former elite prosecutor, reports that "a majority of top-echelon prosecutors . . . tend to cave in to political pressure and are reluctant to pursue cases of corruption out of fear the scandals might lead to the collapse of the governing party" or to "chaos in national politics" (*Japan Times*, October 29, 1992).

Numbers tell a similar story. From 1948 to 1994, Japanese prosecutors indicted forty-one members of parliament for bribery, but since the Occupation ended in 1952, only one member of Japan's political elite has been charged with a serious offense: former Prime Minister Tanaka Kakuei in the 1976 Lockheed Scandal. Political elites are routinely implicated as central figures in corruption scandals, but they are rarely caught in the indictment net. What is more, from 1948 through 1954, prosecutors charged twenty-two of those forty-one members of Parliament, or an average of 3.1 per year. In the forty years since the Ship-building Scandal, prosecutors indicted only nineteen MPs, or less than one every other year. Thus, as measured by indictments of Diet politicians, prosecutors were about seven times more active before 1954 than after (Johnson 1997). Article 14 and Prime Minister Yoshida's *shikiken* directive have exerted a strong "braking effect" on subsequent corruption investigations (Nomura 1988: 154). Limited independence limits indictments. The Recruit and Sagawa Kyūbin scandals further illustrate this truth.

Limited Independence Protects "The Big Evil": Recruit and Sagawa Kyūbin

The Recruit Scandal began on June 18, 1988, when the *Asahi* newspaper uncovered the sale of Recruit Cosmos stocks to Komatsu Hideki, the deputy mayor of Kawasaki City.[6] The scandal ended in August 1989, shortly after the Liberal Democratic Party lost its Upper House majority in a national election. For the

[6] Recruit Cosmos was a major subsidiary of the Recruit telecommunications conglomerate, whose founder and president, Ezoe Hiromasa, tried desperately to buy entry into the inner circle of politics, bureaucracy, and business. For more detailed English accounts of the Recruit scandal, see Holstein (1990), Shiraishi (1990), Yayama (1990), Mitchell (1996), Castberg (1997), and Schlesinger (1997). One of the best Japanese accounts, especially on the role of prosecutors, is Tachibana (1993).

fifteen months it lasted, the Recruit investigation turned Japanese politics upside down. It triggered unprecedented public outrage over "money-power politics." It precipitated the resignation of the Takeshita cabinet. It contributed to the LDP's defeat in the House of Councillors election. It prompted opposition MP Narazaki Yanosuke to videotape a Recruit representative attempting to bribe him with ¥5 million (so Narazaki would not pursue a Diet investigation into Recruit wrong-doing). It revealed that more than forty politicians – including all the top Liberal Democrats and some top opposition leaders – received a total of ¥1.3 billion in Recruit monies (on average, about $250,000 per politician).[7] It led to the indictment and trial of twelve persons, including two Diet politicians – Komeitō MP Ikeda Katsuya and the LDP's Fujinami Takao, who was former Prime Minister Nakasone Yasuhiro's right-hand man. Above all, Recruit generated hopeful predictions, by press and public alike, that bigger fish would be caught and tried – especially Nakasone himself, who in newspaper and television accounts came to personify "the big evil" (*kyōaku*).

But Nakasone was never charged (nor were other tainted LDP elites such as Takeshita Noboru, Miyazawa Kiichi, Watanabe Michio, and Abe Shintarō). Instead, the scandal ended with a whimper, not a bang. On May 25, 1989, Nakasone testified in the Diet, denying any involvement in the scandal, despite strong evidence to the contrary. He resigned from the LDP and from his faction to take symbolic responsibility for the affair, but he did not quit his Diet seat. Three days earlier, Fujinami, his former chief cabinet secretary, had been indicted for accepting bribes of the sort Nakasone was believed to have taken. In the words of one commentator, "It had all hallmarks of a brokered deal, a precisely calibrated settlement. Japanese newspapers were nearly unanimous in complaining that the [prosecutors'] investigation had been aborted, but none of them felt obliged to offer a theory of how this had happened" (Holstein 1990: 116). Here is the missing theory: limited independence limits indictments.

At the eye of the Recruit storm was Yoshinaga Yūsuke, the chief of the Tokyo Special Investigation Division (SID) and therefore the prosecutor in charge of the day-to-day Recruit investigations. While the SID, and Yoshinaga in particular, possessed reputations for independence, they operated under the shadow of Article 14 as their predecessors had done for the thirty-five years since Yoshida saved Satō. The ultimate concern of these prosecutors was that "if they push too far, their independence could be sharply limited" (ibid.: 115). Yoshinaga resisted political influence for months by strategically leaking facts from the investigation to the press. This generated public support for SID to push deeper into the heart of the scandal, but it ultimately proved insufficient. Yoshinaga – and his superiors in the procuracy – realized that moving further would threaten their own relative independence. The procuracy reached, and accepted, the political limit of its independence when Yoshinaga designated the end of May as the deadline for

[7] Former Prime Minister Mori Yoshiro admitted making more than $950,000 by selling Recruit shares he acquired before they went public. At his inaugural press conference as Prime Minister, Mori characterized the deal as a "regular business transaction" (Sims 2000).

completing the investigation. Ostensibly, this was to allow the LDP time to prepare for elections to be held on July 23, but in fact it revealed the bounded nature of the procuracy's independence. As we see below, if Japanese prosecutors had been as independent as their Italian counterparts, they would not have stopped when they did. The Occupation reformers built accountability into the postwar prosecution system in order to reduce the risk of prosecutorial abuses. It worked. But as often happens with legal reforms, the cure created a new problem by making it difficult for prosecutors to charge political elites with crimes. As a result, instead of being tried for the crime of bribery, "the big evil slept" (Tachibana 1993: 559).

Soon after indictments were issued in the Recruit scandal, the Sagawa Kyūbin Scandal began to take shape. At the center was Sagawa President Watanabe Hiroyasu, who confessed to paying off over 100 politicians, including many of the big names implicated in Recruit. The biggest name was Kanemaru Shin, the LDP vice president and "shadow shogun" who received some $4 million in Sagawa payoffs.[8] Hoping to end the issue as Nakasone had done, Kanemaru resigned from his LDP post. Unlike Nakasone, however, he admitted wrongdoing when he acknowledged violating the Political Funds Control Law (PFCL) by not reporting Sagawa's political "contribution." Prosecutors indicted Kanemaru for the PFCL violation without even bothering to interview him about the crime. This outraged large segments of society, who rightly perceived that less prominent offenders rarely get treated so deferentially. Some 30,000 citizens filed complaints with the Tokyo District Prosecutors Office, reproving prosecutors for the "special treatment" accorded Kanemaru (Mukaidani 1993). Satō Michio, a top prosecutor executive, believed prosecutors acted so timorously in the face of potential political intervention that he wrote an acerbic editorial in the *Asahi* newspaper rebuking his colleagues for betraying the principle of impartiality by giving Kanemaru "special treatment." The public uproar not only forced Kanemaru to quit his Diet seat, it spurred prosecutors to investigate him further. Raids on Kanemaru's home uncovered over $50 million in gold bars, cash, and debentures. In March 1993, six months after Satō's editorial, prosecutors charged Kanemaru and his political secretary, Haibara Masahisa, with tax evasion.[9] Kanemaru got caught, but only after he resigned from politics and only after prosecutors were severely criticized for doing what they had routinely done in the postwar era: "adjust" to political exigencies.

An Exception That Illustrates the Rule: Tanaka Kakuei and the Lockheed Scandal

The indictment of former Prime Minister Tanaka Kakuei in 1976 is the most publicized prosecution in Japanese history (MacDougall 1988; Kubo 1989; Johnson 1995). It is also heralded as the procuracy's biggest success (Nomura 1991: 117; Mukaidani 1993: 63; Hotta 1999). Given the procuracy's limited independence,

[8] At least fifty other politicians allegedly received about $800,000 each (Castberg 1997).

[9] Kanemaru died during the trial; Haibara was convicted.

how was it possible to indict and convict the original "shadow shogun," the most powerful politician in postwar history? To put it differently, how did prosecutors acquire sufficient independence to charge the man who dedicated his life to the syllogism that if "democracy is numbers" and "numbers are money," then "democracy is money" (Tachibana 1993: 10)?

Though some commentators believe Lockheed is exemplary proof that prosecutors "are independent of political and other influences" (MacDougall 1988: 227; Tsuchiya 1995: 4), such conclusions are misguided and misleading. Their chief defects are a preoccupation with Tanaka's lofty status and a corresponding disregard for the importance of the other political actors in the Lockheed story, particularly Prime Minister Miki Takeo.

Tanaka was prime minister from July 1972 until December 1974. He was forced to resign when Tachibana Takashi, then a freelance investigative journalist, published two exposés in the monthly *Bungei Shunjū* that detailed Tanaka's dubious financial dealings. The Japanese press largely ignored these articles because the financial improprieties they revealed were neither surprising nor illegal. When an American reporter at the Tokyo Foreign Correspondent's Club pressed the issue during a Tanaka press conference, however, the story got launched internationally. Soon, Japan's "insider journalists" could no longer ignore the matter. Led by the *Asahi* newspaper, the mainstream press began to magnify Tanaka's so-called gray transactions. The consequent criticism forced Tanaka to resign the premiership just four months after Richard Nixon had resigned as U.S. president (Farley 1996: 147).

Because the LDP's faction leaders could not agree on whom to install in Tanaka's place, they delegated the decision to Shiina Etsusaburō, one of the party's oldest and most venerated politicians. The LDP "grudgingly accepted Shiina's unexpected recommendation" that Miki Takeo be made prime minister in order to deal with what Shiina called "the greatest crisis in LDP history" (Curtis 1988: 162). This became known as the "Shiina arbitration." Tanaka was not indicted for the dubious dealings described in Tachibana's articles, but Miki's ascent to premier proved to be the beginning of his end. Eighteen months later, Miki enabled prosecutors to pursue Tanaka when hearings before Idaho senator Frank Church's Subcommittee on Multinational Corporations revealed that A. Carl Kotchian, vice chairman and former president of the Lockheed Aircraft Corporation, had paid then Prime Minister Tanaka $3 million in bribes in order to obtain Tanaka's help in selling the company's airplanes to All Nippon Airways. American media coverage of Kotchian's testimony quickly crossed the Pacific and established the Lockheed Scandal as Japan's number-one news story of 1976.

At the outset of the Lockheed investigation, Miki declared, "Even if we have to risk the honor of Japanese politics, it is necessary to clarify the truth about this problem. To the best of their abilities, prosecutors must gather evidence and, where there are legal violations, strictly dispose of the guilty" (Mukaidani 1993: 66). Still, no matter how persistently Miki expressed his resolve to pursue the investigation, "it was simply not believed . . . that really high ranking politicians would be snared" in the procuracy's net (Fisher 1980: 134). Indeed, most observers believed "prosecutors' hands were tied," in fact if not in Miki's proclamations, by the Article 14 provision that Prime Minister Yoshida had used to save Satō Eisaku in 1954 and that now made Prosecutor General Fuse Takeshi an agent of Prime Minister Miki (Kawai 1979: 18). When prosecutors actually arrested and indicted Tanaka in August 1976, the nation was shocked and LDP leaders were outraged (Fisher 1980: 134). LDP leaders, including Shiina, the politician who annointed Miki premier, were so "furious with Miki for not stopping Tanaka's arrest" that they "pressed forward their 'down with Miki' (*Miki oroshi*) campaign" and drove him from office just four months after Tanaka's indictment (Curtis 1988: 98, 163).

These events raise two critical questions. First, was Miki powerless to stop prosecutors, or did he allow and even encourage them to "get" Tanaka despite the wishes of other LDP leaders? Second, if Miki permitted Tanaka's arrest and indictment, why did he pursue a course of action that antagonized his supporters and cost him the post he had coveted for nearly a decade (Fisher 1980: 238)?

There is substantial evidence that Miki could have stopped prosecutors if he had wanted to protect Tanaka (Hotta 1999: 50). Although Article 14 had not been used openly since the 1954 Ship-building Scandal, few doubted its influence on other investigations or questioned its relevance for Tanaka's case. If Miki wanted to use it, this was the shield that could protect Tanaka from indictment. Further, Miki consistently promised not to interfere in the investigation and on numerous occasions urged prosecutors to do their utmost to "clarify the truth" about Tanaka's alleged misconduct (Fisher 1980: 110, 284; Mukaidani 1993). That his statements were more than the *tatemae* one so often hears from Japan's public officials is made clear by a little-known episode in the Lockheed Scandal. Late in the investigation, Miki received a telephone call from a man claiming to be Prosecutor General Fuse and imploring the prime minister to stop the arrest of another prominent LDP politician who had been implicated in the scandal, future Prime Minister Nakasone Yasuhiro. Miki listened to the caller's pleadings for almost an hour but repeatedly "expressed his desire that such decisions be left to the investigative authorities."[10] Still more compelling evidence of Miki's capacity to control prosecutors is evident in the reaction of other LDP leaders. The intensity of their anger at Miki and their determination to remove him from office speak more convincingly about Miki's capacity to protect Tanaka than did Miki's own pronouncements about the necessity of an independent investigation.

So, if Miki could have intervened to save Tanaka, why didn't he? A comprehensive study of the Lockheed Scandal describes four of Miki's motivations (Fisher 1980). First, Miki refused to invoke Article 14 because he believed a thorough investigation was "morally correct and proper." Miki was widely known and respected as "Mr. Clean" in the dirty world of Japanese politics. Ironically, he was made prime minister and forced from office for the same reason: because he was

[10] Subsequent events revealed that the caller was in fact Kitō Shiro, an assistant judge of the Kyoto District Court. The *Yomiuri* newspaper printed the text of the conversation on October 23, 1976. On November 1 it announced that Kitō confessed that he, not Prosecutor General Fuse, had telephoned Miki (Fisher 1980: 133; Kubo 1989: 62).

perceived to be incorruptible. Second, Miki believed that a thorough investigation would reduce the power of his antagonists in the LDP and thereby redound to his own political advantage. That he miscalculated does not alter the nature of his ex ante belief (Hotta 1999). Third, Miki sensed that political intervention in the Lockheed investigation would damage the LDP's electoral prospects in coming elections. Since the LDP's percentage of the popular vote had declined steadily since 1958 and rapidly since 1971, his perception seemed more reasonable at the time than it did ten years later, when the LDP seemed electorally invincible. Finally, as the Lockheed investigation progressed, "public opinion became a source of vital support to Miki." Journalists noted that the Tanaka case was "one of the rare occasions when genuine popular feeling has played a vital role in Japanese politics" (Fisher 1980). With the public on his side, Miki felt empowered to act on his duty to do the right thing. As Miki told an interviewer during the "down with Miki" campaign that drove him from office, "I don't want to be prime minister indefinitely. . . . My responsibilities are to the Diet, not to the LDP. I, not the LDP, am prime minister of Japan" (Curtis 1999: 3).

In sum, the procuracy remained permeable to political control throughout the Lockheed investigation. Tanaka's case is "the exception that proves the rule" because of the preferences of Mr. Miki, the politician who possessed both de facto and de jure authority to permit or forbid arrest and indictment, and because of the public support Miki received to act on his instincts. Once Miki decided to let prosecutors pursue the former prime minister, no one could quash the prosecution's case.[11] Throughout, Lockheed prosecutors remained attached to the Article 14 leash and therefore under control of their political principal (Ramseyer and Rosenbluth 1993). This time, however, they were given sufficient slack to get their target. As agents, prosecutors still possessed limited independence. What proved decisive was the identity of their principal, Prime Minister Miki. "Another politician might not have demonstrated the same steely resolve. . . . Decisions made by individuals . . . are the direct cause of what happens in politics" (Curtis 1999: 3, 172). Such decisions are not inevitable. Structure constrains, but agency matters, too. People are not replaceable parts. Miki played a principal role in the Lockheed case. As a result, prosecutors had enough independence to satisfy the first major requirement of a corruption prosecution.[12]

[11] Tanaka's power grew after he was indicted. Between his prosecution in 1976 and his stroke in 1985, Tanaka was able to install allies as prime minister and "friendly" ministers of justice in four successive cabinets. After his indictment, however, it was too late for even Tanaka's staunchest supporters – such as Minister of Justice Hatano Akira (1982–83) – to quash the criminal case (Tachibana 1993: 18; Hatano 1994).

[12] Prosecutors satisfied the second requisite of successful prosecution (evidence) by receiving from Japan's Supreme Court a one-time-only pass to offer immunity to A. Carl Kotchian, Tanaka's chief accuser. Until that point, Japanese law had never been interpreted to confer on prosecutors the authority to grant immunity from indictment in exchange for testimony. In 1995, the Supreme Court reversed its 1976 ruling by holding illegal the procuracy's end run around the immunity restriction. Tanaka had many defenders even after conviction. He died in 1993, however, while his appeal was still before the Supreme Court. Subsequent decisions by the Supreme Court and the National Tax Agency leave little doubt about his guilt (Hotta 1999).

The Extreme Independence of Italian Prosecutors: The Tangentopoli Scandal

If limited independence limits indictments, Italy illustrates the converse: extreme independence enables prosecutors to charge crimes of corruption on a vast scale. In Italy, almost absolute priority has been given to the value of prosecutorial independence. At the same time, since independence implies reduced responsiveness to authority, Italy manifests a near total disregard for the value of democratic accountability (Di Federico 1995). Descriptively, independence and unaccountability constitute the core traits of the Italian system of prosecution (Guarnieri 1995; Nelken 1996; Burnett and Mantovani 1998; Colombo 1999; della Porta and Vannucci 1999; Rossetti 2000). Causally, these traits explain why Italian prosecutors were able to indict some 1,200 suspects in the Clean Hands investigation, or 100 times more charges than Japanese prosecutors instituted in Recruit.

As Recruit and Lockheed did for Japan, the Clean Hands case revealed "structural corruption" in the Italian polity. It thereby produced "the most serious political crisis in the history of the Italian Republic" (della Porta and Vannucci 1999: 2, 13). The scandal began on February 17, 1992, when Milan magistrate Antonio Di Pietro arrested Mario Chiesa, a Socialist and the director of a major Milan charity. Di Pietro, who became the leading figure in Tangentopoli and the most popular public official in Italy, charged Chiesa with taking kickbacks from funeral homes for delivering cadavers from his charity's nursing home. As happened to many suspects in the scandal, Chiesa was held in preventive detention for several weeks until he confessed and turned state's evidence. This was the opening act of Operation Clean Hands. The curtain fell on April 21, 1996, when the successor to the Italian Communist Party, the Democratic Party of the Left, won a national election that made it the dominant partner in a coalition government. During the intervening fifty months, more than 5,000 people were investigated, including over 250 former and present members of parliament. Five former premiers were indicted: Giuliano Amato, Giulio Andreotti, Silvio Berlusconi, Bettino Craxi, and Arnaldo Forlani. Thus far, of the 1,200 persons indicted in Clean Hands, courts have convicted 549 and acquitted 150.[13]

Tangentopoli has been called a "coup d'état" executed by a small group of unelected magistrates "whose methods were new but whose fundamental character differs little from a courtier's plunging a knife into the back of the king" (Burnett and Mantovani 1998: 1). On this view, a few radical Milan magistrates aimed to overthrow the ruling regime and succeeded so fully that the standard Italian

[13] Italian criminal justice moves slowly. The normal trial rhythm is about two hearings per case per year. An average trial takes nine or ten years to resolve; complicated trials last longer. In Tangentopoli, more than half of acquitted defendants were exonerated because the statute of limitations expired (Burnett and Mantovani 1998: 20; Colombo 1999), and by 2005, about 60 percent of Mani Pulite trials will have to be barred because the statute of limitations will have been reached (Colombo 2002). Recent reforms have not helped: moving from a written to an oral system of evidence has made Italian trials even slower. The overall result is that "virtually none of the thousands of defendants" charged in Operation Clean Hands are now in jail (Stille 2001).

political annual could accurately declare "the party system which defined the post-war Republic no longer exists" (ibid.: 217). Gone were the Christian Democrats, the Craxi Socialists, the Liberals, the Social Democrats, and the Republicans.

Although the "coup view" captures part of the Tangentopoli truth, it is significantly overstated. The magistrates' methods did stretch the meaning of due process beyond recognition. Indeed, the ability to employ (and abuse) investigative techniques unavailable to Japanese prosecutors is one reason Tangentopoli took a higher trajectory than scandals in Japan.[14] Moreover, the Milan pool of magistrates did manifest a high degree of politicization (della Porta and Vannucci 1999: 132). In an action reminiscent of "prosecutorial fascism" in prewar Japan, Francesco Borrelli, the chief magistrate of the Milan pool, spoke openly of the need for greater prosecutorial power in the Italian political mix, even asserting that because Italy's politicians could not be trusted to run the country right, perhaps the magistrates should take over the job (Burnett and Mantovani 1998: 257, 297). Likewise, when Prime Minister Silvio Berlusconi was issued a notification of investigation (*avviso*) in November 1994, magistrates chose to do it (and leak it) while Berlusconi was in Naples hosting a United Nations conference on criminality (ibid.: 178).

Despite these excesses, Operation Clean Hands was "*not* an attempt to overthrow the State in the cause of a new group or class, or even in the name of a new ideal" (Nelken 1996: 95). It was instead "a revolution conducted within the law," conducted largely by prosecutors and enabled by an old ideal that became increasingly salient in the three decades before Clean Hands began (Gilbert 1995). That ideal is the independence of law and the insulation of legal magistrates from party politics.

The extreme independence of Italy's magistracy rests on five institutional pillars. First, the legacy of fascism prompted the framers of the 1948 Constitution to sever the tie that previously linked magistrates to electoral politics through the Ministry of Justice (Di Federico 1995: 14). This response to the problem of "prosecutorial fascism" is just the opposite of what occurred in Japan, where reform of Article 14 explicitly connected prosecutors to party politics through the Ministry of Justice.

Second, the postwar constitutional assembly envisaged the institution of a self-governing body of prosecutors and judges called the Higher Council of the Magistracy (CSM). It took twelve years, but when the CSM was established in

[14] Italian prosecutors routinely employed four methods for gathering evidence that are rarely used by their Japanese counterparts. First, prosecutors relied on *pentiti*, or "repentant persons," whose main characteristics are a willingness to talk and the ability to point the finger of blame at others. The use of *pentiti* to build cases resembles the use of plea offers and grants of immunity by American prosecutors. Second, preventive detention (or the threat of detention) in Italy's squalid prisons induced many suspects to believe their only avenue to freedom was through becoming a *pentito*. Third, the publication (or leakage) of *avviso di garanzia* (notifications sent to citizens that they are being investigated) helped mobilize public support for aggressive investigations and provided clues and cues to potential *pentiti* about the kinds of information magistrates sought. Finally, wiretaps, such as the one used to corner Mario Chiesa at the start of *Mani Pulite*, generated damning evidence of guilt (Burnett and Mantovani 1998: 19, 36, 42, 45).

1959, it greatly increased the internal and external independence of magistrates (Guarnieri 1995: 93). The CSM makes all decisions concerning magistrate careers, including recruitment, promotion, pay, discipline, and retirement. Twenty of its thirty-three members are elected by the magistrates themselves (Burnett and Mantovani 1998: 18). To reduce the influence of politics on the magistrates' performance, the CSM has separated questions of salary and status from the work magistrates do. Instead, magistrates are guaranteed automatic progression based simply on years of service. Similarly, selection for higher judicial office is based mainly on seniority, not merit (Nelken 1996: 100). The result is that Italian prosecutors possess far more autonomy from external control than do their Japanese counterparts.

Third, Article 112 of the constitution prescribes the legal principal of mandatory prosecution, whereby prosecutors *must* institute indictment for all criminal violations. Thus, unlike prosecutors in Japan, Italian magistrates have no choice but to file criminal charges when there is sufficient evidence of guilt; they do not have authority to withhold charges in order to serve "the public interest" or the rehabilitation of offenders. Italy's postwar constitutional assembly believed independence and compulsory prosecution – two faces of the same coin – would guarantee the precept of the equality of all citizens – including corrupt officials – before the criminal law (Di Federico 1995: 15). This noble ideal has the powerful practical effect of shielding Italian prosecutors from criticisms that they have misused or abused their discretion. Having none, how can they?[15]

Fourth, a series of laws passed by Parliament between 1960 and 1990 "further accentuated the independence of prosecutors" by strengthening the magistracy's system of self-government (ibid.: 15). These laws had four major effects:

- They reinforced the seniority principle for promotions and job assignments so that all forms of professional evaluation were essentially abandoned.
- They granted magistrates salaries, pensions, and retirement bonuses that are by far the highest in public service and that increase automatically year after year.
- They made it impossible for magistrates to be transferred to other offices unless they themselves request it.
- They conferred on prosecutors full control over police investigations.

These legislative changes, which ended in the late 1980s, help explain the timing of the massive Clean Hands operation. Indeed, the investigation began in earnest only

[15] Despite laws requiring Italian prosecutors to charge all criminal violations, prosecution in Italy "is *de facto* largely discretionary just as much as in other countries, and perhaps more" (Di Federico 1995: 18). But if the attempt to outlaw discretion can be attacked as a mere myth, it is a myth with profound practical consequences. Most important, the principle (and myth) of mandatory prosecution helps shield prosecutors from criticism (Nelken 1997).

after magistrates had enhanced their independence from politics and consolidated their control over police.[16]

The final pillar supporting the extreme independence of Italian prosecutors – the commercialization of the Italian media in the late 1980s – further explains the timing of Tangentopoli. Before commercialization, many media were government owned and controlled. Commercialization produced greater independence from government and more competition. In turn, these changes spurred aggressive reporting, often strongly supportive of vigorous, and vigorously independent, prosecution (Giglioli 1996; Stille 1999). In Japan's Recruit Scandal, prosecutor Yoshinaga strategically leaked investigative facts to the media in order to generate public support and deflect or delay political intervention. His leaks had limited success. In Tangentopoli, prosecutor leaks were not only more numerous, they also found a more welcome reception among print and electronic media that eagerly amplified the disclosures (Burnett and Mantovani 1998: 254). In this way, the invigorated Italian media engendered public support – and sometimes unwarranted assumptions of guilt – that simultaneously damaged the image of politicians and sustained prosecutors throughout Operation Clean Hands (Guarnieri 1995: 101).

These pillars of prosecutorial independence are rooted in the soil of Italy's political culture of distrust. It has long been recognized that Italian corruption "is a by-product of the lack of trust among its citizens and between citizens and the state" (Banfield 1958; Heidenheimer 1996: 339; della Porta and Vannucci 1999: 11). Efforts to build a system for controlling and punishing corruption arise from, and have been shaped by, the same distrust (Nelken 1994: 229). The bedrock belief is this: because government officials cannot be trusted to execute the impersonal obligations incumbent on their roles, they must be policed by an actor – the magistracy – that lies outside the sphere of official influence. Of course, the "long tradition of collusion" between magistrates and politicians reveals there is a gap between the principle of prosecutorial independence and the practice of prosecuting corruption, but the gap does not diminish the fact that the Italian magistracy is the most politically independent prosecutor organization in the world (Guarnieri 1995). Moreover, debate over the need to hold Italian magistrates more accountable is conditioned by the fear that greater accountability would bring prosecutors under control of the corrupt executive (Nelken 1997).

[16] Three background causes help explain the timing of Tangentopoli. First, Italy's economic recession made the rising costs of political corruption unsustainable. Second, changes in the international economic environment (especially Europe's economic and monetary integration) generated important shifts in behavior. As Italian banks became subject to international regulation, for example, politicians may have been forced to direct their bribes into channels that were easier for prosecutors to identify. Third and most important, the party system's basis of legitimacy collapsed when the Cold War ended. In the April 1992 election, the governing parties saw their share of the vote decline to 48.8 percent. As the ruling coalition's parliamentary power declined, so did its capacity to refuse prosecutorial requests to suspend the immunity of legislators (*le richieste di autorrizzazione a procedere*). This change "greatly facilitated the 'Clean Hands' investigation" (Golden 1999: 12, 47; della Porta and Vannucci 1999: 266; Nelken 1996: 102).

Regents, Revolutions, and the Costs of Independence

The prosecutorial independence that made Tangentopoli the biggest corruption scandal in the history of Western democracies has found admirers in many countries and emulators in France, Spain, and Greece (Burnett and Mantovani 1998: 235, 264; della Porta and Vannucci 1999: 2).[17] To be sure, there *is* much to esteem in the Clean Hands case. The ideal of equality under the law was pressed to a limit seldom seen in corruption investigations, and the prosecutors' independence curbed "the perverse ascending spiral of corruption and inefficiency" in Italian society (della Porta and Vannucci 1999: 269). These are significant achievements. In result if not intent, prosecutors helped "unblock" a political system that had been obstructed for decades by corruption and clientelism (Nelken 1996: 107). Different analysts appraise this consequence differently, but it is beyond debate that Clean Hands nearly eliminated an entire political class (Guarnieri 1995; Di Federico 1996; Nelken 1996; Burnett and Mantovani 1998; della Porta and Vannucci 1999).[18]

However, the cost of extreme independence was high, and the price was paid in the currency of other democratic values. During Clean Hands, a small group of Italian magistrates possessed immense unchecked power.[19] They frequently abused it. Preventive detention was used to coerce confessions and cooperation from suspects and witnesses. Suspects were cruelly mistreated throughout the pretrial process, causing many magistrates to be reviled for their investigative excesses (Nelken 1995: 6). Yet the abuses continued. Similarly, magistrates' failure to safeguard the secrecy of investigations by strategically leaking *avviso* to the press resulted in irreversible damage to the reputations of people who were always legally and sometimes factually innocent.

Magistrates justified their methods in two ways. Practically, the chief of the Milan pool of magistrates, Francesco Borelli, argued that the shock of preventive detention produced "positive results" (Burnett and Mantovani 1998: 50).[20]

[17] Extreme independence also enabled a larger proportion of Italian magistrates to participate in the Clean Hands case. By December 1993, about 400 magistrates had engaged in the investigations, or about 5 percent of the entire magistracy (Nelken 1996: 111). In contrast, Tokyo's Special Investigation Division seldom operates with more than fifty prosecutors, or about 3 percent of Japan's procuracy. Still, considering the huge size of Tangentopoli, the number of Italian magistrates remains relatively small, too small to explain the difference in scale between the Clean Hands and the Lockheed, Recruit, or Sagawa Kyūbin investigations.

[18] In 1994, in the middle of the Clean Hands investigation, 70 percent of the winning candidates in the general election for Parliament were newcomers. By contrast, in Japan only about 20 percent of the winners in the 1993 and 1996 elections were newcomers (*Asahi Shinbun*, January 10, 2000).

[19] Prosecutors and judges belong to the same organization, and many magistrates switch from one function to the other during their careers. As a result, prosecutors are little checked by their judicial siblings in the magistracy. This pattern has been called "structural collusion between prosecutors and judges" (Guarnieri 1995: 102).

[20] In May 1993, magistrate Borelli publicly declared, "Ours is a legal and wise revolution which has lasted a little more than a year. Remember that the French Revolution began in 1789 and was completed only in 1794." In the service of this revolution, Borelli launched a radio appeal to mobilize

Theoretically, magistrate Gherardo Colombo (1997), considered part of the "political brains" of Clean Hands, articulated a "Regency Theory" of prosecution (*la teoria della reggenza*), which asserts that since corruption hurts everyone, any means to defeat it is in the common interest. In this view, because the other powers of state were delegitimized by corruption, "it is left to the magistracy to assume the regency" of state powers (Burnett and Mantovani 1998: 52).

Pronouncements of "revolutions and regents" threaten the principle of separation of powers enshrined in the Italian constitution. They also reveal the biggest price paid for Italy's prosecution system. Both internally (vis-à-vis other magistrates) and externally (vis-à -vis other political actors), Italian prosecutors possess extreme independence. Ironically, the independence that enables corruption prosecutions also enables the politicization and personalization of those prosecutions (Guarnieri 1995: 107; Di Federico 1996: 20). In effect, independence has two incarnations: as shield, preventing outside intrusions into prosecutorial decision making, and as shelter, concealing decisions motivated by political orientations, alliances, and ambitions (Burnett and Mantovani 1998). In Operation Clean Hands, Italian prosecutors were both highly independent and highly politicized. Like the creators of America's Independent Counsel Act, the architects of the Italian prosecution system attempted to ensure independence in order to ensure equality under law. They both discovered (or should have discovered) that extreme independence comes attached to a Siamese twin: politicization.

Conclusion

The independence of Italian prosecutors enables them to identify and condemn crimes of corruption – to police illicit linkages between state and society – more strictly than can their less independent counterparts in Japan. As is evident in the four cases examined here – Ship-building, Recruit, Sagawa, and Lockheed – prosecutors in Japan operate in an institutional environment that leaves them susceptible to outside political control. Since 1955, LDP leaders have routinely tried to manipulate the institutional structure of prosecution in order to exert political control over prosecutors and thereby protect party members and their cronies from indictment. They have often succeeded. Independence enables indictments; limited independence limits them. This is the main empirical conclusion of this tale of two systems.[21]

But independence is not an unqualified good; it is rather like an axe. It can be a *tool*, indispensable for achieving values such as equality under the law, but

"all the anonymous informers of Italy." Those who do not inform, the chief magistrate asserted, "actually support the criminals" (Burnett and Mantovani 1998: 120).

21 Japan is hardly unique in conferring limited independence on prosecutors. Indeed, limiting independence by securing accountability is the chief justification for the peculiarly American practice of electing local prosecutors (Pizzi 1993: 1336). Limited independence also constrains prosecutors in Germany and France, two other countries from which Japan has borrowed legal institutions (Blankenburg 1996: 285; Provine 1996: 230).

it is an effective tool only when tempered by accountability. When not so tempered, independence can be a *weapon* for personalizing and politicizing law enforcement, thereby damaging the very values – equality, impartiality, public trust, and effective government – that it is meant to serve. This truth, of course, is not merely a Clean Hands message; it is the teaching of post-Watergate America and of Japan's own prewar history of prosecutor fascism (Yasko 1979; Toobin 1999).

The dangers posed by extreme independence are especially significant because most societies have more mechanisms for holding politicians accountable than they have for controlling prosecutors. In democratic countries, elections, the media, and public opinion constrain and restrain politicians' behavior, and no one argues that politicians should be "independent" of the citizens they represent. Outside the United States, by contrast, no prosecutors are elected, and in countries like Japan where crime has not been a chronic problem, prosecutors are relatively insulated from media, public, and other forms of scrutiny (Johnson 2002). One salutary result is that Japanese prosecutors confront little of the fear, fury, and wishful thinking that have driven American criminal justice policy in increasingly punitive directions. That insulation, however, comes linked to a serious risk: that prosecutors will exercise their abundant discretion for personal or political ends. Postwar reforms such as Article 14 provide safeguards against that danger.

My normative conclusion – that independence should be qualified by accountability – is amply illustrated by events in contemporary America, where "independent prosecutors" and other institutional features of "the anticorruption project" have unintentionally but unquestionably undermined public trust and impeded effective government by proliferating scandals, eroding privacy, constraining discretion, distorting priorities, and causing delays (Ginsberg and Shefter 1999; Lewis 1999a). Animated by a noble vision of corruption-free government, America's "pursuit of absolute integrity" has had corrosive consequences for civil society and public administration. Notably, it has done so without contributing much to the prevention or detection of corruption (Anechiarico and Jacobs 1996). Indeed, the ersatz scandals emerging all over America obscure our vision of serious corruption and impair our capacity to distinguish the mere "appearance of impropriety" from serious misconduct (Garment 1991). When everything is a scandal, nothing is (Morgan and Reynolds 1997).

And when everything is scandalized, confidence in government declines. Citizen distrust of government is a trend throughout the democratic world (Pharr and Putnam 2000). If the health of democracy depends on the state of civil society and if civil society consists of "sustained, organized social activity" that is made possible by trust (Pharr, this volume), then this is a troubling trend. The primary source of public disaffection is neither the policy performance of leaders nor shifts in the stock of social capital. It is the corrosive effects of corruption – and perceptions of corruption – on the bonds that link citizens to their leaders and to political institutions (della Porta 2000; Pharr 2002). Since sustaining democracy requires, above all, public trust, "fostering responsible leadership" is indeed "a critical issue for the next millenium" (Pharr 2000: 34). Prosecutors must pursue that end. At the same time, because the pursuit of absolute integrity undermines the public trust on which civil society and democracy depend, fostering accountable law enforcement may be as important a need in the new millenium as fostering responsible political leadership.

That independence should be tempered by accountability is a lesson insufficiently appreciated by critics of Japan's procuracy who rightly lament the corruption in Japanese politics but wrongly attribute it to law enforcement deficiencies (Kubo 1989; Mukaidani 1993; Tachibana 1993). The failure to learn this lesson is important for at least two reasons.

First, those who cannot remember the past may be condemned to repeat it. In their enthusiasm for greater prosecutorial independence, critics of the procuracy overlook lessons from Japan's own history about the need to hold prosecutors, no less than politicians and bureaucrats, accountable. Prosecutors in Japan wield huge control over life, liberty, and reputation. Their discretion is tremendous. Today, they are far more governed by the rule of law – and by the imposition of effective inhibitions on their power – than they were fifty years ago.[22] Prosecutorial independence is both necessary *and* dangerous, and mechanisms of accountability are a bulwark against the dangers. The reforms culminating in Article 14 may not have struck a perfect balance between independence and accountability, but it is a reasonable, decent balance that leaves prosecutors neither highly independent nor highly dependent, and it is certainly an improvement over prewar practice. Political reforms in Japan have frequently reflected "transwar continuities" and the law of unintended consequences (Dower 1999). Article 14, and its overt and covert uses in postwar scandals, comprise one area where there is significant historical discontinuity – and generally for the better. Under the current system, prosecutors are far more accountable than they were in the prewar years, both indirectly, through the political mechanisms described above, and directly, through the influence of public opinion. Civil society's influence was evident, for example, in the Finance Ministry and Bank of Japan scandals of 1998. After months of investigation and the indictment of five elite bureaucrats for bribery, prosecutors closed down the case, in large part because of mounting public criticism that they should let the country's economic mandarins try to steer the debt-ridden, dormant economy back on track. People even coined the term "prosecutors' recession" in order to implicate the procuracy in the nation's economic woes. Prosecutors were further rebuked for a rash of suicides seemingly induced by the investigations (Bondy 1997). They responded accordingly, by backing off (WuDunn 1998).

Second, the singular stress on prosecutorial independence has diverted attention from other means of holding Japan's leaders accountable. As others have noted,

[22] Japan's prewar prosecutors were harshly criticized as "fascist runaway horses" bent on "changing the world" by "purifying politics" (Matsumoto 1981: 313). Even scholars who laud prewar prosecutors for carving out "an autonomous sphere of influence" recognize that their chief goal often was to advance their own political fortunes by "seeking political advantage wherever it might be found" (Yasko 1979: 67).

"the criminal justice approach to corruption is not sufficient" (Rose-Ackerman 1999: 193). Under the present system of limited independence, even the most vigorous prosecution efforts – such as the Lockheed investigation that snared Tanaka Kakuei – will not change the rudiments of Japan's "money-power politics" (Schlesinger 1997: 108). In prosecution as in cuisine, Japan is not Italy. An Italian-style "revolution within the law" is impossible in Japan precisely because limited independence makes it so. If corruption is to be better controlled and Japan's political leaders are to be held more accountable to the rule of law, then one of two things must occur. On the one hand, Japan could travel the Roman road by creating institutions like those that enabled Italian prosecutors to "unblock" their corrupt political system. While some commentators advocate such changes (Hotta 1999), significant movement in this direction is unlikely to occur any time soon, not least because the politicians who must enact the laws would thereby create the inconvenient prospect of "massive indictments," as foreseen by Ozawa Ichirō and other politicians (Schlesinger 1997: 266).

The other approach to corruption control seems more promising. Despite what many see as a "crisis of accountability" in Japan – and probably because of it – there are signs that civil society is itself assuming greater responsibility for policing corruption and ensuring the responsiveness of government officials (French 2000b). The trend is evident in a number of places. In May 1999, for example, after sustained lobbying by many citizen groups, Japan's Diet enacted an Information Disclosure Law that has the potential to increase the accountability of leaders by revolutionizing people's access to official information (Machlachlan 2000). This is a particularly welcome development given that the other "institutional intermediary" examined in this book – the mass media – "have frequently worked together with, or on behalf of, [Japan's] political core," seldom conducting the kind of tough investigative reporting that could help expose and control corruption (Freeman, this volume).

Likewise, the watchdog activities of Japan's 3,000 or so "citizen ombudsmen" have resulted in the return to public coffers of hundreds of millions of misspent tax dollars and major reductions in the hoary practice of *kankan settai*, or bureaucrats' entertaining each other at taxpayer expense (Efron 1998).[23] In addition, popular culture, as reflected in hit films such as *Minbō no onna* (*Woman Mob Fighter*) and *Jubaku* (*Spellbound*), increasingly emphasizes the necessity and the capacity of ordinary Japanese people to redeem corrupt institutions of governance through collective action (Sterngold 1992). Finally, following the lead of South Korea's Internet-based "No to Corruption" campaign, the Tokyo-based civic group "Citizens Solidarity/Wave 21" has created a website where citizens can nominate candidates deemed "unqualified" for reelection to the Diet. Of the six characteristics that define "unqualified," three can be construed as proxies for corruption: "the privatization of politics," "participation in money politics," and

[23] For example, ombudsman Gotō Yūichi, a forty-eight-year-old baker, has singlehandedly badgered Tokyo city hall into returning to public coffers some $8 million in misspent funds (Efron 1998).

"prior criminal convictions." As of this writing, of the twenty-two candidates regarded as most unfit to govern, twenty-one are members or former members of the LDP. Four of those have criminal records.[24]

Following scandals, Japanese citizens have generally "played their role in fighting corruption" by withholding votes from tainted candidates (Reed 1999: 186). They appear to be "playing their role" all the better now, and not just at the ballot box. If civil society in Japan continues to expand and diversify, as some in this volume predict, then this trend will continue. It, too, would be a welcome development. Japan "needs new types of civil society organizations" in order to better control corruption in the twenty-first century (Tsujinaka 2000). This is one lesson of the transnational "anti-corruption eruption," wherein citizens around the world "are mobilized as never before to demand greater transparency and to hold to account those entrusted with power" (Eigen 2001: 6). Japan's civil society appears to be one participant among many in this global movement. Wrongdoers should be punished, but it is unrealistic to rely mainly on prosecutors to root out corruption. The first function of prosecution is to attract notice and public support – to mobilize civil society – not to solve the underlying problems (Rose-Ackerman 1999: 226). In turn, a more vibrant civil society will make it possible for prosecutors to come closer to realizing the imperatives of the rule of law: government by and under law. One hopes it will also help to steer prosecutors between the Scylla of extreme independence and the Charybdis of unaccountability.

[24] In South Korea's anticorruption campaign preceding the midterm parliamentary election of April 13, 2000, civic groups urged voters to reject 86 candidates. They did well: more than two-thirds (59 out of 86) of the blacklisted candidates were defeated (French 2000a). In the capital city of Seoul and its vicinity, 19 out of 20 blacklisted candidates failed to be elected. South Korean civil organizations blacklisted politicians in previous elections as well (Yoon 2000: 197). On Japan's analogous "Expel Political Misfits" and "Make Them Lose" movement, see the Citizens Solidarity homepage (http://nvc.halsnet.com/jhattori/rakusen). Before the Lower House election of June 25, 2000, one of Japan's largest daily newspapers, the *Asahi Shinbun* (April 18, 2000), noted that "the South Koreans' resolve not to let incompetent and corrupt politicians get elected holds a lesson worth learning," but concluded that "it may be difficult to mount a similar campaign in Japan." That prediction proved too pessimistic. By election day, the "Make Them Lose" homepage had received more than 286,000 hits, a very high number for Japan. At the polls, the Liberal Democratic Party suffered a "severe election setback," while the opposition Democratic Party made "dramatic gains" and a "huge advance" (French 2000d). The *Asahi* declared that the election was "in effect a defeat for the LDP." The loss of 38 LDP seats from the party's preelection strength was the biggest shift since the party lost 36 seats in the 1983 Lower House election following former Prime Minister Tanaka Kakuei's conviction in the Lockheed bribery trial. Of the first 25 blacklisted candidates, seven lost, six of whom were from the LDP. The core of the Democrats' campaign, like the theme of the "Make Them Lose" movement, was an attack on the LDP's prolific pork-barrel spending and influence peddling. The appeal worked especially well in urban districts among voters who benefited little from the LDP's lavish spending. For background about Japan's blacklist campaign, see *Asahi Shinbun* (May 11, 2000), Saitō (2000), and French (2000c). See also Iitake and Karasaki (2000) on the recent formation of the Politicians Evaluation Conference (Seijika Hyōtei Kaigi), a group of Japanese intellectuals, journalists, and writers who rate politicians on their ability to fulfill campaign promises.

V

GLOBALIZATION AND VALUE CHANGE

13

Trust and Social Intelligence in Japan

Yamagishi Toshio

For most theorists, the concept of civil society extends beyond institutions to include specific, constitutive values, and among the most important of those values is trust. Adam Seligman (1992: 147), for example, observed that "the concept of social trust is essential to any idea of civil society, in the West as in the East." Although many scholars and pundits have assumed otherwise (e.g., Fukuyama 1995), both surveys and experiments consistently demonstrate that levels of general trust in people and society are not high in Japan. In fact, they are appreciably lower in Japan than in the United States. Why are Americans more trustful than Japanese, and what are the implications of this difference? I seek to answer this question by means of empirical research, and I conclude that different kinds of social intelligence are adaptive in American and Japanese society. Driven by a variety of factors, including economic trends such as globalization, Japanese society is changing, however, and with it the incentives that advantage different kinds of social intelligence, their attendant attitudes of trust, and the resulting shape of civil society. In sum, Japan is moving from a security-based society in which individuals pursue cautious, commitment-forming strategies to a trust-based society in which individuals pursue more open, opportunity-seeking strategies.

Are Japanese More Trustful Than Americans?

It is often claimed that business practices in Japan are based on trust to a much greater degree than in the West, where business practices are more heavily based on contracts. It is also claimed that social relations in Japan depend more heavily on trust than in the United States. This view is so widely shared that it is fair to say that it is the accepted wisdom.

Surveys do not support this accepted wisdom, however. Instead, they consistently demonstrate that Americans have a stronger tendency to trust others than do Japanese. My own study (Yamagishi 1988a) found that the average level of general trust of 852 American students was conspicuously higher than that of 212 Japanese students. Another study (Yamagishi and Yamagishi 1989), which reported the questionnaire responses of 167 American and 165 Japanese students, revealed that Americans have a stronger belief that people are generally honest. A more systematic survey (Yamagishi and Yamagishi 1994), which used both student samples and randomly selected samples from the general population, confirmed that Americans exhibit a higher level of general trust than Japanese. The difference was consistent among students, general citizens, and individuals of either sex.

In these studies, a trust scale developed by the author and his associates was used to measure the trust respondents felt toward other people in general.[1] We must always wonder whether questionnaires correctly measure respondents' general trust – an issue inherent in any use of questionnaires – but the General Trust Scale used here was fairly successful in predicting the actual behavior of participants in a series of experiments (e.g., Yamagishi 1986, 1988a, 1988b, 1992; Yamagishi and Satō 1986; Yamagishi and Cook 1993, Yamagishi et al. 1996; Kakiuchi and Yamagishi 1997). Thus, what the General Trust Scale measures is not an abstract belief; rather, the results of those studies indicate that a respondent's level of general trust as measured by the scale has a very strong influence on his or her actual behavior.

The first two studies used student samples from only Hokkaidō University and the University of Washington, and the samples in the third study were limited to residents of Seattle and Sapporo. Even so, a study conducted by the Institute of Statistical Mathematics used representative national samples of 1,571 American and 2,032 Japanese respondents and arrived at similar findings. First, when asked, "Do you think you can put your trust in most people or do you think it's always best to be on your guard?" 47 percent of the Americans responded, "People can be trusted." In contrast, only 26 percent of Japanese respondents gave that answer (in 1978, and 31 percent in 1983). Similarly, when asked, "Do you think that other people are always out to make use of you if ever they see an opportunity, or do you think that's not true?" 62 percent of the Americans answered, "Not true." Only 53 percent of the Japanese answered the same way (in 1978, and 59 percent in 1983). Moreover, 47 percent of the Americans responded, "People try to be helpful" to the question, "Would you say that most of the time people try to be helpful or that they are mostly just looking out for themselves?" Only 19 percent of the Japanese gave the same answer (in 1978, and 24 percent in 1983).

Although Japanese society is thought to boast stable, long-lasting social relations that rest on strong mutual trust, these studies found Japanese to be *less* trustful of others in general than Americans. Why? This is the first problem I

[1] In Yamagishi and Yamagishi's survey (1994), for example, the level of respondents' general trust was measured by the average of responses to the following six statements: "Most people are basically honest," "Most people are trustworthy," "Most people are basically good and kind," "Most people are trustful of others," "I am trustful," and "Most people will respond in kind when they are trusted by others."

would like to answer, but before offering my answer, we must examine differences in trustfulness more carefully.

Are Trustful People More Perceptive Than Distrustful People?

We generally regard trust in others as desirable but, at the same time, we worry about the possibility of being cheated or exploited by others. When we see someone around us trust others too quickly, we might hint at the possibility of being cheated or look down on such a person as naive, especially when he or she is not very close to us. We learn the accepted wisdom that clever people do not trust others easily or, conversely, that individuals who trust others too easily are naive people who know little of the world. Yet experimental evidence challenges this accepted wisdom.

Experiments on Sensitivity to Information

The first evidence comes from a series of experiments conducted by Kosugi and Yamagishi (1998). A booklet distributed to test participants contained fifteen scenarios in which a target person might behave selfishly and betray other people's trust. Participants were asked to predict whether the target person would act in a trustworthy manner in each scenario. The goal of the experiment was to gauge whether estimations of the target person's trustworthiness would vary among people with different tendencies to trust others in general. Participants were divided into high and low trusters on the basis of their scores on a trust scale included in a postexperiment questionnaire.

Information about the target person as well as about the situation was provided. For example, "A is a person who does not say thanks to people who have been kind to him or her" or "A cuts into line at the supermarket." The point was to see how estimations of the target's trustworthiness would change with the provision of such information. Two types of information about the target person were provided, positive information suggesting potential trustworthiness and negative information revealing the potential lack of it. Figure 13.1 graphs how estimations of the target person's trustworthiness changed with the provision of positive information (graph on left) and negative information (graph on right). The starting point of each graph indicates the mean probability estimation by high and low trusters that the target person would act in a trustworthy manner when no information about that person was provided. Without information, high trusters were more likely to think that the target person would act in a trustworthy manner than were low trusters. This indicates that the General Trust Scale used to classify participants reflected fairly well the extent to which they think an unspecified partner would act in a trustworthy manner.

Having thus demonstrated the reliability of the General Trust Scale, let us turn to differences in how sensitive high and low trusters are to information revealing potential trustworthiness. It is generally believed that low trusters are more sensitive to negative information and high trusters to positive information. In other words,

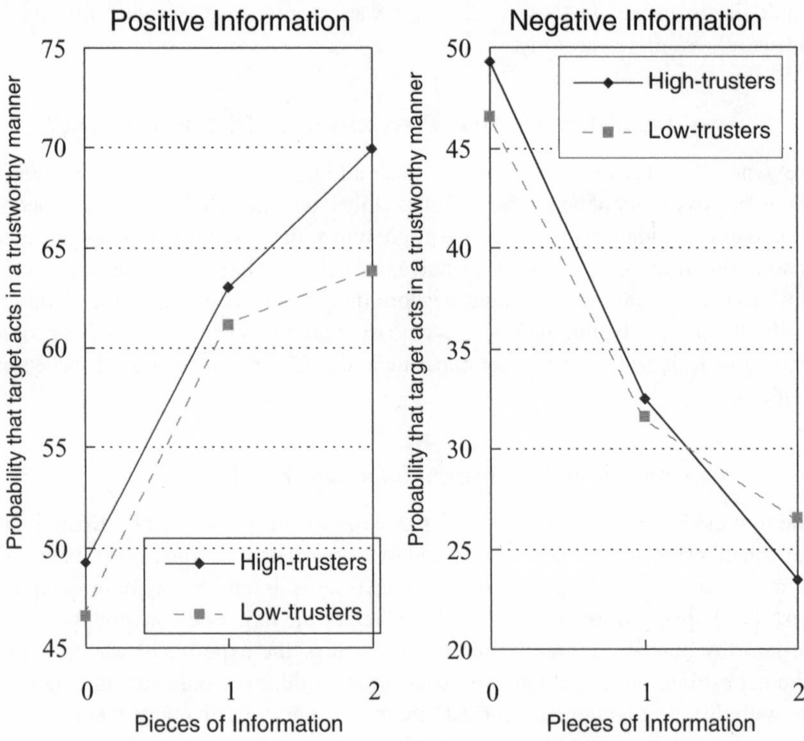

Figure 13.1 The effect of positive or negative information on high and low trusters' estimations of a target person's trustworthiness (Kosugi and Yamagishi 1998).

low trusters, who are always suspicious of others, would discount a target person's trustworthiness given the slightest doubt. Conversely, high trusters would have faith in a target person's trustworthiness with even a little positive evidence.

Do experimental results support this expectation? As the left-hand side of Figure 13.1 reveals, both high and low trusters raised their estimations of the target person's acting in a trustworthy manner when positive information was provided. As expected, when positive information was provided, high trusters raised their estimations of the target person's trustworthiness more rapidly than did low trusters. This difference in sensitivity to positive information did not reach the level of statistical significance, however.[2] As the right-hand side of Figure 13.1 reveals, on the other hand, both high and low trusters reduced their estimations of the target person's trustworthiness when negative information was provided. And contrary to the accepted wisdom, not only did high trusters respond more quickly to negative information than did low trusters, but the difference in sensitivity to negative information was statistically significant. Thus, high trusters responded more sensitively

[2] Unless otherwise noted, all correlations are statistically significant at the level of $p < .05$.

to positive *and* negative information. They were more attentive or cautious, and more sensitive to information revealing either potential trustworthiness or the lack of it.[3]

Experiments on Predictions of Others' Behavior

Although the experimental results detailed above conflict with our intuitive view of high and low trusters, there is an alternative explanation for these results: it is possible that high trusters in these experiments were more credulous than low trusters and took the words of the experimenter at face value. To eliminate this alternative explanation, we conducted additional experiments.

Participants in this experiment (Kikuchi, Watanabe, and Yamagishi 1997) were asked to decide whether or not to give money to their partner in a Prisoner's Dilemma situation. ("Prisoner's Dilemma" refers to a relationship in which cooperation yields a more desirable outcome than defection for both partners, but defection yields a more desirable outcome for each partner than one-sided cooperation, and mutual defection yields the least desirable outcome for the two.) Participants were provided with ¥800 yen (about $8) before the experiment started. They were then paired with other participants and played a Prisoner's Dilemma game with each partner. Each time, the participant was asked to give ¥100 to the partner or to take ¥100 from the partner. The ¥100 given by a participant was doubled by the experimenter before being awarded to the partner. Thus, both participants received ¥200 when each gave ¥100 to the other. Because each participant gave ¥100 and received ¥200, this yielded a profit of ¥100 for both. On the other hand, when a participant took ¥100 from his or her partner, that ¥100 became the participant's, and the partner's loss was also doubled by the experimenter. Thus, if both participants took ¥100, each earned ¥100, but simultaneously suffered a loss of ¥200, resulting in a net loss of ¥100.

The purpose of this experiment was to examine participants' accuracy in predicting whether other people would give money to their partner (cooperate) or take money from their partner (defect) when faced with a Prisoner's Dilemma situation. To this end, participants had a group discussion of garbage collection issues before they participated in the experiment. Although they were told that the discussion session was a part of another study and was totally independent of the experiment that followed, the real purpose of this session was to give participants an opportunity to get to know each other. Would a group discussion of thirty minutes provide them with the cues they needed to predict others' choices?

A more important question we wanted to pursue was whether the participants' level of general trust would have any relationship to the accuracy of their predictions of other participants' choices. According to the accepted wisdom, high

[3] In a second experiment, the maximum number of pieces of information provided rose from two to three, the number of scenarios rose from 15 to 16, and the number of participants fell from 257 to 75. This second experiment largely replicated the findings of the first, especially the finding that high trusters are more sensitive to negative information than low trusters.

trusters are naive and credulous people who can easily be deceived, so it is the low trusters who should be able to predict other people's choices more accurately. But given the previous experimental result demonstrating that it is high trusters who are more sensitive to information about others, we predicted that it is they who would predict others' choices correctly.

Each participant was informed that he or she was paired with several other participants, but was not told whom those partners were. The participant was then asked to decide whether to give or to take ¥100 from the unknown partner. It was thus impossible to base the choice on attitudes toward a specific partner, and the decision to give or to take money was expected to reflect the participant's general character. Those participants who gave ¥100 were considered to have a strong tendency toward forming cooperative relationships or to have an altruistic tendency. Anonymity was almost completely guaranteed not only vis-à-vis other participants, but also vis-à-vis the experimenter. After having decided to give or take ¥100, participants were told which two of the other five participants they had been matched with. They were then asked to predict whether the two partners had themselves decided to give or to take ¥100 in the experiment. To encourage the participant to take this exercise seriously, an additional bonus of ¥100 was provided for each correct prediction.

This experiment's results are illustrated by the three bars labeled "Kikuchi et al. 1997" in Figure 13.2. Accuracy was calculated by crediting participants with half a point when the partner acted as predicted and no points when the partner did not. As Figure 13.2 plainly shows, high trusters were more accurate in predicting other participants' behavior than medium or low trusters, and the difference was statistically significant. Despite the accepted wisdom that people who trust others are naive and gullible, this experimental result indicates that high trusters are actually prudent people who are more sensitive to information revealing other people's potential trustworthiness.

This surprising finding has been repeatedly confirmed by a series of replication experiments whose results are also displayed in Figure 13.2. The second experiment was a close replication of the experiment detailed above; the other four experiments differed from the first two in that they investigated trustworthiness assessments among people who had known each other for some time. For example, participants in experiment UH96 were sophomores who belonged to the same academic program (that is, smaller units within a department) at Hokkaidō University. They had spent about a year in the program and gotten to know each other fairly well. Two groups of participants were involved, nineteen sophomores from program A and fourteen sophomores from program B. Almost everyone in each program participated in the experiment. Aside from the fact that participants were acquaintances, the experimental setting was almost identical to that of the experiment described above. First, participants were told they would play a Prisoner's Dilemma game with one randomly selected student without knowing whom that partner would be. They were then asked to decide whether to cooperate or defect. Finally, they predicted whether each of the other students from the same program had chosen to cooperate or defect. They also answered a postexperiment

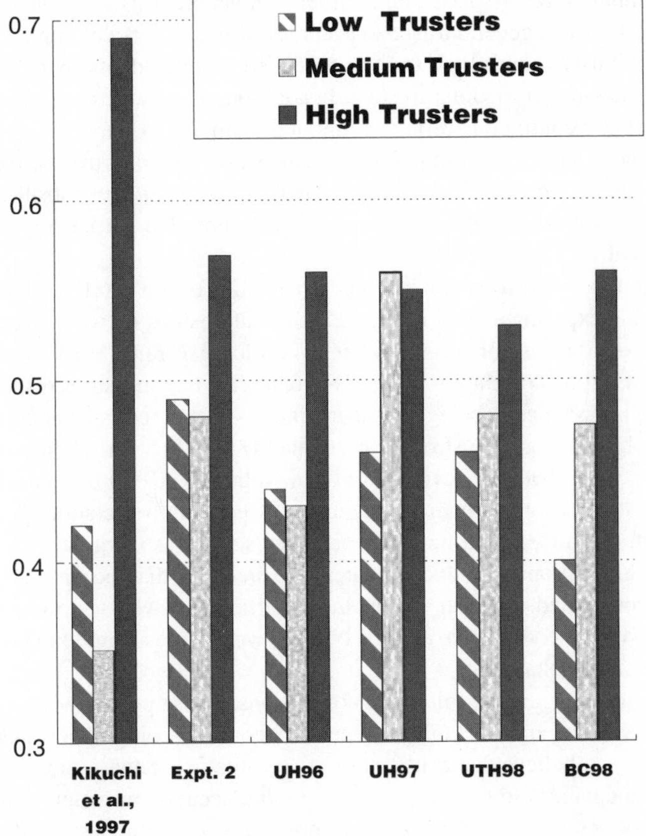

Figure 13.2 Low, medium, and high trusters' accuracy in predicting others' choices in Prisoner's Dilemma experiments.

questionnaire that included items related to general trust and other psychological traits.

We calculated the accuracy of each person's predictions of other participants' choices.[4] The overall accuracy of predictions was 0.48. That is, participants' predictions of the behavior of fellow students from the same academic program were only as good as random guessing. But when we divided participants into low,

[4] In this experiment, the overall cooperation rate was 0.47, but there was a considerable difference in the cooperation rate and the level of general trust in the two groups. The cooperation rate was 0.38 and the average level of general trust 3.02 in program A, while the former was 0.53 and the latter 3.64 in program B. We then had to deal with the following potential problem. Suppose high trusters expected other people to be cooperative. They would then enjoy a high accuracy score in program B, where a majority actually had cooperated, even if the high trusters had indiscriminately predicted that everyone would be cooperative. To avoid this problem, accuracy of prediction was calculated as the unweighted average of the proportions of correct predictions for actual cooperators and defectors.

medium, and high trusters based on their level of general trust, we found that the relationship between general trust and accuracy of prediction was similar to what we had previously found: high trusters predicted other students' behavior more accurately than low or medium trusters. In addition, when we treated the level of general trust as a continuous variable without dividing it into three categories, the correlation between accuracy of prediction and level of general trust was 0.48. This correlation coefficient did not change much (to $r = .41$) when we controlled for the participant's program and the number of people whom the participant evaluated as cooperative.

In addition to the relationship between predictions of trustworthiness and general trust, this experiment also examined the relationships between accuracy of predictions of trustworthiness and other psychological traits. Particularly noteworthy is the strong correlation ($r = .43$) with a scale that measures respondents' belief in the importance of being honest and fair to others. Accuracy of predictions of trustworthiness was also strongly correlated ($r = .55$) with a Sense of Interdependence Scale that was developed by Jin Nobuhito (1997) to measure one's belief that establishing and maintaining mutually cooperative relations is in one's self-interest.[5] Finally, the participant's accuracy score was marginally correlated ($r = .32$) with the proportion of classmates who predicted that the participant him- or herself cooperated. In other words, those participants who were regarded by their classmates as cooperative and trustworthy were more accurate in predicting other classmates' behavior.

These results suggest the following conclusions. Those people who believe in human benevolence and trust others in general, consider being honest and fair to others important, believe that cooperation is a profitable strategy, and are considered by acquaintances to be trustworthy are more accurate in gauging the trustworthiness of people around them than people who belittle honesty and fairness as meaningless, believe that being kind to others brings no good, and are considered by acquaintances to be untrustworthy. Similar results were found in the other experiments included in Figure 13.2.

Necessary Distinctions

Trust versus Assurance

Japanese society and business are characterized by networks of stable relationships of commitment that provide insiders with assurances of mutual cooperation. *Keiretsu* (business groups) and lifetime employment are good examples of such relationships. It is the stable nature of the relations constraining the people or organizations involved that provides assurance that partners will meet their commitments. In the absence of such relation-based constraints on behavior, as in

[5] Scale rankings were based on responses to four statements: "Society is built on mutual dependency among people," "In order to be successful in society, mutual cooperation is necessary," "Being kind to others will eventually help oneself," and "Those who care only about their own benefit will eventually lose out."

artificially created experimental groups, Japanese feel insecure about the honesty of other people, people who might behave in an unrestrained manner. This explains why Japanese respondents reveal a lower level of trust in others in general than do Americans.

To explain this difference, I distinguish between trust and "assurance of security," the former being based on inferences of character and the latter on incentives (see Yamagishi and Yamagishi 1994; Yamagishi 1999). I use the example of "a thousand needle machine" that is surgically implanted in one's throat and releases the needles whenever a promise is broken. Imagine that someone has been implanted with such a machine. Anyone who knows this will believe that this person will never intentionally break a promise even if he has broken countless promises in the past. One's acting on the belief that such a person will keep his promises is based not on his noble character or one's warm feelings toward him but on the benefit derived from one's action. It is this assurance of security, not trust, that is provided by stable relations in which social uncertainty is low. Although the accepted wisdom is that people trust each other more in Japan than in America, they are actually being assured that their partners are constrained by the nature of their relationship not to betray them. Survey results revealing a lower level of trust among Japanese than Americans can be understood in light of this distinction. While the accepted wisdom actually hits on assurance in the constraining power of social relations in Japan, surveys gauge trust in human nature, which is something else entirely.

Trust versus Gullibility

Although the distinction between assurance of security based on incentives and trust in human benevolence explains why Americans are more trustful than Japanese, explaining why high trusters are more accurate in evaluating other people's trustworthiness than low trusters requires another conceptual distinction. Julian Rotter (1980) distinguished between general trust, which is a default expectation of other people's trustworthiness, and gullibility, which involves a lack of responsiveness to information suggesting a potential lack of trustworthiness in others. Logical independence does not preclude a causal relationship between the two, however; one cognitive activity may still affect the other. One possible causal relation is that gullible people, who do not pay proper attention to signs of untrustworthiness, come to distrust everyone because they are often victimized. Generalized distrust can thus be a learned defense strategy: it is better for socially oblivious people to regard everyone indiscriminately as a thief and avoid entering into risky social interactions if they are to avoid being victimized in such interactions.

Such a defensive strategy is not advisable for everyone, however, because it incurs costs. Generalized distrust leads to social isolation or to commitment relations with a limited circle of partners; other opportunities are forsworn. For gullible people, paying this cost might be a better choice than exploring such opportunities and being victimized. But if one is reasonably skillful at detecting signs of untrustworthiness in risky yet potentially profitable social interactions, generalized distrust is not an advantageous strategy. For socially adept people, a willingness to enter into such social interactions is better than isolation, and the experience of success in such interactions (despite some bad experiences) helps them to develop generalized trust, which makes them even more willing to enter into such interactions. There is also a mutually reinforcing relationship between generalized distrust and gullibility or lack of social intelligence. Social obliviousness makes people victims, leading to generalized distrust, which prevents people from entering into social interactions and thus from taking advantage of opportunities to develop the social skills that would reduce their vulnerability.

In sum, for people unable to detect signs of untrustworthiness in others, the best strategy is to assume that *all* strangers are untrustworthy and to seek the security of long-lasting commitment relations at the cost of forgone opportunities. In contrast, more socially perceptive people can afford to assume other people's trustworthiness in the absence of damning evidence and can leave the security of stable relations to pursue better opportunities outside that small circle because they can pull out of risky relations at the first sign of risk.

Two Types of Social Intelligence

We can make sense of the experimental findings reported above in terms of two strategies to deal with social uncertainty and opportunity costs and the two types of "social intelligence" associated with those strategies. I define social intelligence as the general ability to solve problems to adapt to one's social environment.

Since the inception of scientific research on the subject, many people have pointed out that there are various types of intelligence. There is a long history of debates over what kinds of intelligence exist and whether it is meaningful to speak of "general" intelligence. After a period of neglect, social intelligence has recently attracted the attention of many researchers (see Kihlstrom and Canter 2000 for a brief overview of this research). Howard Gardner (1983), for example, distinguished among linguistic, logical-mathematical, spatial, musical, bodily-kinesthetic, and personal intelligences. According to this theory, the importance of any one type of intelligence depends on what is necessary for adaptation within a given culture. Because Gardner's "personal intelligence" is the ability to understand oneself and others, it is equivalent to social intelligence in the context of this chapter. Robert Sternberg (1988) also argued that it is not the academic problem-solving skill measured by IQ tests or the creative intelligence to handle new problems adaptively that is needed under certain circumstances, but the intelligence to handle oneself and others successfully within everyday social relations. The "emotional intelligence" popularized by Daniel Goleman (1995) – the ability to control emotion, understand other people, and keep social relations smooth – is broadly equivalent to social intelligence (cf. Mayer, Salovey, and Caruso 2000).

It is possible that the experimental findings presented here – high trusters are more sensitive than low trusters to information suggesting untrustworthiness and can assess trustworthiness more accurately – may be interpreted as an indication that high trusters are more socially intelligent than low trusters. Of course, being sensitive to information suggesting untrustworthiness or the ability to use such information successfully to discern trustworthiness is only one aspect of social intelligence, which is a more general ability to manage social relations successfully in order to achieve one's goals. But it is an important aspect of social intelligence. The question then arises: Are low trusters social idiots? Experimental evidence suggests otherwise, indicating that low trusters are socially intelligent in their own way. In other words, high and low trusters have different *types* of social intelligence.

The last four experiments included in Figure 13.2 measured how accurately participants assessed the nature of interpersonal relations (i.e., who liked or disliked whom) among their classmates in addition to how accurately they predicted other participants' behavior. As noted above, high trusters were generally more accurate than low trusters in predicting other participants' choices when faced with a Prisoner's Dilemma. Even so, high trusters were no more accurate than low trusters in assessing the nature of interpersonal relations, and this finding was consistent in all four of the experiments.

In interpreting these findings, it is important to note that participants did not know who their partners were when they played a Prisoner's Dilemma game. Thus, they could not draw on their knowledge of interpersonal relations to predict other participants' behavior. They could not reason that "he would cooperate with me because he likes me" or that "she would defect on me because she hates me." What they predicted, rather, was another person's behavior that was not constrained or guided by the nature of particular interpersonal relations. I call such behavior "relation-unconstrained." Although high trusters proved to be good at predicting such relation-unconstrained behavior, they were no better than low trusters in assessing the nature of interpersonal relations.

These experiments provided other interesting findings. In addition to the General Trust Scale, we used another psychological scale that measured *dis*trust. This General Distrust Scale measured a participant's belief that not trusting others is socially more intelligent than trusting. We presented participants with two Japanese proverbs: "It's best to regard everyone as a thief" (*Hito wo mitara dorobō to omoe*) and "You will never meet a demon as you go through the world" (*Wataru seken ni oni wa nai*), and measured participants' responses to the two.[6] It turned out that strong believers in the thief proverb were more accurate in assessing the nature of interpersonal relations among their classmates than believers in the more benign proverb.

Those findings present us with an interesting contrast. Whereas high trusters are good at predicting relation-*unconstrained* behavior (others' behavior toward anonymous partners), low trusters are good at assessing interpersonal relations and

[6] We asked five questions: (1) which proverb represents reality better, (2) whether believers in the first or second proverb are wiser, (3) which believers are more gullible, (4) which believers are more likely to succeed in the world, and (5) whether entrepreneurs who build a business on their own are more likely to be believers in the first or second proverb. The answers to these questions were added in such a way that the higher the score, the greater the participant's belief in the first proverb.

predicting relation-*constrained* behavior. Predictions of relation-unconstrained behavior could not rely on the nature of interpersonal relations (e.g., she will cooperate with him because she likes him); in predictions of relation-constrained behavior, participants forecast whether each of the other participants would have cooperated or defected if he or she had known that they were partners. Their answers to this question were then compared with the answer their partners gave when asked whether they would have cooperated or defected if they had known whom their partner was. The correspondence between the participant's answer to the first question and the partner's answer to the second question measured the participant's accuracy in predicting relation-constrained behavior. Here, participants could use their knowledge of interpersonal relations (e.g., she would have cooperated if she had known I was her partner because I know she likes me). Again, low trusters were more accurate in predicting other participants' relation-constrained behavior, which was consistent with the previous finding concerning the relationship between distrust and accuracy of relational assessment. These findings indicate that people who have accurate information about interpersonal relations and are good at predicting relation-dependent behavior tend to be believers in the proverb, "It's best to regard everyone as a thief."

To find out how the General Distrust Scale helps us understand the second finding, we analyzed data on 467 respondents from several studies that administered the scale. Five categories of items were found to be related to either or both the General Trust and Distrust Scales. The first category consists of items drawn from the Needs for Interdependency Scale developed by Jin (1997; Jin and Shinotsuka 1996), which measures a respondent's belief that cooperation is an effective means of advancing one's self-interest and that other people are willing to cooperate. The pattern of correlations indicates that believers in the thief proverb do not consider cooperation particularly important to advancing their self-interest, while high trusters do.

The second category consists of items taken from Kamahara, Higuchi, and Shimizu's (1982) Locus of Control Scale, which measures the belief that one can determine one's future. Believers in the thief proverb have a lower sense of self-efficacy than high trusters. The third category consists of items that measure social risk avoidance. Believers in the thief proverb tend to avoid socially risky relationships, while high trusters do not. The fourth category consists of items taken from Kudō and Nishikawa's (1983) translation of the revised UCLA Loneliness Scale (Russell, Peplau, and Cutrona 1980). Believers of the thief proverb are lonelier than high trusters. The final category consists of items taken from Wada Makoto's (1991) Social Skill Scale, which measures the belief that one has the ability to build relationships and deal with interpersonal problems. Believers in the thief proverb think they lack such social skills, while high trusters tend to think they possess them.

These items, especially those included in the last three categories, tend to be correlated with accuracy of relational assessment and accuracy of prediction of relation-constrained behavior in the same direction as the General Distrust Scale. That is, those people who are good at detecting the nature of interpersonal relations and predicting relation-constrained behavior tend to be timid and lonely, and they feel they lack social skills.

Opportunity Seeking and Commitment Formation

We can make sense of our experimental findings in terms of two strategies to deal with social uncertainty and opportunity costs: *opportunity seeking* versus *commitment formation*. Opportunity seekers look outside secure commitment relations and invest cognitive resources in developing the ability to predict other people's behavior in an open environment. They can afford to maintain a high level of general trust. Commitment formers, on the other hand, pay opportunity costs in exchange for the security that commitment relations provide and invest cognitive resources in assessing interpersonal relations. They are good at detecting who would be an ally – and everyone else is regarded as a potential enemy. The characteristics of high trusters (i.e., the correlations between general trust and the perceived need for cooperation to achieve one's interests, the sense of self-determination, the lack of social risk avoidance, and the low level of loneliness) are indicative of opportunity seekers who leave the security of commitment relations to pursue better opportunities. Conversely, the characteristics of believers in the thief proverb (i.e., the lack of a perceived need for cooperation or a sense of self-determination, social risk avoidance, loneliness, and the lack of social skills) are likely characteristics of individuals who prefer not to deal with people outside their commitment relations.

Which strategy people adopt depends on the opportunities open to them. An opportunity-seeking strategy is more adaptive in a social environment in which commitment relations entail large opportunity costs, so the social-explorer type of social intelligence is more likely to prosper there. This type of social intelligence is characterized by an ability to evaluate character or predict other people's relation-unconstrained behavior, a willingness to take social risks as indicated by a high level of general trust, and probably cognitive role taking. In contrast, a commitment formation strategy is more adaptive in a social environment in which commitment relations do not entail large opportunity costs, so the commitment-former or security-seeker type of social intelligence will prosper there. This type of social intelligence is characterized by an ability to detect relations, generalized distrust, social-risk avoidance, and probably an ability to read faces.

I have collected some very interesting and provocative data on this issue. Figure 13.3 shows the relationship between the relative standing (*hensachi*) of fourteen Japanese colleges (including two junior colleges) and the average level of general trust found among 2,790 of their students.[7] The correlation between the relative standing of a college and the average trust score of its students was 0.68. In other words, the students of elite colleges are more likely to be high trusters than are the students of low-ranking colleges. This belies the popular belief that students in elite colleges are narrow-minded egoists. Furthermore, belief in the

[7] Average trust scores are not the average of raw scores, but deviations from the base college after controlling for the proportion of female students.

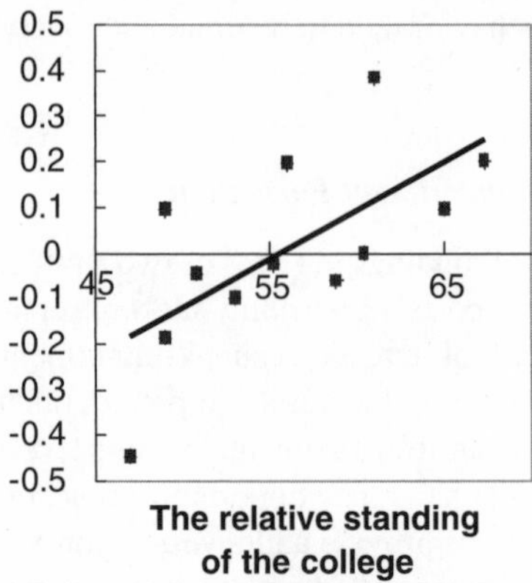

Figure 13.3 The relationship between the relative standing of colleges and the average trust score of their students.

thief proverb was negatively correlated with the relative standing of a college, with $r = -.71$. That is to say, students of low-ranking colleges are more likely to believe the thief proverb.

These correlations indicate that elite college students' social environment, especially their anticipated social environment, is characterized by open opportunities. For these students, closing doors to various opportunities by assuming the worst of everyone is not a profitable strategy. In contrast, future opportunities are not as open for students of low-ranking colleges. For them, the cost of closing doors to various opportunities by distrusting people is much smaller.[8]

Concluding Remarks: The Revenge of the "Progressive Intellectuals"?

Because Japanese society is currently facing a rapid growth in the opportunity costs incurred by commitment relations, an opportunity-seeking strategy is becoming more advantageous than a commitment formation strategy. The contrast between commitment-former and opportunity-seeker types of social intelligence is reminiscent of the distinction Robert Putnam (2000) makes between bonding

[8] An alternative interpretation is possible. According to this interpretation, the students of elite colleges are mostly from well-to-do families and they naively believe in human benevolence because they have not experienced the consequences of nasty social encounters. In contrast, students of low-ranking colleges are mostly from less well-to-do families, and they may have had bad experiences because they have not done as well in school in the past. Given their bad experiences, they do not believe in human benevolence. This explanation fails to explain why the correlations do not exist among college freshmen, however. Among freshman, the correlation between the relative standing of colleges and the average trust score of their students is only 0.07, and the correlation with the Thief Score is $-.22$, but the alternative explanation would predict much stronger, not weaker, correlations among these students. The correlations apparently emerge while students spend time at college.

and bridging types of social capital. Bonding social capital promotes cohesion and cooperation within a bounded social group and helps people "get around." The strong commitment relations that provide security and the basis for mutual cooperation discussed in this chapter are an example of such bonding social capital. Bridging social capital, on the other hand, helps people emerge from closed social circles to explore outside opportunities. It is, Putnam argues, the kind of social capital that helps people "get ahead."

Putnam and I are dealing with the same set of phenomena from two different, though not necessarily opposing, perspectives. Putnam treats bonding and bridging social capital as two types of social relations that people invest in developing. I treat commitment formation and opportunity seeking as two types of strategies or sets of activities. In other words, Putnam emphasizes the end product of people's pursuing certain strategies, while I emphasize the strategies themselves. Clearly, we need to pay attention to both the end product and the process that produces it. One advantage of conceptualizing the difference in terms of types of social intelligence is that each type represents a full configuration rather than isolated psychological traits. Changing one trait at a time will not work; a change in social intelligence requires changing the entire configuration at once. Although the current increase in the opportunity costs of commitment relations provides grounds for such change, because of the equilibrium nature of social intelligence (i.e., the fact that traits do not change singly), this will not happen automatically.

Despite our methodological differences, I also want to highlight the resemblance between my argument and the advocacy of civil society and citizenship (*shimin shakairon*) immediately after Japan's defeat in the Second World War by such "progressive intellectuals" (*shinpoteki bunkajin*) as the historian of political thought Maruyama Masao (see Barshay, this volume) and the social psychologists Shimizu Ikutarō, Hidaka Rokurō, and Minami Hiroshi. They were all ardent advocates of transforming Japanese from feudalistic subjects into modern, independent citizens.

The advocacy of such a transformation dominated the postwar intellectual climate and won enthusiastic acceptance from the general public during the 1950s and, to some extent, the 1960s. It lost its popularity among the general public during the 1970s and 1980s, however, in the shadow of support for the "Japanese system" that was credited with the country's postwar economic development. Reflecting the rapid growth of the 1960s and the 1970s, it came to be widely accepted that this economic success was the product of uniquely Japanese ways of organizing labor and business that derived from a collectivist culture. The meaning of the term "collectivism" shifted from subjugation to authority and the group, as it was conceived by progressive intellectuals in the 1950s, to voluntary cooperation for the sake of the general welfare. Group loyalty and the pursuit of long-term goals rather than a chase for immediate, individual profits were said to be the strength of the "Japanese system." The pursuit of individual self-interest that characterized Western culture, champions of the "Japanese system" claimed, was largely responsible for the end of Western hegemony, at least in the economic sphere. An implication of this was that we were lucky *not* to have listened to the progressive intellectuals, who wanted Japanese to abandon a collectivist culture for an individualistic mentality. Such plaudits for collectivist culture and a uniquely Japanese system have faced serious challenges, however, especially since the collapse of the "bubble economy" in the early 1990s.

As I discussed above, a commitment-forming strategy undoubtedly has advantages over an opportunity-seeking strategy, the most important of which is its reduction of transaction costs. The postwar Japanese system, which promoted and was promoted by stable interpersonal as well as interorganizational relations, certainly enjoyed this advantage, especially when opportunity costs were relatively low. Whether such a system helps or hinders economic efficiency depends on the ratio of savings in transaction costs to increases in opportunity costs. My guess is that the economic and social uncertainty attendant on dealing with noncommitment partners was much higher in the 1950s and the 1960s than it is now, given that the transparency and accountability of social, political, and economic institutions were much more limited then. In such a situation, commitment formation was an efficient strategy to protect oneself from the exploitation that might have resulted from noncommitment relations. The collectivist nature of the "Japanese system" was thus advantageous during the 1950s and the 1960s.

Although the subsequent shift in the balance between transaction and opportunity costs derived from many sources, the decline in seniority-based corporate promotions has been critical. Seniority-based promotion encourages employees to invest in the development of firm-specific skills and promotes efficient and decentralized teamwork, but management must ensure employment stability – ideally, through lifetime employment – to induce employees to accept low salaries while they are young. The dual provision of seniority-based promotion and lifetime employment greatly reduces employees' outside opportunities because of the loss of seniority attendant on every job change.

Seniority-based promotion was economically feasible during the 1950s and 1960s, when Japan's demographic structure ensured a large supply of young employees and rapid economic growth promised continued firm expansion. Employers could promise future promotions and salary increases. As baby boomers began to age and economic growth dwindled in the 1990s, however, employers could no longer offer seniority-based promotions to everyone. Without the prospect of higher future salaries, which had kept employees from looking for work elsewhere, it is now more rational for them to seek better working conditions whenever they present themselves. With outside opportunities growing more attractive and workers increasingly likely to leave, it becomes less profitable for employers to enhance employees' ability through on-the-job training, so they begin hiring more people on spot markets, thus *further* increasing the opportunities of employees who might seek to change jobs.

Other changes in the economic climate are heightening opportunity costs, especially the rapid development of the global economy. A good example of this is found in the procurement of parts for automobile assembly. The traditional system of procurement from *keiretsu* affiliates was regarded as a great asset in the Japanese auto industry because it encouraged investment in relation-specific assets and promoted flexibility. The merits of this system are now being reconsidered given the cost savings that sometimes accrue from deserting *keiretsu* firms and turning to new partners, often foreign firms that can offer highly competitive prices.

The tipping of the balance toward opportunity costs is most clearly visible in the economic sphere, but the same trend can be observed elsewhere. Although strongly committed marriages make possible investment in relation-specific assets such as those needed for raising children, the lack of outside opportunities prevents unhappily married couples from getting divorced. Many unhappy individuals, especially women, refrain from seeking a divorce and remain even with partners they hate. This practice of being emotionally divorced while keeping the household intact (*kateinai rikon*) is thought to be widespread in Japan. An increase in outside opportunities for such couples, in the form of either independent sources of income or potential alternative partners, will induce some of these unhappy couples to split. As the advantages of an opportunity-seeking strategy become more visible, the commitment-forming strategy is losing its appeal for many Japanese in a wide range of activities

This situation did not exist in the 1950s and 1960s, when progressive intellectuals advocated the nurturing of independent citizens. That was a time when a commitment-forming strategy was more advantageous in many spheres of life. The current tipping of the balance between transaction and opportunity costs toward the latter is providing grounds for the emancipation of people from the shackles of collectivist practices. The time is finally ripe, it seems, for progressive intellectuals' call for the transformation of commitment formers into opportunity seekers.

14

Building Global Civil Society from the Outside In? Japanese International Development NGOs, the State, and International Norms

Kim Reimann

Civil Society, the State, and International NGOs

The current revival of interest in the concept of civil society has proceeded in several phases since the 1970s, with shifts in how the term is used (Keane 1998). In all academic discussions of civil society – as should be clear from chapters in this volume – the question of state-society relations and the degree to which society comprises a sphere autonomous from the state have been the central issues (Keane 1988b, 1998; Gellner 1991; Seligman 1992). When the term "civil society" first reappeared in academic discourse in the context of new dissident movements in Eastern Europe in the 1970s and then later in the context of democratic transitions in that region, it was used to portray society as separate from and in conflict with the state (Keane 1988b; Rau 1991; Miller 1992).

This chapter seeks to advance this debate and show how institutions of civil society can be both separate from and partly dependent on the state for growth. Although civil society needs to be understood in relation to the state, it does not necessarily stand in opposition to it (Schwartz, this volume). Nongovernmental organizations (NGOs) and nonprofit organizations – in many ways the quintessential institutions of civil society – provide clear illustrations of this fact, and recent studies have shown how complicated and interdependent their relations with the state often are. As Theda Skocpol (1999: 70) has noted, "The story of American voluntarism has been clearly one of symbiosis between state and society – not a story of society apart from, or instead of, the state." This state-society symbiosis has been especially true in the case of international development nongovernmental organizations (IDNGOs), which strive to reduce poverty and improve socioeconomic conditions in developing countries.

Japan's IDNGOs are of great interest to this ongoing debate. First, Japanese IDNGOs have lagged behind Western ones in development, number, and scale (see Fig. 14.1). According to recent data collected by the Japan NGO Center for International Cooperation (JANIC), the average income of the main 217 IDNGOs

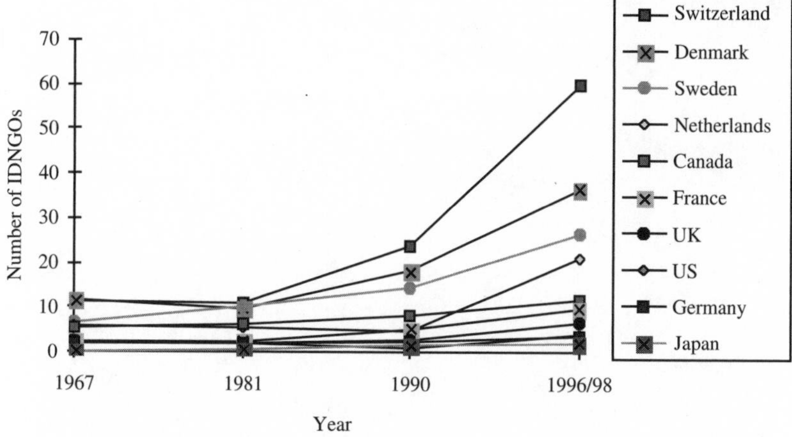

Figure 14.1 Number of international development NGOs, 1967–1996/98 (per million). *Sources:* OECD 1967, 1981, 1990, 1996, 1998; OECD and ICVA 1967.

profiled in its 1998 *NGO Directory* was $808,909 (JANIC 1998b: 41). In contrast, the average revenue of the 153 major American IDNGOs listed in the 1998 InterAction member directory was $25.72 million (InterAction 1998). Japanese IDNGOs also have much smaller staffs, fewer and less dispersed overseas offices, and a much smaller physical presence abroad. OISCA and Japan Sōtōshū Relief Committee, two of the larger Japanese IDNGOs, have budgets of $14.5 million and $6.5 million, staffs of 463 and 183, and offices in 19 and 3 countries, respectively. In contrast, CARE and World Vision, the two largest American IDNGOs, have budgets of $371.9 million and $303.6 million, staffs of 10,000 and 15,000, and overseas offices in 63 and 88 countries, respectively.

At first glance, this is a surprising observation because Japan has many of the important "ingredients" considered to be necessary for the emergence and growth of IDNGOs. In the international relations literature, for example, scholars interested in international NGOs have emphasized that they tend to form in democratic, economically developed nations with high levels of education and global economic interaction (Skjelsbaek 1971; Keohane and Nye 1972; Boli and Thomas 1999). A wealthy nation with a democratic political system, Japan has a well-educated population with one of the highest literacy rates in the world, has been the world's top foreign aid donor since 1989, and is now highly integrated in the world economy.

Despite this surprising pattern of laggard development, it is also important to note that IDNGOs in Japan have boomed in number since the mid-1980s, going from a handful of groups to forming a new nonprofit sector of more than 300 organizations (see Fig. 14.2). This is a significant change in the development of global civil society in Japan and one that deserves analytical attention.

Although these two observations – a pattern of delayed IDNGO formation relative to the West and the recent emergence of increasing numbers of IDNGOs

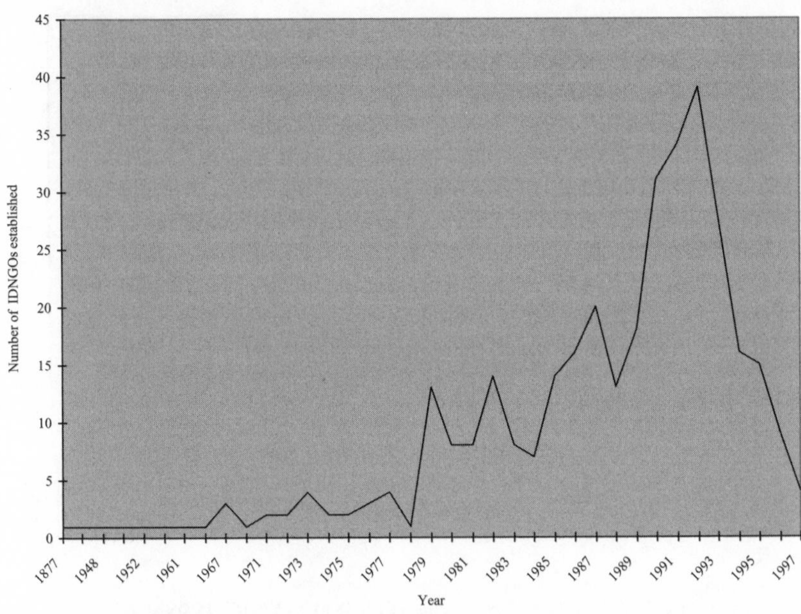

Figure 14.2 Growth of Japanese international development NGOs, 1877–1997 ($N = 347$). *Source:* JANIC 1996a, 1998a.

in Japan – appear contradictory, they are in fact two sides of the same story of how states interact with civil society organizations to promote or discourage their formation. On the one hand, in contrast to the more supportive postures of many other Organization for Economic Cooperation and Development (OECD) countries, Japan's policies long discouraged IDNGO formation, and this more restrictive political environment helps explain why Japanese IDNGOs have lagged in scale and timing. Shifts in Japanese policies since the late 1980s in the form of new support funds, on the other hand, are an important factor behind the proliferation of new IDNGOs in the past decade. The growth of IDNGOs in the late 1980s and 1990s must be understood in this context of changing state policies: as was the case in North America and Europe, the growth of global civil society in Japan has relied on cooperative relations with the state.

Given this context and the importance of state policy to the formation and growth of IDNGOs, this chapter focuses on why policies suddenly changed in Japan in the early 1990s. Considering the Japanese state's long-standing practice of excluding IDNGOs, why did various ministries officially start to promote them as "broader-based participation of people" (Ministry of Foreign Affairs (MOFA) 1994)? This question is particularly puzzling because there was little domestic pressure on the government to adopt the new policies. Few Japanese knew what an IDNGO was in the late 1980s and early 1990s, and the popular image of NGOs at the time was not favorable. With the exception of a few insiders, most Japanese IDNGOs were very suspicious of the government and did not lobby it for money (as IDNGOs have historically done in the West). Considering the lack of domestic demand, why did officials suddenly feel the need to embrace IDNGOs as partners?

The central thesis of this chapter is that to understand the changes that have occurred in government-IDNGO relations in Japan in the 1990s, one must turn to the international arena and international norms. Without a push from the outside, the idea of including and forming partnerships with tiny citizen-organized IDNGOs may not have occurred the way it did. In particular, rising international interest in the role of IDNGOs and in "participatory development" (and later in "civil society") led to stronger state-IDNGO cooperation in other industrialized nations, putting pressure on Japan in the 1990s to reexamine its own relationship to society and somehow to show that it also had an active IDNGO sector.

After providing a more detailed examination of the role of state policies in supporting the growth of IDNGOs and how policies have changed in Japan, this chapter demonstrates how the international environment can be a powerful force for bringing about changes in state policies. Drawing on the theoretical insights of recent studies of norm diffusion and socialization in the international relations literature, this chapter identifies the emergence of a new international norm in the 1980s and 1990s regarding the role of IDNGOs as partners to the state. It then traces the inclusion of this new norm into Japanese state policy and shows how international actors and ideas helped provided new opportunities for civil society actors interested in international development in the 1990s. Returning to the question of state-society relations, the chapter concludes with a discussion of IDNGO autonomy and the role of the state in promoting social organization and action.

State-Society Relations in International Development and Japan's Changing Policies

State policies have affected the formation and size of voluntary organizations by providing (1) an enabling climate by means of legal and fiscal arrangements and (2) direct state support in the form of subsidies, grants, contracts, and in-kind goods or services (Fremont-Smith 1965; Smith and Lipsky 1993; Salamon 1995; Pekkanen 2000b and this volume). This has certainly been the case for IDNGOs. From their emergence at the beginning of the twentieth century, IDNGOs have worked together with their governments and been recipients of government assistance (Smith 1990; Smillie 1995; Chabbott 1999).

Until very recently, the political environment in Japan was not very conducive to the formation of IDNGOs. Unlike most major industrialized countries, where legal institutions and state funding have provided active support to IDNGOs since the 1960s or earlier, state policies and institutions in Japan tended to hinder the formation of independent, voluntary groups. The difficulty of obtaining legal status and preferential tax treatment, for example, made it very hard to establish state-recognized organizations and to collect contributions (Menju and Aoki 1995;

Imata, Leif, and Takano 1998; Pekkanen 1999, 2000b).[1] Lack of access to the bureaucratic process and official development assistance (ODA) policy-making structure cut groups out of the policy loop, and the general attitude of officials toward IDNGOs was one of condescension and disdain (Yonemoto 1994). Finally, there were few public funds for Japanese IDNGO projects overseas. Given this less supportive climate, it has been far more difficult for IDNGOs to form and grow in Japan.

Starting in 1989, however, Japanese state policies toward IDNGOs began to change. The most significant policy shift was the creation in several ministries and agencies by the early 1990s of funding schemes for IDNGO projects in developing countries. Table 14.1 lists the four main officially sponsored funding programs for IDNGOs. In addition to these programs, much smaller programs for IDNGOs – training programs, joint study missions, and small project grants – were also set up during this same period at the Ministry of Agriculture, Forestry and Fisheries, the Ministry of Health and Welfare, and the Ministry of Construction, as well as by local governments coordinated by the Ministry of Home Affairs (MOFA 1996b). In recent years, MOFA-inspired programs have expanded considerably. In 1999, MOFA included NGO emergency relief activities as part of its emergency grant aid, and the Japan International Cooperation Agency (JICA) launched the Development Partnership Program, a contract-style project-funding scheme that pays NGOs, universities, and other nonprofit organizations to implement JICA technical assistance projects. MOFA also introduced three small programs in 1999 aimed at strengthening NGO capacity: the consultant system, the seminar system, and the researcher system. In 2002, MOFA programs to support Japanese NGOs were further reorganized and expanded under the new catch title the "Rainbow Program" to include more support for administrative costs and larger grant amounts for single projects.[2]

Although MOFA had provided funds to a small group of IDNGOs prior to 1989, these groups were very few in number and had the state stamp of approval in the form of public-interest corporation (*kōeki hōjin*) legal status. Unlike these previous subsidies to IDNGOs, the new NGO funding programs set up in 1989 and the early 1990s were open systems that funded not only groups with legal status, but also the large majority of IDNGOs with no legal status.[3] Almost no public funds went to IDNGO projects in the 1980s; by 1997, however, there were 701 IDNGO projects that received some form of official or officially organized funding. This is a big

[1] Compared with IDNGOs in most countries, which go through simple filing procedures to register as nonprofits or charities, 90 percent of all IDNGOs in Japan prior to 1998 did not have legal status and were not eligible for tax breaks or deductions on contributions. See JANIC (1998b).

[2] See http:www.usjapanonline.org/news/news_show.htm?doc_id=4809, accessed December 11, 2001.

[3] This situation is starting to change. With passage of the NPO Law in 1998 and easier, transparent procedures for obtaining legal status, for example, MOFA decided in late 2001 that legal status (as either an NPO or a public-interest corporation) would be a requirement for all NGOs applying for funding under their new "Rainbow Program." See http:www.usjapanonline.org/news/news_show.htm?doc_id=4809, accessed December 11, 2001.

Table 14.1 *Japanese Government Support for NGOs, 1991–2000 (U.S. $ million)*

Ministry or agency	Program (year established)	1991	1992	1993	1994	1995	1996	1997	1998	1999	2000
Ministry of Foreign Affairs (MOFA)	NGO Subsidies Scheme (1989)	2.5	3.1	4.0	4.9	6.9	9.1	10.9	10.5	15[a]	23.3[a]
	Grassroots Grants Program (1989)	4.5	6.4	9.1	13.6	27.3	40.9	45.5	51.8	63.6	77.3
Ministry of Posts and Telecommunications	Postal Savings for International Volunteers (POSIVA) (1991)	9.2	23.6	21.0	22.6	25.6	14.3	9.7	11.3	10.7	5.9
Japan Environment Corporation	Fund for Global Environment (EA) (1993)	–	–	3.7	5.7	5.9	6.1	6.6	6.7	6.7	6.1
Total		16.2	33.1	37.8	46.8	65.7	70.4	72.7	80.3	96.0	112.6

[a] These figures include new MOFA programs for Japanese NGOs in the areas of emergency aid and capacity building as well as a new contract system for Japanese NGOs at the Japan International Cooperation Agency (JICA).

Sources: Government pamphlets and internal government documents, various years. For MOFA subsidies: http://www.mofa.go.jp/mofaj/gaiko/oda/seisaku/seisaku_4/sei_4f.html; for MOFA grassroots grants: http://www.mofa.go.jp/mofaj/gaiko/oda/seisaku/seisaku_4/sei_4f.html, accessed July 18, 2001. For JICA: http://www.jica.go.jp/partner/index.html#project, accessed June 30, 2001. For JFGE: internal documents. For POSIVA: http://www.yu-cho.yusei.go.jp/ volunteer-post/english/a2.htm, accessed July 18, 2001.

shift from the pre-1990s period, and most IDNGOs have come to view the state as a funding source. By the mid-1990s, in fact, 48 percent of the 347 IDNGOs listed in JANIC's NGO 1996 and 1998 directories received some sort of state-sponsored funding.

Explaining Changing State Policies: The Role of International Norms and Ideas

If changing state policies help explain why more IDNGOs started to form in Japan in the 1990s, what helps explain the sudden change in the government's attitude? These shifts in state policy are puzzling for two reasons. First, they appeared rather abruptly in the early 1990s and were not in response to domestic demands. Although a few "insider" IDNGOs were pushing for more government funding from MOFA, for example, there was no consensus or mobilized action by IDNGOs, and many IDNGOs were, if anything, suspicious of government cooptation (Japan NGO Center for International Cooperation (JANIC) 1989; London 1991: 126–27). Second, the new programs were somewhat incomplete and brought with them contradictions in state policies. Legal problems and lack of fiscal incentives, for example, continued to remain a major issue for IDNGOs in the 1990s, and the state was still quite restrictive compared with other OECD countries in this respect. The new NGO grants, however, have gone mainly to IDNGOs with no legal status – the very same groups that the government seemed to be attempting to discourage or restrict.

To understand the changes that have occurred in state-IDNGO relations in Japan in the 1990s, one must turn to international norms. Without a push from the outside, the idea of including and forming partnerships with tiny citizen-organized IDNGOs may not have occurred in the precise way it did. In particular, rising international interest in the role of IDNGOs and "participatory development" that led to stronger state-IDNGO cooperation in other industrialized countries put pressure on the Japanese government to reexamine its own relationship to society and somehow show that Japan, too, had an active IDNGO sector. Although Japanese bureaucrats were suspicious of many IDNGOs, international criticism of Japanese ODA forced them to reconsider the importance of IDNGOs in terms of both living up to an international standard and winning public support for ODA.

International Norms and Pressure as a Source of Policy Change

In recent years, an increasing number of international relations scholars have focused on international norms and the ways in which international structures and ideas influence how states define their interests (Nadelmann 1990; Finnemore 1996; Florini 1996; Katzenstein 1996; Finnemore and Sikkink 1998). Constructivists and sociological institutionalists, for example, have focused on models of international institutions and their socializing role in spreading rationalistic culture and organizations (McNeely 1995; Finnemore 1996; Meyer et al. 1997). According to this explanation, international institutions and actors are independent mediums through which new ideas and norms are diffused on a global scale (McNeely 1995; Finnemore 1996). New norms are introduced by norm entrepreneurs, gradually institutionalized in international law and organizations, and then diffused to member states desirous of showing that they conform to international standards and are thus members in good standing of international society (Finnemore and Sikkink 1998). With the increasing globalization of economies, norms have had new opportunities to spread not only through international organizations such as the United Nations, but also through increasing transnational contacts among governments. As Anne-Marie Slaughter (1997) has argued, transgovernmentalism – a dense web of transnational governmental networks that deal with the nitty-gritty details of policy coordination – is another growing source of policy cooperation and the sharing of ideas and norms among countries.

This process of socialization of international norms is possible because states feel it necessary to be validated as full members of international society (Finnemore and Sikkink 1998). This works in several ways. At the most basic level, by following international norms and standards, states gain legitimacy in the international arena as members of international society and receive a "seal of international approval" from international organizations (Claude 1966; Finnemore and Sikkink 1998). Second, as more states adopt the norm, peer pressure to join and be part of the club can compel states to conform (or at least make the appearance of conforming) to international practices and standards of behavior. Third, obtaining this international legitimation can also prove important to a state's domestic audience and constituencies. In an era of increasing awareness by domestic actors of alternatives and norms promoted at the international level, states may feel the need to harmonize policies with international standards to gain legitimacy at home (Finnemore and Sikkink 1998). Finally, states are also motivated by esteem concerns and sometimes choose to follow norms so that they will look good in the eyes of other states and feel pride or self-esteem (ibid.).

Japan has a rich tradition of paying attention to international cues and borrowing models from abroad that dates from at least the Meiji Restoration in 1868 (Westney 1987; Duus 1998). In the past several years, a few scholars of Japan have started to analyze how international norms promoted by international actors have affected both state policy and state-society relations there. In her study on how immigrants' rights found in U.N. conventions and international law were slowly incorporated into Japanese domestic policies, for example, Amy Gurowitz (1999) has argued that international norms provided NGOs and other societal actors with a source of legitimacy previously denied them. In the area of environmental policy, Miranda Schreurs (1997) has examined how heightened international attention to environmental issues in the 1990s led to shifts in Japan's global environmental policies and the state's general attitude toward environmental NGOs in Japan. As both Gurowitz and Schreurs emphasize, Japan's rise as an economic superpower in the 1980s put pressure on it to prove its worth as a member of international society and to show that it follows international norms. This new opening to international norms, in turn, has provided NGOs and other societal actors in Japan with greater legitimacy and a new source of access to the policy-making process.

A similar dynamic of norm diffusion has occurred in the field of international development and accounts for much of the shift in the early 1990s toward a more cooperative state attitude toward IDNGOs in Japan. This has been a two-step but interactive and ongoing process. First, at the international level of bilateral and multilateral aid organizations, the creation of a paradigm of IDNGOs and NGOs as manifestations of people participation in development started in the 1980s and unfolded in the 1990s (Dichter 1999). Second, as this new international norm spread through various international organizations, state officials in Japan increasingly saw it in their interests for both international and domestic purposes to promote more "citizen-level" ODA activities. In the following sections, I trace this two-step process and show how a new international context influenced the creation of the new NGO support programs of the early 1990s in Japan.

The Rise of IDNGOs in International Organization and Development Debates in the 1980s and 1990s

Starting in the 1980s and blossoming in the 1990s, a new-found interest in and promotion of the role of IDNGOs and NGOs in international development can be clearly seen in the programs and rhetorical language of both bilateral aid agencies and multilateral organizations (Dichter 1999). During these two decades, IDNGOs were legitimized as actors in the official international community and came to represent the "people participation" or "civil society" component of international development.

Bilateral ODA Programs. Although most OECD nations started to include IDNGOs in their official foreign aid programs in the 1960s and early 1970s (Brown and Korten 1991), a clear shift toward more active state cooperation with NGOs started in the 1980s, when state funding and subsidization of overseas projects performed by IDNGOs and NGOs increased dramatically (Smillie 1999). Between the mid-1970s and the mid-1980s, OECD nations and multilateral institutions increased their support to IDNGOs tenfold, bringing about changes to groups that until that time had relied largely on private donations and funds (Hellinger 1987; van der Heijden 1987; Clark 1991; Dichter 1999). The percentage of total IDNGO funds deriving from official sources rose from 1.5 percent in 1970 to 7 percent in 1974, 26 percent in 1976, 33 percent in 1982, and 37 percent in 1986 (Clark 1991).

Together with this new funding came a new normative rationale for the necessity of supporting NGOs. During the 1980s, numerous aid agencies commissioned studies on the role of IDNGOs and NGOs in international development (OECD 1988; Schneider 1988; Brown and Korten 1991), and these evaluations all pointed to the comparative advantages of having NGOs implement projects. From these studies and from an increasing number of works written about IDNGOs and NGOs, a "standard line" on the desirability of including IDNGOs and NGOs in ODA entered international discourse. IDNGOs and NGOs became the preferred alternative vehicles for foreign aid thanks to their ability to reach directly the poorest in developing countries, lower cost and higher effectiveness, greater flexibility and innovative approaches to various problems, ability to mobilize popular groups and increase popular participation, small scale, emphasis on self-help projects, and ability to raise public understanding and support for ODA spending (OECD 1988; Brown and Korten 1991; Clark 1991).

With the end of the Cold War and the spread of democracy in former socialist states, these trends were taken to an even higher level in the 1990s, when official interest in IDNGOs and NGOs blossomed into the even more normatively charged rhetoric of "people participation" and "civil society."[4] Dubbed by some critics (e.g., Edwards 1994) as the "New Policy Agenda," IDNGOs and NGOs were now regarded as providing ideal institutions for both the neoliberal economics and the democratic theory being promoted by the advanced industrial democracies. On the one hand, as service providers that reach the poor, IDNGOs provided an antidote to market and government failure; on the other hand, as organizations with connections to and roots in local populations, IDNGOs and NGOs were also seen as vehicles for democratization and components of a thriving civil society (Smillie 1995; Hulme and Edwards 1997). This renaissance of interest in civil society among both bilateral and multilateral aid agencies resulted in a new surge of funding for all sorts of NGOs as well as a new normative glorification of them as agents of democracy.

Multilateral Aid Institutions. Just as state-IDNGO relations were deepening at numerous bilateral aid agencies, NGOs were also coming of age in international institutions and organizations. Starting in the 1980s in organizations such as the World Bank and then spreading in the 1990s to a whole array of U.N. organizations, IDNGOs became partners with and recipients of official funds from numerous multilateral institutions (Pratt and Stone 1994). At the World Bank, more publicized NGO programs and policy dialogues were set up in the 1980s (Beckman 1991; Smillie 1999), which were followed in the 1990s by a proliferation of initiatives that transformed the Bank into a more active promoter of NGOs. This included new grant programs for local NGOs, the promotion of NGOs in Bank dealings with lender country governments, and further reinforcement of the idea of IDNGOs and NGOs as "participatory" and civil society actors in its various publications (World Bank 1991, 1992, 1996a, 1997; Alger 1994). Outside the World Bank, interest in partnering with IDNGOs and NGOs gathered steam in the mid- to late 1980s at numerous U.N. organizations involved in development issues.[5]

Finally, paralleling the rising interest in IDNGOs among its member nations, the OECD also began to display a more active interest in including IDNGOs and

[4] As IDNGO observer Ian Smillie (1999: 22) noted, "It is a safe bet that more books appeared on NGOs during the first half of the 1990s than was the case of the whole previous two decades."

[5] U.N. agencies with new or expanded NGO programs include the Food and Agriculture Organization, the International Fund for Agricultural Development, the U.N. Children's Fund, the U.N. Development Fund, the U.N. Development Fund for Women, the U.N. High Commissioner for Refugees, and the World Food Program.

NGOs in ODA policies in the 1980s. The OECD's Development Assistance Committee (DAC) began collaborative efforts with IDNGOs in 1986 and 1988 (OECD 1988) and started a series of publications on NGOs in international development (OECD 1990, 1992–94, 1996–98; Smillie and Helmich 1993, 1999). NGOs were increasingly mentioned in DAC annual reports as "partners in the development field" (DAC 1989–91a), and with the adoption of "participatory development" as the new official emphasis of international development for the 1990s (DAC 1989, 1990), IDNGOs and NGOs became part of a new normative framework that would be institutionalized in member states' ODA policies through DAC initiatives and follow-ups. In 1992 and 1993, DAC adopted a policy statement and "orientations" on participatory development and good governance that emphasized the role of NGOs (DAC Expert Group on Aid Evaluation 1997). These orientations were meant to be incorporated by DAC member nations in their ODA policies, and subsequent DAC reviews took them into account when evaluating the ODA policies of each country. The adoption of these orientations thus provided a way in which NGO partnerships with the state in the area of international development were institutionalized, internationally promoted, and monitored for compliance.

International Norms and Changing State Policies in Japan

This international context provides the crucial background for understanding why Japanese state officials began to reexamine their relations with IDNGOs and created new NGO grant programs in 1989 and the early 1990s. Two factors in particular stand out and combine to provide a logical explanation for such a shift. First, because Japan was an outlier among industrialized nations in the 1980s – it was the only OECD country that did not have a visible NGO component in its ODA policy, and its IDNGOs were much smaller in number and size than IDNGOs in other industrialized countries – it was under pressure to make changes that would somehow bring it in line with international practices and standards. Second, in the mid- to late 1980s, Japan became an economic superpower and was under an international spotlight. International criticisms of its so-called self-serving policies and rising expectations of global leadership pressured Japan to prove that it was making contributions to international society. These two factors converged temporally to produce an external push toward greater state-IDNGO cooperation. A closer examination of the origins and evolution of the four main funding schemes for IDNGOs reveals the importance of international norms and the international context.

MOFA Programs. Because they are part of Japan's ODA policies, MOFA's NGO Project Subsidies Program and Grassroots Grants Program are the programs closest to international institutions and norms concerning international development. Looking at the creation of these two programs, it is evident in official documents that both the international promotion of IDNGOs and rising criticism of Japan's ODA policies were important factors in the initial decision to extend official funds to IDNGOs.

To begin with, as participants in DAC and other international institutions, MOFA officials were aware of the rising interest in IDNGOs in the 1980s and felt pressure to "catch up" with the West both in setting up a more open NGO subsidy and grant system and in having a larger and more effective IDNGO sector. MOFA started to express an interest in including NGOs in ODA programs in its annual ODA publications in the mid-1980s – precisely when the OECD and aid agencies in OECD countries were looking to NGOs as a more democratic and effective way of providing aid (MOFA 1987, 1989). As proof that MOFA officials were paying attention to the international discourse on IDNGOs at the time, from about 1987, MOFA's annual ODA reports started to mention the advantages of NGOs in precisely the same terms found in the international development literature and OECD reports. In the 1988 *Japan's ODA* report (MOFA 1988), the need to adopt a program similar to those of OECD countries was clearly stated:

> In the U.S. and in European countries, co-financing systems by which ODA funds are extended to small-size development projects implemented by NGOs constitute Government's most basic support measures for NGOs. It is generally recognized that support for NGOs with ODA funds is a useful way of taking advantage of their characteristics and promoting effective development assistance. Though there is great expectation for the introduction of such a system, it is necessary to carefully study the experiences of Western countries in this regard.

This reference reflected the behind-the-scenes planning of the NGO Projects Subsidies scheme. MOFA's other program, the Grassroots Grants Program, was also established in part due to the influence of international models (Association for the Promotion of International Cooperation (APIC) 1985) and "the fact that other donor countries receive major foreign policy benefits from their schemes" (MOFA 1989).[6]

The other major inspiration for new government funding for Japanese IDNGOs in the 1980s was growing international and domestic criticism that Japanese ODA was overly commercial and closed. As Alan Rix (1993) and Susan Pharr (1994) have noted, Japan's rise as an economic and ODA superpower in the 1980s brought with it increasing attention to and criticism of how its ODA was implemented. International criticism of Japanese aid as overly commercial, lacking a philosophy, and environmentally destructive, several ODA "scandal" exposés in the Japanese press in the mid- to late 1980s, and pressure from a small group of activists and academics in Japan pushing for more responsible ODA policies prompted concern among government officials about the public image of Japan's ODA.

With this background of rising criticism in mind, an advisory council was set up in 1987 by Prime Minister Nakasone Yasuhiro to examine ways of improving Japan's ODA policies. The council's final report recommended government

[6] The decision to create the Grassroots Grant Program was largely a response to an ODA review done by the Management and Coordination Agency (MCA) in 1988 that suggested the establishment of a small-scale grant cooperation system. The report gave only a general idea of what sort of system to set up and did not target support of NGOs in particular. Thus, MOFA's decision to highlight this program as another means to support NGOs may have been influenced by international debates on the role of local NGOs at the time (see MCA 1988).

funding of NGO projects overseas, and the ODA Fourth Medium Target released in June 1988 took this report into account by specifying improved cooperation with NGOs as one of its goals (APIC 1995). Thus, by 1988, concerns felt by policy players at a variety of levels about criticism of Japan's ODA programs came to be linked with improvements that would make its ODA appear more open and (in the language of the OECD) more people participatory. With its new stated goal of "economic cooperation with public participation," MOFA's 1989 ODA report (MOFA 1989) was a clear statement of this linkage. Including Japanese IDNGOs into ODA also provided a new human face to Japanese aid, meeting criticisms that Japanese ODA was "characterless" – lacking philosophy – and "invisible" – involving money but no people (MOFA 1989; Rix 1993; interview with Saotome Mitsuhiro, director, NGO Assistance Division, Economic Cooperation Bureau, Ministry of Foreign Affairs, December 12, 1997).

The expansion of MOFA's two programs in the 1990s also involved and reflected the ongoing influence of international norms and actors. With the growing importance of civil society in international development circles in the 1990s, international actors paid even closer attention to IDNGOs in Japan. In particular, DAC and the United States were active promoters of IDNGOs as partners in development throughout this period.

DAC's active promotion of participatory development and good governance in the 1990s provided a very specific and institutionalized source of international pressure for more cooperative state-NGO relations in Japan. With the adoption of guidelines on participatory development and good governance in the early 1990s, DAC started to report on ODA policies in member countries regarding the degree to which they were promoting these new democratic principles. In this context, DAC reviews of Japanese ODA in the 1980s and 1990s started to point to the need for better support of NGOs in Japan. A 1990/91 DAC aid review of Japan (DAC 1991b) noted in its section on participatory development that "NGO programs remain relatively modest by DAC standards," and the 1992/93 DAC review (DAC 1993) also mentioned that "Japan's assistance through NGOs (0.8 percent in 1989) has been among the lowest of the DAC Members." In its 1995 annual review of Japanese ODA programs (DAC 1996), DAC reviewers recommended that NGOs be used more extensively and that steps be taken to provide a better legal status for Japanese IDNGOs. DAC's 1999 peer review of Japan (DAC 1999) also strongly recommended increased NGO support and involvement in ODA programs and policies. As these reports have entered the domestic debate on ODA reform within Japan, they have lent greater legitimacy to IDNGOs and provided useful resources for actors interested in promoting greater government support of IDNGOs in Japan (Economic Planning Agency (EPA) 1997a; Nijūichi Seiki 1998; Sangiin Kokusai Mondai ni kan suru Chōsakai 1998).

In addition to the OECD, the United States was also an active outside promoter of Japanese IDNGOs in the 1990s by means of the so-called Common Agenda. Launched in 1993, the Common Agenda for Cooperation in Global Perspective is an effort at U.S.-Japan bilateral collaboration on global projects and coordination of foreign policy. A good example of transgovernmentalism (Slaughter 1997), the

Common Agenda initiative has brought together officials from a whole range of bureaucratic agencies and provided a venue for the sharing of information and ideas.

In the international development areas of health and the environment, U.S. officials from the U.S. Agency for International Development (USAID) have actively promoted the use of IDNGOs and NGOs in Common Agenda projects (interview with Paul E. White, minister counselor for development cooperation, American Embassy, Tokyo, January 30, 1997). At first, Japan was hesitant about including NGOs in these projects, but by the late 1990s, IDNGOs from both the United States and Japan had become active participants in the Common Agenda process. In 1992, for example, when a joint U.S.-Japan biodiversity project in Indonesia (which eventually became a Common Agenda project) was being discussed, the Japanese side resisted the idea of including an NGO. At the insistence of USAID, however, it eventually went along with it. The talks went well and the resulting project proved to be a learning experience for MOFA officials that changed their view of IDNGOs. From that point on, NGOs were included in more Common Agenda projects without reservations from the Japanese side (White interview, 1997). At first, most of the NGOs involved were American, but as new projects were started, the United States suggested inclusion of more Japanese NGOs, and Japanese officials themselves started to feel that it would look bad if Japan did not have its own civil society representatives at the table.[7]

The Environment Agency and the Japan Fund for Global Environment. As was the case for MOFA programs for IDNGOs, the origins of the Japan Fund for Global Environment (JFGE) were not domestic but more a reflection of international politics and norms, in this instance those of the U.N. Conference on Environment and Development (UNCED) held in Rio de Janeiro in 1992.[8] The idea to create a fund for IDNGO environmental projects overseas came from an international civil servant, and JFGE is a good example of how Japan was searching in the late 1980s and early 1990s for new, internationally acceptable ways of contributing to international society. Through the international channel of UNCED and international actors, Japanese IDNGOs were given a new source of state funding for their overseas projects.

[7] Throughout the 1990s, various Common Agenda seminars and roundtables held in Washington and Tokyo brought together not only Japanese and American officials but Japanese and American NGOs. These events all highlighted the importance of NGOs in solving problems in their issue areas and forced the Japanese government to round up its own NGO representatives. These meetings included a series of U.S.-Japan NGO seminars and workshops on HIV/AIDS in the mid-1990s, a U.S.-Japan NGO Forum on Population and Related Global Issues in 1997, the U.S.-Japan Partnerships on Environmental Awareness and Education Workshop in 1997, the U.S.-Japan Common Agenda Civil Society Workshop in 1998, the U.S.-Japan Common Agenda Open Forum in 1998, and the U.S.-Japan Common Agenda Civil Society Organization Forum in 2000.

[8] Considering that most environmental NGOs were very suspicious of the government, it would have been unlikely for them to take the initiative in the late 1980s or 1990–91 to request the creation of such a fund. There is no evidence of lobbying by environmental IDNGOs for state funding for their overseas projects.

JFGE was part of a larger shift in environmental policies in Japan in the late 1980s during the period leading up to the UNCED gathering. Prime Minister Takeshita Noboru underwent a sudden "green" transformation and pushed for reversals in Japan's previous global environmental policies. A prominent component of this green transformation was the creation of several global initiatives that would show Japan's international leadership in the area of the environment (Schreurs 1996). Although the JFGE was one of these international initiatives, the idea to set up a fund that would give money to NGOs originated not in Japan but at the United Nations during talks Takeshita had with UNCED Secretary General Maurice Strong (JANIC, *Kokoro* 1993). It was Strong, an international actor steeped in the norms of the day, who provided the initial idea for the fund.

Considering that Takeshita was a conservative politician who felt no great love for NGOs in Japan – if anything, he viewed them as troublemakers – the JFGE is a fund whose creation clearly demonstrates how international politics can override national norms and create new opportunities for domestic civil society.

Ministry of Post and Telecommunications: The Government Organizes IDNGO Philanthropy. The origins of the Ministry of Post and Telecommunications (MPT)'s POSIVA program are less directly related to international organizations and events than the MOFA programs and the JFGE, but they, too, were rooted in a desire to prove that Japan was committed to contributing to international society and following international norms.

At the start, MPT was interested in a new idea for the 1990s that would revitalize consumer interest in postal savings accounts. In 1989, MPT set up an outside advisory study group composed mainly of university professors to draft recommendations for a "Vision of Postal Savings in the 1990s" (interviews with Nishida Hiromitsu, public relations chief, Postal Savings for International Voluntary Aid Office, Postal Savings Bureau, Ministry of Post and Telecommunications, July 18 and October 7, 1997). In its 1990 report (MPT 1990), the study group recommended using an "international volunteer" postal savings account as a way to raise interest in international society and "participation consciousness." With its 24,000 post offices extending into both urban areas and the rural hinterlands, the postal system was an ideal way to reach citizens, the report argued. The fact that MPT chose NGOs as the channel through which Japanese citizens could contribute to international society is interesting given that most MPT officials had probably never heard of NGOs in 1989. The choice reflects the need perceived by many Japanese in the late 1980s – including the study group that made the recommendations – that Japan show more active leadership and engagement with the world.

Conclusion: Civil Society Organizations as "Partners" of the State

As scholars of nonprofit and voluntary organizations have recently argued, relations between civil society and the state are complex and often defy simplistic "society versus state," "society instead of the state," or "society autonomous from the state" approaches. In contrast to the autonomous image of civil society found in much of the literature, this chapter has tried to show that societal groups are rarely completely free from the influence of the state and often work with – not against – it. States choose which sorts of groups they want to promote by means of their legal and fiscal policies, and these choices create an environment that either encourages or stifles certain types of society-based activity. As Robert Pekkanen argues in this volume, civil society organizations are shaped by an institutional and political environment that is largely framed by the state.

With their many ties to state and intergovernmental organizations, IDNGOs are perfect examples of this phenomenon. They are also a type of civil society organization whose international expansion has been supported by many industrialized states and by international organizations. The dramatic growth in number and scale of IDNGOs in OECD countries in the 1980s and 1990s paralleled an equally dramatic growth in funding of NGOs by bilateral and multilateral aid agencies. Although these groups also relied on voluntary support from the general public, the availability and use of government funding by a substantial number of IDNGOs makes it hard to view this sector as existing completely autonomous from or in opposition to the state.

Such observations naturally lead to the question of autonomy and the costs to IDNGO independence of accepting state money. At what point do IDNGOs become instruments of the state? With the amount of official funding available to IDNGOs in industrialized countries increasing from the 1970s to the 1990s, observers and practitioners in the West have been grappling with the potential dangers inherent in becoming a partner of the state. Legitimate worries about the risks of IDNGOs losing their original mission as they conform to state funding requirements or restrictions have been borne out in cases where IDNGOs have shifted their geographical focus or type of assistance to match state funding opportunities (Lissner 1977; van der Heijden 1987; Smillie 1995, 1999). When IDNGOs follow the money in this way, they also risk turning into strategic instruments of foreign policy, as was the case for state-funded American IDNGOs operating in Vietnam in the 1960s (Lissner 1977; Roberts 1986). The other obvious potential cost of becoming a partner to the state is the silencing effect: IDNGOs that are heavily reliant on state funds are likely to be far less critical of state policy. As a group, IDNGOs have in fact tended to be less critical of government policies (Smillie and Helmich 1999).

Writers who have called attention to the strength of the Japanese state will be equally skeptical of state motives and the autonomy of Japanese IDNGOs that accept state funding. In light of the dominance enjoyed by the state and marketplace (Hardacre 1991), Japan has been characterized as a society with little room for an independent civil society, and persuasive studies demonstrate how the Japanese state has been able to coopt civil society organizations for state purposes (Garon 1997 and this volume). Given that close to half of the IDNGOs listed in JANIC's 1996 and 1998 NGO directories received some sort of government funding, the question about autonomy vis-à-vis the state is very relevant. How have these issues of autonomy and cooptation played out in Japan?

So far, there has been evidence in Japan for relatively greater IDNGO autonomy as well as for increasing state control. To begin, compared with the levels of support given to IDNGOs in other OECD countries, the total amount of funding provided by the state in Japan is not large and remains a relatively small proportion of total income for IDNGOs as a whole (Miyake 1999). In contrast to the United States, Germany, the Netherlands, Sweden, Switzerland, and Norway, where state funds comprised one-quarter to two-thirds of total IDNGO income in the mid-1990s (Smillie and Helmich 1999), official funds amounted to only 13 percent of total Japanese IDNGO income in 1996 (JANIC 1998b). On average, the top ten IDNGOs in Japan in the mid-1990s were less than half as dependent on state funding as the top ten IDNGOs in the United States, with an average of 15.6 percent of their funding coming from official sources compared with an average dependency of 39.3 percent among the U.S. IDNGOs (InterAction 1998; JANIC 1998a). Of the 217 IDNGOs surveyed by JANIC, the majority of them (90 percent) received less than 30 percent of their income from official sources (JANIC 1998b).

Funding in Japan does not seem to be overly biased toward politically conservative groups: Japanese IDNGOs that have received state funding do not seem to fall into any clear ideological category. As in all countries, service IDNGOs in Japan have tended to focus more on delivering services than on political advocacy, but there are cases of left-of-center Japanese IDNGOs that have simultaneously received official funding and actively participated in advocacy efforts criticizing Japanese ODA policies.[9] Because the tools available to the state for control and cooptation are more numerous for public-interest corporations (*kōeki hōjin*) than for groups with no legal status, the fact that a majority of state-funded IDNGOs do not have legal status is evidence that they are less likely to be direct instruments of the state. Seen from this perspective, Japanese IDNGOs seem to face fewer problems and risks of losing autonomy than their counterparts in other OECD countries.

Looking beyond state funding to the larger environment for NGOs in Japan, however, the picture starts to look more like one of a strong state that has influenced the capacity of IDNGOs by limiting the resources available to them. Although less dependent on state funding than IDNGOs in many other OECD countries, Japanese IDNGOs have lacked many of the basic tools for raising funds from the general public commonly used in North America and Europe. Until very recently, the fact that groups could not get legal status or tax breaks on contributions has meant that independent fund raising in Japan and gaining legitimacy in the eyes of the public

[9] For example, Japan International Volunteer Center (JVC) and the Shanti Volunteer Association (SVA) have simultaneously received government funds and criticized ODA policies through participation in advocacy networks such as Mekong Watch, People's Forum on Cambodia, and Tokyo NGO Forum on the Asia Development Bank. Among environmental groups that have received JEC grants, the following groups have engaged in advocacy activities critical of government policy: Japan Tropical Forest Action Network, Friends of the Earth Japan, Kikō Forum, A SEED Japan, Earthday Japan, JVC, SVA, Mekong Watch, Japan Committee for Negroes Campaign, and the Fukuoka NGO Forum on the Asian Development Bank. Because most of these groups have continued to be vocal critics, the silencing effects of funding do not yet seem to be very significant.

have not been easy. Such factors have dampened the ability of IDNGOs to carve out a strong, independent position vis-à-vis the state and made them increasingly reliant on state funds for growth.

Although there are few cases of outright interference by state officials in IDNGO operations and activities in Japan, there have been costs associated with taking state funds. Because most funding schemes cover little or no project overhead costs and require rigid reporting procedures, the use of government funds has at times strained IDNGO capacity and limited the flexibility of activities. In the early years of the MOFA program, IDNGOs complained about limits on the type of projects eligible for funding because such limits controlled what kind of aid IDNGOs could provide. The situation has improved over the years, however, and seems to have been less of a problem in the IDNGO programs run by MPT and Japan Environmental Corporation (JEC). More serious than these programmatic concerns is the greater vulnerability of an increasing number of IDNGOs to unpredictable changes in government funding. The huge decline in the volume of the POSIVA program due to a fall in interest rates in 1996 and 1997 led to sudden drops in funds for many IDNGOs, forcing them to cut staff and reduce or terminate other projects (Miyake 1999).

Although there appear to be a few cases of IDNGOs serving as agents of the state in countries with which Japan has limited or strained diplomatic relations (e.g., Myanmar), for the most part the strategic use of IDNGOs by the Japanese government appears to be minimal and limited to public relations toward the outside world. With a few exceptions, Japanese IDNGOs are simply too small in their operations to be considered serious tools for foreign policy goals. Although some observers have argued that Japanese IDNGOs are used instrumentally by the state (Potter 1999), there is little evidence that state-funded IDNGO projects differ greatly from independently funded IDNGO projects.

Beyond the obvious public relations boost provided by partnering with IDNGOs, it is in fact unclear exactly what the state in Japan expects to get out of this new relationship with society actors. This ambiguity makes sense given the international origins and inspiration of the various IDNGO support programs and is what makes Japan a particularly intriguing case. As this chapter has tried to show, state-IDNGO cooperation in Japan in the 1990s came about not as a result of domestic demand or a clearly formulated state plan to use IDNGOs but as a reaction to international pressure promoting civil society and the use of IDNGOs in development. Unlike previous studies on the effects of foreign pressure (*gaiatsu*) on Japan, which have focused primarily on economic policies (e.g., Orr 1990; Schoppa 1997), this study has tried to illustrate how more diffuse international factors such as international norms can have transformative effects on state policies and state-society relations. In many ways, the 1990s were a fascinating learning period for both government officials and IDNGOs. Although state-civil society partnerships in international development are still in their early stages in Japan and many tensions remain, the new dialogue and cooperation between IDNGOs and the state is an important first step in the evolution of global civil society in Japan.

15

Conclusion: Targeting by an Activist State: Japan as a Civil Society Model

Susan Pharr

The concept of civil society inspires, irritates, or confounds depending on the context and whose judgment is brought to bear.[1] Civil society consists of sustained, organized social activity that occurs in groups that are formed outside the state, the market, and the family. Such activity on the part of groups and individuals cumulatively creates a domain of discourse, a public sphere. Nonstate, nonmarket, nonfamily actors and activities are myriad in any society, however, and there will inevitably be debates over what to include and exclude in considering that vast sphere in which people come together to create social life and public discourse. But these uncertainties should not obscure the value of a concept that offers a powerful analytical tool for thinking about the associational landscape that exists in any given country, the forces that shaped it, the nature of social experiences within the various groups that comprise it, and the ways in which these terrains vary across nations.

Building on the existing literature on organized social life there, civil society provides precisely such a tool for analyzing associational life in Japan. A rich tradition of scholarship traces the country's early civic legacy in the feudal era and before (see Garon, this volume). The social science literature on modern Japan since the onset of the modern era in 1868 – and the chapters of this book – reveal a wide array of protest movements, neighborhood associations, big-business organizations, farmers' cooperatives, women's groups and movements, small-enterprise associations, labor unions, right-wing groups, old people's groups, citizens' and

[1] I express appreciation to the international students who took my graduate seminar in fall 2000 on "Civil Society West and East" (co-taught with Grzegorz Ekiert) and my junior seminar on "Civil Society in Asia" in spring 2001, from whom I learned a great deal; to Steven Benfell, William Cole, Neil DeVotta, Grezgorz Ekiert, Sheldon Garon, Inoguchi Takashi, Ben Kerkvliet, Kuroda Kaori, Robert Mitchell, Robert Putnam, Richard Samuels, Frank Schwartz, Theda Skocpol, and Patricia Steinhoff for comments at various stages that contributed to my work for the chapter; and to Daniel Aldrich, Kage Rieko, John Kuczwara, and Jeffrey Newmark for their able research assistance.

consumer movements, and all manner of organizational life, depending on the period under discussion. They also offer theories and evidence about how particular groups and movements interact with the state and how they are organized internally (Muramatsu and Krauss 1987, 1990; Upham 1987; Tsujinaka 1988, 1996; Okimoto 1989; Pharr 1990; Ramseyer and Rosenbluth 1993; Schwartz 1998). The civil society approach provides a framework for analyzing these disparate groups and relationships more systematically and comprehensively. It suggests how and why the nature of Japan's civic life has changed over time and how it may change in the future.

To make an analysis of civil society useful from a comparative-politics standpoint, we argue that the scope of inquiry should be as broad as possible. Much of the popular discourse and, indeed, a significant part of the academic literature on civil society have gone in the opposite direction and adopted a narrow focus, thereby excluding great swaths of associational life. For many commentators, civil society is simply a fashionable term for public advocacy, and they, along with many others, define entire categories of groups out of civil society. Pointing to the early Western European origins of the concept, in which private associations developed in space wrested from a powerful and all-embracing Catholic Church, or to the contemporary role of the Church in countries such as Italy, or to basic Islamic precepts, some commentators exclude religious organizations from a modern-day definition of civil society (Putnam et al. 1993; Gellner 1994). Holding that civil society groups must be public interest-oriented rather than self-regarding, others exclude all economic groups, from labor unions to industry associations. Still others require some level of "civility"; to qualify, groups must operate within preestablished "rules of a 'civil' nature" (Shils 1991).

For anyone who seeks to apply the concept of civil society across borders and outside the Western European settings where it first took shape, none of these exclusions makes sense, however. The role of Catholic Church–related organizations in Latin America and in the transition from state socialism to democracy in Eastern Europe, for example, suggests the inappropriateness of excluding religious groups (Kubik 2000). Similarly, to neglect the role of Islamic groups in countries such as Indonesia and Egypt is to ignore major, and indeed often dominant, outlets for social activism (Hefner 1997). Leaving out economic groups presents similar problems. Obvious examples include the parts played by labor movements in democratic transitions in Poland, South Korea, and elsewhere, and by business groups as increasingly autonomous civic interests in the Middle East (Koo 1993; Ekiert and Kubik 1999; Bellin 2002).

A repugnance for groups – skinheads, the Ku Klux Klan, or religious extremists – that violate laws and/or transgress the norms of democratic discourse and conduct makes it tempting to set a minimum requirement of "civility." Such a requirement ultimately undermines the utility of the civil society concept as a tool of historical and comparative analysis, however. Where there is no legitimate space for challenges to authoritarian or totalitarian governments, for example, groups seeking a voice almost inevitably violate laws or rules along the way, with postwar student movement organizations in predemocratic South Korea and Falun Gong in contemporary China constituting obvious examples. To deny rule-breaking groups the status of civil society actors is thus to ignore the roles they play as organized, nonmarket, nonstate, nonfamily groups attempting to operate under oppressive conditions.

We argue, then, for using civil society not as a rallying call or as a salute to groups that challenge the state but, drawing on the work of Philippe Schmitter (1997) and others, as a neutral term that encompasses all kinds of social groups, organizations, and movements so long as they meet certain minimal tests:

- *dual autonomy* in that they be "relatively independent of both public authorities *and* private units of production and reproduction" (i.e., firms and families);
- *capacity for collective action* in defense of or in pursuit of their interests and concerns;
- *nonusurption* in that they do not seek to replace state agents or to run the polity;
- *voluntary in nature*, at least to the extent that membership or inclusion is not coerced.[2]

These criteria permit a number of legitimate exclusions. Civil society is *not* the same thing as society; as Philip Nord (2000: xiv) observed, it "occupies a smaller swatch of territory." The family, the workplace, and informal groups lie outside it, as do spontaneous uprisings such as riots. It also excludes informal activities, the stuff of daily life that goes on all around us, whether in salons and cafes or at dinner parties and picnics. Although these kinds of activities create social capital – defined as "social networks and the norms of reciprocity and trustworthiness that arise from them" (Putnam 2000: 19) – and thus provide a basis for building associational life, informal activities in themselves are not a part of civil society, which consists rather of sustained, organized group activity.

Furthermore, the criteria listed above should not be regarded as absolutes. Despite the assumptions that underlie much popular writing on civil society and nongovernmental organizations (NGOs), total autonomy from the state is relatively rare among major civic groups today even in those nations thought to have vibrant civil societies. State funding constitutes the lion's share of income for a large number of domestic and international NGOs in many European countries, for example (Reimann, this volume). Even in the United States, with its attachment to limited government, the federal government had by the 1970s become "the largest single source of direct and indirect revenues for nonprofits" (Hall 2000: 3). Thus, a nation's associational landscape properly includes a number of groups

[2] The first three of these criteria, which distill points made in a large body of literature, come directly from Philippe Schmitter (1997: 240). The fourth criterion, emphasized by Robert Putnam (1993) in his work on social capital in Italy and Susanne Rudolph (2000) in her work on civil society in India, appears to be crucial if we are to apply the term "civil society" to non-Western settings. I do not, however, support a purist notion of volunteerism in that there may be some degree of social pressure to join a whole variety of groups, including, for example, Parent-Teacher Associations in the United States.

with varying degrees of proximity to the state as long as they still enjoy a measure of autonomy from it.

The civil society framework we offer in this book therefore embraces a large number of organizations that have been wholly excluded in many previous discussions of Japan's civil society: neighborhood associations in most periods of their history, including today; religious groups; business and industry associations; consumer groups, which some theorists would exclude because of their proximity to the marketplace; and labor unions, indeed, even enterprise unions, which, despite their close ties to firms, have the *potential*, as Suzuki Akira argues in this volume, to "offer a rich associational life for their members" even if they do not necessarily achieve it. The public role of many of these groups (e.g., consumer cooperatives, enterprise unions, and religious organizations) is small; the market overshadows or entangles them (Maclachlan, Suzuki, and Hardacre, this volume). Not only is the voice of religious groups weak in public debate over moral issues, for example, but their role in service provision – which looms large in many countries, including the United States – is minimal (Hardacre, this volume). Nevertheless, only when all such groups come under the lens does Japan's civil society take shape.

Pathways to Civility

How do civil societies first emerge? The essence of the notion of civil society is that it encompasses social activity that arises in a space that exists *outside the state, but in some kind of relationship to it*. Many countries, including Japan, have rich civic legacies that long predate modern statehood. In Japan's case, the feudalism of the previous Tokugawa era (1603–1868) gave rise to numerous forms of associational life that served as precursors to civil society and opened up at least some measure of space for public discourse (Garon, this volume). Civil society does not require democracy; indeed, some civil society groups can be bad for democracy. But it *does* require the existence of a modern state. Premodern settings, however much they may create the conditions for the rise of civic life, lack "modularity," the relative freedom of people to "combine into effective associations and institutions, without these being total, many-stranded, underwritten by ritual, and made stable through being linked to a whole set of relationships" (Gellner 1995: 41). In the Japanese context, what can meaningfully be called civil society thus emerged only with the collapse of feudalism and the rise of the Meiji state after 1868.

As this volume attests, Japan's path to civil society has been bumpy and at times uncertain. Rapid industrialization swept citizens into new roles and identities during the Meiji era, and a modern civil society and public sphere took shape and then expanded and diversified in a relatively permissive environment until century's end. Industrialization, along with the dramatic opening to the West that preceded it, raised a host of new issues for popular debate and created new reasons for people to form associations and indeed to challenge the state. After 1900, however, the autonomy and spirited resistance of civil society in the previous three decades diminished; thereafter, "civil society and the state were considerably more intertwined" as the state sought "to organize society on its own terms"(Garon, this volume). Civil society continued to develop and diversify through the early 1930s, but in fits and starts, as state policies promoted some groups, such as business associations, but repressed others with such measures as the Peace Preservation Laws, which restricted oppositional groups. Prewar civil society peaked in the era known as Taishō democracy (1918–31), when the environment in which all but the most extreme groups operated became relatively permissive. From the early 1930s through 1945, however, in an atmosphere of increasing censorship, firings of university professors who strayed from the nationalist line, arrests of communists, and rising militarism, civil society took a sharp, state-guided turn to the right.

Associational life was closely monitored, and even informal social activities came under police scrutiny. A foreign resident of Tokyo in the late 1930s recalled in her memoirs how police routinely called at the door to collect from the cook the names of the Japanese artists, musicians, and other guests who flocked to her Viennese parents' dinner parties (Gordon 1997: 65). In October 1940, this shift culminated in the formation of the Taisei Yokusankai, or Imperial Rule Assistance Association (IRAA), which forced the dissolution of almost all independent organizations, from business federations to women's groups, and their mutation into "patriotic associations." With the powerful Home Ministry at the helm, the state orchestrated this new patriotic federation through "a hierarchical series of cooperative councils" extending down to the prefectural and even local levels (Fletcher 1979: 59). The IRAA became an arm of the state, "assist[ing] the government in policy research, in the carrying out of orders, and in mobilizing public support for official policy" (Minichiello 1984: 115).

As Andrew Barshay observes in this volume, civil society prior to 1945 lacked "broad moral and conceptual legitimacy." Not until military defeat discredited the imperial system and "significantly eroded the moral statue of the state and the attendant category of imperial subjecthood" did the notion of citizenship come out of the "ideological shadows." Except during the brief period of IRAA ascendancy, civil society survived, however, with the associational landscape shaped rather than suppressed by the regulatory and moral environment surrounding it. From its low point in the wartime years, civil society sprang back to life during the Allied Occupation (1945–52), diversified in a newly created democratic context that guaranteed basic civil liberties, and surged ahead. The pluralism of associational life has grown steadily since.

This volume highlights at least eight distinctive features of Japan's postwar civil society:

- Producer groups predominate. Industry associations, other business groups, and agricultural cooperatives are remarkably large and highly organized compared with most other interest group sectors in Japan and with their counterparts in the United States.
- Labor and consumer organizations are far weaker relative to producer groups and comparable organizations in the United States and most countries in Western Europe.

- Religious organizations play an extraordinarily weak role in service provision and in public discourse over moral questions compared with the role of the religious groups in a great many countries, including the United States, many countries in Western Europe, virtually all Latin American nations, and most countries with significant Islamic populations.
- Political advocacy groups have been strikingly underrepresentated in the overall composition of civil society until quite recently and are weak in number, membership size, and funding compared with the situation in most advanced industrial nations.
- Horizontally organized, grassroots social movements such as environmental, consumer, and student groups have figured large in Japan's postwar civic life, mirroring trends in Western Europe, where "new social movements" have played significant roles; indeed, they constitute a major form of public advocacy in Japan. But compared with the United States, for example, relatively few such movements have metamorphosed into permanent public-interest organizations with large professional staffs that pursue public-policy agendas.
- In Japan's public sphere (that discursive realm in which political and social issues get aired and debated), according to many critics, the mass-media establishment appears to work "together with, or on behalf of, the political core – capturing, subverting, misleading, or alternatively ignoring the political periphery . . . " (Freeman, this volume; cf. Krauss 1996), and marketplace considerations loom large (Hardacre, this volume).
- There exist a surprisingly small – if growing – number of international NGOs despite the wide range of Japan's commitments abroad, including its standing as one of the world's largest aid donors and funders of international organizations.
- As an overarching and defining feature, a close symbiotic relation between an activist state and civil society colors and contours, to varying degrees and in different ways, the day-to-day activities of virtually the full range of civil society actors.

Pathways Compared: Japan and Western Europe

Recent work on the emergence of civil societies in Western Europe suggests that Japan's path has been far more typical than observers might suspect. Although the groundwork was laid far earlier in many countries, civil societies did not emerge across late eighteenth- and nineteenth-century Europe smoothly and gradually, but in "bursts" in which the "mix of organizational forms mutate[d]," just as in Japan (Nord 2000: xvi–xviii). According to Nord, key "moments of metamorphosis" came after 1815, when the repressive conditions following the Congress of Vienna curtailed prospects for the development of independent organizations, but they did not deter the appearance of upper-class men's clubs and circles, while the lower classes built "neighborhood-based networks of self-help." Although this wave of civic activism came to an abrupt end as authorities reacted to the revolutions of 1848, a mainly middle-class (but also working-class) "mania for associations" took hold in the 1860s and 1870s, giving rise to professional associations, fraternal societies, trade unions, and cooperative movements and opening up political life to the masses. At century's end, there appeared widespread religious-based peasant mobilization and labor activism.

As in Japan, these developments did not depend on guarantees of civil liberties or legal recognition: "For much of Europe for most of the century, civil society made its way outside the law" (Nord 2000: xix). In Germany, for example, for most of the nineteenth century, the "right to organize for political purposes was still restricted, confined to males of a certain minimum age who had to give authorities notice of their activities and subject themselves to police control," while "supralocal organizations were banned altogether" (Tenfelde 2000: 87). The greatest gains occurred not from de jure recognition, but in windows created by de facto tolerance (Bermeo 2000: 243) – an apt characterization of civil society's flowering in Taishō Japan. Repression had similar effects in Europe and Japan, "strangl[ing] associational energies" and giving a "boost to clandestine modes of organizations" (Nord 2000: xix). The growth of markets spurred associational life in both Europe and Japan even if state repression and corporate strategies constrained trade unionism far more in the latter than the former. With its turn to the right in the 1930s, Japan was fully in step with European trends that took the civil societies of Germany and Italy from florescence to fascism. Nor were the extremes of Japan's IRAA an aberration, for they parallel developments elsewhere in the Axis sphere: Nazi *Gleichschaltung* (coordination) "meant the absolute destruction of a free and voluntary associational life" (Tenfelde 2000: 103).

At other points, however, the paths followed by Western Europe's and Japan's civil societies diverged sharply. A central difference is timing. A late emergence from feudalism in the mid-nineteenth century put Japan centuries behind key Western European nations, if we are to believe the claim of Robert Putnam et al. (1993) that "the civility of some societies is shrouded in the mists of time." Another key difference is the role of religion. The Catholic Church and other religious groups loomed large in shaping nineteenth-century European civic life. For example, the Catholic Church catalyzed rural mobilization in Belgium, Germany, and Northern Italy, among other places, at the end of the nineteenth century (Nord 2000). Indeed, although they are numerous and active in Japan today, religious groups continue to play a larger role in Europe (and the United States), particularly in service provision and in public debate over moral questions. But the central difference between Japan and Europe undoubtedly lies in the role of the state.

The State of Civil Society

The reawakening of interest in the notion of civil society in the 1980s resulted from developments in Eastern Europe, the Soviet Union, and Latin America, where protest groups and movements arose to challenge authoritarian or crumbling totalitarian regimes. Perhaps due to these origins, much of the literature – and almost all popular writing – casts the state in the role of antagonist to civil society and recognizes little room for the state in fostering civic life. And indeed, according to Nord, in Europe, where civil societies first took shape, "what stands out . . . is how small a part the state had in the process." Driving changes across the continent were forces from below: "protean but organized opinion whose energies might be diverted or hemmed in but never stanched" (Nord 2000: xix, xx).

A great deal of recent research has fundamentally challenged this view, holding that the state plays a powerful role in shaping the associational landscape. From the earliest days of American nationhood, civic groups rarely arose in opposition to the state and wholly in isolation from it, Theda Skocpol argues. Instead, the government actively "encouraged the proliferation of voluntary groups linked to regional or national social movements" (Skocpol 1999: 33; 1996). Furthermore, it is government policies or a desire for a greater share of public goods and services that often spark the birth of citizens' groups. Alternatively, as Nord (2000: xix) acknowledges even while downplaying the role of the state in the rise of civil societies in nineteenth-century Europe, "repressive conjunctures" at times configured "the expansion and forms of civic activism." State policies and laws – from tax policies to postal rates – mold civil society in critical ways. Focusing more narrowly on the state's coercive arm (i.e., the police, judiciary, and military), Nancy Bermeo (2000: 242) sees three possible relations between such agencies and any given civic group: they may "provide legal sanctions," outlaw it, or "simply tolerate the group, ignoring the letter of the law." This new stream of research suggests a broad range of roles the state may play in shaping the associational landscape.

The question, then, is not *whether* the state plays a role in the evolution of civil society, but *which* roles it plays. Four possibilities stand out. The state may *inspire* civic activism, such as when groups mobilize in response to state policies (or the lack of them) or opportunities to secure or retain goods or services. It may *enable* the formation of groups by means of a wide range of policies, such as guaranteeing citizens' right of free association; extending various benefits, such as favorable tax treatment and preferential mail rates; or failing to enforce the law where the legal environment for group formation is restrictive. It may *constrain* or *bar* group formation by means of repressive measures or by creating high hurdles to gaining access to resources. And while it is necessary to distinguish state-sponsored groups from state organs, it may actively *create* or *sponsor* associations. By means of such measures, states configure civil society, and by selectively applying these measures to particular groups or categories of groups, they mold it.

This process is hardly unidirectional, and it is sorely mistaken to claim state primacy. The activities of civil society groups and voices from the public sphere can and do have profound effects on governments. In democracies, for example, the principal of accountability creates much space for civil society groups to criticize, derail, and modify state policies and to transform political institutions over time. Even authoritarian regimes can be forced to respond to protest groups and

ACTIVIST STATE, POLICIES APPLY BROADLY	**ACTIVIST STATE, POLICIES ARE TARGETED**
19th c. France, state socialist systems, U.S. since the 1970s	20th c. Japan, interwar Germany and Italy
PERMISSIVE STATE, POLICIES APPLY BROADLY	**PERMISSIVE STATE, POLICIES ARE TARGETED**
19th c. Britain, 19th and early 20th c. U.S.	19th c. Germany, Meiji Japan until around 1900

Figure 15.1 State orientations toward civil society and the scope of state policies: four possibilities.

movements, as developments in Eastern Europe and South Korea over the past few decades attest. But the role that states play in contouring the associational landscape over time should not be underestimated.

Activist versus Permissive States, Broad versus Targeted Policies

States differ significantly in their *orientation* toward civil society and in the *scope* of their policies. Regarding orientation, states may be *activist*, implementing a wide range of policies that affect civil society groups. Most if not all advanced industrial democracies today, including the United States, actively foster civil society by means of their tax policies for nonprofits and the substantial funding they make available to groups. They thus fall into the activist camp. The policies of activist states need not boost civil society, of course. History – and indeed, the contemporary world – is replete with examples of states that have intervened into virtually every nook and cranny of associational life to contain, control, or obliterate it, state socialist systems being prime examples. Alternatively, states may be merely *permissive*, providing an environment in which groups can operate fairly freely, but offering little in the way of support beyond guaranteeing basic rights of free association.

Regarding scope, the policies of most advanced industrial democracies today apply *broadly*, affecting the larger community of civil society associations in more or less the same way (e.g., tax policies that benefit all nonprofits equally). State policies may also be *targeted* or segmented, however, so that specific groups or categories of groups are treated one way, while others are treated differently.

When these criteria are combined, four different possibilities emerge, and examples of each abound (see Fig. 15.1). Nineteenth-century Britain provides an example of a permissive state whose policies, based on a "jealously guarded rule of law," applied broadly and were gradually extended to new groups (including, by the 1820s, trade unions). The "legal space" for associational life expanded to the point that "the controls on association characteristic of countries like France were totally absent" (Morris 2000: 112, 113). Nineteenth-century Germany was also toward the permissive end of the continuum. Writing in the 1830s, Karl Immermann observed that virtually everybody belonged to some group, "be it an art society, an association to improve prisoners . . . , a shareholders' company or something else" (quoted in Tenfelde 2000: 86). But a patchwork quilt of rules permitted some groups while restricting or barring others.

These broad characterizations create strange bedfellows. In post-1970 America, nineteenth-century France, and state socialist systems, activist states applied their policies broadly, in the U.S. case to promote civic life and in the other cases to constrain it. For example, a nineteenth-century activist French state used its authority broadly to control "all and not just some of the associations"; it was not until 1901 that it waived its authority to bar citizens from founding associations (Huard 2000: 135, 136).

The Emergence of State Activism: Prewar Japan

Where is Japan situated in this typology? *Perhaps the most striking feature of Japan's civil society over the past century, dating from around 1900, has been the degree to which the state has taken an activist stance toward civic life, monitoring it, penetrating it, and seeking to steer it with a wide range of distinct policy tools targeted by group or sector.*

State activism was a regular feature of twentieth-century Japan, whatever the political arrangements at the time. Until 1945, the basic right of free association was not guaranteed; and even during the interlude of Taishō democracy, a legal framework based on a notion of imperial subjecthood rather than citizen rights continued to prevail. State policies, both in the past and today, continue to be highly segmented or targeted. In an extraordinary burst of activism, the Meiji state singled out producer groups to engineer their development. Observing that chambers of commerce dotted the associational landscape of Western countries and seeing a way to increase government access to business, the state ordered the Bureau of Commercial Development to study foreign examples and design a plan to guide firms in forming them. The government subsidized them with the 1890 Chambers of Commerce Act (Ishida 1968: 301). Similarly, while the Meiji state busily established enterprises (that it later sold off) in heavy industry, munitions, mining, and other fields, it just as actively set about encouraging business to form trade associations in "those industries that the government wanted to see grow quickly" (Schaede 2000: 235).

Semiofficial associations proliferated. State activism reached deep into the countryside with the formation of the Imperial Agricultural Association, one of many producer-oriented civil society groups formed under the government's aegis or with its approval. Another paramount example was neighborhood associations, numbering 298,000 today, that then and now engage citizens in neighborhood clean-ups, crime watches, park maintenance, the distribution of safety information, and other activities. Although many such associations originated as independent groups that sprang up to meet local needs, by the early decades of the twentieth century, the national bureaucracy guided their activities and promoted their spread (Garon and Pekkanen, this volume).

Whatever their origins, these new associations stood well apart from the kinds of state-controlled associations found in twentieth-century totalitarian systems. Although they hardly served as channels for interest articulation in the same manner as their foreign models, the state saw a need for their participation in policy-making (Ishida 1968: 302). Their relationship with the state was deeply symbiotic, but for the most part, they were encouraged and guided, not controlled, and the space between the state and the association expanded or contracted, depending on the era.

Consistent with the notion of targeting, Japan's prewar state had distinct policies for an astonishingly broad range of associations. While it sponsored and even subsidized the development of producer associations, it suppressed trade unions. Restrictions on political advocacy groups and activities began to appear relatively early in the Meiji period. In 1880, for example, the government decreed that "no political association . . . may advertise its lectures or debates, persuade people to enter its ranks by dispatching commissioners or issuing circulars, or combine and communicate with other similar societies"(Scalapino 1953: 65). Other restrictive measures included the Book Censorship Law of 1869, the Press Law of 1875, the Libel Law of 1875, and the Police Regulations on Public Meeting of 1880 (Henderson 1968: 419). The Peace Preservation Law of 1887 gave police the authority to seize anyone within a seven-mile radius of the Imperial Palace if such a person gave evidence of "scheming something detrimental to public tranquility," a law that soon led to the arrests of political activists (Moore 1966: 294).

Thus, the state treaded heavily on the prewar associational landscape. The preferred method of Japan's leaders was not suppression, but rather cooptation and guidance. The result was a patchwork of relationships between the state and all manner of groups. Not until the creation of the IRAA in 1940 was there a concerted, but ultimately short-lived, state effort to craft a uniform approach to civil society.

State Activism and Targeting: The Postwar Era

After Japan's defeat, so many groups arose or reestablished themselves that its associational world became a very different place. The Allied Occupation (1945–52) represented one of the most extensive experiments with democratization and legal overhaul ever attempted, and the success of that effort is indisputable. According to the ratings developed by Freedom House, Japan stands alone in Asia among those nations with the highest possible scores for political rights and civil liberties.

But even in this new environment in which freedom of association is fully guaranteed, an approach characterized by state activism coupled with targeted policies has continued. Indeed, it has shown striking durability despite the profound changes Japan has undergone. Although freedom of assembly and the right to form associations are guaranteed under Article 21 of Japan's 1947 constitution, nonprofit organizations per se lack legal standing. Gaining standing as a "public-interest legal person" (*kōeki hōjin*), as defined by Japan's Civil Code (which dates from 1896), has until recently required clearing high, successive hurdles (see the Introduction and Pekkanen, this volume).

While outright denials were rare, there were no clear standards for approval, and no legal obligation for administrative agencies to disclose information on existing public-interest corporations so that new groups could easily learn what was required of them (Amemiya 1999: 135–36). Until 1998, when a new Nonprofit Organization (NPO) Law was passed, the maze of paths for different types of groups and the regulations surrounding each were astonishing. Ninety laws provide for some 130 types of public-interest corporations, and Japan's activist state was present at every stage of the application process. Approval came with a "discretionary screening function, close supervision of operations, and sanctioning power" (Pekkanen, this volume). Perversely, with so many supervisory agencies involved, the more flexible the association and the broader its range of activities, the more difficult it was to win approval. Furthermore, the benefits of winning initial approval were hardly automatic. To enter into contracts, acquire real estate, and be eligible to receive tax-deductible contributions, an organization had to incorporate, but it then had to clear the additional hurdle of gaining status as a "special public interest-promoting" corporation. As of the mid-1990s, only 3.4 percent of public-interest corporations qualified (Amemiya 1999: 136, 144).

Gaining tax-exempt status remains quite difficult. Although a new law that passed on March 28, 2001, and took effect October 1 of that year allows individuals and firms who make donations to recognized nonprofit organizations to deduct their contributions from their taxes, qualifying for such status still presents formidable obstacles for many organizations. As of April 2002, only eleven out of an estimated 6,700 eligible organizations had applied, and only five of these had qualified (Matsubara 2002: 2–3). Thus, unless there is further loosening of legal provisions, many if not most civil society groups are likely to remain ineligible for the kind of tax-deductible contributions that are the lifeblood of their counterparts in many other advanced industrial democracies.

Consequences: Environmental Groups in Japan and the United States

The broader consequences of these state policies for structuring associational life may be suggested by comparing the development of one sector of civil society – environmental groups – in the United States and Japan from the late 1960s to the present. The comparison is especially apt because environmentalism arose in the two countries at roughly the same time, and it initially took similar forms. In both nations, the late 1960s was a period of intense environmental activism, and by the early 1970s (marked in 1970 in the United States by Earth Day and in Japan by the "Pollution Diet" session that approved fourteen antipollution measures), a broad range of environmental issues were on local and national agendas. Since that time, both countries have made significant environmental gains, but numerous problems remain, and new problems regularly call for policy remedies (McKean 1981; Pharr and Badaracco 1986; Upham 1987; Schreurs 2002).

Despite these common origins and striking parallels, the two countries could not look more different thirty years later when it comes to the civic communities that have formed around environmental issues. In the United States, groups of citizens with environmental concerns readily gained tax-exempt, nonprofit status under section 501(c)(3) of the tax code. In a signal victory for public-advocacy groups, a 1976 revision of the U.S. tax code boosted their cause by allowing 501(c)(3) groups to devote up to 20 percent of their budget to lobbying. By Earth Day in 1990, twelve highly visible national environmental organizations with a combined membership of 3 million and sizable professional staffs had emerged and were headquartered in Washington, D.C., eleven of them founded after 1970. They employed a total of 88 professional lobbyists, and eight of the twelve organizations boasted annual budgets exceeding $1 million. The Nature Conservancy alone had a budget of $156 million (Mitchell, Mertig, and Dunlap 1992: 223, 228). While certain groups, such as Greenpeace, favored direct action, most had become regular participants in the policy-making process.

In Japan, the situation was entirely different. Although some 1,500 to 3,000 citizens' groups had organized to press for pollution control by the early 1970s, most of them had faded from the scene by the 1980s (*Asahi Shinbun*, May 21, 1973, cited in Pempel 1982: 232; Schreurs 2002). Those groups that remained or formed thereafter faced the numerous institutional barriers detailed above. According to Tanaka Yukio, the group's founder, Friends of the Earth, for example, never even tried to gain nonprofit status when it formed in 1979. Not only were its prospects for approval dim, but the association was unwilling to submit to the kind of ministry supervision that accompanied that status. Miranda Schreurs (2002) found that 80 percent of the NGOs listed in a key Japanese directory as engaging in at least some environmental activity internationally in 1992 had combined individual and organizational memberships of under 2,000. Although civic groups certainly exist today and they push for environmental improvements, their memberships remain small. Lobbying is permitted, but without access to tax-deductible contributions, and most groups lack the resources to take on more than one or two issues at a time.

Tables 15.1 and 15.2, which compare the top ten environmental groups that currently engage in lobbying in the two countries, reveal civic worlds that are quite distinct. The average membership of the top ten U.S. environmental groups in 2000 was almost 700,000, while the comparable figure for Japan was under 20,000. Thus, American groups' average membership size was *35 times* larger, and their average budget was *over 20 times* that of Japanese groups.

Similarly, depending on their particular mix of activism or permissiveness and on the scope of their civic policies, other nations – all of them democracies responding to a common set of issues, in this case, environmental problems – can end up with different-looking civic realms. Germany, too, gave birth to a major environmental

Table 15.1 *The Top Ten Environmental Lobbying Groups in the United States by Membership and Budget*

Organization	Members	Budget
National Wildlife Federation	4,000,000	$102,053,000
Sierra Club	600,000	$52,000,000
National Audubon Society	550,000	$131,663,815
National Parks and Conservation Association	460,000	$19,551,000
Natural Resources Defense Council	400,000	$30,632,992
Defenders of Wildlife	381,568	$18,149,269
Environmental Defense Fund	300,000	$33,500,000
Wilderness Society	190,000	$16,052,132
Izaak Walton League	50,000	$4,000,000 (proposed for 2001)
Friends of the Earth	30,000	$3,000,000 (2000)
Average	696,157	$41,060,221

Source: Data are from the organizations' websites and annual reports. Missing information was collected by means of phone calls to staff members. Figures for membership are for 2000. Budget figures are for 1999 unless otherwise indicated. In some cases, membership is for "membership and supporters."

Table 15.2 *The Top Ten Environmental Lobbying Groups in Japan by Membership and Budget*

Organization	Members	Budget[a]
Let's Get Together for Minamata	32,000	$900,000 (2000)
Japan Ecological Society	31,000	$1,141,740
Fukagawa's Society for Health and Sanitation	28,246	$21,000
Kanagawa's Green Trust Foundation	26,367	$2,278,260
OISCA, International	19,500	$10,100,000 (2000)
Ecological Preservation Society of Saitama	18,000	not available
Nature Conservation Society of Japan	15,275	$2,244,400
Society for Beautifying Kasumigawa	10,000	$20,180
Takahata Town Sanitation Union	6,367	$48,980
Greenpeace Japan	5,400	$1,025,000
Average	19,216	$1,975,507

[a]Budget calculations made at an exchange rate of $1 = ¥100.
Source: Data are from Japan Fund for Global Environment 1998. The data dates from the mid-1990s unless otherwise indicated. Missing information was collected by means of fax and e-mail correspondence with staff members.

movement in the 1970s, and decades later, its far-ranging civic activism helps explain why Germany's environmental community looks more like America's than Japan's. It is well established and large, and with the rise of the Green Party, it enjoys a powerful voice in policy making. As in the United States, German groups acquired tax-free status with relative ease, and their memberships soared. By 1985, Deutscher Naturschutzring, an umbrella organization for conservation groups, had a membership of 3.3 million (Schreurs 2002).

One can point to many policies in the advanced industrial democracies that help explain how state activism contours the civic landscape. According to Robert Mitchell, for example, the introduction of bulk mail rates, which paved the way for direct-mail fund raising, offers one of the single best explanations for how mass-membership environmental organizations grew in America. As early as 1971, the National Audubon Society was sending 2 million pieces of mail annually (Mitchell et al. 1992). In contrast, as Pekkanen notes (this volume), the absence of such breaks in Japan makes reaching potential members through mailings extremely costly. Access to the policy-making process obviously constitutes another critical factor. By the 1970s, changes in American administrative law gave groups standing to take part on a routine basis "in administrative proceedings to determine the implementation of the laws" (Mitchell et al. 1992: 228). This access has granted environmental lobbyists a recognized role in debates over environmental impact, the standards to be applied, and so on.

Different Strokes for Different Folks: Boosting Civic Life for Producers

At the same time the postwar Japanese state threw a battery of obstacles in the path of environmental groups (along with consumer and women's organizations and numerous other types of civic associations), it used a wide range of policy tools to craft an entirely different associational landscape for producer organizations. While nonprofit organizations faced countless impediments to their gaining a solid legal foothold, for-profit corporations encountered few such difficulties. The same goes for industry or trade associations, for which the agency with jurisdiction is typically quite clear and the procedures are well established. Furthermore, because of the relatively early retirement age of Japan's bureaucrats and the widespread practice of their seeking comfortable perches in the private sector once they leave office (*amakudari*, or "descent from heaven"), ministries are apt to look with great favor on industry associations and the possible openings they create. As Tsujinaka Yutaka demonstrates (this volume), the broad result is a "long-lasting predominance of business associations" that over the period 1951–99 accounted for one-third to one-half of the total of organizations with "establishments" (a headquarters and staff). Only in the 1980s were business organizations eclipsed in number by a broad category of interest groups made up in part of civic associations. In the United States, civic associations and labor organizations overwhelmed business associations in numbers over roughly the same period.

Industry associations flourish in Japan. While a great many citizens' groups squeeze into crowded offices in seedy buildings or operate out of homes because they lack the legal standing necessary to rent space and rely heavily on volunteers to carry out their work, the leading industry associations operate in spacious, well-decorated quarters and employ large professional staffs. The community of organizations representing producer interests has thrived as a result of numerous targeted measures. Generous tax deductions for business entertaining sustain the social networks on which associational life in the business world is built (Witt 2000), for example. Indeed, even in the recessionary 1990s, total annual entertainment expenses for Japanese companies remained well above $50 billion (Asashi Shinbun 1999a: 94). Business treads heavily on the civic terrain in other ways as well. Although contributions from individuals to public-interest associations are not tax deductible in Japan, corporate donations generally are, giving firms far more influence than individuals in social life and policy making. Furthermore, such donations "are not confined to causes for the public good but also include, for example, the purchase of tickets for political fundraisers" (Amemiya 1999: 145). As Helen Hardacre has shown (1991), yet another legacy of the powerful role played by business in civic life is a public sphere heavily dominated by marketplace issues.

Close ties bind the business side of the civic world to politics and policy making. Dense social networks founded on school ties and well-established habits of consultation link business people and government officials. Despite the widely shared assessment that major business organizations such as Keidanren (Federation of Economic Organizations) now play a smaller role in policy making than in the past, their influence is still formidable and in many spheres well outside of their narrow self-interest. When the Liberal Democratic Party embarked on a major initiative of judicial reform, the party soon turned to Keidanren for recommendations in May 1998, for example. Just one month later, the party published a report that closely mirrored many of Keidanren's recommendations (Miyazawa 2001a, 2001b).

Targeting in the Civic Realm: The Institutional Origins of State Choices

Thus, targeted policies by an activist Japanese state have crafted a particular associational landscape in Japan. It is clear, as Skocpol holds and as Pekkanen argues here, that the legal and regulatory frameworks contour the civic terrain, whatever the setting. The remaining question, then, is *why* the Japanese state made the policy choices it did. The best explanation is an institutionalist one. Choices initially made in the Meiji era, when the state responded to the rise of new social groups unleashed by rapid modernization, proved quite durable. A major original impetus for these choices undoubtedly sprang from "developmentalism," the commitment of Japan's national leadership to advancing economic growth in a late-developing nation. This commitment dates back to the Meiji era and was renewed in 1945 after Japan's catastrophic defeat.

Established before Japan began to develop its response to emerging civic life, this national priority guided the state's selection of policy tools for dealing with civil society. In the Meiji period, for example, the Civil Code provisions Japan's leaders drafted for regulating for-profit corporations were modeled on those found in German law, which permitted easy incorporation. The laws dealing with nonprofit corporations, on the other hand, were based on those found in the civil codes of France and Italy, which took "a relatively obstructionist stance" toward such groups and subjected them to bureaucratic control (Yamaoka 1999: 163–64). Targeting was in evidence from the start, that is to say. Meanwhile, fostering and even subsidizing a range of private economic groups, from industry associations to chambers of commerce, represented a useful way to advance Japan's developmental agenda in the 1880s and 1890s.

An institutionalist explanation of Japan's postwar trajectory makes complete sense. In 1940, after all, Japan's wartime government had dissolved all interest groups when it created the Imperial Rule Assistance Association; and when it came to associational life, the postwar state in many ways confronted a blank slate. Operating in the context of a newly established democratic system founded on the notions of citizens' rights and freedom of association, Japan's postwar leadership might well have abandoned targeting and adopted broad policies for contouring the new associational terrain. After all, a great many incentives arising out of the new political environment would have supported such a shift. But they did not change course. Instead, they not only retained the 1896 Civil Code and maintained its elaborate maze of paths to nonprofit status, but as new types of groups appeared, they added yet more bends and turns by bringing an expanding number of bureaucratic agencies into the approval process. Meanwhile, as in the prewar era, these same leaders selected another, quite different set of policy tools to boost associational life in the economic realm and to shepherd groups representing the business community into the postwar policy-making process.

An institutionalist explanation thus offers a compelling framework for understanding the remarkable continuity in Japan's civic policies over more than a century. What sparked the initial, Meiji-era choices? The economic imperative was clearly central. Under the slogan "Rich nation, strong army" (*fukoku kyōhei*), Japan's leaders subordinated other objectives to pursue rapid economic development in what they took to be a dangerous world. In such a context, promoting business interests that advanced their program while constraining potentially disruptive social forces undoubtedly struck them as prudent. Norms shaped in the prior era of Tokugawa feudalism, in which protests were steadfastly repressed, also supported this strategy, however.

Ideas coming out of the dominant moral tradition provided support for leaders' selection of tools in the same way that liberal ideas were critical in shaping state responses to early manifestations of civic life in the West. In Western Europe, the rise of civil society was closely associated with the development of a tradition of autonomous individuals who were entitled to operate in a domain of social life outside the state (Gellner 1995; Hall 1995; Nord 2000). After Japan's opening to the West in the Meiji era, these same notions found advocates in Japan as well, and they fueled many citizens' push for a voice and for the creation of a public sphere. These same ideas infused the many Western models that Japan's Meiji leaders studied when assembling their policy tools for responding to civic ferment. But it should come as no surprise that rival ideas derived from indigenous moral precepts mingled with the liberal doctrines embedded in Western legal codes. As Barshay attests (this volume), many notions associated in the West with the rise of civil society were wholly alien to Japanese thought at the start of the Meiji era, and they were not all that well understood even by their Japanese advocates. Furthermore, concerned that liberal ideas would fuel antigovernment movements, the state acted relatively quickly to check their spread by suppressing Western books on philosophy and morals and by mandating the adoption of textbooks based on Confucian moral precepts (Iokibe 1999: 70–71).

The single most important idea reflected in the Japanese government's approach to associational life was a Confucian notion of the proper relation between state and society. Although liberalism posits a clear division between the two, Confucianism does not. As Tu Wei-Ming (2000: 263) has argued, in the Confucian vision, civil society does not represent space between family and the state that stands in an oppositional relation to both; rather, it offers "mediating cultural institutions that allow a fruitful articulation between family and state." Society is "subsumed under the state" (Koo 1993: 238) and entrusted to the care and protection of leaders. State power is itself subordinate to a higher moral authority, but rulers, not subjects, are expected to define the public good. Confucian thought allows private interests to be pursued as long as they do not interfere with the public interest as defined by rulers, and it is the rulers' duty to monitor such interests closely to advance the common good (Yamamoto 1999: 8). A high value is placed on social harmony, and a negative view is taken of conflict and thus of confrontational conduct on the part of social groups (Pharr 1990).

All of these ideas, embedded in Tokugawa beliefs and practices, were available to Meiji leaders. Whether they deeply believed these ideas or merely used them strategically to justify their actions can be debated, but in the end, it is beside the point for an institutionalist interpretation. Leaders in Japan, like leaders everywhere, selected from the "tool kit" of ideas available to them at that particular historical juncture (Swidler 1986; Benfell 2002). Contrary to what social constructivists would claim, their selection was hardly random. A sense of crisis – an urgent perceived need to maintain domestic control in order to play catch-up with the West in the Meiji era and to secure recovery from wartime devastation in the immediate aftermath of the Pacific War – undoubtedly drove the choices they made from the options available to them, leading to what Steven Benfell (2002) has called, in another context, "punctuated transformations in institutions."

At both junctures, the choices they made also operated to secure their own positions. In selecting French and Italian over German models for civil code provisions governing citizens' groups, they chose measures that provided maximum bureaucratic control over such groups. Furthermore, in applying the new civil code, they construed their authority to go beyond the mere authorization of groups to extend to regular bureaucratic guidance of their activities. They could readily justify this on the basis of widely accepted ideas. The common prewar practice of turning to "private" groups, such as neighborhood associations, to carry out state activities similarly reflected these views. And early state activism to help create and subsidize business associations was consonant with the supposition that organizing "private" interests is a natural and legitimate activity of the state.

Japan's Civic Legacy as It Affects Civil Society Today

A pattern of state activism coupled with targeting has operated in a wide variety of settings over the course of many years in Japan. In the new context created by military defeat and the devastation of the war's aftermath, Japan's postwar political and bureaucratic leadership, choosing from among the options available to them, elected once more to keep a tight leash on civil society and secure their own power in the process. Consonant with the idea of permeable rather than demarcated boundaries between state and society, bureaucrats routinely turn to carefully chosen civic groups as "social partners" in issue areas such as social welfare (Estévez-Abe, this volume). In so doing, the state has often chosen to create auxiliary associations *(gaikaku dantai*) that, despite their quasigovernmental status, are treated as part of the nonprofit sector under Japanese law and indeed have become part of the policy-making process as authoritative representatives of society. Japan's civic legacy is reflected in a style of discourse in which state officials often use "mutual exhortation" and urge "a communal way of self-realization" (Tu 2000: 263).

Other examples abound. Having to seek bureaucratic approval to gain nonprofit status is normal in the advanced industrial democracies, but the degree and types of bureaucratic supervision that come into play once approval is granted reflects Japan's particular civic legacy. As Iokibe Makoto (1999: 52) has observed:

> Even today, few public-interest corporations (*kōeki hojin*) are completely independent of the government.... There are numerous occasions... when the government calls upon the support and cooperation of people or groups in the private sector in order to fulfill public goals or needs. In these endeavors, ... the scope and purpose of their activities can unfold only within areas prescribed and determined by the powers that be.

A leading critic of the Japanese state's heavy influence on civil society has called this pattern a "public-equals-official schema" that is founded on officials' assumption that "public" space is theirs to oversee and maintain (Yamamoto 1999).

Although it has many critics in Japan today, such thinking is hardly confined to officials. As Patricia Maclachlan demonstrates (this volume), consumer groups in the early postwar period readily cooperated with government authorities in a state-sponsored, "grassroots" New Life Movement (Shin Seikatsu Undō) to "modernize" citizens' attitudes and encourage a strong work ethic. And although local consumer groups later became far more active and independent, "passive dependence on government initiatives" has largely prevailed at the national level. Members' motives for cooperation are mixed, Maclachlan notes. On the one hand, they feel "morally obligated" to work closely with a state that is "purportedly acting in the best interests of the 'people's economy.'" On the other hand, they cooperate to win state financial resources and to secure legitimacy in a society that distrusts groups that question authority. Other advocacy groups share consumer groups' concerns about gaining legitimacy from a public that (like officials) remains distrustful of protest activities. The ideal model of protest that operates in Japan and that has been conditioned by Japan's civic legacy sets exceedingly high hurdles for civic groups that hope to reach out to gain public support for their cause (Pharr 1990).

Understanding Civil Societies

Studying the choices that leaders make and the institutional framework arising from them is essential for understanding any nation's associational landscape. At critical junctures, leaders, in effect, lay down pipes across the civic terrain and shape the flow of its future development. State actions are hardly the be-all and end-all, of course. The nature of associational life and, indeed, the impetus to form associations in the first place are affected by a wide variety of forces (e.g., education, economic transformations, internationalizing trends, technological change) independent of state intervention in the civic realm. And the actions of social actors, from neighborhood groups to NGOs, can prompt or accelerate changes in the regulatory status quo, as Japan's recent reforms governing nonprofit status demonstrate. Nevertheless, the choices leaders make and the regulatory frameworks that result from them are central for explaining why some states – including Japan, the United States, and many other liberal democracies – choose an activist orientation toward civil society and seek to shape it with a wide variety of possible tools or are merely permissive and play a minimal role in determining the rules of the game for civic participation. The civic legacies that result also explain why states forge civic policies that apply widely, as in the United States, or instead target their strategies, treating various sectors or groups quite differently, as in Japan.

In addition, looking closely at choices of institutions helps one to identify significant differences among countries that end up with similar orientations and policy tools (see Fig. 15.1). In its extreme state activism vis-à-vis civil society, for example, the prewar Japanese state (particularly from 1930 until 1945) appears at first glance to have much in common with state socialist systems. In both cases, state penetration of social life was extremely deep and had strong ideological underpinnings. But whereas activist states in socialist Eastern Europe and the Soviet Union sought to obliterate any and all manifestations of an independent civil society (Havel 1985; Ekiert and Kubik 1999), the activist Japanese state, guided by a different civic legacy, generally sought to encompass and shape them.

The analytic framework presented here offers a way to study states and civil societies across a wide range of nations, including those in Asia that so far have rarely been examined on more than a country-by-country basis. Japan's experience is a particularly useful guide in the latter endeavor because a pattern of state activism combined with targeted policies can almost certainly be found in Taiwan, South Korea, Singapore, Thailand, Indonesia, and Malaysia. Relative permissiveness guided by targeted policies arguably appears to characterize Pakistan, Sri Lanka, and Nepal. Permissive states with broadly applicable policies are in short supply in Asia; the best examples are probably India, the Philippines, and possibly Hong Kong. Meanwhile, the Japanese state's orientation in the 1930s, with its extreme activism and broad monitoring of a wide spectrum of groups, has parallels in Asia's state socialist and hard authoritarian systems, such as China, Vietnam, and Laos, with the extremes represented by Myanmar and North Korea. As Japan's experience indicates, national patterns may change over time in response to globalization, regime change, and other forces. Thus, while the basic pattern holds, the direction of change in Japan is toward activism combined with broadly applicable policies. The analytical lens presented here and brought to bear on Japan's experience offers a means to understand and link disparate associational landscapes across borders.

Bibliography

Aera. 1997. "Hitori ichi man en zeikin yamawake: Nōgyō yosan musabaru riken kōzō" (¥10,000 Yen in Taxes for Each [Taxpayer]: The Structure of Agricultural Budget Greed). *Aera* (April 28–May 5): 24–27.

Alexander, Jeffrey C. 1997. "The Paradoxes of Civil Society." *International Sociology* 12 (2): 115–33.

Alexander, Jeffrey C. 1998. "Introduction: Civil Society I, II, III: Constructing an Empirical Concept from Normative Controversies and Historical Transformations." In *Real Civil Societies: Dilemmas of Institutionalization*, ed. Jeffrey C. Alexander. London: Sage Publications.

Alger, Chadwick F. 1994. "Citizens and the UN System in a Changing World." In *Global Transformation: Challenges to the State System*, ed. Yoshikazu Sakamoto. Tokyo, New York: U.N. University Press.

Allinson, Gary D. 1989. "Politics in Contemporary Japan: Pluralist Scholarship in the Conservative Era: A Review Article." *Journal of Asian Studies* 48 (2): 324–32.

Allinson, Gary D. 1993. "Introduction" and "Analyzing Political Change: Topics, Findings, and Implications." In *Political Dynamics in Contemporary Japan*, ed. Gary D. Allinson and Sone Yasunori. Ithaca, N.Y.: Cornell University Press.

Allinson, Gary, and Sone Yasunori, eds. 1993. *Political Dynamics in Contemporary Japan*. Ithaca, N.Y.: Cornell University Press.

Amano Masako. 1996. *Seikatsusha to wa dare ka* [Who is the *seikatsusha*?]. Tokyo: Chūkō Shinsho.

Ambaras, David R. 1998. "Social Knowledge, Cultural Capital, and the New Middle Class in Japan, 1895–1912." *Journal of Japanese Studies* 24 (1): 1–33.

Amemiya Takako. 1998. "The Nonprofit Sector: Legal Background." In *The Nonprofit Sector in Japan*, ed. Yamamoto Tadashi. Manchester, U.K.: Manchester University Press.

Amemiya Takako. 1999. "Nonprofit Law Reports: Japan." In *Philanthropy and Law in Asia: A Comparative Study of the Nonprofit Legal Systems in Ten Asia Pacific Societies*, ed. Thomas Silk. San Francisco, Calif.: Jossey-Bass.

Amenomori Takayoshi and Yamamoto Tadashi. 1998. "Introduction." In *The Nonprofit Sector in Japan*, ed. Yamamoto Tadashi. Manchester, U.K.: Manchester University Press.

Anechiarico, Frank, and James B. Jacobs. 1996. *The Pursuit of Absolute Integrity: How Corruption Control Makes Government Ineffective*. Chicago, Ill.: University of Chicago Press.

Aoki Masahiko, and Ronald Dore, eds. 1994. *The Japanese Firm: The Source of Competitive Strength*. New York: Oxford University Press.

Aoki Masahiko and Okuno Masahiro, eds. 1996. *Keizai shisutemu no hikaku seido bunseki* [Comparative Institutional Analysis of Economic Systems]. Tokyo: University of Tokyo Press.

Apter, David, and Sawa Nagayo. 1984. *Against the State*. Cambridge, Mass.: Harvard University Press.

Arato, Andrew. 1981. "Civil Society Against the State: Poland, 1980–81." *Telos* 47: 23–47.

Arato, Andrew. 1990. "Revolution, Civil Society and Democracy." *Praxis International* 10 (1/2): 24–38.

Arato, Andrew, and Jean Cohen. 1988. "Civil Society and Social Theory." *Thesis Eleven* 21: 40–64.

Archambault, Edith. 1997. *The Nonprofit Sector in France*. Manchester, U.K., and New York: Manchester University Press.

Asahi Shinbun. 1999a. *Japan Almanac* 1999. Tokyo: Asahi Shinbun.

Asahi Shinbun. 1999b. "Survey: Some Words Are Difficult." May 3. http://www.asahi.com/english.html.

Asahi Shinbun. 2000a. "Climate for Political Change Still Cold and Cloudy in Japan" (editorial). January 10. http://www.asahi.com/english.html.

Asahi Shinbun. 2000b. " 'Inadequate' Candidates Hit Back: LDP Tops 'Bad' List." May 11. http://www.asahi.com/english.html.

Asahi Shinbun. 2000b. "Triumph of a 'No to Corruption' Campaign" (Vox Populi, Vox Dei). April 18. http://www.asahi.com/english.html.

Asano Kiyoshi and Shinoda Takeshi. 1998. "*Gendai sekai no 'shimin shakai' shisō*" ["Civil Society" Thoughts in Contemporary Society]. In *Fukken suru shimin shakai ron* [Revival of the Civil Society Argument], ed. Yagi Kiichirō, Yamada Toshio, Senga Shigeyoshi, and Nozawa Toshiharu. Tokyo: Nihon Hyōronsha.

Asanuma Banri. 1985. "The Contractual Framework for Parts Supply in the Japanese Automotive Industry." *Japanese Economic Studies* 15: 54–78.

Association for the Promotion of International Cooperation (APIC) [Kokusai Kyōryoku Suishin Shōkai]. 1985. *Tōjōkoku no minkan kōeki soshiki (NGO) jittai chōsa* [A Survey of the State of NGOs in Developing Countries]. Tokyo: APIC.

Association for the Promotion of International Cooperation (APIC) [Kokusai Kyōryoku Suishin Shōkai]. 1995. *Wagakuni NGO ni tai suru shien taisei chōsa* [A Survey of Support Programs for Japanese NGOs]. Tokyo: APIC.

Atoda Naosumi, Amenomori Takayoshi, and Ohta Mio. 1998. "The Scale of the Japanese Nonprofit Sector." In *The Nonprofi Sector in Japan*, ed. Yamamoto Tadashi. Manchester, U.K.: Manchester University Press.

Bagdikian, Ben. 1987. *The Media Monopoly*. 3rd ed. Boston: Beacon Press.

Banfield, Edward C. 1958. *The Moral Basis of a Backward Society*. New York: Free Press.

Bayart, Jean-François. 1986. "Civil Society in Africa." In *Political Domination in Africa: Reflections on the Limits of Power*, ed. Patrick Chabal. Cambridge, U.K.: Cambridge University Press.

Beckford, James. 1985. *Cult Controversies: The Societal Response to the New Religious Movements*. London: Tavistock.

Beckman, David. 1991. "Recent Experiences and Emerging Trends." In *Nongovernmental Organizations and the World Bank: Cooperation for Development*, ed. Samuel Paul and Arturo Israel. Washington, D.C.: World Bank.

Beer, Lawrence Ward. 1984. *Freedom of Expression*. Tokyo: Kodansha International.

Beetham, David. 1998. "Market Economy and Democratic Polity." In *Civil Society: Democratic Perspectives*, ed. Robert Fine and Shirin Rai. London: Frank Cass.

Bellin, Eva. 1995. "Civil Society in Formation: Tunisia." In *Civil Society in the Middle East*, 2 vols., ed. Richard Augustus Norton. Leiden: E. J. Brill.

Bellin, Eva. 2002. *Stalled Democracy: Capitalist Industrialization and the Paradox of State Sponsorship in Tunisia*. Ithaca: Cornell University Press.

Bendix, Reinhard, John Bendix, and Norman Furniss. 1987. "Reflections on Modern Western States and Civil Societies." In *Research in Political Sociology*, vol. 3. Greenwich: JAI Press.

Benfell, Steven T. 2002. "The Politics of Reconstructing National Identity in Postwar Japan." Manuscript.

Bennett, John, and Ishino Iwao. 1955. *Paternalism in the Japanese Economy: Anthropological Studies of Oyabun-Kobun Relations*. Minneapolis: University of Minnesota Press.

Bentley, Arthur F. 1908. *The Process of Government: A Study of Social Pressures*. Chicago, Ill.: University of Chicago Press.

Berger, Gordon Mark. 1977. *Parties Out of Power in Japan, 1931–1941*. Princeton, N.J.: Princeton University Press.

Berger, Suzanne, and Ronald Dore, eds. 1996. *National Diversity and Global Capitalism*. Ithaca, N.Y.: Cornell University Press.

Berkman, Lisa, and Kawachi Ichirō. 2000. *Social Epidemiology*. New York: Oxford University Press.

Berman, Sheri. 1997. "Civil Society and the Collapse of the Weimar Republic." *World Politics* 49 (3): 401–29.

Bermeo, Nancy. 2000. "Civil Society after Democracy: Some Conclusions." In *Civil Society before Democracy: Lessons from Nineteenth-Century Europe*, ed. Nancy Bermeo and Philip Nord. Lanham, Md.: Rowman and Littlefield.

Berry, Jeffrey M. 1977. *Lobbying for the People*. Princeton, N.J.: Princeton University Press.

Berry, Jeffrey M. 1998. "The Rise of Citizens Groups." In *Civic Engagement in American Democracy*, ed. Theda Skocpol and Morris P. Fiorina. Washington, D.C.: Brookings Institution Press.

Berry, Mary Elizabeth. 1998. "Public Life in Authoritarian Japan." *Daedalus* 127 (3): 133–65.

Bestor, Theodore C. 1989. *Neighborhood Tokyo*. Stanford: Stanford University Press.

Bestor, Victoria Lyon. 1999. "Reimagining 'Civil Society' in Japan." *Washington-Japan Journal* (special issue, spring): 1–10.

Blaney, David L., and Mustapha Kamal Pasha. 1993. "Civil Society and Democracy in the Third World: Ambiguities and Historical Possibilities." *Studies in Comparative International Development* 28 (1): 3–24.

Blankenburg, Erhard. 1996. "Changes in Political Regimes and Continuity of the Rule of Law in Germany." In *Courts, Law, and Politics in Comparative Perspective*, ed. Herbert Jacob et al. New Haven, Conn.: Yale University Press.

Boli, John. 1999. "Global Civil Society and USA/Japan Involvement." In *Civil Society: New Agenda for U.S.-Japan Intellectual Exchange*. Tokyo: Japan Foundation Center for Global Partnership.

Boli, John, and George M. Thomas. 1999. "Introduction" and "INGOs and the Organization of World Culture." In *Constructing World Culture: International Nongovernmental Organizations Since 1875*, ed. John Boli and George M. Thomas. Stanford, Calif.: Stanford University Press.

Bondy, Christopher. 1997. "Scapegoat Suicide: An Analysis of Suicide Related to Scandal in Postwar Japan." Master's thesis, University of Hawaii at Manoa.

Boyer, Robert, and J. Rogers Hollingsworth, eds. 1997. *Contemporary Capitalism: The Embeddedness of Institutions*. New York: Cambridge University Press.

Braibanti, Ralph J. D. 1948. "Neighborhood Associations in Japan and Their Democratic Potentialities." *Far Eastern Quarterly* 7 (2): 136–64.

Braisted, William R., trans. 1976. *Meiroku Zasshi: Journal of the Japanese Enlightenment.* Cambridge, Mass.: Harvard University Press.

Bratton, Michael. 1989. "Beyond the State: Civil Society and Associational Life in Africa." *World Politics* 41 (3): 407–30.

Bratton, Michael. 1994. "Civil Society and Political Transitions in Africa." In *Civil Society and the State in Africa*, ed. John W. Harbeson, Donald Rothchild, and Naomi Chazan. London: Lynne Rienner.

Brehm, John, and Wendy Rahn. 1997. "Individual-Level Evidence for the Causes and Consequences of Social Capital." *American Journal of Political Science* 41 (3): 999–1023.

Broadbent, Jeffrey. 1998. *Environmental Politics in Japan: Networks of Power and Protest.* Cambridge, U.K.: Cambridge University Press.

Brown, L. David, and David C. Korten. 1991. "Working More Effectively with Nongovernmental Organizations." In *Nongovernmental Organizations and the World Bank: Cooperation for Development*, ed. Samuel Paul and Arturo Israel. Washington, D.C.: World Bank.

Bryant, Christopher G. A. 1993. "Social Self-Organisation, Civility and Sociology: A Comment on Kumar's 'Civil Society.'" *British Journal of Sociology* 44 (3): 397–401.

Bryant, Christopher G. A. 1995. "Civic Nation, Civil Society, Civil Religion." In *Civil Society: Theory, History, Comparison*, ed. John Hall. Cambridge, U.K.: Polity Press.

Bull, Hedley. 1977. *The Anarchical Society: A Study of Order in World Politics.* London: Macmillan.

Bullock, Robert. N.d. *Politicizing the Developmental State: Agriculture and the Conservative Coalition in Postwar Japan.* Forthcoming.

Bunkabu shūmuka. 1997. "*Shūkyō dantai ni okeru kōeki katsudō*" [Public Service Activities by Religious Organizations]. *Bunkachō geppō* 351 (12): 14–16.

Bunkachō, ed. 1998. *Heisei jūnenban shūkyō nenkan* [Religions Yearbook of 1998]. Tokyo: Gyōsei.

Burnett, Stanton H., and Luca Mantovani. 1998. *The Italian Guillotine: Operation Clean Hands and the Overthrow of Italy's First Republic.* Lanham, Md.: Rowman & Littlefield.

C's (Shimin Katsudō o Sasaeru Seido o Tsukuru Kai). Various dates. *C's nyūsuretaa.* Tokyo: C's.

Calder, Kent C. 1988. *Crisis and Compensation: Public Policy and Political Stability in Japan, 1949–1986.* Princeton, N.J.: Princeton University Press.

Calhoun, Craig. 1992. "Habermas and the Public Sphere." In *Habermas and the Public Sphere*, ed. Craig Calhoun. Cambridge, Mass.: MIT Press.

Calhoun, Craig, ed. 1992. *Habermas and the Public Sphere.* Cambridge, Mass.: MIT Press.

Calhoun, Craig. 1993. "Civil Society and the Public Sphere." *Public Culture* 5 (2): 267–80.

Campbell, John C. 1989. "Bureaucratic Primacy: Japanese Policy Communities in an American Perspective." *Governance* 2 (1): 5–22.

Campbell, John C. 1992. *How Policies Change: The Japanese Government and the Aging Society.* Princeton, N.J.: Princeton University Press.

Campbell, John C. 1996. "Media and Policy Change in Japan." In *Media and Politics in Japan*, ed. Susan J. Pharr and Ellis Krauss. Honolulu: University of Hawaii.

Campbell, John C. 2000. "Long-Term-Care Comes to Japan." *Health Affairs* 19 (3): 26–39.

Campbell, John C., and Ikegami Naoki. 1999. *Long-Term Care for Frail Older People: Reaching for the Ideal System.* New York: Springer.

Campbell, John C., with Mark A. Baskin, Frank R. Baumgartner, and Nina P. Halpern. 1989. "Afterword on Policy Communities: A Framework for Comparative Research." *Governance* 2 (1): 86–94.

Carapico, Sheila. 1996. "Yemen Between Civility and Civil War." In *Civil Society in the Middle East*, 2 vols., ed. Richard Augustus Norton. Leiden: E. J. Brill.

Carapico, Sheila. 1998. *Civil Society in Yemen: The Political Economy of Activism in Modern Arabia*. Cambridge, U.K.: Cambridge University Press.

Carothers, Thomas. 1999. "Civil Society: Think Again." *Foreign Policy* 117: 18–29.

Castberg, A. Didrick. 1997. "Prosecutorial Independence in Japan." *UCLA Pacific Basin Law Journal* 16: 38–87

Chabbott, Colette. 1999. "Development INGOs." In *Constructing World Culture: International Nongovernmental Organizations Since 1875*, ed. John Boli and George Thomas. Stanford, Calif.: Stanford University Press.

Chazan, Naomi. 1992. "Africa's Democratic Challenge." *World Policy Journal* 9: 279–307.

Chessa, Cecilia. 2000. "State Subsidies, Civil Society, and the Anti-Liberal Milieu in East Germany: A Case of Unintended Consequences." Presented at the annual meeting of the American Political Science Association, Washington, D.C.

Chung, Young-Soo, and Elise K. Tipton. 1997. "Problems of Assimilation: The Koreans." In *Society and the State in Interwar Japan*, ed. Elise K. Tipton. London: Routledge.

Clark, Ann Marie, Elisabeth J. Friedman, and Kathryn Hochstetler. 1998. "The Sovereign Limits of Global Civil Society: A Comparison of NGO Participation in UN World Conferences on the Environment, Human Rights, and Women." *World Politics* 51 (1): 1–35.

Clark, John. 1991. *Democratizing Development*. London: Earthscan Publications.

Claude, Inis. 1966. "Collective Legitimization as a Political Function of the United Nations." *International Organization* 20: 367–79.

Clausing, Jeri, and Rebecca Fairley Raney. 1998. "More Members Are Plugged In, But Few Are Making Connections." *New York Times* (online), January 15 (accessed June 11, 2000). http://www.nytimes.com/library/cyber/week/011598congress.html.

Cohen, Jean. 1995. "Interpreting the Notion of Civil Society." In *Toward a Global Civil Society*, ed. Michael Walzer. Providence, R.I.: Berghahn Books.

Cohen, Jean L., and Andrew Arato. 1992. *Civil Society and Political Theory*. Cambridge, Mass.: MIT Press.

Colombo, Gherardo. 1997. *Il vizio della memoria* [The Vice of Memory]. Milan: Feltrinelli Press.

Colombo, Gherardo. 1999. "Global Crime, Corruption, and Accountability: Investigations into Corruption in Milan." Presented at Tufts University, Boston.

Colombo, Gherardo. 2002. "Mani Pulite? 60% Will Vanish by Being Barred by Limitation." *Corriere Della Sera*, February 5, trans. Transparency International Daily Corruption News Full Text Service.

Corrado, Anthony. 2000. *Campaigns in Cyberspace: Toward a New Regulatory Approach*. Washington, D.C.: Aspen Institute.

Crozier, Michel, Samuel P. Huntington, and Watanuki Jōji. 1975. *The Crisis of Democracy: Report on the Governability of Democracies to the Trilateral Commission*. New York: New York University Press.

Curtis, Gerald. 1975. "Big Business and Political Influence." In *Modern Japanese Organization and Decision-Making*, ed. Ezra Vogel. Berkeley: University of California Press.

Curtis, Gerald. 1988. *The Japanese Way of Politics*. New York: Columbia University Press.

Curtis, Gerald. 1997. "A 'Recipe' for Democratic Development." *Journal of Democracy* 8 (3): 139–45.

Curtis, Gerald. 1999. *The Logic of Japanese Politics: Leaders, Institutions, and the Limits of Change*. New York: Columbia University Press.

DAC Expert Group on Aid Evaluation. 1997. *Evaluation of Programs Promoting Participatory Development and Good Governance: Synthesis Report*. Paris: OECD.

Dahl, A. Robert. 1991. *Modern Political Analysis*, 5th ed. Englewood Cliffs, N.J.: Prentice-Hall.

Dash, Samuel. 1999. "Why the Independent Counsel Law Deserves to Live." *New York Times*, February 17, sec. A.

Deguchi, Masayuki. 1999. "A Comparative View of Civil Society." *Washington-Japan Journal* (special issue, spring): 11–20.

Deguchi, Masayuki. 2000. "Not for Profit: A Brief History of Japanese Nonprofit Organizations." *Look Japan* 45 (526): 18–20.

della Porta, Donatella. 1996. "Actors in Corruption: Business Politicians in Italy." *International Social Science Journal* 149: 349–64.

della Porta, Donatella. 2000. "Social Capital, Beliefs in Government, and Political Corruption." In *Disaffected Democracies: What's Troubling the Trilateral Countries?*, ed. Susan J. Pharr and Robert D. Putnam. Princeton, N.J.: Princeton University Press.

della Porta, Donatella, and Alessandro Pizzorno. 1996. "The Business Politicians: Reflections from a Study of Political Corruption." *Journal of Law and Society* 23: 73–94.

della Porta, Donatella, and Alberto Vannucci. 1999. *Corrupt Exchanges: Actors, Resources, and Mechanisms of Political Corruption*. New York: Aldine de Gruyter.

Dellinger, Walter. 1999. "A Too-Independent Counsel." *New York Times*, February 24, sec. A.

Dentsū Sōken, eds. 1996. *NPO to wa nani ka* [What Is an NPO?]. Tokyo: Nihon Keizai Shinbunsha.

Development Assistance Committee (DAC). 1989–91a. *Development Cooperation: Efforts and Policies of the Members of the DAC*. Paris: Organization for Economic Cooperation and Development (OECD).

Development Assistance Committee (DAC). 1991b. "Aid Review 1990/91: Report by the Secretariat and Questions for the Review of Japan." Paris: OCDE/GD (91) 198.

Development Assistance Committee (DAC). 1992a. "DAC and OECD Public Policy Statements on Participatory Development/Good Governance." Paris: OCDE/GD (92) 67.

Development Assistance Committee (DAC). 1992b. *Development Assistance Manual: DAC Principles for Effective Aid*. Paris: OECD.

Development Assistance Committee (DAC). 1993. "Aid Review 1992/93: Report by the Secretariat and Questions for the Review of Japan." Paris: OEDE/GD (93) 119.

Development Assistance Committee (DAC). 1995. *Participatory Development and Good Governance*. Paris: OECD.

Development Assistance Committee (DAC). 1996 and 1999. "Development Cooperation Review Series: Japan." Paris: OECD (96) 13 and (99) 34.

Diamond, Larry. 1999. *Developing Democracy: Toward Consolidation*. Baltimore: Johns Hopkins University Press.

Dichter, Thomas. 1999. "Globalization and Its Effects on NGOs: Efflorescence or Blurring of Roles and Relevance?" *Nonprofit and Voluntary Sector Quarterly* 28 (4) supplement: 38–58.

Di Federico, Giuseppe. 1995. "Prosecutorial Independence and the Democratic Requirement of Accountability in Italy: Analysis of a Deviant Case in Comparative Perspective." In *The Role of the Public Prosecutor in Criminal Justice According to Different Constitutional Systems*. Reports presented to the ancillary meeting held at the Ninth United Nations Congress on the Prevention of Crime and the Treatment of Offenders, Cairo.

Domon Takashi. 1996. *Nōkyō daihasan* [The Great Collapse of Nōkyō]. Tokyo: Tōyō Keizai Shuppansha.

Doner, Richard, and Ben Schneier. 1999. "Business Association and Economic Development." Working paper, Institute for Policy Research, Northwestern University.

Dore, Ronald P. 1958. *City Life in Japan*. Berkeley: University of California Press.

Dore, Ronald P. 1959. *Land Reform in Japan*. Oxford: Oxford University Press.

Dore, Ronald P. 1987. *Taking Japan Seriously: A Confucian Perspective on Leading Economic Issues*. Stanford, Calif.: Stanford University Press.

Dore, Ronald P. 1989. "*Kōporatizumu ni tuite kangaeru*" [Thinking about Corporatism]. *Leviathan* 4: 120–46.

Dower, John W. 1999. *Embracing Defeat: Japan in the Wake of World War II*. New York: W. W. Norton.

Duus, Peter. 1998. *Modern Japan*. Boston: Houghton Mifflin.

Economic Planning Agency (EPA). 1981–98 (annual). *Minkan hieiri dantai jittai hōkoku* [Report on the Conditions of Private Nonprofit Organizations]. Tokyo.

Economic Planning Agency (EPA), Economic Cooperation Policy Study Group. 1997a. "*Jizoku kanō na keizai kyōryoku ni mukete*" (Toward Sustainable Economic Cooperation). Tokyo.

Economic Planning Agency (EPA), Social Policy Bureau. 1997b. *Shimin katsudō repōto: Shimin katsudō dantai kihon chōsa hōkokusho* [Report on Citizen Activities: Report on a Basic Survey of Citizen Activity Organizations]. Tokyo: Ministry of Finance.

Economic Planning Agency (EPA). 1998. *Nihon no NPO no keizai kibo* [The Economic Scale of Japan's Nonprofit Organizations]. Tokyo: Ministry of Finance.

Edwards, Michael. 1994. "International Non-Governmental Organizations, 'Good Government' and the 'New Policy Agenda': Lessons of Experience at the Program Level." *Democratization* 1 (3): 504–15.

Efron, Sonni. 1998. "Disgusted Public Balks at Japan Inc." *Los Angeles Times*, February 8, sec. A.

Eggertsson, Thrainn. 1990. *Economic Behavior and Institutions*. New York: Cambridge University Press.

Ehrenberg, John. 1999. *Civil Society: The Critical History of an Idea*. New York: New York University Press.

Eigen, Peter. 2001. "Introducing the Global Corruption Report." In *Global Corruption Report 2001*, ed. Robin Hodess, with Jessie Banfield and Toby Wolfe. Berlin: Transparency International.

Eisenstadt, Shmuel N. 1995. "Civil Society." In *The Encyclopedia of Democracy*, ed. Seymour Martin Lipset. Washington, D.C.: Congressional Quarterly.

Ekiert, Grzegorz, and Jan Kubik. 1999. *Rebellious Civil Society: Popular Protest and Democratic Consolidation, 1989–1993*. Ann Arbor: University of Michigan Press.

Elias, Norbert. 1978. *The Civilizing Process: The Development of Manners*. Trans. Edmund Jephcott. New York: Urizen Books.

Elias, Norbert. 1988. "Violence and Civilization." In *Civil Society and the State: New European Perspectives*, ed. John Keane. London: Verso.

Elshtain, Jean Bethke. 1997. "Not a Cure-All." *Brookings Review* 15 (4): 13–15.

Estévez-Abe, Margarita. 2002. "Negotiating Welfare Reforms: Actors and Institutions in the Japanese Welfare State." In *Restructuring the Welfare State*, ed. Bo Rothstein and Sven Steinmo. New York: Palgrave Macmillan.

Etō Mikiko. 1996. "*Jichitai no seisaku keisei nōryoku*" [Local Governments and Their Policymaking Capabilities]. *Kikan gyōsei kanri kenkyū* 6 (74): 3–14.

Evans, Peter B. 1992. "The State as Problem and Solution: Predation, Embedded Autonomy, and Structural Change." In *The Politics of Structural Adjustment: International Constraints, Distributive Conflicts, and the State*, ed. Stephan Haggard and Robert R. Kaufman. Princeton, N.J.: Princeton University Press.

Evans, Peter B. 1995. *Embedded Autonomy: States and Industrial Transformation.* Princeton, N.J.: Princeton University Press.

Executive Office of the President, Office of Management and Budget. 1987. *Standard Industrial Classification Manual.* Springfield, Va.

Falk, Richard. 1993. "The Infancy of Global Civil Society." In *Beyond the Cold War: New Dimensions in International Relations*, ed. Geir Lundestad and Odd Arne Westad. London: Oxford University Press.

Farley, Maggie. 1996. "Japan's Press and the Politics of Scandal." In *Media and Politics in Japan*, ed. Susan J. Pharr and Ellis S. Krauss. Honolulu: University of Hawaii Press.

Feldman, Ofer. 1993. *Politics and the News Media in Japan.* Ann Arbor: University of Michigan Press.

Fenno, Richard F., Jr. 1978. *Home Style: House Members in Their Districts.* Boston: Little, Brown.

Field, Stewart, and Caroline Pelser, eds. 1998. *Invading the Private: State Accountability and New Investigative Methods in Europe.* Brookfield, Vt.: Ashgate-Dartmouth.

Finnemore, Martha. 1996. *National Interests in International Society.* Ithaca, N.Y.: Cornell University Press.

Finnemore, Martha, and Kathryn Sikkink. 1998. "International Norm Dynamics and Political Change." *International Organization* 52 (4): 887–917.

Fisher, Lawrence. 1980. "The Lockheed Affair: A Phenomenon of Japanese Politics." Ph.D. diss., University of Colorado at Boulder.

Fisher, Louis. 1999. "Yes! An Independent Counsel Is Needed." *Law Matters*, Winter 1999: 1.

Flaherty, Darryl. 1999. "Organizing for Influence in Meiji Japan: Associations of Advocates and Their New Middle Politics." Presented at the annual meeting of the Association for Asian Studies, Boston.

Fletcher, Miles. 1979. "Intellectuals and Fascism in Early Showa Japan." *Journal of Asian Studies* 39 (1): 59.

Florini, Ann. 1996. "The Evolution of International Norms." *International Studies Quarterly* 40 (3): 363–89.

Florini, Ann M. 2000. "Lessons Learned." In *The Third Force: The Rise of Transnational Civil Society*, ed. Ann M. Florini. Washington, D.C.: Japan Center for International Exchange and Carnegie Endowment for International Peace.

Francks, Penelope. 1998. "Agriculture and the State in Industrial East Asia: The Rise and Fall of the Food Control System in Japan." *Japan Forum* 10 (1): 1–16.

Fraser, Nancy. 1992. "Rethinking the Public Sphere: A Contribution to the Critique of Actually Existing Democracy." In *Habermas and the Public Sphere*, ed. Craig Calhoun. Cambridge: MIT Press.

Fraser, Robert, ed. 1992. *Western European Economic Organizations: A Comprehensive Reference Guide.* Essex, U.K.: Longman.

Freeman, Laurie. 2000. *Closing the Shop: Information Cartels and Japan's Mass Media.* Princeton, N.J.: Princeton University Press.

Fremont-Smith, Marion. 1965. *Foundations and Government: State and Federal Law and Supervision.* New York: Russell Sage.

French, Howard W. 2000a. "Leader's Party Gains Seats in South Korean Vote, as Do Rivals." *New York Times*, April 14, sec. A.

French, Howard W. 2000b. "Japan Debates Culture of Covering Up." *New York Times*, May 2, sec. A.

French, Howard W. 2000c. "Lone Voice No Longer, Japan Gadfly Catches On." *New York Times*, June 18, sec. A.

French, Howard W. 2000d. "Japan's Governing Party Suffers Severe Election Setback." *New York Times*, June 26, sec. A.

Fujii Tadatoshi. 1985. *Kokubō fujinkai* [National Defense Women's Association]. Tokyo: Iwanami Shoten.

Fujisawa Kenji. 1978. "*Ōte seitetsujo honkō rōdōroku no saihen tōya*" [Reorganization and Training of Labor Force in Steel Mills of the Major Steel Firms]. In *Gendai Nihon no tekkō rōdō mondai* [Labor Problems of Steelworkers in Contemporary Japan], ed. Michimata Kenjirō. Sapporo: Hokkaidō Daigaku Tosho Kankōkai.

Fujita Teiichirō. 1988. "Local Trade Associations (*Dōgyō Kumiai*) in Prewar Japan." In *Trade Associations in Business History*, ed. Yamazaki Hiroaki and Miyamoto Matao. Tokyo: University of Tokyo Press.

Fukuyama, Francis. 1995. *Trust: The Social Virtues and the Creation of Prosperity*. New York: Free Press.

Fuller, Lon. 1969. *The Morality of Law*. New Haven, Conn.: Yale University Press.

Furusei Yukihiro and Hirose Katsuya. 1996. *Intaanetto ga kaeru sekai* [How the Internet is Changing the World]. Tokyo: Iwanami Shinsho.

Gardner, Howard. 1983. *Frames of Mind: The Theory of Multiple Intelligences*. New York: Basic Books.

Garment, Suzanne. 1991. *Scandal: The Culture of Mistrust in American Politics*. New York: Anchor Books.

Garon, Sheldon. 1987. *The State and Labor in Modern Japan*. Berkeley: University of California Press.

Garon, Sheldon. 1996. "Social Knowledge and the State in the Industrial Relations of Japan (1882–1940) and Great Britain (1870–1914)." In *States, Social Knowledge, and the Origins of Modern Social Policies*, ed. Dietrich Rueschemeyer and Theda Skocpol. Princeton, N.J.: Princeton University Press.

Garon, Sheldon. 1997. *Molding Japanese Minds: The State in Everyday Life*. Princeton, N.J.: Princeton University Press.

Garon, Sheldon. 2000. "Luxury Is the Enemy: Mobilizing Savings and Popularizing Thrift in Wartime Japan." *Journal of Japanese Studies* 26 (1): 41–78.

Garon, Sheldon, and Mike Mochizuki. 1993. "Negotiating Social Contracts." In *Postwar Japan as History*, ed. Andrew Gordon. Berkeley: University of California Press.

Gelb, Joyce, and Margarita Estévez-Abe. 1998. "Political Women in Japan: A Case Study of the *Seikatsusha* Network Movement." *Social Science Journal of Japan* 1 (2): 263–79.

Gelb, Joyce, and Marian Lief Palley. 1982. *Women and Public Policies*. Princeton, N.J.: Princeton University Press.

Gellner, Ernest. 1991. "Civil Society in Historical Context." *International Social Science Journal* 43 (129): 495–510.

Gellner, Ernest. 1994. *Conditions of Liberty: Civil Society and Its Rivals*. New York: Allen Lane/Penguin Press.

Gellner, Ernest. 1995. "The Importance of Being Modular." In *Civil Society: Theory, History, Comparison*, ed. John Hall. Cambridge, U.K.: Polity Press.

Gerlach, Michael. 1992. *Alliance Capitalism: The Social Organization of Japanese Business*. Berkeley: University of California Press.

Gibbs, Michael Hallock. 1980. "The Labor Movement at the Yahata Steel Works, 1945–1957." Ph.D. diss., University of California at Berkeley.

Giglioli, Pier Paolo. 1996. "Political Corruption and the Media: The Tangentopoli Affair." *International Social Science Journal* 149: 381–94.

Gilbert, Mark. 1995. *The Italian Revolution*. Boulder, Colo.: Westview Press.

Giner, Salvador. 1985. "The Withering Away of Civil Society?" *Praxis International* 5 (3): 247–67.

Ginsberg, Benjamin, and Martin Shefter. 1999. *Politics by Other Means: Politicians, Prosecutors, and the Press from Watergate to Whitewater*. New York: W. W. Norton.

Gluck, Carol. 1985. *Japan's Modern Myths: Ideology in the Late Meiji Period*. Princeton, N.J.: Princeton University Press.

Gluck, Carol. 1992. "Introduction." In *Showa: The Japan of Hirohito*, ed. Carol Gluck and Stephen Graubard. New York: W. W. Norton.

Gold, Thomas B. 1990. "The Resurgence of Civil Society in China." *Journal of Democracy* 1 (1): 18–31.

Golden, Miriam A. 1999. "Competitive Corruption: Factional Conflict and Political Corruption in Postwar Italian Christian Democracy." Paper presented at the meeting of the MacArthur Research Network on Inequality and Economic Performance, MIT, October 1–3.

Goleman, Daniel. 1995. *Emotional Intelligence: Why It Can Matter More Than IQ*. New York: Bantam Books.

Gordon, Andrew. 1989. "Business and the Corporate State: The Business Lobby and Bureaucrats on Labor, 1911–1941." In *Managing Industrial Enterprise: Cases from Japan's Prewar Experience*, ed. William D. Wray. Cambridge: Council on East Asian Studies, Harvard University.

Gordon, Andrew. 1991. *Labor and Imperial Democracy in Prewar Japan*. Berkeley: University of California Press.

Gordon, Andrew. 1993. "Contests for the Workplace." In *Postwar Japan as History*, ed. Andrew Gordon. Berkeley: University of California Press.

Gordon, Andrew. 1997. "Managing the Japanese Household: The New Life Movement in Postwar Japan." *Social Politics* 4 (2): 245–83.

Gordon, Andrew. 1998. *The Wages of Affluence: Labor and Management in Postwar Japan*. Cambridge, Mass.: Harvard University Press.

Gordon, Beate Sirota. 1997. *The Only Woman in the Room: A Memoir*. New York: Kodansha International.

Gotō Akira. 1976. *Tennōsei to minshū* [The Emperor System and the People]. Tokyo: University of Tokyo Press.

Gotō Michio. 1996. "'*Hi shimin shakai' kara 'Nihongata taishū shakai' e*" [From "Non-Civil Society" to "Japanese-Style Mass Society"]. In *Gendai Nihon shakai ron* [Theories of Contemporary Japanese Society], ed. Watanabe Osamu. Tokyo: Rōdō Junposha.

Graber, Doris A. 1986. "Press Freedom and the General Welfare." *Political Science Quarterly* 101 (2): 257–75.

Gramsci, Antonio. 1971. *Selections from the Prison Notebooks*. Trans. Quintin Hoare and Geoffrey Nowell Smith. New York: International Publishers.

Groth, David Earl. 1996. "Media and Political Protest: The Bullet Train Movements." In *Media and Politics in Japan*, ed. Susan J. Pharr and Ellis S. Krauss. Honolulu: University of Hawaii Press.

Guarnieri, Carlo. 1991. *Magistratura e politica in Italia* [The Magistracy and Politics in Italy]. Bologna: Mulino.

Guarnieri, Carlo. 1995. "The Political Role of the Italian Judiciary." In *Deconstructing Italy: Italy in the Nineties*, ed. Salvatore Sechi. Berkeley: University of California International and Area Studies.

Guarnieri, Carlo. 1997. "Prosecution in Two Civil Law Countries: France and Italy." In *Comparing Legal Cultures*, ed. David Nelken. Brookfield, Vt.: Dartmouth Publishing.

Gurowitz, Amy. 1999. "Mobilizing International Norms: Domestic Actors, Immigrants and the Japanese State." *World Politics* 51 (3): 413–45.

Habermas, Jürgen. 1989. *The Structural Transformation of the Public Sphere: An Inquiry into a Category of Bourgeois Society*. Cambridge, Mass.: MIT Press.

Habermas, Jürgen. 1992. "Further Reflections on the Public Sphere." In *Habermas and the Public Sphere*, ed. Craig Calhoun. Cambridge, Mass.: MIT Press.

Habermas, Jürgen. 1998. *Between Facts and Norms: Contributions to a Discourse Theory of Law and Democracy*. Trans. William Rehg. Cambridge, Mass.: MIT Press.

Hadenius, Axel, and Fredrik Uggla. 1996. "Making Civil Society Work, Promoting Democratic Development: What Can States and Donors Do?" *World Development* 24 (10): 1621–39.

Haley, John O. 1998. *The Spirit of Japanese Law*. Athens: University of Georgia Press.

Hall, Ivan P. 1998. *Cartels of the Mind: Japan's Intellectual Closed Shop*. New York: W. W. Norton.

Hall, John A. 1995. "In Search of Civil Society." In *Civil Society: Theory, History, Comparison*, ed. John Hall. Cambridge: Polity Press.

Hall, John A. 1998. "Genealogies of Civil Society." In *Democratic Civility: The History and Cross-Cultural Possibility of a Modern Political Ideal*, ed. Robert W. Hefner. New Brunswick, N.J.: Transaction Publishers.

Hall, Peter A. 1986. *Governing the Economy: The Politics of State Intervention in Britain and France*. New York: Oxford University Press.

Hall, Peter Dobkin. 1987. "A Historical Overview of the Private Nonprofit Sector." In *The Nonprofit Sector: A Research Handbook*, ed. Walter W. Powell. New Haven, Conn.: Yale University Press.

Hall, Peter Dobkin. 2000. "Philanthropy, the Welfare State, and the Transformation of American Public and Private Institutions, 1945–2000." Working paper, Hauser Center for Nonprofit Organizations, Harvard University.

Hann, Chris. 1996. "Introduction: Political Society and Civil Anthropology." In *Civil Society: Challenging Western Models*, ed. Chris Hann and Elizabeth Dunn. New York: Routledge.

Harbeson, John W. 1994. "Civil Society and Political Renaissance in Africa" and "Civil Society and the Study of African Politics: A Preliminary Assessment." In *Civil Society and the State in Africa*, ed. John W. Harbeson, Donald Rothchild, and Naomi Chazan. London: Lynne Rienner.

Hardacre, Helen. 1991. "Japan: The Public Sphere in a Non-Western Setting." In *Between States and Markets: The Voluntary Sphere in Comparative Perspective*, ed. Robert Wuthnow. Princeton, N.J.: Princeton University Press.

Hardacre, Helen. 1995. "Aum Shinrikyō and the Japanese Media: The Pied Piper Meets the Lamb of God." New York: Institute Reports, Columbia University.

Hardacre, Helen. 1996. "Shinmeiaishinkai and the Study of Shamanism in Contemporary Japanese Religious Life. " In *Religion in Japan: Arrows to Heaven and Earth*, ed. Peter Kornicki and Ian McMullen. Cambridge, U.K.: Cambridge University Press.

Hardacre, Helen. 1999. "Historical Perspectives on Japanese New Religions and the Media." Presented at the annual meeting of the Japanese Studies Association of Canada, Montreal.

Harootunian, Harry D. 1974. "Between Politics and Culture: Authority and the Ambiguities of Intellectual Choice in Imperial Japan." In *Japan in Crisis: Essays on Taishō Democracy*, ed. Harry D. Harootunian and Bernard S. Silberman. Princeton, N.J.: Princeton University Press.

Hasegawa Kōichi. 1991. "*Han genshiryoku undō ni okeru josei no ichi: Posuto Cherunobiru no 'atarashii shakai undō'*" [The Position of Women in the Anti-Atomic Energy Movement: A Post-Chernobyl "New Social Movement"]. *Leviathan* 8: 165–84.

Hatano Akira. 1994. *Tsuno o tamete ushi o korosu koto nakare: Kensatsu kenryoku wa kokumin no teki ka* [Straightening the Horns But Killing the Cow: Is Prosecutor Power the People's Enemy?]. Tokyo: Kobunsha.

Havel, Vaclav, et al. 1985. *The Power of the Powerless: Citizens Against the State in Central-Eastern Europe*. New York: M. E. Sharpe.

Hayashi Chikio, ed. 1997. *Genzai Nippon no hieiri hōjin* [Nonprofit Corporations in Contemporary Japan]. Tokyo: Sasakawa Heiwa Zaidan.

Hayashi Shuzō. 1972. *Kōeki hōjin kenkyū nyūmon* [Introduction to Public-Interest Legal Person Research]. Tokyo: Kōeki Hōjin Kyōkai.

Heclo, Hugh. 1978. "Issue Networks and the Executive Establishment." In *The New American Political System*, ed. Anthony King. Washington, D.C.: American Enterprise Institute.

Hefner, Robert. 1997. "Islamization and Democratization in Indonesia." In *Islam in an Era of Nation-States: Politics and Religious Renewal in Muslim Southeast Asia*, ed. Robert Hefner and Patricia Horvatich. Honolulu: University of Hawaii Press.

Hefner, Robert W. 1998. "On the History and Cross-Cultural Possibility of a Democratic Ideal." In *Democratic Civility: The History and Cross-Cultural Possibility of a Modern Political Ideal*, ed. Robert W. Hefner. New Brunswick, N.J.: Transaction Publishers.

Heidenheimer, Arnold J. 1996. "The Topography of Corruption: Explorations in a Comparative Perspective." *International Social Science Journal* 149: 337–48.

Hellinger, Doug. 1987. "NGOs and the Large Aid Donors: Changing the Terms of Engagement." *World Development* (15) supplement: 135–43.

Henderson, Dan Fenno. 1968. "Law and Political Modernization in Japan." In *Political Development in Modern Japan*, ed. Robert E. Ward. Princeton, N.J.: Princeton University Press.

Herbst, Susan. 1994. *Politics at the Margin: Historical Studies of Public Expression Outside the Mainstream.* Cambridge, U.K.: Cambridge University Press.

Higuchi Kenji. 1977. "*Sengo chūshō kigyō undō no tenkai*" [Development of the Postwar Small- and Medium-Sized Industry Movement]. In *Soshiki mondai to chūshō kigyō* [Organizational Problems and Small- and Medium-Sized Industry], ed. Katō Seiichi, Mizuno Takeshi, and Kobayashi Yasuo. Tokyo: Dōyūkan.

Hirano Yoshitarō. 1934. *Nihon shihonshugi shakai no kikō* [The System of Japanese Capitalist Society]. Tokyo: Iwanami Shoten.

Hirano Yoshitarō. 1944. *Minzoku seiji no kihon mondai* [Basic Issues in Ethno-National Politics]. Tokyo: Koyama Shoten.

Hirata Kiyoaki. 1969. *Shimin shakai to shakaishugi* [Civil Society and Socialism]. Tokyo: Iwanami Shoten.

Hirata Kiyoaki. 1989. "*Keizaigakusha Uchida Yoshihiko – Sono fūkaku to sakuhin*" [Uchida Yoshihiko, Economist: His Style and Works]. In *Watakushi no naka no Uchida Yoshihiko* [Uchida Yoshihiko as We Knew Him]. Tokyo: Iwanami Shoten.

Hirata Kiyoaki. 1994a. "*Gendai shimin shakai to kigyō kokka*" [Contemporary Civil Society and the Enterprise State]. In *Gendai shimin shakai to kigyō kokka* [Contemporary Civil Society and the Enterprise State], ed. Hirata Kiyoaki. Tokyo: Ochanomizu Shobō.

Hirata Kiyoaki, ed. 1994b. *Gendai shimin shakai to kigyō kokka* [Contemporary Civil Society and the Enterprise State]. Tokyo: Ochanomizu Shobō.

Hirschman, Albert O. 1973. *Exit, Voice and Loyalty*. Cambridge, Mass.: Harvard University Press.

Hiwatari Nobuhiro. 1991. *Sengo Nihon no shijō to seiji* [Market and Politics in Postwar Japan]. Tokyo: University of Tokyo Press.

Hollingsworth, J. Rogers, Philippe Schmitter, and Wolfgang Streeck, eds. 1994. *Governing Capitalist Economies: Performance and Control of Economic Sectors*. New York: Oxford University Press.

Holstein, William. 1990. *The Japanese Power Game: What It Means for America*. New York: Charles Scribner's Sons.

Honma Masaaki and Deguchi Masayuki. 1996. *Borantia kakumei* [The Volunteer Revolution]. Tokyo: Tōyō Keizai Shinpōsha.

Honneth, Axel. 1993. "Conceptions of 'Civil Society.'" *Radical Philosophy* 64: 19–22.

Hoshino Eiichi. 1970. "*Iwayuru kenri naki shadan ni tsuite*" [On So-Called Unincorporated Associations]. In *Minpō ronshū* [On the Theory of the Japanese Civil Code], vol. 1. Tokyo: Yuhikaku.

Hotta Tsutomu. 1999. *Kabe o yabutte susume: Shiki rokkido jiken* [Break Down the Walls and Move Forward: A Personal Account of the Lockheed Case], 2 vols. Tokyo: Kōdansha.

Howell, David L. 2000. "Visions of the Future in Meiji Japan." In *Historical Perspectives on Contemporary East Asia*, ed. Merle Goldman and Andrew Gordon. Cambridge, Mass.: Harvard University Press.

Huard, Raymond. 2000. "Political Association in Nineteenth-Century France: Legislation and Practice." In *Civil Society before Democracy: Lessons from Nineteenth-Century Europe*, ed. Nancy Bermeo and Philip Nord. New York: Rowman and Littlefield.

Hulme, David, and Michael Edwards. 1997. "NGOs, States and Donors: An Overview." In *NGOs, States and Donors: Too Close for Comfort?*, ed. David Hulme and Michael Edwards. New York: St. Martin's Press.

Huntington, Samuel P. 1968. *Political Order in Changing Societies*. New Haven, Conn.: Yale University Press.

Huntington, Samuel P. 1991. *The Third Wave: Democratization in the Late Twentieth Century*. Norman: University of Oklahoma Press.

Hyōdō Tsutomu. 1982. "*Shokuba no rōshi kankei to kumiai*" [Workplace Labor-Management Relations and Unions]. In *Sengo rōdō kumiai undō shi ron* [A History of the Postwar Union Movement], ed. Shimizu Shinzō. Tokyo: Nihon Hyōronsha.

Ibusuki Makoto. (N.d.). "Update to Japanese Law via the Internet." http://www.llrx.com/features/japan2.html.

Iitake Kōichi and Karasaki Tarō. 2000. "Few Willing to Challenge Relatives of Lawmakers." *Asahi Evening News*, May 22.

Ikado Fujio, ed. 1993. *Senryō to Nihon shūkyō* [The Occupation and Japanese Religion]. Tokyo: Miraisha.

Imata Katsuji. 1999. "Civil Society in the U.S. and Japan: Polar Opposites." *Washington-Japan Journal* (special issue, spring): 21–28.

Imata Katsuji. 2001. "Players That Make Up the Nonprofit Sector." Presented at the workshop of the Japan Foundation Center for Global Partnership, Tokyo, June 12.

Imata Katsuji, Elissa Leif, and Takano Hiroyuki. 1998. "Structural Impediments of Japan's Nonprofit Sector: Overcoming the Obstacles to Increased Nonprofit Collaboration with Japan." Presented at the annual meeting of the Association for Research on Nonprofit Organizations and Voluntary Action, Seattle.

Inaba Michio, Onō Shōji, Shōda Akira, Nakamura Kii, and Hanahara Jirō. 1979. "*Shōhisha mondai no arikata*" [The State of Consumer Issues]. *Jurisuto zōgen sōgō tokushū* 13: 6–25.

Inoguchi Takashi. 2000. "Social Capital in Japan." *Japanese Journal of Political Science* 1 (1): 73–112.

Inoki Takenori. 1995. "Japanese Bureaucrats at Retirement: The Mobility of Human Resources from Central Government to Public Corporations." In *The Japanese Civil Service and Economic Development*, ed. Hyung-Ki Kim, Michio Muramatsu, T. J. Pempel, and Kozo Yamamura. Oxford: Clarendon Press.

Inoue Egyō. 1969. *Shūkyō hōjin hō no kisoteki kenkyū* [A Basic Study of the Religious Corporations Law]. Tokyo: San'ichi Shobō.

Intaanetto hyakusho 2001. 2001. Tokyo: Impress Corporation and Access Media International.

InterAction. 1998. *Member Profiles, 1997–98*. Washington, D.C.: InterAction.

Iokibe Makoto. 1999. "Japan's Civil Society: An Historical Overview." In *Deciding the Public Good: Governance and Civil Society in Japan*, ed. Yamamoto Tadashi. Tokyo: Japan Center for International Exchange.

Iriye Akira. 1967. *Across the Pacific: An Inner History of American-East Asian Relations.* New York: Harcourt, Brace and World.

Irokawa Daikichi. 1985. *The Culture of the Meiji Period.* Trans. and ed. Marius Jansen. Princeton, N.J.: Princeton University Press.

Ishida Hirohide. 1963. "*Hoshutō no bijon*" [The Conservative Party's Vision]. *Chūō kōron* January: 88–97.

Ishida Takeshi. 1968. "The Development of Interest Groups and the Pattern of Political Modernization in Japan." In *Political Development in Modern Japan*, ed. Robert E. Ward. Princeton, N.J.: Princeton University Press.

Ishida Takeshi and Ellis S. Krauss. 1989. "Democracy in Japan: Issues and Questions." In *Democracy in Japan*, ed. Ishida Takeshi and Ellis S. Krauss. Pittsburgh, Pa.: University of Pittsburgh Press.

Ishida Takeshi and Kang Sangjung. 1997. *Maruyama Masao to shimin shakai* [Maruyama Masao and Civil Society]. Yokohama: Seori Shobō.

Ishii Kenji. 2000. "*Nihonjin no 'shūkyō dantai' ni tai suru ishiki to jittai ni tsuite*" [Japanese Attitudes Toward Religious Organizations]. *Chūō chōsahō* 510 (4): 1–4.

Ishikawa Masumi. 1984. *Deita sengo seiji shi* [Data on Postwar Political History]. Tokyo: Iwanami Shoten.

Itagaki Kuniko. 1992. *Shōwa senzen, senchūki no nōson seikatsu: Zasshi 'Ie no hikari' ni miru* [Farm Life in the Shōwa Era as Seen in the Magazine *Ie no hikari* Before and During World War II]. Tokyo: University of Tokyo Press.

Itō Shūhei. 1996. "*Shakai fukushi ni okeru riyōsha sanka*" [User Participation in Social Welfare]. In *Shimin sanka to shakai fukushi* (Civic Participation in Social Welfare), eds. Shakai Hoshō Kenkyūjo. Tokyo: University of Tokyo Press.

Ivy, Marilyn. 1993. "Formations of Mass Culture." In *Postwar Japan as History*, ed. Andrew Gordon. Berkeley: University of California Press.

James, Estelle. 1987. "The Nonprofit Sector in Comparative Perspective." In *The Nonprofit Sector: A Research Handbook*, ed. Walter W. Powell. New Haven, Conn.: Yale University Press.

James, Estelle. 1989. *The Nonprofit Sector in International Perspective*. New York: Oxford University Press.

The Japan Federation of Steelworkers Unions (Tekkō Rōren). 1980. *Tekkōgyō no rōshi kankei to rōdō kumiai* [Industrial Relations and Labor Unions in the Steel Industry]. Tokyo: Nihon Rōdō Kyōkai.

The Japan Federation of Steelworkers Unions (Tekkō Rōren). 1981. *Tekkō rōren undō shi – 30-nen no ayumi* [A Thirty Years' History of the Japan Federation of Steel Workers Unions]. Tokyo: Japan Federation of Steelworkers Unions.

Japan Fund for Global Environment. 1998. *Kankyō dantai sōran: Heisei 10 nendo ban* [Directory of Environmental Organizations in Japan, 1998]. Tokyo: Nihon Kankyō Kyōkai.

Japan NGO Center for International Cooperation (JANIC). *Kokoro* newsletter. Various dates. Tokyo: JANIC.

Japan NGO Center for International Cooperation (JANIC). 1996a. *Directory of Non-Governmental Organizations in Japan 1996.* Tokyo: JANIC.

Japan NGO Center for International Cooperation (JANIC). 1996b. *NGO Deita Bukku '96* [NGO Data Book, 1996]. Tokyo.

Japan NGO Center for International Cooperation (JANIC). 1998a. *Directory of Non-Governmental Organizations in Japan* 1998. Tokyo: JANIC.

Japan NGO Center for International Cooperation (JANIC). 1998b. *NGO deita bukku* [NGO Data Book]. Tokyo: JANIC.

Jin Nobuhito. 1997. "*Shakaiteki aidentitii riron no saikentō to shūdannai gokeisei ni kan suru jisshō kenkyū*" [Reconsidering Social Identity Theory: An Empirical Study of Within-Group Reciprocity]. Ph.D. diss., Hokkaidō University.

Jin Nobuhito and Shinotsuka Hiromi. 1996. "*Sōgo izonsei ninchi to kyōryoku keikō*" [Perception of Interdependency and the Cooperative Tendency]. In *Dai37kai Nihon Shakai Shinrigakkai taikai happyō ronbunshū* [Proceedings of the 37th Annual Meeting of the Japanese Social Psychological Association]. Sapporo: Japanese Social Psychological Association.

Johnson, Chalmers. 1978. *Japan's Public Policy Companies*. Washington, D.C.: American Enterprise Institute–Hoover Policy Studies.

Johnson, Chalmers. 1982. *MITI and the Japanese Miracle: The Growth of Industrial Policy, 1925–1975*. Stanford, Calif.: Stanford University Press.

Johnson, Chalmers. 1995. "Tanaka Kakuei, Structural Corruption, and the Advent of Machine Politics in Japan." In *Japan: Who Governs? The Rise of the Developmental State*, ed. Chalmers Johnson. New York: W. W. Norton.

Johnson, Chalmers. 1999. "The Developmental State: Odyssey of a Concept." In *The Developmental State*, ed. Meredtih Woo-Cumings. Ithaca, N.Y.: Cornell University Press.

Johnson, David T. 1997. "Why the Wicked Sleep: The Prosecution of Political Corruption in Postwar Japan." Japan Policy Research Institute, Working Paper No. 34 (June).

Johnson, David T. 1999. "*Kumo no su ni shōchō sareru Nihon hō no tokushoku*" [Japan's Legal Cobweb]. Trans. Tanaka Hiraku. *Jurisuto* 1148 (January 1–15): 185–89.

Johnson, David T. 2002. *The Japanese Way of Justice: Prosecuting Crime in Japan*. New York: Oxford University Press.

Johnston, David. 1999. "With Counsel Law Expiring, Attorney General Takes Reins." *New York Times*, June 30, sec. A.

Jurisuto. 1997. "*NPO hō no kentō*" [Investigating the NPO Law]. *Jurisuto* 1105: 4–20.

Kabashima Ikuo. 1999. "*1998-nen san'in sen – Jimintō wa naze maketa ka?*" [The 1998 Upper House Election –Why Did the LDP Lose?]. *Leviathan* 25 (Fall): 78–102.

Kage Rieko. 2001. "Why Volunteer? Explaining the Micro-Level Foundations of Civil Society." Ph.D. diss. Prospectus, Harvard University.

Kakiuchi Riki and Yamagishi Toshio. 1997. "*Ippannteki shinrai to izondo sentakugata shūjin no jirenma*" (General Trust and the Dilemma of Variable Interdependency). *Shakai shinrigaku kenkyū* [Japanese Journal of Social Psychology] 12: 212–21.

Kamada Toshiko. 1994. "'Japanese Management' and the 'Loaning' of Labour: Restructuring of the Japanese Iron and Steel Industry." In *Global Japanization?* ed. Tony Elder and Chris Smith. London: Routledge.

Kamahara Masahiko, Higuchi Kazunori, and Shimizu Naoharu. 1982. "Locus of Control *shakudo no sakusei to shinraisei, datōsei no kentō*" [Construction of Locus of Control Scale and Its Reliability and Validity]. *Kyōiku shinrigaku kenkyū* [Japanese Journal of Educational Psychology] 30: 302–07.

Kamimura, Naoki. 2001. "Japanese Civil Society, Local Government, and U.S.-Japan Security Relations in the 1990s: A Preliminary Survey." In *Nationalism and Citizenship III* (Japan Center for Area Studies (JCAS) Occasional Paper No.11), ed. Chieko Kitagawa Otsuru and Edward Rhodes.

Kasfir, Nelson. 1998. "The Conventional Notion of Civil Society: A Critique." *Commonwealth and Comparative Politics* 36 (2): 1–20.

Kasza, Gregory J. 1988. *State and Mass Media in Japan, 1918–1945*. Berkeley: University of California Press.

Kasza, Gregory J. 1995. *The Conscription Society*. New Haven, Conn.: Yale University Press.

Katzenstein, Peter J. 1987. *Policy and Politics in West Germany: The Growth of a Semi-Sovereign State*. Philadelphia, Pa.: Temple University Press.

Katzenstein, Peter J., ed. 1996. *The Culture of National Security: Norms and Identity in World Politics*. New York: Columbia University Press.

Kaufmann, Franz-Xaver. 1991. "The Blurring of the Distinction 'State versus Society' in the Idea and Practice of the Welfare State." In *Guidance, Control, and Evaluation in the Public Sector*, ed. Franz-Xaver Kaufmann et al. New York: Walter de Gruyter.

Kawabe Nobuo. 1994. *Sebun irebun to keiei shi* [7-Eleven and Management History]. Tokyo: Yukikaku.

Kawai Nobutarō. 1979. *Kensatsu tokuhon* [A Prosecutor's Manual]. Tokyo: Shōji Hōmu Kenkyūkai.

Kawakami Shin'ichirō. 1999. "*NPO to janarizumu*" [NPOs and Journalism]. In *Nippon no NPO 2000* [Japan's Nonprofit Organizations, 2000], ed. Nakamura Yōichi and Nihon NPO Sentaa. Tokyo: Nippon Hyōronsha.

Kawamura Masayoshi. 1996. *Atarashii kōreisha fukushi* [New Elderly Welfare Services]. Kyōto: Minerva.

Kawanishi Hirosuke. 1992. *Enterprise Unionism in Japan*. Trans. Ross E. Mouer. London: Kegan Paul International.

Kawanishi Hirosuke. 1998. "*Horon shingata rōdō kumiai no doko*" [Supplementary Argument: The Current Status of New-Type Unions]. *Nihon rōdō shakai gakkai nenpō*, no. 9.

Kawashima Takeyoshi. 1948. *Nihon shakai no kazokuteki kōsei* [The Familistic Organization of Japanese Society]. Tokyo: Gakusei Shobō.

Keane, John. 1988a. *Democracy and Civil Society: On the Predicaments of European Socialism, the Prospects for Democracy, and the Problem of Controlling Social and Political Power*. London: Verso.

Keane, John. 1988b. "Introduction" and "Despotism and Democracy: The Origins and Development of the Distinction Between Civil Society and the State, 1750–1850." In *Civil Society and the State: New European Perspectives*, ed. John Keane. London: Verso.

Keane, John. 1998. *Civil Society: Old Images, New Visions*. Stanford, Calif.: Stanford University Press.

Keck, Margaret E., and Kathryn Sikkink. 1998. *Activists Beyond Borders: Advocacy Networks in International Politics*. Ithaca, N.Y.: Cornell University Press.

Keeler, John T. S. 1985. "Corporatist Decentralization and Commercial Modernization in France: The Royer Law's Impact on Shopkeepers, Supermarkets and the State." In *Socialism, the State and Public Policy in France*, ed. Philip G. Cerny and Martin A. Schain. London: Methuen.

Keizai Kikakuchō and Kokumin Seikatsu Kyoku. 1999. *Handobukku shōhisha '99* [The 1999 Consumer Handbook]. Tokyo: Keizai Kikakuchō.

Kenny, Michael. 1999. "Marxism and Regulation Theory." In *Marxism and Social Science*, ed. Andrew Gamble, David Marsh, and Tony Tant. Urbana: University of Illinois Press.

Keohane, Robert O., and Joseph S. Nye. 1972. "Transnational Relations and World Politics: An Introduction." In *Transnational Relations and World Politics*, ed. Robert O. Keohane and Joseph S. Nye. Cambridge, Mass.: Harvard University Press.

Kihlstrom, John F., and Nancy Cantor. 2000. "Social Intelligence." In *Handbook of Intelligence*, ed. Robert J. Sternberg. Cambridge, U.K.: Cambridge University Press.

Kikkawa Takeo. 1988. "Functions of Japanese Trade Associations before World War II." In *Trade Associations in Business History*, ed. Yamazaki Hiroaki and Miyamoto Matao. Tokyo: University of Tokyo Press.

Kikkawa Takeo. 1995. "*Chūkan soshiki no henyō to kyōsōteki kasen kōzō no keisei*" [The Transformation of Intermediary Associations and the Formation of Oligopolies]. In *"Nihonteki" keiei no renzoku to danzetsu* [Continuity and Discontinuity in "Japanese-Style" Management], ed. Yamazaki Hiroaki and Kikkawa Takeo. Tokyo: Iwanami Shoten.

Kikuchi Masako, Watanabe Yoriko, and Yamagishi Toshio 1997. "*Tasha no shinraisei handan no seikakusa to ippanteki shinrai: Jikken kenkyū*" [Judgment Accuracy of Other's Trustworthiness and General Trust: An Experimental Study]. *Jikken shakai shinrigaku kenkyū* [Japanese Journal of Experimental Social Psychology] 37: 23–36.

Kimoto Kinya. 1986. *Gendai shōhisha hō no kōzō* [The Structure of Contemporary Consumer Law]. Tokyo: Shinhyōron.

Kingdon, John W. 1984. *Agendas, Alternatives, and Public Policies*. Boston: Little Brown.

Kisala, Robert. 1997. "Reactions to Aum: The Revision of the Religious Corporations Law" *Japanese Religions* 22 (1): 60–74.

Kitazawa Masakuni. 1968. "*Ningen – Sono botsuraku to saisei: Kyūshinteki kōzōshugi no ningenkan*" [Human Beings – Their Fall and Revival: A Radical Structuralist Perspective on Human Beings]. *Tenbō* 111: 16–36.

Kitazawa Masakuni. 1975. "Militarism Under the Cloak of Management Society." *Japan Intepreter* 9 (3): 324–30.

Knight, Jack. 1992. *Institutions and Social Conflict*. New York: Cambridge University Press.

Kobayashi Kyōichi. 1994. "*Nihon no shōhisha undō shi: Kansai shufuren no zenshi*" [The History of the Japanese Consumer Movement: The Prehistory of the Kansai Chifuren]. *Gekkan shōhisha* (April).

Kobayashi Kyōichi. 1995a. "*Nihon no shōhisha undō shi: Yamataka Shigeri to Chifuren zenshi*" [The History of the Japanese Consumer Movement: Yamataka Shigeri and the Prehistory of Chifuren]. *Gekkan shōhisha* (July).

Kobayashi Kyōichi. 1995b. "*Nihon no shōhisha undō shi: Chifuren seiritsu no keiei*" [The History of the Japanese Consumer Movement: The Management of the Establishment of Chifuren]. *Gekkan shōhisha* (November).

Kobayashi Takasuke, et al. 1996. *Shūkyō to hō* [Religion and Law]. Tokyo: Kitaki Shuppan.

Kofusha Shuppan. 1996. *Shimin media nyūmon – Anata ga hasshinsha* [An Introduction to Citizen Media: You Can Be a Publisher]. Tokyo: Kofusha Shuppan.

Kokugakuin Daigaku Nihon Bunka Kenkyūjo, ed. 1990. *Kindaika to shūkyō būmu*. [Modernization and the Religion Boom]. Tokyo: Dōbōsha Shuppan.

Kokumin Seikatsu Sentaa. 1997. *Sengo shōhisha undō shi* [A History of the Postwar Consumer Movement]. Tokyo: Ministry of Finance.

Komatsu Hiroshi. 1968. *Sagyōchō seido [The New Foremen System]. Tokyo: Rōdō Hōrei Kyōkai.*

Koo, Hagen. 1993. "Strong State and Contentious Society." In *State and Society in Contemporary Korea*, ed. Hagen Koo. Ithaca, N.Y.: Cornell University Press.

Koschmann, J. Victor. 1978. "Soft Rule and Expressive Protest." In *Authority and the Individual in Japan: Citizen Protest in Historical Perspective*, ed. J. Victor Koschmann. Tokyo: University of Tokyo Press.

Kosugi Motoko and Yamagishi Toshio. 1998. "*Ippanteki shinrai to shinraisei handan*" [Generalized Trust and Judgments of Trustworthiness]. *Shinrigaku kenkyū* [Japanese Journal of Psychology] 69: 349–57.

Krauss, Ellis S. 1974. *Japanese Radicals Revisited: Student Protest in Postwar Japan*. Berkeley: University of California Press.

Krauss, Ellis S. 1980. "Opposition in Power: The Development and Maintenance of Leftist Government in Kyoto Prefecture." In *Political Opposition and Local Politics in Japan*, ed. Kurt Steiner, Ellis S. Krauss, and Scott C. Flanagan. Princeton, N.J.: Princeton University Press.

Krauss, Ellis S. 1996. "Portraying the State: NHK Television News and Politics." In *Media and Politics in Japan*, ed. Susan J. Pharr and Ellis S. Krauss. Honolulu: University of Hawaii Press.

Krauss, Ellis S. 2000. *Broadcasting Politics in Japan: NHK and Television News*. Ithaca, N.Y.: Cornell University Press.

Krauss, Ellis S., and Bradford L. Simcock. 1980. "Citizens' Movements: The Growth and Impact of Environmental Protest in Japan." In *Political Opposition and Local Politics in Japan*, ed. Kurt Steiner, Ellis S. Krauss, and Scott Flanagan. Princeton, N.J.: Princeton University Press.

Kubik, Jan. 2000. "Between the State and Networks of 'Cousins': The Role of Civil Society and Noncivil Associations in the Democratization of Poland." In *Civil Society before Democracy*. Ed. Nancy Bermeo and Philip Nord. Lanham, Md.: Rowman and Littelefield.

Kubo Hiroshi. 1989. *Nihon no kensatsu* [Japan's Prosecutors]. Tokyo: Kōdansha.

Kudō Tsutomu and Nishikawa Masayuki 1983. "*Kodokukan ni kan suru kenkyū (1): Kodokukan shakudo no shinraisei, datōsei*" [A Study of the Feeling of Loneliness (I): The Reliability and Validity of the Revised UCLA Loneliness Scale]. *Jikken shakai shinrigaku kenkyū* [Japanese Journal of Experimental Social Psychology] 22: 99–108.

Kumar, Krishan. 1993. "Civil Society: An Inquiry into the Usefulness of an Historical Term." *British Journal of Sociology* 44 (3): 375–95.

Kumar, Krishan. 1994. "Civil Society Again: A Reply to Christopher Bryant's 'Social Self-Organisation, Civility and Sociology.'" *British Journal of Sociology* 45 (1): 127–31.

Kumazawa Makoto. 1989. *Nihonteki keiei no meian* [The Bright and Dark Sides of Japanese-Style Management]. Tokyo: Chikuma Shobō.

Kurita, Ken. 1994. *Nihon no rōdō shakai* [The World of Labor in Japan]. Tokyo: University of Tokyo Press.

Kusano Atsushi. 1992. *Daitenhō: Keizai kisei no kōzō* [The Large Stores Law: The Structure of Economic Regulation]. Tokyo: Nihon Keizai Shinbunsha.

Labaton, Stephen. 1999. "What a Difference a Scandal Makes." *New York Times*, March 7, sec. A.

Lange, Peter, George Ross, and Maurizio Vannicelli. 1982. *Unions, Change, and Crisis: French and Italian Union Strategy and the Political Economy, 1945–1980*. London: Allen and Unwin.

LeBlanc, Robin M. 1999. *Bicycle Citizens: The Political World of the Japanese Housewife*. Berkeley: University of California Press.

Levi, Margaret. 1996. "Social and Unsocial Capital: A Review Essay of Robert Putnam's *Making Democracy Work*." *Politics and Society* 24 (1): 45–55.

Levy, Jonah D. 1999. *Tocqueville's Revenge: State, Society, and Economy in Contemporary France*. Cambridge, Mass.: Harvard University Press.

Lewis, Anthony. 1999a. "Back to a Republican System." *New York Times*, July 6, sec. A.

Lewis, Anthony. 1999b. "The Prosecutorial State: Criminalizing American Politics." *American Prospect* 42: 42–47.

Lewis, Jonathan. 2000. In *SSJ-FORUM* [Social Science Japan Forum] (online), June 8. http://www.iss.u-tokyo.ac.jp/SSJForum.

Lewis, Michael. 1990. *Rioters and Citizens: Mass Protest in Imperial Japan*. Berkeley: University of California Press.

Lipschutz, Ronnie. 1992. "Restructuring World Politics: The Emergence of Global Civil Society." *Millennium* 21 (3): 389–420.

Lipset, Seymour Martin, Martin Trow, and James Coleman. 1956. *Union Democracy: The Inside Politics of the International Typographical Union*. New York: Free Press.

Lissner, Jorgen. 1977. *The Politics of Altruism: A Study of the Political Behavior of Voluntary Development Agencies*. Geneva: Lutheran World Federation.

LoBreglio, John. 1997. "Revisions to the Religious Corporations Law: An Introduction and Annotated Translation." *Japanese Religions* 22 (1): 38–59.

London, Nancy. 1991. *Japanese Corporate Philanthropy*. New York: Oxford University Press.

Lynn, Leonard H., and Timothy J. McKeown. 1988. *Organizing Business: Trade Associations in America and Japan*. Washington, D.C.: American Enterprise Institute.

MacDougall, Terry. 1988. "The Lockheed Scandal and the High Costs of Politics in Japan." In *The Politics of Scandal: Power and Process in Liberal Democracies*, ed. Andrei S. Markovits and Mark Silverstein. New York: Holmes & Meier.

Machida City Kōreika Shakai Sōgō Keikaku Suishin Iinkai. 1997. "*Shimin sankagata kōreisha fukushi katsudō dantai chōsa*" [Organizational Survey of Civic Activities in Welfare Services for the Elderly]. Typescript.

Machida City Kōreika Shakai Sōgō Keikaku Suishin Iinkai. 1998. "*Shimin sankagata kōseisha fukushi katsudō ni kan suru kentō hōkokusho*" [Report on the Activities of Civic Participatory Welfare Services for the Elderly]. Typescript.

Maclachlan, Patricia L. 1999. "Protecting Producers from Consumer Protection: The Politics of Products Liability Reform in Japan." *Social Sciences Japan Journal* 2: 2.

Maclachlan, Patricia L. 2000. "Information Disclosure and the Center-Local Relationship in Japan." In *Local Voices, National Issues: The Impact of Local Innovation on Japanese Policy-Making*, ed. Sheila A. Smith. Ann Arbor: University of Michigan Press.

Maclachlan, Patricia L. 2002. *Consumer Politics in Postwar Japan: The Institutional Boundaries of Citizen Activism*. New York: Columbia University Press.

Makino Jirō. 1999. "Network Powerlessness, National Irrationality, and the Correlation Between the Two." *Center for Cyber Communities Initiative News Letter* (online). Summer (accessed June 10, 2000). http://www.ccci.or.jp/newsletter/99summer_e/issues.html.

Management and Coordination Agency (MCA). 1988. "*ODA no genjō to kadai – Sōmuchō no daiichi gyōsei kansatsu kekka: Mushō shikin kyōryoku, shijutsu kyōryoku*" [Current State and Issues of ODA – MCA's First Administrative Inspection Report: Grant Aid Cooperation and Technical Cooperation]. Tokyo: Management and Coordination Agency.

March, James G., and Johan P. Olsen. 1995. *Democratic Governance*. New York: Free Press

Marshall, Thomas H. 1977. *Class, Citizenship and Social Development*. Westport, Conn.: Greenwood Press.

Maruyama Masao. 1961. *Nihon no shisō* [Japanese Thought], ed. Iwanami Shinsho. Tokyo: Iwanami Shoten.

Maruyama Masao. 1963. *Thought and Behaviour in Modern Japanese Politics*. London: Oxford University Press.

Maruyama Masao. 1966. *Gendai seiji no shisō to kōdō* [Thought and Action in Contemporary Politics]. Expanded ed. Tokyo: Miraisha.

Maruyama Masao. 1998. *Jikonai taiwa* [Dialogues with Myself]. Tokyo: Misuzu Shobō.

Maruyama Masao, Satō Noboru, and Umemoto Katsumi. 1983. *Gendai Nihon no kakushin shisō* [Renovationist Thought in Contemporary Japan]. Tokyo: Gendai no Rironsha.

Marx, Karl. [1867] 1990. *Capital*, vol. 1 Trans. Ben Fowkes. London: Penguin/New Left Books.

Masamura Kimihiro. 1990. *Sengo shi* [Postwar History], vol. 2. Tokyo: Chikuma Shobō.

Masumi Junnosuke. 1968. *Nihon seitō shi ron* [A History of Japanese Political Parties], vol. 4. Tokyo: University of Tokyo Press.

Masumi Junnosuke. 1985. *Gendai seiji: 1955-nen igo* [Contemporary Politics since 1955]. Tokyo: University of Tokyo Press.

Masumi Junnosuke. 1988. "The 1955 System in Japan and Its Subsequent Development." *Asian Survey* 28 (3): 286–306.

Mathews, Jessica T. 1997. "Power Shift." *Foreign Affairs* 76 (1): 50–66.

Matsubara Akira. 2002. "*Konmei suru seiji no ugoki*" [Confusing Political Drift]. *C's nyūsuretaa* [C's Newsletter]. April 25.

Matsui Kantarō. 1997. "*Jichitai kōreisha fukushi shisaku no hiyō hikaku ni kan suru sentaku no kanōsei*" [Choices and Possibilities for Comparative Costs of Local-Level Elderly Welfare Policies]. Typescript.

Matsumoto Ichirō. 1981. "*Kensatsu fassho*" [Prosecutor Fascism]. In *Gendai no kensatsu: Nihon kensatsu no jittai to riron, hōgaku seminaa zōkan*. 16 (August): 313.

Matsumoto Sannosuke. 1978. "The Roots of Political Disillusionment: 'Public' and 'Private' in Japan." In *Authority and the Individual in Japan: Citizen Protest in Historical Perspective*, ed. J. Victor Koschmann. Tokyo: University of Tokyo Press.

Matsushita Keiichi. 1978. "Citizen Participation in Historical Perspective." In *Authority and the Individual in Japan: Citizen Protest in Historical Perspective*, ed. J. Victor Koschmann. Tokyo: University of Tokyo Press.

Matsuzaki Tadashi. 1982. *Nihon tekkō sangyō bunseki* [An Analysis of the Japanese Steel Industry]. Tokyo: Nihon Hyōronsha.

Matsuzaki Tadashi. 1991. "*Tekkō sōgi (1957–1959 nen)*" [Labor Disputes in the Iron and Steel Industry, 1957–59]. In *Nihon no rōdō sōgi (1945–80 nen)* [Labor Disputes in Japan, 1945–80], ed. Rōdō Sōgishi Kenkyūkai. Tokyo: University of Tokyo Press.

Mayer, John D., Peter Salovey, and David Caruso. 2000. "Models of Emotional Intelligence." In *Handbook of Intelligence*, ed. Robert J. Sternberg. Cambridge, U.K.: Cambridge University Press.

McAdam, Doug, John D. McCarthy, and Mayer N. Zald. 1996. "Introduction." In *Comparative Perspectives on Social Movements: Political Opportunities, Mobilizing Structures, and Cultural Framings*, ed. Doug McAdam, John D. McCarthy, and Mayer N. Zald. Cambridge, U.K.: Cambridge University Press.

McCarthy, John D., and Mayer N. Zald. 1977. "Resource Mobilization and Social Movements: A Partial Theory." *American Journal of Sociology* 82 (6): 1212–41.

McElvoy, Anne. 1997. "A Time to Choose, Again." *Times Literary Supplement* 4940: 30.

McKean, Margaret. 1981. *Environmental Protest and Citizen Politics in Japan*. Berkeley: University of California Press.

McKinsey Group (Japan). 1993. *Manufacturing Productivity*. Tokyo: McKinsey Group.

McNeely, Connie L. 1995. *Constructing the Nation-State: International Organization and Prescriptive Action*. Westport, Conn.: Greenwood Press.

Menju Toshihiro and Aoki Takako. 1995. "The Evolution of Japanese NGOs in the Asia Pacific Context." In *Emerging Civil Society in the Asia Pacific Community: Nongovernmental Underpinnings of the Emerging Asia Pacific Regional Community*, ed. Yamamoto Tadashi. Singapore and Tokyo: Institute of Southeast Asian Studies and the Japan Center for International Exchange.

Merton, Thomas. 1966. *Conjectures of a Guilty Bystander*. New York: Image Books.

Meyer, John W., and Michael T. Hannan. 1979. "National Development in a Changing World System: An Overview." In *National Development and the World System: Educational, Economic, and Political Change, 1950–1970*, ed. John W. Meyer and Michael T. Hannan. Chicago, Ill.: University of Chicago Press.

Meyer, John W., John Boli, George M. Thomas, and Francisco O. Ramirez. 1997. "World Society and the Nation-State." *American Journal of Sociology* 103 (1): 144–81.

Michimata Kenjirō. 1974. "*Tekkō rōdō undō ni okeru uyokuteki chōryū*" [The Rise of Rightist Trends in Japanese Iron and Steelworkers' Unions]. In *Rōdō undō no shindankai* [A New Stage for the Labor Movement], ed. Rōdō Undō Shi Kenkyūkai. Tokyo: Rōdō Junpōsha.

Migdal, Joel S., Atul Kohli, Vivienne Shue, ed. 1994. *State Power and Social Forces: Domination and Transformation in the Third World*. New York: Cambridge University Press.

Miller, Robert F. 1992. "Introduction." In *The Developments of Civil Society in Communist Systems*, ed. Robert F. Miller. Sydney: Allen and Unwin.

Milly, Deborah. 1999. *Poverty, Equality and Growth: The Politics of Economic Need in Postwar Japan*. Cambridge, Mass.: Harvard University Asia Center.

Minichiello, Sharon. 1984. *Retreat from Reform: Patterns of Political Behavior in Interwar Japan*. Honolulu: University of Hawaii Press.

Ministry of Foreign Affairs (MOFA). 1987–97. *Japan's ODA*. Tokyo: Ministry of Foreign Affairs.

Ministry of Foreign Affairs (MOFA). 1996b. *'96 NGO shien gaido bukku* [Guidebook for Supporting NGOs, 1996]. Tokyo: Ministry of Foreign Affairs.

Ministry of Posts and Telecommunications (MPT). 1990. *A Vision of Postal Savings in the 1990s*. Tokyo: Ministry of Posts and Telecommunications.

Minkan Kōeki Sekutaa Kenkyūkai, ed. 1997. *Minkan kōeki sekutaa no zentaizo* [A General View of Private Public-Interest Corporations]. Tokyo: Zaidan Hōjin Kōeki Hōjin Kyōkai.

Mitchell, Richard H. 1996. *Political Bribery in Japan*. Honolulu: University of Hawaii Press.

Mitchell, Robert C., Angela G. Mertig, and Riley E. Dunlap. 1992. "Twenty Years of Environmental Mobilization: Trends Among National Environmental Organizations." In *American Environmentalism: The U.S. Environmental Movement, 1970–1990*, ed. Riley E. Dunlap and Angela G. Mertig. Philadelphia, Pa.: Taylor and Francis.

Miyake Takafumi. 1999. "A Subcontractor or a Partner? Opportunities and Constraints of Partnerships Between ODA and NGOs." Presented to the Advanced Development Management Program, Sophia University and FASID, Tokyo.

Miyamoto Matao. 1988. "The Development of Business Associations in Prewar Japan." In *Trade Associations in Business History*, ed. Yamazaki Hiroaki and Miyamoto Matao. Tokyo: University of Tokyo Press.

Miyao Takahiro. 2000. *Nihongata jōhōka shakai* [A Japanese-Style Informatized Society]. Tokyo: Chikuma Shinsho.

Miyata Yoshiji. 1991. "*Tekkō rōren no gekidō*" [The Great Transformation of the Japanese Federation of Steelworkers Unions]. In *Shōgen kōsei sengo rōdō undō shi* [An Oral History of the Postwar Labor Movement], ed. Morioka Takeo and Naka Mamoru. Tokyo: SBB Shuppankai.

Miyazaki Ryūji. 1984. "*Senzen Nippon no seiji hatten to rengō seiji*" [Political Development and Coalition Politics in Prewar Japan]. In *Rengō seiji I* [Coalition Politics I], ed. Shinohara Hajime. Tokyo: Iwanami Shoten.

Miyazawa Setsuo. 2001a. "The Politics of Judicial Reform in Japan: Judiciary, Lawyers, Legal Education, and Legal Aid." In *Japanese Law in Context: Readings in Society, the Economy, and Politics*, ed. Curtis J. Milhaupt, J. Mark Ramseyer, and Michael K. Young. Harvard East Asian Monograph No. 198. Cambridge, Mass.: Harvard University Asia Center.

Miyazawa Setsuo. 2001b. "Politics of Judicial Reform: Will It Deliver?" Presented at the weekly seminar of Harvard University's Program on U.S.-Japan Relations, Cambridge, Mass.

Moore, Barrington, Jr. 1966. *Social Origins of Dictatorship and Democracy*. Boston: Beacon Press.

Morgan, Peter W., and Glenn H. Reynolds. 1997. *The Appearance of Impropriety: How the Ethics Wars Have Undermined American Government, Business, and Society*. New York: Free Press.

Morita Akira. 1967. "*Yahata Seitetsu ni okeru rōdōsha shihai*" [Control Over Workers at Yahata Steel]. *Gekkan rōdō mondai* 111: 59–71.

Morris, Robert J. 2000. "Civil Society, Subscriber Democracies, and Parliamentary Government in Great Britain." In *Civil Society before Democracy: Lessons from Nineteenth-Century Europe*, ed. Nancy Bermeo and Philip Nord. New York: Rowman and Littlefield.

Mukaidani Susumu. 1993. *Chiken tokusobu* [The Public Prosecutor Office's Special Investigation Division]. Tokyo: Kōdansha.

Murai Jun. 1995. *Intaanetto* [Internet]. Tokyo: Iwanami Shinsho.

Murai Jun. 1998. *Intaanetto II* [Internet II]. Tokyo: Iwanami Shinsho.

Murakami Shigeyoshi. 1980. *Japanese Religion in the Modern Century*. Trans. H. Byron Earhart. Tokyo: University of Tokyo Press.

Murakami Yasusuke. 1984. *Shin chūkan taishū no jidai* [The Age of the New Middle Mass]. Tokyo: Chūō Kōronsha.

Muramatsu Michio. 1994. *Nippon no gyōsei* [Public Administration in Japan]. Chūkō Shinsho.

Muramatsu Michio and Ellis S. Krauss. 1987. "The Conservative Policy Line and the Development of Patterned Pluralism." Vol. 1 of *The Political Economy of Japan*, ed. Kōzō Yamamura and Yasukichi Yasuba. Stanford, Calif.: Stanford University.

Muramatsu Michio and Ellis S. Krauss. 1990. "The Dominant Party and Social Coalitions in Japan." In *Uncommon Democracies: The One-Party Dominant Regimes*, ed. T. J. Pempel. Ithaca, N.Y.: Cornell University Press.

Muramatsu Michio, Itō Mitsutoshi, and Tsujinaka Yutaka. 1986. *Sengo Nihon no atsuryoku dantai* [Pressure Groups in Postwar Japan]. Tokyo: Tōyō Keizai Shinpōsha.

Murō Tadashi. 2000. "*Shirarezaru kyōsei kaishū meguru kōbo*" [The Vicissitudes of Forcible Conversions]. *Tsukuru* 333 (3): 136–47.

Murobushi Tetsurō. 1981. "*Kensatsu to seiji: Kenryoku chukaku to no kōbō*" [Prosecutors and Politics: Battles with the Core Authorities]. *Gendai no kensatsu: Nihon kensatsu no jittai to riron* [Contemporary Criminal Investigation: The Reality and Theory of Japanese Criminal Investigation]. *Hōgaku seminaa zōkan* 16: 265–72.

Murobushi Tetsurō. 1988. *Oshoku no kōzō* [The Structure of Corruption]. Tokyo: Iwanami Shoten.

Nadelmann, Ethan A. 1990. "Global Prohibition Regimes: The Evolution of Norms in International Society." *International Organization* 44 (4): 497–526.

Najita Tetsuo. 1987. *Visions of Virtue in Tokugawa Japan: The Kaitokudō Merchant Academy of Osaka*. Chicago, Ill.: University of Chicago Press.

Nakamura Yōichi and Nihon NPO Sentaa, eds. 1999. *Nippon no NPO 2000* [Nonprofit Organizations in Japan, 2000]. Tokyo: Nippon Hyōronsha.

Nakane Takashi. 1996. *Shin shūkyō hōjin hō: Sono haikei to kaisetsu* [The New Religious Corporations Law: Background and Explanation]. Tokyo: Daiichi Hōki.

National Institute for Research Advancement (NIRA). 1995. *Shimin kōeki katsudō no sokushin ni kan suru hō to seido no arikata* [The Laws and System Regarding the Promotion of Citizen Public Interest Activities]. Tokyo: NIRA.

National Institute for Research Advancement (NIRA), ed. 1994. *Shimin kōeki katsudō kiban seibi ni kan suru chōsa kenkyū* [Research Report on the Support System for Citizen's Public-Interest Activities]. Tokyo.

Neary, Ian. 1989. *Political Protest and Social Control in Pre-War Japan: The Origins of Buraku Liberation*. Atlantic Highlands, N.J.: Humanities Press International.

Negroponte, Nicholas. 1995. *Being Digital*. New York: Alfred A. Knopf.

Nelken, David. 1994. "Whom Can You Trust? The Future of Comparative Criminology." In *The Futures of Criminology*, ed. David Nelken. Thousand Oaks, Calif.: Sage Publications.

Nelken, David. 1995. "Stopping the Judges." Paper presented at the Center for the Study of Law and Society, Boalt Hall School of Law, University of California at Berkeley.

Nelken, David. 1996. "The Judges and Political Corruption in Italy." *Journal of Law and Society* 23: 95–112.

Nelken, David. 1997. "Studying Criminal Justice Comparatively." In *The Oxford Handbook of Criminology*, 2nd ed., ed. Mike Maguire, Rod Morgan, and Robert Reiner. New York: Oxford University Press.

Nelken, David, and Michael Levi. 1996. "The Corruption of Politics and the Politics of Corruption: An Overview." *Journal of Law and Society* 23: 1–17.

Nenkan Jiten Henshūshitsu, ed. 2000. *Chiezō: Asahi gendai yōgo* [Chiezō: Asahi Contemporary Terminology]. Tokyo: Asahi Shinbunsha.

New York Times. 1996. "Virtual Japan: Plenty of On-Ramps and Little Traffic." *New York Times*, July 27–28, Cybertimes section.

Newell, Susan. 1997. "Birth Control and the Population Problem." In *Society and the State in Interwar Japan*, ed. Elise K. Tipton. London: Routledge.

Nielsen, Kai. 1995. "Reonceptualizing Civil Society for Now: Some Somewhat Gramscian Turnings." In *Toward a Global Civil Society*, ed. Michael Walzer. Providence, R.I.: Berghahn Books.

Nihon Bengoshi Rengōkai. 1999. "*Ikensho: Hanshakaiteki na shūkyō katsudō ni kakawaru shōhisha higai nado no kyūsai no hōshin*" [Position Paper: Guidelines for the Relief of Victimized Consumers in Cases of Anti-Social Religious Activity]. http://www.nichibenren.or.jp/sengen/iken/9907–02.htm.

Nihon Bengoshi Rengōkai Shōhisha Mondai Taisaku Iinkai, ed. 1999. *Shūkyō toraburu no yobō, kyūsai no tebiki* [Handbook for the Prevention and Relief of Problems Regarding Religion]. Tokyo: Kyōiku Shiryō Shuppankai.

Nihon Hōsō Shuppan Kyōkai. 1980. *Nihon no shōhisha undō* [The Japanese Consumer Movement]. Tokyo: Nihon Hōsō Shuppan Kyōkai.

Nihon Intaanetto Kyōkai. 2000. *Intaanetto hakusho 2000* [Internet White Paper, 2000]. Tokyo: Impress Corporation and Access Media International.

Nihon Intaanetto Kyōkai. 2001. *Intaanetto hakusho 2001* [Internet White Paper, 2001]. Tokyo: Impress Corporation and Access Media International.

Nijūichi Seiki ni Mukete ODA Kaikau Kondankai [Council on ODA Reforms for the 21st Century]. 1998. *Final Report*. Tokyo: Nijuichi Seiki ni Mukete ODA Kaikau Kondankai.

Nippon Steel Union. 1985. *Chōsa jihō* [Research Report]. No. 26.

Nishimura Ichirō. 2000. *JEN, kyū Yūgo to ayunda 2,000 nichi* [JEN, 2,000 Days in the Former Yugoslavia]. Tokyo: Kōsei Shuppan.

Nitta Michio. 1979. "*Kumiai yakuin no senbatsu to yōsei*" [The Selection and Education of Union Officials]. *Shakai kagaku kenkyū* 30 (4): 248–77.

Noda Takao, 2000. "*Kōan Chōsachō motoshokuin ga kataru Aum shin hō no uragawa*" [The Other Side of the New Aum Laws According to a Former Employee of the Public Security Investigation Agency]. *Tsukuru* 333 (3): 80–89.

Nomura Jirō. 1988. *Nihon no kensatsu: Saikō no kenryoku no uchigawa* [Japan's Prosecutors: The Backstage Activities of the Ultimate Authority]. Tokyo: Kōdansha.

Nomura Jirō. 1991. *Nihon no saibankan* [Japan's Judges]. Tokyo: Kōdansha.

Nomura Jirō. 1994. *Nihon no kensatsu* [Criminal Investigation in Japan]. Tokyo: Hyōronsha.

Nomura Jirō. 1996. *Kensatsu no hanseiki: Sengo 50-nen no jitsuzō* [A Half-Century of Prosecutors: An Empirical Account of the Postwar Years]. Tokyo: Waseda Keiei Shuppan.

Noonan, John T., Jr. 1984. *Bribes: The Intellectual History of a Moral Idea*. Berkeley: University of California Press.

Nord, Philip. 2000. "Introduction." In *Civil Society before Democracy: Lessons from Nineteenth-Century Europe*, ed. Nancy Bermeo and Philip Nord. New York: Rowman and Littlefield.

Norris, Pippa. 2001. *Digital Divide: Civic Engagement, Information Poverty, and the Internet Worldwide*. New York: Cambridge University Press.

Norton, Augustus Richard. 1995. "Introduction." In *Civil Society in the Middle East*, 2 vols., ed. Richard Augustus Norton. Leiden: E. J. Brill.

Nōsei Jaanarisuto no Kai, ed. 1996. *Sutaato shita shin-shokuryō hō* [The New Food-Supply Law Has Begun]. Tokyo: Nōsei Jaanarisuto no Kai.

Ohara Shakai Mondai Kenkyūjo. 1999. *Nihon no rōdō kumiai 100-nen* [One Hundred Years of Japanese Labor Union History]. Tokyo: Junposha.

Okabe Aki. 1986. *Pasokon shimin netowaaku* [Citizen's Computer Networks]. Tokyo: Gijutsu to Ningen.

Okabe Aki. 2000. "English Publications from Ohdake Foundation" (accessed July 23, 2000). http://www.igc.org/ohdakefoundation/telecom/overview.html.

Okimoto, Daniel I. 1989. *Between MITI and the Market: Japanese Industrial Policy for High Technology*. Stanford, Calif.: Stanford University Press.

Oku Mumeo. 1988. *Nobi akaaka tō: Oku Mumeo jiden* [Brightly Burning Brush Fires: The Autobiography of Oku Mumeo]. Tokyo: Domesu Shuppan.

Okudaira Yasuhiro. 1996. *Kore ga habō hō* [This Is the Anti-Subversive Activities Law]. Tokyo: Kadensha.

Olson, Mancur. 1982. *The Rise and Decline of Nations: Economic Growth, Stagflation, and Social Rigidities*. New Haven, Conn.: Yale University Press.

Organization for Economic Cooperation and Development (OECD). Various years. *Agricultural Policies, Markets, and Trade: Monitoring and Outlook*. Paris: OECD.

Organization for Economic Cooperation and Development (OECD). 1981. *Directory of Non-Governmental Organizations in OECD Member Countries Active in Development Cooperation*, 2 vols. Paris: OECD.

Organization for Economic Cooperation and Development (OECD). 1988. *Voluntary Aid for Development: The Role of Non-Governmental Organizations*. Paris: OECD.

Organization for Economic Cooperation and Development (OECD). 1990. *Directory of Non-Governmental Development Organizations in OECD Member Countries*. Paris: OECD.

Organization for Economic Cooperation and Development (OECD). 1992. *Directory of Non-Governmental Environment and Development Organizations in OECD Member Countries*. Paris: OECD.

Organization for Economic Cooperation and Development (OECD). 1993. *Human Rights, Refugees, Migrants and Development: Directory of NGOs in OECD Countries*. Paris: OECD.

Organization for Economic Cooperation and Development (OECD). 1994. *Population and Development: Directory of Non-Governmental Organizations in OECD Countries*. Paris: OECD.

Organization for Economic Cooperation and Development (OECD). 1996. *Directory of Non-Governmental Organizations Active in Sustainable Development, Part I: Europe*. Paris: OECD.

Organization for Economic Cooperation and Development (OECD). 1997. *International Cooperation for Habitat and Urban Development: Directory of NGOs in OECD Countries*. Paris: OECD.

Organization for Economic Cooperation and Development (OECD). 1998. *Directory of Non-Governmental Organizations Active in Sustainable Development, Part II: Australia, Canada, Japan, Korea, New Zealand, United States*. Paris: OECD.

Organization for Economic Cooperation and Development (OECD) and International Council of Voluntary Agencies (ICVA). 1967. *OECD-ICVA Directory: Development Aid of Non-Governmental Non-Profit Organizations*. Paris: OECD.

Orr, Robert M. 1990. *The Emergence of Japan's Foreign Aid Power*. New York: Columbia University Press.

Ouchi Tsutomu and Saeki Naomi, eds. 1995. *Seifu shokkan kara Nōkyō shokkan e: Shinshokuryō hō o tō: Nihon nōgyō nenpō 42* [From Government Food Control to Nōkyō Food Control: Questioning the New Food Supply Law: Japan Agricultural Yearbook 42]. Tokyo: Nōrin Tōkei Kyōkai.

Pateman, Carole. 1988. "The Fraternal Social Contract." In *Civil Society and the State: New European Perspectives*, ed. John Keane. London: Verso.

Patrick, Hugh T., and Thomas P. Rohlen. 1987. "Small-Scale Family Enterprises." In *The Political Economy of Japan*, vol. 1: *The Domestic Transformation*, ed. Kozo Yamamura and Yasukichi Yasuba. Stanford, Calif.: Stanford University Press.

Pekkanen, Robert. 1999. "Civil Society in Japan." Presented at the annual meeting of the Association of Asian Studies, Boston.

Pekkanen, Robert. 2000a. "*Hō, kokka, shimin shakai*" [Law, the State, and Civil Society]. *Leviathan* 27: 73–108.

Pekkanen, Robert. 2000b. "Japan's New Politics: The Case of the NPO Law." *Journal of Japanese Studies* 26 (1): 111–48.

Pekkanen, Robert. 2000c. "Law, the State, and Civil Society." Presented at the annual meeting of the Association of Asian Studies, San Diego.

Pekkanen, Robert. 2000d. "Theories of Civil Society: How Japan Fits." Presented at the annual meeting of the American Political Science Association, Washington, D.C.

Pekkanen, Robert. 2001a. "A Less-Taxing Woman? New Regulation on Tax Treatment of Nonprofits in Japan." *International Journal of Not-for-Profit Law* 3 (3): 1–7.

Pekkanen, Robert. 2001b. "An Analytical Framework for the Development of Civil Society and the Nonprofit Sector." Washington, D.C.: Aspen Institute, Nonprofit Sector Research Fund Working Paper Series.

Pekkanen, Robert. 2002a. "Civil Society in Japan." Ph.D. diss., Harvard University.

Pekkanen, Robert. 2002b. "Japan's Dual Civil Society and Democracy." Presented at the "Civil Society and Political Change in Asia" conference, Honolulu, H.I.

Pekkanen, Robert. 2003. "The Politics of Regulating the Nonprofit Sector." In *The Voluntary and Non-Profit Sector in Japan: An Emerging Response to a Changing Society*, ed. Stephen Osborne. London: Routledge.

Pekkanen, Robert, and Karla Simon. 2003. "The Legal Framework for Voluntary and Not-for-Profit Activity." In *The Voluntary and Non-Profit Sector in Japan: An Emerging Response to a Changing Society*, ed. Stephen Osborne. London: Routledge.

Pelczynski, Zbigniew A. 1988. "Solidarity and 'The Rebirth of Civil Society' in Poland, 1976–81." In *Civil Society and the State: New European Perspectives*, ed. John Keane. London: Verso.

Pempel, T. J. 1974. "The Bureaucratization of Policymaking in Postwar Japan." *American Journal of Political Science* 18: 647–64.

Pempel, T. J. 1978. "Japan's Foreign Economic Policy: The Domestic Bases for International Behavior." In *Between Power and Plenty: Foreign Economic Policies of Advanced Industrial States*, ed. Peter J. Katzenstein. Madison: University of Wisconsin Press.

Pempel, T. J. 1982. *Policy and Politics of Japan: Creative Conservatism*. Philadelphia, Pa.: Temple University Press.

Pempel, T. J. 1993. "From Exporter to Investor: Japanese Foreign Economic Policy." In *Japan's Foreign Policy after the Cold War: Coping with Change*, ed. Gerald Curtis. Armonk, N.Y.: M. E. Sharpe.

Pempel, T. J. 1998. *Regime Shift: Comparative Dynamics of the Japanese Political Economy*. Ithaca, N.Y.: Cornell University Press.

Pempel, T. J., and Tsunekawa Keiichi. 1979. "Corporatism Without Labor: The Japanese Anomaly." In *Trends Toward Corporatist Intermediation*, ed. Philippe C. Schmitter and Gerhard Lehmbruch. Beverly Hills, Calif.: Sage Publications.

Pérez-Díaz, Víctor M. 1993. *The Return of Civil Society: The Emergence of Democratic Spain*. Cambridge, Mass.: Harvard University Press.

Pérez-Díaz, Víctor M. 1995. "The Possibility of Civil Society: Traditions, Character and Challenges." In *Civil Society: Theory, History, Comparison*, ed. John Hall. Cambridge, U.K.: Polity Press.

Pérez-Díaz, Víctor M. 1998. "The Public Sphere and a European Civil Society." In *Real Civil Societies: Dilemmas of Institutionalization*, ed. Jeffrey C. Alexander. London: Sage Publications.

Peterson, M. J. 1992. "Transnational Activity, International Society, and World Politics." *Millennium* 21 (3): 371–88.

Petracca, Mark P., ed. 1992. *The Politics of Interests: Interest Groups Transformed*. Boulder, Colo.: Westview Press.

Pharr, Susan. 1981. *Political Women in Japan: The Search for a Place in Political Life*. Berkeley: University of California Press.

Pharr, Susan J. 1990. *Losing Face: Status Politics in Japan*. Berkeley: University of California Press.

Pharr, Susan J. 1994. "Japanese Aid and the New World Order." In *Japan, a New Kind of Superpower?* ed. Craig C. Garby and Mary Brown Bullock. Washington, D.C.: Woodrow Wilson Center Press.

Pharr, Susan J. 1997. "Political Ethics and Public Trust in Industrial Democracies." *Centerpiece* 11 (1): 3–5, 8.

Pharr, Susan J. 1999. "Is Social Capital Always . . . Capital? Civic Engagement vs. Clientelism in Japan." Presented at the annual meeting of the Association for Asian Studies, Boston.

Pharr, Susan J. 2000. "Corruption and Public Trust: Perspectives on Japan and East Asia." Honolulu, H.I.: East-West Center Working Papers, Politics and Security Series.

Pharr, Susan J. 2002. "Public Trust and Corruption in Japan." In *Political Corruption: Concepts and Contexts*, ed. Arnold J. Heidenheimer and Michael Johnston. New Brunswick, N.J.: Transaction Publishers.

Pharr, Susan J., and Joseph L. Badaracco. 1986. "Coping with Crisis: Environmental Regulation." In *America versus Japan*, ed. Thomas K. McCraw. Boston, Mass.: Harvard Business School Press.

Pharr, Susan J., and Ellis Krauss, eds. 1996. *Media and Politics in Japan*. Honolulu: University of Hawaii Press.

Pharr, Susan J., and Robert D. Putnam, eds. 2000. *Disaffected Democracies: What's Troubling the Trilateral Countries*. Princeton, N.J.: Princeton University Press.

Pickert, Mary Alice. 1999. "Endangered Service: The Decline of Volunteer Firefighters in Japan." Presented at the Ph.D. Kenkyūkai Conference of the International House of Japan, Tokyo.

Pickert, Mary Alice. 2001. "Dis-Embedding the State? The Transformation of the Intermediate Sector in Japan." Presented at the annual meeting of the Association for Asian Studies Annual Meeting, Chicago.

Pizzi, William T. 1993. "Understanding Prosecutorial Discretion in the United States: The Limits of Comparative Criminal Procedure as an Instrument of Reform." *Ohio State Law Journal* 54: 1325–73.

Poggi, Gianfranco. 1978. *The Development of the Modern State: A Sociological Introduction*. Stanford, Calif.: Stanford University Press.

Politics Online. 1998. *.netpulse* 2 (16), August 18 (accessed June 11, 2000). http://www.politicsonline.com/netpulsearchives/216netpulse.html.

Posner, Richard A. 1999. *An Affair of State: The Investigation, Impeachment, and Trial of President Clinton*. Cambridge, Mass.: Harvard University Press.

Poster, Mark. 1995. "The Net as a Public Sphere?" *Wired* 3 (11).

Potter, David. 1999. "NGOs and Japan's Role in Post–Cold War Asia." In *Weaving a New Tapestry: Asia in the Post–Cold War World*, ed. William P. Head and Edwin G. Clausen. Westport, Conn.: Praeger.

Powell, Walter W., ed. 1987. *The Nonprofit Sector: A Research Handbook*. New Haven, Conn.: Yale University Press.

Powell, Walter W., and Elisabeth S. Clemens, eds. 1998. *Private Action and the Public Good*. New Haven, Conn.: Yale University Press.

Pratt, Brian, and Adrian Stone. 1994. *Multilateral Agencies and NGOs: A Position Paper*. Occasional Paper Series 1 (1). Oxford, U.K.: INTRAC.

Pratt, Edward E. 1999. *Japan's Proto-Industrial Elite: The Economic Foundations of the Gōnō*. Cambridge, Mass.: Harvard University Asia Center.

Price, Richard. 1998. "Reversing the Gun Sights: Transnational Civil Society Targets Land Mines." *International Organization* 52 (3): 613–44.

Prime Minister's Office. Various years. *Kōeki hōjin hakusho* [Public-Interest Person White Paper]. Tokyo: Ministry of Finance.

Provine, Doris Marie. 1996. "Courts in the Political Process in France." In *Courts, Law, and Politics in Comparative Perspective*, ed. Herbert Jacob et al. New Haven, Conn.: Yale University Press.

Przeworski, Adam, and John Sprague. 1986. *Paper Stones: A History of Electoral Socialism*. Chicago, Ill.: University of Chicago Press.

Putnam, Robert D. 1995. "Bowling Alone: America's Declining Social Capital." *Journal of Democracy* 6 (1): 65–78.

Putnam, Robert D. 2000. *Bowling Alone: The Collapse and Revival of American Community*. New York: Simon and Schuster.

Putnam, Robert D., with Robert Leonardi and Raffaella Y. Nanetti. 1993. *Making Democracy Work: Civic Traditions in Modern Italy*. Princeton, N.J.: Princeton University Press.

Pyle, Kenneth B. 1973. "The Technology of Japanese Nationalism: The Local Improvement Movement, 1900–1918." *Journal of Asian Studies* 33 (1): 51–65.

Ramseyer, J. Mark, and Frances McCall Rosenbluth. 1993. *Japan's Political Marketplace*. Cambridge, Mass.: Harvard University Press.

Raney, Rebecca Fairley. 1999. "FEC Allows Matching Funds for Online Donations." *New York Times* (online). June 10 (accessed June 11, 2000). http://www.nytimes.com/1999/06/11/technology/11campaign.html.

Rau, Zbigniew. 1991. *The Reemergence of Civil Society in Eastern Europe and the Soviet Union*. Boulder, Colo.: Westview Press.

Rauch, Jonathan. 1994. *Demosclerosis: The Silent Killer of American Government*. New York: Times Books.

Raz, Joseph. 1979. *The Authority of Law: Essays on Law and Morality*. Oxford, U.K.: Oxford University Press.

Reed, Steven R. 1999. "Political Reform in Japan: Combining Scientific and Historical Analysis." *Social Science Japan Journal* 2: 177–93.

Reed, Steven R., with Ieiri Tomonori, Okumura Matsuko, Rokkaku Kōji, Tabata Shuichi, Tabira Kenji, and Takeuchi Masao. 1996. "Political Corruption in Japan." *International Social Science Journal* 149: 395–405.

Reich, Michael R. 1984. "Crisis and Routine: Pollution Reporting by the Japanese Press." In *Institutions for Change in Japanese Society*, ed. George DeVos. Berkeley: Institute of East Asian Studies.

Reimann, Kim. 2000. "Civil Society and Official Development Assistance: International Politics, Domestic Structures and the Emergence of International Development NGOs in Japan." Presented at the annual meeting of the International Political Science Association, Quebec City.

Reimann, Kim. 2001a. "Building Networks from the Outside In: International Movements, Japanese NGOs and the Kyoto Climate Change Conference." *Mobilization* 6 (1): 69–82.

Reimann, Kim. 2001b. "Riding the International Wave: Sustainable Development, Advocacy NGOs and Official Development Assistance (ODA) Policy in Japan in the 1990s." Presented at the annual meeting of the International Studies Association, Chicago.

Rheingold, Howard. 1997. *The Virtual Community*. http://www.rheingold.com/vc/book.

Rheingold, Howard. 1998. *The Virtual Community* (accessed August 2000). http://www.rheingold.com/uc/book/7.html.

Richardson, Bradley. 1997. *Japanese Democracy: Power, Coordination, and Performance*. New Haven, Conn.: Yale University Press.

Richardson, Bradley, and Scott C. Flanagan. 1984. *Politics in Japan*. New York: Harper Collins.

Rix, Alan. 1993. *Japan's Foreign Aid Challenge: Policy Reform and Aid Leadership*. London: Routledge.

Roberts, Hibbert R. 1986. "The Domestic Environment of AID-Registered PVOs: Characteristics and Impact." In *Private Voluntary Organizations as Agents of Development*, ed. Robert Gorman. Boulder, Colo.: Westview Press.

Robins-Mowry, Dorothy. 1983. *The Hidden Sun: Women of Modern Japan*. Boulder, Colo.: Westview Press.

Rōdōshō (Ministry of Labor). 1964. *Rōdō kumiai kihon chōsa* [Basic Survey of Labor Unions]. Tokyo.

Rōdōshō (Ministry of Labor). 1978. *Shiryō rōdō undō shi* [Materials on the History of the Labor Movement]. Tokyo.

Rōdōshō (Ministry of Labor). 1988. *Rōdō kumiai kihon chōsa* [Basic Survey of Labor Unions]. Tokyo.

Rohlen, Thomas P. 1980. "The Juku Phenomenon: An Exploratory Essay." In *Journal of Japanese Studies* 6 (2): 207–42.

Rohlen, Thomas P. 1983. *Japan's High Schools*. Berkeley: University of California Press.

Rose-Ackerman, Susan. 1999. *Corruption and Government: Causes, Consequences, and Reform*. New York: Cambridge University Press.

Rosenbluth, Frances McCall. 1996. "Internationalization and Electoral Politics in Japan." In *Internationalization and Domestic Politics*, ed. Robert Keohane and Helen Milner. New York: Cambridge University Press.

Rossetti, Carlo. 2000. "The Prosecution of Political Corruption: France, Italy, and the United States – A Comparative View." Institute of Sociology and Political Studies, University of Parma, Italy. Typescript.

Rotter, Julian B. 1980. "Interpersonal Trust, Trustworthiness, and Gullibility." *American Psychologist* 35: 1–7.

Rudolph, Susanne Hoeber. 2000. "Civil Society and the Realm of Freedom." *Economic and Political Weekly* 35 (20): 1762–69.

Ruoff, Kennth James. 2001. *The People's Emperor: Democracy and the Japanese Monarchy, 1945–1995*. Cambridge, Mass.: Harvard University Asia Center.

Russell, Dan, Letitia A. Peplau, and Carolyn E. Cutrona. 1980. "The Revised UCLA Loneliness Scale: Concurrent and Discriminant Validity Evidence." *Journal of Personality and Social Psychology* 39: 472–80.

Saitō Jun. 2000. "Blacklist Drive Takes on the System." *Asahi Evening News*, June 5.

Saitō Michiko. 1988. *Hani motoko*. Tokyo: Domesu Shuppan.

Saitō Michiko. 1993. "*Senjika no josei no seikatsu to ishiki* – Shufu no tomo *ni miru*" [Women's Lives and Consciousness in Wartime – As Seen in the Magazine *Shufu no tomo*]. In *Bunka to fashizumu* [Culture and Fascism], ed. Akazawa Shirō and Kitagawa Kenzō. Tokyo: Nihon Keizai Hyōronsha.

Saitō Takao. 1995. "*Kome bijinesu to shōsha*" [The Rice Business and Trading Companies]. *Shokun* 27 (5): 133–42.

Saki Ryuzō. 1969. *Tekkō teikoku no shinwa* [The Myth of the Steel Empire]. Tokyo: Sanichi Shobō.

Salamon, Lester M. 1994. "The Rise of the Nonprofit Sector." *Foreign Affairs* 73 (4): 109–22.

Salamon, Lester M. 1995. *Partners in Public Service, Government-Nonprofit Relations in the Modern Welfare State*. Baltimore, Md.: Johns Hopkins University Press.

Salamon, Lester M., and Helmut K. Anheier. 1994. *The Emerging Sector*. Baltimore, Md.: Johns Hopkins Comparative Nonprofit Sector Project, Institute for Policy Studies, Johns Hopkins University.

Salamon, Lester M., and Helmut K. Anheier. 1996. *The Emerging Nonprofit Sector: An Overview*. New York: St. Martin's Press.

Salamon, Lester M., and Helmut K. Anheier. 1997. *Defining the Nonprofit Sector: A Cross-National Analysis*. Manchester, U.K.: Manchester University Press.

Salamon, Lester M., and Helmut K. Anheier. 1998. "Social Origins of Civil Society: Explaining the Non-Profit Sector Cross-Nationally." *Voluntas: International Journal of Voluntary and Nonprofit Organizations* 9 (3): 213–81.

Salamon, Lester M., Helmut K. Anheier, Regina List, Stefan Toepler, S. Wojciech Sokolowski, and Associates, eds. 1999. *Global Civil Society: Dimensions of the Nonprofit Sector*. Baltimore, Md.: Johns Hopkins Comparative Nonprofit Sector Project.

Samuels, Richard. 1987. *The Business of the Japanese State: Energy Markets in Comparative and Historical Perspective*. Ithaca, N.Y.: Cornell University Press.

Sangiin Kokusai Mondai ni kan suru Chōsakai (Upper House Research Group on International Issues). 1998. *Taigai keizai kyōryoku ni kan suru iinkai chōsa hōkokusho* [Report of the Subcommittee on Foreign Economic Cooperation]. Tokyo.

Sasakawa Heiwa Zaidan. 1992. *Nihon no kōeki hōjin* [Japan's Public-Interest Corporations]. Tokyo.

Sasaki-Uemura, Wesley. 2001. *Organizing the Spontaneous: Citizen Protest in Postwar Japan*. Honolulu: University of Hawaii Press.

Satō Koji and Kinoshita Tsuyoshi. 1992. *Gendai kokka to shūkyō dantai* [The Contemporary State and Religious Organizations]. Tokyo: Iwanami Shoten.

Satō Seizaburo and Matsuzaki Tetsuhisa. 1986. *Jimintō seiken* [Liberal Democratic Party Power]. Tokyo: Chūō Kōronsha.

Scalapino, Robert A. 1953. *Democracy and the Party Movement in Prewar Japan: The Failure of the First Attempt*. Berkeley: University of California Press.

Schaede, Ulrike. 2000. *Cooperative Capitalism: Self-Regulation, Trade Associations, and the Antimonopoly Law in Japan*. New York: Oxford University Press.

Schattschneider, E. E. 1988. [1960]. *The Semi-Sovereign People*. New York: Harcourt Brace Jovanovich.

Scheiner, Irwin. 1970. *Christian Converts and Social Protest in Meiji Japan*. Berkeley: University of California Press.

Schlesinger, Jacob M. 1997. *Shadow Shoguns: The Rise and Fall of Japan's Postwar Political Machine*. New York: Simon & Schuster.

Schmitter, Philippe C. 1993. *Some Propositions About Civil Society and the Consolidation of Democracy*. Vienna: Institut für Hohere Studien.

Schmitter, Philippe C. 1997. "Civil Society East and West." In *Consolidating the Third Wave Democracies: Themes and Perspectives*, ed. Larry Diamond, Marc F. Plattner, Yun-han Chu, and Hung-mao Tien. Baltimore, Md.: Johns Hopkins University Press.

Schmitter, Philippe C., ed. 1977. *Corporatism and Policy-Making in Contemporary Western Europe*. London: Sage Publications.

Schmitter, Philippe, and Wolfgang Streeck. 1981. "The Organization of Business Interests: Studying the Associative Action of Business in Advanced Industrial Societies." Typescript.

Schneider, Bertrand. 1988. *The Barefoot Revolution: A Report to the Club of Rome*. London: Intermediate Technology Publications.

Schoppa, Leonard J. 1997. *Bargaining with Japan: What American Pressure Can and Cannot Do*. New York: Columbia University Press.

Schreurs, Miranda A. 1996. "Domestic Institutions, International Agendas and Global Environmental Protection in Japan and Germany." Ph.D. diss., University of Michigan.

Schreurs, Miranda A. 1997. "Conservation, Development, and State Sovereignty: Japan and the Tropical Forests of Southeast Asia." In *State Sovereignty: Change and Persistence in International Relations*, ed. Sohail H. Hashmi. University Park: Pennsylvania State University Press.

Schreurs, Miranda A. 2002. *Environmental Politics in Japan, Germany, and the United States*. New York: Cambridge University Press.

Schudson, Michael. 1992. "Was There Ever a Public Sphere? If So, When? Reflections on the American Case." In *Habermas and the Public Sphere*, ed. Craig Calhoun. Cambridge, Mass.: MIT Press.

Schwartz, Frank J. 1998. *Advice and Consent: The Politics of Consultation in Japan*. New York: Cambridge University Press.

Scott, James C. 1972. *Comparative Political Corruption*. Englewood Cliffs, N.J.: Prentice Hall.

Seligman, Adam. 1992. *The Idea of Civil Society*. New York: Free Press.

Seligman, Adam. 1995. "Animadversions upon Civil Society and Civic Virtue in the Last Decade of the Twentieth Century." In *Civil Society: Theory, History, Comparison*, ed. John Hall. Cambridge, U.K.: Polity Press.

Selznick, Philip. 1957. *Leadership in Administration: A Sociological Interpretation*. New York: Harper and Row.

Serizawa, Hisayoshi. 1984. "*1960 Nendai kōhanki no tekkō kumiai undō*" [The Union Movement in the Steel Industry in the Second Half of the 1960s]. *Kōchi tandai shakai kagaku ronshū* 47: 99–194.

Serizawa, Hisayoshi. 1988. "*Tekkō sangyō ni okeru rōdō undō to shōsūha undō*" [The Labor Movement and the Minority Movement in the Steel Industry]. *Rōdō hōritsu junpō* 1204: 4–27.

Shakai Chōsa Kenkyūjo. 1997. *Shimin katsudō kihon chōsa* [A Basic Survey of Citizen Activities]. Tokyo.

Shakai Hoshō Kenkyūjo, ed. 1996. *Shimin sanka to shakai fukushi* [Civic Participation and Social Welfare]. Tokyo: University of Tokyo Press.

Shaw, Martin. 1994. "Civil Society and Global Politics: Beyond a Social Movements Approach." *Millennium* 23 (3): 647–67.

Shils, Edward. 1991. "The Virtue of Civil Society." *Government and Opposition* 26 (1): 3–20.

Shimazono Susumu. 1995. "In the Wake of Aum: The Formation and Transformation of a Universe of Belief." *Japanese Journal of Religious Studies* 22 (Fall): 381–416.

Shimizu Hiroko. 2000. "Strategies for Expanding the Nonprofit Sector in Japan: An Assessment of the Potential and Constraints on Nonprofit Organization Use of Volunteers and Paid Staff." Presented at the International Philanthropy Fellow Seminar, Center for Civil Society, Johns Hopkins University, Baltimore, Md.

Shimizu, Makoto. 1994. "*Shōhisha no kenri: Sono igi to jūyōsei*" [Consumer Rights: Their Significance and Importance]. *Hōritsu jihō* 66 (4): 14–18.

Shimizu Shinzō. 1982. "*Sengo rōdō kumiai undō shi josetsu*" [An Introduction to Historical Analysis of the Postwar Labor Movement]. In *Sengo rōdō kumiai undō shi ron* [The History of the Postwar Labor Union Movement], ed. Shimizu Shinzō. Tokyo: Nihon Hyōronsha.

Shinoda Toru. 1989. *Seikimatsu no rōdō undō* [The Labor Movement at the End of the Century]. Tokyo: Iwanami Shoten.

Shipper, Apichai. 1999. "Reconstructing Reality: Foreign Workers and Secondary Associations in Japan." United Nations University, Institute of Advanced Studies Working Paper 75, Tokyo: United Nations University, Institute of Advanced Studies.

Shirai Taishirō. 1983. "A Theory of Enterprise Unionism." In *Contemporary Industrial Relations in Japan*, ed. Shirai Taishirō. Madison: University of Wisconsin Press.

Shiraishi Kōjirō. 1990. "The Recruit Scandal and 'Money Politics' in Japan." Harvard University Program on U.S.-Japan Relations, Occasional Paper 90–10.

Shōda Akira. 1989. *Shōhisha undō to jijitai gyōsei* [The Consumer Movement and Local Administration]. Tokyo: Hōken Shuppan.

Shūkan Tōyō Keizai. 1996. "*Nōkyō to nōsei*" [The Agricultural Cooperatives and Agricultural Policy]. April 20: 67–73.

Shūkyō to Shōhisha Bengodan Nettowaaku, ed. 1996. *Shūkyō meimoku ni yoru akutoku shōhō* [Corrupt Commerce Under the Name of Religion]. Tokyo: Rokufū shuppan.

Sievers, Sharon L. 1983. *Flowers in Salt: The Beginnings of Feminist Consciousness in Modern Japan*. Stanford, Calif.: Stanford University Press.

Silverberg, Miriam. 1990. *Changing Song: The Marxist Manifestos of Nakano Shigehara.* Princeton, N.J.: Princeton University Press.

Sims, Calvin. 2000. "Yoshiro Mori, a Loyal Party Man." *New York Times*, April 6, sec. A.

Skjelsbaek, Kjell. 1971. "The Growth of International Nongovernmental Organization in the Twentieth Century." *International Organization* 25 (3): 420–42.

Skocpol, Theda. 1985. "Bringing the State Back In: Strategies of Analysis in Current Research." In *Bringing the State Back In*, ed. Peter B. Evans, Dietrich Rueschemeyer, and Theda Skocpol. Cambridge, U.K.: Cambridge University Press.

Skocpol, Theda. 1996. "Unraveling from Above." In *Ticking Time Bombs*, ed. Robert Kuttner. New York: New York University Press.

Skocpol, Theda. 1997a. "America's Voluntary Groups Thrive in a National Network." *Brookings Review* 15 (4): 16–19.

Skocpol, Theda. 1997b. "The Tocqueville Problem." *Social Science History* 21 (4): 455–79.

Skocpol, Theda. 1999. "Advocates Without Members: The Recent Transformation of American Civic Life." In *Civic Engagement in American Democracy*, ed. Theda Skocpol and Morris P. Fiorina. Washington, D.C.: Brookings Institution Press.

Skocpol, Theda, and Morris P. Fiorina. 1999. "Making Sense of the Civic Engagement Debate." In *Civic Engagement in American Democracy*, ed. Theda Skocpol and Morris P. Fiorina. Washington, D.C.: Brookings Institution Press.

Skocpol, Theda, with Marshall Ganz, Ziad Munson, Bayliss Camp, Michele Swers, and Jennifer Oser. 1999. "How Americans Became Civic." In *Civic Engagement in American Democracy*, ed. Theda Skocpol and Morris P. Fiorina. Washington, D.C.: Brookings Institution Press.

Skocpol, Theda, Marshall Ganz, and Ziad Munson. 2000. "A Nation of Organizers: The Institutional Origins of Civic Voluntarism in the United States." *American Political Science Review* 94 (3): 527–46.

Slaughter, Anne-Marie. 1997. "The Real New World Order." *Foreign Affairs* 76 (5): 183–97.

Smillie, Ian. 1995. *The Alms Bazaar: Altruism under Fire – Non-Profit Organizations and International Development*. London: IT Publications.

Smillie, Ian. 1999. "At Sea in a Sieve? Trends and Issues in the Relationship Between Northern NGOs and Northern Governments" and "The World Bank." In *Stakeholders: Government-NGO Partnerships for International Development*, ed. Ian Smillie and Henny Helmich. London: Earthscan.

Smillie, Ian, and Henny Helmich, eds. 1993. *Non-Governmental Organizations and Governments: Stakeholders for Development*. Paris: OECD.

Smillie, Ian, and Henny Helmich, eds. 1999. *Stakeholders: Government-NGO Partnerships for International Development*. London: Earthscan.

Smith, Brian H. 1990. *More Than Altruism: The Politics of Private Foreign Aid*. Princeton, N.J.: Princeton University Press.

Smith, Dennis Mack. 1998. *Modern Italy: A Political History*. Ann Arbor: University of Michigan Press.

Smith, Steven Rathgeb, and Michael Lipsky. 1993. *Nonprofits for Hire: The Welfare State in the Age of Contracting*. Cambridge, Mass.: Harvard University Press.

Smith, Thomas C. 1970. "Ōkura Nagatsune and the Technologists." In *Personality in Japanese History*, ed. Albert M. Craig and Donald H. Shively. Berkeley: University of California Press.

Sone Yasunori. 1993. "Structuring Political Bargains: Government, Gyokai and Markets." In *Political Dynamics in Contemporary Japan*, ed. Gary Allinson and Sone Yasunori. Ithaca, N.Y.: Cornell University Press.

Sone Yasunori et al. 1985. *Shingikai no kiso kenkyū: Kinō, taiyō ni tsuite no bunseki* [Basic Research on *Shingikai*: An Analysis of Their Functions and Conditions]. Tokyo: Keio University.

Sonni, Efron. 2000. "Online Is Off Limits to Japan's Politicians." *Los Angeles Times* (online), June 19. http://www.latimes.com/news/nation/2000619/t000058094.html.

Soranaka Seiji, Hasegawa Kōichi, Katagiri Shinji, and Terada Ryōichi. 1991. *Shakai undō ron no tōgō o mezashite: Riron to bunseki* [Toward a Synthesis of Social Movement Theories: Theories and Analysis], 2nd ed. Tokyo: Seibundō.

Sōrifu [Prime Minister's Office]. 1997. *Kourisha tenbōtō ni kan suru yoron chōsa* [Public-Opinion Survey Concerning Small-Retail Shops]. Tokyo: Sōrifu.

Sōrifu [Prime Minister's Office]. 1998. *Yoron chōsa nenkan* [Public Opinion Survey Yearbook]. Tokyo: Naikaku Sōri Daijin Kanbō Kōhokushitsu.

Sōrifu [Prime Minister's Office]. Various years. *Shokuseikatsu nōson no yakuwari ni kan suru yoron chōsa* [Public-Opinion Surveys Concerning the Roles of Food and Farm Villages]. Tokyo: Sōrifu.

Stepan, Alfred. 1985. "State Power and the Strength of Civil Society in the Southern Cone of Latin America." In *Bringing the State Back In*, ed. Peter B. Evans, Dietrich Rueschemeyer, and Theda Skocpol. New York: Cambridge University Press.

Stepan, Alfred. 1988. *Rethinking Military Politics: Brazil and the Southern Cone*. Princeton, N.J.: Princeton University Press.

Sternberg, Robert J. 1988. *The Triarchic Mind: A New Theory of Human Intelligence*. New York: Viking Press.

Sterngold, James. 1992. "Japan Takes on the Mob and the Mob Fights Back." *New York Times*, June 15, sec. A.

Stille, Alexander. 1999. "Emperor of the Air: Berlusconi Owns Italian Politics, But He Wants More." *The Nation* (November 29): 16–20.

Stille, Alexander. 2001. "Making Way for Berlusconi." *New York Review of Books*, June 21.

Streeck, Wolfgang. 1983. "Between Pluralism and Corporatism: German Business Associations and the State." *Journal of Public Policy* 3 (3): 265–84.

Streeck, Wolfgang, and Philippe Schmitter, eds. 1985. *Private Interest Government: Beyond Market and State*. London: Sage Publications.

Strom, Stephanie. 2000. "Japanese Widely Assume Truth Is Hidden." *New York Times*, April 5, sec. A.

Sugimoto Yoshio. 1997. *An Introduction to Japanese Society*. Cambridge, U.K.: Cambridge University Press.

Sugiyama Mitsunobu. 1993. "*Nihon shakai kagaku no sekai ninshiki – Kōzaha, Ōtsuka shigaku, Uno keizaigaku o megutte*" [Understandings of the World in Japanese Social Science – The Cases of "Lecture Faction" Marxism, Ōtsuka-School Historiography, and Uno-School Economics]. In *Nihon shakai kagaku no shisō* [Japanese Social Science as Thought], ed. Yamanouchi Yasushi et al. Tokyo: Iwanami Shoten.

Sugiyama Mitsunobu. 1995. "'*Shimin shakai' ron to senji dōin – Uchida Yoshihiko no shisō keisei o megutte*" ["Civil Society" Discourse and Wartime Mobilization: On the Intellectual Formation of Uchida Yoshihiko]. In *Sōryokusen to gendaika* [Total War and the Transition to the Contemporary Era], ed. Yamanouchi Yasushi, Narita Ryūichi, and J. Victor Koschmann. Tokyo: Kashiwa Shobō.

Sunstein, Cass R. 1999. "An Office with an Incentive for Zealotry." *New York Times*, February 17, sec. A.

Supreme Commander for the Allied Powers (SCAP). 1951. "Local Government Reform." In *History of the Nonmilitary Activities of the Occupation of Japan*. Historical Monograph No. 6. Tokyo: SCAP.

Suzuki Akira. 1997. "The Polarization of the Union Movement in Postwar Japan: Politics in the Unions of Steel and Railway Workers." Ph.D. diss., University of Wisconsin at Madison.

Suzuki Akira. 2000. "The Transformation of Visions of Labor Unionism: Internal Union Politics in the Japanese Steel Industry in the 1960s." *Social Science Japan Journal* 3 (1): 77–93.

Swidler, Ann. 1986. "Culture in Action: Symbols and Strategies." *American Sociological Review* 51 (2): 273–86.

Szücs, Jenö. 1988. "Three Historical Regions in Europe." In *Civil Society and the State: New European Perspectives*, ed. John Keane. London: Verso.

Tabata Hirokuni. 1991. "*Gendai Nihon no kigyō, shakai, kokka*" [Corporations, Society, and the State in Contemporary Japan]. In *Gendai Nihon shakai 5: Kōzō* [Contemporary Japanese Society 5: Structure], ed. Tokyo Daigaku Shakai Kagaku Kenkyūjo. Tokyo: University of Tokyo Press.

Tachibana Takashi. 1993. *Kyōaku vs. Genron* [The Big Evil vs. the Press]. Tokyo: Bungei Shunjū.

Takabatake Michitoshi. 1975. "Citizens' Movements: Organizing the Spontaneous." *Japan Intepreter* 9 (3): 315–23.

Takano Kazuyoshi. 1996. "*Borantia katsudō no kōzō*" [The Structure of Volunteer Work]. In *Shimin sanka to shakai fukushi* [Civic Participation and Social Welfare], ed. Shakai Hoshō Kenkyūjo. Tokyo: University of Tokyo Press.

Takao Yoshihiko. 1993. *Ura kara mita Tōkyō Chiken Tokusobu* [Behind the Scenes of the Tokyo Public Prosecutors Office's Special Investigation Division]. Tokyo: Eru Shuppansha.

Takashima Zen'ya. 1950. "*Shakai kagaku to wa nani ka*" (What Is Social Science?). In *Shakai kagaku no kiso riron* [Basic Theories of Social Science]. Tokyo: Kōbundō.

Takechi, Hideyuki. 1993. "*Fukushi kōsha ni yoru zaitaku sabisu*" [Home Care Services by Parapublic Agencies]. In *Daisan sekutaa no kenkyū* [A Study of the Third Sector], ed. Tsunao Imamura. Tokyo: Chūō Hōki.

Takechi Hideyuki. 1996. "*Seifu to hieiri dantai*" [Government and the Nonprofit Sector]. In *Shakai fukushi ni okeru shimin sanka* [Civic Participation in Social Welfare], ed. Shakai Hoshō Kenkyūjo. Tokyo: University of Tokyo Press.

Tanaka Hirohide. 1982. "*Nihonteki koyō kankō o kizuita hitotachi – Komatsu Hiroshi shi ni kiku* (2)" [People Who Built Japanese-Style Employment Relations: Hearing from Mr. Komatsu Hiroshi (2)]. *Nihon rōdō kyōkai zasshi* 276: 56–70.

Tarrow, Sidney. 1996. "Making Social Science Work across Space and Time: A Critical Reflection on Robert Putnam's *Making Democracy Work*." *American Political Science Review* 90 (2): 389–97.

Tarrow, Sidney. 2000. "Mad Cows and Social Activists: Contentious Politics in the Trilateral Democracies." In *Disaffected Democracies: What's Troubling the Trilateral Countries?* ed. Susan J. Pharr and Robert D. Putnam. Princeton, N.J.: Princeton University Press.

Taylor, Charles. 1989. "Cross-Purposes: The Liberal-Communitarian Debate." In *Liberalism and the Moral Life*, ed. Nancy Rosenblum. Cambridge, Mass.: Harvard University Press.

Taylor, Charles. 1990. "Modes of Civil Society." *Public Culture* 3 (1): 95–118.

Tekkō Rōdō Tsūshin. 1968. "*Kumiai yakusen o kaishaha dō miru ka*" [How Companies Regard Union Elections]. *Tekkō rōdō tsūshin* 12: 2.

Tenfelde, Klaus. 2000. "Civil Society and the Middle Classes in Nineteenth-Century Germany." In *Civil Society before Democracy: Lessons from Nineteenth-Century Europe*, ed. Nancy Bermeo and Philip Nord. New York: Rowman and Littlefield.

Tilly, Charles. 1979. "Repertoires of Contention in America and Britain, 1750–1830." In *The Dynamics of Social Movements*, ed. Mayer N. Zald and John D. McCarthy. Cambridge, Mass.: Winthrop.

Tilton, Mark. 1996. *Retrained Trade: Cartels in Japan's Basic Materials Industries*. Ithaca, N.Y.: Cornell University Press.

Tochimoto Ichisaburō. 1996. "*Shimin sanka to shakai fukushi gyōsei*" [Civic Participation and Social Welfare Administration]. In *Shakai fukushi ni okeru shimin sanka* [Civic Participation in Social Welfare], ed. Shakai Hoshō Kenkyūjo. Tokyo: Tokyo University Press.

Tocqueville, Alexis de. 1988. *Democracy in America*. Trans. George Lawrence, ed. J. P. Mayer and Max Lerner. New York: Harper and Row.

Tokyo Metropolitan Government, ed. 1996. *Gyōsei to minkan hieiri dantai (NPO): Tōkyō no NPO o megutte* [Public Administration and Private Nonprofit Groups: On Tokyo NPOs]. Tokyo.

Toobin, Jeffrey. 1999. *A Vast Conspiracy: The Real Story of the Sex Scandal That Nearly Brought Down a President*. New York: Random House.

Transparency International. 1999. "1999 Bribe Payers Index; 1999 Corruption Perceptions Index." http://www.transparency.de/documents/cpi/index.html.

Trentmann, Frank. 2000. "Introduction: Paradoxes of Civil Society." In *Paradoxes of Civil Society: New Perspectives on Modern German and British History*, ed. Frank Trentmann. New York: Berghahn Books.

Tsebelis, George. 1990. *Nested Games: Rational Choice in Comparative Politics*. Berkeley: University of California Press.

Tsuchiya Shin'ichi. 1995. "Experiences and Practical Measures Aimed at Combating Corruption Involving Public Officials." Presented at the Asia Crime Prevention Foundation, Tokyo.

Tsujinaka Yutaka. 1988. *Rieki shūdan* [Interest Groups]. Tokyo: University of Tokyo Press.

Tsujinaka Yutaka. 1989. "'*Fukushi shakai' no mosaku to Nihon no fukushi dantai no genzai*" [The Future of "Welfare Society" and the Current Status of Japan's Welfare Organizations]. In *Nenpō seijigaku*, ed. Japanese Political Science Association. Tokyo: Iwanami Shoten.

Tsujinaka Yutaka. 1996. "Interest Group Structure and Regime Change in Japan." In *Maryland/Tsukuba Papers on U.S.-Japan Relations*, ed. I. M. Destler and Satō Hideo. College Park: University of Maryland.

Tsujinaka Yutaka. 1997. "*Nihon no seiji taisei no bekutoru tenkan*" [Vector Change in Japan's Political Regime]. *Leviathan* 20: 130–50.

Tsujinaka Yutaka. 1998. "*Seijukugata shimin shakai to NPO/NGO shimin katsudō dantai*" [Mature Civil Society and NPO/NGO Citizen's Activities Groups]. In *NIRA seisaku kenkyū* 11 (9): 16–23.

Tsujinaka Yutaka. 1999a. "*Gendai Nippon no rieki dantai to seisaku nettowaku, 1–12*" [Interest Associations and Policy Networks in Contemporary Japan, 1–12]. *Senkyo* 52 (1–12).

Tsujinaka Yutaka. 1999b. "*Kanryōsei nettowaku no kōzō to henyō*" [The Structure and Transformation of Bureaucratic Networks]. In *Gendai Nippon no gyōsei* [Public Administration in Contemporary Japan], ed. Mizuguchi Kaneto and Mabuchi Masaru. Tokyo: Bokutakusha.

Tsujinaka Yutaka. 2000. "Japan's Civil Society Organizations in a Comparative Perspective." Presented at the "Global Perspectives on Civil Society in Japan" conference, Honolulu.

Tsujinaka Yutaka, ed. 1999a. *Dantai no kiso kōzō ni kan suru chōsa (Kankoku) J-JIGS Codebook* [Cross-National Survey of Civil Society Organizations and Interest Groups in Korea: Codebook of the Korean Survey]. Leviathan Database.

Tsujinaka Yutaka, ed. 1999b. *Dantai no kiso kōzō ni kan suru chōsa (Nippon) J-JIGS Codebook* [Cross-National Survey of Civil Society Organizations and Interest Groups in Japan: Codebook of the Japanese Survey]. Leviathan Database.

Tsujinaka Yutaka, ed. 2001a. *Dantai no kiso kōzō ni kan suru chōsa (Amerika) US-JIGS Codebook* [Cross-National Survey of Civil Society Organizations and Interest Groups in the U.S.A.: Codebook of the U.S. Survey]. Leviathan Database.

Tsujinaka Yutaka, ed. 2001b. *Dantai no kiso kōzō ni kan suru chōsa (Doitsu) G-JIGS Codebook* [Cross-National Survey of Civil Society Organizations and Interest Groups in Germany: Codebook of the German Survey]. Leviathan Database.

Tsujinka Yutaka, ed. 2002. *Gendai sekai no shimin shakai rieki dantai: 1 Gendai Nippon hen* [Civil Society and Interest Groups in the World, vol. 1: Contemporary Japan]. Tokyo: Bokutakusha.

Tsujinaka Yutaka and Mori Yūji. 1998. *Gendai nihon ni okeru rieki dantai no zonritsu yōshiki* [Interest Groups in Contemporary Japan]. Tsukuba: Tsukuba Hōsei.

Tsujinaka Yutaka, Chung-Hee Lee, and Jaeho Yeom. 1998. *Nikkan rieki dantai no hikaku bunseki* [A Comparative Analysis of South Korean and Japanese Interest Associations]. *Leviathan* 23: 18–49.

Tsūsanshō (MITI). 1997. *Chūshō kigyō hakusho* [Small and Medium-Sized Enterprises White Paper]. Tokyo.

Tsūsanshō (MITI). 1998. Unpublished internal report. Tokyo.

Tu Wei-Ming. 2000. "Multiple Modernities: A Preliminary Inquiry into the Implications of East Asian Modernity." In *Culture Matters: How Values Shape Human Progress*, ed. Lawrence E. Harrison and Samuel P. Huntington. New York: Basic Books.

Uchida Yoshihiko. [1946] 1989. "*Narōdoniki to marukusushugi – Reinin riron seiritsu no ichi sōwa*" [The *Narodniki* and Marxism: A Note on the Formation of Leninist Theory]. In *Uchida Yoshihiko chosakushū* [Collected Works of Uchida Yoshihiko], vol. 10. Tokyo: Iwanami Shoten.

Uchida Yoshihiko. [1948] 1989. "*Senji keizaigaku no mujunteki tenkai to keizai riron*" [The Contradictory Development of Wartime Economics and Economic Theory]. In *Uchida Yoshihiko chosakushū* [Collected Works of Uchida Yoshihiko], vol. 10. Tokyo: Iwanami Shoten.

Uchida Yoshihiko. [1953] 1989. *Keizaigaku no seitan* [The Birth of Economics]. In *Uchida Yoshihiko chosakushū* [Collected Works of Uchida Yoshihiko], vol. 1. Tokyo: Iwanami Shoten.

Uchida Yoshihiko. 1967. *Nihon shihonshugi no shisōzō* [An Intellectual Portrait of Japanese Capitalism]. Tokyo: Iwanami Shoten.

Uchida Yoshihiko. 1970. "Japan Today and *Das Kapital*." *Japan Interpreter* 6 (1): 8–28.

Uchida Yoshihiko. 1993. *Sakuhin to shite no shakai kagaku* [Social Science as Literary Work]. Tokyo: Iwanami Shoten.

Ullman, Claire F. 1998. "Partners in Reform: Nonprofit Organizations and the Welfare State in France." In *Private Action and the Public Good*, ed. Walter W. Powell and Elisabeth S. Clemens. New Haven, Conn.: Yale University Press.

United Nations Development Program (UNDP). 1990, 1992, 1993, and 1999. *Human Development Report*. New York: Oxford University Press.

Upham, Frank. 1987. *Law and Social Change in Postwar Japan*. Cambridge, Mass.: Harvard University Press.

van der Heijden, Hendrik. 1987. "The Reconciliation of NGO Autonomy: Program Integrity and Operational Effectiveness with Accountability to Donors." *World Development* 15 (supplement): 103–12.

Varty, John. 1998. "Civic or Commercial? Adam Ferguson's Concept of Civil Society." In *Civil Society: Democratic Perspectives*, ed. Robert Fine and Shirin Rai. London: Frank Cass.

Verba, Sidney, Norman H. Nie, and Jae-On Kim. 1978. *Participation and Political Equality: A Seven-Nation Comparison*. Cambridge, U.K.: Cambridge University Press.

Vogel, Steven K. 1996. *Freer Markets, More Rules: Regulatory Reform in Advanced Industrial Countries*. Ithaca, N.Y.: Cornell University Press.

Wada Jun. 1999. "Civil Society in Japan Through Print and Statistical Data." In *Deciding the Public Good: Governance and Civil Society in Japan*, ed. Yamamoto Tadashi. Tokyo: Japan Center for International Exchange.

Wada Makoto. 1991. "*Taijinteki yūnōsei ni kan suru kenkyū: Non baabaru sukiru shakudo oyobi sōsharu sukiru shakudo no sakusei*" [A Study of Interpersonal Competence: Construction of a Nonverbal Skill Scale and Social Skill Scale]. *Jikken shakai shinrigaku kenkyū* [Japanese Journal of Experimental Social Psychology] 31: 49–60.

Wade, Robert. 1992. "East Asia's Economic Success: Conflicting Perspectives, Partial Insights, Shaky Evidence." *World Politics* 44 (2): 270–320.

Walker, Jack L. 1977. "Setting the Agenda in the U.S. Senate: A Theory of Problem Selection." *British Journal of Political Science* 7: 423–55.

Walker, Jack L., Jr. 1991. *Mobilizing Interest Groups in America: Patrons, Professions, and Social Movements*. Ann Arbor: University of Michigan Press.

Walthall, Anne. 1998. *The Weak Body of a Useless Woman: Matso Taseko and the Meiji Restoration*. Chicago, Ill.: University of Chicago Press.

Walzer, Michael. 1991. "The Idea of Civil Society: A Path to Social Reconstruction." *Dissent* 38 (2): 293–304.

Walzer, Michael. 1992. "The Civil Society Argument." In *Dimensions of Radical Democracy: Pluralism, Citizenship, Community*, ed. Chantal Mouffe. London: Verso.

Wapner, Paul. 1995. "Politics Beyond the State: Environmental Activism and World Civic Politics." *World Politics* 47 (3): 311–40.

Waswo, Ann. 1988. "The Transformation of Rural Society, 1900–1950." In vol. 6 of *The Cambridge History of Japan*, ed. Peter Duus. Cambridge, U.K.: Cambridge University Press.

Watanabe Osamu.1991. *Kigyō shihai to kokka* [The Control of Enterprises and the State]. Tokyo: Aoki Shoten.

Weber, Max. 1949. "'Objectivity' in Social Science and Social Policy." In *The Methodology of the Social Sciences*, ed. Edward A. Shils and Henry A. Finch. New York: Free Press.

Weber, Max. 1952. *The Protestant Ethic and the Spirit of Capitalism*. New York: Charles Scribner's Sons.

Weisbrod, Burton A. 1988. *The Nonprofit Economy*. Cambridge, Mass.: Harvard University Press.

Weisbrod, Burton A., and Mark Schlesinger. 1986. "Ownership Forms and Behavior in Regulated Markets with Asymmetric Information." In *The Economics of Nonprofit Institutions: Studies in Structure and Policy*, ed. Susan Rose-Ackerman. Oxford: Oxford University Press.

Weller, Robert P. 1998. "Horizontal Ties and Civil Institutions in Chinese Societies." In *Democratic Civility: The History and Cross-Cultural Possibility of a Modern Political Ideal*, ed. Robert W. Hefner. New Brunswick, N.J.: Transaction Publishers.

Wesolowski, Wlodzimierz. 1995. "The Nature of Social Ties and the Future of Postcommunist Society: Poland after Solidarity." In *Civil Society: Theory, History, Comparison*, ed. John Hall. Cambridge, U.K.: Polity Press.

Westney, Eleanor. 1987. *Imitation and Innovation: The Transfer of Western Organizational Patterns to Meiji Japan*. Cambridge, Mass.: Harvard University Press.

Wheeler, Mark. 1997. *Politics and the Mass Media*. Cambridge, Mass.: Blackwell.

White, Gordon. 1994. "Civil Society, Democratization and Development (I): Clearing the Analytical Ground." *Democratization* 1 (3): 375–90.

Wilson, Graham. 1985. *Government and Business: A Comparative Introduction*. London: Macmillan.

Wilson, Graham. 1992. *Business and Politics: A Comparative Introduction*. London: Macmillan.

Wilson, Sandra. 1997. "Angry Young Men and the Japanese State: Nagano Prefecture, 1930–33." In *Society and the State in Interwar Japan*, ed. Elise K. Tipton. London: Routledge.

Witt, Michael. 2000. "Networking, Consulting, Poaching: Corporate Reconnaissance in the Trilateral Economies." Ph.D. diss., Harvard University.

Wolfe, Alan. 1997. "Is Civil Society Obsolete? Revisiting Predictions of the Decline of Civil Society." *Brookings Review* 15 (4): 9–12.

Wolferen, Karel van. 1989. *The Enigma of Japanese Power: People and Politics in a Stateless Nation*. New York: Alfred A. Knopf.

Wolferen, Karel van. 1991. "An Economic Pearl Harbor?" *New York Times*, December 2, sec. A.

Wood, Ellen Meiksins. 1990. "The Uses and Abuses of 'Civil Society.'" In *Socialist Register 1990*, ed. Ralph Miliband, Leo Panitch, and John Saville. London: Merlin Press.

Wood, James E., Jr. 1993. "Government Intervention in Religious Affairs: An Introduction." In *The Role of Government in Monitoring and Regulating Religion in Public Life*, ed. James E. Wood, Jr., and Derek Davis. Waco, Tex.: J. M. Dawson Institute of Church-State Studies, Baylor University.

Woodward, William P. 1972. *The Allied Occupation of Japan 1945–1952 and Japanese Religions*. Leiden: E. J. Brill.

World Bank. 1991, 1992, 1996a, and 1997. *World Development Report*. New York: Oxford University Press.

World Bank, Participation and NGO Group, Poverty and Social Policy Department. 1996b. *The World Bank's Partnership with Nongovernmental Organizations*. Washington, D.C.: World Bank.

WuDunn, Sheryl. 1998. "Japan's Corruption Fighter Is Shunted Aside." *New York Times*, August 14, sec. A.

Yahagi Toshiyuki. 1994. *Kombiniensu sutoa shisutemu no kakushinsei* [Possibilities for Reforming the Convenience Store System]. Tokyo: Nihon Keizai Shinbunsha.

Yahata Steel. 1980. *Yahata seitetsujo 80-nen shi bumon shi gekan* [The 80-Year History of Yahata Steel Works: The History of Departments, vol. 2]. Yahata Seitetsujo.

Yamada Moritarō. [1934] 1992. *Nihon shihonshugi bunseki* [An Analysis of Japanese Capitalism]. Ed. Iwanami Bunko. Tokyo: Iwanami Shoten.

Yamada Toshio. 1987. "Les Tendances du marxisme japonais contemporai" [Tendencies in Contemporary Japanese Marxism]. *Actuel Marx* 2: 34–44.

Yamada Toshio. 1994. "*Kigyō shakai to shimin shakai*" [Corporate Society and Civil Society]. In *Gendai shimin shakai to kigyō kokka* [Contemporary Civil Society and the

Corporate State], ed. Hirata Kiyoaki, Yamada Toshio, Katō Tetsurō, Kurosawa Nobuaki, and Itō Masazumi. Tokyo: Ochanomizu Shobō.

Yamagaki Masahiro. 2000. "*Nihongata 'rōdōkumiaishugi' undō to sono kiketsu*" [Japanese-Style "Labor Unionism" and Its Consequences]. *Ohara shakai mondai kenkyūjo zasshi* 498: 19–42.

Yamagishi Midori and Yamagishi Toshio. 1989. "Trust, Commitment, and the Development of Network Structures." Presented at the workshop for the "Beyond Bureaucracy Research Project," December 18–21, Hong Kong.

Yamagishi Toshio. 1986. "The Provision of a Sanctioning System as a Public Good." *Journal of Personality and Social Psychology* 51: 110–16.

Yamagishi Toshio. 1988a. "Exit from the Group as an Individualistic Solution to the Public Good Problem in the United States and Japan." *Journal of Experimental Social Psychology* 24: 530–42.

Yamagishi Toshio. 1988b. "The Provision of a Sanctioning System in the United States and Japan." *Social Psychology Quarterly* 51: 265–71.

Yamagishi Toshio. 1992. "Group Size and the Provision of a Sanctioning System in a Social Dilemma." *Social Dilemmas: Theoretical Issues and Research Findings*, ed. Wim B. G. Liebrand, David M. Messick, and Henk A. M. Wilke. Oxford: Pergamon Press.

Yamagishi Toshio. 1998. *Shinrai no kōzō: Kokoro to shakai no shinka geimu* [The Structure of Trust: The Evolutionary Games of Mind and Society]. Tokyo: University of Tokyo Press.

Yamagishi Toshio. 1999. *Anshin shakai kara shinrai shakai e: Nihongata shisutemu no yukue* [From a Security-Based Society to a Trust-Based Society: The Future Direction of the Japanese System]. Tokyo: Chūō Kōron Shinsha.

Yamagishi Toshio and Karen S. Cook. 1993. "Generalized Exchange and Social Dilemmas." *Social Psychology Quarterly* 56: 235–48.

Yamagishi Toshio and Satō Kaori. 1986. "Motivational Bases of the Public Goods Problem." *Journal of Personality and Social Psychology* 50: 67–73.

Yamagishi Toshio, Watabe Motoki, Hayashi Nahoko, Takahashi Nobuyuki, and Yamagishi Midori. 1996. "*Shakaiteki fukakujitsusei no moto de no shintai to komittomento*" [Trust and Commitment Under Social Uncertainty]. *Shakai shinrigaku kenkyū* 11: 206–16.

Yamagishi Toshio and Yamagishi Midori 1994. "Trust and Commitment in the United States and Japan." *Motivation and Emotion* 18: 129–66.

Yamaguchi Jirō. 1997. *Nihon seiji no kadai* [Themes of Japanese Politics]. Tokyo: Iwanami Shoten.

Yamaguchi Noboru and Takahashi Kōji, eds. 1993. *Shimin sanka to kōreisha kea* [Civic Participation and Elderly Care]. Tokyo: Daiichi Hōki.

Yamaguchi Yasushi. 1992. "*Shin shimin sengen*" [A New Citizens' Declaration]. In *Shimin jiritsu no seiji senryaku* [Political Strategy for Autonomous Citizens], ed. Yamaguchi Yasushi, Takarada Zen, Shindō Eiichi, Mizusawa Hiroki. Tokyo: Asahi Shinbunsha.

Yamakawa Katsumi. 1985. "*Shimin ishiki no henyō to shisei no kadai*" [Changes in Citizen Consciousness and Topics in City Policies]. *Toshi mondai* 76 (3): 3–13.

Yamamoto Akira. 1982. *Nihon seikatsu kyōdō kumiai undō shi* [A History of Japan's Lifestyle Cooperative Movement]. Tokyo: Nihon Hyōronka.

Yamamoto Kiyoshi. 1981. *Jidōsha sangyō no rōshi kankei* [Labor-Management Relations in the Auto Industry]. Tokyo: University of Tokyo Press.

Yamamoto Kiyoshi. 1990. "'*Infōmaru soshiki' ni kan suru ichi kōsatsu (2): Kō Denki ni okeru jirei o chūshin to shite*" [An Analysis of "Informal Organization" Based on the Case of Kō Electronics]. *Shakai kagaku kenkyū* 42 (2): 113–59.

Yamamoto Kiyoshi. 1991. "*Daikigyō no rōshi kankei*" [Labor-Management Relations in Large Enterprises]. In *Gendai Nihon shakai 5 kōzō* [Contemporary Japanese Society, vol. 5: Structure], ed. Tokyo Daigaku Shakai Kagaku Kenkyūjo. Tokyo: University of Tokyo Press.

Yamamoto Tadashi, ed. 1995. *Emerging Civil Society in the Asia Pacific Community*. Tokyo: Japan Center for International Exchange.

Yamamoto Tadashi. 1998. "The State and the Nonprofit Sector in Japan" and "Current Issues and Future Agenda." In Yamamoto Tadashi, ed., *The Nonprofit Sector in Japan*. Manchester, U.K.: Manchester University Press.

Yamamoto Tadashi. 1999. "Emergence of Japan's Civil Society and Its Future Challenges." In *Deciding the Public Good: Governance and Civil Society in Japan*, ed. Yamamoto Tadashi. Tokyo: Japan Center for International Exchange.

Yamamoto Tadashi, Iokibe Makoto, Irie Akira, Ōta Hiroko, and Yoshida Shin'ichi. 1998. *Kan kara min e no pawa shifuto: Dare no tame no kōeki ka* [The Power Shift from Bureaucratic State to Civil Society: The Public Interest for Whose Benefit?]. Tokyo: TBS Britannica Japan.

Yamamoto Taketoshi. 1989. "The Press Clubs of Japan." *Journal of Japanese Studies* 15: 371–88.

Yamaoka Yoshinori. 1999. "Recent Trends in the Non-Profit Sector in Japan, Including Background on the New NPO Law." In *Civil Society: Japanese Experiment and American Experience*, ed. Ruri Kawashima and Betty Borden. New York: Japan Society.

Yamauchi Naoto. 1997. *Nonpurofito ekonomii* [The Nonprofit Economy]. Tokyo: Nippon Hyoronsha.

Yamauchi Naoto, ed. 1999. *NPO Deetabukku* [NPO Databook]. Tokyo: Yuhikaku.

Yamauchi Naoto, Shimizu Hiroko, S. Wojciech Sokolowski, and Lester M. Salamon. 1999. "Japan." In *Global Civil Society: Dimensions of the Nonprofit Sector*, ed. Lester M. Salamon, Helmut K. Anheier, Regina List, Stefan Toepler, S. Wojciech Sokolowski, and Associates. Baltimore, Md.: Johns Hopkins Comparative Nonprofit Sector Project.

Yasko, Richard. 1979. "Bribery Cases and the Rise of the Justice Ministry in Late Meiji–Early Taisho Japan." *Law in Japan* 12: 57–68.

Yayama Tarō. 1990. "The Recruit Scandal: Learning from the Causes of Corruption." *Journal of Japanese Studies* 16 (1): 93–114.

Yokota Katsunori. 1995. "'*Sankagata fukushi' to seikatsu kurabu undō*" ["Participatory Welfare" and the Livelihood Club Coop Movement]. *Sōgō Kea* 5 (12): 25–28.

Yonekura Seiichirō. 1993. "*Gyōkai dantai no kinō*" [Functions of Trade Associations]. In *Gendai Nihon keizai shisutemu no genryū* [The Fountainhead of Contemporary Japan's Economic System], ed. Okazaki Tetsuji and Okuno Masahiro. Tokyo: Nihon Keizai.

Yonemoto Shōhei. 1994. *Chikyū kankyō mondai to wa nani ka* [What Is the Global Environment Problem?]. Tokyo: Iwanami Shinsho.

Yoon Sangchul. 2000. "[The] Anticorruption Movement in Korea: Focusing on International Influence and Internal Political Context." *Korea Journal* 40 (3): 185–216.

Yoshida Shin'ichi. 1999. "Rethinking the Public Interest in Japan: Civil Society in the Making." In *Deciding the Public Good: Governance and Civil Society in Japan*, ed. Yamamoto Tadashi. Tokyo: Japan Center for International Exchange.

Yoshimi Yoshiaki. 1987. *Kusa no ne no fashizumu* [Grassroots Fascism]. Tokyo: University of Tokyo Press.

Young, Louise. 1998. *Japan's Total Empire: Manchuria and the Culture of Wartime Imperialism*. Berkeley: University of California Press.

Zadankai [Roundtable]. 1989. "*Seiji no no gendō to nōgyō: Nōson no shinro*" [Agriculture and the Motor of Politics: The New Way for Farm Villages]. *Zenshin* (June).

Zielenziger, Michael. 1996. "Rigid Campaign Rules Keep Japanese Politics off Internet." *San Jose Mercury News*, October 14.

Author Index

Subject Index